CRY ALOUD,
SPARE NOT

To Beverly Boland
Thanks for your
friendship + help.
God bless.
Stephen E. Dove
Jer. 33:3

CRY ALOUD, SPARE NOT

The Story of W. E. Dowell
1914-2002

Stephen E. Dowell

PILGRIMAGE ROAD PRESS
SPRINGFIELD, MISSOURI

Cry Aloud, Spare Not: The Story of W. E. Dowell
© 2017 by Stephen E. Dowell
Pilgrimage Road Press
Springfield, Missouri
All rights reserved. Published 2017.

Cover design by Eowyn Riggins
Design consultation by Ryan Allison
Cover photos courtesy of the John E. Craig, Jr., family
Layout by Penoaks Publishing, http://penoaks.com

ISBN: 978-0-9969892-8-2

All scripture references are from The Holy Bible. Edited by C. I. Scofield, Authorized King James Version, Oxford UP, 1945.

To the Dowell family tree.
I love you forever. God loves you more.

Table of Contents

Foreword by Bill Dowell Jr.

This book tells the story of an exceptional man of God. I loved him and looked up to him with great admiration. But I knew him in a way that most other admirers did not. Dr. W. E. (Bill) Dowell was my "Daddy."

In writing this introduction, I reflected back upon the many memories I had of my dad. Our happy times together were plentiful. Dad was frequently gone for revival meetings and other speaking engagements, but when he came home he always had a gift for me and my brother and sister. The good times went far beyond trinkets, however. Dad was also careful to make time in his busy schedule for his family. One time we spent two weeks in a primitive cabin in Northern Michigan where we had to draw our own water to cook and drink and had to use an outhouse when needed. He took us to a nearby lake to swim and fish. On another occasion we spent a week in Old Mexico. It was on that trip, at Acapulco, that I was introduced to waterskiing. I also remember his taking us all to Carlsbad Cavern, and the Grand Canyon, and Hoover Dam, and the Painted Desert, and many other places on vacations together. At Christmas time on one occasion, he dressed up like Santa Claus and surprised us all. He had a great sense of humor.

Dad owned a private plane with another man in the church. It was a small two-seater private plane, with one seat in the front and one in the back. It was controlled with a stick in front of each seat. As I recall, you had to start the plane manually by giving the propeller a spin. Dad flew to his meetings in that airplane, and one time he had to make an emergency landing in a field. When he was ready to take off again, some cows were in the way, so the man that he was traveling with got out to chase the cows away, and a wind suddenly flipped the plane over on its back with Dad inside. Fortunately no one was hurt.

Dad and I also had our own adventures in that airplane. On one occasion, when I was quite small, Dad and I flew together in his plane to Joplin, Missouri, to see an air show. I rode in the front seat, and he rode in the back seat. The air show was great. Then on the way home, Dad tried his best to get me to fly the plane. We were five thousand feet in the sky, and Dad was right there in the back seat to compensate for anything that went wrong, but I was too frightened of crashing to touch that stick.

Even so, I treasured such times with my dad. My dad was good to me. When I was on a boys' basketball team playing at the YMCA, he bought me a beautiful pair of basketball shorts and a shirt. They stood out from what the others were wearing, and unfortunately some kid stole them while I was in the shower. But Dad never complained. Dad also took me with him fishing and hunting and bought me a 20-gauge shotgun and later a .22 rifle. We hunted for quail, squirrels, and rabbits. I remember one time going fishing with him and staying in a tent all night on a river bank. I learned to cast a line using a rod and reel that he bought me. On several occasions, Dad and I drove to St. Louis to see the St. Louis Cardinals play. That was exciting. Dad loved sports. Years later, he took my young daughter to see the Cardinals play, and they too shared in a sweet memory. They sang together on the way, "Goodbye, My Sweet Mary Ann," and laughed and laughed.

Yet with all the fun, my dad had a very serious side. He could be strict, which meant no movies, no dancing, no smoking, no gambling, and no cussing. He did not even want me going skating at the rink because he termed that "dancing on wheels." He did not want me playing Monopoly because it used dice, and he didn't want me to get caught up in gambling with dice.

My dad was quick to let me know when I did wrong, even using a belt when it was needed. Once at the dinner table something was said that hurt my feelings, and I started crying. Dad rebuked me and told me to grow up. On another occasion, when I was talking and cutting up with my friends during a church service, he called me down publicly, saying, "The first thing I want to say tonight is . . . Billy, shut-up." I knew that I would get a spanking for that one, so I hurried home at the end of the service (we lived right next door to the church), and I took a belt and spanked myself on the legs. When Dad got home, I told him I had already spanked myself, so he didn't need to spank me. I actually got by with that on that occasion. But even when my father was doing the spanking, I never questioned his love.

On one occasion, I walked into my father's bedroom before noticing that Dad was stretched out on the bed crying and praying to God. I did not fully understand why at the time, but I always knew my dad was a devout man who cared about the souls of others. I have vivid memories of him preaching and holding tent revivals in Springfield. Those meetings lasted two or even three weeks. Then after those tent revivals, we had river baptisms for the many who were saved. Usually, those baptisms occurred on Ross Owens's farm down on the James River. Other baptisms were held at the Sac River north of town.

Dad was not just a preacher at the church, however. His concern for the spiritual wellbeing of others extended even to the members of his own household. He led me to Christ when I was a young boy. He then baptized me a couple weeks later at the High Street Baptist Church. When I surrendered to preach at age sixteen, Dad left the pulpit and came down and knelt by my side at the altar and prayed with me as I gave my life and ministry to God.

My dad was also there to watch out for me as I grew in the Lord. When I was in grade school, I learned about evolution, and I came up with the idea on my own that maybe God created everything by a process of evolution. When I expressed the idea to

Dad, he became visibly upset, and I knew that "theistic evolution" was an evil idea. Later, when I was in a secular college, I was toying around with the idea of Calvinism, and Dad grew angry with those who were influencing my theology. He made it quite clear that this was heresy.

Run-ins with my dad were rare, however. Mostly, I remember my father as a happy, good-natured man, who loved and cared for his family. He enjoyed sports, and quite often he played on his harmonica. He also grilled steaks out on his patio whenever there was a special occasion. When I met the girl of my life in Borger, Texas, Dad, along with my mother, my brother, my sister, and Earl Smith, drove to Borger for the wedding. Dad performed the ceremony. He then lent me his new Oldsmobile 98 for my new bride and me to take on our honeymoon. After that, Dad found an affordable home for us to rent in Springfield, and he hired me on the staff at High Street Baptist Church. I served there for the first five years of our married life while I was finishing degrees at both Missouri State University (Southwest Missouri State College at the time) and Baptist Bible College.

It was my father who called for my ordination to the ministry in 1960. He also arranged for many of his close friends to be on the ordination council. Those men included Dr. G. B. Vick, John Rawlings, and nine other great pastors whose names on my ordination certificate I have always treasured.

I later worked for my dad again, first as a professor at Baptist Bible College and then as his co-pastor for many years at Baptist Temple in Springfield, Missouri. Dad was not only a great preacher and leader, he was a great boss. We never once had any conflict, though I knew he was in charge.

When I succeeded my father as pastor of Baptist Temple, our roles shifted, yet Dad always respected my pastoral leadership. He was willing to do anything I asked of him, whether it was preaching, participating in our debt retirement celebration, or giving me advice, guidance, and prayer. But never once did he try to undermine my authority. On one occasion, a man came to him over some issue in the church, and Dad simply told him that he would have to talk to the pastor about that. To me, my dad was the ideal father, pastor, leader, friend, and encourager. I have no bad memories at all of my dad.

I am glad my son Stephen decided to write this biography of Dad. Stephen knew his grandfather very well, but he has gone far beyond his personal observations about him in the development of this work. His research has included lengthy interviews with Dad's closest friends, co-workers, and family members. He has also explored many print resources and has traveled to various places to gain further insights. This book reads like a novel, but it is well documented.

W. E. Dowell makes a worthy subject for such a study. Dad conducted revival meetings all over the world and was instrumental in bringing thousands to Christ. Dad rubbed shoulders with many of the great ministry leaders of his generation. His friends included John Rawlings, Wendell Zimmerman, David Cavin, Art Wilson, and of course his closest friend and associate, Earl Smith. Dr. G. B. Vick, pastor of the Temple Baptist Church in Detroit, was another close personal friend. In fact, Dad frequently preached at Temple as a guest speaker. Vick's church averaged over 3,800 in weekly attendance, though this was long before the era of megachurches. My dad also pastored several great churches of his own. One of those was the High Street Baptist Church, which reached a membership of five thousand under his leadership. It was the largest church in Missouri at that time.

Dad served as an important part of a great movement of fundamental Baptists. He served as the first president of the Baptist Bible Fellowship International (BBFI), a network of pastors and missionaries. The BBFI is the largest independent Baptist association in America and has grown to represent more than eight thousand churches worldwide. Dad also played a vital role in the life of the Baptist Bible College (BBC). He helped found BBC in Springfield, Missouri, in 1950, and he was named the college's executive vice president in 1968. Then in 1976, Dad became BBC's second president. Enrollment at the college peaked at more than two thousand students during the years he was there.

It was Dad's association with BBC that helped my father to build a rapport with so many of the preachers that came after him. BBC's original classes were held in the facilities of the High Street Baptist Church while Dad was still the pastor there. Consequently, he served as pastor and mentor to many up-and-coming young leaders, men like Jerry Falwell, who went on to found Thomas Road Baptist Church and Liberty University in Lynchburg, Virginia. No one pastor has had greater influence than my father did over so many other pastors and missionaries.

Something else that made my father unique was his association with Dr. J. Frank Norris. Norris was the influencer in my father's early life. Norris was a very controversial leader in Ft. Worth, Texas, but when my father was a young preacher, he was greatly affected by Norris. Dad emulated Norris in his strong stand against the evils of his day. My dad fought against the liquor crowd, "lewd literature," and other corrupting influences. In Springfield, Dad had a major role in preventing beer from being sold at the fairgrounds. He opposed dancing on the square when President Harry Truman came to town. He attacked Drury College for having a noted liberal theologian speak on their campus.

As a consequence of such efforts, Dad, like Norris, became a controversial figure to the people around him. Yet my father never backed down. Dad believed the Bible is the inspired, inerrant Word of God, and he stood on that authority when he preached. One of my father's oft-used phrases was "Let there be no mistake about it," and his dogmatic delivery caught the attention of many. Dad spoke out boldly from the pulpits of his churches and over his radio and television programs, denouncing the things that he firmly believed were destructive to our society and harmful to Christianity. He also spoke eloquently, with few notes, and he often "shot from the hip" with ad lib remarks in his sermons. Dad was frequently quoted in the newspaper as he opposed the ungodly influences of his day. Many times he also appeared in public debates representing the "fundamental Christian perspective." Then at one historic gathering of fundamentalists in 1984, Dad even shared a platform with President Ronald Reagan. In short, my father was a man of influence. He was either greatly loved or greatly hated, but there was never any question about what he stood for. Dad never wavered from his fundamentalist beliefs.

This book tells my father's story in a clear and interesting way. Dad was bold and courageous in opposing societal evils, yet at the same time he was a gentle man with a great compassion for "lost and dying souls." This writer captures both of those dimensions, presenting an amazing story of one of the truly great men and preachers of the twentieth century. I'm happy that I can call that man my father. Dad's influence in my life; in the life of my younger brother, Clyde Dowell; in the life of my older sister, Janet Rodgers; and in the lives of countless others is unparalleled. And my prayer is that you, too, will be blessed as you visit the pages of the life of W. E. Dowell.

Bill Dowell Jr.
Springfield, Missouri
2017

Preface

"Dowell, you say? Are you any relation to–?" I did not need to hear the end of the statement. I knew what was coming. The same question popped up frequently in the city of Springfield. I heard it from store clerks, restaurant personnel, teachers, neighbors. And when I answered, "He's my grandfather," there was almost always a reply. "I attended his church years ago." "We used to listen to him on the radio." "He officiated at my daughter's wedding." "He baptized me." "My sister got saved under his preaching."

Such comments never made me feel that my grandfather was famous, but it was clear to me that he was a man of influence. Even when our family left Missouri to go on vacation, we routinely ran into people with connections to Granddad's ministries back in Springfield. And why should that surprise us? Churches the world over had been influenced by his work.

But truth be told, when I was growing up, I was never quite sure what the big deal was. Why did so many people admire him? To me, he was just Granddad. Throughout much of the 1970s and 80s, I was a member of my grandfather's church. I heard him preach on a regular basis, but I heard a lot of other preachers as well. And I could not honestly say that I preferred his preaching over theirs.

Then in the mid-1980s, I finally saw it. I was sitting in the choir loft during a service at Springfield's Baptist Temple, and my grandfather started to preach. Granddad had been battling a string of illnesses for several years, and his lack of strength often showed when he got up to speak. But not on this day. I do not remember my grandfather's subject matter or anything that he said during the course of that message. I just remember thinking, "Oh. Now I get it." He spoke with such power and authority. Even a cynical college student like me had to sit up and take notice. The Spirit of God was upon him. I observed the same thing the following week. And the week after that.

Granddad's vigor did not last, of course. Eventually his sermons returned to the more ordinary variety that I had been accustomed to. I have since reached the conclusion that even his "ordinary" sermons outstripped many of the sermons preached by other preachers. But in those days my palate was too spoiled by spiritual steak to appreciate what I was feasting upon. I have never forgotten, however, the epiphany that came to me that day in the choir loft. For a brief time, I caught a glimpse of my grandfather in his prime. And I was truly impressed.

I remain impressed even today. But this book was not written to heap praises on my grandfather. It was written to observe the workings of God in his life. In many ways, W. E. Dowell was quite ordinary. He had humble beginnings, and even after he rose to prominence as a minister, he remained accessible and down to earth. No one knew that better than his family members.

Yet without question God managed to accomplish great things through this man. God took the things that made my grandfather so very human, and He turned them into a thing of beauty. In God's hands, this ordinary life became extraordinary. Indeed, as I reflect upon my grandfather's life, I note that his accomplishments glisten even brighter against a woolen humanity.

My hope is that the reader will better appreciate God's handiwork by getting to know my grandfather as he really was. To that end, I have made an effort to bring this story to life. Most of the chapters begin with a fictionalized account of some real event. All of the invented material is rooted in fact, but I readily admit taking some dramatic license. I have added imagined details and even some original dialogue. Italics have been incorporated to help distinguish my dialogue creations from quotations. I trust that the reader will embrace this storytelling device.

I have also done my best to research my subject and to present what I know about him in as truthful a manner as I know how. This story is true, and from start to finish, the telling of this tale is aimed at making Dowell and his God more accessible. One of the ways we learn and grow is by reflecting on those who have gone before us. And I believe W. E. Dowell's story reveals what God can do in the lives of real people— ordinary people—if we will simply remain close to Him. That, dear reader, is a valuable lesson. May we learn it well.

Acknowledgments

I am indebted to the many friends and family members who contributed personal reflections to help make this book a reality. Many of their names are scattered throughout this text. Although several of those individuals are now in Heaven, their kindnesses have not been forgotten. My dear grandmother, Nola Dowell, though she has been gone many years, has remained a constant helper in this project because of her meticulous recordkeeping.

I also received gracious assistance from the Southern Baptist Historical Library and Archives in Nashville, TN, from the G. B. Vick Memorial Library on the campus of Baptist Bible College in Springfield, Missouri, and from the staff of the *Baptist Bible Tribune*.

I am likewise grateful for the warm encouragement that I received from my pastor, Mark Rounsaville, and for the access he gave me to my grandfather's sermon recordings at Baptist Temple. Pastor and author David R. Stokes helped me further, offering some much-needed publishing advice.

Above all, I must acknowledge my wife, Robin, and my parents, Bill and Joan Dowell, for their many contributions and for their assistance in editing the text. Their unwavering support and encouragement—together with the love of our three children, Matt, Nicole, and Isaac—have always meant the world to me.

PART 1: DAYBREAK

Chapter 1: *Albin*

Nothin' but sky.

In every direction the sprawling landscape ended in a brassy sky. The farmer huffed as he walked. In Coleman County, Texas, July's endless days and cloudless canopy give the adjective *breathtaking* a double edge. Stroll out under that sky long enough and its coppery bowl might just clamp down on top of you.

Suffocatin'.

The farmer sighed. The sun's rays were carefully baking the grassy plains and dirt roads of Central Texas. The farmer took a red handkerchief to his brow as he made his way out of an emerald field and onto one of those roads.

Gonna be a good year for cotton, though. Maybe one of the best.

Then he chuckled.

Better be. Got another mouth to feed.

Albin pulled the rag to the other side of his face as he started down the road. His walk was more of a lumber, but he added gracefulness to the movement by whistling a hymn in cadence with his stride. He was doing his best to ignore the heat. Some folks might have cursed the discomfort, but Albin never could. Glancing up at the sun, he said cheerfully:

"The heavens declare the glory of God."[1]

This farmer might utter the scriptures aloud anytime an apt passage crossed his mind. And this happened often. Farming was a necessity for Albin—a way of life—but it was not his life. He had what the neighbors down the road may have referred to as a "higher calling." That, of course, meant that he was a man of God, or more specifically, a Southern Baptist preacher.

Albin's specialty was taking charge of the tiny churches scattered throughout rural Texas, particularly those that were facing some sort of difficulty. He would come in, resolve the problems, build up the congregation, and then turn the church over to a permanent pastor and move on to the next location. He also engaged in extensive evangelistic endeavors, conducting frequent revival meetings in nearby towns. It was meaningful work, though Albin knew it was not the easiest life for his wife Lizzie and their nine—or we should say, now, ten—children.

The thought of having ten children made this farmer whistle through his teeth.
Ten mouths to feed. Have to get used to the sound of that.

The last of Albin's children had arrived earlier this same day, and the proud father's heart was full of rejoicing, though a casual observer might not have noticed. Albin was an even-tempered man by nature. Still, the farmer silently celebrated his son's birth as he marched toward his unpainted farmhouse. Albin could not help but thank his God for this blessing, and as he did, some of his other blessings came into view. The youngest ones were chasing one another around the yard. A family dog studied the children from the shade of the front porch, and Albin likewise drank in this sight. Nine-year-old Ruth, the fifth child in the family, was mothering the young brood around her. She served as the dividing line between the older siblings in the family and the littlest ones. Ruth's three older brothers were occupied with farm chores elsewhere. And fifteen-year-old Bertha—the only daughter in the family older than Ruth—was indoors tending to the needs of the new baby, their mother, and the busy family kitchen. So naturally Ruth played mother to the ones that remained.

Albin loved them all, every last member of the clan. They had a good life together. The Dowell family never had much money, and they never lived in any one place more than five years, but even so, there remained an innocent happiness in their meager and rootless existence. The children of this family belonged to what Tom Brokaw would later dub "the greatest generation."[2] And who could disagree? Their generation overcame much more adversity than most of us will ever see. Albin and Lizzie's tenth child started life near the beginning of the First World War. He would marry and start his family at the height of the Great Depression, and he would be twenty-seven years old when his country entered the Second World War. And this says nothing of the personal battles he would experience. Hardships lay ahead of all of these children. Yet for them, such things seem to have been a recipe for courage, tenacity, faith—all the foods that make a generation exceptional.

William Edgar.

As Albin approached the yard, he tried out the name that he and Lizzie had attached to their newborn. Like the names of some of their other children, *William* was a family name. It had previously belonged to one of Albin's uncles, one of his cousins, and even one of his brothers—a boy who died in infancy.

Yessir, I think the name William is gonna do real good. Or I should say—do well.

Albin grinned out of one side of his mouth and relished his pun. The farmer's surname was pronounced like the name of a dowel rod, but folks unfamiliar with the pronunciation often turned it into "do well" or "dole" or something else. The family learned to embrace these blunders.

Albin wiped his brow again, concluding that the summer heat would serve as an annual reminder of his youngest son's birthday. He gave the date added weight by pronouncing it aloud:

July the eighth, nineteen hundred and fourteen.

This child would be the last of Albin and Lizzie's offspring. To put it in biblical terms, their quiver was full.[3] The next youngest in the family was Gladys. She was just two and a half years old. Then there were two boys, Albin Theodore and Joe. After them came Eunice, who was a year younger than Ruth. But this pack of playmates did not give their father so much as a glance as he strutted across their play-filled yard, a fact that he could not fail to notice.

Isn't that somethin'?

The children's inattention left Albin more amused than offended, yet he instinctively noted a spiritual application.

Don't you know the children of God get jus' that same way many a time? The Father comes and goes, and not a one of 'em looks up to see what He's about.

Albin filed this sermon illustration in the back of his mind as he climbed into the shade of his front porch. He stopped next to a pair of sleeping cats, and with his damp handkerchief, he began to scrape some of the soil off his hands.

Well, it's Wednesdee. Better be gettin' ready for prayer meetin'.

It went without saying that Lizzie would not be attending that meeting. She and the baby needed their rest. Albin could have used a little rest himself, but there was not much hope of that.

Must be about my Father's business.

The preacher sighed and stepped through the screen door. As he did, he turned for one more glimpse of his little ones out under that Texas sky. He marveled once again over the number of arrows now in his quiver.

Ten of 'em—just like ol' Job in the Bible.

Albin chuckled at this, thinking it best not to take the analogy too far. Instead, he reminded himself matter-of-factly:

Well ol' Job, he was mighty blessed.

A baby's cry was now ringing out from a back room. The sound of that tenth arrow brought a bright smile to the preacher's face.

We'll surely have a pile of blessings to praise God for down at the prayer meetin' tonight, now, won't we?

Like so many preachers of bygone eras—D. L. Moody, R. A. Torrey, and others—Albin McLinic Dowell was known to most folks only by his initials. He was Reverend A. M. Dowell. He and his family were living at a place called Red Bank when this tenth child was born. Red Bank was southwest of Dallas, some fifteen miles south of Brownwood—in other words, the middle of nowhere.

But Albin did not stay there or anywhere else very long. Too many churches needed his care. During his thirty-five year career as a pastor, A. M. Dowell ministered at Voss, Gouldbusk, Liberty, Brown Ranch, Vega, Wildorado, Bushland—a host of places that few people have ever heard of. One of his largest congregations was at Macon, Texas, east of Dallas. Then at a place called Cleo, he launched a new church. That congregation later disbanded, however.[4]

Little else about the life and work of Albin Dowell is of much consequence. He was respected but never famous. In many ways he lived the same humble life that his parents had lived. His father, Louis Marion Dowell, had likewise worked as a migrant minister-farmer. Marion, as he was known to contemporaries, began his life in Tennessee, yet his preaching ministry spread across Missouri, Arkansas, and eventually, East Texas.

Marion's decision to enter the gospel ministry left an important mark on this family tree. The decision came during a distinctly transformational time in US history, the period known as the Reconstruction. Like the rest of America, the Dowell family was then picking up the pieces after the Civil War, coping with their losses but also carving a new path toward the future. Marion had been a resident of central Missouri when the war broke out. Then in 1863 he left to serve the Union Army alongside two of his brothers. He and his Arkansas bride, Eliza, had been married just two years when he bid her farewell to join Company C of the Eighth Regiment of the Missouri Volunteer Cavalry. Interestingly, this regiment was "[o]rganized at Springfield, Mo,"[5] a city that would one day hold great significance for his Texas-born grandson, William.

Of greater importance to Marion's generation, however, was the fact that in 1863, the same year he enlisted, the Eighth Regiment took part in the victorious capture of Little Rock.[6] This was a landmark victory for Union forces, yet Marion paid a very personal price for it. Among the 382 men lost to this regiment was Marion's older brother, John Dowell. He had contracted German measles at Little Rock, and at his own request, was discharged to die at home.[7] The disease took him just a week after he reached Missouri. Two weeks after that, John's wife also fell to the illness. Marion and Eliza became the adoptive parents of the couple's two surviving children, James and Mary Ann.

Marion himself was discharged from the army in July 1865. He was just twenty-four years old when he returned to Missouri from Little Rock. His discharge papers indicate he was five feet, ten and a half inches tall, and had a dark complexion. Yet this cursory description reveals little about the man that Marion was becoming. War had changed this rugged young soldier's life forever, not only because of his wartime experiences but also because of the readymade family that awaited him after his discharge.

Yet further changes lay ahead. In November 1866, just a year and a half after Marion came home, Eliza gave birth to the couple's first child, Rosetta Deborah. Near the time of Rosetta's birth, Marion seems to have reached a spiritual crossroads. Though few details have been preserved, family records show that the same month his daughter was born, Marion "united with the Baptist Church by baptism."[8] Then, just a few months after his baptism, Eliza too united "with the Baptist Church August 1867 by baptism."[9] Suddenly the Dowell family was headed in a new direction. As one family member put it, they were now traveling the "pilgrimage road."[10]

A further development in Marion and Eliza's journey occurred in 1873. It was then that Marion announced he had been called by God to become a preacher of the gospel. Apparently the news came as a surprise to some in the family. A letter sent from Marion's older brother James is laced with plenty of skepticism:

> Well Marion you stated in your letter you had turned out trying to preach. That is a good work to engage in if you feel it is your duty to do so and feel competent to accomplish any good by it. I will say I wish you the best of success. And I hope

*that you may improve rapidly by applying yourself properly and that the time may
come when you may be able to do honor to your self and to the cause of religion.
But I fear unless you are well gifted that your education is too limited to succeed
very well.*[11]

Marion managed to set aside such cautions, it seems, for family records indicate
that he was licensed to preach at the Mount Zion Baptist Church in Jamestown,
Missouri, in 1873. And he never abandoned that calling. No longer were the Dowells
merely traveling the pilgrimage road. Now they were leading others down that same
path.

In 1875, Marion moved his family by covered wagon to East Texas. Albin, who had
been born in Moniteau County, Missouri, was just four years of age. Though the exact
circumstances prompting the family to make this move are unknown, the Dowell family
resettled in Madison County, Texas, where Marion purchased a farm with funds from
his Civil War pension.[12] He also established himself as a full-fledged minister of the
gospel, receiving ordination at the Kickapoo Missionary Baptist Church of Madison
County in 1876.[13]

Thus began Marion and Eliza's spiritual pilgrimage, a trek that would have a
remarkable influence on the destinies of their descendants. In fact, of the eleven
children this couple produced—six girls and five boys—three followed their patriarch into
ministry. Others served and followed the Lord in other ways. Grandchildren, great
grandchildren, and even great-great grandchildren have been similarly impacted. Marion
and Eliza's faith put this family on a new trajectory. And though they could not have
foreseen the significance of their decisions, this couple's simple obedience to God's call
set off a chain of events that would have eternal implications.

That's right, son. G'on, now.

As Marion's grandson William wailed in the back room, Albin stood smiling at the
screen door and calling scriptures to mind. He could not help himself, for the Bible was
second nature to him. With a grin, he spouted the words that his mind had
involuntarily summoned up:

"Cry aloud, spare not—"[14]

The irony of this phrase from Isaiah 58 made Albin chuckle.

Perhaps that'll be the text of this evenin's message.

The farmer now sat on a wooden bench next to the front door and started
removing his boots. Though Albin had an excellent grasp of scripture, he himself was
still relatively new to the clergy. He had not been licensed to preach until 1909, just five
years before William's birth. Then in 1910, he was ordained into ministry at the
Pilgrim's Rest Baptist Church in Coleman County.[15] By then, this farmer was already in
midlife—close to forty years old—and he was the father of eight children. He was also
living more than two hundred miles away from Marion's East Texas homestead. Had
God summoned Albin late in life? Or had this man, like Jonah, struck out on his own
in an attempt to escape God's call? The only thing that can be said with certainty is that,
up until 1909, Albin Dowell forged a life devoted to farming, not ministry.

But then in the first decade of the twentieth century, Albin's own pilgrimage road took a new turn. Circumstances surrounding his entry into the ministry have passed out of memory, but we do know that his father, Marion, died in 1904. That news came to Albin from East Texas, a town called Normangee back in Madison County. Did the end of Marion's life help usher Albin to his own spiritual crossroads? Was this son somehow inspired to take up his father's mantle? It is difficult to say. But whatever the case, within a few years, A. M. Dowell had shifted his focus from farming to preaching. And when he did, he seems to have made what the Baptists call "a full and complete surrender."[16] Or to borrow a biblical image, he put his hand to the plow and never looked back.[17] Though Albin continued to farm throughout his life, he was now a preacher of the gospel above all else.

Albin was still relishing the sound of William's cry as he rested his bare feet on the floor of his farmhouse. He chuckled again at that verse in Isaiah:

Yes, sir. You just go right on. So says the scripture, "Lift up thy voice like a trumpet."[18]

The late afternoon sunlight was pouring over the threshold to soothe Albin's toes, and the farmer-preacher leaned his head up against the wall to soak up this and other blessings. If, in that moment, Albin speculated about what lay ahead, he probably underestimated the extent of the Lord's goodness. God would grant him thirty-one more years to proclaim the gospel message and to light the way for others on the pilgrimage road. In fact, young William would be among those fellow travelers. But William would not merely be guided by his father's light. Like the sun-fed cotton crops in Albin's fields, he would be nourished daily under his father's glow. Albin Dowell's example would instill in this child a hunger for the scripture, a passion to live by faith, and perhaps most obvious, a zeal to preach the truth to others. One day soon, just as Albin and Marion had done in their generations, this boy, William, would rise up and answer the call of God upon his own life. And when that day finally came, he would harness the power of his voice to do exactly what he was born to do—cry aloud and spare not.

Chapter 2: *Lizzie*

*L*ooky there.

It was the middle of the night, well past one o'clock. Unlike the others in her household, Elizabeth Artie Dowell—Lizzie, as they called her—was wide awake. Her tenth child was just a day and a half old, and he was resting in a cradle a few steps away from her bed. Lizzie had slipped out of bed and crawled across the floor to her child's side. Now she was staring into his face.

Sleepin' away.

The baby gurgled, and the farmer's wife bit her lower lip to stifle a laugh.

Sweet thang.

He opened one eye a bit.

Well, hello there, William.

In later life, this child would be known as Bill, even to his mother, but for the moment he was still tiny enough to be thought of as William. Lizzie rested a hand on his forehead to help him go back to sleep.

People in Lizzie's community knew her as "Mother Dowell,"[1] and certainly she was that. Her daughter Gladys remembered her as "a good housekeeper." Bill raved that she was "one of the finest cooks I ever saw." He added, "My mother made the best sausage."[2] Yet there was much more to Lizzie's mothering than cleaning and cooking. She was the family's nurturer, a kind and gentle caregiver.

Lizzie was not at all what one would assume judging from her outer shell. In an 1890s portrait with Albin and their firstborn, Ernest, Mother Dowell appears quite stern. All three of the subjects in this photograph wear on their faces the familiar solemnity that characterizes most nineteenth-century portraits. Since early cameras required long exposure times, subjects found it easier to remain motionless if they did not smile. Even so, as Lizzie stands beside her seated husband, one hand on his shoulder, her expression seems inordinately grim. Albin's presence is notably warmer. He is the dominant figure in the composition, both in size and in personality. His broad mustache and knee-high boots lend the farmer a mountain man's ruggedness. But he is also interesting and inviting. There is a marked tenderness emanating from his eyes. He is both solemn and approachable.

Lizzie, by contrast, has a look that is off-putting. She is the image of plainness. She wears that floor-length skirt that we have come to associate with prairie wives. There are no signs of jewelry about her, and her face is equally unadorned. The corners of her mouth are permanently downturned. Adding to the unpleasantness is the fact that Lizzie's hair has been pulled tightly to the top of her head, exposing a large set of ears—the same ears that each of her children, including William, would eventually inherit from her.

On Lizzie, however, these unflattering traits accentuated an innate awkwardness in front of a camera. Nothing could have felt less natural to this woman than to be the object of such unwanted attention. Lizzie's youngest son often employed the word *humble* when he described his mother, and the term seems strikingly well suited to the woman standing in the portrait. Dowell said his mother never ate at a restaurant, not only because she was poor but also because she would have been too embarrassed to have somebody else serve her. Even in later life, Lizzie Dowell was marked by a timid self-consciousness. In a 1943 letter to her son, Lizzie struggled to express herself saying, "excuse this writing I am neverous maby you can read it [sic]."[3] It seems clear, then, that the stoic face that Lizzie wears in her family portrait was not the mark of sternness. Instead, it was a mark of diffidence. Though Mother Dowell was a consummate nurturer, she lacked confidence. Her own great worth was incomprehensible to her.

Mama's going to take real good care of you, William.

Across the room from William's cradle, Albin was sleeping in the couple's high bed. The busyness of the week had finally caught up with him, and he was slumbering soundly. A little too soundly, Lizzie thought. Tucking the baby's blanket around her sleeping child, Lizzie said:

Not sure how you can sleep at all, your daddy snorin' so awful.

Albin suddenly snorted, and Lizzie shot a sour look at the noisemaker. But Albin was not the least bit perturbed by her glance. After another snort, the mother took a more direct approach:

Pipe down over there!

Her hoarse reprimand was enough to rouse the sleeping giant momentarily—just enough to interrupt his snoring. Then, after the noise subsided, Lizzie returned her attention to the cradle.

Mother Dowell was no pushover when it came to her children. This normally reserved woman had an instinctive assertiveness when it came to the wellbeing of her little ones, and there was nothing she would not do for them. "I've seen her save up all year to buy herself a coat that she needed so bad, and ended up buying me a little suit and some other things that I needed," her youngest son recalled.[4]

One of Dowell's earliest memories was a day when he and his mother were walking across a field—"coming home from an errand we'd run." Dowell shared this recollection with his mother years later, and she was amazed that he had any memory of it. "She swears I was just two and a half years old," he said. But the memory was vivid. "Suddenly we were attacked by a great big ol' hawk. He was crippled and that made him defensive, and so he fought us. Tried to." The frightened young boy would never forget what happened next. Lizzie snatched up a stick lying nearby, and before her son's eyes, she bludgeoned the life out of that aggressive hawk.[5]

This mother's watchful care of her young ones also included firm and steady discipline. Though she was a tiny woman, Lizzie demonstrated great skill in her use of the peach tree switch. Both Dowell and his sister Gladys confessed to receiving "a lot of spankings" from her.[6] Dowell recalled, "One time she got a little excited, I guess. I guess I agitated her quite a little bit, and she was whipping me until her hand got away from her and she caught me around the neck. And that little ol' keen peach tree switch just raised a clear blister around my neck." Even as Dowell chuckled over the memory, pity entered into his voice when he described his mother's remorse: "And she was so sorry about that."[7]

The Dowell home was a thoroughly loving place, yet Albin and Lizzie had high expectations. They kept a tight rein on the children, their son said, and good behavior was a must. "You got home by a certain time at night. You let them know where you are and where you're going. All those things. They kept tabs on the kids."[8]

Lizzie's bedroom had grown quiet.

See there? You and yer daddy is both sleepin' good now.

Kneeling next to her infant child, Mother Dowell noticed for the first time just how much the baby and the slumbering father resembled one another. This observation softened that natural frown on her face, for Lizzie loved both of these men. And time would prove that the father and son shared many qualities. Indeed, Dowell's own description of Albin seems equally applicable to himself. "He had a sense of humor," the younger Dowell said, "but he was an extremely serious man."[9] Albin, like his son, was no stick-in-the-mud. He enjoyed many seasons of fun and laughter with his family. The younger Dowell recalled his father's warm presence at holiday gatherings, in particular. One family photograph shows Albin dressed in a suit and tie while playfully poised atop a riding toy—a child-sized tractor. This was the man that youngsters like William were so easily drawn to.

Such frivolities notwithstanding, it is clear that Albin Dowell devoted most of his time to earnest pursuits. This preacher had a sense of purpose, and he resisted idleness. He was diligent and determined in his ministry, ever mindful of accomplishing the Lord's work. In this, too, the son bore the father's likeness. Albin did not retire from pastoring until two years before his death, yet even then he remained hard at work. A short time after Albin's retirement, Lizzie wrote a letter to their son, describing how his father was spending his seventy-second birthday: "We have moved our house 4 blocks north the church we surely proud. . . . Will build a room across the back of house and have a bath room and toilet. . . . Albin is diging the ditch for the water pipe and don't have time to write."[10]

This was ever the case. Rest, relaxation, family time—these had to be eked out of Albin's never-ending work schedule. Even so, his diligence was never a cause for resentment. Lizzie and her children remained deeply loyal to Albin, mindful of the love that motivated his work. More than that, they valued the work itself. Young William grew up with many fond memories of accompanying Albin to revival meetings, experiences that helped him gain an appreciation for his father's "serious" side. Albin brought to every situation a commanding presence, Bill recalled, an aura of passion and intensity. And these qualities, perhaps even more than Albin's playfulness, won the boy's deep admiration:

> *I remember I went with him to a church—I don't remember where it was—and he was holding a meeting, of course. I was just a small boy at that time, but I was old enough to know and understand things. But two men, as they went out the church, . . . got on the outs with each other and they started fighting, and I remember my big dad as he stepped up and just walked right up between 'em and pushed 'em. And I thought, "Boy, what a dad. What a dad." And then they made up and got right with the Lord and went on their way.*[11]

Dowell respected his father's work in the ministry, and in many ways he benefitted from it. Yet he acknowledged that he and his family sacrificed much for the Lord's work. He remembered, in particular, the burden that Albin's busy schedule placed upon his mother. Evangelistic meetings took Albin away from the family for weeks at a time, and in those times, Lizzie was left to manage things at home. She often had to face the challenges of farming and parenting alone. The weight of that responsibility made Dowell's mother more stoop-shouldered with each passing year, he said.

Albin's absences also had another effect. Since Lizzie did most of the parenting, she loomed larger and larger as an influence in her youngest son's life. She became his stabilizing force—and a very good one. "My mother was the one that I always went to when I needed some comfort," her son said. In his eyes, Lizzie's manner, spirit, and overwhelming presence in his life elevated her to a status that approached sainthood. In his adult life, Lizzie's son commonly described her as "an angel." "If she ever did anything wrong," he said, "I didn't see it. I know she did, but she was one of the most saintliest women."[12]

Dowell's most enduring memory of his mother seems modeled after the "virtuous woman" that is pictured in Proverbs 31. "I have vivid memories," he said, "of her doing chores like churning for butter and things like that, and just singing up a storm. She wasn't a singer. You couldn't have forced her to sing a solo, but she would sing around the house—'What a Friend We Have in Jesus' and all those great old hymns."[13]

The infant in front of Lizzie stirred a bit, and she soothed him by placing her hand upon his chest. Perhaps it was then that William first heard his mother sing those familiar lyrics:

What a friend we have in Jesus,
All our sins and griefs to bear.
What a privilege to carry
Everything to God in prayer!
O what peace we often forfeit,
O what needless pain we bear. . . .

As Lizzie stroked William's tiny body, the child's outstretched hands balled up into fists and then seemed to relax. Lizzie suspended her song when she sensed that the baby had been adequately comforted. Now the room was quiet again, and Lizzie filled the silence with a conversation that only she could hear. She spoke to the unseen Friend that had been referenced in her song:

You made a fine one this time, Lord. Fine as they come.

Lizzie spied a twitching in her baby's right hand.

And he's strong, too!

These words made William smile—or so the mother pretended. She teased her son for eavesdropping on a private prayer:

And, Lord, you oughta hear that stinker bellow. Why, I don't believe I have ever heard such a racket.

Lizzie shared a laugh with her God. Then she said with a smile:

Yes, Lord, I'd say he's gonna have a voice just like his daddy.

The baby squirmed a bit when she said this, and without a thought, Mother Dowell adjusted the blanket that was covering him. She then pacified the infant with the last lines of her song:

All because we do not carry
Everything to God in prayer.

This was just how it went with Lizzie. Spirituality was intertwined with the mundane. God went with her through every moment of her life, the ordinary as well as the sublime. And the Lord was as real to Lizzie as the infant lying in front of her. As William grew up, this deep faith affected him. It introduced him to a genuine intimacy with His Creator. Just as Albin's hard work and dedication inspired zeal, Lizzie's heart for the Lord exposed young William to the kind of sweet fellowship that is possible only between a redeemed child and a Heavenly Father.

Lord—

Lizzie's voice now broke the silence. She prayed with the same boldness that she would later exhibit in that fight against the hawk. One had to wonder if it was through prayer that she had learned the kind of fearlessness that was necessary to protect and discipline ten children.

I asked you for a baby boy, and you gave him to me. Thank you.

Lizzie's words were clear and direct. There was no lack of confidence in Mother Dowell now. Never had a mother's thanksgiving sounded more purposeful. But then again, this was not merely a prayer of thanksgiving. It was also a prayer of commitment.

Now, I want to give him back to you.

This was the real reason Lizzie Dowell had come to the cradle.

If it be your will, Lord, I ask that you make him a preacher.

Lizzie had come to make an offering, so with those words, she presented her tenth child to the Lord. A proper Baptist tithe was paid, one might say. Just as Hannah had once done with the prophet Samuel, Lizzie was now giving her infant son into the Lord's service.

Amen.

Mother Dowell died thirty-one years after she prayed that prayer. During her funeral service in Dimmit, Texas, the officiating minister related the story of Lizzie's late-night visit to the cradle. Lizzie had confided the story to her minister, but until the day of her funeral, none of the Dowell children had ever heard it. Dowell himself took a particular interest in the tale, though he found the minister's telling of the story a bit unsatisfying. The preacher did not say which son Lizzie had prayed over, only that it was "one of her sons."[14] In one of his own sermons, Dowell later recalled his reaction to the minister's remark. "This stirred a tremendous curiosity in my mind," he said, "because I had two brothers that were preachers, too." Indeed, three of the family's six boys—Ernest, Joe, and Bill—all followed their father and grandfather into the ministry. So after the funeral concluded, Dowell felt compelled to approach the minister. "I could not refrain from it," Dowell told his audience. "After the graveside service was over, I went up to this preacher and I said, 'Are you free to tell me who that baby was?'" Dowell's strong voice then quivered as he described the minister's reply: "He slipped his arm around my shoulder and he said, 'Bill, it was you.'"[15]

The youngest Dowell was a man in his early thirties when both parents finished their time on Earth. Albin died in the spring of 1945; Lizzie's death came just nine months later. By that time Dowell was already pastoring his sixth and largest church. Yet even so, the loss of his parents seems to have been a pivotal moment for him. Many of his greatest achievements occurred after their deaths, and it may be that the experience of parting with Albin and Lizzie helped spur him on to such victories. Throughout his life, Dowell attributed the blessings that he experienced to his parents' influence. "There's been a good many times," he told one congregation, "when I've reached a place where I almost felt that the sky was made out of brass and I wasn't getting through. And I cried out and said, 'Oh God, if you can't hear me, please hear my mother's prayer. She gave me to you when I was born.'"[16]

An article written soon after Albin's death captures the feelings that Dowell had toward his parents. "Mother and Dad were reading through the Bible in their evening devotions, when death separated them," the article states. "I am so thankful I was reared in that kind of a home."[17] But Dowell's response went beyond thanksgiving. Just as Lizzie's grateful heart had once prompted her to present a late-night offering to the Lord, Dowell's appreciation for his parents' influence now urged him to honor their memory by recommitting himself to the Lord's work. He published an account of that recommitment in his church's newspaper:

> Dad believed the Bible and had no patience with those who compromised its precious truths. His admonition to me was constantly, "Bill, preach the Word."
> As I stood in the First Baptist Church of Dimmitt, Texas that day and looked upon his face for the last time until the morning of the resurrection, it seemed that his mantle fell upon me, and I could hear him speak again, "Bill preach the Word." I bowed my head and from the deepest sincerity of my heart I promised God and him that I would continue to hold the blood-stained banner of

Jesus Christ high until I, too, shall hear the welcome voice of the Savior say "Come up higher."[18]

Albin and Lizzie Dowell would have been proud to hear their son express such a commitment. More than that, they would have delighted to see him fulfill the promise. And this he did—faithfully—for the remainder of his long and fruitful life. But of course, a man of God can never begin his life as a man. First, he must experience this world as a boy.

Chapter 3: *Boy in the Outhouse*

A teenage farm boy sat on the edge of a bed, pulling on a pair of boots. Even as he did, he nudged his much younger brother. The toddler was still fast asleep.

Git up, Bill'ards.

This was the nickname with which Louis Dowell jibed his youngest sibling throughout childhood. These two brothers enjoyed a special bond, Dowell said, because Louis always paid considerable attention to him. They especially loved to laugh together. "He was always pulling jokes on me," the younger brother noted.[1]

This day was no different. Louis pounced on an empty spot on the bed, the spot normally occupied by Bill's slightly older brother, Joe.

Looky here. Joe's already up and sittin' at the table. You gonna let him eat your eggs?

Louis bounced up and down on the mattress, working hard to shake Bill from his slumber, but to no avail. The boy peeked through his eyelids yet stubbornly refused to budge.

Dowell had fond memories of all his siblings. The older ones were like surrogate parents, he said, and the younger ones were like playmates. Bill, Joe, and Gladys were all close in age, so these three, in particular, shared many good times. The fact that they had similar personalities and interests added to their closeness. With Joe, Bill shared not only a boyhood bed but also a talent for singing and eventually a knack for public speaking. Joe traveled with a gospel quartet as an adult, and like his younger brother, he also served as a preacher. Gladys, on the other hand, shared Bill's love of sports, perhaps even more so than Joe. Even she admitted that she had been something of a tomboy growing up. "My sisters," Gladys confessed, "they'd be in the house crocheting and quilting and stuff like that, but I didn't like to do things like that. I wanted to be out playing ball."[2]

Though Dowell lived apart from his siblings throughout most of his adult life, he never missed an opportunity to visit these family members whenever he was passing through the regions where they lived. His siblings also came to visit him, and they communicated with each other through letters and telephone calls as well. Dowell believed his family's blood ties were made stronger by the spiritual bond they all shared. He once wrote to his sister Ruth, saying, "We have been very fortunate as a family. All of our brothers and sisters have been Christians and our mother and dad."[3]

But Dowell made no pretense about his family's sinless perfection. Despite their Christian upbringing, the Dowell family's children behaved—and misbehaved—just like the children in any other household. With a Cheshire cat's grin, Dowell recalled that, in his early life, Joe and Gladys were not merely his principal playmates, they were also his chief antagonists. He admitted that rivalries developed among them, making each one eager to get the others into trouble. In a joint interview with Gladys, Dowell said, "We'd do anything to get something on the other one."[4] Gladys countered, saying the mischief was a little more one-sided from her perspective. "Sometimes he'd make up a story and tell it just to get me," she said, pointing an accusing finger at her younger brother.[5]

Hey, Bill'ards! You listenin' to me?

Louis jabbed the sleeping boy's ribs.

Better not let Lester catch you sacked out like that.

Lester was the second oldest son in this family, the one between Ernest and Louis. As an adult, Lester became a wheat farmer and a deacon in the Baptist church. He was also a family man. He was the sibling who cared for Albin and Lizzie during their last days. This special care for his family was evident even during Bill's boyhood. After their oldest brother, Ernest, married and entered the ministry, Lester became the de facto man of the house whenever Albin was away. For Bill, who was only two years old when Ernest married, Lester became like a second father. "He'd discipline me," Dowell said. "I'd go out with him or something, working, and I'd do something wrong—Brother, he'd discipline me. He'd spank me. Now I took it from him just like I would my parents 'cause I looked up to him so much."[6]

Louis began to tease.

Ohhhh, is that Lester I hear comin'?

Young Bill rubbed his eyes.

Ohhhh, Bill'ards. You're in for it now.

The boy suddenly shot up in the bed.

Louis beamed, delighted that he had successfully roused the boy. He picked up his straw hat off the floor and bounced toward the door, saying:

Better git out of that bed. Cotton's not gonna pick itself, y'know.

Then to finish the ruse, Louis leaned out of the doorway and called down the hall:

Isn't that right, Lester?

Young Bill instantly darted out of bed and scuttled across the floor to the hallway. But when he peered down the corridor, he found that Lester was nowhere in sight. Louis then cackled at the youngster's gullibility, and with that, the lanky tormenter ran down the hall. Bill stood in a daze. He might have been more agitated over the ruse had a more pressing matter not grabbed his attention. In fact, part of him was glad that Louis's remark *had* been a hoax. At least now, the boy thought to himself, he could make a detour to the family outhouse on his way to the breakfast table.

Breakfast came early in the Dowell household, especially at harvest time. Although Albin's farms were never large, there was always plenty of work to do. Everyone in the family pitched in at harvest. "We'd get up before daybreak," Dowell recalled. "We'd eat our breakfast and go out and pick a sack full of cotton. Have to strike a match to weigh it just about."[7] It was not uncommon for Albin to hire Mexicans to help with the work, but the children of the family also assisted. The youngest children—Joe, Gladys, and Bill—had the job of picking the largest cotton blossoms, since these blossoms were somewhat easier for their tiny fingers to grasp.

Bill was a regular part of the family's labor force from his earliest days. He recalled participating in the full gamut of farm duties, everything from shucking corn to tending the animals. "We had horses and cows. Sometimes we'd have sheep. There was a lot of chickens," he said. "After I grew up, I did most of the plowing and planting."[8] Even years after he had entered adult life, Dowell could give a detailed description of his boyhood plowing implement: "I had a little sweep on a plow that went ahead of a planter and opened up a furrow and then the planter dropped the seed into the furrow. Then I had two little sweeps behind that went along behind and covered up the furrow."[9] The long days spent behind that plow and a team of mules were likewise never forgotten, Dowell said.

But Dowell admitted that not all of his boyhood days were so arduous. When the farm work was completed, Bill and his siblings frequently joined their friends at a nearby swimming hole. Dowell remembered "baptizing" other boys as part of this water sport, one evidence of the kind of influence that his family's culture was having upon him. On weekends, in addition to regular church attendance, Bill might take in a western film at the local theatre or attend a nearby party. On the subject of these parties, Dowell was quick to note, "They didn't dance, but they played party games."[10] This was the preacher's not-so-subtle way of clarifying that his boyhood social events were of the wholesome, Baptist variety.

Intermixed with such unexceptional life experiences, Dowell said, were some boyhood moments that held greater significance. Indeed, these were the moments that helped this youngster come to terms with a matter that many children never consider: human mortality. One such moment occurred while Dowell was coming home from one of those weekend social gatherings with his friends. He and another boy had gone to the party on horseback because the event was being held several miles from their homes. The boys reached their destination without incident, but on the way back, they foolishly decided to engage in a moonlit horserace. "What we didn't know," Dowell explained, "is that two or three days before, the rain had washed out part of the road."[11] As soon as the riders reached that washed-out section of their darkened route, their horses stumbled, sending both boys flying onto the ground. Dowell landed on his left ear and was knocked unconscious for several minutes. Then when he awoke, he suffered from amnesia, he said, and was unable to tell his friend even who he was or where he lived. The other boy, who was in better shape, managed to help Bill back to his horse. And fortunately, the amnesia dissipated by the time the boys reached the Dowells' home. Even so, Bill knew that he had narrowly escaped a serious injury, perhaps even death.

Death was a topic that Dowell heard about often during his early life. The death of his grandmother Eliza, Albin's mother, occurred when he was just nine years old. Then there was an earlier experience, when Bill was just four years old, that left a profound impression. The Dowell family was living in Dallas at that time, and though the youngest Dowell retained few memories about the episode, he did recall the basic facts. His eight-year-old brother, Albin Theodore, became seriously ill, and sadly, the boy did not recover. Albin and Lizzie's ten children were suddenly reduced to nine. Dowell remembered seeing his brother's lifeless body as it lay in repose in the family's living room. A great sense of loss came over him, he said, as he stood there studying the corpse. He went on to confess that this feeling never left him.

No doubt Albin Theodore's death was still fresh on everyone's mind when Bill was himself stricken with a boyhood illness. Dowell said he became bedfast after contracting this sickness from a banana that he ate. "It just wrecked my body," he said. "I battled that thing for close to six weeks. I decided I could get up one day. I was feeling better and decided I'd get up. I didn't stop to think what happens to you in six weeks." Dowell said his body had lost the strength to walk. "I tried to walk and I fell flat on my face," he said. "Took me a little while to learn how."[12]

Dowell recovered from that illness with a fresh appreciation for life's fragility. Though he was yet a boy, he was beginning to grasp the fact that man's days upon the earth are numbered. The scriptural warning that "it is appointed unto men once to die" became a lesson that young Bill could not escape.[13] Indeed, he heard some version of it almost every time he entered the doors of the church. "I remember back during World War I," Dowell recounted in one of his sermons. "I was young then, but . . . I heard many a preacher say from the pulpit that they weren't sure but what this wasn't the Battle of Armageddon."[14] For Bill, every sermon seemed to be a reminder that life on earth would one day come to an end. And though this child did not consider such things deeply, much of his boyhood was spent absorbing the reality of death.

In 1924, Bill, now age ten, engaged in an important conversation with his brother Ernest about what comes after death. Ernest, the oldest Dowell child, was a devout young man who had followed their father into ministry. In fact, Ernest was conducting a joint revival with Albin that same week. This revival was held at a church just west of Canyon, Texas, where Dowell's family was then living. And during the course of those meetings, the young evangelist became concerned—"burdened," as the Baptists like to say—for his ten-year-old brother. Ernest knew that this child had not yet received Christ as savior.

Upon returning from his revival meeting one afternoon, Ernest decided to approach Bill about his spiritual condition. He found him playing in the back yard of the Dowells' farm house.[15] "Bill," Ernest began, "have you ever thought about your need of Christ?"

The child replied frankly, "No, Ernest, I haven't exactly."

This response was a sincere one. Although Bill had grown up under his father's preaching and had experienced several brushes with death, he had never yet given serious consideration to the state of his own soul. Yet Ernest's question changed all of that. "He said, 'Christ loves you and wants to save you,'" Dowell recalled.[16]

This conversation was brief but meaningful. Ernest did not urge or cajole, Dowell said. Nor did he need to. After all, Bill had grown up under the sound of biblical preaching. He was well acquainted with the Bible's teachings on the subjects of sin, judgment, and salvation. Bill had heard many times the message that our souls live under the curse of sin and that this curse brings with it not only our physical death but also eternal separation from God.

Bill also knew how to respond. He had often sat in those revival meetings, listening to Albin and Ernest as they admonished congregants to apply Christ's blood to the doorposts of their lives. Jesus paid the penalty for sin upon the cross, these ministers proclaimed, and because of His sacrifice, sinners could have their guilt washed away, enabling them to enter God's presence unashamed. But there was one requirement, the revivalists warned. This free gift of salvation must be accepted. Every man, woman, and child must *personally* receive God's gift by accepting Christ as savior before it is too late.

As Ernest stood in the yard talking with his younger brother, that familiar message took on a fresh meaning. The truth of the gospel began to sink in, and Bill realized that he could not be saved by his father's faith. Nor could he be saved by his brother's faith. If he wanted to accept God's saving grace, he would have to come to God himself.

Writing about this day years later, Dowell said Ernest "gave to [him] very clearly and plainly the plan of salvation." But that was all. "[H]e did not press me," Dowell wrote. "He said 'When you feel God is dealing with you about this, don't fight it, accept Him as your Savior.'"[17]

And with that, the older brother walked away, perhaps expecting Bill to return to his recreation. Bill, too, expected to pick up his playtime where he had left off.

But Dowell said he had "lost interest" in playing. His mind was now elsewhere. "The words of my brother kept coming to me, and I kept thinking about it and finally I realized I had reached the age when I understood that I was a sinner and I needed to accept Jesus Christ as my Savior."[18] So that was when the boy took his brother's advice not to delay the matter any longer.

In public accounts of his salvation experience, Dowell usually glossed over the end of this story, saying, "I found a place of seclusion and got on my knees."[19] To Dowell, it seemed too undignified, perhaps even sacrilegious, to admit that the most significant turning point in his life took place in the family outhouse. Yet it did. In a personal interview, he confided with a chuckle, "I wanted to find a place where I felt like I'd be secure, [where] no one would be coming, interfering or bothering me. So I went to the outhouse, locked the door, got down on my knees in the outhouse and accepted Christ as my savior."[20]

The humble setting for this event, unbeseeming though it was, could not diminish the sincerity of a boy's prayer. And even if onlookers would have mocked the ridiculousness of it all—a sinner kneeling at "the throne"—such irony was lost on a ten-year-old Bill Dowell. This was a hallowed moment. For the remainder of his life, Dowell pointed to that day as the time when he accepted the forgiveness of Almighty God. "I accepted the Lord Jesus as my Saviour," Dowell wrote in 1980, "and I could hardly wait to get to church the next service and publicly tell about it."[21] With new confidence, then, this child was ready to face his future, in death as well as in life.

A few days later, Bill was immersed by his father in baptism at a nearby creek. Ernest was among the onlookers watching from the banks that day, no doubt with tear-filled eyes. Ernest's actions—his obedience to the Spirit's promptings—had changed this boy's eternal destiny. And not surprisingly, this shared experience brought these two brothers closer than ever. Ernest's interest in Bill served to forge a special bond between them, and for many years afterward, the older brother served as a spiritual mentor to Bill. Indeed, in the coming decade, Ernest would influence many of Bill's most important life decisions. The youngest Dowell had begun a new journey upon that old pilgrimage road. And as he set out on this new adventure, he considered himself blessed to have Albin, Lizzie—and now Ernest—alongside him to help guide his steps.

Chapter 4: *The Driver's Seat*

You *git his hands, and we'll git his legs!*
There was a sudden commotion in the schoolyard. A band of freckled boys was closing in on young Bill. The ringleader barked an order at the tallest boy in the group.

Make sure no one is watchin'!

The tall boy then cast an eye toward the school building. The facility was too large to be called a one-room schoolhouse, though it was still a small rural school.

Coast is clear. Who's got the rope?

To Bill's horror, one of the hoodlums stepped up behind him, rope in hand. A couple of other boys grabbed him hard and began to laugh.

C'mon, now. Hold still, Preacherrr!

Their twangy elongation of the name made it clear that this was a term of derision. The leader shouted his next command in that same voice.

Hitch him to the post. Hurry it up!

And they did.

Dowell told an audience in 1957, "I have actually had fifteen boys hog-tie me, tie me to a post." Dowell explained that when his tormenters finished their knots, they joined hands and began dancing around, laughing and jeering at him for being a preacher's kid. It was merely a schoolyard prank, but Dowell confessed that few boyhood experiences were more traumatic for him. "It did something to my young heart and my young mind," he told his listeners.[1]

Schooling for Bill Dowell began at the age of six. He entered the first grade in Voss, Texas, south of Abilene, though he attended several schools throughout the central and eastern parts of that state. His father's frequent moves meant that he was the perennial new kid in the class. He was an average student, often earning B's and C's, yet he always viewed himself as a "rough country boy."[2] He also came to believe that, no matter where his family went, he would be denigrated for being the son of a preacher. Albin's occupation made his children a prime target for bullying. Bill's sister Gladys testified that she experienced similar prejudice. "I grew up with an inferiority complex," she said, "because I'd been called just an old preacher's kid." She explained that, in schoolyard lore, this meant that the Dowell children "wouldn't amount to anything."[3]

Bill learned to survive these trials by adopting an aggressive persona. "I had to either whip or get whipped [by] the biggest bully in the school before they'd accept me," he said. "I'd have to fight them so they'd let me alone. It didn't really matter too much whether you won the fight, just so you held up for yourself."[4] He added that sometimes school officials unwittingly facilitated these boyhood scraps. "At noon they permitted us to have boxing matches," Dowell explained. And some of these school-sanctioned sporting events devolved into something else. Recalling one match he had against a particularly disagreeable classmate, Dowell said:

> *This guy—we hadn't gotten along too well—I think we was in love with the same girl or something. We hadn't gotten along too well. . . . So the time came when I got teamed up with this boy that I wanted to lick anyway. And he wanted to lick me. We put those gloves on and, boy, we pounded each other, I tell you, till they finally just stopped us. We had blood on us when we got through. We weren't boxing; we were fighting.*

Then Dowell added with a chuckle, "And the funny thing about it, after that we became friends."[5]

Bill was a likable boy, never truly hot-tempered, though at times he did have to keep his adolescent aggressions in check. In one instance, he and a friend were walking home from school, and as they approached Dowell's house, they found themselves in a dispute. "We got mad," Dowell said. The cause of the argument was long forgotten, but Dowell could not forget the blows that it precipitated. "We pulled our coats off and just waded into it. We were really fighting," he said. "And we looked suddenly, and we saw Lester coming up the trail toward us. And we straightened ourselves up real quick and patted each other on the back, you know. Lester came up and said, 'What are you two guys doing?' We said, 'Aw, we was just playing.'"[6]

Dowell admitted that he was not always so successful at summoning up such self-control. "My dad aggravated me one time. I was sharpening a hoe, and he just kept on and kept on and kept on. He said, 'That's not the way to do it. Let me show you how to do it. Do it this way.'" Eventually the son's frustration reached a boiling point. "I finally looked over at him, and I threw the hoe down at his feet and I said, 'I'm leaving!'" And with that, Bill stormed off the property. "I took off the entire day," Dowell recalled.[7]

When evening came, the prodigal regained his composure enough to return home, but he could not bring himself to face his father. "They told me, when I got back, Dad was sitting on the porch reading the Bible. And they said he'd been reading the Bible all afternoon." But Bill did not go to him. He was too remorseful. Instead the two opted to bury the incident silently. "From that day on he was just my old dad again," Dowell said with a shrug.[8]

The tool-sharpening episode seems to have brought about a change in Bill's relationship with his father. "It was his first realization," Dowell explained, "that this is not a kid anymore. This fellow's come of age."[9] And indeed, Bill was quickly approaching manhood. He was beginning to voice opinions and to forge a personal identity. He was also learning to venture out away from his family and into the world. For Bill, this journey was both thrilling and troubling.

Like most boys, Dowell acquired an interest in sitting in the driver's seat—both literally and figuratively—at an early age. He witnessed the dawn of the automobile era. Indeed, Dowell confessed that his first memories of transportation involved horses, not horsepower. He said that the older men in the family usually did the driving in those days. "We didn't go a lot of places. To church and places like that. In the early part of my life, we rode either in a buggy or a wagon. Or I think maybe we had a hack one place." And he added a note of clarification about his use of the word *hack*: "That's just a little larger buggy."[10]

But as Bill grew older, those buggy rides with the family were replaced not only with different modes of transportation but also with greater independence. "I got a chance to make a trip one time when I was in high school," he said. "We got a chance to go on a train—a whole delegation to the state fair in Dallas, Texas. That was my first experience riding a train." And Dowell delighted in such adventures. "The fair was fabulous," he raved.[11]

Such experiences filled him with a thirst for more of the same. He and a boyhood friend even concocted an idea for a homemade vehicle. That idea yielded some very happy rewards. Dowell explained:

> *He and I, of course, we lived on farms next to each other. We were just real good friends. We dated together and we thought we'd do something novel. So we got us a girlfriend apiece, and on the farm that I was living on there was two [broken down] buggies. And this was beyond buggy days, but there was two buggies and we got enough parts off of one to fix one buggy that was just real good, a real fine buggy. And we'd go out and date in that buggy. All the girls wanted to go with us to get a buggy ride.*[12]

Now a teenager, Dowell was discovering what it meant to sit in the driver's seat. And he liked it. His affinity for it grew even stronger, he said, once he was introduced to the automobile. "My dad found an old Westcott," Dowell recalled. "That was the first car we had. I learned to drive a little on that Westcott by getting in it and backing it out of the garage." Then later, Albin replaced his Westcott with a Model T Ford. "That's the one I learned to drive," Dowell said with a lift of the eyebrows. "I thought I was really something, going to see my girlfriend in a Ford."[13]

The perks of sitting in the driver's seat were plentiful, Dowell discovered, yet so were the challenges. As this youngster puttered toward manhood, the pilgrimage road ahead of him became tricky to navigate. Where would he go? What would he do? Dowell pondered a variety of career choices during those years. For a time, he seriously considered taking up a career as a cowboy. He had worked a brief stint on a cattle ranch, and he said the experience afforded him much of the excitement that he found so enjoyable in western films and novels. He recalled herding cattle across rivers and open territory, and occasionally even rescuing the animals from quicksand.[14] Consequently, he wondered if he might make a life out of that sort of work.

But even as Dowell was wrestling with such thoughts, his family moved back to Madison County in East Texas. This was the same area where Albin had grown up, and in fact, Albin still had siblings living in Normangee, a town just eleven miles from the Dowell family's new farm. By this time, nearly all of Albin's other children were married and gone. Bill, however, was still in high school and was living with his parents, assisting his father with the operation of their farm.

This was how a coach at a nearby high school came to meet young Dowell. In the summer of 1932, the summer just before Bill's senior year, he was out picking cotton in his father's fields, and he looked up to see a square-jawed visitor walking toward him. The man introduced himself as Dewitt Holleman, coach of the football Panthers over in Normangee. "He was getting the football team together," Dowell said.[15] Holleman was scouting area farms for new players, and he had spotted Bill's large frame out in the field. Holleman immediately struck up a conversation.

Although Dowell had never played on a football team, he was athletic. In fact, Bill had a love for all kinds of sports, particularly basketball. He had also been successful in baseball, tennis, and several school track events, including the 440 and the high jump. Thus, it took little persuasion to interest the teenager in a spot on the Normangee football team. The only concern was the distance. Bill was set to start his senior year at a different high school, one that was considerably closer to home. How could he manage to go to a school eleven miles away?

Dowell said Holleman was undaunted by the obstacle, especially after he learned that Dowell had several family members living in Normangee. Holleman assured Bill that, if his parents would allow him to move into town, the rest would work itself out. Holleman would see to it that he had a place on the team and a place to live. So, at the first opportunity, Bill brought Holleman's proposal to his father's attention. And to the son's delight, Albin raised no objections. "He decided it'd be all right," Dowell piped.[16]

Dowell spent the next year living in Normangee with his aunt and uncle, Runie and A. J. Martin. The experience was transformative. Dowell played right halfback for the Normangee Panthers, and he became fast friends with a cousin, DeWitte Dowell, quarterback for the Panthers and the son of Albin's brother James. DeWitte and Bill became inseparable. "I loved him like a brother," Dowell told one audience.[17]

That year was a far cry from the times when Bill had been mocked as a preacher's kid and tethered to a post. Holleman's 1932-33 recruits enjoyed a unique camaraderie, and the memories that Dowell made while wearing that number fifteen jersey were cherished ones. "We never lost a game my senior year," Dowell once bragged to a newspaper reporter.[18] The Panthers won the district championship that year, having been scored upon only one time during the entire season. And even decades later, Dowell proudly displayed a Panther team photo on his office wall.[19] Indeed, in 1978, Dowell attended a team reunion, where he and his Panther teammates met up with Coach Holleman and honored him for the special contribution he had made to their lives forty-five years earlier.

Dowell's senior year had been a triumphant one, and it had brought this teenager both the independence and the kind of acceptance he had longed for. Yet even so, Dowell admitted that those rewards came at a price. In his effort to win popularity, he had also compromised some of the values he had known as a child. "I did a little drinking the last year I was in high school," Dowell confessed in an interview. He elaborated on his lapse of character by describing some early encounters with whiskey. "I despised the stuff," he said. "Most of the time I didn't drink it; I just made the boys think I did. They'd pass the bottle around, and I'd take it and put my thumb over the bottle and act like I was drinking it. Then I'd say, 'Whew.' But I really never did like it."[20]

Regardless of how much he swallowed, however, Bill's participation in such gatherings put him at odds with both his faith and the law. He was well versed in the Baptist position on drinking. He was also aware that Prohibition remained in full swing. The national ban on alcohol would not officially end until six months after Dowell's graduation. Thus, no matter how the boy tried to look at it, his actions were illicit. And while he may have succeeded in avoiding the taste, he could not avoid what was happening within his own conscience.

Those drinking incidents were part of a larger pattern in this young man's life. Other vices were plaguing Bill's conscience as well. Dowell confessed that he became a regular smoker during high school. This was a habit he had picked up when he was sixteen, he said. Compared to alcohol, tobacco carried a lesser stigma among the Christians in rural Texas. Indeed, Dowell's own preacher-father chewed tobacco regularly and also smoked cigars on occasion. It was Albin who had introduced Bill to tobacco, though he did it as a practical joke. One time when Bill told his father that he wanted to try chewing, Albin took out a pouch and offered it to him. The boy reached for a large hunk of the black goo and squeezed it into his mouth, and soon afterward, much to Albin's delight, Bill's face turned green.

Dowell said his father's prank had been enough to cure him of further interest in chewing tobacco, but it did not diminish the appeal of tobacco's other forms. To Bill, smoking represented a rite of passage. After all, many of the men that he knew, including many of the men of his father's church, were regular smokers. Dowell admitted, however, that the broad acceptance of smoking in his community did not diminish a certain shame that he felt when he took up the habit. And this explains why he kept the activity hidden from his parents. "I did it on the sly," Dowell confessed.[21]

Cigarette smoking, like whiskey drinking, had become a weapon in a subtle rebellion that was smoldering within this young man. And his activities were less about reaching adulthood than they were about proclaiming selfhood. Bill was seizing control of a life that rightfully belonged to God. And the struggle brought him misery. In a sermon, Dowell recalled the inner turmoil he experienced while living with his aunt in Normangee:

For one solid year I tried to fit back into the world, and I couldn't. There was no way. I did some things I shouldn't do, and God rebuked me for it, and He kept me from going into sin very deeply at all. But I was trying. I was away from home. I was among those who lived that way. I was a football star. I wanted to be popular, and I tried to be. The least little thing that I did that I knew was wrong, when I got to my bedroom that night, I got down and wept and said, "Oh, God, forgive me. This is not for me. I can't do it. It's not my nature. It's not my nature."[22]

Remorse notwithstanding, Dowell remained conflicted about living the Christian life throughout that final year of high school. Even after he graduated in the spring of 1933, he was "semi-backslidden," he said.[23] Bill also found himself mired in aimlessness. Like the rest of the country, this boy was facing a precarious future. Franklin Delano Roosevelt had taken office just three months before Dowell's graduation, and the Great Depression was now well underway. For Dowell, the high school joyride had reached an abrupt end, and the road ahead seemed dark and treacherous.

After graduation, Dowell left Normangee and moved back to his parent's farm. He then spent the summer of his nineteenth birthday participating in a desperate attempt to save Albin's crops from an invasion of grasshoppers. The family stretched long ropes across their endangered plants and then walked through the fields, hoping to shoo away the swarms that had been spawned by the drought. But despite these efforts, much of the harvest was lost.

As Bill sat in his father's Model T Ford studying those ravaged fields, the driver's seat was never less comfortable, and the word *Depression* seemed an apt name for the times. Dowell's journey over those last several months had put distance between him and the One who wanted to pave his pilgrimage road, and consequently, the horizon ahead of him looked entirely bleak. Bill wondered if the hardships that he had experienced back on the schoolyard might pale in comparison to the ones that manhood would bring. For his own sake, he hoped this would not be the case.

Chapter 5: *A Walk with Nola*

Texas voices rang out in Ernest and Bessie's modest home:

S-i-le-n-t night, h-o-ly night—

This was Merkel, Texas, a few miles west of Abilene. Ernest Dowell was pastoring a church there now, the North Side Missionary Baptist Church.

A-ll is calm, a-ll is bright—

This was indeed a bright moment, perhaps because of its contrast to the desperate conditions of the Depression. The singers in the room seemed oblivious to the national gloom. They were too busy rejoicing. To them, this was the music of angels. They would have contended, no doubt, that their nasally Texas drawl lent the melody its proper angelic tone. And the volume, too, was just as it should be. None of that high-church inhibition here; these singers ignored the song's lullaby lyrics and belted out the tune like the boisterous Baptists they were.

Round yon virgin mother and Child—

Over in one corner of this crowded room sat Bill's brother Joe, hand-in-hand with his new bride Katherine. This couple had been married just five months, a fact that any keen observer might easily have deduced. Bill's other siblings—together with their young families—were likewise packed into this room.

A Christmas tree adorned one end of this gathering place. The tree's aroma seemed to carry the family's music. As was customary, this tree had been fresh-cut and dragged in from a nearby grove of evergreens. A similar tree was on display in Ernest's church. In those days, Christmas was inextricably linked to the church. Ernest's congregation even made it a practice to exchange gifts, just as families do. Those festivities had concluded earlier that same evening.

Holy Infant so tender and mild—

The people at this gathering were strictly kinfolk, however. Dowell recalled that there was always singing at these celebrations. For one night out of the year, the normally downturned corners of the singers' mouths became a little less severe.

Sleep in heavenly p-e-a-c-e—

As this family of singers belted out the penultimate phrase, their chins lifted in unison. Then as if they had rehearsed it, those same chins followed the tune downwards to complete the song:

S-l-e-e-p in heavenly peace.

Christmas reunions were a treasured tradition for the Dowell clan. Most years the family came together for three or four days, and like other Americans, they exchanged gifts and enjoyed a turkey feast. Dowell remembered the music in particular. "All of my family would sing," he said.[1] The family often sang a cappella, though Dowell also remembered times when they used a piano. During one period, Albin and Lizzie even owned an organ.

Santa Claus was another regular part of this family's Christmas fun. Though the bearded man's gifts might strike today's children as paltry, Bill never noticed. As a youngster, Bill had delighted in the jump ropes and tin horns and storybooks that he received. One of his favorite gifts was a curved harmonica given to him by his parents. "Cost about fifteen cents," Dowell remarked in an interview. Even so, it became a treasured possession. "It was on that harmonica that I learned to play the French harp," Dowell said. "I was really proud of that thing. I finally got my tongue where it could pick out a tune." [2] Dowell carried that skill with him throughout his life, and as an adult, he entertained many of his preaching audiences, particularly those at Christian youth camps, with the lively tunes he played on his harmonica.

Just before Albin carved up the traditional Christmas turkey, the Dowell family would always gather around their father and listen to him read the nativity story from the Bible. Then at the close of the reading, Albin led his family in prayer. He was always careful to pray for each of his family members by name, Dowell said.

After the meal concluded, Bill and the other men of his family routinely embarked on hunting expeditions. Dowell recalled participating in some of these outings back on the plains of central Texas. "[T]here was a lot of lakes up there," he said. "There was just scads of ducks—bunches of ducks—on the lakes, and we'd go duck hunting." For the youngest boy in the family, these day trips yielded both excitement and consternation. "I remember I had a shotgun," Dowell explained with a laugh, "and I couldn't get that thing to aim right to save my life. . . . Looked like you could just shoot into 'em and get 'em—and I guess that's what I did, just shot into 'em. I think I crippled one, but I didn't get any."[3]

As Bill sang carols with his family in 1933, he was filled with the usual holiday excitement. But his feelings that year had little to do with hunting ducks. Bill was intent on a different sort of hunt, one that had started earlier that same night over at the North Side Missionary Baptist Church.

Christmas Eve fell on a Sunday that year, and so, throughout the day, Bill and the rest of the visiting relatives had attended services at Ernest's church. Joe, Gladys, and Bill also attended a late-afternoon youth service. Dowell said he and his siblings arrived at that youth meeting to find several long benches squeezed around the room's only source of heat, a potbellied stove. Joe and Bill sat next to each other on one side of the room; Gladys mingled with some girls across the aisle.

A dark-haired girl in her early twenties soon came and sat next to Gladys. She introduced herself as Nola Mae Callahan, leader of the youth group. Gladys and Nola were close to the same age, somewhat older than the others who were attending the class, and these two struck up a fast friendship. Nola was quite pleased to meet one of her pastor's relatives, and as she and Gladys chatted, she asked her new friend about the others who were visiting with her. "Who's that?" Nola asked with a nod toward Bill. "That's my brother," Gladys replied.[4]

Once the class got underway, another conversation started up, this one on the other side of the aisle. According to the youngest brother, the exchange began without words. Joe started making mischievous grins at him and glancing at him out of one corner of his eye. Bill pretended not to notice at first, but then he felt a sharp nudge in his side. There was no need to ask what Joe's clowning was all about. Nola Callahan was now standing at the front of the group, and no young man could miss the fact that she was stunningly beautiful. As her photographs still attest, she had the features of a Hollywood starlet, not a Texas farm girl.

Dowell sat with his arms folded and shot Joe a disapproving look, as if to rebuke him for misbehaving in church, but Joe was not deterred. Dowell later wondered if his brother's poor manners had been less irreverent than they initially seemed. After all, Bill had been flirting with waywardness for more than a year, and Joe knew it. Perhaps the older brother sensed a need to look out for him.

Joe may also have recognized that the young woman standing in front of them had much more to offer his brother than beauty. As Nola taught the young people that night, she exuded confidence, independence, and most importantly, a love for the Word of God. Joe was impressed—so much so that he leaned over to his bachelor brother and whispered, "If I was a little younger and not married, I'd marry that girl."[5]

Bill's lips now tightened a bit. And for a moment he lost the ability to suppress a smile. To him, Joe's remark was an unabashed challenge: *I dare you to try to win her.* It now felt as if the erstwhile cowboy's honor were on the line. So with a brazen look Bill whispered back, "Y'know, I might just do that."[6]

Dowell said he followed up those words with immediate action. As the congregants began to disperse at the end of that evening, Bill followed Nola and Gladys out of the church building and imposed himself on their company. He persuaded Gladys to introduce her new friend to him, and then, as part of that conversation, he learned that Gladys and Nola were planning to escort one another home. Nola's family, it turned out, lived only a short distance away from the church and not far from Ernest and Bessie's place.

Dowell's oversized ears perked up at this revelation. According to Nola, "He spoke to me just pretty quick and says, 'Well Gladys, you don't have to walk her home. I'll walk her.'"[7] And to Bill's delight, Nola consented. The two of them set out on a journey that night that would last for more than sixty-seven years.

As they walked together on that Christmas Eve, Bill and Nola began to get better acquainted. Bill soaked in every tidbit about his new girl. He learned that Nola was born on November 14, 1912, making her nearly a year and a half older than him. She was the middle child of seven siblings—four brothers and three sisters. She was an active and fun-loving person, who, like him, had grown up on a farm. Her family was originally from Goree, Texas, but they later moved to Merkel.

Nola enjoyed a special closeness with her mother, a spirited woman named Noma Lea. The reason for this bond was probably due to the fact that Nola was the youngest of the family's three girls. She would ever be Noma Lea's little girl. Even after Nola was grown, Noma Lea commonly employed pet names for Nola in her letters, names like "Baby Girl," "Doodle Bug," and (most often) "Honey." Once when she was a child, Nola contracted a case of the measles, which later turned into a serious bout with pneumonia. It was Noma Lea who painstakingly nursed her daughter back to health. "You were such a delicate little doll, and oh how sick you were," Noma Lea recalled in a letter, "and it seemed impossible that you could live." The attending physician treated the ailment by prescribing "a plaster made up of ammonia, camphor, turpentine, and pure lard."[8] All the while, the doctor warned Noma Lea that excessive use of the plaster could bring her daughter permanent harm. No one was more delighted than Noma Lea when her daughter finally recovered.

Nola's father, Sanford Jesse Callahan, was more reserved than his wife. He was a quiet, hard-working man. Nola long remembered toiling alongside him in the maize and cotton fields. "I'd drag those heavy, big, long sacks behind me," she said, referring to her days of picking cotton. "And when it was full I'd throw it over my shoulder and carry it."[9] Nola was never afraid of hard work, yet for her, farming was particularly exhausting. Sanford's high expectations did not make it any easier.

Nola never forgot her father's blustery consternation whenever she and the other Callahan children failed to take their labors seriously. More than once, Nola heard her father scold them for loafing on the job or for whining about some task. One of Sanford's most colorful outbursts incorporated a familiar image from those nearby lakes. "Dad and one of my brothers and sisters and I were chopping weeds, you know, around the cotton plants," Nola related in an interview. "And we got tired and got to talking." Nola said that she and her siblings soon stopped to lean against a fence, one foot propped up. Meanwhile, Sanford, unaware of what was happening, continued working and making his way down a row of cotton plants. Only after he got some distance away did he look up and realize that his children were not at his heels. The red-faced Sanford shouted back to his children, "You all get to work!" Then he added in disgust, "Standin' there like a bunch of ducks lookin' for thunder!"[10]

Nola cackled as she remembered her father's phrasing. Though she had not always enjoyed working in those farm fields, she maintained a deep affection for her dad. When he died of a heart attack in July 1965, "she grieved herself into the hospital," one daughter-in-law recalled.[11] Such was the bond that Nola shared with her father. Just as Albin had influenced Bill, Sanford's loving care for his family had left a deep impression on his youngest daughter.

Nola was particularly grateful that her father had made it a practice to take his family to church. In one account, she wrote that she "never knew anything during childhood but to go to church on Wed. nights & Sunday at our Southern Bapt. ch." Indeed, church events were the Callahan family's principle diversion. "If another church or denomination was in a revival," Nola wrote, "Mother, Dad and us 7 children would pile in our Model T Ford and attend the services."[12] Many of those revivals, she said, lasted three or four weeks straight, and often they were held outdoors under tents or brush arbor shelters. The Callahans, like many Depression-era families, delighted in the excitement that such diversions afforded.

It was also during one of those revival meetings that Nola, as an eleven-year-old girl, decided to become a Christian herself. "We were attending a Nazarene revival," she wrote, "and I became under strong conviction of the Holy Spirit for the first time. I felt that if I did not go to the altar, repent, and trust the Lord Jesus Christ as my Lord and Savior, I would die that night and sink into hell." The young pragmatist opted to go to the altar, a decision that brought her great relief. She rose from her prayer with an exuberant heart. "[E]veryone that was saved that night was asked to tell what God did for them," Nola recalled. "My testimony was, 'I'm saved and sanctified, and I'm determined to go through!'" The following Sunday Nola visited a nearby lake, where she was baptized by her Baptist pastor.[13]

From that time on, Nola was affected by a "strong desire" to render service to God as a missionary or nurse. So deep was her newfound passion for Christ that, at times, she became the Callahan family's most vocal champion for Christian living. Indeed, a few months after she met Bill, she voiced concern over a growing inconsistency in her parents' church attendance. This apparent loss of interest was likely tied to some of the family's personal difficulties. Even Nola had seen the toll that the Depression had taken on them. Remembering one devastatingly bad crop yield, Nola described a dark mood that came over her household. "I can never forget the worried look and the tone of conversation," she wrote.[14] But that was not all of the trouble. Sanford's father, George, had also fallen into bad health and had to come live with the family. He stayed with the Callahan family for about two years until he eventually passed away.

These difficulties must certainly have played a part in the Callahan's slow drift from church. Yet Nola could see only the empty pews. Whatever her parents' reasons, their absence from church greatly bothered her. In a letter to Bill, she wrote, "I'm very sorry Mother and Dad haven't a very great desire to go. Pray with me that they will be interested as they should be. It hurts me terribly if I just cannot go to the house of God, and to think so many people have opportunity after opportunity to go and yet don't. How can they do that?"[15]

In time, Nola's prayers and persistence seem to have paid off. Her parents became quite active in the church later in life. For many years Sanford helped with the maintenance of his church's facilities. He even took a job for a time as a church caretaker. And Noma Lea likewise became involved in regular church operations. For as many years as she was able, she volunteered to work in the annual Vacation Bible School. Then in her closing years, she often wrote to Nola to share the latest church news as well as the salvation stories of those who had joined her church congregation. For Nola, who loved the church almost as much as her own family, this news could not have been more pleasing.

Nola's spiritual strength also proved to be a great encouragement to the boy who went walking with her in 1933. "She was very, very active in that church," Dowell observed. "And her life influenced me in the right direction a great deal." Then he added, "She was a woman of faith."[16]

But during his Christmas visit in 1933, Bill had worried that his relationship with this girl would be short-lived. After all, Bill was only in Merkel for the holidays. When the celebration ended, he and the others would make their way back to their respective homes. What would happen then?

As it turned out, those worries were quickly allayed. On the day that Bill's family was preparing to travel back to Madison County, a group of friends and family gathered around the Dowells' car to say their final farewells. Nola was among the crowd. And as they stood talking, Ernest spoke up and said, "Bill, you don't have to go back home, do you? You don't have anything to do. Why don't you just stay with us awhile?" Bill tried to mask his instant enthusiasm, but Nola saw through it. "They had to twist his arm about like you had to twist my arm," she jibed.[17] And when the conversation ended, Bill quickly unpacked his belongings from the automobile and moved in with Ernest and Bessie.

Dowell never again lived with his parents. Albin and Lizzie returned to Madison County, and their son remained in Merkel under the capable guardianship of his brother and sister-in-law. Indeed, this proved to be a significant turning point in Dowell's journey. Suddenly a boy's aimlessness was replaced with a man's sense of direction. And even if, for the moment, his compass was fixed on a young lady, Bill's life was once again moving in a positive direction on the pilgrimage road. Eight months later he and Nola would start a new life together as husband and wife, joining their hearts not only for a life of marriage but also for a life of ministry.

Part 2: Morning Hours

Chapter 6: *Surrender*

His elbow propped atop the open car window, Bill bounced along in Ernest's well-used black Ford. Ernest was doing the driving. For a long while these two travelers rode silently. Then Ernest cleared his throat.

You awake?

What?

Thought maybe you was sleepin'.

Nah.

This was May of 1934, four months before the Dowells' wedding. The sun was already high in the sky, and Ernest's Ford was staggering in the Texas wind. The driver had to keep a firm grip on the steering wheel just to keep the vehicle on the road. In Bill's estimation, his brother was only marginally successful at this. Indeed, Ernest's carefree driving suggested to Bill a man barely cognizant of their vehicle's constant zigzagging. Bill coped with the swerving by keeping his gaze locked on the horizon ahead of them. When Ernest noticed his stare, he said:

I s'pose you're thinkin' about your sweetheart.

Bill grinned a sheepish answer:

I'll be anxious to see her, all right.

Although Bill and Nola were not yet married, they were now fully in love. Ernest seized a chance to needle his brother about that:

I just hope she hasn't forgotten you.

Bill did not dignify this remark with a reply, but he did shoot his brother an indignant look. Ernest responded with a lift of the eyebrows and another swerve on the road.

The Dowell brothers had spent the last two weeks in Fort Worth and were now returning to Merkel. They did not talk much on the journey home. They were too tired from their trip. They were also lost in their thoughts. They looked forward to sharing their experiences with Bessie and Nola.

Quite a meetin', huh, Bill?

It took Bill a moment to answer, but a sudden jolt from the road shook free his response:

Yup. Sure was. . . . Most remarkable thing I ever witnessed.

Ernest thought his younger brother seemed uncharacteristically soft-spoken that day. Or else the wind was just making it difficult to hear.

Say again?

This time Bill spoke up.

I said it was quite an experience for me.

Ernest nodded. Straight winds were roaring across the road. The wind had been pushing at Ernest's vehicle ever since the two men left Fort Worth. A poetic observer would have posited that summer's manhood was blasting away at the childhood of spring. But the young man sitting in Ernest's passenger seat was oblivious to any such poetry. Like most nineteen-year-olds, he was feeling this change of seasons without paying attention to any of it. There was too much else to ponder—his girl, his trip—not to mention the new direction his life was taking now that he had moved to Merkel.

Bill was also preoccupied, at least for the moment, with a prayer. He was asking the Lord to keep Ernest's rickety Ford on the road. It seemed to him that Ernest should have been praying the same thing, but if he was, Bill did not see much sign of it. Each time the older brother spoke, he overcame the wind's roar by turning his head toward Bill. He also employed the kind of volume that was normally reserved for his revivals. Bill would have preferred a little less volume and a little more attentiveness, but this never came.

Ernest shouted again:

Yes, it's a powerful thing when God's people come together and let the Holy Spirit come upon them, I'll say that!

This enthusiastic remark referred to the brothers' two weeks in Fort Worth. The statement sounded much too Pentecostal to be coming from a Baptist preacher, but neither of these travelers gave that a second thought. They were still reeling from all that had transpired. The men had gone to Fort Worth to attend a semiannual training for preachers known as the Premillennial Bible School. The conference was hosted by the First Baptist Church and her larger-than-life pastor, J. Frank Norris. Norris had launched the Bible school only a few years earlier, but already his classes were drawing hundreds of participants. Thousands more, mostly laypeople from the Fort Worth area, attended the evening revival services that ran concurrently with the daytime sessions.

Author Billy Vick Bartlett described Norris's training, saying it was "ostensibly for the enlightenment of fundamental Baptist preachers in the general areas of church building, Biblical scholarship, and the nuances of the modernistic threat."[1] Whatever the purpose, a young Bill Dowell found it nothing short of electrifying.

Bill shouted back a reply:

Amen to that!

This answer felt awkward to Bill, as if he had borrowed the words from a much older man. He was still new to his preacher-boy identity. At times it felt as though he was clomping around in his father's boots. Never had this young man imagined that he would pursue such a career. He once told an audience:

Now preaching was one thing I determined I wouldn't do. My father was a preacher. I was raised in a pretty rough part of Texas, attended some schools where they delighted in taking it out on preachers' sons especially. . . . [S]o I determined I would never subject my family to that sort of treatment. I purposed in my heart there were two things I wouldn't do. One, I didn't want to farm. I don't mind the work so much but I just don't like to be out by myself. I like to work with people, to be around people, I didn't want to farm. The second was, I didn't want to preach. I determined that I was not going to preach.

Dowell concluded this tale with an ironic punch line: "So the Lord let me farm until I started preaching!"[2]

That story made Dowell laugh in retrospect, but the humor had been lost on him in May of 1934. Back then, he was just trying to hang on for the ride—the one in the Ford as well as the one on the pilgrimage road. With encouragement from Ernest and Nola, Bill's faith had been undergoing rapid growth. Already he had become a mainstay at the North Side Missionary Baptist Church. An undated news clipping published soon after Dowell's arrival at Merkel illustrates just how quickly he had found his niche. "We are ordering about 50 new song books for our Sunday afternoon singing class," the article reported. "Bill Dowell was elected president of the class. Nola Mae Callahan was elected secretary. Sister Frank Carr is our pianist. We are hoping every member of the class will be present every Sunday."[3]

God was doing exciting things in Ernest's church, and no one was feeling the effects more than the pastor's brother. Indeed, just two months after coming to the church, the teenager made an unexpected announcement. It happened on a cold night as Ernest's congregation was gathered "around an old-fashioned coal stove in a big tabernacle with a gravel floor."[4] Ernest brought a message that night about the necessity of every man being yielded to God. And despite the frigid temperatures, the fire of the sermon got through. Dowell recounted the experience, saying:

At the close [Ernest] gave an invitation. He said, "I don't know; perhaps there is someone here tonight who needs to surrender to God, someone whom God has laid His hand upon and who needs to surrender." The Spirit of God moved upon my heart and soul and I stood with tears streaming down my cheeks. I said, "I must surrender tonight to preach the Gospel, for I feel as the Apostle Paul once expressed it, 'Woe is unto me if I preach not the Gospel.'"[5]

No one was more surprised by this announcement than Bill himself. "I didn't feel worthy to be a preacher," he confessed. The "inferiority complex" that had shadowed Dowell since boyhood left him with a sense of inadequacy that, until that moment, had made a life in the ministry unthinkable.[6] Yet the Lord finally dissuaded him of that self-opinion.

Dowell never looked back after that, in part because his brother never gave him the chance. Ernest scheduled the teenager to preach just two weeks after his surrender. It was an assignment that filled the him with apprehension. "I was exceedingly nervous," Dowell said. "I was afraid that I'd get up there and preach ten minutes and have to quit."[7] Dowell said he hedged his bets by crafting a sermon with some built-in flexibility: "I chose a subject, 'God's Call,' and I went back to the beginning and talked about God's call to Adam and God's call to Abraham and went right on through the Bible."[8] It was an accordion-like outline, both expandable and collapsible, ensuring that the message would be neither too long nor too short. And it worked. A twinkle came into Dowell's eye when he thought back on his use of the device. "It made pretty easy preaching," he said.[9]

But young Dowell had been less sure of himself on the night that he stood up to preach at the North Side Missionary Baptist Church. Ascending that wide platform for the first time, Bill carried with him his Bible, a brief set of notes, and a stomach full of butterflies. If onlookers failed to notice the butterflies, it was only because Bill had dabbled enough in public speaking to know how to hide them. One of his favorite high school memories had been conducting mock trials in a civics class. Bill had felt quite successful during those exercises. Indeed, he relished the experience so much that he briefly entertained the idea of pursuing a career as a lawyer.[10]

Bill also excelled in declamation when he was in school. He explained declamation, saying, "You memorized a speech, someone else's speech. You'd memorize it and give it. That was declaiming."[11] Such presentations were then delivered as part of a competition. Dowell's declamation entry had been a work by noted orator Robert Ingersoll.[12] Dowell chortled as he looked back on that selection. "Bob Ingersoll was an *atheist*," he said with his chin tucked to his chest. This irony had been completely lost on him as a student. "I didn't think about it until years later," he said with a laugh. Rather, Dowell chose Ingersoll's text based solely on the quality of the literature. And according to him, it was "a real oratorical speech." He also maintained that his presentation of it went well. "I put myself into it and won first place," Dowell recalled. Then he added, "And I was proud of myself."[13]

Victories such as these may have emboldened the novice preacher as he made his way up to Ernest's modest wooden pulpit.[14] They did not, however, make him fearless. Dowell said his nerves bothered him so badly that he struggled to speak almost as soon as he began. "I was so nervous till my mouth got dry," he said.[15] And making matters worse was the fact that a water pitcher had been tantalizingly placed at the far edge of the platform. The tormented young preacher was loath to interrupt his own sermon, but the cotton growing in his mouth made this oasis too powerful to resist. "I finally just quit and walked over there and poured me a glass of water," he said flatly, "and went back and took that message up where I left off."[16]

Dowell confessed that, at the time, this interruption felt deadly. Yet in the end it proved well worth the embarrassment. With his thirst now quenched, Bill's lips were finally freed. He preached for a full twenty minutes, he said. And when he concluded his sermon, he saw the fruit of his labors. Dowell extended an invitation, asking his listeners to accept "God's Call" just as the Bible characters in his sermon had done. And he was overwhelmed by the response. Many in the crowd, including one of

Dowell's own brothers-in-law, came forward to make spiritual decisions at the church altar. For the first time, Bill saw what it meant to be used by God.

A news article published later that week incorporated some rather unremarkable language to sum up what had transpired during that service. "Last Sunday was a cold and disagreeable day," the article reported, "yet we had a fine congregation at our church services. Sunday night Bill Dowell preached for us." To this, the article added a word of encouragement for the young preacher: "Bill is growing in grace and knowledge of the word of God. He says with Paul, 'Woe is unto me if I preach not the gospel.'"[17]

This was the extent of the write-up. There were no glowing reviews of the speaker and no superlatives used to describe the altar call that had followed the sermon. Still, Dowell held onto the clipping for the rest of his life. To him, this night had been special. Though he still considered himself unworthy to be identified with someone like the Apostle Paul, Dowell considered his calling to preach no less divine. Indeed, he often referred to it as "the highest calling on earth."[18]

This reverence for his calling may have helped to spur the rapid Christian growth that Dowell experienced during those early months of 1934. Soon after he started preaching, he put away cigarettes for good. While many in his culture would have accepted the habit, even upon the lips of a preacher, Dowell said his conscience would not permit him to continue the practice. "I couldn't associate smoking with preaching," he said.[19] For him, preaching was serious business. "When God lays His hand upon a man and says, 'I have chosen you,'" Dowell remarked in one sermon, "He has placed upon that man the highest honor that could possibly be placed upon him." Then he added, "Along with that honor, He gives to that man the greatest responsibility that any man can possibly have."[20]

Bill's appreciation for that responsibility may have grown during his visit to Fort Worth. It was certain that he would have much to tell Nola about what he had learned from J. Frank Norris. And he was eager to do so. Perhaps he was reviewing the things he wanted to share even as he was riding westward in Ernest's Ford. Whatever the case, Bill was once again shaken from his thoughts when Ernest interrupted to say:

Hey, Bill, okay with you if we stop? Gonna need some gasoline before long. Oh yeah, and we can get some lunch, too—if you want.

The teenager's raging appetite had been primed for lunch since mid-morning, but he had been trying to conceal the fact. Now Ernest's toothy grin and sarcastic tone made it obvious that the older brother had not been fooled a bit. That being the case, Bill gladly dropped his façade.

Well, if you say so! You're the driver!

And with that, the two hungry preachers puttered toward the next town.

Chapter 7: *Fort Worth*

O land of rest, for thee I sigh!
    When will the moment come
    When I shall lay my armor by
And dwell in peace at home?

Ernest kept time to his song by tapping his palm on the steering wheel. A full belly had put this pastor in a good mood. Bill had been similarly affected, and he could not resist joining his brother on the chorus:

We'll work till Jesus comes,
We'll work till Jesus comes—

The Dowell men sang at full volume, which was considerable, and young Bill relished the moment. He imagined that his duet with Ernest was ringing out across the whole territory. He halfway prayed that it would. His newly invigorated relationship with the Lord, now further energized by the things he had experienced in Fort Worth, gave him a new passion for preaching the gospel message to others.

We'll work till Jesus comes,
And we'll be gathered home!

Bill noticed that the prairie winds had shifted while they were eating lunch and that Ernest's old Ford was now sailing with ease. In fact, the wind seemed to be coaxing their car along. Bill imagined that these gusts were the Lord's hand hastening their journey back to Merkel. For this, he was most grateful. At last his two-week separation from his sweetheart would end.

Bill and Nola had corresponded by mail almost daily during Bill's stay in Fort Worth, but this did little to cure their lovesickness. Midway through his Bible school training Bill wrote to Nola, saying, "I get so lonesome for you at times I almost decide to come home. But in the midst of it all, I am happy because I know that you love me and will be waiting when I return."[1]

Bill did his best to cope in the meantime. He hoarded Nola's daily missives, and he read and re-read every word. The lean years of the Depression afforded few treasures, but correspondence from a sweetheart ranked among them. As Bill rode back in Ernest's Ford, his trouser pockets were fully padded with the letters he had received.

Bill had parted from Nola on Monday, April 30, 1934, and he and Ernest had then made the one-hundred-and-seventy-mile journey to Fort Worth. Once there, Bill did his best to concentrate on his Bible training. The jam-packed itinerary and the exciting atmosphere at the First Baptist Church helped keep his mind off of his separation from his girl. First Baptist was touted as the world's largest congregation, with a reported membership of twelve thousand.[2] More impressive still was the church's legendary pastor, J. Frank Norris. In addition to leading the church, Norris was a noted evangelist, author, radio personality, and the editor of a weekly newspaper called *The Fundamentalist*, which boasted a circulation of over sixty thousand.[3]

Bill and Ernest lived at Norris's church during their time in Fort Worth. The majority of the students attending the Bible school were poor men from rural places, so Norris helped these impoverished men by providing them with some modest accommodations.[4] For one dollar, guests could secure a spot on one of the five hundred cots filling Norris's Sunday school building.[5] Free meals were also provided. R. O. Woodworth, one of Norris's former associates, quipped that in order to take advantage of the church's hospitality "nearly every bum in Fort Worth became a Baptist preacher the week of the schools."[6] G. Beauchamp Vick, another ministry partner, had a similar recollection. Vick noted the distinctive odor that struck him as he passed by the living quarters of Norris's ragtag clientele. "[T]he stench was so bad that walking down the halls (of the Sunday school building) was an ordeal," he said.[7]

For Dowell's part, any such unpleasantness was forgettable. The wide-eyed farm boy was either too unrefined or too awestruck to pay any attention to it. He was more interested in the agenda than the aroma. As Dowell sat on the edge of his cot after his first day of training, he tried to capture the experience for Nola:

> *Excuse the writing. I am writing on my knee. . . . We had a wonderful service tonight. Dr. Rector gave us a lecture on first chapter of Acts. Then Dr. Norris gave us a lecture. After the service Dr. Frank Norris called a lot of us boys up and gave us some tracts on "What Must I Do to Be Saved," and sent us out over the town to the "beer" joints to deliver them and talk to the drunken men (and "women" too), about their souls. It really is a thrilling and interesting work.*[8]

The ratification of the Twenty-First Amendment in December 1933 had ended Prohibition, and Norris responded by sending his 1934 Bible school students out on late-night "raids." Each evening Norris's men visited local bars and other night spots so that they might minister to the wayward souls occupying those establishments. On May 2, the *Fort Worth Press* published a front-page story about the raids under a headline that read, "Prayer Heard at Night Club Tables. Patrons Stare into Beer Steins as Young Pastors Search for Converts."[9] Another story appeared in the *Star-Telegram* on May 3. That story began:

"Where He Leads Me I Will Follow," sang 70 young ministers as they marched into beer halls under sidewalks where layers of tobacco smoke floated, into domino parlors and into pool halls last night.

Business came almost to a standstill as old, familiar songs were sung. Hats came off. A few of the patrons joined in singing.

The reception ranged all the way from the proprietor at one place who stood at the stairs and shook hands with each man to a woman at a table who called out, "Goody and go to hell."[10]

Dowell reveled in these adventures. "I am certainly having a spiritual feast," he told Nola.[11] And in another letter, he said, "We surely are having some glorious experiences. I have had the joy of seeing many souls saved, and been instrumental in leading several to Christ. How happy it makes me to see a soul saved."[12]

Dowell was unaware that a local newspaper back home had picked up the *Fort Worth Press* article and had leaked some of his news before he got the chance. "Dearest Bill," wrote Nola, "I've just received your kind and sweet letter. Probably you will be surprised to hear that I knew of your movement yesterday (about the crusading in the beer-joints). The Abilene Paper reported it. . . ."[13] Nola then went on to comment about a portion of the article that she and other members of their church had found particularly interesting. It was a portion that referred to Bill by name. The article stated:

Other members of the salvation "raid" buttonholed drinkers at the bar.

One hospitable soul insisted he was a Christian but was "unhappy." Groping for his hip pocket, he brought out an unlabeled bottle and offered Bill Dowell, 19-year-old Merkel evangelist, a drink.

Young Dowell handed him a tract.

"I'll read this 'il book in the morning, but I'll still be an unhappy man," the imbiber said mushily.[14]

In response to the report, Nola relayed to Bill a playful message from their fellow church members. "[T]he paper did not state whether you took the drink offered you or not," she wrote, "so they said they were surely going to tease you about that when you returned."[15]

As always, Dowell could not help smiling whenever he thought of his sweetheart. How eager he was to see her again. Riding along in Ernest's Ford, he tried to hasten his much anticipated reunion with her by picking up the tempo of his duet with Ernest:

To Jesus Christ I fled for rest;

He bade me cease to roam—

Ernest grinned at his brother's zest but was determined not to be outdone. He matched Bill's tempo and added a bit of harmony.

And lean for comfort on His breast

Till He conduct me home.

After the intense schedule at the Bible school, these two singers were glad to let loose. The breakneck pace of the previous two weeks had been thoroughly exhausting. Bill had taken a brief illness in the midst of it all, something for which he earned a scolding from Nola. "I still love you," she snipped in a letter, "but I fear you have been keeping something from me. Bro. Rister has been telling us a lot of things. Dear, why haven't you told me of your being sick?"[16] The cause of Dowell's illness may have been a downpour that came during one of those late-night tavern raids. "Many of the young evangelists were without coats and hats," the *Fort Worth Press* reported. "They strode thru a rainstorm and soon were dripping."[17]

But young Dowell seems to have cared little about such setbacks. Nor did he let it keep him from his training. Some observers have cast aspersions on the educational value of Norris's schools, but Dowell himself found the experience life-changing. More than forty years after he attended the Premillennial Bible School, he wrote, "When history is finally written, no doubt it will record that the beginning of the greatest fundamentalist movement in history started when Dr. Frank Norris started week-long Bible conferences and invited preachers and laymen from all over the nation to attend."[18]

This assessment stands in stark contrast to Billy Vick Bartlett's characterization of the training. Bartlett called it "fundamentalism at its worst."[19] Citing an interview with his grandfather, G. B. Vick, Bartlett said, "Although the meetings were referred to as 'schools,' they were actually Chautauqua-like Bible conferences but not approaching the Chautauqua in educational quality. They were promotional rather than educational and actually depreciated the function of formal education."[20]

Bartlett's appraisal has some validity, no doubt, yet the picture seems less than complete. Evidence suggests that Norris's training was not entirely devoid of substance. Dowell retained in his library a printed copy of Norris's 1933 lecture "Fifteen Signs of the Second Coming of Christ," a work that rebuts such overly dismissive criticisms. This lecture, though limited in its depth, does manage to provide a systematic overview of Pre- and Post-Millennialism, the Rapture, the Great Tribulation, the Battle of Armageddon, and a range of other eschatological topics.[21] It also explores some of the major religious controversies of the day as well as some important Baptist doctrines. For novice Christian workers like Dowell, such content must have been greatly enriching.

But Norris's training served another educational purpose as well. It exposed students to some of the nation's greatest fundamentalist visionaries. The 1934 roster of speakers included not only J. Frank Norris but also such notables as W. B. Riley and John R. Rice. Together these men delivered lectures on subjects as wide-ranging as church administration and Old Testament history. Norris himself taught through the entire books of Genesis, the Gospel of John, and Revelation. Lectures began at 8 a.m. and continued throughout the day and evening, Monday through Saturday. "I get up in the morning," Bill wrote to Nola, "hurriedly eat my breakfast, and rush over for the first lecture. At noon I eat my lunch and hurry back for services, and they last the rest of the day. Then I eat supper and hurry back for night services. As soon as night services are over we go out on personal work until about 12 or half past 12 o'clock."[22]

Bill's singing unexpectedly morphed into a wide-mouthed yawn:

Are we there yet?

Ernest's reply set off a lighthearted exchange:

Won't be long now.

It's already been long.

Yeah, but it was worth it.

Bill had to agree. While Norris's school may not have offered a formal education in any modern sense of the expression, it certainly offered an informal one. Indeed, these classes were the only real Bible training Dowell ever received. And he cherished the experience. In the end, Norris's training may have imparted a kind of knowledge that was more caught than taught. And a certain nineteen-year-old from Merkel seems to have caught a great deal.

The brothers now picked up their song where they had left off:

We'll work till Jesus comes,

We'll work till Jesus comes,

We'll work till Jesus comes,

And we'll be gathered home![23]

Chapter 8: *Dr. Norris*

Ernest's black Ford was still slicing through the Texas dust. The two brothers had somehow managed to pass the time with their hymn singing, and now their long trip was nearing an end. Merkel was just minutes away.

Feeling playful, Bill turned to Ernest and said:

Do you s'pose Dr. Norris would enjoy our singing?

Ernest answered:

Oh, I don't know. We're not so bad.

Bill picked up the banter from there:

Probably not ready for his radio program just yet.

Well, that's why we was rehearsin'.

Maybe we could preach for him instead.

Think you could do it like he does?

This question fired Bill up.

Oh, I can tell it to people straight, all right. That's what Dr. Norris does. And that's a whole lot better than tickling people's ears—which is what a lot of 'em do.

Ernest smiled at his youngest brother's fervor. Then he said:

I think we might just turn you into a fundamentalist.

A seminal part of Dowell's experience in Fort Worth had been his introduction to Baptist fundamentalist J. Frank Norris. Even as a young man, Dowell could see that this preacher's reputation was well deserved. Norris, known to many as "The Texas Tornado," was nothing short of sensational.[1] His confrontational speaking style made him both captivating and controversial. And Norris relished controversy. He used it to generate publicity for himself and his work. In the pulpit and in the media, Norris regularly skewered his many doctrinal and philosophical foes. This list included the liquor establishment, the Catholic Church, Fort Worth city officials, the Northern and Southern Baptist Conventions, and Baylor University. Norris also targeted many of his one-time allies. As Bartlett observes, Norris developed a penchant for burning bridges: "Beginning about 1930, his life became a violent series of breaks with most of his former associates, accompanied by mutual denunciations."[2]

Although Norris's vitriol earned him many detractors, this preacher's charisma also won him a large number of stalwart supporters. These individuals viewed Norris as a man of exceptional courage and conviction, and they remained deeply loyal to him, even dismissing allegations of his sometimes unscrupulous behavior. In fact, long before Dowell ever met up with him, Norris had weathered two major scandals wherein he had been accused of criminal activity. These accusations would have poisoned the careers of many ministers, but that was not the case with Norris.

The first of these scandals erupted in 1912, just a couple of years after Norris became pastor of First Baptist. It grew out of a battle Norris had waged against a string of eighty prostitution houses. These establishments littered a district of downtown Fort Worth that had become known as Hell's Half Acre. Norris alleged that city leaders were a party to the illicit activities of Hell's Half Acre, and he lashed out at those leaders for their involvement. His efforts then set off a series of bizarre events. One account of the scandal summarizes it this way:

> *Norris used his Sunday evening sermons to expose and humiliate the men who owned Hell's Half Acre. He advertised sensational sermon titles like, "The 10 Biggest Devils In Town And Their Records Given." Overflow crowds attended the services where Norris named the persons who profited and the city officials he believed were their cohorts.*
>
> *That summer [1911] he erected an enormous tent in a vacant lot near the Half Acre and preached a series of sermons on its sins and challenged the city to enforce the law. He also attacked the liquor industry and brought major Prohibition leaders to help. The city mayor, W. B. Davis, had the tent removed because Norris had not obtained permission to use the lot.*
>
> *Norris then attacked the city administration, and in January, 1912, Davis threatened to have Norris hung. Two days later a fire was discovered at First Baptist Church, but was quickly put out. Three days after that, two shots were fired through the church study windows where Norris was working. On February 4, an explosion and fire burned the church to the ground. A month later, the Norris family escaped harm when their home was also burned.*[3]

This is where the story takes an unexpected turn. Investigators charged Norris himself with setting the fires. "It was alleged that he wanted to build a new [church] building and used the controversy to cover his guilt." Was Norris the victim of enemy attack, or had this master manipulator capitalized on a controversy in order to acquire an enlarged facility for his church? Both views were argued vigorously in court. Yet in the end, Norris's version won the day. "[T]he preacher was acquitted by order of the judge."[4]

Exonerated of any wrongdoing in the arson case, Norris went on to rebuild both his church and his reputation. But then, more than a decade after the first scandal, there came a second criminal investigation. This time the charge was murder. This latest crisis erupted when Norris shot and killed an adversary in his church office at First Baptist. According to one source, "Norris had been conducting a running battle with the Roman Catholic mayor of Fort Worth over Norris's charges that the mayor had illegally favored a Catholic organization."[5] Bartlett details what transpired in the wake of that battle:

> On Saturday, July 17, 1926, D. E. Chipps, a wealthy Fort Worth lumberman and a personal friend of [Mayor] Meacham's, marched into the office of Norris's downtown church, warned him to desist from his exposé of Mayor Meacham, and turned to leave. Upon reaching the door he whirled and thrust his hand into his back pocket, a gesture that was still pregnant with implication in the unsophisticated cowtown. Norris, watching out of the corner of his eye, lifted what was later described as "the night watchman's gun", and fired three shots into Chipp's massive frame.[6]

Had Norris acted in self-defense? This would be a difficult argument for the preacher to make. As Dowell himself observed, "A mystery that I suppose has never been solved is the fact that no gun was found on Mr. Chips [sic]."[7] The ensuing investigation revealed that Norris had taken the life of an unarmed man who was standing across the room from him. On that point there was no dispute. The only real question was whether this preacher could emerge from such a scandal unscathed. Amazingly Norris seems to have done so.[8]

After Norris was charged with murder in 1926, his supporters came to his aid. "His devoted congregation quickly raised funds for his defense, at one time collecting $16,000 in cash in a washtub." Then Norris mounted a vigorous defense in court, insisting "that he had been threatened on the telephone and, fearing for his life, defended himself by killing his visitor." And once again, the court found his story credible. "Norris was acquitted on the first ballot by the jury, who agreed that it really was a case of self-defense."[9] For a second time, then, J. Frank Norris had escaped from a personal and legal quagmire.

What is most remarkable in all of this is that Norris's public support flourished both during and after these scandals. Supporters stood with him no matter what. Author David Stokes describes Norris, saying, "He became a composite personality, blending some Billy Sunday with a touch of P. T. Barnum, and with a little William Randolph Hearst thrown in."[10] This seems an accurate description. Part preacher, part showman, Norris always seemed to know how to sway public opinion, or at least some of it, in his favor. Even if his tactics were sometimes suspect, the sheer force of his personality won him the respect of many. This preacher was not always right, but he was always dogmatic. And his crowds loved him for that.

Of course, those early scandals in Norris's career were ancient history by the time the Dowell brothers attended the Premillennial Bible School. By then, Norris had become more popular than ever, and large numbers were flocking to Fort Worth for an opportunity to study under him. In fact, just days before that 1934 training began, Norris boasted in *The Fundamentalist* that his church had received "more than three times as many letters" from students who were seeking to enroll that year.[11] Then, during the second week of classes, Norris reiterated the school's success, publishing a report that said students had traveled from twenty-seven different states to attend his meetings.[12] Why all of this interest? The answer was J. Frank Norris. Norris's lion-like boldness had made him an icon, and preachers everywhere were eager to see him roar in his natural habitat. Norris's once-regional celebrity had now spread to other parts of the nation.

Norris's expanding appeal was likewise seen in the relationship that he was forming with the northern city of Detroit. During the early 1930s. Norris conducted a series of successful revival meetings in that city. Now those meetings were opening a new door of opportunity, one that would eventually affect Dowell as well. This chain of events began when Norris was contacted by the leaders of Detroit's Temple Baptist Church. The men informed Norris that their pastor, Albert G. Johnson, was retiring and that they wanted Norris to consider becoming their new pastor.[13]

Temple was a solid church, averaging 761 at the time, yet it was considerably smaller than Norris's church in Fort Worth.[14] Still, the invitation to pastor this church was not without its appeal. Temple was located in one of the north's most important industrial centers, and Detroit's booming auto industry made this a strategic city for any preacher interested in drawing large audiences and influencing American society.

For Norris, there was also another attraction: his presence in Detroit would outrage the leaders of the Northern Baptist Convention. Members of that Convention had vehemently opposed Norris's revival meetings in Detroit, charging that his coming would mean nothing but trouble. And they had good reason for saying so. It was no secret that Norris wanted to mount a campaign against the Northern Baptists just as he had done with the Southern Baptists. As far as he was concerned, the heresies of these two groups were indistinguishable. Norris commonly lumped the conventions together using the derogatory phrase "denominational machine."[15] So it went without saying that, if Norris set up a permanent ministry in Detroit, he would expend a great deal of effort to throw a wrench into that machine.

Yet would this celebrated preacher seize the opportunity? The leaders at Temple were operating under no misapprehension. Norris had built a sizable empire in Fort Worth, and they knew there was little chance that Norris would want to give it all up. So they did not ask him to. Instead they proposed that Norris pastor both congregations simultaneously. Norris would commute between the two works, the one in Detroit and the one in Fort Worth, and he would use other men to fill his two pulpits whenever he was away.

The idea was preposterous, yet in March of 1935, Norris demonstrated that he was just brash enough to try it. He installed his long-time ministry partner, Louis Entzminger, as his on-site associate in Detroit. Entzminger's job was to manage the church's day-to-day operations and also to preach when Norris was away. The arrangement got off to a rocky start, however. Though Entzminger had his strong points, great preaching seems not to have been one of them. "[H]e could preach any place . . . in the world empty," one contemporary said.[16] As a result, Temple Baptist began to flounder, and many church members began attending services only when

Norris was there to do the preaching. After about a year, Norris summoned Entzminger back to Fort Worth and replaced him with a new associate, G. Beauchamp Vick.[17]

Vick had once served as a highly successful lay leader under Norris in Fort Worth, yet more recently he had been doing evangelistic work, serving under Wade House and also Mordecai Hamm.[18] Norris believed Vick had the right skill set to run a church. As biographer Mike Randall put it, Vick had proven abilities in "organization, planning, public relations, finance, music, leadership, and attention to detail."[19] Best of all, Vick could preach.

Vick's new title in Detroit was "general superintendent," though his duties quickly outstripped that unimpressive name. Vick not only managed Temple, he ran it. And he became a key figure behind the pulpit. Randall continues his account, saying, "When Norris couldn't be at church to preach on Sunday, which was often, Vick was responsible to either preach or invite another preacher to fill the pulpit." According to Randall, Vick's duties at the church were essentially "the same as a pastor's."[20]

This new partnership proved highly successful for both Norris and Temple Baptist Church. Indeed, with Vick's help, Norris's unprecedented dual pastorate would continue until 1950.[21] By that time, Temple would be averaging over 3800 in Sunday school attendance.[22] And though Vick played a significant role the church's growth, it was Norris who won the acclaim. As Norris himself was fond of stating, the combined membership of his two churches meant that no pastor on earth had a larger following than he did.

Norris was, indeed, a powerhouse of a leader. One observer called him a "spellbinder," saying, "He had a 'mystical' power over audiences, a remarkable facility in earthy idiom."[23] Many of Norris's contemporaries noted the same thing. On one occasion in 1939, when Norris tried to resign from Temple Baptist due to the strain of his responsibilities, his resignation was refused. The deacons insisted he was too valuable to let go. In fact, forty-seven years after Norris's death, a newspaper in Fort Worth named him among the city's "Top 100 Movers and Shakers."[24] This was a preacher who left an indelible mark.

Little wonder, then, that a young man like Dowell would be swept up by the charisma of this larger-than-life leader. In 1977, Dowell wrote that the training he received under Norris had been of "great profit" to him.[25] Dowell expressed similar sentiments the year he exited Norris's Bible school. Near the end of that 1934 session, Norris published in *The Fundamentalist* comments that had been submitted by some of his recent pupils. Dowell was quoted as saying, "I am surely enjoying the Bible School. It has increased my knowledge of the Bible and made me more apt to teach the Word of God. I rejoice in being instrumental in God's hands of leading lost souls to Christ here in Ft. Worth. I thank God for his goodness."[26]

So impressed was Dowell by the things he had experienced in Fort Worth that he returned for another session of Norris's Bible school just six months later. His published comments after that second session illustrate the ongoing influence Norris was having upon him. "This is the second Bible School I have been privileged to attend," Dowell wrote. "I have gained a deeper knowledge of the 'Word of God.' I have been preaching only eight months, but through these Bible Schools I have been enabled to gain knowledge, experience and training that I have been unable to get elsewhere." Then, as the writer continues, he seems to parrot some of Norris's own rhetoric:

> *I have been told what great opportunity could be mine, as a young preacher if I would line up with the Convention. I answer back and say I am not taking orders from any Convention or group of Modernists. I am taking orders from Jesus Christ, and as long as this body God has given me can stand, I am going to fight sin and preach the Gospel of Jesus Christ plus nothing and minus nothing. I thank God for this school.*[27]

It would seem that the son of a Southern Baptist preacher was now spouting defiance against the denominational machine. Dowell had come under the spell of the spellbinder.

Unquestionably, Norris's training instilled in Dowell not only an understanding of scripture and a passion for evangelism but also a measure of fundamentalist pugilism. Though Dowell would never expend much energy attacking other Christian groups (unlike Norris), this young preacher did adopt many of Norris's basic attitudes and philosophies. And equipped with these, Dowell quickly branded himself as an independent fundamental Baptist, a badge he would proudly wear throughout his ministry. It was J. Frank Norris who helped him discover that identity.

Have you been to Jesus for the cleansing power?
Are you washed in the blood of the Lamb?

As another boisterous duet took off, Bill and Ernest's shared rejoicing defied explanation. If Bill had tried to put it into words, he might have said that his cup was running over.

He patted his thigh in rhythm as he sang.

Are you fully trusting in His grace this hour?
Are you washed in the blood of the Lamb?–

Bill now wondered if Paul and Silas had experienced similar rapture when they sat singing at midnight in the Philippian jail. Bill assured himself that they had. And this thought reminded him of something he had read in one of Nola's letters. "The church received yours and Bro. Dowell's letter," Nola wrote. "We were surely glad to get it." Nola then invoked the name of that same New Testament apostle that Bill had just been pondering. "It made me think of Paul when writing to the churches," she said. "In our lesson this morning, Paul sent Timotheus to the church at Thessalonica to learn of their welfare. He came back with this report that they loved and desired to see Paul as much as Paul longed to go to them. Then when your letter was read I felt as if I was going to just weep for joy."[28]

A smile came over Bill's face as he thought about Nola's words. It was not merely her mention of Paul or the sentiment that Nola had expressed that pleased him. It was the realization that Nola shared his love for the Bible. Like him, she was a student of scripture. When she opened up the Word, she too heard a Voice echoing back a message of immediacy, a message about her life and times. Bill loved her all the more for that.

As the young traveler sat reflecting on this thought, the town of Merkel appeared on the horizon. Bill's heart pounded when he saw it, and he momentarily forgot that Ernest was sitting next to him in the car. But then, singing and patting the letters in his pocket, the young man slowly came back to himself. Or did he? Somehow Bill seemed different now.

Are you washed—
In the blood,
In the soul-cleansing blood of the Lamb?—

Bill's overflowing joy was making his head sway from side to side as he belted out that last jubilant chorus. A new confidence had also come over his face.

Are your garments spotless?
Are they white as snow?
Are you washed in the blood of the Lamb?[29]

Ernest spotted that new confidence when Bill turned to him and said:

Y'know, Ernest? I don't believe Paul and Silas could have sung that song one bit better.

The older brother did not know what had brought on this comment, but he had to agree.

Well, now that you mention it, I think you may be right!

And to this Ernest added a wink and a smile.

Chapter 9: *Merkel*

*O*h. . . . *Now isn't that somethin'.*

Bessie bit her lower lip as she admired the scenery in a gold-framed oil painting. She was struck by the serenity of it all, a glassy lake reflecting the pink sunlight above. Two mountain peaks standing in the distance were likewise bouncing off the water.

Sure don't see mountains like those in Texas.

Birds dipped their wings in the lake, but that was the only hint of any movement. All else was still.

What a beautiful place. So peaceful and relaxin'.

Even though the terrain of this scene was markedly different from anything in Texas, its tranquility reminded Ernest's wife of some of the watering holes near Merkel. Throughout the warm months, Merkel's young people loved to refresh themselves at a place called Mulberry Creek. In fact, soon after Bill left for his first Bible school training in Fort Worth, some of Nola's girlfriends orchestrated a trip to Mulberry Creek for a sunrise breakfast. Or at least they tried. "[O]ur parents said no after we had fixed for it," Nola complained in one of her letters. "We had planned to go in swimming too. They said if one of us got in deep water or had a cramp the rest knew too little about rescuing to save her, so our plans were blasted."[1]

Sweet Nola sure loves the water. . . .

As Bessie continued studying the vista, she noticed a lone fisherman sitting in a canoe out on the lake. He wore a broad-brimmed hat, and his long cane pole extended over the water.

I imagine Bill would like the fisherman. He could imagine that it was him—fishin' up a big one for Nola to fry.

Bessie chuckled.

Oh, and it's got so much blue. Such a pretty blue.

The scene was covered by a vast turquoise sky. There were clusters of trees on the periphery—tall, slender evergreens trying to hold it all in. Yet this sky could not be contained. Indeed, the blue's dominance made Bessie think of that old expression:

Something old, something new, something borrowed—

She did not even finish the saying. She turned to the merchant and piped:

I'll take it. I think it's perfect. Somehow it just makes me think of "Home Sweet Home."

Bessie then reached into her purse and pulled out a small sum of money to hand to the shopkeeper. He rang up the purchase as Bessie continued studying her painting.

Handing back the change, the man said:

You got a pretty one, all right.

This was when Bessie leaned over the counter and whispered:

It's gonna be a weddin' gift. Don't you tell nobody.

The painting that Bessie selected was not large, but to her it seemed an ideal size for the small living space in the back of her home. Bill and Nola would be renting that space after their wedding. They would have three rooms—a bedroom, a dining room, and a bathroom—for the grand sum of three dollars a month.

Bessie dangled her purse from her forearm and carefully lifted her oil painting off the counter, saying:

I think they will just love it, don't you?

She was already walking away before the man had a chance to reply. It mattered little what the shopkeeper thought. Besides, this was all she could afford. Given the state of the economy, any gift at all was a sacrifice. The truth was that Ernest and his siblings had been forced to pool their meager resources just to manage this purchase. Bessie called back to the shopkeeper as she strode through the store's open doorway:

Hope to see you in services on Sunday!

Then she bounced down the sidewalk.

Bill and Nola's wedding ceremony took place on September 2, 1934. It followed the morning worship services at North Side Missionary Baptist Church. Ernest officiated, and nearly every member of the congregation attended. It was a simple ceremony. There were no bridesmaids or groomsmen, no photographers, and there would be no honeymoon vacation afterwards. Such were the constraints of the Great Depression.

The Dowell's nuptials followed an eight-month courtship. That was all the time it took for the love-at-first-sight romance to blossom into a lifelong commitment. Indeed, Nola had confessed deep feelings for her beau even during his first visit to Fort Worth. "I want you to hurry back to me, so I can start living and enjoying life again," she pined in a letter. "I feel that I'm only existing, that a better half of me has disappeared, and so it has."[2] These two lovers had determined to view their separation as a test of their commitment, so Bill wrote back to inform Nola that he had passed the test with ease. "You said one time you would like for us to be separated for a short while to see if my love for you would last," he said. "My darling each day I love you *more*."[3]

For a while Bill and Nola worried that this test of theirs might be extended through the summer months. Nola learned while Bill was away that her parents were considering a three-month trip to California. Nola's mother had relatives living in California, and employment opportunities there might help tide the family over during the lean days of the Depression. Nola nervously wrote to Bill, "Wouldn't it be awful if we went before you returned?"[4]

In the end, the California trip was delayed, perhaps due to the illness of Nola's married sister, Jewell. Nola also wrote about that: "I told you in my last letter that Jewell was getting along fine. Well they had to call the Dr. this morning. So Mother and Dad had her brought over here (on a stretcher). Mother couldn't keep from going into another room and crying as it looked so pitiful, almost like a corpse. Her side is hurting awfully bad."[5]

Jewell eventually recovered from that illness, but Nola took from her sister's experience an important lesson, one which she forthrightly declared to Bill. She explained that she had been deeply offended when Jewell's husband refused to cancel an out-of-town trip in the midst of his wife's health crisis:

> *Bill, please don't ever leave me when I'm sick, especially if it's only a pleasure trip as he went on. I almost cried, and I did inwardly, when he came in to tell her about it. She asked him not to go, as she was so sick and weak. He's funny and absolutely crazy. I wouldn't put up with a man that didn't care any more about me than that. And since you have all my heart's love, I'm asking you now, to please, don't treat me so cruel as that. . . .*[6]

Such remarks make it evident that Bill and Nola were now pondering the depth of their commitment to each other. And as it turned out, these thoughts were prompted not only by their separation but also by the efforts of some rival suitors. With amusing candor, Nola broached that subject in another letter:

> *Then last Wed. night, Will Huffman was at prayer meeting, and by the way, while speaking of him, he has fallen off 19 lbs. and he surely shows it too. He does not look very well yet. Anyway, I'll bet he would have liked to walk home with me, but I didn't give him a chance. Did I imagine you said, 'Cruel!'? I may be but if you love a person and am planning to be his bride, I can't help but think of only him, and cannot bear to go with someone else, even if I did do such a thing in the past.*[7]

Nola's too-fervent insistence that she had no interest in Will Huffman is as comical as it is sweet, though she sounds less like the object of a serious rivalry than she does a lovesick girl trying to squelch a hoped-for rumor. But Nola's suspicions about Will Huffman were not entirely unfounded, as one of her later letters confirms. In that letter she relates how Huffman made a presumptuous attempt to steal her companionship, walking alongside her uninvited as she made her way home from church services. "[A]nd of course he would start a conversation," she groused. Here again Nola defended her honor, describing how she thwarted Will's advances by altering her usual route home from church. "I made a complaint about the sun being so hot," she wrote, "and as soon as we came to the turn at the alley I turned in."[8]

Yet this was not the end of such nuisances. Only a few days later, whispers began about Nola's associations with yet another interested boy. She explained the circumstance to Bill, saying:

I have been accused of going with Homer R. in swimming just because he went along with me and my brother and sister and cousins, but I wasn't with him any more than I was anyone else, not as much, if anything. I also heard that if we didn't come before the church and apologize for going in swimming (with my brother and cousins) a certain party was going to withdraw their membership. I heard all this, so it may and again it may not be only a joke. I am not bothered one bit about it, for everything was carried on as nice as could be. So let them withdraw if that's the way they feel. I'm not going in again if someone no more kin than Homer R. goes, but that's that, for the present.[9]

And to this she added flatly, "'Ol Will asked to see me home last night, but I would not hear of such folly. May and Travis escorted me home."[10]

Nola's indignation aside, nothing of any importance seems to have come of these courtship dramas. And for his part, Bill seems to have remained unaffected by all of it. "So Homer and Will are fighting over you now are they?" he teased in one letter. "Well just so they keep hands off!"[11] A day later he joked again, "I surely do miss you. I don't guess Homer and Will are missing me much though."[12]

Of course, interspersed with these frivolous exchanges is evidence that Bill and Nola were giving earnest thought to sharing a married life together. Each wanted to be worthy of the other's love. In a serious mood Bill wrote, "I think often of our last evening together, and the many happy hours I have spent with you and the sweet memories causes me to have a greater determination to be what God would have me be, and a man you will be proud to call your own."[13] Then in another letter he declared, "My highest ambition is to be an obedient minister of the gospel. My next greatest ambition is to win and claim Nola Mae Callahan as my bride. If you are a good prophet, write and tell me if I shall gain victory or lose the fight. God grant that I shall win. With you I could conquer the world. Without you I could never be happy."[14]

Nola's writings show similar concern for giving God the preeminence in their relationship. "I have always longed for a man," she confided, "someone that loved God above all things and had that desire in his heart and soul to be a preacher of the Gospel. I know, absolutely know that I can always be happy with you."[15] Elsewhere she wrote of a conversation she had with a sister about her anticipated marriage to Bill: "Estell asked me this morning if I was going to do everything I could (when we are married) to encourage you in the work and be an inspiration to you, or be the opposite as some preacher's wives do (I have a cousin, a preacher, and his wife doesn't want him to be). Of course I was going to do the affirmative, because I'm very interested in doing service for the Lord."[16]

Nola was sincere in this. Her interest in spiritual matters was anything but fleeting. As a girl of eleven years old, she had stepped on a broken fruit jar while playing in the yard with some cousins. The glass cut the main artery in her left foot, leaving Nola unable to walk for the next six months. She made the best of the circumstance, however, by reading through the entire New Testament. "For a child of eleven years that was pretty good," she said of the experience.[17]

This interest in the Bible never abated. Indeed, one of Nola's greatest disappointments over Bill's trip to Fort Worth was the fact that she would miss out on the spiritual training herself. She confessed her jealously, saying, "I do so love to read and study the Bible, and I enjoy and am so happy when I'm in company of God's people who enjoy and are really striving to do his will."[18] Nola made sure that she did not miss the next such opportunity. When Bill made his second trip to Fort Worth soon after their wedding, she went with him. Her reaction to the experience was recorded alongside Bill's in *The Fundamentalist*:

> *This Bible School has helped me to stir up the gift that is within me to the extent that I desire to make the statement that Paul made in writing to the Philippians, "For to me to live is Christ, and to die is gain." Not only to make it, but to live the statement. I have been made to realize that God still exists, and His power and glory can still be manifested in his people. My great desire is that this Bible School will continue to spread and be a blessing to all.*[19]

The Dowells' mutual commitment to the Lord would bring them many joys as they started their new life together. But of course, there would also be challenges, especially in those early days. For Nola, one of the greatest challenges proved to be the frequent periods of separation from her husband. Unlike that shared visit to Fort Worth, day-to-day married life was often spent apart. Soon after the Dowells wed, Ernest published an article on the happenings at the North Side Missionary Baptist Church, saying "Bill Dowell preached for us last Sunday morning and the church elected him as assistant pastor." Then Ernest added a note about some ambitious plans the brothers had made: "Bill and I will enter into a continued evangelistic work; going out from this good church, we will have a revival going on all time and establish good churches in every city."[20]

Bill and Ernest's evangelistic efforts soon became not only a part of their ministry but also a part of their livelihood. Meanwhile, Nola was left alone at home. In November of 1934, the young wife described in a letter to her husband the deep despair that had come over her as she watched him depart for a ministry engagement. "I fell across the bed," she wrote, "my heart was breaking, it seemed that you had died and I would never see you again. I wept bitter tears. . . . I feared I would have hysterics as I did one night, on the day of Minnie Peterson's death." Then as she continued, Nola described an unusual encounter that helped to free her from those tears:

> *I was weeping heartbreakingly again when a knock sounded. I answered the door. The man said he saw me thru the window crying, and asked me what I was crying for. I told him and he told me not to cry, but be a brave little girl and pray for my husband. He said a preacher's wife had a hard life to live, and that it was a very important life. He bought 50¢ worth of old jewelry from me. When he started to leave he said, "Do not cry any more but go read your Bible and pray for your good husband." Said that would do more good that anything.*[21]

Nola took the man's advice and found it to be effective. Reading the Bible and praying were indeed good medicine for her despondency, though she did not go so far as to call them antidotes. In truth, Nola never fully conquered those feelings of loneliness and anxiety. She did learn to cope with them, however. Bill's ministry meant that he was frequently away from her, and Nola acknowledged the importance of his work. She also acknowledged the importance of her role as the preacher's wife. And in that confidence, she learned to carry on in her husband's absence.

During that first year of marriage, Nola learned many such lessons. At every turn, it seemed, her former way of life was being rewritten. Her grandfather, George G. Callahan, who had been living with her family for two years, passed away about the same time that she and Bill were married. Then, not long afterward, Nola's parents and several of her brothers and sisters decided to move away from Merkel. They migrated from Texas to California, where the economic opportunities were said to be more plentiful. Nola and Bill stayed behind.

The Dowells took the opportunity to exit their tiny apartment in Ernest's home and to rent the Callahans' vacant house. This only magnified Nola's sense of isolation, however. The family that had once shared this home with her was now missing.

Nola's despondency was compounded by the financial difficulties that she and her husband began to face. The congregation at North Side was small, averaging only eighty to ninety people, so Bill earned little from his church work. On Mother's Day in 1934, Nola reported an exceptional attendance of a hundred and fourteen people, yet even then, the entire offering totaled just one dollar and twenty-five cents.[22]

Such circumstances made it impossible for the Dowells to survive on Bill's associate's income alone. To make ends meet, Bill also had to work as a farmhand. His employer was a man named Armstrong, a local physician who also owned a large farm. Armstrong hired Bill at a wage of one dollar and twenty-five cents a day, and this meager pay meant that Bill had to work constantly in order to survive. Dowell worked an average of eleven hours per day, he said. Recalling the experience, he told some students, "We made some sacrifices in every area during those days, but we were happy because we knew we were in God's will. I have often said that I would take nothing for this experience, but I would not want to go through it again at any price."[23]

From Nola's perspective, Bill was always either in the fields or at the church or on the road conducting an evangelistic meeting. She coped with her loneliness as best she could, first by channeling her energies into her love of music. She took piano lessons all through that winter, and since she did not yet own a piano (in later life, she kept a spinet in her living room), she made daily trips to the frigid church tabernacle to practice her lessons. She later gave up the instrument, preferring to sing music more than to play it.

Nola then took up a new hobby: gardening. She harvested and canned twenty-eight quarts of produce that year, she said. All of them went bad except for one. The disastrous experience caused her to give up that hobby too. She never gardened again.[24]

What sustained this preacher's wife thereafter was simply the Lord's goodness. And despite the many challenges, Nola could see that God's blessings on her family were abundant.

On January 6, 1935, Ernest moderated a committee of Baptist preachers as they interrogated Bill for his ordination into the gospel ministry. Ordination would formalize the call that Bill had already heard from God. It would also lend credibility to his ministry, making further opportunities possible. Shortly after Dowell was ordained, an article described some of those fresh opportunities: "Brother Bill Dowell, who has been ordained but a few months, is filling Brother Shepherd's pulpit at Sweetwater each Sunday. They are having some wonderful services there. . . . Bill is also preaching over the radio at Dublin each Monday from 11:45 to 12:15 and from 1 to 1:30."[25]

The Dowells also found themselves blessed in their own church. Whenever Bill was not preaching elsewhere, he and Nola were faithfully continuing their work with the youth of North Side Missionary Baptist. During one warm-weather revival, Bill invited the youth to meet with him out under a tree before each service. Together they prayed that God would bless the evening's service and that souls would be saved. Dowell recalled that, of their own accord, some members of his youth group began asking God for specific numbers of converts. Dowell did not think the practice was wise, but he also did not want to discourage the fervent prayers of his young charges. So he said nothing. And to his amazement, God honored and answered those prayers each night. Even when, on one occasion, the total number of converts fell short of the requested number by one soul, Dowell and his young charges refused to be discouraged. They rejoiced and went home, Dowell said, only to learn the next day that an additional soul had accepted Christ after the conclusion of the service.[26]

At the end of 1935, the Dowells experienced one more important blessing. That was when Nola gave birth to their first child, a nine-pound girl whom they named Noma Lea Janet. This child, who would become known as Janet (pronounced like *Janette*), was delivered at home on December 13. Her father assisted Dr. Armstrong in the delivery, as did one of Nola's sisters-in-law, Deta Callahan.

Janet's arrival meant more changes for Nola. Writing many years later, Nola reflected on the experience of becoming a mother. "It was so different" she said. "[I]t was like reading a book and then taking up another one, altogether different, in every way."[27] But that new book was far from over. Indeed, further changes lay yet ahead. On the heels of Janet's arrival, the Dowells learned that Ernest and Bessie were planning to move to Hobbs, New Mexico, to undertake a new ministry. And in the wake of their departure, Bill would receive his first call to become a pastor, serving in his brother's stead at North Side Missionary Baptist.

Bill's salary from North Side now increased to three dollars per week. Even so, the Dowells found that their income was not sufficient to support a family of three. For several months Bill continued working both as pastor and farmhand, doing his best to provide for Nola and Janet. But their existence was a meager one at best. Consequently, just six months after Bill became the pastor of North Side, he decided his family needed a fresh start.

Dowell said that he and Nola found new direction in a letter that came in the mail. "I got a letter one day from my wife's father, saying they were coming back to Merkel on a trip and that if we would like to do it, we could sell everything and arrange to return with them to California."[28] Dowell accepted that invitation. In August of 1936, with only a few personal possessions—among them a cherished oil painting that they had received as a wedding gift—Bill and Nola migrated with their eight-month-old daughter to the Golden State. They settled in the town of Tulare, where they hoped to find a new home with new opportunities. They would not be disappointed.

Chapter 10: *Eighteen Faces*

Bill examined the line of faces in front of him—eighteen of them in all—staring back at him with expressionless eyes. These faces were spread across a pew in the First Baptist Church of Tulare, California. The man on the end of the row stood up with his hat in his hands and said:

I wonder if we might have a word with you.

The inquiry made the preacher curious, if not altogether anxious.

We heard you preach tonight, and we'd like to ask you a few things.

Questions from church people still made this young preacher's heart race. "I felt very limited in my knowledge of the Bible," Dowell once confided. "I felt very uneasy that someone would ask me a question about the Bible that I couldn't answer. I had the idea that if you were a preacher—particularly if you were a pastor—I had the idea that you ought to be able to answer any question anybody would ask you about the Bible." He added, "I learned better later."[1]

Yet at this point in his life, Dowell was still a novice. Despite having experience as the pastor of North Side Missionary Baptist and as a revival speaker, this young preacher's confidence was easily shaken. "I used to hold revivals," he said, "and I'd take me an armload of books—sermon books, particularly, by some of the great preachers— and I'd work on those sermons. Day by day I'd prepare a sermon for that night. But I still felt very limited in an extensive knowledge of the Bible."[2]

Dowell's speaking engagement at Tulare had not been a revival meeting. He had been filling the pulpit, as preachers like to say, for an absent minister. The absentee was a pastor who had recently been wed and was now away on his honeymoon. This pastor's invitation to Dowell was the first preaching opportunity that Dowell had received since leaving Texas a few months earlier. And he was happy to have it. The preacher who invited him even placed an announcement in the newspaper advertising Dowell's name.

Dowell hoped that he had not made a bad impression. He and Nola were still newcomers to Tulare, a farming community north of Bakersfield. Their first few months in central California had been spent getting settled and finding enough work to provide for their family. They had carried few possessions with them from Texas, so most things had to be purchased after they got settled. With the help of Noma Lea and some other Callahan family members, even Nola was able to take a job to help meet their needs.

Nola left Janet in the care of these family members and worked alongside Bill out in the cotton fields. Bill recalled that one of their first priorities had been to earn enough money to buy clothing suitable for church.[3]

Bill was subconsciously securing the top button of his new suit coat as he stood in the aisle of the First Baptist Church. Glancing at the solemn-looking assembly sitting in the pew, he forced a smile and answered them:

Why, certainly. What can I do for you folks?

The man clutching his hat then began an explanation:

See, we heard that you was going to be here tonight and that you was going to fill in for the regular preacher. That's why we come over.

The "regular preacher" was a Southern Baptist man, but Dowell did not quibble over that. Though Dowell had aligned himself ideologically with the independent Baptist movement, he was never belligerent toward Southern Baptists. He just could not be a part of their movement. Dowell, like J. Frank Norris, believed the denominational machine was a contraption in need of an overhaul. Historian Mike Randall sums up Norris's point of view, saying, "Norris had removed himself from the Baptist Conventions because of the toleration of evolution in their schools, the sympathy for communism by some of their leaders, the hoarding of missions monies by their headquarters, and the dictatorship over local churches by denominational leaders."[4]

Norris also railed against the Southern Baptist Convention for embracing modernist views—views that tended to subjugate scripture to rational explanation. This was a charge that Dowell believed had merit. In the 1920s and 30s, Sunday School literature distributed by the Southern Convention drew sharp criticism from independent Baptists for making statements that seemed to explain away the Bible's miracles. "I had a [Southern Baptist] teacher's quarterly that said that a trade wind opened the Red Sea for Moses," Dowell once told a reporter. "'[O]ne quarterly said that salty lava from a volcano enveloped [Lot's wife] and gave her the APPEARANCE of a pillar of salt.'"[5]

Dowell's contempt for such teachings could not have been clearer. Independent Baptists like him vehemently objected to efforts aimed at rationalizing the miracles of God. To them, such thinking subordinated a supernatural Creator to human reasoning. "The Bible says what it means and means what it says," Dowell maintained. "We don't try to change the Bible. We believe that these things happened in the way that the Bible says they happened." This, in Dowell's view, was the essence of fundamentalism. "We use the word fundamentalism," he said, "to distinguish us from modernism or theological liberalism. Some modernists deny the divine inspiration of the Scriptures, the Virgin Birth, they even question the reality of the new birth. We cannot have fellowship with those who deny these fundamental truths."[6]

As Dowell studied the folded arms of the eighteen people now addressing him, he wondered if he had been summoned over for a theological debate. As a guest in another man's pulpit, it had certainly not been Dowell's intention to stir up any controversy. Despite his views about the Convention, he knew and respected many Southern Baptist Christians, the newlywed pastor at Tulare among them. Dowell told an audience in

1965, "My father was a pastor in Southern Baptist Convention churches for 50 years. I could not help but have a very soft spot in my heart for Southern Baptists. They perhaps won more souls to Christ and built some great institutions in their time, and I give them credit for all that they've done."[7]

Ironically, Dowell's father, though he never left the Southern Baptists himself, may have instilled in Dowell the courage of conviction that eventually led to his son's departure from the Convention. Like Bill, Albin was a fundamentalist at heart, believing that the Bible says exactly what it means. By example, Albin taught his son to live life according to the Bible's teachings, even when this meant turning away from preconceived notions. In one sermon, Dowell described how his father's personal study of scripture led Albin to reexamine some long-held views about tithing, the practice of giving one-tenth of one's income to the church. Dowell said:

> *Years ago my dad, when he was a young preacher, decided that all laypeople are supposed to tithe, but the preacher wasn't supposed to tithe because he gave his whole life. He gave everything he had. And then he was reading the Bible one day and it talked about them giving the tithes to the Levites—who were the preachers—and then it said, "And the Levites tithed of the tithe." And so my dad had to back up a little bit and said, "Well God expects us to tithe, too."*

Dowell added, "I would say God *especially* expects the preacher to tithe. . . . You follow me as I follow Christ!"[8]

Albin's careful reading of scripture and his adherence to Biblical teachings, hallmarks of the fundamentalist, quickly found their way into his son's life and ministry as well. Indeed, Dowell's break with the Southern Baptist Convention represents one of the first exercises of that devout spirit that he inherited from his father. "I'm glad about the time I started preaching," Dowell said in one sermon, "because of some convictions I had, I made my stand and became an independent Baptist. I've never been sorry. I know that I did right. I know that God led me in it."[9]

The man standing in the aisle of the First Baptist Church now cleared his throat.

Anyway, when we read in the paper that you was going to be here today, some of us got together and said we'd like to hear what you had to say.

The man gestured to those who were seated.

These folks—all of us come over from Corcoran. See, there's not a Baptist church where we live, but we'd like there to be—a good soul-winning type church, see? And we thought maybe you'd be the one to get it going.

Corcoran was a small town southwest of Tulare, a short drive by car. This group of visitors told Dowell that they had been praying for over a year that God would send a preacher to organize a church in their city. "What they did not know," Dowell explained many years later, "was that I had been praying daily in a hay barn near our home for God to open a door for me to begin a new work."[10]

When Dowell heard what the Corcoran delegation wanted, his eyes suddenly lit up. He then engaged them in a lively conversation, and by the end of it, he had agreed to visit Corcoran to conduct a revival. Dowell told them he would use that revival meeting as a means of gauging God's direction regarding the new church. And so he did. The outcome of that episode was captured in a news article published March 1, 1937:

> *Rev. William E. Dowell, a 23-year-old Texas farmer, has been chosen pastor of the newly-organized Baptist Church in Corcoran, which was formed in January at the close of revival services conducted by the youthful cleric.*
>
> *The services are being held in the Seventh Day Adventists' Church on Sherman Avenue until such time as the young congregation can erect a church of its own.*
>
> *Nineteen charter members joined the congregation at its inception and a large number of others have joined since.*[11]

The Dowells moved to Corcoran in 1937, and Bill then became the full-time pastor of the newly formed First Baptist Church, a work unaffiliated with any denominational convention. Nola was, by this time, expecting the family's second child, so money remained tight. Still, Dowell's salary was sufficient to rent a small living space. The Dowells had one room to live in, and they shared a bathroom and kitchen with the home's other occupants. "We were poor, but happy in the Lord's service," the preacher said.[12]

Dowell enjoyed his ministry in Corcoran. He praised this church for its emphasis on soul-winning.[13] He also appreciated the lovingkindness that this congregation showed toward him and his family. On April 23, 1937, the church acknowledged their young pastor by presenting him with a token of appreciation: a Bible. The brown, leather-bound book was an Oxford edition of the Authorized King James Version (KJV), which was the only rendering of the Bible familiar to English-speaking Christians at the time. The KJV remained Dowell's version of choice even after other versions became widely available, and he never preached from any other translation.

Dowell also grew attached to this particular copy of the Bible. Though he used many other Bibles during the course of his preaching ministry, the one given to him by the First Baptist Church of Corcoran remained in his possession throughout his life. An inscription inside the front cover bears the name of its recipient: "Presented to W. E. Dowell." This was the moniker Dowell adopted throughout his ministry. It was a professional name by which audiences around the world would one day know him, though the name bore little significance when it was first inscribed in the front of his Bible. Dowell was still honing his craft in those days, a fact that even his Bible attests. Indeed, signs of this young preacher's development are evident throughout the pages of that book.

For instance, a sermon outline penciled opposite the title page reminds the observer that Dowell was yet new to sermon-making. The sermon's title, written in large flowing handwriting, is "Look unto Me," a phrase borrowed from Isaiah 45:22: "Look unto me, and be ye saved, all the ends of the earth: for I am God, and there is none else." As a rule, Dowell did not write his sermon outlines on the pages of his Bibles, yet he was never too particular about where and how he recorded them. Sermon notes might be written on almost any size paper, though his favorite material seems to have been a half-sheet page that fit neatly between the pages of the scriptures. Even at the end of his life, many of the sermon outlines in his files remained handwritten. Others had been typed by his secretaries.

It was common for Dowell to give titles to his sermons. He often advertised upcoming messages by announcing the titles in advance, a technique he may have picked up from J. Frank Norris. Dowell's titles were crafted to stir up the listener's curiosity or interest. Representative titles include:

- Can the Spirit of God Communicate with the Spirit of Man?
- What a Saved Person Can Lose
- Why It Pays to Live Right
- Does the Bible Teach Once Saved Always Saved?
- Evils That Curse Our City and What Can Be Done
- God's Perfect Bookkeeping System
- The Horrors of Hell That's Never Been Told
- When Will Peace Come? *or* Four Reasons Why We Cannot Have Peace on Earth Now

Years later Dowell would teach his Bible college students that a well-rounded preaching ministry requires a pastor to vary his approach to sermon development. He recommended that preachers employ in their arsenal a combination of expository, textual, and topical outlines. His personal favorite seems to have been the textual form, the one represented by the outline of "Look unto Me." Textual outlines take their main points from a single part of scripture, often a single verse, though subordinate ideas may be developed using other passages. Dowell liked to stick closely to a text. Invoking Spurgeon, Dowell would say, "I don't defend the Bible. It's like a lion. I just turn it loose and it defends itself."[14]

Dowell's handwritten outline for "Look unto Me," enumerates four brief points taken from that passage in Isaiah 45:

(1) Greatest possible blessing (salvation)
(2) At least effort (for a look)
(3) Offered to largest number (all the Earth)
(4) Upon the highest authority (I am God)

This example is typical of Dowell's sermon content. Though later outlines usually included subpoint development and some additional scripture references, Dowell's speaking notes tended to be sparse. A brief set of main points seems to be all that was needed for this preacher to speak to an audience for his typical thirty to forty minutes.

Dowell's opening text for a sermon might be an entire chapter of the Bible or, as with "Look unto Me," a single verse. Dowell then fleshed out the points of his messages with scripture references and modern day examples. He often included in his presentations references to unnamed or hypothetical individuals: "There was a missionary some years ago in Africa . . ." or "I heard of a lady one time . . ." or "Suppose someone came to you and said. . . ." Personal observations from Dowell's rural upbringing also made their way into his messages. "You can take a sheep and throw him in a mud puddle," he told one audience as he was explaining the human sin nature, "and, man alive, he'll get up and run for all he's worth. He's miserable in it. He don't like mud. But you get a hog and put him in a mud puddle, and he'll lie down in it. Why? That's his nature."[15] In another sermon Dowell queried, "Does it seem logical that a black cow can eat green grass and give white milk?" To this he answered, "It's not logic; it's faith that brings salvation."[16]

In Dowell's advice to young preachers, he said a minister should be well read, especially about history and current events.[17] Dowell believed such reading could produce valuable sermon material. And Dowell himself often incorporated such content into his messages. In 1968 he opened a message about salvation saying:

> Recently there appeared startling headlines announcing a heart transplant from a dead person to a living person. A person who has just died. That heart is taken out and transplanted in another body whose heart is damaged and who [is a] person with no hope or little hope of living unless there is this transplant. There's been not one example, but there's been several cases recently where this has been undertaken; and in one case especially, South Africa, the man is still living and the doctors say the operation has been successful.[18]

Dowell used the story to segue to his text, Jeremiah 24:7: "And I will give them an heart to know me, that I am the LORD: and they shall be my people, and I will be their God: for they shall return unto me with their whole heart." Dowell found that newsy tidbits often made an effective means of introducing such truths, and for that reason, he was a regular reader of newspapers and other types of literature.

Dowell also took sermon materials from other sources. He peppered many sermons with pithy phrases like those found scribbled in his 1968 pocket date book:

- "Successful folks don't just entertain thoughts, they put them to work."
- "The full and honorable use of today is the best preparation one can make for tomorrow."
- "May God break my heart with the things that break the heart of God."

These one-liners may have been gleaned from other preachers, Christian periodicals, or even church marquees. Whatever their source, Dowell found them meaningful enough to jot down, and from time to time, he would inject them into one of his messages. In a sermon entitled "Doing Something about It," Dowell invoked one such turn-of-a-phrase: "Someone has said the business of the true preacher is to comfort the afflicted and afflict the comfortable." Then at another point in this message, he quipped, "The same sun melts snow and hardens clay and I say to you, my friends, the

Word of God will either melt your heart and make you into a fruitful Christian or it will harden your heart and bring you under the hand of God's judgment. . . ."[19]

Dowell's sermons also employed levity when it suited him, though humor was never a major component of Dowell's speaking style. Lighthearted stories were more the exception than the rule. A story that almost certainly did find its way into a sermon is one found handwritten on a page in his brown Bible: "Baptist preacher preached for Methodist. He drank the water the Meth. preacher had prepared for baptizing 16 candidates. The report went out that the Bapt. preacher drank enough water to Baptise [sic] 16 candidates." Another humorous anecdote discovered in his personal notes says this: "A woman was disturbed because she had reached thirty and was not married. She mentioned her concern to her pastor. He said, 'God's plan is one man for one woman. You can't improve on that.' She said, 'I don't want to improve on it. I just want to get in on it.'"

Dowell had no reservations about incorporating humor into his sermons, but he tended to be a serious-minded speaker as a rule. He purposed to move people rather than to entertain them. His high school study of Robert Ingersoll, Daniel Webster, and others may have helped shape this mindset. On a blank page in his high school textbook, Dowell wrote, "Eloquence is the speech of one who knows what he is talking about & is earnest." And inside the back cover, he wrote, "True oratory is not the spirit of denunciation but to give out the truth. It should lead the hearer to denounce himself."

Dowell's high school teacher had the students practice what they were learning by composing original paragraphs that would "arouse in the listener the feeling indicated."[20] Students were given particular feelings that they must try to evoke in their writings. Targeted responses included contempt for cheating and the courage to live one's convictions. Dowell's writings for these assignments have not survived, but it would appear he learned the lessons well. And perhaps as a result, his preaching was always more likely to prick the listener's conscience than to tickle his funny bone.

Dowell's manner of speaking may likewise have been rooted in that high school training. As a student, Dowell had worked hard to maximize the impact of his oratory. He was taught that attention to the voice and body was an essential part of the speaker's preparation. Dowell's high school notes include this statement: "Effective speaking is not for exhibition but for communication. It commands attention in order to win response."[21] And Dowell embraced the maxim. He later taught his preaching students not to overlook in their preparations any potential hindrance to effective communication, including those that might seem outward or superficial. Regarding hygiene, Dowell instructed, "The minister, of all men, should take scrupulous care of his person." On the matter of dress, he said, "Avoid gaudiness, excessive trinkets and jewelry, and anything else which would attract undue attention to the wearer." And with regard to "noble carriage," Dowell taught, "It will require effort to stand straight, walk erect, and be impressive in form and movement, but it will add weight and force to one's message."[22]

Dowell modeled such principles. At just over six feet, his large frame easily commanded the attention of his audience. His hair, parted on the left, was always neatly slicked back. As he approached the pulpit, he confidently popped a breath mint into his mouth to help moisten his tongue. Then, standing with heels together on the platform, he began his message. To many in his audience, he seemed the essence of "noble carriage."

At the beginning of Dowell's messages, his mighty hands often rested in his pockets or drummed the sides of the pulpit. Then as his presentation unfolded, those hands took on new force and power. Dowell's signature gesture was extending his right hand toward the audience, often with his long index finger pointed. This he used to punctuate his most important statements. In preparation for the move, Dowell cocked his arm with his palm next to his ear. The suspended hand might wave there for several seconds in anticipation of a coming crescendo in his voice. But then, when that crescendo came, the gavel came down with dramatic emphasis. One of Dowell's ministry associates commented that the gesture "gave a whole new meaning" to the well-known advertising slogan "Reach out and touch someone."[23]

More memorable than Dowell's physical presentation, however, was the speaker's unforgettable vocal delivery. As with his mannerisms, certain speech patterns came to be expected. Prominent catchphrases in Dowell's arsenal included "Make no mistake about it," "Oh, hear me!" and "I say this carefully, but I say it deliberately." Also heard were the occasional errors in grammar and pronunciation left over from his rural upbringing. He made frequent use of the non-word *cain't*, for instance. He also brought a distinctly Texan pronunciation to words like *normal*, *apostasy*, and *hypocrisy*, rendering them instead as "narmal," "apostasay," and "highpocrisy."

Such quirks notwithstanding, this speaker's vocal delivery could never be described as unpolished. Dowell knew how to use his voice to get through to an audience. Even in high school, his oratorical training placed great emphasis on the declaimer's vocal technique. Dowell's high school text, *Natural Drills in Expression*, contains more than two hundred "tone drills," exercises by which students explored the vocal intonations associated with "Delight," "Disdain," "Exultation," "Mirth," "Praise," "Sadness," "Urging," etc.[24] Dowell and his classmates were assigned to spend fifteen minutes each day on such exercises, and the teacher supplemented the textbook's drills with other interpretive practices, including tongue twisters (e.g., "big black bugs blood," and "round and round the rugged rock the ragged rascal ran") as well as dramatic words and phrases (e.g., "Go! Fire! Stop, halt, joy! Come! Yes. No. W-e-l-l. Ship ahoy. Charge.").[25]

In his sermons, Dowell put all of this training to use with dramatic effect. At times he assumed the voices of biblical characters, as he did when he spoke on the elder brother from the story of the Prodigal Son. Dowell voiced the brother's bitterness, saying, "He chose to leave! Let him stay gone!"[26] A more common use of this oratorical training may be found in Dowell's rhythmic patterns. Mirroring the great orators of his generation, Dowell often gripped the listeners' ear through repetitions. "You can't sin and be a soulwinner," begins a typical passage in one sermon. "[Y]ou can't live a compromising life and be a soulwinner; you can't go out and patronize the things of the world, the honky tonks, the beer gardens, the theatres and dance halls and all of these things that are wrong and sinful in the sight of God, and things that will wreck your influence, and expect to be a soulwinner."[27]

Dowell's most notable vocal characteristic, however, was always his volume. Dowell had a thunderous resonance. A favorite adjective employed by those who remembered his powerful voice was the word *booming*. ". . . I am quite sure he never learned to whisper," one man said.[28] Another associate joked that when Dowell asked the blessing over a meal in a restaurant, he "blessed everyone's food."[29] Reportedly, Dowell's prayers could bring all activity in a restaurant to a halt: "Everyone stopped talking, the servers would stop serving, customers would stop moving about."[30]

Dowell was likewise a boisterous preacher. His sermons were not a continuous shout, but his voice was naturally loud, and his preaching included frequent spikes in volume. He once gave a scriptural rationale for his volume. Invoking the first verse of Isaiah 58, he said: "You wonder why I preach so loud, don't you? Well, I'm going to give you a scriptural answer. It says, 'Cry aloud!' That's the first two words. 'Cry aloud, spare not, lift up thy voice like a trumpet, and shew my people their transgression, and the house of Jacob their sins.'"[31] Ministry Associate Keith Stoller recalled another defense that Dowell gave for his volume. Dowell argued that his preaching, boisterous though it was, was mild compared to Christ's. After all, Dowell reasoned, Christ preached to a crowd of five thousand without a microphone.[32]

In actual practice, Dowell contrasted his loud cries with a variety of other volumes. For example, in his message "Divine Invitation," Dowell used a low growl when he said, "You don't have God in your life."[33] Dowell's slow, dramatic intonation of the statement seems intent on screwing the words to the listeners' conscience. In other instances, Dowell preceded or followed his bursts of volume with silence. He would pause, often for two or three seconds at a time, as if to give his meaning time to soak in.

Dowell was unapologetic about such dramatic intensity. Indeed he believed the importance of his message demanded nothing less. He remarked in one sermon:

> A man said sometime ago concerning a certain church, 'I enjoy attending that church, it is so soothing to my conscience—it is so restful, the preacher has a very quiet voice and he says such pleasing things and I can just sit there and listen to him and almost go to sleep.' I thought pretty seriously in my own heart, though I did not say it, 'Brother if you will come over and hear me preach it won't be so restful—it won't be so soothing to your conscience.'[34]

But even if Dowell's sermons failed to soothe, they did manage to influence. One of Dowell's admirers, Kevin Carson, recalled hearing Dowell preach in 1990. In the course of the message, Dowell said, "I'm going to say something and I am not ashamed to say it, Jesus loves you and died for you." Recalling the statement, Carson said he was struck by the way Dowell introduced "the simple Gospel message with personal authority."[35] That personal authority had much to do with Dowell's ability to influence others from the pulpit. Dowell wielded not just a mighty voice but also a life that honored his personal relationship with the Lord. Another note that Dowell jotted down in his Bible said this: "Pastor should say come on not go on." And Dowell seems to have heeded that admonition. His manner, vocal delivery, and content all blended together with his life, resulting in a single, coherent message: "come on."

Five months after Dowell received that brown Bible at the First Baptist Church of Corcoran, he once again stood in front of his congregation to preach. As his message drew to a close, he may have quoted the lyrics to some poignant or inspirational hymn. He often did this. Just before his standard closing line—"May we stand with our heads bowed"—he would invoke the words of songs like "Amazing Grace," "In the Garden," and "Work for the Night is Coming." With these, he made one last appeal for his listeners to respond to his message. This was a technique that, like so many others Dowell employed, he had seen used to great effect in the pulpit ministry of J. Frank Norris.

Dowell was keen to impact the souls of California the way that Norris had done it in Texas. "I've had one tremendous temptation throughout my entire ministry," Dowell confessed to one audience. "Every time I stand in the pulpit, if there is one sinner in that crowd, I want to preach to that one sinner and ignore everybody else."[36] Dowell said he eventually learned the importance of tempering that zeal:

> *I used to try to convict sinners. I had some of the greatest stories. I had some of the most convincing arguments. I had some of the most persuasive words that I used to try to convict people of sin. Then suddenly I discovered that isn't my job. My job is not to convict sinners. When He—the Holy Spirit—is come, He will reprove the world—or convict the world—of sin, of righteousness, and judgment. Not me, the Holy Spirit.*[37]

Dowell was still learning such lessons as he preached in his church in Corcoran on September 19, 1937. His trademark speaking traits, too, were still in development—all except his vocal strength, which had been gifted to him by God. Yet listeners may have noted an extra measure of fervor in Dowell's voice that morning. Dowell received word that his second child was about to be born. Indeed, Nola was already at the hospital in Tulare, and Bill, once he finished preaching, was then rushed to be with her. Since the Dowell family did not yet own a vehicle, two ladies from the church provided the necessary transportation. And by the end of that whirlwind day, Bill and Nola were the parents of a baby boy: William Edgar Dowell, Jr.

Perhaps it was in the corridors of that Tulare hospital that Dowell opened up his brown Bible and circled in pencil a statement found in Exodus 32: "Consecrate yourselves to day to the LORD, even every man upon his son, and upon his brother; that he may bestow upon you a blessing this day."[38] Dowell recognized the vital importance of consecration. According to Moses, it was the means of securing God's richest blessings for the Israelites and their children. Dowell believed the principle applied just as much to the New Testament Christian. And though Dowell was young and poor and had little influence in the world, he was convinced that his continued faithfulness would be blessed. Indeed, it was evident that the Lord's blessings were already upon him. In his first year in California, he had been given a new church, a new Bible, and a new son. He now waited eagerly to see what blessings lay yet ahead.

Chapter 11: *Open Doors*

A white-haired preacher in the front row stood up.

I move that the nominations cease.

Two rows back, a preacher wearing a black tie lifted his hand in agreement.

I second the motion.

The secretary seated behind them barely had enough time to jot down the meeting minutes before a well-dressed man continued from the platform.

We have a motion and a second to cease the nominations.

This was the annual gathering of the Missionary Baptist Association of California, a cooperative venture of likeminded pastors and churches within the American Baptist Association. The regional group had been organized in the early 1930s, and approximately a dozen churches were now sending delegates to its sessions. Meetings were always hosted by a participating church.

The speaker on the platform continued with the procedural formalities.

All in favor? . . . Any opposed?

As the delegates of this organization met together, they carried out a range of activities including sharing Christian literature, endorsing training institutions, and approving new missionaries to support. They also conducted business pertaining to their own governance.

Nominations for the new moderator have ceased, and we will now proceed to a vote.

Dowell first attended one of these sessions as a visiting preacher in March 1937. Leaders of the group had learned of his new independent Baptist church up in Corcoran and, perhaps as a means of winning Dowell's active participation in their organization, they invited him to bring a message to their group at a meeting down in La Habra, a town southeast of Los Angeles. The strategy seems to have worked. The following year, April 1938, Dowell's church in Corcoran made application for admission into the association. Their participation in the organization has continued even into the twenty-first century.[1]

All those in favor of appointing the nominee as the new moderator of the Missionary Baptist Association of California please signify by raising your right hand.

The secretary wrote furiously. Then the speaker announced:

Let the record show that the association has selected the Reverend W. E. Dowell as state moderator.

Like the other pastors who attended Missionary Baptist Association (MBA) meetings, Dowell found that he benefitted not only from the group's shared undertakings but also from the preaching and camaraderie that took place when the preachers met together. "[W]e stood for the same things," he said, "and I thoroughly rejoiced because I made so many new friends."[2] Dowell remained an active part of the organization for the next several years, ultimately winning a term as the group's leader. And in 1940 he also taught in the Pamona Bible Institute, a school that the association had recently organized.[3]

Dowell's involvement with the MBA also facilitated a new direction in his ministry. In 1938, the pastor of the First Missionary Baptist Church of La Habra resigned his post, causing the congregation to go in search of a new pastor. Church members remembered Dowell's 1937 sermon, and a delegation from the church made the two hundred mile journey from La Habra to Corcoran to renew their acquaintance. "They sent some folks up and heard me preach at my own church at Corcoran," Dowell said, "and then they came to me and asked me if I'd consider coming down to try out as a pastor."[4] Dowell agreed to seek the Lord's direction in the matter, and after preaching a second time down in La Habra, he accepted a unanimous call from the church to relocate.

Though the La Habra church was not large, it was an established congregation running over eighty in attendance. For the Dowells, this meant an improved standard of living. The family even managed to purchase an automobile, the first they had ever owned.

This change in circumstances also helped to relieve some of the strain the family had been experiencing in Corcoran. Of particular concern had been Nola's unstable health. "At the time when Bill Jr. was a baby," Nola wrote in a personal journal, "I got so run down that I became anemic, got so weak that I could hardly lift my arms." Nola said the persistence of her illness prompted a chiropractor to make a surprising recommendation. "He recommended that I get some beer because it would create an appetite for food," she said. Suddenly the teetotaling minister's wife faced a dilemma: to drink or not to drink. "We bought two or three cans and set them in the refrigerator," she confessed. Yet downing the contents was another matter. The beer sat in the refrigerator untouched for several days because, even with a doctor's orders, Nola could not overcome her aversion to alcohol. Ultimately, the preacher's wife refused the medicine altogether. "I decided I could not partake of it," she said, "so I poured it down the sink drain."[5]

Life was better in La Habra, however. There was more money, and the family finally had their own transportation. They also had a good church. The La Habra congregation welcomed its new pastor in July 1938, hosting a birthday picnic to celebrate Bill's twenty-fourth birthday. A news article reporting on the affair said, "The minister was thoroughly surprised after accepting an invitation to be the guest of Mr. and Mrs. Ludy at an outdoor dinner at Hillcrest park, and on arrival found [sixty of] his members assembled and ready to extend birthday greetings."[6]

This warm welcome reinvigorated the Dowell family, and they were soon pouring all their energies into their new ministry, a work that proved highly fruitful. During Dowell's time in La Habra, church attendances grew, and construction of a new church building was completed. Dowell also initiated a weekly radio ministry that aired each Sunday morning from a station in Long Beach, KGER. This radio ministry, together with Dowell's work in the Missionary Baptist Association, gave him broad exposure, which in turn helped to make him a sought-after evangelist.

La Habra was also important to Dowell for another reason. It served as the birthplace for the final member of his family. About a year after the Dowells moved, Nola announced that she was expecting the family's third child. This boy, born at home on February 23, 1940, was given the name Clyde Paul.

Clyde's arrival signaled further challenges for Nola. Even though she delighted in her role as a mother, she confessed that she found this phase of her life to be "involved and strenuous."[7] That "book" of parenthood that she had taken up when she set aside her girlhood back in Merkel was now proving to be an all-consuming tale. She missed the active role that she had once played in the work of the church, most of all her involvement in church music. Since childhood, Nola had immersed herself in vocal performance, singing her first duet in church at the age of six and then attending Stamps Quartet singing conventions as a teen.[8] Now, as a mother of three, Nola found that merely attending church services was a chore. Church nurseries were yet unheard of, so while Bill preached, Nola spent her time in the pew managing three children under the age of five. "Many times," she admitted, "I received nothing but the peace of God in my heart from just being in the house of God on Sunday."[9]

There were other frustrations for this preacher's wife as well. Staying busy at home was no longer a challenge, but Nola experienced renewed feelings of loneliness and isolation, particularly when her husband left to conduct a revival meeting or to attend a session of the Missionary Baptist Association. Dowell was away on one such a trip in the spring of 1940 when Nola decided to take her three children to a park for a much-needed outing. When they arrived at the park, she was greeted by several young couples who were playing baseball together. Then to Nola's delight, they invited her to join in their fun. She leapt at the chance, but her participation proved to be short lived. "I hit the ball, got to second base, slid and fell and broke my arm," she said.[10] Not only was Nola unable to finish the game, but for several weeks thereafter, she would be required to carry out her mothering responsibilities with the use of one arm instead of two. "Marrying a preacher is not always a 'bed of roses,'" she concluded matter-of-factly.[11]

Nola did see a silver lining in such hardships, however. "I had to learn to stand on my own two feet," she said.[12] Though Nola would have welcomed her husband's constant companionship, she resigned herself to the fact that Bill's ministry would pull him away from their family often. Out of necessity, then, she learned independence. And those closest to her would attest that she learned the lesson well. Nola could be bold, blunt, and even headstrong. She could also be delightfully adventurous. During time, this preacher's wife became a top-notch amateur tennis player, a licensed .... pilot, and a quartet singer performing on radio and in front of large audiences. She also developed a love for driving, and in her later years she traveled throughout the US equipped with a CB radio. When she made such trips, she placed men's hats in the back window of her car to convince would-be attackers that she was not traveling alone. This habit said less about her fearfulness than it did about her ability to pick up helpful hints from magazines and newspapers. Nola never had a particularly fearful nature. Indeed, the only time this author ever traveled at a speed in excess of one hundred miles per hour was when Nola Dowell was behind the wheel. She thought it would be a thrill. And it was.

Nola's husband, too, had a favorite anecdote about his wife's boldness. His story featured an event from the late 1970s. It happened when Missouri Governor Kit Bond was speaking in Ozark, Missouri. Bond was speaking in defense of a controversial amendment to the U.S. Constitution, the Equal Rights Amendment (ERA). The amendment—a measure that would ostensibly protect women from discriminatory practices—had been passed by Congress in 1972. However, it still needed the approval of thirty-eight states to become law. Bond wanted Missouri to be among those states; many Christians did not. Fundamentalists, in particular, saw the amendment as an assault on the distinct roles of men and women established by the Bible.

After Governor Bond addressed his audience in Ozark, he invited listeners to ask questions. It was then that Nola, an opponent of ERA, rose to her feet. She reportedly quoted to the governor several scriptures from the epistles written to Titus and Timothy, and then she said, "In view of what the Word of God says, how can you be here doing what you're doing?" Governor Bond began his response, saying, "Well, Ma'am, I'm afraid I don't know much about the Word of God—." But the preacher's wife interrupted: "Well, Sir, in view of the fact that you're going to represent all the people of Missouri, don't you think you ought to learn something about it?"[13] Even Nola's husband was taken aback by her words, though he could not help admiring her gumption. Nola was no women's libber, but she most certainly knew how to stand on her own two feet. And no one appreciated that quality more than he did.

While Nola was discovering this independence back in La Habra, her young husband was likewise growing and maturing. "God used this church," Dowell said, "— my experiences there—to teach me how to lean on the Lord and depend upon the Lord." Dowell related one experience as an example. "I got the feeling at one particular time that I wasn't as concerned, interested in soul-winning as much as I ought to be," he said. The young pastor decided to address the problem head on:

> I dismissed myself to my wife, told her I might not be back till real late, that there was no limit to how late I might stay. I went to the church office, and I had almost an all-night prayer meeting. And I was begging God to give me a burden for souls. Finally, I heard a voice—it wasn't a voice, but it was as clear as a voice—said, "If you want to be concerned about lost people, get up and go out where they are and start talking to them and start witnessing to them."[14]

Dowell said a family he wanted to reach then came to mind, and he immediately purposed to visit their home with the gospel:

> [W]ithin a week or so, I led that entire family to Christ. And my interest, of course, was renewed, and I realized one of the major lessons that God has taught me–that if you want a burden for souls, get out where souls are and witness to them, and He'll give you a burden for them. You don't necessarily get a burden just by staying and praying and saying, "Lord, give me a burden," and waiting until He gives you a burden. You get up and go.[15]

Another experience in La Habra was likewise influential in shaping Dowell's evangelistic outlook. Nola came to him one day, saying, "I think I'd better let you read this telegram, Honey." It was from some family members back in Texas. "She handed it to me," Dowell said, "and I opened up that telegram, and I'll never forget the words: 'Your cousin, DeWitte Dowell, was accidentally killed in a bar in Houston, Texas.'"[16] The young man had bled to death after being shot in the hip and wrist in a dispute over an eight dollar gambling debt. He was survived by a wife and a ten-month-old daughter.[17]

This news devastated Dowell. "Like a flash it went through my mind," Dowell recalled in one of his sermons, "You loved DeWitte. You were always together. But never one time–never one time did I witness to DeWitte Dowell." Dowell's thoughts went back to his senior year and the many days that he and DeWitte had spent together playing for the Normangee Panthers. It horrified Dowell that he had not been a better Christian example to his best friend. "I was backslidden," Dowell confessed with tears, "but I was saved." The preacher also recalled what he told his wife after reading the telegram. "I stood there just almost frozen like a statue. Finally I held my hands out like this to my wife, and I said, 'Honey, the blood of DeWitte Dowell is on those hands. And I'll never have a chance–I had a chance. He's in Hell tonight. And I'm responsible.'"[18]

Such experiences left a lasting impression on Dowell. They also affected his ministry. He called the First Missionary Baptist Church of La Habra "one of the most evangelistic churches that I ever pastored,"[19] a characteristic no doubt owing to the pastor. "We'd hold revival meetings and pack the place out to standing room," Dowell recalled. "Sometimes they'd have to go and borrow chairs from another church in order to seat the people who were coming. And we just had the altar filled continually."[20] For Dowell, the church at La Habra became the most fruitful ministry he had yet seen.

But then, in the spring of 1940, Dowell was presented with a new ministry opportunity. He received an invitation from a prominent church in a nearby city, the Lynwood Missionary Baptist Church. Lynwood was thirty minutes west of La Habra, and although the congregation there had not actively participated in the Missionary Baptist Association, they had heard of Dowell and knew enough about him to extend a call for him to be their pastor. Dowell accepted.

Dowell said he came to Lynwood with mixed emotions. In a news article, he explained, "It was with great hesitation that we left our former field of service, . . . for the Lord was blessing in such a marvelous way, but in accepting our present pastorate, we know that God was leading and that we are in His will. God works in a mysterious way His wonders to perform."[21] And with that, Dowell went to work building his fourth church.

Almost immediately after Dowell took the Lynwood church, this ministry began to flourish. Two months after he came, a news report went out:

> The Lynwood Church is enjoying, in an unusual way, the blessings of God. During the past two months, 30 new additions have come into the Church, 8 by baptism. Notwithstanding the summer weather, the attendance has more than doubled. The Bible School is holding to the 200 mark, and [in] the preaching service both morning and evening, the church auditorium is crowded to capacity.[22]

Another favorable write-up appeared in the local newspaper in January 1941: "Rally Day at the First Missionary Baptist Church of Lynwood last Sunday brought out a record attendance at both Sunday school and church services." The article continued, "The Baptist Young People's Union of the church, which has grown the past six months from about 12 members to 40, are carefully preparing weekly programs that will be of interest to young people. They propose by prayer, personal visitations and hard work, Reverend Dowell stated further, to double that number this year."[23]

As it turned out, these blessings at Lynwood were part of a mixed bag. Dowell quickly learned that the nature of the Lynwood congregation had been affected by her former leader. Some individuals in the church "had ideas," Dowell said. "They were a Baptist church by name," he explained, "but they'd had an interdenominational pastor, and he left his mark upon them."[24] Before long, the new pastor's leadership met with some resistance.

Dowell said his trouble at Lynwood began when he withheld church membership from a couple that had asked to join his church. At the close of one of the services, a man and his wife expressed a desire to join, but Dowell learned that the couple had been baptized by a famed Pentecostal preacher Aimee Semple McPherson. Dowell maintained that McPherson's baptism identified these converts with Pentecostal beliefs and practices, ideas radically different from the teachings of his church. In Baptist phraseology, McPherson's baptism was "alien immersion," invalid for the purpose of uniting with a Baptist church. So Dowell turned the couple down. "I wouldn't accept them," he said. If they wished to become a part of his congregation, they would need to be re-baptized.

Dowell briefly discussed these things with the newcomers at the end of that service, deferring their request for membership and asking for an opportunity to meet with them in their home to more fully counsel them on the matter of baptism. However, his actions were met with immediate opposition. Alien immersion had never been an issue under the former pastor, so "some in the church kind of challenged me a little," Dowell said, "not openly, but after the service was over."[25]

Dowell stood his ground, however. Later in the week, he met with the prospective members, and when they learned that they had to be re-baptized in order to join the church, they withdrew their application for membership. In turn, a group of about ten church members, disgruntled over Dowell's handling of the episode, also withdrew their membership.

Dowell said the majority of the Lynwood church "stood solidly" behind him during that initial conflict, but he noted that he faced further problems as time went on. A broad undercurrent of insubordination ran through this congregation, he said. Dowell attributed some of these attitudes to the social status of the families who attended. "[This church] had some of the big businessmen in the city," he explained. "It was well represented as far as the city was concerned." That affluence, according to Dowell, clouded the congregation's judgment with regard to the proper workings of the church. "They wanted to be looked up to in the city, and they wanted me to fit into their program instead of them fitting into my program," he said.[26]

As a result, less than a year after coming to Lynwood, Dowell decided to resign his position. "I didn't have to resign," he said. "They wanted me to stay." But Dowell believed this was the Lord's will for him. Just as he had acted in faith when he accepted the call to come to Lynwood, Dowell now tendered his resignation believing that it was time for him and his family to go. "I resigned," he said, "because I determined that what I was going to do, I was going to start an independent Baptist church in the Los Angeles area where I could grow and build."[27]

Had it been a mistake for Dowell to go to Lynwood in the first place? It was impossible not to wonder. Yet a life-altering event that occurred during his time there seems to answer the question. In November of 1940, Dowell traveled from Lynwood to Springfield, Missouri, a city of about sixty-five thousand inhabitants. He was there to conduct a two-week revival for Charley Dyer, pastor of the High Street Fundamental Baptist Church. As it happened, some of Dowell's church members in Lynwood had previously lived in Springfield and had attended the High Street Church. Once they moved to California, this family made mention of their new pastor to friends back in Springfield. Their high praise of Dowell led Dyer to invite him to come to Springfield as a guest evangelist.

Dowell sent Nola and his children a letter soon after he reached the Missouri town:

Well we are in our hotel in Springfield. Have a very nice place. This is Monday 5 min. until 8 a.m. Yesterday was a great day. We preached in the morning to about 800 or 900, and in the evening to over a 1000. Charley baptized a large group in the beautiful large natural stone baptistery. It is the most beautiful baptistery I have seen. We had 5 glorious conversions and 3 other additions to the Church. Every one was so happy. I had perfect liberty. The Church is indeed ready for a meeting. Everyone is expecting a great meeting, and are working to that end. We had 657 I believe in Sunday School yesterday. A record attendance for the Sunday School. Pray much for us.[28]

During this visit, Dowell and Dyer struck up an immediate friendship. Elsewhere in his letter Dowell said, "Dear old Charley is a prince of a fellow to work with." And that feeling appears to have been mutual. Dowell even reciprocated his friend's speaking invitation by bringing Dyer to Lynwood for a revival just two months later. Nola had to miss that Lynwood meeting. All three of her young children came down with whooping cough and scarlet fever just before the revival began. "My husband had to make a choice to cancel the revival or be quarantined out of the house," Nola recalled. In the end, the Dowells agreed that quarantine was the best option. Bill brought groceries to the family doorstep, and Nola stayed indoors with the children and "became a real nurse."[29]

Meanwhile the mutual admiration between Dowell and Dyer continued to grow. And in retrospect, Dowell considered this providential. Despite the ups and downs at Lynwood, God used his time there to bring him and Dyer together. The full significance of their association would not become evident for some time, but even in 1940, Dowell sensed its importance. He made a curiously prophetic remark in another part of that letter he sent to his family from Springfield. "This meeting is going to mean a lot to me," he said.[30] And he was right.

Even so, Dowell's friendship with Dyer had to be set aside when Dowell resigned his position at Lynwood. Dowell's full attention now needed to be directed at the organizing of a new church. This undertaking went remarkably well, Dowell said. He secured a meeting place in South Gate, a community just north of Lynwood, meeting in the "old Topsy building." Dowell explained, "It was a night club." The Topsy building on Long Beach Boulevard was vacant at the time, and Dowell relished the notion of transforming this former drinking establishment into a church. He also found that the facility was ideal for his needs: "It was right downtown between Huntington Park and South Gate. . . . And it was well-known all over that country. Ol' Topsy. Beautiful building. Roomy." Even better was the price. "We got it cheap. Got it for about a hundred dollars a month," Dowell recalled.[31]

Dowell was still being heard on Station KGER each Sunday morning, so he used his radio broadcasts to publicize the new church plant. "I had enough folks that knew me that I didn't have to look for members of that church," Dowell said. "When I announced that we were going to start a new church, we had some forty or fifty people that immediately said they wanted to be a part of it."[32] Thus, in the spring of 1941, the South Gate Fundamental Baptist Church was organized with more than forty charter members. Dowell admitted that some of these were former members from his Lynwood congregation, but he quickly added, "I did not split the [Lynwood] church. I begged the members there to stay. Nevertheless I had some thirty that came and asked for admittance into our new church that we started."[33]

Dowell was optimistic about the potential he saw in this new church. He explained that he had done "a lot of survey work" going into the project and that it seemed to him these efforts were going to pay great dividends. "The church was very evangelistic," he observed. "It was a good location. I had a lot of people, had a lot of room. I got the building reasonable. And I thought, well, I'll just stay here."[34]

But then, within weeks of launching his new church, Dowell received a surprising telephone call. "[J]ust as we got to going real good," Dowell said, "I got a call from Charley Dyer in Springfield. He said, 'Bill, I'm leaving the High Street Baptist Church and I want you to be the next pastor if God leads you.'" Dyer, who had founded High Street just five years earlier, felt that the Lord was leading him into full-time evangelism. He assured Dowell that there were no problems in the church and that no one was asking him to leave. "He just felt like his work there was over," Dowell said.[35]

Dowell was instantly torn by this invitation. On the one hand, the South Gate church was only a few weeks old and had great potential. On the other hand, Dowell's visit to Springfield had been an impactful one. Dyer's congregation was quite large, and it, too, was an important opportunity. After consideration, Dowell answered Dyer's offer with a counterproposal. "If the Lord leads in it, I'll consider [your invitation] under one condition," Dowell told Dyer, "if you'll come out and stay with [the South Gate congregation] until they are able to get a pastor and get going good."[36] To Dowell's great pleasure, Dyer liked the idea. Moving to the west coast to work with a small congregation seemed the ideal transition into Dyer's new calling as an evangelist. And if it meant Dowell would take the reins at High Street, it would be worth it.

Having reached an agreement, then, the two preachers waited to see how the Holy Spirit would lead in their respective congregations. Among independent Baptists, it is not the pastor who chooses his replacement, but the people of the church. And that being the case, both Dowell and Dyer went about the business of asking God to direct their people wisely. The preachers selected August 1941 as the time to put their plan into motion. The first order of business would be for Dyer to resign. After that, Dowell would return to the corner of High and Prospect, this time to present himself as a candidate.

Chapter 12: *Corner of High and Prospect*

Bill grasped the top of the steering wheel and turned onto a dark, deserted street. As the car rounded the corner, he playfully nettled his wife:

And you said we'd never make it—

Shhh.

She didn't even bother to scold him. Bill knew full well that there were three sleeping angels occupying the back seat. Nola turned to check on them, and fortunately for Bill, nobody was stirring. He began again, this time lowering his voice to a whisper:

We'll be there any minute.

Uh-huh . . .

A yawn interrupted her reply. Then she added:

Praise the Lord.

The words were more a sigh than a celebration. Bedraggled by the long journey to Springfield, Nola had gained a new appreciation for simple comforts—like beds, for instance. Even now she was wishing she could crawl into the one that she had left back in California.

Bill whispered again:

What time is it?

It's almost one o'clock in the morning.

Nola did not need to check her watch; she had been monitoring it for the last several hours. Nola was ever mindful of the time. In later life she often wore two watches on the same arm, keeping the faces tucked on the underside of her wrist instead of on the back of it. No one really understood why she did any of this. For Nola's family members, the habit was just one of her many endearing quirks.

But the preacher's wife was not bothering with a watch just now. Instead she was digging around in the floorboard in search of her black purse. She produced it momentarily and began probing inside to find a tube of lipstick to moisten her lips. It peeved Bill a little that Nola was fussing over a tube of lipstick instead of soaking in the town. By contrast, he was leaning over the wheel of his car, studying the rows of dark houses lining the moonlit street. It was impossible not to dream of the future.

Nola smacked her lips, knocking her husband back to the present. Then Bill was struck with an idea.

Hey, you want to see it?

See what?

The church—

Another shush from Nola reminded Bill to whisper. He tried again with reduced volume:

Our new church building. You want to see what it's like, don't you?

How are we going to see anything this time of night?

Bill grinned and pulled the top of his steering wheel, rounding another corner. Nola was busy packing away her lipstick. Her head was still buried in her purse when Bill guided the car to the curb and set the vehicle's parking break.

Well, there it is.

At last Nola looked up. She stared through her window into the night. The late summer moon seemed to be hanging directly behind the roof of the church building causing her to have to squint to make out what she was seeing. Her husband raised an impish set of eyebrows in anticipation.

So what do you think?

When Nola's eyes finally adjusted to the silhouette in front of her, she drew in a little gasp. For an instant she forgot about waking the children.

I thought you said it was a big church!

Already Bill was chuckling, but he stifled his laughter in order to ask:

What's the matter?

Then came a sharp reply:

You mean to tell me that tiny little building is our new church?!

Bill knew better than to drag out the gag any longer. His fit of laughter soon would have betrayed him anyway. He leaned toward Nola's window as if he were just then noticing the little church next to their car.

Oh that? Nah. That's the Church of Christ.

The prankster then pointed to a considerably larger building.

Our church is there, down at the other end of the block.

And so it was.

This was 1941. The Dowell family arrived at the High Street Fundamental Baptist Church near the end of summer. As promised, Dowell had returned to Missouri a few weeks earlier to candidate before the church and to seek God's direction. During that visit he had also conducted a weekday revival meeting in the nearby town of Lebanon. Then on Sunday he preached at High Street. After Dowell's first Sunday back in Springfield, the congregation, following Pastor Dyer's recommendation, asked to put the preacher's candidacy to a church vote. Dowell gave permission for the vote, and he received a nearly unanimous call, with only two dissenting ballots. Still, Dowell was uncertain about making the move. "I'd just started the work in California," he said, "and I felt a little bit fearful of me leaving the work."[1]

Dowell told the congregation that he would respond to their invitation the following Sunday, and throughout that week, he prayed for God's blessings upon the upcoming Sunday services. He decided this would be the best means of confirming the Lord's clear direction. When that Sunday morning came, however, the Lord's direction was anything but clear. "We had a great service, but I felt hampered and uneasy," he said. "I didn't feel the freedom and liberty that I normally had." So Dowell delayed his response once again. "At the close of the service, I said, 'I'm sorry but I can't give you my answer. I'll try my best to be able to give you my answer tonight.'"[2]

Dowell spent that whole afternoon in prayer, and when he returned for the evening service, his prayers were answered. "It was a great crowd that came out, and I preached, and God gave me a lot of liberty and freedom," Dowell said. The preacher was most impressed by what took place after his sermon concluded: "When I gave the invitation people just flocked down to the altar. A great number of people were saved that night." And with that, Dowell was satisfied that the Lord wanted to use him in this place. At the close of the service, he addressed the crowd with full confidence: "I'm happy to announce I'm going to accept your offer to become pastor of this church."[3]

The Dowell family then sold everything that would not fit into the back of their car and made the move from California to Missouri, relocating to a two-story frame house on the corner of High and Ramsey. They lived just across the street from the church building. This residence was the first of several homes the family would occupy in Springfield. The second came not long afterward. The Ramsey house, though it was spacious, had a floor plan that proved a challenge for Nola. "All bedrooms, clothes closets, and chest of drawers, all upstairs," she lamented in her personal notes.[4] The ailing young housewife was continuing to struggle with a loss of appetite and weight, and she found that running up and down the stairs of their new home only made matters worse. The family doctor advised Bill to find a floor plan that would ease the strain of Nola's household duties. So by 1943, the Dowells had moved to a different house, this one located at 2127 North Prospect, just south of the church facilities. The Dowell family would remain at that location until the mid-1950s.

Even as the Dowells were settling into this new life in Springfield, Charley Dyer was making his way to South Gate to assume the leadership of the congregation that Dowell had left behind. Dowell and Dyer's pulpit swap had worked seamlessly. Dyer "stayed with [the South Gate church] about three years until it was established," Dowell recalled.[5] The transition went so smoothly that Dowell soon invited Dyer back to High Street to preach to his former congregation. Such an invitation, Dowell reasoned, would assure congregants of his and Dyer's mutual good will.

Yet during Dyer's visit, something unexpected happened. "As [Charley] came to the platform," Dowell said, "the people stood." Dyer was greeted with a boisterous standing ovation as he came to speak. For Dowell, it was no surprise to him that the people loved their former preacher. He was a dynamic, good-looking speaker with an impressive ability to quote long passages of scripture. What was more, he "had started the church and led most of [its members] to the Lord," Dowell said.[6]

What did surprise Dowell was his own reaction to the crowd's exuberance. His spirit was deeply troubled by the affection his people showed for Dyer. After all, none of them had ever stood to welcome Bill Dowell to the pulpit. "I felt almost for the first time in my life the terrible, uncomfortable feeling of jealousy," Dowell confessed.[7]

Dowell's heart ached over the matter. Though his jealous reaction was uncharacteristic, he also knew it was wrong. "It alarmed me and I determined to rid myself of it," he said. So after Dyer returned to California, Dowell prayed over the situation and hashed out a plan. A series of upcoming meetings on Dowell's calendar meant that he was going to be away from High Street for four straight Sundays. This circumstance, Dowell concluded, would be the perfect opportunity to mount a direct assault on his fleshly feelings. "I deliberately invited Bro. Dyer to fill the pulpit for those four Sundays," Dowell said.[8]

Dowell claimed that this decision brought about an immediate release. As soon as that second invitation to Dyer went out, his former feelings dissipated. Moreover, the Lord rewarded his humble spirit with fresh encouragement. "When I returned [from my meetings], the people gave me a great ovation and were happy to have me back," Dowell said. "All jealously was gone."[9]

Of course, even greater blessings were in store for Dowell during his tenure at High Street. One of the first of these was a renewed association with J. Frank Norris. Throughout the 1930s, Norris had been steadily expanding his empire of independent Baptists, first forming a fellowship of likeminded pastors in 1931,[10] then hosting a series of Bible schools like those Dowell had attended, and finally, in 1939, establishing a year-round seminary, the Fundamental Baptist Bible Institute.[11] By 1941 Norris's network of pastors, a group called the World Fundamental Baptist Missionary Fellowship (WFBMF), had active supporters in thirty-six states.[12] Even Charley Dyer had been a part of it. In fact, while Dyer was at High Street, he had been elected to serve as a state representative for the organization in Missouri.

Many others, like Dyer, had likewise been convinced to become a part of Norris's efforts. Norris pointed out to his peers that joining a fellowship was far better than taking orders from the denominational machine. As Bartlett explains, fellowships allow each church to determine "what programs it will support and to what degree it will support them."[13] For fundamentalists, such autonomy was highly prized, making it easy for Norris to rally them to his causes, especially those related to mission work and Christian education.

Norris was more powerful than ever when the Dowells reached Springfield in 1941. The combined membership of First Baptist in Fort Worth and Temple Baptist in Detroit now exceeded sixteen thousand,[14] and it was commonly reported that Norris was pastor of the two largest churches in the United States.[15] Norris's new seminary was likewise experiencing a measure of success and was producing a steady stream of recruits for his fundamentalist army. Then, too, Norris had won many friends in high places. Norris had a knack for that. Already in his career this celebrated pastor had rubbed shoulders with preachers like Billy Sunday, W. B. Riley, T. T. Shields, and Mordecai

Ham. Back during the famed Scopes Trial, Norris had been a friend and ally of William Jennings Bryan. Even J. C. Penney had been a guest at Norris's church.

Some of Norris's latest admirers were the top auto executives in Detroit. Their admiration could be seen in the generous company favors that they routinely bestowed upon Norris.[16] This pastor had friends in politics as well. Norris spoke by invitation to the state legislatures of both Texas and Georgia,[17] and he considered himself a personal friend of Cordell Hull, who served as US Secretary of State from 1933 until 1944.[18] On a trip to the Holy Land, Norris had even been granted a personal interview with the Grand Mufti, then head of the Moslem world.[19] So renowned was this preacher that Sinclair Lewis, winner of the 1930 Nobel Prize for Literature, once visited the First Baptist Church in Fort Worth merely out of curiosity. After the visit, Lewis remarked, "I have never seen before so many people at church at once."[20]

Of course, Norris's prominence did not always aid his causes. In the case of the WFBMF, the founder's prestige tended to undercut the organization's legitimacy. Critics belittled Norris's group, calling it a "one-man movement."[21] This was a characterization Norris found particularly distasteful. Norris had nothing but contempt for the ecclesiasticism of the Northern and Southern Baptist Conventions, so he bristled at the notion that the pastors in the WFBMF were somehow his underlings. To combat the criticism, he seeded his movement with many leaders. At his behest, for instance, statewide fellowships like the one Dyer had participated in were organized. Norris also led the WFBMF to select national officers. Though Norris himself remained the unofficial overlord of the fellowship, he touted these organizational initiatives as proof that the WFBMF was much more than a one-man movement. This was a grassroots uprising.

Norris kept his grass growing by remaining on the lookout for new men to enlist in his causes, so it was little surprise when Norris began courting the new pastor at High Street. Yet Norris was not the first to take notice of Dowell. Indeed, Dowell's initial recognition in the WFBMF took place while Norris was out of the country on a highly publicized tour of Europe. Acting as a self-appointed American diplomat, Norris had gone to assess the crisis in Europe and to weigh in on the question that was then occupying the thoughts of every American: Should the United States enter World War II? To facilitate this mission, Norris obtained letters of commendation from Secretary of State Hull and other Roosevelt cabinet members. And equipped with these, Norris secured not only his safe passage but also a personal audience with British Prime Minister Winston Churchill.

Norris left for his trip on September 2 and was scheduled to return on a Pan American Yankee Clipper on October 6. Not coincidentally, his return would correspond with the start of the 1941 meeting of the WFBMF, set for October 5-12 in Fort Worth. Members of Norris's fellowship would be waiting eagerly to hear from him. Throughout his journey, Norris had documented his experiences in letters and cablegrams, and many of his writings had been published in his weekly paper, *The Fundamentalist*. In addition to detailing his forty-five minute interview with Churchill, Norris reported being given a tour of the bomb damage in London. He also wrote about preaching one night in Charles Spurgeon's bombed-out Metropolitan Tabernacle. Norris boasted that, despite ongoing air raids and a war-time blackout, he preached before a capacity crowd. He also reported on visits to other parts of Europe, including Scotland, where he spent time with a prominent preacher named Jock Troup. In praise of Troup, Norris wrote that he was "the biggest and most influential minister in Scotland and preaches to the largest crowds of anybody in all Great Britain."[22]

Several reports about Norris's travels appeared in major newspapers across Europe and the US. The most notable of these was the one that revealed Norris's conclusion about US involvement in the war. Norris put his findings in a cablegram to President Roosevelt, and then he forwarded a copy of that cablegram to the *London Evening Standard*. The article in the *Standard* said this: "'Formal declaration of war only thing that will finish Hitlerism,' are the opening words of a cablegram sent from London by Dr. J. Frank Norris, Baptist pastor of the two largest churches in the United States, to President Roosevelt."[23]

Although it is doubtful that either the cablegram or Norris's tour of Europe had any bearing on US history, his trip did generate a good bit of buzz among his fellowship's constituency. In fact, just as Norris's cable to Roosevelt was hitting the presses, Norris's supporters were gathering back in Fort Worth for the start of the national meeting. Anticipation over Norris's report was attracting a larger-than-usual crowd. Dowell himself was among the throng that was there to hear it. As had been the case when Dowell attended those earlier Fort Worth Bible schools, the itinerary for this conference was jam-packed. The published speaking schedule for the week included a daily lineup of Norris's closest associates, though Norris himself retained the rank of featured speaker. "The Preacher" (as Norris was often called) was slated to speak no less than three times each day throughout the conference.[24]

As this fellowship meeting was getting underway, however, word came that storms over the Atlantic Ocean had delayed Norris's flight back home. Suddenly, conference organizers had to scramble. No one knew when Norris's Clipper might be cleared to make the return trip across the Atlantic, and it seemed that each report that came saying Norris was finally off the ground was quickly followed by another report stating that he had been turned back again. And so it went throughout the week, forcing fellowship leaders to proceed without their featured speaker. For Dowell, this development proved providential. Norris's absence meant that preachers who were not originally slated to speak were invited to fill vacant timeslots. Dowell was among those added to the roster.

As these lesser-known speakers stepped up to the pulpit one by one, the tenor of the fellowship meeting began to change. Something like a revival broke out. The looming war had produced a mood that, though not somber, was particularly solemn. "It was a deeply Spiritual meeting," one preacher said, "for the reason that the days of distress and wreck and ruin are so appalling that everybody felt keenly the responsibility of finding a more effective way of reaching lost humanity."[25] Each new speaker delivered a divine challenge that seemed perfectly suited to the hour, and the audience sat enrapt, forgetting momentarily that their revered leader was absent. In fact, near the end of the week, the assembly received the disturbing news that a Clipper over the Atlantic had gone down in mid-flight. Prayers went up for Norris's safety, but the preaching continued from morning to night uninterrupted.

There was great rejoicing when delegates finally learned that Norris was safe and sound aboard a different Clipper, and that he would be making a dramatic landing in Texas on Sunday, October 12, the last day of the national meeting. Interest in what Norris would have to say was now running so high that meeting planners secured Farrington Field from the Fort Worth public schools for that closing session. Over fifteen thousand people filled this stadium to hear Norris's address.[26]

Once Norris made it back to the States, all attention was back on him. Yet no one who had attended the preceding week's meetings could forget the great moving of God that they had experienced. The young speakers who had stepped up to the pulpit were hailed as "brilliant."[27] Indeed, one pastor wrote, "I think I know preaching and teaching, and I was amazed every day at a new star that would arrive on the scene." The writer concluded that Norris's delay had been "providential, for if he had arrived sooner everybody would have been interested, and properly so, in what he had to say having just come from war-torn Europe." As it happened, the Clipper's delay gave the delegates, instead of a meeting with J. Frank Norris, an encounter with Almighty God. "What fellowship!" the writer raved. "What 'In honor preferring one another'!"[28]

Dowell's ministry was a beneficiary of that great meeting. Recalling the experience Dowell said, "I left the building that morning after I preached with a pocketful of invitations for meetings and so forth. And then they asked me to preach again the next afternoon on a broadcast program."[29] The most significant invitation, however, came from G. Beauchamp Vick, Norris's general superintendent at Temple Baptist. Vick, who was once described by Louis Entzminger as "the greatest layman in Christian service I have ever known,"[30] was a dynamic leader in his own right. And of course, Vick was also one of Norris's closest ministry associates. So for Dowell, it was a singular honor when Vick approached him at the fellowship meeting and said, "I want you to come up and preach for us at the Temple Baptist Church."[31]

Dowell said he was quick to accept Vick's invitation, but he also confessed that he was "fearful" as he went to Detroit a few weeks later to fulfill that speaking obligation. This would be a pivotal moment in his career, and Dowell knew it. He said his feelings of trepidation were ultimately allayed by Vick. "I went up, and he made me feel like a king," Dowell said. "He boosted me before the church, took me around to see all the Sunday school departments and so forth. And I had a fabulous service and some forty-two people saved that Sunday morning. And four or five that night."[32] The experience forged one of Dowell's most treasured ministry relationships, one that would endure until Vick's death in 1975. Dowell became a regular guest evangelist at Temple, and for many years he preached there six or eight Sundays out of the year.

But Dowell's affiliation with Vick also affected him in another way. It brought him to the attention of J. Frank Norris. After Norris delivered his war report to the crowd at Farrington Field, he went on tour to several cities across the nation making similar presentations. Among his scheduled stops was a visit to the congregation at Temple. Norris visited his church on November 2, intending to leave Detroit afterwards by airplane. Yet his plans had to be revised when executives from the Chrysler Corporation presented him with a new automobile. To get the vehicle home, Norris now needed to make an unexpected road trip from Detroit to Fort Worth.

When Vick learned of Norris's revised plans, he approached Norris with a suggestion. "Beauchamp suggested that I stop at Springfield and preach for Bill Dowell," Norris said in an article. "[Vick] was so superlative in his praise of this young preacher of only twenty-seven, having heard him in the Bible School three weeks before, I decided to stop if it was convenient to Bill."[33] Suddenly the celebrated J. Frank Norris was on his way to Springfield. For Dowell, it was both an honor and a nightmare. Norris's impromptu visit was set for Tuesday, November 4, just two days after Norris left Detroit. In that short amount of time, Dowell was expected to come up with an audience for the famed preacher to address. The young preacher dared not disappoint.

Dowell immediately went to work promoting the event, mostly through radio announcements. And fortunately his listeners responded. According to Norris's article about the visit, High Street's auditorium and even its basement were filled to capacity.[34] The visit also received front-page coverage in a Springfield newspaper the next day.[35] In the following issue of *The Fundamentalist*, Norris lauded Dowell for his efforts. "I don't want to praise any man," he wrote, "but I do want to thank the Lord for such a heroic, high standing, clean-cut young Timothy. He has heart, brain, soul, and a giant body." Norris was further pleased when Dowell offered him a "nice check" at the close of his stay. Regarding the gift, Norris added a note of clarification. "They wanted to give me an offering," he said, "but I had them turn it to the Bible Institute."[36]

Norris's write-up about Dowell suggests not only that he was impressed by the young preacher but also that he had aspirations for expanding their association. "It was discussed," Norris continued in his article, "that in the not distant future we would have a three day state wide meeting at the High Street Fundamental Baptist Church."[37] Suddenly Dowell was a rising star in Norris's court. Though Dowell had been virtually unknown a few weeks earlier, he was now an ally of one of the nation's most powerful preachers.

This budding relationship between Dowell and Norris laid a foundation for many other significant events yet to come, and for that reason, it represents one of the most significant turning points in Dowell's career. But like other turning points in this story, the origin of the events seems more divine than human. Plane delays, automobile gifts, impromptu speaking engagements—these were not the doings of any man. Instead, they evoke the words of Psalm 37: "The steps of a good man are ordered by the Lord."[38] Dowell's steps, it would appear, were being carefully orchestrated by Heaven. And even he could not imagine where those steps would lead next.

Chapter 13: *The Light That Shines Farthest*

This was a difficult moment. A troubled member of High Street Church sat across the desk from Dowell in his office, one of his hands nervously clutching the back of his other hand as he spoke.

I'm asking you not to do it. . . .

Like the majority of Dowell's congregation, this man was a blue collar sort, plainly dressed in a pair of dungarees and a drab cotton shirt. Dowell studied the man's eyes and could see tears clinging to his lower lashes. The pastor leaned forward in his chair, resting his arms on his desk. His booming voice became surprisingly gentle.

It's a hard time, I know. And I can tell you that I've wrestled with this decision a good deal—

The man did not wait for Dowell to finish.

No one's gonna think any less of you, Brother Dowell.

The man's interruption was unexpected. Under ordinary circumstances a church member would have been more deferential in the company of his pastor. Such was the reverence the people of this generation had for their clergymen. In this instance, however, the church member was uncharacteristically outspoken. He pulled a red handkerchief from his shirt pocket and was now daubing his eyes. He then took a breath to calm himself, though his voice still trembled with emotion.

I . . . and a lot of other men in this church . . . we're not going to be here. Could be for a very long time . . . and we don't know when we'll be back . . . or if . . .

Those last words caught Dowell off guard. In fact, he had to clear the emotion from his own throat before he could respond. Dowell could sense that this man was truly frightened. So moving were the man's tears that, at first, Dowell missed the point of his pleas. Dowell thought the man was worried about his pastor's wellbeing. And in that thought, Dowell tried to offer him some comfort:

We've—we've all got to understand something, my friend, now more than ever. The Scripture makes it plain that we don't any of us have the assurance of another day.

Sharing such biblical truths had become second nature for Dowell, but in this case it was also a means of coping with his own uncertainties. When all else in the world was confusion and upheaval—and it was—the Word of God remained firm and familiar territory. Declaring its truth gave the preacher a calm confidence as he continued:

Look. I appreciate your concern for me. But I might die here just as well as there. Just like you. And it might be that I could do a lot of good over there. I'm able-bodied, and I'd be ready to minister to the troops whenever there was an opportunity. God can take care of me. And the fact of the matter is, I want to serve my country. You can understand that, can't you?

World War II had come to the United States with the bombing of Pearl Harbor on December 7, 1941, less than six months after the Dowells arrived at High Street Church. In the days that followed the attack, Dowell and his loved ones, like most Americans, sat beside their living room radio listening to Roosevelt's declaration of war. They then braced themselves for the coming battle and for what this might mean to their way of life. Scores of men from Springfield were summoned up for duty, many of them from High Street's congregation. At first, only single men and married men without children were drafted, but by 1943 fathers were also being called up to serve. Dowell was keen to serve alongside them. "I felt very strongly about going into the army," he said.[1]

Dowell originally sought to enlist as a chaplain. He made an inquiry about the possibility only to discover that he lacked the educational requirements necessary to serve in that capacity. Thereafter he determined to enter as a buck private.

But, Brother Dowell, what good is it going to do us to win this war if we don't have something to come home to?

By now the man in Dowell's office was nearly yelling. He was ashamed to have spoken so forcefully to his preacher, but he was glad to have asked the question. And suddenly Dowell realized that the man's distress was not merely a sign of concern for his pastor's wellbeing.

Still wiping tears, the man said:

Our children . . . our wives . . . they're going to need you here.

As a minister, Dowell received a 4-D draft classification exempting him from military service. Even so, Dowell found it difficult to stay at home when so many others were serving. "Just about nearly all of our fine young men was going into the service," Dowell said in an interview. "And I remember how strongly I felt about it." At one point Dowell proposed taking a leave of absence from the church so that he might enlist in the army. It was the servicemen in his congregation who opposed the idea. They were adamant that their pastor remain in Springfield. "They said, 'We'll do the fighting; you do the taking care of our families.'"[2]

In time Dowell recognized the magnitude of what they had asked him to do. "It placed upon me a tremendous responsibility," he said, "because those men were trusting me, so to speak, with their families. To minister to them and comfort them. Some of those men that left would not be coming back, and they wanted a strong man in the pulpit pastoring their families while they were gone."[3] So Dowell stayed. He resolved that he would not only defend the home front but that he would do it honorably. He set aside thoughts of serving in the military and instead poured himself into the ministry at High Street as a soldier for the Lord.

Always near the top of this soldier's battle objectives was keeping the spiritual fires of his church well kindled. Dowell scheduled a revival meeting at High Street for February 1942, just weeks after the US entered the war. A layman named Oscar T. Hicklin led the congregational music for that meeting. Hicklin had been with the church almost since it began, and he gave "of himself and his talent untiringly," Dowell said in a newsletter article. Another layman, Ray Hunt, led the church choir. "Ray is an accomplished musician," Dowell wrote, "and has taught singing schools in many places through-out [sic] the state."[4] Equally important to this revival meeting was a certain preacher boy in the church, Warren Norton. Though Norton neither led the music nor preached, he was ever fervent in his service to the Lord. And Norton's efforts during that 1942 revival would impact High Street's ministry for many decades to come. It was he who invited a pair of his friends to the revival, Earl and Genevieve Smith.

The Smiths, an amiable couple, readily accepted Norton's revival invitation, and they were impressed by what they experienced—especially by the church's lively and inspiring music. Though Earl did not consider himself highly trained in music, he did admit a knack for it. "I played a trumpet for six years during school and kind of knew the basics," he said in an interview.[5] Smith also possessed what Dowell would later describe as "a beautiful golden tenor voice."[6] High Street's revival piqued Earl and Genevieve's interest, and they continued visiting the church for several more weeks. Then, within six months, they became church members—and active ones at that. "Every time you opened the doors, I was there," Earl said. This he always followed with a joke: "I'd have gone to ladies' meetings if they'da let me."[7]

Earl and Genevieve Smith were still newlyweds in 1942. Earl made eighteen dollars a week as a grocery store meat cutter, and like so many other young couples in the church, he and his wife barely scraped by. Because of this, it became routine for the Smiths and others to do their socializing at church. After services, they would stand around talking with friends, sometimes for long periods. "We didn't have any money to go [out to] eat," Smith explained.[8]

Not everyone delighted in this practice, Smith said. In fact, the old church janitor, a man named Dodson, grew exasperated over it. "He said, 'Earl if you're gonna stand around here and talk,' he said, 'I'm gonna give you a key. You lock up.'"[9] And Dodson eventually followed through with the threat. Smith was given a key to lock up the church facility, and this, said Smith, was the first of many unofficial duties he was assigned at High Street. He and Genevieve, one-time newcomers to the church, were now insiders. Warren Norton's revival-time invitation had earned for this congregation not only a pair of workhorses but also a set of lifelong friends.

Even as God was moving such key personnel into the church, High Street's pastor was experiencing a growing burden to reach people outside the church walls. Dowell once admitted that, during his early ministry, it was not uncommon for him to leave his pulpit and weep if his preaching did not result in conversions.[10] A similar fervor now drove Dowell as he built his new ministry in Springfield. Church growth would prove challenging, however, given the wartime circumstances. For every new member that joined, Dowell said, there was another member that left either to serve on the battlefront or to work in wartime factories. Dowell had to resign himself to the fact that the war would limit his congregation's size. Instead of working to build a larger audience, he put his efforts into seeing people saved.

Dowell found that the adversity of the hour aided him in this cause. The war seemed to spark a kind of spiritual awakening in the US. Writing in February 1944, Dowell said, "There is a great revival on in practically every Fundamental Baptist Church in the State of Missouri; yea, and throughout the nation."[11] On this subject he could speak with authority; he had personally witnessed the spread of these revival fires in his efforts as a traveling evangelist. So hectic was Dowell's personal speaking schedule that, by the mid-1940s, he had purchased a Piper Cub airplane to facilitate his frequent travels. Both he and Nola took flying lessons and obtained pilot's licenses in order to fly it. Dowell was now constantly on the go, and wherever he went, he found Christians aflame with the Spirit of God.

Dowell seized this moment back at High Street by launching a variety of evangelistic ministries, efforts that would prove highly profitable. "The church grew powerfully in a spiritual way," Dowell said.[12] One of Dowell's initiatives was a ministry targeting the soldiers of nearby Fort Leonard Wood. Many of the soldiers spent Saturday nights carousing on Springfield's city square. High Street's members capitalized on that opportunity by frequenting the square in search of the lost. "And we urged them," Dowell remembered. "We had boys go down to the square and meet all these boys and invite them out to the service the next day." The added incentive was free food. "They'd come to the service, and then we'd feed them after the service," he explained. "[W]e won a lot of those boys to the Lord."[13]

Another successful initiative of this period was one that was suggested to Dowell by High Street's lay youth leader, a stockyard worker named Lee McLean. McLean proposed that the young people of the church team up with Dowell to conduct weekly evangelistic meetings all across southwest Missouri. "The young people sold me on the idea," Dowell said.[14] After securing a church or school building in one of the neighboring communities, Dowell would announce on radio that he and his young evangelistic team were coming to town on the following Thursday night. Then week by week they would take their traveling ministry to rural places throughout southwest Missouri.

The formula for these youth meetings was simple. Dowell would preach the sermon and his teenage collaborators would handle everything else. And the meetings were a huge success. "The place would be packed," Dowell said.[15] Of course, Dowell made no mention of the fact that these "packed" rural venues were often very small. To him, the size of the facility was immaterial. Dowell's son-in-law, Bernie Rodgers, once traveled with him to such a meeting and recalled how Dowell "preached as hard to the small group [as] he did to large groups."[16] Earl Smith agreed. "If we had fifty people, he'd preach like there were a thousand," Smith said.[17]

What mattered to Dowell was the spiritual harvest. Recalling those Thursday night outings, Dowell said, "We had scores of people saved from these meetings."[18] Indeed, he counted these youth-sponsored events among the most fruitful meetings of his career.

And his teenage collaborators could not have been more energized by the experience. Their partnership with Dowell fostered not only their spiritual growth but also a deep loyalty for their pastor, outcomes that would benefit High Street for years to come.

One other important outreach strategy of this period was High Street's revival meetings. Dowell hosted successful meetings in both the summer and winter months. During the summer of 1943, Dowell rented a plot of ground near the center of Springfield, where he erected a tent for his first city-wide tent revival. He wrote an article to promote the event, saying: "May I urge you in this dark hour in which we are living, when armies are marching and our boys are being killed by the thousands, when our very homes and churches are being attacked. I say! God help us every one to join hands together in a great city-wide soul-winning campaign with a prayer upon our hearts that literally hundreds will turn to Jesus Christ and be saved."[19] In response to this appeal, people from all over the area congregated night after night under a tent that measured 60 feet by 120 feet.[20] "We'd order a tent that would seat under the tent probably around twelve hundred," Dowell recalled. "But we'd have as high as two thousand or twenty-two hundred people that would come. We'd put them all around the tent."[21]

High Street's tent revivals continued with great success for twelve straight years. On one occasion, Dowell recalled, some celebrities even showed up: "Bette Davis and her fourth husband, whom she had just married." In July 1950, Davis and her *All About Eve* co-star, Gary Merrill, traveled to Juarez, Mexico, to obtain quick divorces from their respective spouses. The couple was then married in Mexico on July 28, after which they drove their black Cadillac convertible from El Paso back to New England. On July 30, the last night of Dowell's three-week tent revival in Springfield, Davis and Merrill made an unpublicized stop at the tent near the intersection of Glenstone Avenue and St. Louis Street. Speaking many years later, Dowell said that he had spotted this couple in the crowd but had not recognized them. And those in his congregation who did recognize them were more interested in their souls, it seems, than their autographs. "One of our personal workers went to [Davis] during the invitation," Dowell explained, "and asked her if she was a Christian." To this question the brash Hollywood star took offense. "What do you think I am," she snapped, "a heathen?"[22]

Although the lives of Davis and Merrill may not have been transformed by their tent revival experience, many others who attended Dowell's summer meetings were forever changed. "We had literally hundreds of souls that were saved in those meetings," Dowell reported. And at the end of those campaigns, High Street celebrated God's blessings with a river baptism. Church member Ross Owens owned a farm on the nearby James River, and for many years crowds of up to fifteen hundred people drove out to that picturesque site south of Springfield to watch Dowell immerse his latest converts. "We'd baptize as high as sixty and seventy people at a time at the end of those tent revivals," Dowell recalled.[23]

Of course, Dowell's church held additional meetings during the wintertime. These, too, proved fruitful. In February 1944, guest evangelist Roland C. King preached to "overflow crowds" in the High Street auditorium "night after night in spite of gasoline and tire rationing, and some bad weather."[24] Though King's revival was conducted indoors, enthusiastic church members refused to confine this event to the four walls of their building. Auxiliary meetings soon began springing up off site. Dowell wrote about these meetings, saying:

> *Besides the services here at the church, we went into Oberman's factory for several noon day services where a number were gloriously saved. And through the kind invitation of Bro. Lee McLean, one of the men at the Union Stock Yards, we had an early morning service at the Union Stock Yards where a large number of cattle men from all over the country listened attentively to the simple Gospel of Jesus Christ. When the invitation was given, several big-fisted, rugged cattle men with tears streaming down their cheeks, raised their hand requesting prayer for their salvation.*[25]

Dowell found that guest speakers like Roland C. King were often effective in attracting crowds and in partnering with him to reach lost souls. For that reason, special guests became a regular feature of High Street's evangelistic strategy. Through the years Dowell's guests included such notables as Dallas Billington, Robert T. Ketcham, Jack Schuler, J. Harold Smith, and G. B. Vick. Evangelist Roy Kemp drew crowds to the church using a "500-foot Technicolor chart" to outline the prophetic events found in the Book of Revelation. Then in 1951, John Rawlings preached a winter revival that produced a hundred new church members.[26] Even many years later, Rawlings remembered Dowell's reaction to the meeting: "[He] said it was the greatest revival he had ever been in."[27]

One speaker who seems to have had exceptional appeal to Dowell's wartime audience was Fred Donnelson, missionary to China. Donnelson and his family had been engaged in a fruitful ministry in and around Hangchow when the war broke out. Yet even after it appeared that a Japanese invasion of China was imminent, Donnelson refused to abandon his work. He stayed in China, and in time, he and his family became trapped behind enemy lines. They were soon placed under house arrest and, later, into a Japanese internment camp. The Donnelsons endured seven months of harsh conditions in the camp, though J. Frank Norris made several trips to Washington to try to free them. Then in the fall of 1943, the Donnelsons were finally repatriated. They began their return voyage on September 19, and seventy-four days later, the emaciated family arrived back on American soil.

This was a welcome Christmas present both for the Donnelson family and for the war-weary Christians who had been following their story. The Donnelsons were viewed as heroes, and independent Baptist churches across the nation—including High Street—wanted an opportunity to hear their story firsthand and to celebrate their repatriation. Dowell scheduled Fred Donnelson to speak to his church on January 2, 1944.

For this event, Dowell secured Springfield's largest auditorium, the Shrine Mosque. Such a large venue was fully warranted. Even though the night was snowy, people poured into the arena. The headline on the front page of Dowell's next newsletter read,

"3700 People in Evening Service to Hear Dr. Fred Donnelson." The building had been "packed to capacity," Dowell said.

There were plenty of accolades for the Donnelsons that evening. Dowell reported that Mayor Carr delivered "a welcome address," and that "most of the county and city officials" were also present to honor the Donnelsons. But better than any of that, as far as Dowell was concerned, was the fact that the meeting helped to spread the gospel both at home and abroad. An "offering of $546.00 was taken for China missions," Dowell wrote. "As soon as the war is over, Dr. Donnelson plans to return to China with twenty other Missionaries, and enough money to build great Baptist churches all over China."[28]

One of Fred Donnelson's favorite missionary slogans was this: "The light that shines farthest shines brightest at home." Dowell seems to have taken those words to heart. Soldier Dowell's wartime strategies launched High Street into an era that he would later describe as "perennial revival."[29] Indeed, it seems apparent that Dowell's efforts were the catalyst for High Street's most outstanding period of growth, a period that would last long after the end of the war.

But Dowell's strategies also served another purpose. They helped make the war more bearable. Despite the toll that this conflict was having, servicemen from High Street could fight with confidence, knowing that a light was brightly shining back in Springfield. High Street, like the Allied forces, was now on a road to victory. And this brought comfort to Dowell's fellow soldiers, helping to assure them that their own homecomings would one day be as joyful as the Donnelsons'.

Chapter 14: *Watchdog*

The cigarette smoke might have been sliced with a knife.

You havin' a good time?

Dowell tried not to choke on his words. He leaned toward a pair of teenage boys, one tall and one not, and he rested his elbows on the countertop so that he would be able to hear their reply over the music. The preacher wanted to appear casual; instead he looked uncomfortable and not at all preacher-like. Though he wore a slight smile on his face, his eyes were narrower than usual. If the room had not been so dimly lit, the look on his face might have made the youths in front of him feel uneasy. As it was, the boys did not even notice him. They continued drumming their fingers to the music, oblivious to his presence.

Dowell repeated himself:

You boys havin' a good time?

The taller youth was snacking on something out of a paper bag. He had just popped another large handful into his mouth when he realized that Dowell was addressing them. He elbowed his brown-haired friend and then sputtered as he choked down a laugh. Meanwhile the brown-haired kid tried to form a response:

Huh? Oh yeah. Sure.

The boys rolled scampish eyes at one another. The taller boy, wearing a dopey grin on his face, continued munching. The other boy suddenly reached for the paper bag, and his friend yanked it away. Dowell was still hoping to carry on a conversation with them, so he waited patiently for the boys to finish scuffling.

Do the two of you come here very often?

The tall boy stood upright, as if to make a reply.

Um . . .

The second boy finished his friend's thought:

Just every now and then.

Dowell nodded to acknowledge what the brown-haired boy had said; then he averted his eyes, gazing off into the crowd. The preacher was eager to ask additional questions, but he did not want to make the boys suspicious. As he stood there pondering what to say next, the brown-haired boy spoke up again:

Mostly Saturdays. We see a lot of our friends here usually.

The boy's relaxed tone made the conversation feel less awkward now. Dowell took advantage of the opening. Forcing a smile, he said:

Is that right?

The tall boy answered this time.

Yeah. There's always gobs of people here on Saturdays.

Dowell was doing his best to remain nonchalant, and he used the palm of his hand to slick down the back of his hair. A moment later he asked:

So what are you guys, anyway? Sixteen? Fifteen?

The tall one shot his hand into the air like a Boy Scout ready to take an oath.

I am. I'm fifteen.

Dowell bobbed his head. Then he turned the other boy.

You too?

The boy hid his fingers in his pockets and shrugged.

Nah. Not yet. I will be, though. Next birthday.

On any other day Dowell would not have been caught dead in a night club. He approved of neither drinking nor dancing. Moreover, he admonished the people of his church to eschew such practices. It was the boys standing in front of him—and the many others in Springfield just like them—that had drawn him into this place.

Since the beginning of the war, youth-related problems (loosely termed "juvenile delinquency") had evolved into a serious public concern in Springfield. The city's newspapers had documented a wave of incidents: auto thefts, youths brandishing weapons, underage drinking. And additional reports were cropping up with alarming frequency. Were these problems attributable to the absence of soldier dads? Pastor Dowell had to wonder. All that was certain was that a man in his position could not remain silent while scores of young people in his community were going astray. Dowell was, after all, a soldier at home.

Dowell did not enjoy battles, yet he was never afraid to wage them. Indeed, he believed that all Christians are engaged in a conflict, one that has raged for centuries. It is not a battle "against flesh and blood," Dowell would have argued; it is a spiritual warfare.[1] He saw the Hitlers and Mussolinis of the world as mere puppets of a more sinister dictator, the Devil. And the battlefields of Europe and Asia were but one outcropping of a much larger conflict. A different manifestation of this battle could be found in the cities and homes of America. And Dowell believed that if he stood idly by while such battles were raging, the Lord would hold him accountable for it. So he took up his sword.

Dowell characterized the battles that he engaged in as moral fights. He was standing for righteousness, and against sin. In his mind, no preacher who was worth his salt would do any less. "I don't like to offend people," he once said, "but if the Word of God offends them, there's nothing I can do about it. Because I'm going to preach the Word of God, and I'm going to cry out against sin wherever it's found, because the Bible condemns it."[2]

Dowell's campaign against juvenile delinquency is one of the earliest examples of his efforts to battle the sin in his city. His target, in this instance, was not so much the youthful offenders as it was the city's officials. Dowell had been pleased when city leaders implemented a strict new curfew to try to address the juvenile delinquency problem. He agreed that the first step to getting teens under control was getting them off the streets. Under this new ordinance, issued in 1944, people sixteen and under would no longer be allowed out on the streets past 10:00 p.m. This seemed to Dowell a wise and reasonable step. But after this law was passed, news came that the curfew was not being kept. Dowell learned that many teens were openly defying the curfew and were, in fact, frequenting local nightclubs. Most alarming of all was the report that no one in authority was making any effort to stop it.

So Dowell decided to go and assess the situation for himself. "I took witnesses with me," he said, "and I made a tour of the nightclubs." Dowell and a couple of other men in the church stayed out until midnight investigating the reports that he had heard. "And I saw all kinds of teenagers on the floor of those nightclubs dancing with older people," he testified.[3] Dowell said he even spoke to some of the youths, careful not to reveal his purpose. He learned that some of them were as young as fourteen years old. And for him, this outrage could not be ignored.

Taking out an ad in the local newspaper a few days later, Dowell announced that he would be preaching a sermon exposing "the fact that the curfew law was not being kept."[4] And then on the following Sunday night, Dowell stood before a packed auditorium presenting the details of his nightclub experiences. In that message he also decried the adults, including negligent law enforcement officials, who were contributing to his city's ongoing moral decay.

When Dowell preached this message, many people of Springfield sat up and took notice. His words quickly earned him a reputation as a preacher who was unafraid to speak the truth. His was not a Sunday-only religion; this pastor's faith had legs. It walked boldly into places that no one expected a preacher to go. Furthermore, no segment of Dowell's society, not even a city official, was exempt from his scrutiny.

While Dowell was still in the midst of this war on delinquency, he preached a second controversial sermon. This time he took aim at a group of school teachers. In October of 1944, the Southwest Missouri Teachers Association (SMTA) held a major convention in Springfield. This annual event attracted hundreds of teachers to the city, and each year local merchants targeted these educators, filling the newspapers with ads that announced special sales coinciding with their conference. But in 1944, local merchants also did something else. On Thursday, October 12, the Associated Retailers of Springfield treated conventioneers to a social gathering, a late-night dance held at the Shrine Mosque.

A published announcement for this dance caught Dowell's attention, not to mention his ire. In advance of the event, sponsors sent out an appeal in the local newspapers on behalf of the SMTA's mostly female constituency. Since wartime conscription had drained the city of so many men, party planners were concerned that there would be a shortage of dance partners for the women who attended the event. The ad urged all available "males" from the area to come and help make the dance a success.[5]

In Dowell's opinion, this flew in the face of common decency. It could not have sent a worse message to the city's youth, he thought. The notion of teachers—supposed role models—openly drinking, dancing, and partying with strange men made the preacher wince. "So I preached on 'Southwest Missouri Teachers Association Openly Encourages Juvenile Delinquency,'" he said flatly.[6] Just as Dowell had done after his nightclub raid, he now announced his controversial sermon title in the local newspaper. The ad appeared two days after the teachers' dance. It appeared under the headline "Will the Teen Age Group have confidence in Jitterbug Teachers?" As part of the ad, Dowell pointedly stated, "While young America dies on the battlefield, teachers dance and mourn the lack of males." Dowell then concluded his announcement, saying, "Night owling . . . defies the teaching of God, the church, and the Christian home."[7]

The night after the ad appeared, Dowell stood before another packed audience and delivered the promised diatribe, denouncing the deplorable example that had been set by the teachers. Dowell said his remarks instantly "caught fire."[8] On the front page of the next day's *Springfield Leader and Press* appeared an article entitled "Teachers Call Their Dancing 'Innocent Fun.'" The article published details about Dowell's criticisms, even quoting a statement from his sermon. "Notwithstanding that a curfew law was recently enacted in Springfield to get our youngsters off the street," Dowell was quoted as saying, "these teachers come along and set just the opposite example."[9] The news report then went on to defend the teachers and to discredit Dowell. The journalist went so far as to comment, "Mr. Dowell is not a member of the Springfield Ministerial Alliance and it was clear his attack did not represent the attitude of the city's clergy."[10]

Dowell was unperturbed by the newspaper's take on his message. He was hearing a very different reaction from many others in the community. "I got letters from all over the country commending me for the stand that I made," he said.[11] A week after his sermon, the *Springfield News and Leader* ran in its editorial section some of the many letters it had received on the matter, letters both for and against Dowell's position. One detractor referred to the matter as the "'publicity seeking' expostulations of one Baptist minister."[12] Another rebuked Dowell for exacerbating an ongoing teacher shortage. But a third respondent submitted this rather compelling statement expressing a different point of view:

> I happen to be one of the teachers who attended the convention given for the Southwest Missouri Teachers. I must say from the bottom of my heart I am ashamed to admit that I was present at such a, might I say, "hell hole"?
>
> No, I'm not a member of the High Street Fundamental Baptist church, nor have I ever attended this church, although I do think Pastor W. E. Dowell definitely had the right to make a mountain out of a mole hill, as Louis W. Reps [of the Chamber of Commerce] put it.
>
> . . . I stayed a short while and during my stay I saw enough out of some of the teachers that if the students they teach could have seen them, the youngsters would no longer have confidence in their teachers.

. . . I'm proud that we have one preacher in the city of Springfield that has Guts enough to speak what he knows is right. It really is a shame that some churches have preachers that are too much of a coward to teach what they know is right, but they're afraid the members of their church might disapprove.

. . . Reverend Dowell, my hat is off to you. I admire you for being the only preacher in the city of Springfield to speak what is in his heart.[13]

Looking back, Dowell said that this sermon won him "lots of friends" and also "some very, very bitter enemies."[14] Yet like his sometime mentor J. Frank Norris, Dowell never made apology for stirring up such controversy. Indeed, Norris regularly drew large crowds by promising to reveal secrets and to expose corruption. He was even known to add a bit of theatricality to ensure his services were suitably sensational (e.g., producing a live monkey to denounce evolution[15] or shredding a Russian flag to condemn Communism[16]). Dowell's preaching never approached that level of showmanship, but like Norris, Dowell did relish the effect that controversial preaching had on the size of his audiences. This was part of what motivated his controversial preaching, he confessed. "One of the main reasons that I had was to get crowds out, get people out— lost people," Dowell said. "People will come hear something like that."[17] Sensational subjects were bait with which the preacher went fishing for men. Dowell explained his use of the strategy:

A lot of people confessed that they came to hear me preach just to hear what I was going to say. When they got there, I preached a gospel sermon. I'd open it by telling about my experiences, about the nightclub, that the curfew was not being kept and [the young people] were being permitted to carry on. And I'd go through all this, and then I'd preach a great gospel sermon. We'd have folks pile down the altar and get saved just from the sermon.[18]

The similarity to J. Frank Norris is hard to miss. One biographer said Norris "would 'raise hell' for the first twenty minutes or so to get the attention of the people, then settle in and preach the old-time gospel."[19] Where Dowell and Norris differed, it seems, was in Norris's seemingly unquenchable thirst for a fight. Dowell was no warmonger. "I don't believe in just cooking something up," Dowell said. "I used sensational subjects when there was something sensational taking place."[20]

Dowell's controversial preaching drew many people from the community into his church. It also helped to define his ministry and to brand him as a man of integrity. "I began to be looked upon by a lot of people here in the city as the watchdog of the city," Dowell said, "because I noted the controversial issues, and I made a stand on them."[21] Even those who did not attend Dowell's church took notice. Eldon Harmon was then just a boy living in Dowell's neighborhood, though his family had never been a part of the High Street congregation. "My folks didn't go to church," Harmon explained in an interview. Yet in the summertime, when the windows of the unairconditioned church were opened up, the Harmon family would listen to Dowell's preaching from the porch of their home. "There was several people in the neighborhood who would just sit out there on the porches, listen to him from the porch," Harmon recalled.[22]

Another boy in the city, future US Attorney General John Ashcroft, was similarly affected by Dowell's presence in his community. Ashcroft, too, was unaffiliated with High Street, yet in a 1984 letter to Dowell, he wrote, "Since my boyhood days on the north side of Springfield I have felt the impact of your spiritual leadership on my life. The city was different (better) because of you, my high school was different (better) because of you, our home was different (better) because of your testimony and your witness and ministry."[23]

Of course, the real power of Dowell's preaching was in its message, not in its controversy. While controversy sometimes bolstered Dowell's prominence in the community, he did not fight for selfish reasons. He fought as a soldier fights, to defeat an enemy. A sermon from the spring of 1945, "Why the Coming of V-Day Has Been Prolonged," reveals the spiritual eyes with which Dowell viewed the world around him. In that message, he stated:

> *As I see our own beloved nation following in the foot-steps of France in desperation my very soul cries out, oh, America turn to God before the same terrible fate that has befallen these other nations who mocked God befalls us! God has always used war as a scourge to whip His people back into line. God help us to see this one terrible truth. This present war with all of its tragedies is the result of our nation forgetting God.*[24]

The moral battles that Dowell waged in his sermons were intended to help people see that "terrible truth." Dowell believed that someone had to be courageous enough to shine a spotlight on the sin of the age. And if no one else would do it, he would.

Dowell's message was not just about sin, however. It was also about hope. Dowell unmasked the problem so that he could offer his listeners the solution. In that same "V-Day" sermon, Dowell went on to say, "I am so glad that in the midst of all the darkness and chaos of this present hour, there is a light, shining like the star of Bethlehem that pierces the darkness to guide men aright."[25] Dowell concluded his message with these words of hope:

> *Wherever man might be—on the cruel bleak mountain side of some far flung battlefield, hurling through space in a modern bomber, sailing the high seas, struggling in a death grip with the enemy in the islands of the South Pacific, or here at home quietly reading this article, if by faith he will look through the darkness of his own soul to Jesus Christ, and with a cry for mercy, trust in that Saviour, the blessed light of God will shine into his soul and the darkness will flee like the dew before the early rising sun.*
>
> *Some time ago I was called into a home to visit a man who was an habitual drunkard, whose home was almost on the rocks. I will never forget his pleading eyes as he looked up into my face and said, "I have made a wreck of my life, I am*

a slave to liquor, my home is broken, I am ruined, there is no hope." His little wife was sitting in the corner weeping. She had suffered so much at his hands she felt she could go no farther. My heart broke within me. I sat down by his side and opened the precious word of God and said, "My dear friend there is hope in this book and in the Christ this book reveals." The poor man looked up hopelessly and cried, "But I have gone too far. My sins are too great!" I slowly began to read the words of Jesus, "I came not to call the righteous but sinners to repentance" and then I read, "For the son of man came to seek and to save that which was lost." Then I turned over to Isa. 1:18 "Come let us reason together, saith the Lord: though your sins be as scarlet they shall be as white as snow; though they be red like crimson, they shall be as wool." Then I turned over to 1 John 1:7 "But if we walk in the light as he is in the light, we have fellowship one with another and the blood of Jesus Christ his Son cleanseth us from all sin."

Suddenly he grasped the meaning of those precious promises, and out of an heart of gratitude cried "O, that means me doesn't it?" I said, "yes that means you." Then he looked up and said, "Oh, but what can I do to obtain this wonderful salvation?" I turned over to John 1:12 and began reading, "To as many as received him to them gave he the power to become the sons of God, even to them that believe on his name." He cried out of his sin-burdened soul and said, "I will receive Him now." As on our knees we prayed the light of God burst forth in his soul and he came to his feet saying, "It is real! God has forgiven me. I have peace I have never known before. It is wonderful!" And there he promised his wife that, with God's help, they would begin a new life.

O, my friend, you too can have peace and joy if you will renounce your sins and trust in Jesus Christ as your personal Saviour.[26]

The same month that Dowell preached that sermon, he himself had to lean upon the Peace That Passes All Understanding. On March 17, 1945, Dowell received a 3:00 a.m. telephone call. His sister-in-law was on the other end of the line, and she said, "Bill, Dad passed away this morning."[27] Dowell's father, Albin, had died.

Dowell found solace in the knowledge that his father had accepted Christ and that Albin, like the Apostle Paul, had fought a good fight. What lay ahead of Albin Dowell was a crown of righteousness.[28] It was this hope that sustained Dowell as he watched his father's casket being lowered into the ground a few days later. And Dowell wanted nothing more than for others to have that hope, too. He understood that this was the real reason he fought. Though the conflicts were sometimes bitter, victory was worth the price.

Less than six months after Albin's death, Dowell received some more sobering news: United States forces had dropped the atomic bomb on Hiroshima and Nagasaki. The war had reached an end. For Dowell, the news brought deep emotion, if not celebration. The devastation in Japan served as a reminder that victory had come at a high price. "I felt so deeply about it until I just wanted to get away," Dowell said. So Dowell drove himself out to the hangar where his Piper Cub was stored, and he spent the afternoon flying down to the city of Branson and circling the August sky. "[I] just meditated," he said.[29]

Of course, the spiritual battle that Dowell had been waging would go on long after the end of World War II. There would be no surrender in that conflict, not until the return of Christ. But in the meantime, Dowell and others would fight on, praying that their efforts, like those of the Allied troops, would ultimately benefit humanity. In this, Dowell remained hopeful. In fact, now that the war was over, he had good reason to believe that the work of his church would take on new life. The prospects for a better tomorrow, Dowell thought, were as bright as those green Ozark hills beneath his plane. Perhaps the war's conclusion was not so much an end as it was a beginning.

Chapter 15: *Earl*

*L*ast *night I lay a-sleeping*
  There came a dream so fair,
  I stood in old Jerusalem
Beside the temple there.
I heard the children singing,
And ever as they sang,
Methought the voice of angels
From heav'n in answer rang.
Methought the voice of angels
From heav'n in answer rang.

August 1945 had just begun, as had the city-wide tent revival sponsored by High Street Fundamental Baptist Church. A soloist stood singing on the platform under the tent. The tent that year was pitched at the corner of Boonville Avenue and Division Street, just blocks away from the city square.

Jerusalem! Jerusalem!
Lift up your gates and sing,
Hosanna in the highest!
Hosanna to your King!

At one end of the tent, just in front of the wooden platform, a long dark-stained bench stretched across a rolled-out carpet. This was the mourner's bench, a bench reserved for those who would, at the end of each evening's service, kneel, repent, and meet Jesus. It was the only spot under the tent that was not currently occupied. Even the wooden folding chairs, now scattered four and five rows deep around the outside of the tent, were all taken. Some onlookers simply stood. Everywhere one looked there were more people, each one of them decked out in his or her Sunday best—hats, ribbons, suit coats, neckties—as if oblivious to the meeting's rugged outdoor setting. Some of the women also brought sweaters along in case the night air became too chilly. Like the mourner's bench in front of them, the congregants' faces seemed to anticipate the evening's climax, the time when sinner and Savior would finally be reconciled.

And then methought my dream was chang'd,
The streets no longer rang,

Hush'd were the glad Hosannas
The little children sang.
The sun grew dark with mystery,
The morn was cold and chill,
As the shadow of a cross arose
Upon a lonely hill.
As the shadow of a cross arose
Upon a lonely hill.

Some of the little ones seated at the front of this crowd entertained themselves by scuffing their feet on the sawdust floor. The rest of the audience sat with eyes glued to the soloist on the platform. Anything less would have seemed disrespectful. After all, this singer was wearing the uniform of the United States Army Air Force.

Jerusalem! Jerusalem!
Hark! How the angels sing,
Hosanna in the highest!
Hosanna to your King!

The singing soldier and his wife had recently been transferred from North Carolina to California, but on their way to their new post, they stopped by Springfield to visit their beloved family and friends. Just a few days later Pastor Dowell would be flying above the Ozark hills pondering the bombing of Japan, but as of yet, that event was still in the future. For the moment, names like Enola Gay and Hiroshima and Nagasaki were unknown to these people. And oh how they prayed for a speedy end to the war.

As the crowd listened to the solo, the singer on the platform became a symbol of the many husbands, fathers, brothers, and sons that were still fighting on their behalf. Then, as if sensing the crowd's emotional state, the piano accompaniment hit a minor chord. Even the distracted children on the front row paused to listen.

And once again the scene was chang'd;
New earth there seemed to be;
I saw the Holy City
Beside the tideless sea;
The light of God was on its streets,
The gates were open wide,
And all who would might enter,
And no one was denied.
No need of moon or stars by night,
Or sun to shine by day;
It was the new Jerusalem
That would not pass away.
It was the new Jerusalem
That would not pass away.

As the pianist began pounding the victorious marching chorus one last time, a man outside the tent shouted, "Glory!" and a chorus of others from across the audience echoed with "Amen!" and "Bless God!" and "Hallelujah!" A cluster of women in the makeshift choir loft began simultaneously reaching for their handkerchiefs. Meanwhile, the tenor soloist held nothing back.

Jerusalem! Jerusalem!
Sing for the night is o'er!
Hosanna in the highest!
Hosanna for evermore!
Hosanna in the highest!
Hosanna for evermore![1]

Many years after that meeting, the singer, Earl Smith, discussed his memory of that experience. When he finished singing, Smith said, "what wasn't shoutin' was cryin'."[2] The Holy Spirit had done His work, and hearts were now receptive to the call of God upon their lives. In short, revival had come to the revival tent.

Earl Smith had been drafted into the Army Air Force back in August 1943, only about a year after he and Genevieve first joined High Street. He was then shipped off to Greensboro, North Carolina, for basic training, where he took and passed the "butcher's trade test."[3] His wife later joined him in North Carolina.

The Smiths were happy to serve their country but were also saddened to be away from the church that they had come to love. Earl wrote a letter to the Dowells during his training, saying, "Sundays are pretty rough on me."[4] Then in another heartfelt letter Smith wrote, "All the boys are gone to town tonite except myself and 3 more. I'd sure like to be in Spfd. tonight and get up in the morning and come to High St. I'm looking forward to being right in with you before too long. But folks, you can't know how much I miss you. I get so hungry for all of you. It's hard to stand. But I know it's best I'm here. Rom. 8:28."[5]

Smith's military stint served as a test of his spiritual mettle. He was suddenly surrounded by men of different beliefs and values, and he sometimes struggled to know how to react. "All they want to do is play cards and shoot craps," he once wrote. "I try to remember that I'm no better than they and still keep myself clean. I don't indulge with them, and I try not to condemn them. There's a lot of Catholic boys here. Of course they just do any way." Smith said he took refuge from it all in a diversion of his own making. "One thing we do," he continued, "there's some boys here that like to sing, and I brought my song books (2, Fav. Songs and Hymns) and we sang a lot of old songs."[6]

Within a short time, Smith found, his fellow soldiers not only learned of his faith but also grew to respect him for his clean living. "The boys here have given me their money (some of them) so they won't gamble it away," he wrote. "I won't allow any gambling in our tent."[7] In another place Smith wrote, "I've moved in bks 423. I was in 424. Some in there called me Parson. The main one that called me that likes me real well. He asked me to pray for his mother who's in the hospital in Springfield. I told him I would and did."[8]

Yet even as this young soldier was striving to honor Christ with his life, he admitted wrestling with deep feelings of guilt over the lack of boldness in his Christian witness. Smith wrote candidly:

I feel like the Lord will let me come back to High St. I don't know why. I'm not doing anything for him here. I've really failed him so far. I haven't give up yet. But the Lord is going to throw me overboard if I don't get in gear. The boys like and respect me, but I'm not talking to them and winning them to Christ. I hope I can do better. I know all of you are praying for me, but I'm not doing enough myself. I've got to get in gear and I know it. The Lord's going to do me like He did Jona (sic) and I deserve it.[9]

Perhaps in these letters Dowell recognized a kindred spirit. For all their evangelistic fervor, Dowell and Smith were both rooted in remarkably humble soil. Many who witnessed their public ministries would later characterize them as zealous, passionate, and unwavering. Yet they themselves knew they were men, not saints. One of Dowell's admirers once said, "He was a wonderful friend who never dipped his colors."[10] Dowell was not always so sure. In a 1957 sermon, he described a faltering moment he experienced even as a young pastor at High Street:

It should never have happened, but it taught me a lesson. I was called to the home of a very prominent person in Springfield who was sick. I had never met that person, and I knew the family was high in society. I visited the person. When I got ready to leave I wanted to say, "Let's have a word of prayer." But the old Devil said to me, "They wouldn't appreciate that here in this fine mansion. This person has probably never prayed. They wouldn't appreciate your wanting to have prayer in their home. You had better say, 'God bless you, and I hope you get well,' then go on about your business. You'd better not antagonize this person by asking to have prayer."

I have to confess to you—this has been many years ago—I left that home without prayer. Later this person said to a friend, "I enjoyed Brother Dowell's visit very, very much, but I was terribly let down that he didn't have prayer before he left."[11]

Like the Apostle Peter, Bill Dowell and Earl Smith both heard the cock crow from time to time. As in the Bible story, the sound always harbingered a dawning, a heavenly light arriving to rebuke some inner darkness. But just as it was with Peter, these two men were quick to recognize their faltering and to return to the Lord's bosom. Far from thinking themselves better than others, they were both highly cognizant of personal failings. They shared a humility—an authenticity—that served them well in their respective ministries. It may also have served to meld their hearts one to another. "I doubt seriously if any other two men have had the relationship that we had," Smith once said.[12]

Dowell and Smith's long association traced its origin back to the war years. Earl and his wife had joined the church back in 1942, and Dowell stayed in touch with them over the next three years as Smith served his country. Dowell reflected on those years of military service, observing that Smith "gave his talents to the Lord and was used in a marvelous way in different parts of the United States where he was stationed. He did evangelistic singing and radio work in North Carolina and worked with a 'Gospel Team' in Fresno, California, traveling all over that part of the country singing for 'Youth For Christ' meetings and other special evangelistic services."[13]

In Dowell's estimation, Smith served both his country and his Lord with honor, and Dowell admired the Christ-like spirit that characterized Smith as he emerged from his military experiences. By the summer of 1945, when the Smiths came through Springfield on their way to California, Dowell knew that he wanted Smith on his team. After Smith finished his solo that night under the tent, Dowell stepped to the pulpit and posed a question to the audience: "'How many would like to hire this young man to come work for us full time when he gets back?'" To that, the congregation replied with "ten thousand amens," Smith said. Recounting the incident, Smith added wryly, "That was my first hint."[14]

Smith was discharged the following February, and Dowell quickly hired him as a full-time assistant. "His duties here at the church will be many," Dowell promised in his church newspaper. Smith was given charge of the radio ministry music and was also asked to assist Oscar Hicklin and Ray Hunt in carrying out other music responsibilities. "Besides all of this," Dowell wrote, "he will assist in our Sunday School; teach whenever he is needed and during the week go from house to house doing personal visitation and soul winning work."[15]

Though Smith was earning a wage of just forty-five dollars a week from the church, he quickly became the go-to man in church operations. As Bill Dowell Jr. remembered it, "Dad preached, and Earl pretty well took care of the business of the church." Dowell Jr. illustrated his meaning, saying, "If there was going to be a revival meeting, Earl took care of ordering the tent, getting men together, building the platform, spreading sawdust shavings, getting the benches and the wiring and the signs. Earl took care of all the detail work. . . . Dad would be the idea man, but Earl was the detail man."[16]

Of course the most crucial detail managed by Smith was High Street's music. Smith recalled how his role in that arena evolved over time. In July 1946, only weeks after Smith was hired, Oscar Hicklin contacted Dowell and told him that, due to some throat trouble he was having, he was resigning from his song-leading responsibilities. Smith said Dowell immediately came to him in the nursery and told him, "'You'll be leading singing from here on.'" Then about a year later, the layman in charge of High Street's choir, Ray Hunt, likewise turned his duties over to Smith. Looking back, Smith was glad for the gradual way he had taken on these responsibilities. "[I]t was a blessing in disguise," Smith confessed. "I wasn't ready for all of it."[17]

Smith always adopted a self-deprecating tone when he spoke about his work in music. "Thought I'd butcher meat," he used to joke; "instead I butchered music."[18] Yet the jest belies Smith's considerable ability. Dowell's newspaper ads for High Street's services routinely promoted a forty-five minute musical program. And Smith coordinated it all. Smith built a large choir (more than a hundred and fifty voices by 1950), and he also encouraged the formation of many small groups. Nola sang in several of those ensembles, including a mixed quartet that also included Smith, and an all-female quartet that was accompanied on the piano by Nola's teenage daughter, Janet.

Singing in such groups became some of Nola's most treasured memories in the church. "Between my 30th and 40th years, *I had the time of my life*," she once wrote. "The children were not dependent on me for about everything, my health was better, I was doing the thing I loved so much—giving out the message of God in song, singing in the choir, in duets, singing trios, quartets, both girls quartet and mixed quartet."[19] Janet, too, recalled her mother's delight in participating in such activities. "Many times they would meet at our house to practice and practice and practice," Janet said. Even when the pianist's fingers grew exhausted from playing, "They all never wanted to stop," Janet noted.[20]

Under Smith's leadership, quartets became a particular specialty at High Street. Such groups worked well as crowd pleasers, Smith learned. At one point, High Street was home to two different men's quartets, and Smith made the most of them. "If I really wanted to tear the house down," he noted, "I'd put them both together." High Street's audiences could not get enough of such music. "They'd fall in the aisle," Smith said.[21]

Of course, Smith's signature group was a men's quartet originally known as the Gospel Four, later renamed the Beacon Quartet. This group not only ministered in the church but also produced albums and, for thirteen years, its own radio program. On one occasion, Nola herself stepped in to sing with them. Smith gave few details about this last-minute substitution. He simply said, "My first tenor got drunk, and I had to let him go."[22]

Such a reaction was instinctive for Smith. This musician had no interest in presenting mere performances. For him, the music had to be authentic, emanating first and foremost from the heart. Smith's commitment to that philosophy resulted in a music program whose greatest successes occurred more off the platform than on. As Smith once told his music students, "I don't care how good your music is, if it doesn't touch people in the heart, you've failed." And Smith became a master at reaching the hearts of congregants. Though he did not recommend the practice to other church music leaders, Smith never followed a set schedule in his services. "All I wanted was the first [song]," he confided. "I picked me one to start with." The remainder of the service unfolded as the music director saw fit. This meant that instrumental accompanists had to remain alert and that scheduled vocalists were called to platform "when the time was right." For Smith, the practice left the door open for a kind of Spirit-led immediacy. "Somehow or other it worked," he said.[23]

In a 1993 interview Smith contrasted himself to music ministers who viewed congregational singing as "a necessary evil." "To me, I enjoyed it," he said. "It was the highlight of my music program." In Smith's mind, music possessed an emotional potency that communicated directly to the heart. "It'll put a baby to sleep and it'll calm a wild animal," he said. "That's why it's important. The big thing in the music program is to get the crowd ready to preach to." And Smith took that responsibility seriously. "I had a preacher ask me one time out in the foyer of the old church," Smith said,

"'What's the secret to this church?'" To that, the song leader replied, "Good preaching and visitation." Then Smith added, "But not very many successful churches get that way without a good, lively music program."[24]

While Smith's focus on the heart must surely have been one key to his success, sheer exertion seems to have been another. During one of High Street's tent revivals, after some particularly boisterous congregational singing, Smith whispered to Dowell, "'Bill, I wish I could get them to sing like that in church.'" To that Dowell replied, "Well, if you work at it as hard as you did tonight, you might."[25] When Smith led singing, he thought of the congregation standing in front of him as a great choir. He then worked to evoke from them the kind of singing that he loved best, the kind that flows from the heart. Yet this required total commitment from the song leader, Smith believed. He once marveled at a music director he saw holding a hymnal in one hand while trying to lead the congregation with the other. To Smith, such half-heartedness was incomprehensible. "Man, I led with my toenails," Smith barked.[26]

Throughout Smith's career, his exuberance made him a beloved figure at High Street as well as a favorite at many revivals and fellowship meetings. "The biggest thrill of it all," Smith said, came in 1984, when Jerry Falwell, famed televangelist and founder of the Moral Majority and Liberty University, invited Smith to Washington, DC, to lead the congregational singing at an event called Baptist Fundamentalism '84. "We had twelve thousand the first night," Smith recalled, "fifteen the second night, twenty the last night. And I'll never get over hearing that twenty thousand sing 'Wonderful Grace of Jesus.'" Smith credited Dowell—the pastor who had first enlisted him into the ministry—for making such experiences possible. Without him, Smith claimed, "nobody'd ever known who I was."[27]

Smith's feeling of indebtedness toward Dowell probably colored his view of his partner in ministry. Even so, their close working relationship makes Smith's perceptions difficult to ignore. In one statement Smith praised Dowell, saying, "He had more common sense—I'll call it horse sense—than anybody I've ever seen." Then at another point Smith said, "The best preacher and most consistent preacher I've ever heard is Brother Dowell. I've never heard him miss. He didn't always hit a home run, but he never did strike out." Most of all, Smith was impressed by Dowell's "relationship with the Lord." Listeners heeded Dowell's preaching, Smith said, because "there was something about him that you knew he was sincere, knew he was honest. He told it like it was. If it was sin, it was sin. He called it by name."[28]

According to Smith, Dowell's authenticity was also evident in the way he treated those around him. Smith recalled attending national fellowship meetings and seeing Dowell's reaction when Smith received accolades for his singing. In Smith's opinion, many of Dowell's peers in the ministry would not have tolerated being upstaged by an associate. Yet Dowell showed no such thirst for glory. Just the opposite, Smith said. "If they'd show me a little attention," Smith claimed, "you'd think his buttons would pop off his coat."[29]

Smith also remembered Dowell as "the ultimate of patience," though Smith sometimes wondered whether this was a strength or a weakness. "In fact, he almost lets people take advantage of him," Smith said. "There was a time or two when he probably should have kicked one or two guys' rear ends and didn't. But he always told me, 'If I'm gonna make a mistake, I'd rather make it that way than the other way.'" Such qualities set Dowell apart in the eyes of Smith. "I'll just say it flat out," Smith blurted. "He's the best man I ever knew. That takes nothing away from anybody else. He's just head and shoulders above anybody else I ever knew. If he told you something, you could take it to the bank. I've known him now fifty years, and I never saw him do anything that I questioned."[30]

Earl Smith and Bill Dowell enjoyed a remarkable mutual regard, and it is clear that this helped to sustain their seventeen-year ministry partnership at High Street. In all that time, Smith said, the two never experienced a conflict: "He never scolded me. As a matter of fact, we never had an argument." What they did experience was a deep and lasting trust, something that facilitated Dowell's ministry in ways both small and great. On the platform of High Street, if the fired-up preacher removed his suit coat, Smith was there to catch it before it hit the floor. "I knew what he was going to do," Smith said. "I could read him like a book."[31]

Smith also made it possible for Dowell to carry on the evangelistic work that was so important to him. In addition to Dowell's frequent engagements at Temple Baptist in Detroit, Dowell had regular speaking invitations from Dallas Billington, Lee Roberson, Bob Jones, Jack Hyles, and others. He conducted several revivals and youth camps each year, and he was a featured speaker at many of the Sword of the Lord soul-winning conferences orchestrated by John R. Rice. For Dowell, these engagements were as much a part of his calling as pastoring. The ministry he was ordained to, Dowell always insisted, was that of the pastor-evangelist. "Even when giving instructions to the preacher," Dowell explained to one audience, "God said put this down: 'Do the work of an evangelist!'"[32]

Smith's able assistance meant that Dowell was able to pour himself into these evangelistic endeavors without worrying about losing ground at the church. "Sometimes Brother Dowell would be gone for two or three weeks in a row," Smith noted. When that happened, it fell to the associate to carry on the ministry at home. According to Smith, Dowell looked to him as someone who could "carry on when the quarterback was gone." And Smith never dropped the ball. "You want a full night's work," Smith said with a laugh, "you teach the teachers at 6:30, speak at prayer meeting at 7:30, and rehearse the choir at 8:30. That's tougher than plowing." Then he added, "But it was fun."[33]

Smith was once asked about the private side of his relationship to Dowell, and he was candid to admit that the social interaction between the two men was limited. "We didn't have time," he explained. "I probably wasn't at his home more than once a year, twice a year, and vice versa." Over the years these men did manage to share several fishing and golfing experiences. And then on Saturday afternoons, they regularly went to the YMCA to play basketball. Their physical aggressiveness on the court took some opponents by surprise, Smith said. No one expected a pair of ministers to play competitively. "One fellow said we were the roughest players they ever played against," Smith recalled.[34]

Smith also remembered something else about those visits to the YMCA. Two of the men that he and Dowell played against eventually came to faith in Christ. And this may reveal as much as anything about the true nature of Smith and Dowell's friendship. They never stopped ministering. Neither of these men knew how to take off his ministry hat. Even during times of recreation, business and pleasure seemed to intermingle. Smith, who had a great love for the game of baseball, remembered attending just one professional baseball game with his longtime ministry partner. They attended a game up in St. Louis, Smith said. But even that was part of a ministry trip. "I was getting him up there to catch transportation to Detroit," Smith said.[35]

Smith and Dowell enjoyed a lifelong friendship, and while their ministry at High Street went through periods of difficulty, their friendship never did. In fact, Smith testified that "when the valleys would get a little deeper," the pair of them would sometimes contemplate leaving High Street and going into evangelistic work together. "And I think we could have made it," he said. Then he qualified the statement, saying, "But that was just times when we had our dauber down."[36]

In actuality, both of these men found their ministry at High Street highly rewarding. Smith affirmed that he would have done it all again, "heartaches and all."[37] And Dowell shared this sentiment. After all, nothing else could have been so rewarding to these men as pointing others to Christ. That common purpose is what has linked the careers of Dowell and Smith not only to High Street but also to one another. These choice servants formed a team that was specially appointed to share in a great work. And as time would tell, their efforts would yield remarkable rewards at the High Street Fundamental Baptist Church.

Chapter 16: *Not by Might, nor by Power*

Madam, may we help you?

The woman could hardly believe her ears. His voice sounded strikingly familiar, like the one she had heard so many times before on the radio. But it had never sounded so close before. Or so gentle. There was not even a hint of fire and brimstone.

Madam?

She was too frightened—too mortified—to look up.

It couldn't be him.

With this thought, she tried to rein in her heavy sighs, but instead they grew more severe. Now she had to bury her face more deeply in her trembling hands, and as she did, her shoulders began to quake with her weeping. She felt as if every person standing in that large congregation was staring directly at her.

What am I doing? Why am I making such a fool out of—

A hand on her shoulder interrupted this thought, reminding her that someone in front of her was waiting for a response.

But he doesn't know about me. He can't.

The woman was only half right. It was true that the preacher did not know her name. He had never yet even had a good look at her face. He knew nothing about her background or about what had prompted her tears. He later speculated that something someone had read or taught in one of his Sunday school classes that morning had somehow pricked her heart, but it was impossible to say for sure. All the preacher knew was that, as he had looked out over his congregation on that Sunday morning, a woman standing in the crowd had a need. Her sobs made this abundantly clear. So, without knowing any of the details, the preacher responded.

Now, in the midst of that vast crowd, this man was offering his aid. The woman was so distraught that she found it difficult to formulate a response, but at last she managed to put together the words:

I want to be saved![1]

This was the spring of 1946. That same year Harry Truman and Winston Churchill would make a joint appearance at Westminster College over in Fulton, Missouri. Dowell made the one-hundred-and-fifty-mile drive to hear Churchill's speech. The March 5 event drew forty thousand people, but Dowell did not much mind the crowd. He wanted "to see that great big old bulldog and hear him speak," he said. Churchill introduced the world to the phrase "iron curtain" that day. Dowell's summary of the momentous occasion was simply, "I enjoyed it."[2]

More important to Dowell was what was happening in Springfield. In that postwar era there was an unmistakable spirit of revival abiding on the High Street Fundamental Baptist Church. Earl Smith had recently joined Dowell's staff, but as of yet Oscar Hicklin was still the congregational song leader. In fact, Hicklin was leading the opening song for the eleven o'clock worship service when Pastor Dowell spotted that weeping woman standing to his left. While the people all around him sang, Dowell walked off of the platform and made his way over to her. It was an instinctive move, nothing premeditated or calculated, which explains why the woman's statement to him—"I want to be saved"—caught him a bit off guard. There were yet songs to be sung, announcements to be made, and a sermon to be preached. The "invitation" would come after those things. As any Baptist preacher knows, the invitation is the culmination of the day's labors. But as of yet, those labors had barely begun. In fact, Preacher Dowell had not so much as approached the pulpit.

In reply to the woman's plea to be saved, the befuddled pastor asked awkwardly:
When?

He later chuckled as he reflected on his question. "I don't know why I said that," he confessed, "but I did."[3]

Perhaps it was because the situation was so unusual and unexpected, one might daresay supernatural. Whatever the case, the nameless woman's emphatic reply shook the preacher loose from his momentary hesitation. She answered:
I can't wait. I've just got to be saved. I want to be saved now!

And that was all it took. Dowell recognized a moving of the Holy Spirit when he saw it. He often reminded his listeners "behold, *now* is the accepted time; behold, *now* is the day of salvation."[4] Dowell viewed procrastination as one of Satan's most effective weapons. And on this day, he determined to have none of it. He said:
Come on. Let's go to the altar.

As the congregation sang, Dowell ushered the weeping woman to the front of the church and tapped another woman to go and pray with her and to show her from the scriptures how to be saved. He assumed, as the pair left the auditorium, that the rest of his morning would continue as normal. But then, when he reached the platform again, he realized the Holy Spirit was still at work:

> I got back in the pulpit and I looked, and all heaven fell down on that service that morning. People were weeping. I felt so strongly about it, I turned to the song leader and said, "Sing an invitation song." And so he started singing the invitation song. And people began to break loose from that auditorium and began

to stream down the aisles to the altar. One or two of them fell on the way down under conviction. They had to pick them up and help them to the altar. I've never seen a service where there was such deep conviction as there was in that service. They kept streaming down until nearly one o'clock.[5]

This, Dowell said, is what revival looks like.[6] When the Spirit of God had finished His business that day, the church "had a little time of rejoicing," and Dowell dismissed the service.[7] The sermon that he had prepared for that morning was never preached.

Dowell was the first to acknowledge that the blessings experienced at High Street under his leadership could not be explained in human terms. It certainly could not be attributed to his own abilities. Dowell, like the rest of his congregation, was the beneficiary of an often inexplicable outpouring of God's power. Dowell spoke to a group of preachers at a 1957 Sword of the Lord Conference and admitted that there were even times in his ministry when he had seen a lesser sermon bring about greater results. "I knew that what I had said in that sermon didn't sound as good as what I had said in the other sermon," he confessed, "but when I gave the invitation men and women began to flock down to the altar with broken hearts." Then quoting Zechariah 4:6, Dowell told his listeners why he thought this had occurred: "Not by might, nor by power, but by my spirit, saith the Lord."[8]

By the mid-1940s, High Street was seeing the Holy Spirit do a mighty work, and even the pastor himself, it seemed at times, could do nothing more than to stand idly by and watch. Of course, in truth, Dowell never stood idly by. Indeed, he chided preachers who did. In that same 1957 sermon he said:

A lot of preachers never take time to plan anything. They don't even plan a revival. I have been invited to hold revival meetings in certain churches, and I would get there and say to the pastor, "What do you have in mind? What advertising have you done?"

"Well, we have been announcing it for two or three Sundays from the pulpit."

"Put an ad in the paper?"

"No."

"Put out any handbills?"

"No."

"Have it announced on the radio and television?"

"No. We have just been announcing it and we thought everybody would find out about it."

"What calls do you have for us to make?"

"We are just about caught up on our calls. We have made most of them."

I found out he didn't have a thing planned for revival. He hadn't taken time. He had been too busy doing something else.

Listen! Speaking from a human standpoint, two things are essential if you are going to be in the work of God. One is, plan your work; the other is, work your plans. You've got to do both.[9]

In this regard, Dowell clearly practiced what he preached. Visiting evangelist Roy A. Kemp recalled working alongside Dowell in 1948. "The truth is," said Kemp, "that there is no such thing as a great, aggressive, soul winning missionary church without, first of all, an aggressive, spirit-filled and world-visioned pastor. Such is Bill Dowell." Kemp illustrated by saying, "Before I went the pastor wrote me for my mats in order that he might give it the widest publicity. When I arrived on Monday night my eyes beheld the greatest Monday night crowd that I have seen in the United States of America—and I have been to 99 places in two years. And the attendance kept up through the fifteen nights." Kemp credited Dowell for this success. "Humanly speaking," said Kemp, "he is the one dynamo that makes the church go."[10]

When Dowell looked back on the beginning of his ministry at High Street, he admitted, "I had a tremendous ambition to build a church."[11] Indeed, even though the war slowed his church's numerical growth in those early days, Dowell still set his sights on specific attendance goals. High Street averaged 421 in Sunday school during his first full year there,[12] but Dowell determined to build that number to one thousand. Dowell's city-wide tent revivals, beginning in 1943, were one of the many strategies employed in this effort. And by 1944—despite the hindrances of war—Dowell was making significant progress toward his attendance objective. In February of that year, he wrote:

Our Sunday School has grown to such proportions that we are hardly able to seat the great crowds of Bible loving men, women, boys and girls that are attending. Application is being made for a priority; to begin immediately on a Sunday school building, to take care of our overflow crowds. What a testimony during this hour of defeatism, when so many are complaining about having to preach to empty wood yards. What is the answer? The world is hungry for the pure, unadulterated word of God; preached and taught in power and demonstration of the Holy Spirit. To Jesus Christ be all the glory and honor, both now and for ever more. Best of all, souls are being saved in every service. Last Sunday, throughout the day, there were 15 glorious conversions and many additions to the church. There were 688 in Sunday School and the attendance is growing rapidly.[13]

In this same article Dowell attempted to explain the reasons for his church's rapid growth. "What is the secret of the overflow crowds and of the great success of the High Street Church?" he asked. "This question is upon the lips of thousands throughout the Ozark Empire today." Then in answer to his question, Dowell listed some of the qualities that made his church unique:

First, the church was founded upon the word of God, with Jesus Christ as its only head; the Holy Spirit as its only administrator; and the winning of souls, and baptizing them, and teaching them as their only mission. The second reason is the large number of consecrated capable, Bible teachers and workers throughout the church and Sunday School. The third reason is the lack of formality in the church. People do not feel cramped. There is a spirit of freedom and liberty in our services that is remarkable indeed. No cut and dried program, no social affairs, no pie suppers, no banquets, or such, but like the Apostle Paul we preach Jesus; no big I's, or little you's, but we are all equal in the Lord. The fourth reason is that we really believe in men and women being saved. We have an old-fashioned altar where sinners are invited to come and fall upon their face, and repent of their sins and put their faith and trust in Jesus Christ. We do not ask them to shake hands with the preacher and join the church. We invite them to accept Jesus Christ, and be born again by His spirit.[14]

This fourth reason seems to have had a particular bearing on the success of Dowell's ministry at High Street. Frequent revivals and an ongoing emphasis on evangelism made the salvation of souls paramount in the mind of every member. Even Dowell's children were affected. All three of them were saved and baptized under Dowell's ministry at High Street during the 1940s. The youngest child, Clyde, recalled having to tug at his father's pant leg up on the church platform because, at the age of six, he went unnoticed as he made his approach during Dowell's invitation. Yet even at that early age, Clyde knew he needed a savior. "Having heard my dad preach about salvation every Sunday morning, even as a young kid, I was very aware that everyone had to be saved to go to heaven" Clyde said.[15] Father and son prayed together that morning at a bench near the front of the auditorium, and when they stood up again, Clyde's need had been met.

Clyde's older brother, Billy, had similarly accepted Christ just two years earlier. After a service in the annual tent revival, Bill, Jr., and the rest of the family visited a nearby A&W restaurant, where they enjoyed "root beer served in frosty glass mugs." The seven-year-old happily downed his drink, but then as he traveled home again, the boy's thoughts returned to the preaching he had heard earlier in the evening. It was not until the family was sitting around their living room conversing before bed that young Billy finally blurted, "Dad, how does a person know they have been saved, after they are saved?"[16] The boy's father took his cue at once, and after providing some answers to Billy's questions, Dowell and his wife knelt beside their middle child in the living room as he, too, prayed to accept Christ.

The oldest child, Janet, came to Christ at the close of High Street's Mother's Day service in 1942. During the invitation, Nola spotted her tearful daughter coming down the aisle, so she left her place in the choir loft to go and pray with her. Then, after the morning service had ended, Janet raced to share the news of her salvation with her daddy. In fact, as it turned out, he was just one of many people that Janet wanted to tell. "Young as she was," Dowell told one audience, "she stood up in the street all afternoon, and everyone that stopped, she said, 'I was saved this morning. I took Jesus as my Savior this morning.'"[17] It struck Dowell that his daughter had inherited a bit of his own evangelistic zeal. And no parent could have been prouder.

Dowell's fervor for evangelism was having a similar effect on High Street's entire membership. When Evangelist Kemp visited High Street, he noted some unusual characteristics within this congregation:

> I have never seen so many adult men per ratio of membership in my whole ministry as I saw at the High Street Baptist Church. When the pastor has to be away for a few days there are so many consecrated and humbly willing, until it is never a matter of "who" will lead, but a question of "which" will step in and fill the breach. They remind me of a big family of flesh brothers—these men—except that they get along even better!

Kemp further noted a spirit of evangelism that permeated High Street's entire congregation. "The fact that they never lost sight of the importance of soul-winning impressed me," Kemp wrote. "This was not only true as they attended and prayed for soul winning power upon the regular series on Revelation, but it was equally true at the Young People's Meeting and the Women's Meeting—I spoke to both—and every public prayer was bathed with compassion for the salvation and baptism of converts."[18] Dowell's leadership had galvanized this church in a shared vision aimed at reaching lost souls in their community.

Of course, Dowell's successes at High Street must also be attributed to the faithfulness of his members. Charley Dyer had trained High Street's congregation well, and when Dowell came to the church in 1941, he already had a church that was highly committed to evangelism. A woman named Ethel Martin, for instance, was then head of the Women's Prayer Meeting. This group had been organized by charter member Bessie Oliver back in 1936, and it was still going when Dowell left High Street in 1963. From its earliest days, the Women's Prayer Meeting had as its purpose not only praying for lost souls but also going out and finding them. A memory book published in 1967 describes the group's origins:

> There was no church visitation at the time, [but] a church congregation was needed, therefore the first [women's] meetings were very brief, no singing. The women had prayer then went out, as the Bible instructs, by twos, inviting people to come hear the old-time Gospel, emphasizing the fact, only the Bible was taught in Sunday School. Many came and found Christ is so real. Not only were souls saved at church; but many were led to the Lord in their homes, at jail, and in the county home.[19]

Visiting evangelist David A. Cavin described his 1948 encounter with the Women's Prayer Meeting, calling it "one of the high-spiritual experiences of my life."[20] And Dowell, too, saw its considerable value.

During the 1940s, Dowell made an effort to harness these evangelistic efforts. For him, it was not enough to reach lost souls; people also needed to be discipled. Dowell insisted that a vibrant Sunday school was the key to stimulating real Christian growth—growth that would give long-term meaning to High Street's outreach efforts. And in this regard, Dowell's leadership at High Street seems to have differed from his predecessor's. Charley Dyer's Sunday school attendance had been considerably lower than the attendance in his preaching services. Dowell set about to invert those statistics, and he did so by emphasizing Sunday school attendance above all else.

Dowell's efforts soon paid off. By the end of the war, Sunday school attendance at High Street was approaching the one-thousand mark. Indeed, this growth necessitated a new two-story Sunday school space, a building that was dedicated in 1945. This building was promptly filled to capacity, so Dowell announced plans for another addition to the Sunday school plant. He also set fifteen hundred as the church's new Sunday school attendance goal. Dowell published an article in May 1946 entitled "How the High Street Fundamental Baptist Church Will Build a Sunday School of Fifteen Hundred." In it he proclaimed, "The High Street Fundamental Baptist Church has a vision as never before. We will not stop until we have built a Sunday School of fifteen hundred in Springfield. Then we will take a new grip and head for the two-thousand mark."[21]

Dowell's published strategies for reaching his attendance target included further organizing the Sunday school and initiating a new Monday night visitation program inspired by Acts 5:42: "And daily in the temple, and in every house, they ceased not to teach and preach Jesus Christ." To Dowell, following scripture's model was the only way to build a church. He candidly admitted that he was not well educated in any particular method of church administration. "I just had to take what I'd picked up through the years," he confessed.[22] Yet Dowell had confidence in the Lord's plan. "With hundreds of personal workers going out through the city of Springfield," he boldly declared, ". . . we will build a Sunday School of fifteen hundred."[23] In this, Dowell seems to have intuited a key principle of church growth: people reach people. Years later Dowell elaborated on his strategy, saying, "It had to do with multiplying by dividing. The best way to multiply is to divide—divide our classes and start new classes. The more people you have teaching, the more people you'll have come to Sunday school. It's just common reasoning."[24]

Dowell now maximized his church's outreach by making Sunday school growth the primary focus of all efforts. It was the focus not only of personal contacts but also of the church's print and broadcast media. As early as 1942, High Street was producing its own monthly newspaper, a publication loosely modeled after *The Fundamentalist*. Originally named *The Guide to Light*, later *The Soul Winner*, these four-page circulars gave a wider audience to Dowell's "red-hot evangelistic sermons and practical Bible teaching and helpful suggestions."[25] The contents of the newspaper were largely sermons and doctrinal articles (composed with the aid of Dowell's Dictaphone), but the publication also included poems and pithy quotations taken from a variety of outside sources. And of course, each issue contained frequent references to the exciting happenings at the High Street Fundamental Baptist Church. For Dowell, this was but one more means of reaching people outside the church walls. Indeed, statements printed in the paper openly encouraged subscribers to share their copies of the publication with friends and neighbors in the hopes of reaching new people and bringing them into the Sunday school.

Dowell also reached a large audience with the advertisements he placed in the Saturday editions of Springfield's morning and evening newspapers. These ads, often four inches high by three columns wide, almost always featured a photograph of Dowell along with promotional language aimed at enticing readers to visit his church.

- No Formality – Deep Spirituality[26]
- The plainest preaching you ever heard.[27]
- Springfield's Soul Winning Center[28]

These ads were also used to announce upcoming sermon topics, especially sensational ones, and at times they were tools for publicizing Dowell's latest Sunday school attendance and goals. For example, an ad that appeared November 30, 1946, announced, "859 present last Sunday – Help us make it 1,000 by Christmas." Then all through December, new attendance numbers were posted in Dowell's weekly ads as the church crept toward the one thousand mark: 869 on December 1, 926 on December 8, 1027 on December 15, and 1078 on December 22. Did Dowell's ads make the difference? It is impossible to be certain. Yet the impressive growth suggests that the preacher's advertising dollars were well spent.

Even more impactful than Dowell's print media outreach, however, was his presence on the radio. Having experienced the fruit of radio broadcasts in California, Dowell was quick to secure timeslots on the airways as soon as he moved to the Midwest. Throughout the 1940s, Dowell's voice was broadcast over stations KWTO and KGBX, and later KTTS. He could be heard each weekday for thirty minutes, and on Sunday mornings his services were carried live from High Street's auditorium. And the impact of this regional exposure is hard to overstate. People throughout the region, even those who were unaffiliated with Dowell's church, grew to respect his ministry. One such individual was the young announcer who introduced Dowell's radio program on KTTS, Bob Barker, future host of the television game show *The Price is Right*. Barker was then a college student attending Drury College in Springfield, and he worked his way through school as a radio announcer. He would not soon forget the radio preacher that he encountered back in the 1940s. Recalling Dowell in 2006, Barker wrote, "He was a colorful, charismatic and dedicated man of God."[29]

One of the more enduring fruits of Dowell's radio ministry was a congregation that formed in Springdale, Arkansas. Though this town was located more than a hundred and thirty miles away from Springfield, a group of Christians living there contacted Dowell after listening to his broadcasts on the radio. The group told Dowell that they had no pastor of their own but that they regularly met around a radio to listen to him preach. After Dowell made their acquaintance, he began commuting to Springdale to hold meetings with them on Tuesday nights. In fact, converts from this ministry periodically traveled up to Springfield to be baptized at High Street's facility. Then, with Dowell's help, this congregation was organized as the Temple Baptist Church in 1950, calling Duane Pringle to be its first pastor.[30]

Dowell's efforts to build his Sunday school were yielding impressive results, both near and far, yet these efforts did not always endear his church to others. Ethel Martin recalled visiting house to house with other High Street women and having many doors slammed in her face. One resident went so far as to tell her "she would rather go to Hell than to High Street."[31]

Dowell, too, faced such animosity. Some of his harshest critics, he said, were other preachers. Dowell suspected he had brought some of that rancor upon himself. Soon after he arrived in Springfield, Dowell refused an invitation to join the local ministerial alliance. "You don't want me," he flatly told the group. He went on to explain to them that he saw little possibility of working together in harmony. Their views on the scriptures were simply too different. "There is no place for compromise when it comes to the Word of God," Dowell maintained.[32]

Dowell suspected that this narrow stance had engendered ill will from some of his fellow pastors. He recalled one Southern Baptist preacher who made it his personal mission to discredit him. In particular, the man wanted to prove that Dowell was exaggerating claims about the size of his audiences at High Street. Describing those efforts, Dowell said:

> He had heard me announce over the radio about the crowds we were having coming out to High Street, and he got with a group of preachers and said, "I'm going to take off Sunday, and I'm going in, and I'm going to attend the service. And I'm going to bring you back an honest report. And we'll find out that preacher's lying." But he got off a little bit late and got to church just a little bit late. It wasn't even a special service—regular Sunday night service. He got there just a little bit late, and he couldn't get in. They had to put him a chair out in the vestibule—they opened the doors where he could see in—because the building was just packed and jammed to standing room.[33]

Dowell's large audiences were no lie, and for that, he made no apology. He delighted in such crowds inasmuch as they helped him spread the gospel message. To that end, Dowell found that even his antagonists sometimes served as allies. In his 1944 article about High Street's rapid growth, Dowell credited "the great number of jealous Baptist preachers in Springfield who advertise us constantly, by telling the people 'that we are not Baptist, and that we are not missionary, and that our 'order' is different; therefore they should stay away from us.'"[34] Dowell noted some of the steps that had been taken by those other pastors to thwart High Street's growth. "The preachers all got together when they saw what was taking place, and voted among themselves not to grant letters to the High Street Fundamental Baptist Church," he explained.[35]

Church letters are commonly used to transfer membership from one body of believers to another, so the decision to withhold such letters was, in effect, a blockade aimed at stopping the flow of members coming into High Street. Yet Dowell found a way around the measure. He announced to his congregation that there was no scriptural dictum requiring that they obtain *any* letters for the transfer of church membership. Thus, High Street could accept members from hostile churches by simply asking the candidates to give a statement of their faith and of their scriptural baptism. And so they did. Thereafter many individuals "joined by statement," and in Dowell's estimation, the only effect the blockade had produced was to usher more people through High Street's doors. Indeed, at the close of his 1944 article, Dowell gleefully reported, "Last Sunday night there were about 400 people from other Baptist churches in our services, and what a joy to have them. They felt at home and said, 'We are coming back again.'"[36]

Dowell's efforts to grow his church were yielding indisputable results, and by the end of the 1940s, High Street's Sunday school attendance would be approaching two thousand. True to his word, Dowell had planned his work and worked his plans. Now, as he always did, Dowell followed up his successes with new plans aimed at furthering that growth. This time, however, his plans had unusual urgency. The ever-increasing crowds at High Street meant that Dowell's congregation could no longer fit under one roof. The church had simply outgrown its old auditorium. So Dowell and his church went to work on their next expansion project, one that would quickly become, not merely a goal, but a necessity.

PART 3: HIGH NOON

Chapter 17: *Expansion*

A haze covered the February sky as a couple hundred church members stood in long dark coats. They were huddled together on the vacant plot of land next to the High Street Fundamental Baptist Church. Adults standing at the back of the crowd had to crane their necks for a better view. Meanwhile, the children standing at the front were paying little attention at all. Instead they were fidgeting with the white cord that hung in front of them. This cord, stretched between wooden posts, served to outline a central courtyard and to keep the frozen onlookers from coming too close.

Ye also, as lively stones, are built up a spiritual house,—

With an open Bible in hand, Earl Smith read these solemn words from 1 Peter 2 into a microphone. He was standing atop a flatbed trailer that was parked alongside the cordoned off plot of land. Smith's quartet had sung from this platform just moments earlier, accompanied by the plunk-plunkery of an upright piano that was positioned at one end of it. Now the yard was quiet as the crowd hushed to listen to the scripture reading.

—an holy priesthood, to offer up spiritual sacrifices, acceptable to God by Jesus Christ.

A patch of loosened dirt was visible in one corner of the courtyard just in front of the trailer. There, several men in suits formed a semicircle: Braden McCroskey, a charter member of the church; Archie Yates, chairman of the deacon board; and Everett Dameron, chairman of the building committee. Also on hand was a pastor friend, Bill McTeer, of the Southside Fundamental Baptist Church across town.

Wherefore also it is contained in the scripture, Behold, I lay in Sion a chief corner stone, elect, precious: and he that believeth on him shall not be confounded.

As Smith read the words, Pastor Dowell took a spade in hand and prepared to turn over the first shovelful of loosened soil. This was February 23, 1949, the day that High Street broke ground for her new auditorium. Though the existing auditorium was barely twelve years old, the church's rapid growth had made a larger meeting space a dire necessity. As early as 1944 Dowell had written in his monthly newspaper, "One of the greatest problems facing the High Street Church at present is making room for the great crowds that are coming. Many are turned away from our Sunday night services, because of insufficient room. Plans are already under way to erect a huge auditorium, with a seating capacity of 2,500, as quickly as materials are released."[1]

Before Dowell could begin serious plans for this project, he had to wait for the wartime rationing of building materials to end. This finally occurred in 1946, so soon thereafter Dowell went to work, commissioning architectural plans and selling bonds to raise money. Dowell's friend Roy Kemp saw the plans for the building in 1948 and described the planned structure as "a mammoth thing and something after the fashion of the Moody Church auditorium in Chicago."[2] Dowell's new auditorium would be one hundred feet wide by one hundred and twenty-six feet long, and it would have a seating capacity that was only slightly less than Dowell's original projection back in 1944. The main floor and balcony would hold about two thousand people, and the choir loft would seat an additional one hundred and eight-two. Architects also left some room for expansion. The balcony could later be reconfigured into a horseshoe shape, if desired, further increasing the auditorium's seating capacity.[3]

As Dowell lifted the first spade of dirt for this project in 1949, he could well imagine that every inch of his new building might one day be needed. Less than a year before the groundbreaking, High Street's Sunday school attendance on Easter topped eighteen hundred. "We had them stacked in every corner," Dowell told a newspaper reporter.[4] High Street's original auditorium could pack in no more than fifteen hundred, so Dowell had to move overflow crowds to an empty space downstairs, where congregants could listen to the music and sermon via loudspeaker. The solution was imperfect, but Dowell thought it better than turning people away.

Dowell eagerly awaited the day when seating such large crowds would no longer be a problem. Indeed, his new facility would alleviate overcrowding not only in the preaching services but also in the Sunday school program. Dowell had added two stories of classroom space since coming to High Street in 1941, but already more space was needed. For that reason, the new auditorium was being erected alongside the existing structure. Dowell planned to preserve the old auditorium and to convert it into Sunday school space.

Unto you therefore which believe he is precious: but unto them which be disobedient, the stone which the builders disallowed, the same is made the head of the corner.[5]

After Smith concluded the scripture reading, Dowell ceremoniously overturned his spade of dirt. And with that, construction of the new auditorium was set in motion. Funds for the $160,000 structure were now waiting in the bank; all that remained was the construction itself.[6] And no one was more eager for it to be completed than the pastor. Just a few weeks after the groundbreaking, the church set yet another attendance record on Easter Sunday: 2,207 in Sunday school. Then, a few weeks later, High Street's city-wide tent revival saw record attendances as well. For Dowell, construction crews could not move fast enough.

High Street conducted a second outdoor ceremony on May 15, 1949, this one to set the cornerstone for the new building. A stonemason in the congregation, Sam Cramer, placed the specially designed stone. Its inscription read

High St. Fundamental Baptist Church
"Jesus Christ Himself Being the Chief Corner Stone"

The church collected several symbolic objects for the ceremony: "a Bible, a history of the church, articles of faith and a small tract written by the church founder, the Rev. Charles W. Dyer of Phoenix, Ariz." These items were then deposited into "a recessed box behind the cornerstone," thus making them a permanent part of the structure.[7] A thousand church members stood outside to watch as the items were packed away and the cornerstone was set in place. Then at the conclusion of the presentation, congregants joined in prayer asking God to hasten the completion of their new building.

Those prayers were answered just eight months later as the much-anticipated auditorium opened its doors on January 8, 1950. An eager crowd scrambled into the building that day to get a good look. Whereas the main entrance to the old second-story auditorium could only be accessed by climbing a large double stairway, all of the entrances to the new structure were at street level. This made the church accessible to all, a fact that Dowell trumpeted in his weekly newspaper ads. Other celebrated features of Dowell's red brick structure included a radiant heating system and a glassed-in nursery with an "amplifier" (allowing mothers to see and hear the services as they cared for their infants). In addition, the building was equipped with a new set of chimes for the church's three-year-old Wurlitzer organ.

Visitors to Dowell's new facility were rightly impressed by such features, though, as churches go, the ornamentation and design of this building were rather unimpressive. Perhaps one of the most eye-catching features was its baptistry. Located directly behind the pulpit, the baptistry showcased a mural painted by Springfield artist Oliver Corbett. "The scene is dominated by a river with two waterfalls, creating an illusory perspective of many miles," begins a newspaper article describing Corbett's art. "Rock work has been built against the setting and actual water, giving the effect of flowing from the river, will come out of the rock into the baptistery."[8]

Apart from this baptistry, however, not much could be said for the new building's opulence. It had no stained-glass splendor, no carved-oak elegance, and no marble stateliness. If High Street's visitors were impressed by anything, it was probably the sheer size of the place. For a city like Springfield—mid-sized at best—this facility was vast.

Guests may also have marveled over the fact that Dowell managed to fill such a space. Dowell touted his new building as the largest church auditorium in the State of Missouri, yet even so, on the day that the new auditorium was dedicated, the facility was packed. Sunday school attendance that day set a new record of 2,549, and Dowell said that even his new auditorium was inadequate to house all the people who came. Describing that day in *The Fundamentalist*, Dowell wrote, "Before the 11 o'clock services began, the new spacious auditorium, balcony and vestibule were packed and jammed, and the ushers and people sitting in their cars that couldn't get in, listening on their radios, said there were a thousand people that were turned away, and this on a cold day with the streets covered with ice."[9]

Among the many civic leaders who attended that dedication service was Springfield Mayor Otis L. Barbarick. Dowell asked Barbarick to give a brief address to the audience as part of the day's activities. Dowell also invited founding pastor Charley Dyer to participate. Dyer rendered an emotional dedicatory prayer that morning. He was present not only for the dedication service but also to conduct the church's first revival meeting in its new facility. This nightly meeting ran for three weeks, and it resulted in fifty-seven conversions as well as a hundred and thirty-one new members for the church.[10] Dowell celebrated these victories in an article he wrote for *The Fundamentalist*, saying, "The pastor and all the members of the church were constrained to cry out in the words of the Psalmist David, 'The Lord has done great things for which we are glad.'"[11]

Yet even Dowell may not have fully grasped the magnitude of this moment. The completion of High Street's new auditorium in 1950 positioned this church for its greatest decade, a period that would culminate in the church's highest average attendance: 2,726 in 1960. Under Dowell's leadership, High Street would become, by far, the largest church in southwest Missouri.[12]

Dowell's success at High Street would also augment his influence among other preachers. Already in the 1940s Dowell had been rising through the ranks of the WFBMF. High Street had twice been selected to host a national fellowship meeting, once in November 1946 and then a second time in April 1950, just shortly after the new auditorium was completed. Dowell had also become a regular speaker at such meetings, something that brought him further acclaim. The energetic thirty-something made a good impression on fellowship audiences, especially on the up-and-coming young preachers in the constituency. One such preacher, Verle Ackerman, heard Dowell preach for the first time in 1946 and was struck by Dowell's obvious "concern for young people."[13] J. Curtis Goldman, another admirer, first heard Dowell speak in 1947, while Goldman was still a student at Norris's seminary in Fort Worth. Recalling his initial reaction to Dowell, Goldman said, "Man, HE is one BIG MAN!" Goldman said that physical impression morphed into something deeper as he listened to Dowell preach. "When I heard him preach the Word of God," Goldman wrote, "I knew then beyond the shadow of a doubt that he was really ONE BIG MAN in every sense of the word!"[14]

Over time, High Street's pastor came to be seen not only as the leader of a great church but also as a leader of other pastors. And this was a trait that also won him the admiration of J. Frank Norris. By this time, Dowell had become a key player in Norris's organization. In July of 1948, Norris wrote to Dowell, inviting him to accompany him on a trip to Palestine. "I have a score of fellows who have been begging to go with me on my next trip," Norris wrote, "but I am writing you first, and nothing would give me greater joy than to have you as a traveling companion."[15] Dowell was flattered by the invitation but had to decline. "I am just not financially able to do so," he said in reply.[16] The trip's fifteen- to eighteen-hundred-dollar price tag was more than Dowell could afford.

Dowell and Norris did share many other experiences, however, and each time they interacted, their mutual admiration grew. Though Norris was thirty-seven years older than Dowell, these two men shared a white-hot fervor for the ministry and a fearless hatred of sin, two characteristics that frequently planted them on the same side in moral and religious battles. In a 1947 sermon delivered at Norris's seminary, for instance,

Dowell lambasted J. M. Dawson, one of Norris's Southern Baptist archenemies. Dawson was the former pastor of the First Baptist Church in Waco, and years earlier, he had been Norris's classmate at Baylor. But by this time, Dawson was serving as executive director of the Baptist Joint Committee on Public Affairs, an organization that championed church-state separation. In 1948, for instance, Dawson's group filed an *amicus curiae* brief for a US Supreme Court case, arguing against some elective religion classes offered at public schools in Illinois.[17] Norris was outraged that Dawson, a preacher himself, would oppose such classes. Yet Dawson did so in the name of church-state separation. And much to Norris's dismay, the Court's eventual decision upheld Dawson's side of the argument.

When Dowell preached at Norris's seminary back in 1947, the animosity between Norris and Dawson already had deep roots. So it goes without saying that Norris would have delighted in Dowell's opening remarks. Dowell explained that Dawson had recently visited Springfield to give a lecture and that Dowell had attended Dawson's address out of curiosity. Then Dowell shared one of Dawson's statements. "As he began his message," Dowell said, "he informed the people that he was not a Communist." To this, Dowell added wryly, "I don't have to tell folks that I am not a Communist; they already know."[18]

No enemy was as universally hated as a communist during those early days of the Cold War, and Norris and Dowell's common views about this subject made them natural allies. As loyal patriots, they felt obliged to root out communist ideas wherever they might be lurking. Norris delivered an anti-communist diatribe in 1947 called "The Communistic Character of the New Deal."[19] Dowell's best-known message of this sort was preached during the early 1960s. It was a sermon called "The Communist Infiltration of the Church."

As the title of Dowell's message suggests, it focused on the perceived threat that communism posed to the local church. Subsequently published as a nineteen-page booklet, this sermon was a reaction to a national news story about a US Air Force manual written by Homer H. Hyde. In this manual, Hyde had made the controversial claim that leaders in the National Council of Churches (NCC) had "pro-communist" affiliations. NCC constituents were outraged by the accusation, but Dowell, never a fan of the interdenominational NCC, sided with Hyde in the matter. "The evidence to substantiate these charges would fill volumes," Dowell said in his sermon.

Dowell then went on to defend his statement, citing quotations from FBI Director J. Edgar Hoover, FBI Informant Herbert A. Philbrick, Radio Commentator Fulton Lewis, Jr., and others. "In one single issue of the DAILY WORKER," Dowell said, "which is the official Communist paper in the United States, there was a report that at a New York City rally to save the Rosenbergs, who were convicted spies, over 2,000 messages asking clemency were distributed and signed by clergymen."[20] Another quotation in this sermon came from Claude C. Williams, a minister within the NCC. Williams told the First Baptist Church in Denver, Colorado, "Denominationally I am a Protestant; religiously I am a Unitarian; and politically I am a Communist."[21]

Dowell could not have had a lower opinion of such ministers. In Dowell's eyes, a man who would stand in a pulpit and sympathize with communism was a threat to all that was holy and decent. Norris felt the same way. With matching fervor, then, Dowell and Norris railed against communism, ecclesiasticism, modernism, and any other threat to the church. The denominational machine had opened the door for such heresies by dismantling biblical authority, and men like Dawson and Williams were now symptoms of a deep-rooted apostasy that was plaguing churches across America. Dowell and Norris believed it was their duty to stop it.

When fighting apostasy, neither Dowell nor Norris pulled any punches. In a letter to C. Oscar Johnson in 1947, Norris wrote, "The Northern Baptist Convention years ago went over boots, bag and baggage to modernism. And a small percent of the hierarchy of the Southern Baptist Convention, like Louie Newton, J. M. Dawson and yourself, have tried unsuccessfully to carry Southern Baptists into this modernistic camp with Northern Baptists."[22] Dowell picked a similar fight in "The Communist Infiltration of the Church." At one point in the sermon, Dowell broadened the scope of his attack, suggesting that the Southern Baptist Convention, though it was not a part of the NCC, was culpable by association. "It should be noted here," Dowell declared, "that while the American (Northern) Baptist Convention is part of the NCC, the Southern Baptist Convention is not. However, many of their leaders are doing everything in their power to lead the convention into the NCC. The Southern Convention invites to their colleges and seminaries many of the rank liberals and modernists affiliated with the NCC to speak at conferences."[23]

Shared views such as these worked like a magnet to draw Dowell and Norris together, and by the late 1940s, Norris began to treat Dowell not merely as an ally in his fights, but as a go-to guy. In fact, the same year that Dowell spoke to Norris's seminary about Dawson, Norris asked Dowell to participate in a plot against the Southern Baptist Convention (SBC). The SBC's May meeting was set to take place in St. Louis, a mere two hundred miles from Springfield, and the organization's president, Louie D. Newton, was up for re-election. Like Dawson, Newton was under fire for having communist leanings. Newton had been interviewed by *Time* magazine about a recent trip that he had made to Russia, and the article reported that Newton was "'brimming with enthusiasm'" for what he had seen in the Soviet nation. Newton was even quoted as saying that "'Baptists stand for the same thing as the Russian government," and that "we should regard Russia as our great ally."[24] Norris was appalled. And according to him, he was not the only one. Writing in *The Fundamentalist*, Norris said, "J. Edgar Hoover stated to a closed session of the American Legion that 'Dr. Louie Newton, President of the Southern Baptist Convention, had given more comfort to the Communists of America than any other man.'"[25]

Seizing this opportunity, Norris immediately made preparations to go to St. Louis to fight Newton's re-election. Norris planned to humiliate Newton and the SBC by delivering an impromptu speech from the floor of their national meeting. Norris would then follow up his attack by hosting a series of his own meetings in a nearby venue. Though he knew he would be shouted down on the floor of the SBC, Norris believed that even a brief outburst from the floor of the convention would attract enough attention to ensure a good audience for his private meetings. And at those gatherings, Norris would have freedom to launch a full-scale attack against Newton and other SBC leaders.

The single greatest threat to Norris's plan was the SBC itself. Norris had tried this same strategy at another Convention meeting a decade earlier—also coincidentally in St. Louis—but had failed miserably. In that earlier instance, Norris had widely publicized his battle plan in advance, announcing the location of his alternative venue and inviting curious SBC delegates to come and hear the evidence that he would be revealing. He had hoped that the publicity would instigate a mass exodus from Convention proceedings. However, when Norris arrived at his venue, he found that the doors of his private room had been padlocked. Purportedly, his ne'er-do-well SBC adversaries had taken notice of Norris's plan and had responded to it with countermeasures. And with no place for his revolutionary fires to burn, Norris's scheme quickly fell apart.

Now ten years later, the Texas Tornado was taking steps to safeguard his plot against any enemy interference. And a key component of his strategy was the element of surprise. For this, Norris enlisted Dowell's help. Writing to Dowell in 1947, Norris said:

> *Without doubt we are in the greatest battle that was ever waged among Baptists and we have them on the run and now is the time to press the battle to the limit.*
>
> *The Southern Baptist Convention meets in St. Louis May 7-14th. I want to rent one of the smaller auditoriums in the huge Municipal Auditorium at St. Louis for the night before the Convention meets. You can secure it, you give the check and get the contract and I'll send you the money.*
>
> *I am planning to go as a delegate myself to the Convention and get up on the platform and make a protest as high as heaven against Louie Newton's endorsement of Moscow.*
>
> *If I do this and make the announcement ahead of time we will have 20,000 Baptists come to see the fight.*[26]

Using Dowell as a front man, Norris secured a room in the same building where the SBC would be meeting. In this way, he would conceal his involvement in the matter until the very end. Norris also contacted his lawyers as an added layer of security. He had them draw up an injunction that would protect the rights of his assembly.[27] Norris even wrote to the manager of the Henry W. Kiel Auditorium with a polite reminder that any interference from his office would be a breach of contract: "Of course, yours is the responsibility," Norris told the manager, "having signed the contract with Mr. W. E. Dowell."[28] One of Norris's allies in St. Louis, Bill Fraser, also visited with that manager on Norris's behalf a few days later. Fraser then sent Norris a wire telling him the manager had given him strong assurances. Dowell's arrangement was "gilt edged and iron clad," Fraser said.[29]

Norris's careful planning of this plot seems to have paid off. The controversy he generated at that SBC meeting drew national attention. The Associated Press picked up the story, and across the country newspapers ran articles like the one that appeared on the front page of the *Chicago Daily News*:

> *A preconvention assembly of Southern Baptist pastors was thrown into brief disorder last night over an attempt of the Rev. Dr. J. Frank Norris of Fort Worth to have Dr. Louie D. Newton of Atlanta, convention president, answer 13 questions of his attitude toward Russia and Communism.*
>
> *Police, who arrived after order was restored, talked separately with the Rev. Norris and the Rev. Dr. M. E. Dodd of Shreveport, La., conference chairman, in a church hallway and left without comment.*
>
> *Rev. Newton began his report on a trip to Russia. Rev. Norris arose and laid a copy of the 13 questions on the rostrum.*
>
> *Outcries from the audience interrupted Norris when he started to read from the list.*
>
> *Newton signaled with upraised arms for the start of a hymn. The assembly of 1,000 ministers arose and sang 'How Firm a Foundation.' Norris joined in on the second verse.*
>
> *Dodd halted the singing with a wave of his hands and attempted to persuade Norris to resume his seat.*
>
> *The shouting went on for several minutes while Norris tried to be heard. Dodd and Newton likewise were unable to restore order.*[30]

Norris's thirteen questions (which Newton ultimately refused to answer) were published in the *St. Louis Globe-Democrat*, the *Star-Telegram* of Fort Worth, and other newspapers. And Norris's four-night rally in the Kiel Auditorium not only went on as planned but also was filled to capacity. Among the spectators there to see it were Bill and Nola Dowell. Nola sent her parents a postcard bearing a photograph of the Municipal Auditorium where the ruckus was taking place. On the back she wrote, "Bill and I are attending the Southern Bapt. Convention and the sideshow of Frank Norris. We are shocked about the trend of the S. B. Convention." She then added matter-of-factly, "Dr. Newton was reelected president. . . ."[31] In spite of Norris's legal posturing and rabble-rousing theatrics—or perhaps because of these—Louie Newton had won another term. Norris had won the battle but lost the war.

What was not lost in all of this was Norris's esteem for Dowell. These two preachers had built a fast friendship. And though it was evident that Norris intended to use their association to his advantage, Dowell too would be a beneficiary in this relationship. In 1949, Norris's seminary conferred on Dowell an honorary doctorate. Then in March 1950, Norris took Dowell and two other fellowship leaders, G. B. Vick and Wendell Zimmermann, on a trip to Mexico City. One of Norris's contacts in Detroit, the president of the Export Division of Chrysler, arranged for their delegation to have a new Chrysler vehicle for the trip. The travelers used this vehicle to visit various mission works supported by the fellowship. Then on the last night of their visit, they were taken by the US Ambassador in Mexico, Walter Thurston, to meet the President of Mexico, Miguel Alemán Valdés.[32]

Dowell had become part of J. Frank Norris's inner circle, and Norris's high regard served not only to usher Dowell into the presence of foreign dignitaries but also to bolster Dowell's reputation within the WFBMF. Indeed, Dowell was selected to become the president of that organization in 1948. Life with the Texas Tornado—at least for the moment—was quite good. But could this friendship be sustained? Norris's interpersonal track record made the prospects seem dubious. Tornados are, after all, one of nature's most unpredictable forces.

Chapter 18: *Into the Spotlight*

Dowell leaned back in his office chair holding the telephone receiver to his ear. A voice on the other end of the line said:

He told us we have to go through you.

Dowell's eyebrows furrowed as he tried to make sense of the statement.

Who did?

The caller replied respectfully:

Dr. Norris.

Dowell then cleared his throat.

So you spoke to Dr. Norris?

But Dowell already knew the answer. The man on the other end of the line answered:

Well, yes. This morning. Tried to, anyway. I barely had the words out of my mouth before he said I was barking up the wrong tree. "It's Bill Dowell that handles missions," he said. "Go talk to him."

As the fellowship grew in strength and numbers—and as J. Frank Norris grew older and increasingly capricious—the politics of the WFBMF became complicated. Relationships with the aging monarch were easily strained, and when that happened, no one was quite sure what Norris would do next. Dowell, of course, enjoyed a great deal of favor from Norris throughout the 1940s, but during that time he also learned about the difficulties of working under him. Norris could issue a demand with one breath and then denounce those who granted it with the next. Year by year, Norris insisted on shedding more and more of his leadership responsibilities, but even as he did, he expected to have full control over the territory he had just given away. In this regard, he was a modern day King Lear, abdicating his throne while still speaking the words, "Only we shall retain / The name and all th'addition to a king."[1]

Norris's kingdom in the 1940s included the First Baptist Church, the Temple Baptist Church, and a fellowship of about three hundred other pastors.[2] It also included Norris's Bible institute, now known as the Bible Baptist Seminary, which Bartlett described as the "most valuable Fellowship possession."[3] Founded in 1939, this seminary had been led by its beloved first president, Louis Entzminger, until 1944.

During those early years, the school grew from a class of sixteen students to a student body numbering well over a hundred.

The seminary's rapid growth delighted fellowship leaders, yet it also presented challenges. President Entzminger, "Entz" as he was known, felt the weight of these challenges more than anyone. It was he who bore the burden of addressing the housing and instructional needs of the growing student body. Entzminger had been an ally of Norris since 1913, but by 1944, he had reached seventy years of age, and the burdens of raising and managing funds were becoming too much for him. He told Norris that, though he was willing to serve in a lesser capacity, it was time for him to step down from the seminary's presidency.

After Entzminger's resignation, Norris made a surprising announcement. Norris said that he himself would assume the presidency. He also said that his son George would be taking his place as pastor of First Baptist Church. Many were shocked by this news, including George. Norris's son was already serving as associate at the church, yet he had been told nothing about Norris's plan before it went public. And upon hearing it, George had immediate concerns. After all, no one knew better than he did that his father found it difficult to surrender the control of anything. Norris's proposal smacked of too-good-to-be-true, especially since nothing in his history with George had suggested that this father could be anything other than autocratic. Norris's biographer, Barry Hankins invoked a 1940 letter from Norris to George to illustrate the general tone of this relationship: "'Find enclosed letter that I want you to take time Sunday morning at 11 o'clock and read to the whole congregation. It doesn't matter what the program is, you hustle everybody in there at 11 o'clock and I don't mean 11:10.'"[4]

History shows that George was right to question whether his father would release the reins of the First Baptist Church. From all accounts, the attempted transition did not go well. "Norris was unable to allow George a free hand in leading the church even after he had named George head pastor," Hankins writes. And this resulted "in a bitter dispute."[5] In fact, George ultimately broke ties with his father, leaving the church and taking a large group of Norris's church members with him. Norris's son then started a new church in another part of Fort Worth.

The break with George did not merely produce a personal loss for Norris and his church; it also created a labor shortage. Without additional help, Norris was going to be left shouldering an extraordinarily heavy load—the church and the seminary—at a relatively advanced age. Norris remained undaunted. He was confident that, if George would not assist him, somebody else would. This was Norris's typical outlook. He could turn any circumstance into a triumph. Vick once said of him, "I have never heard him, even in our private conversations, utter one word of pessimism."[6]

Norris was ever prepared with a fresh idea, and if one plan did not work out, he instantly moved on to the next. During Norris's later life, a steady stream of associates and figureheads came to work for him, and when things did not work out, Norris quickly moved on to someone else. From 1950 to 1952, Norris tapped four different men to serve as either pastor or co-pastor of First Baptist Church, and three of the four men left their new appointments after just a few months. The fourth man, Homer G. Ritchie, was still fresh on the job when Norris died in 1952.

With few (if any) exceptions, then, Norris's associates found that he could be difficult to work with. The domineering tone that Norris took with his son George was the same tone that he used with nearly everyone who worked under him. And like George, many found the treatment unbearable. Yet Norris had no desire to change. When one proposed successor—Tom Malone of Pontiac, Michigan—was approached about replacing Norris at the First Baptist Church, Malone's conditions for accepting the appointment included this demand: "I would have to have full authority as pastor with absolutely no interference from Dr. Norris or any one else."[7] Reportedly, Norris reviewed his conditions and then rescinded the original invitation, choosing instead to move on to the next name on his list.[8]

But Norris always seemed to have a next name on his lists. This was certainly the case when George and Entzminger resigned back in 1944. Their departures set the wheels of Norris's mind in motion, resulting in a fresh batch of offers and invitations. At least one of these went to Dowell. In May of that year, Norris wrote to Dowell with a proposal that left Dowell dumbfounded:

> *The thing I want to write you about, and I am trusting to your good sense not to whisper to any human being for it would cause unnecessary discussion that I am not ready for.*
>
> *I have been praying and longing for a true yokefellow in the pulpit at Detroit. It's a whale of an enterprise we have there and will require my present relation there for many years, but I have more and more to realize that we need a true pastor, a man with preaching ability that can fill the pulpit with me.*
>
> *I am dreaming of two months here and then two months there. There is plenty to do the months I'm there. For example, we have two tremendous classes, bigger than the average congregation.*
>
> *I don't expect you to say "yes," but I certainly don't want you to say "no." Just wanted you to know what is ruminating in my mind. You can speak to me freely but don't speak to anybody else. The Church there put the whole matter in my hands when I went there years ago. It is certainly an opportunity for a young man with capacity to grow and you have that capacity. We never accomplish that tremendous result without feeling our way step by step. I repeat, do not discuss this with any human being for it would defeat any purpose I have in mind.*
>
> *Yours most cordially,*
> *J. Frank Norris*[9]

It seems likely, in retrospect, that Norris's proposal to Dowell had less to do with Dowell than it did with G. B. Vick. As time would prove, Norris and Vick were headed for a serious rift over the control of Temple Baptist Church, and Norris may have already become concerned about Vick's entrenchment among his northern congregation. More importantly, perhaps, Norris wanted and needed a man like Vick to run his seminary in Fort Worth. Norris's overtures to Dowell were likely an attempt to pull Vick away from Temple and into the seminary presidency. And the ploy might have worked if Dowell had been a man of greater personal ambition and lesser loyalty to his friends. But Dowell rejected Norris's proposal:

> *Dear Dr. Norris:*
>
> *Your letter greatly humbled me. You will never know this side of eternity what a blessing you have been to my life.*
>
> *Your great and fearless ministry has been and is a challenge to every young preacher who has a real passion to be used of God.*
>
> *I appreciate the fact that you would even think of me, as a co-worker at Temple. However there are two reasons why I do not feel that such a move would be wise.*
>
> *First, I have a great and growing church here in Springfield. Our Sunday School has doubled the last five months. Since the first of the year we have had 160 additions, over 100 have been saved and baptised. (sic)*
>
> *Besides all of this, Dr. Norris, I am well aware of the fact that I am not capable of holding such a place of responsibility.*
>
> *I do not question the power of God, and I certainly want to be used in as large a capacity as possible. And by His Grace I shall follow as he leads.*
>
> *But I sincerely question my ability to fill such a large position at present.*
>
> *Again may I say I appreciate your confidence, and covet your earnest prayers that I may be used of God, in God's way and at God's place.*
>
> *Sincerely yours,*
> *W. E. Dowell*[10]

Of course, Dowell's lack of interest only prompted Norris to pursue other options. And this he did for the next several years, hounding Vick and Dowell (and probably others) with regular proposals aimed at lightening his personal load and reconfiguring the leadership in his kingdom. In a 1947 letter, Norris wrote to Dowell, ". . . I was not joking with you about taking the presidency of the Seminary. I want to talk to you in all seriousness about it—being joint-pastor here with me and ultimately take over the entire pastorate. Think this over and I will talk to you when I see you."[11] Vick received similar proposals during this same period. To one of these he responded, saying, "To save my life, I cannot see why you or anyone else can seriously consider me for such a position. I am not a school man. I do not know anything about running a school, and never dreamed of any such remote possibility."[12]

Even as Norris was engaging in these maneuverings, however, a separate political chess game was underway, this one involving the fellowship's mission office. Because of the strong stand Norris had taken against the Northern and Southern Conventions, Norris remained sensitive to the charge that his dominance of the WFBMF made his organization every bit as ecclesiastical as those other entities. As early as 1944, Norris wrote to Dowell and said, "You and I have discussed frequently making other centers besides Detroit and Fort Worth. We are indeed growing a great happy Fellowship, and we need to conserve all of our forces and demonstrate that we can be a mighty Fellowship without 'ecclesiastical headquarters' or any ecclesiastical iron bands."[13] Norris wrote again in 1947, "I don't want anything else centered in and around the First Church here. I want to avoid the error of too much centralization."[14] In the same vein, Norris made statements in *The Fundamentalist* expressing an intention to establish new seminaries in cities such as Jacksonville, Springfield, and Detroit.[15] Then, in 1948, Norris wrote to Dowell, saying, "There is only one way to maintain, promote and increase New Testament fellowship–don't let it be run by one man, or any group of men, not even the Directors, myself included."[16] That same year Norris asked Dowell to give him a less prominent place on the speaking roster at a fellowship meeting, saying, "I have been criticized before because I spoke too much and I am going to remove that criticism."[17]

Another tactic that Norris used to defang the charge of ecclesiasticism was relocating the fellowship's mission office away from Fort Worth. The WFBMF operated mission works in China and Mexico, and pastors within the fellowship sent their churches' monthly support for these works through a central clearinghouse. Originally, mission money went directly to the First Baptist Church, but by 1936, Norris decided it would be wise to have the fellowship's funds managed at a designated office off site. Robert White, a San Antonio pastor and the newly appointed president of the fellowship, was asked to oversee this clearinghouse out of his church in San Antonio.

Yet Norris had an apparent change of heart about this move a couple of years after it was made. In 1938, he and White had a falling out, and Norris accused White of "misappropriating Fellowship funds by purchasing a hat out of the Fellowship till."[18] Norris used this small-scale scandal to justify shutting down the San Antonio mission office. Yet instead of bringing the office back to First Baptist or sending it to another church, Norris now opened an independent facility in Chicago's Midland Hotel building. Mission funds "ought not be in the church office," Norris decided.[19]

Norris gave charge of this new office to a personal appointee, a trusted widow from his inner circle, and he believed the new setup would help eradicate any lingering suspicions of impropriety. Unfortunately, Norris remained in control of the entire operation, and in time, Norris and the woman had a "falling out." According to Vick, she vacated her post "in a huff."[20]

Norris was now left scrambling for a replacement. And this was when Vick contacted him with a recommendation. Vick said he knew a couple in Chicago— Reginald and Dorothy Woodworth—whom he considered ideal candidates for running the mission office. The Woodworths had been members of the Temple Baptist Church in Detroit but had moved to Chicago so that Reg might attend the Moody Bible Institute. The Woodworths were both capable managers, and Dorothy even had experience as an executive secretary at General Motors in Detroit. Such business savvy would be a boon for the clearinghouse operation, Vick reasoned.

At Vick's recommendation, then, Norris invited the Woodworths to step in. They oversaw operations at the mission office for the next couple of years. But in 1947, Norris once again began pushing for a shakeup in the leadership of the WFBMF. Still insisting that he must lighten his load, Norris advocated changes at both the seminary and the mission office. He reached out to his allies to help him in these efforts. This time, however, Norris's proposals gained greater traction, largely because of the declining health of both Norris and his wife. In a letter to Dowell, Norris wrote:

> I have jeopardized my health but if I follow my doctor's advice to use common sense, I will be good for many, many years but I must unload every responsibility that others can carry. I have a long hard road yet to go in the strenuous work of our growing Seminary and there are many problems.
>
> During the last few years my wife has had three serious major surgical operations. While she is able to go, yet I feel that I must give her more time in the future than I have in the past.[21]

Norris wrote another time, saying, "I am coming back stronger physically than ever before. I have had a hard fight to bring my blood pressure down, and I am going to get out from under a lot of things."[22]

Dowell and others began to see that the weight of the fellowship was taking its toll on their leader, and for his sake, they knew that Norris's leadership proposals must be given more serious consideration. But that was not all. The teetering financial health of the Bible Baptist Seminary was a second factor that shifted the political winds of the WFBMF. Norris wrote to Vick in 1948, saying, "I have often thought the devil owed me a debt and paid me off with the fellows I turn the finances of the Seminary over to."[23] Not everyone believed Norris's underlings were the source of the trouble. Many in the fellowship felt that Norris himself was to blame for the school's financial woes. Under his administration, funds for the seminary were allowed to intermingle with the general funds of the First Baptist Church. Consequently, some donors doubted whether their contributions were actually reaching the intended purpose.[24]

Much concern, for instance, dogged the fundraising efforts for a proposed dormitory, a building that would be dedicated to the memory of a beloved missionary to China, Mother (Josephine) Sweet. Pastor Scotty Alexander recalled the frustration that he and others experienced over this project's lack of progress. "Year after year we'd gather around that hole in the ground and pray and go home and raise more money and send it to the First Baptist Church," Alexander said. "The next year we'd come back and gather around the same hole in the ground and pray some more. After a while it got ridiculous, and the pastors just got tired of pouring their money down a rat hole." For Alexander, suspicions that his contributions for this project had been either mismanaged or misappropriated were later confirmed when a report came from Norris's secretary, Florence Mattison, saying "that enough money had come in to pay for that dormitory three times."[25]

The skepticism resulting from such reports brought about a decline in the financial support for the Bible Baptist Seminary, and this, according to author Mike Randall, sparked an institutional indebtedness that rose to over a quarter million dollars.[26] Vick, who had served as the president of the fellowship during that time, recalled the seminary's financial predicament, saying, "They owed everybody and his brother."[27] And Vick and others recognized that something had to be done. Though Vick was still quite leery of the idea—"I didn't want it," he told one interviewer[28]—Vick began to give serious consideration to becoming the seminary's next president.

Among the reservations that Vick had about taking this post was the thought that doing so might damage his relationship with Norris. Vick had even related those concerns to Norris. According to Randall, Vick warned Norris that, if he were to accept the seminary's presidency, "he would make changes that Norris would probably oppose, and that he could see the real possibility of conflict because the chain-of-command would be upset."[29] In reply to this, Norris assured him, saying, ". . . responsibility must carry with it liberty of action. . . . [Y]ou have place of first responsibility and with it, absolute freedom."[30]

Vick said these assurances were coupled with other communications from pastors urging him to take the seminary post. They "twisted my arm," Vick alleged.[31] John Rawlings, pastor of the Central Baptist Church in Tyler, Texas, admitted to being one such arm-twister. Rawlings, a trustee of the seminary at the time, warned Vick, "If you don't take it over, the seminary is going to go defunct."[32]

Bowing to pressure, then, Vick worked out an agreement with Norris, and its terms led to a shakeup in Norris's organization in 1947 and 1948. Vick was named co-pastor of Temple Baptist Church as well as the president of the Bible Baptist Seminary. Vick stepped down as president of the fellowship in order to assume these other positions. As Norris had done for so many years, Vick would now commute between Detroit and Fort Worth to carry on his dual responsibilities. To ensure things would run smoothly at the seminary, he was permitted to appoint a business manager to assist him. Vick selected his old friend from the Chicago mission office, Reg Woodworth. The Woodworths would relocate to Fort Worth, and Reg would answer directly to Vick. This, too, was a stipulation in Vick's agreement with Norris.

Of course, these changes within the WFBMF organization prompted other appointments as well. The fellowship now needed a new president, and the mission office needed a new director. For both vacancies, Norris and Vick looked to Dowell. Vick considered Dowell "a natural" for the presidency,[33] and Norris, by this time, had relented on the idea of keeping the fellowship's mission money out of the control of a pastor. Norris had even been somewhat critical of the work the Woodworths had done in Chicago. "I have known and felt very keenly for a long time," Norris wrote to Dowell in 1947, "that we were losing because there was not a responsible supervision and superintendency at Chicago."[34] For that reason, Norris proposed shutting down the Chicago facility and moving the entire operation to Springfield.

As was usually the case, Norris's recommendations were quickly ratified by the rest of the fellowship. By 1948, Vick had become president of the seminary, Dowell had become president of the fellowship, and the mission office had been relocated to Springfield under the charge of Dowell and his mission secretary, Zellota Sage. Norris could not have been happier. "The coming of Beauchamp as president is the greatest joy of my whole life," Norris wrote to Dowell, "and the next is the coming of Reg Woodworth as business manager."[35] In another letter, Norris said, "All the fellows are very happy over Beauchamp's taking the presidency of the Seminary, and it certainly relieves me. While I will do no less, yet I am glad to have the unbroken management and administration of the Seminary to go on."[36] Norris was equally pleased with Dowell's new role: "It has been amazing and wonderful the response that I have had from every section and from everybody on the good news of moving the mission office from Chicago to Springfield. And the happiest thing is it is going to be under your supervision."[37]

Of course, such happiness would be short-lived. Unbeknownst to Dowell, in accepting these new positions, he, Vick, and the others had taken parts in a modern Shakespearean tragedy, with Norris standing in the role of Lear. They were living the actor's nightmare, performing in a play for which they had never rehearsed. Yet, ready or not, these players and their mad king were now in the spotlight. And soon they would carry this drama to its dark, but inevitable, conclusion.

Chapter 19: *The Water Was Boiling*

Dowell drummed his fingers on his desk as he spoke back into the phone. He was still addressing the missionary on the other end of the line:

Well, it makes no sense to me that Dr. Norris doesn't want to make a few calls to help our new missionaries.

The voice on the other end said:

Apparently, he expects you to do it.

Dowell huffed:

Well, of course I should be doing it. And I have been. I've called. I've written letters. I'm doing everything in my power—which includes sending you to Dr. Norris. It seems to me, if Dr. Norris wants this thing to move along any faster, the least he can do is pick up the phone and give Washington a call. They're not much interested in what I have to say, that's for sure.

Despite Norris's ongoing songs of praise for Dowell and others in the late 1940s, many of his co-laborers found him to be an unreliable ally. At times he proved uncooperative. At other times he was downright backstabbing. Consequently, leaders of the WFBMF learned to work around him as best they could, even if Norris did not make this an easy task.

Vick understood these politics as well as anyone. Vick's long association with Norris had resulted in both a high tolerance for Norris's antics and a thick skin to handle his attacks, two things that came in handy once he became president of the seminary. Vick had been asked to bring financial stability to the seminary, and this process became a somewhat painful one. "One of the first official acts of Dr. Vick as president of the seminary," Dowell explained, "was a complete separation of the finances of the school from the First Baptist Church. . . . [B]eing a man of unquestionable integrity, he wanted the records to show where every dime had gone."[1]

Initially, Vick's financial reforms were "tolerated" by Norris, Dowell said, though Norris never was comfortable yielding control.[2] In Vick's first meeting with the seminary's trustee board, Vick insisted on reading a long list of the school's outstanding bills. The move was aimed at making the institution's financial situation fully transparent, but Norris saw it as an affront. After all, the accrued indebtedness had piled up on Norris's watch. Not surprisingly, then, Norris was miffed by Vick's decision to publicly itemize seminary debts. He openly criticized Vick for making such a waste of time, and when Vick overruled Norris's objections, Norris stormed out of the room.[3]

This became the new tone for Norris and Vick's working relationship. According to Bartlett, another impasse occurred between them when Vick disallowed a one thousand dollar reimbursement check requested by Norris. Though Norris said the expenses were incurred as part of "his travels for the school," Norris had provided no documentation for any of the expenditures.[4] And for Vick, such a sloppy approach to finances was unconscionable. Norris's request was denied.

Actions such as these may have made Norris regret his decision to tap Vick as the seminary's president. Bartlett writes that Vick's leadership "no doubt, infuriated 'The Texas Tornado.'"[5] And in Dowell's mind, the only thing that prevented Norris from throwing Vick out of his new position was the fact that Vick was making real progress. "I believe from the very beginning [Norris] planned to get rid of Vick in time," Dowell said. "However, he was patient until most of the seminary debts had been paid."[6]

Vick's success in managing the school's finances was undeniable, even for Norris. Randall summarized the accomplishments, saying, "The long unfinished dormitory was completed; enrollment increased; debt was substantially reduced. By 1950, the debt was down to $135,000, a reduction of $115,000."[7] So Vick was doing precisely what Norris had asked him to do, even if he was sidestepping Norris in the process. And on a professional level, things at the seminary appeared to be on the right track. On a personal level, however, tensions between Norris and Vick continued to mount.[8]

Direct conflicts between Norris and Dowell during this period pale in comparison to the conflicts between Norris and Vick, though they did occur. And like Vick, Dowell had to develop a thick skin for his dealings with Norris. Dowell's new role as fellowship president and mission office director frequently made him an arbiter in Norris's political squabbles, especially those involving Vick. Dowell routinely accompanied Vick to Fort Worth whenever Vick was anticipating a contentious meeting with Norris. Dowell was also involved whenever squabbles arose between Norris and the fellowship's missionaries. Norris expected to dictate his underlings' every move, and missionaries were no exception. Indeed, Norris felt such oversight was his duty. In a letter written soon after Dowell took charge of the mission office, Norris said, "Inasmuch as I was largely responsible for the launching of this mission work, naturally I feel very keenly the responsibility concerning every phase of it."[9]

Out of deference, Dowell usually tried to accommodate Norris's intrusions into his work. Yet Dowell grew alarmed whenever those intrusions seemed to stymie good progress. Norris had particularly strong opinions, Dowell learned, about the work of Fred Donnelson in China. Norris was especially critical of Donnelson for not being more forthcoming about his ministry's finances. At the beginning of 1948, Norris lashed out at Donnelson in *The Fundamentalist* for failing to provide the fellowship with a 1947 audit. In making this attack, Norris left a general impression that Donnelson's activities were not on the up and up. Suddenly Dowell found himself not only mediating a dispute between Norris and Donnelson, but also answering letters from puzzled pastors who were wondering what was really happening to their churches' contributions.

Dowell thought this firestorm would abate when, on April 7, 1948, Dowell supplied Norris with the requested audit from Fred Donnelson. Yet even then, Norris complained that Donnelson's report was incomplete.[10] Dowell quickly realized that Donnelson was out of favor with Norris and that no amount of reporting was going to change that. According to Vick, Norris's problems with Donnelson were less about a financial report and more about control. When the Donnelsons made their triumphant return from that Japanese prison camp, "Norris tried to dictate to Fred what he ought to be doing," Vick said. But Donnelson resisted. ". . . Fred wasn't anybody's . . . weathervane," Vick added.[11]

Norris continued to undermine Fred Donnelson's work at every turn, Dowell said. He used a property in Hangchow as a pawn in the dispute. Donnelson's close associate, the late Mother Sweet, had deeded this mission property to the fellowship upon her death, and Donnelson made efforts to put his son Paul in charge of it. To most observers, Paul Donnelson's family connections and his familiarity with Chinese ministry made him a natural choice for the post. Norris, however, fought the appointment, calling Paul "dead weight."[12]

Once again Dowell was caught in the middle. Norris wrote to him, saying, "I do not believe that Paul is qualified to take charge of that important mission."[13] Then, to ensure that Paul would not be assigned the post, Norris distributed copies of his objections to all of the directors of the fellowship. But Dowell remained puzzled over Norris's assessment of Paul. A pastor who had worked with Paul in the US gave Dowell a high recommendation for him. And Dowell received other positive reports as well.[14]

So for the next several months, Dowell was left to referee a dispute that he never fully grasped. "I am sorry that keeps coming up," Dowell told Norris in one letter, "and I do not understand the reason for it."[15] Norris was obstinate, however. He remained critical not only of Fred's son but also of his son-in-law Bill Logan and, it seemed to Dowell, of the entire Donnelson clan. From Dowell's perspective, Norris was bent on putting an end to Donnelson's ministry in China and on forcing his family back to the US. Yet Dowell vehemently opposed such an idea. Responding to these efforts in a 1948 letter, Dowell said, "I feel that it would be disastrous to try to recall Paul and Bill from China as seemingly was suggested in your letter."[16]

Dowell continued to mediate for the Donnelsons for the next sixteen months, but to little avail. Norris's hostility could not be assuaged. Finally, on January 27, 1950, Norris published a notice on the front page of *The Fundamentalist* declaring that Fred Donnelson was "no longer associated with the Fellowship." In this way, Norris aimed to shut off Donnelson's financial support from fellowship pastors.

Vick and Dowell considered this action utterly self-defeating. Donnelson was the fellowship's single most productive missionary, and without him, the WFBMF might as well remove the word *Missionary* from its title. Vick, who saw Norris's notice before it went to press, tried to lobby against it. "If you [print] that," Vick told Norris, "you'll split this Fellowship." To underscore his point, Vick even threatened to cut off Temple's underwriting of *The Fundamentalist*. "The Temple Baptist Church . . . has no inclination to put $250 a week in the paper that will split our Fellowship."[17] But the words fell on deaf ears.

Now a serious rift began to emerge between Norris and Vick. According to Vick, the Donnelson issue started it all. "Fred Donnelson was the first human focal point of any disagreement between Norris and me," Vick said. Norris's dominance of the fellowship's mission activities had become a serious point of contention. "[T]he only use he had for missions," Vick said cynically, "was to use it as a prize pole to get money—to get people to send in money for the school."[18]

Dowell, too, observed a disconnect between Norris's public support for missions and his behind-the-scenes machinations. For many years, Norris and others had expressed a strong desire to branch out beyond China and Mexico and to start works in other places. Yet whenever such opportunities presented themselves, Norris offered little support. "You'd tell Norris, let's send a hundred missionaries into the field," Dowell recalled, "and he'd try to block every last one of them."[19]

One of Dowell's greatest frustrations came when the fellowship tried to bring its missionary endeavors to the field of Japan. After World War II ended, this was the field of greatest interest to American Christians. In fact, two young couples from the WFBMF— Mr. and Mrs. Ike Foster and Mr. and Mrs. Olson Hodges—had surrendered to work among the Japanese people. It became Dowell's responsibility to help these couples reach their field as quickly as possible. The post-war process for obtaining Japanese visas proved to be cumbersome, however, and the difficulties were compounded by the fact that the WFBMF was trying to send two couples at once. Mission organizations typically sent only one representative into a new field. It was up to that first representative to establish a positive presence, and only then would additional missionaries be accepted.[20]

The WFBMF needed to get around that procedural roadblock, however. Dowell had two missionary families on his hands, not one. And it seemed to Dowell that, with a little string-pulling in Washington, D.C., the Fosters and the Hodges might obtain their visas simultaneously. To that end, Dowell advised the Fosters and the Hodges to contact Norris for help.

Yet when the prospective missionaries reached Norris's office, their inquiries were rebuffed. They were immediately referred back to Dowell, leaving Dowell nonplussed. He was certain there must have been some sort of misunderstanding, and he told the missionary couples, "Go back and see [Norris] again, and tell him that I sent you, and that I requested that—that you come to him, and both couples can go at one time."[21] The candidates followed those instructions, but Norris responded exactly as he had the first time. He would have virtually nothing to do with them.

By the end of it all, Dowell threw up his hands. He was perturbed by Norris's response, but he left the matter alone. The missionaries would have to obtain their clearances using normal channels, and Dowell and the missionaries worked to do just that. Indeed, Dowell considered it a great victory when one of the families, the Fosters, finally secured a set of visas.

Unfortunately, not everyone was rejoicing. Some observers, chiefly members of the Hodges family, were irate to learn that the Fosters' visas had been issued while Hodges's application remained in limbo. Moreover, they believed that Dowell was to blame. Dowell received "a very bitter letter," written by Olson Hodges' father, George Hodges, raking Dowell over the coals for bungling his son's case. George, a prominent pastor in Jacksonville, Florida, said that Norris himself had pinned the blame on Dowell. "If Bill Dowell hadn't been so bull-headed," Norris reportedly told him, "he could have sent them to me, and I could have gotten all four of them over."[22] This remark, of course, did a great disservice to the truth, but Dowell saw no point in confronting Norris about it. He did, however, work to set the record straight with the Hodges family. And in good time, Dowell said, the rift was repaired.

But frustrations such as these were commonplace for those who worked closely with J. Frank Norris. The fortunes of such individuals seemed to rise and fall on Norris's whims, and many times it was difficult to tell which way the wind was blowing. Vick recalled one instance when Norris expressed sharp criticism of Dowell, saying, "As long as I'm pastor and have anything to do with the Temple Baptist Church, I don't want Bill Dowell speaking one time from that pulpit." Reportedly, Dowell's crime had been some public remarks he made about one of his speaking engagements at Temple. "He bragged at the recent Fellowship meeting," Norris railed, "how many [people] he had come forward and compared it with how few I had the Sunday before that."[23] Dowell was baffled when he heard the accusation. "[T]he only time I ever mentioned that," Dowell said, "[was when Vick] asked me to—he asked me to get up and give a testimony, tell what had happened at the Temple Baptist Church the Sunday I was up there. I got up and told exactly what happened, how many converts were there." As for comparing the number of his converts to Norris's number the week before, Dowell maintained it never happened. "I didn't say a word about Norris," Dowell insisted.[24]

Fortunately for Dowell, Vick saw through Norris's charges and stood up for his friend. "I don't know who your informant or misinformant was," Vick said, "but I wish you'd let me have the name because we'll get Bill Dowell together. . . . I haven't heard anything Bill Dowell has said, but that's entirely foreign to his whole makeup." To this Vick added a bit of defiance: "You tell me who that is or else I intend to keep on having Bill Dowell [speak at Temple] just exactly like I have."[25] And according to Vick, this ended the matter.

Of course, many other squabbles would soon follow. Vick, Dowell, and others continued sparring with Norris on a seemingly endless number of issues throughout the end of the 1940s. Though many of these storms blew over quickly, there was no mistaking the fact that life under this monarch was growing increasingly difficult. Even Norris's successor at First Baptist, Homer G. Ritchie, conceded that, during this period, Norris's "spirit evinced a slow but obvious change." Ritchie observed that Norris often "pitted one leader against another and played the ends against the middle. He regularly used *The Fundamentalist*, the most powerful of all independent Baptist publications, to force into submission directors, trustees, faculty members, and Fellowship leaders who opposed him."[26] All the while Norris became increasingly unpredictable. "Norris would oscillate," wrote Ritchie, "from caustic criticism of an individual to high eulogy in succeeding issues of *The Fundamentalist*."[27]

Under such conditions, it is little surprise that the WFBMF would soon be plunged into a great crisis. Norris's "domineering attitude and stubborn spirit"[28] left subordinates with few options. They could stand by and watch tyranny destroy them and their fellowship, or they could rise up against the monarch's despotism. In the end, Norris's own actions dared them to rise. And so they did. As Vick put it, ". . . the water was boiling in the kingdom."[29]

By May of 1950, tensions between Norris and his fellow leaders could no longer be contained, and a full-scale war was ready to erupt. "What took Norris thirty years to establish," laments Ritchie, "was divided and weakened in one day."[30] Norris's tragic drama was now approaching its climax, and standing with him at center stage were Beauchamp Vick and Bill Dowell.

Chapter 20: *So What Do We Do Now?*

Dowell was tromping down a sidewalk toward a busy street corner when a thin young man stepped up behind him.

So what do we do now?

The preacher whirled around to see who was speaking. The youngster before him was barely past puberty, or so it seemed. Dowell thought the undersized lad might be wearing his father's clothes.

The young man spoke nervously:

We—we just want to know what's going to happen. Do you think Mr. Vick and Dr. Norris are going to work things out?

The youth's tie was flopping in the wind, and the end of it was directing Dowell to look over the young man's shoulder. When Dowell glanced up, he saw a band of seminary students assembled in the background. Dowell could not immediately tell how many were in the crowd, but whatever the number, the plate glass windows lining the sidewalk seemed to double it. Worry was written on every face.

This was Fort Worth—Tuesday afternoon, May 23, 1950. Dowell had never anticipated a moment like this one. The schism set ablaze that week was anything but sudden, but the inferno had taken on a life of its own. Student lives were being affected. And their lives were not the only ones.

The mob following Dowell assumed that, since Dowell was standing in the thick of it all, he had answers to their questions. Yet Dowell was just as full of questions as they were. Though he had most definitely taken a side in this uproar, it was not his battle. This battle was between Norris and Vick. And even Dowell did not know how things were going to play out.

The disagreement that erupted during that May Fellowship Meeting of 1950 was a complex one, and one with deep roots. At the heart of it was an ongoing power struggle between Norris and Vick. Although these two men had managed to work together for many years, their coexistence at the Bible Baptist Seminary proved problematic, in part because they both demanded ultimate authority. Vick, like Norris, was a take-charge individual. Even Vick's grandson, Billy Vick Bartlett, saw parallels between the two men. "Vick is a benevolent despot," Barlett wrote, "while Norris was a despot."[1]

Though Vick was the president of the Bible Baptist Seminary, Norris and his ally Louis Entzminger had brought the school into existence. Who should have the ultimate authority? Vick had come into the presidency with the clear understanding that he would be allowed to run the school without interference. But that proved to be a tall order. Vick operated out of Detroit and could be in Fort Worth only a few days each month. Meanwhile the seminary was located in Norris and Entzminger's backyard. Its classes were conducted on the property of the First Baptist Church. Whenever Vick was away, Norris and Entzminger could not help but lord over the seminary. And to many of the school's students, faculty, and staff, Norris ranked somewhere between celebrity and saint. Entzminger, as the cofounder of the institution, was similarly revered. So at the very least, demands made by either of these men left underlings at the seminary feeling caught in the middle.[2]

Vick had tried to ward against potential conflicts before he stepped into the presidency. He had insisted, for instance, that the seminary's finances be handled separately from the finances of the First Baptist Church.[3] Vick wanted to establish fresh transparency in order to restore confidence in the school's financial management. Consequently, he insisted upon regular financial reports, frequent meetings with trustees, and above all, complete accountability within the seminary's business office. And in order to achieve such things, Vick believed there had to be a separation of powers. He wrote to Norris in 1948 to negotiate his terms:

> I would want that one man to have entire charge of the finances and be responsible for the Seminary. I think the man you have there, and whom you so highly regard, Verle Ackerman, is well qualified and entirely dependable.
>
> However I would want him to be entirely responsible for the finances from the time the mail reaches Fort Worth; opening the mail, depositing the money in the bank and issuing checks.[4]

It was Norris who convinced Vick that his wishes would be followed. Continuing that same letter, Vick said, "If I know that I would be just as free to carry out my plans and follow what I consider the leadership of the Holy Spirit in every degree in the Seminary just exactly like I have been here in Temple Baptist Church—that might be the deciding factor in my decision." To this, Norris replied, "The sum of all I want to say is, you have place of first responsibility and with it, absolute freedom."[5]

Over the next two years, however, Norris found it difficult to live up to his end of the bargain. In his mind—and in the minds of many others in the fellowship—he and Entzminger remained the school's ultimate authority figures. Even Norris acknowledged this general perception. Indeed, he had tried to defuse it. One of Norris's oft-proposed solutions to the charge of fellowship ecclesiasticism had been to send seminary students elsewhere to train. At one time, Norris and Entzminger had pushed to open a school in Detroit. It was Vick, Norris said, who resisted the idea.[6] A similar discussion, focused on opening branch institutions, had occurred about the time that Vick became president. Dowell himself had been a part of those conversations.[7] Then, this topic came up again just weeks before the May 1950 fellowship meeting. This was when Norris printed an announcement in *The Fundamentalist* stating his intention to open a branch seminary in Dallas.[8] The fellowship would be better off, Norris consistently maintained, if its power structure could be decentralized.

But that spirit was not driving Norris's actions in the spring of 1950. Far from divesting himself of any power at the Bible Baptist Seminary, Norris was, by this time, making every effort to wrest control of the seminary away from Vick. According to John Rawlings, "He wanted back control of the seminary because Dr. Vick had it operating in the black. There was a great spirit of growth and development in the Fellowship at that time. The fellows had rallied to Dr. Vick's leadership because he was—he was honest in the money matters."[9]

Under Vick, the seminary had become a well-oiled machine. In addition to better financial management, Vick had introduced improvements to the curriculum. He had also put a stop to practices and policies that were interfering with student learning. "Norris used to go in and break up the classes if he wanted to speak to them," Rawlings said. "Dr. Vick had changed that." The seminary was now stronger than ever, and according to Rawlings, Norris wanted it back. So instead of celebrating Vick's accomplishments at the institution, Norris turned on Vick "like a blind rattlesnake," Rawlings said.[10]

Though Rawlings's assessment seems accurate, it may mask some of the complexity of the dispute between Norris and Vick. The trouble between them extended far beyond the seminary itself. It involved not only power and personalities but also other people—bystanders—both the innocent and the not so innocent. In all, at least four strands of history converged to help spawn this conflict. And when they did, a seismic shift occurred, which put the balance of power back in Norris's favor. And so, seizing the moment, Norris made a move to oust Vick from the seminary's presidency, prompting an all-out war.

What were these four strands of history? The first of them was the emergence of a new prince in Norris's kingdom, a Scotsman named Jock Troup. Norris had originally met Troup during a campaign to Troup's homeland in 1936.[11] For many years Troup was the on-site pastor of Tent Hall, the 2200-seat facility in Glasgow that had been built to replace D. L. Moody's revival tent. Norris's visit to this place had produced an enduring friendship between him and Troup. In fact, Troup never forgot Norris's first visit to his home, specifically how Norris had prayed asking God to save the soul of his young son and even to call him into the ministry one day. Troup was so moved by that moment that, after the boy grew up, he arranged to send his son to Norris's seminary in Fort Worth. Troup's son was still a member of the student body in May of 1950.

Troup himself was also in Fort Worth that year. Norris had brought him over from Scotland just after Christmas in 1949. Ostensibly, he came to the States to visit his son and to minister for a time in America. During his stay, several WFBMF churches engaged him to hold special meetings for them. Norris, too, made plans to make the most of his friend's visit. He invited Troup to be a special lecturer at the seminary.[12]

But there was more to this story than what first meets the eye. On January 20, Norris announced in *The Fundamentalist* that Troup would be the seminary's commencement speaker in May.[13] Then on January 27, Norris ran a front-page story announcing that the First Baptist Church had called Troup to be Norris's co-pastor in Fort Worth.[14] Suddenly Troup was Norris's new right-hand man at the First Baptist Church. And for the next three months, Norris celebrated Troup's arrival, routinely trumpeting in *The Fundamentalist* the greatness of both the man and his preaching. Troup was a new hero. And Vick was looking more and more expendable.

A second strand in this political knot relates to a personal crisis within the Vick family. Vick's married daughter, Evelyn Rae Bartlett, had recently been discovered in an adulterous relationship with Vick's Sunday school superintendent, Gordon Bonner. Vick heard incontrovertible proof of the affair when his son-in-law, Billy Bartlett, Sr., played for him some secret wire recordings of conversations between Bonner and Evelyn Rae. News of the affair reached Norris's attention in January of 1950.[15]

Soon after this scandal was uncovered, Evelyn Rae's marriage to Bartlett Sr. ended. The situation was heartbreaking for Vick and his family, yet in addition to coping with its personal toll, Vick had to deal with the implications this matter had for Temple. Bonner was on Temple's payroll, so the matter had to be addressed immediately. Vick approached the circumstance in a manner that he must have considered both righteous and merciful. He ended Bonner's employment at Temple, but then he worked on Bonner's behalf to help him find a new place of ministry. After all, Bonner had been a highly effective Christian leader, and he had also been contrite in his response to his moral failing. Even Norris, after he confronted Bonner, said that Bonner "confessed the whole affair with Evelyn Rae and said, 'I made a mistake and have asked the Lord to forgive me.'"[16] In an attempt to minimize damages, then, Vick began pulling strings to try to win Bonner a new position in a new city, someplace far away from Evelyn Rae. And with Vick's help, Bonner was named superintendent at the Central Baptist Church of Denton, Texas, a large church pastored by Loys Vess.

Vick's crisis was thus addressed, though not fully contained. Even after Bonner's exit from Temple, Vick found that his family remained vulnerable to criticisms. The shame of Evelyn Rae's actions would linger indefinitely, and then there was the question of whether or not Vick had shown good judgment in helping a known adulterer gain a position at another church. Some believed that Bonner's actions with Evelyn Rae were part of a lecherous pattern.[17] Had Vick "palmed" Bonner off on an unsuspecting congregation?[18] And what of all the secrecy surrounding these matters? Did Vick's actions constitute a cover-up? Understandably, Vick had tried to handle the situation with discretion, yet even this left him open to attacks. And once the strife between Norris and Vick came to a head, those vulnerabilities became ripe for the picking.

A third strand leading to the clash between Norris and Vick stemmed from Louis Entzminger's role at the seminary. Although Entzminger had stepped down from the seminary presidency several years earlier, he remained an integral part of the institution. And for Vick, his presence became problematic. In fact, in 1950 Norris charged that

Vick had been trying "to get rid of [Entzminger] on the Seminary faculty" for more than a year.[19] While Vick himself denied that charge, he did not deny suggesting that Entzminger's salary should be reduced. Entzminger was paid twenty-five dollars a week more than the other faculty members at the seminary, a special arrangement that had been set up by Norris before Vick ever became president. The extra pay had been instituted because the elder statesman regularly represented the seminary in churches and special meetings. But Vick grew to dislike the arrangement.

At the very least, Vick thought Entzminger's extra pay should have strings attached. When Vick became president, he agreed to let the special pay continue "provided [Entzminger's] meetings brought in that amount to the Seminary."[20] If Entzminger's travels profited the school financially by at least twenty-five dollars a week, then the school would continue to pay him the extra money. But by 1950, Vick believed that this stipulation was no longer being met. Vick wrote to Norris in April, saying:

> *The last two years, although [Entzminger] has brought in practically nothing to the Seminary, yet he regularly received the $25 week extra even though other faculty members have had to teach his classes repeatedly.*
>
> *Many times the Seminary has had to pay visiting speakers to fill in his place in his classes while Entzminger was away. Yet he received his full $125 weekly.[21]*

Vick had other concerns about Entzminger as well. Entzminger's fundraising efforts, according to Vick, were not only failing to bring money into the school, but they were actually diverting funds away from the seminary and into the coffers of the First Baptist Church. This occurred because Norris, of his own accord, initiated a fundraising effort for a new student dormitory. The project was ostensibly for the benefit of the school, but it was completely out of Vick's control. Even the finished building would be owned and operated by the First Baptist Church, not by the seminary. Yet as Entzminger went out to represent the school, he began promoting Norris's project as if it were a project of the seminary and, more to the point, as if the contributions for it were bound for the school's treasury. This was not the case.

When Vick found out what was happening, he had grave concerns. Vick had expressed approval for Norris's building project when it was first proposed, but he did not foresee how this pet project would eventually conflict with the seminary's other fundraising efforts. Vick now objected to the fact that those who were contributing to the new building were being duped into believing that their monies were going directly to the seminary. Worse still, Vick had heard that Norris was letting Entzminger keep a sizeable portion of the money that he was raising. If true, this meant that Entzminger was receiving money from both the church and the school for his fundraising efforts. And the portion that did not go to Entzminger—an unknown amount—was landing, not in the seminary's coffers, but in the coffers of the First Baptist Church under Norris's control.

To Vick, the whole thing smacked of impropriety, and he was candid in expressing those concerns. When John Rawlings, then-president of the seminary's alumni association, heard that there was friction between Vick and Entzminger, he inquired to find out what was going on. Vick responded forthrightly, saying, "John, he's taking up money and it's not reaching the school."[22] Vick also spelled out his concerns in a letter to Norris:

> I agreed upon his and your request that Entzminger would be allowed to hold outside meetings, and that he would be allowed to take up money for a proposed building project to house students, even though the Seminary would not own the proposed dormitory, nor would they collect rent on the same.
>
> I agreed to that until I found out he was raising money, leaving the impression that it was for the Seminary. Is it true that he got 50 per cent of what he raised on your building program?
>
> I objected to him raising money for that purpose while he made pastors and churches think that it was for the Seminary.
>
> I also objected to his taking money which the churches already had in their treasuries for the Seminary and Entzminger asked pastors to divert this, to the proposed building project in which he and you were interested.[23]

Vick did more than complain, however. He also proposed cutting the extra twenty-five dollars from Entzminger's salary. And this, as it turned out, set off a firestorm. Hearing of Vick's proposed salary reduction, Entzminger, on April 3, 1950, submitted to Vick a resignation letter indicating that, for him, the camel's back had been broken: "Since Reg informed me you intended to reduce my salary I could not retain my self-respect and continue with the Seminary."[24] Entzminger then gave a copy of his letter to Frank Godsoe, the unofficial chairman of the seminary's faculty.[25]

Upon seeing Entzminger's letter, Godsoe took immediate action. He brought Entzminger and the letter before an assembly of the student body. There he made an impassioned plea, charging that the seminary's beloved founder was being cast aside in the closing years of his life. And responsible for it all, Godsoe explained, was a cold and unfeeling dictator, G. B. Vick. Not surprisingly, the students were appalled. In response to what they heard, they voted to send Vick a resolution. They demanded that Entzminger's resignation letter be rejected and that Entzminger be retained at the seminary for life with his pay fixed at a level not less than the present sum.[26]

News of these theatrics now outraged Vick. He considered Godsoe's actions a deliberate manipulation of public sentiment and a distortion of the facts. He also believed that Norris and Entzminger had been complicit in the business. Vick had not fired anyone, nor had he cut anyone's salary. Entzminger's pay reduction had merely been proposed and, in Vick's mind, for good reason. Yet as far as Vick was concerned, the whole episode had little to do with Entzminger's pay. This was about gaining control. Norris and Entzminger resented Vick's interference in their fundraising efforts, and now they aimed to silence him.

Vick responded with venom. He wrote to Norris, saying:

I consider Entzminger's so-called resignation to the student body a childish, foolish blunder, as well as an unethical and deliberate stab in my back.

I cannot conceive of his going before the student body on such a matter without your knowledge and consent. Moreover, I was greatly surprised to learn that in my absence you would go before the student body and even on the radio and leave the impression that I had mistreated Entzminger.

If he doesn't straighten out the whole matter before the students immediately, most certainly he will be out, and I shall tell the student body, trustees, and whomsoever else I deem necessary exactly what I objected to in the financial set-up that Entzminger desires.[27]

Norris, of course, took all of these threats in stride. Indeed, Norris added Vick's correspondence to an arsenal of weapons that he would later draw upon as he waged this political war. In the coming days, Norris would play the role of a compatriot defending the honor of a maligned comrade.[28] And equipped with messages like these, Norris would paint Vick as a calloused usurper who regularly trampled upon everyone who was standing in his way. A statement published in *The Fundamentalist* in June 1950 typifies the rhetoric Norris employed:

Incidentally, the spirit of Beauchamp's telegram has been his attitude and spirit towards me for more than a year.
I never was talked to and so mistreated in my life.[29]

Such indignation notwithstanding, Vick refused to back down. These things were nothing but childish machinations, and Vick was not going to let Norris and his crowd get away with any of it. Vick's friend Reg Woodworth reported that two days after Entzminger submitted his resignation, Entzminger sat across from him sipping a cup of coffee and boasting, "Reg, you had just as well forget all about Detroit. You had better forget all about Beauchamp, Vick [sic]. Dr. Norris is taking over and I am going to be Dean."[30]

Thus, Entzminger's resignation was part of a larger narrative, and in Vick's eyes, Enztminger's role in this story was not so much the maligned comrade as it was the problem child. Indeed, Entzminger had resigned no less than three times during Vick's two years as president. Each resignation had been refused, though Vick sometimes wondered if the institution would have been better off letting him go. Even Norris had grown dismissive of the old man's constant complaining. As evidence, Vick cited a November 3, 1948, letter that Norris wrote to him after Entzminger's second resignation:

I have just had a talk with Entzminger and he says he has written you that he is going to resign. I think it best to accept it. He has been in such an unsettled state of mind and we can't go on that way forever.

He went over everything with me, none of which I can seem to do anything with. He has that peculiar super-sensitiveness that comes to all old preachers. I guess I may have it but I hope somebody will knock me in the head if I get a bad case of it, that I may get over it and have my funeral.[31]

Such remarks were nowhere to be seen in Norris's published statements during the spring of 1950. Norris also made no mention of the efforts that Vick had made to retain Entzminger and to smooth things over with him after these flare-ups. Instead, the articles Norris was now printing in *The Fundamentalist* consistently cast Entzminger as a victim and Vick as the villain. And as this political spin continued, Vick once again found himself in a precarious position.

One final strand of development leading up to the showdown between Norris and Vick, arguably the most significant one, concerns the legal status of the Bible Baptist Seminary. On February 27, Oliver E. Meadows, Director of the Institutional Division at the State Approval Agency in Austin, Texas, wrote to the Bible Baptist Seminary, saying:

> Gentlemen:
> This has reference to your approval issued by the state Veterans Approving Committee, Austin, Texas.
> Current standards for approval require that Theological Schools be accredited by a recognized accrediting association to qualify for approval under Public Law 346, 78th Congress.[32]

Norris referred to this letter as the seminary's "death warrant." And rightfully so, for its implications might have shut the doors of the seminary for good. With the passing of the GI Bill in 1944, veterans around the country had begun enjoying benefits that helped them pay for their educational expenses. Even seminary students received such funds, provided they were attending a "recognized" educational institution. Yet in the years immediately following the war, there had been some provisional leniency in the way institutions were granted such recognition. The bar for approval was set fairly low, and there was little oversight from the government.

By 1950, however, officials were beginning to crack down on who could and could not receive GI Bill monies. Fly-by-night institutions had sometimes preyed upon America's veterans, so new standards were being introduced to ensure that GI Bill money was truly helping those it was intended to help. These new regulations also meant new oversight. In the State of Texas, any institution receiving GI Bill money now had to meet the accrediting standards of one of the following entities: the Southern Association of Colleges, the American Association of Theological Schools, or the State Department of Education. Norris's "death warrant" letter concluded with this statement: "Your approval will remain in force until June 1, 1950, at which time approval under Public Law 346 will be withdrawn unless evidence of accreditation by one of the above listed accrediting associations is presented."[33]

Suddenly Norris had a serious problem. The Bible Baptist Seminary had nearly one hundred and fifty veterans among its student body.[34] If those men could not receive their GI Bill funding, many of them, if not all, would have to discontinue their training. Yet how could the required accreditation be achieved in just three months? And was accreditation even desirable? An outside accrediting body might try to impose standards that Norris and the rest of the fellowship would find objectionable. After all, Norris's great purpose in starting the seminary had been to provide an alternative to denominational schools. He had proudly insulated his institution against modernism by proclaiming the "English Bible" as the school's sole theological textbook. But what would happen if the state began to call the shots?

Norris also had another question. Was the denominational machine perpetrating these new accreditation requirements as a means of shutting him down? Norris speculated that it was. And his instinctive reaction to the smell of any kind of enemy plot was, of course, to fight. So Norris prepared for battle. State officials were welcome to scrutinize any aspect of his seminary they wanted to scrutinize, but if they thought to modify his training or to close his doors, he would fight them to the death. And he would pull out every weapon in his arsenal to do so, especially his connections in Washington, D.C.[35]

For the time being, however, Norris was content to pursue peaceful, or at least civil, negotiations. This he did when he gathered a party of supporters—including Entzminger, John Rawlings, and a professional educator from Rawlings's church—and made a trip to the city of Austin. Together they would testify about the seminary before the Department of Education.

According to Rawlings, Norris's belligerence and constant name-dropping during this meeting nearly torpedoed the whole effort. But in the end, officials chose to overlook Norris's impertinence, and they agreed to send a representative to do an on-site study of the Bible Baptist Seminary.[36]

Now Entzminger took the lead. His long history with the seminary made him the individual most qualified to represent it, so Entzminger was charged with gathering documents, preparing reports, and coordinating the itinerary for the on-site examination. Entzminger's job was to demonstrate that the seminary was a serious institution and not a diploma mill. And he succeeded. A representative of the State, L. A. Woods, soon visited the campus, and not long after that, Norris received a letter from the Commissioner of Education, announcing Woods' findings: the Bible Baptist Seminary was "being placed on the list of approved Schools of Special Subjects."[37]

Norris was overjoyed. "O, what gall and wormwood this is to the Baptist machine," he gloated. "They have done everything on earth, and under the earth to put us out of business. Now they have put us IN business." From Norris's point of view, the seminary had struck oil. "And we have the same rating, the same standing [as] the State University, Baylor University, S.M.U., T.C.U. and all the other U's," Norris raved. "There is no estimating the value, it's not for a year, it's official, it's permanent and the highest that can be given."[38]

Norris and Entzminger's achievement was more than just a victory for the seminary, however. It was also a personal triumph. It gave the two of them a new tactical advantage. Whether by design or by accident, Entzminger had submitted to the State, as part of his documentation, a set of bylaws that gave him and Norris absolute power over the seminary. Vick would argue that these bylaws were bogus. Norris would argue that their submission to the State of Texas had made them incontrovertible. Whatever the case, Norris now believed he had the perfect weapon with which to subjugate Vick. And he intended to use it.

Could the seminary survive such a skirmish? Nobody really knew—least of all Dowell. Like that band of puzzled students, Dowell now found himself standing on a Fort Worth street corner waiting for answers.

Chapter 21: *Philippi*

Motorists sped up and down the street as Dowell stood face to face with that young crowd on the street corner. The weight of the young people's concern began to tug at Dowell's shoulders. He responded by standing a little taller and locking his eyes on the young man directly in front of him. He then mustered (or feigned) the confidence of an army general:

You want to know what we do now? I'll tell you what we do. We keep doing what the Lord tells us to do.

Dowell wished he could have given the boy greater assurances, but there were none to give. So he left the matter as it was, hoping that his brief remark would satisfy this crowd of students. The look of disappointment that swept over their faces told him it did not. The young people's eyes seemed to say:

That's it? That's your grand plan? Don't you have a more precise course of action to offer?

Of course, Dowell did not give these students a chance to ask any of that. The traffic at the street corner had stopped, so the preacher took the opportunity to make his departure. He cut across to the other side of the road, thinking that he had broken free from the crowd. But when he stepped up in front of the corner drug on the next curb, a reflection in a store window told him he was mistaken. The student mob was following behind him.

Their voices rang out:

But what about us?

Are we supposed to go back in there?

What about next year?

Are we even going to have a school to go to?

The May Fellowship Meeting had been thrown into disarray by Norris's recent maneuverings. Of chief concern was the legitimacy of his seminary bylaws. These bylaws, variously cited as the 1945 or 1947 version, had allegedly been in effect since before Vick became president. Unfortunately, the document's contents were also a reflection of that earlier period in the school's history. Article II, Section 1, stated, "The business and property of the corporation shall be managed by a board of three directors, who are as follows: J. Frank Norris of Fort Worth, Texas; Louis Entzminger of Fort Worth, Texas; And Luther C. Peak of Dallas, Texas; who shall act as such for life, unless any should resign." Article II, Section 8, added this: "It shall be the duty of the directors to elect all members of the faculty of the Bible Baptist Seminary. . . ."[1] The seminary had long since abandoned this organizational model, yet Entzminger made no effort to fix the discrepancy before submitting his documentation to the state. And under these bylaws, Norris and Entzminger, as two-thirds of the board of directors, were fully empowered to run the seminary in any manner they saw fit.

Norris published his bylaws in the April 28 issue of *The Fundamentalist*, and Vick immediately recognized the implications. Vick also recognized, or thought he did, a clever use of smoke and mirrors. Vick had never before seen this document, and he believed that Norris had concocted his bylaws for the purpose of ousting him. Norris, in answer to that charge, said that his bylaws had been published in *The Fundamentalist* as early as 1945. However, when Vick tasked some of his staff members to search the archives for evidence, they came up emptyhanded. "[T]hey did not find any trace of these by-laws," Vick said. "As far as I have been able to ascertain, these by-laws, under whose provisions Dr. Norris sought to dominate and absolutely control the Bible Baptist Seminary, had never been published, had never been approved or voted upon by the World Fundamental Baptist Missionary Fellowship which owns the Bible Baptist Seminary, had never been voted on and approved by the trustees of the Bible Baptist Seminary."[2] The whole thing, in Vick's words, had been "cooked up" by Norris as part of a scheme to reclaim power.[3]

None of those charges really mattered to Norris, of course. He had his bylaws, and he intended to use them. In the weeks leading up to the 1950 May Fellowship Meeting, in addition to routinely lauding Entzminger as the savior of the seminary, Norris launched a campaign in *The Fundamentalist* aimed at silencing any who might question— or try to undo—his and Entzminger's newfound authority. Norris wrote in the April 28 edition, "It is no small thing to lead the church to give place to the Seminary under its roof. Beauchamp Vick has said more than once that he would not permit such to be done with the Temple Baptist Church."[4]

As pastor of the seminary's host church, Norris felt entitled to direct the school's operations. Indeed, he now mocked the outlandishness of thinking that it might be any other way. "It would be utterly out of all reason," Norris wrote, "for a body of trustees who have no responsibility for the welfare of the church, to run the Seminary according to their own notions. Property rights are involved and a million dollars' worth of property must be protected for the interest of the church as well as of the Seminary. . . . The charter and by-laws protect both."[5]

Norris also declared his bylaws to be legally binding. Since Entzminger's document was now on record with the Department of Education, Norris argued, the bylaws had become official. Norris wrote to Vick, saying, "We have not paid much attention to the charter and by-laws as a governing document, but we will be compelled to follow this charter and by-laws from now on, since [the seminary] has been recognized on the basis of the charter, the by-laws, the curriculum and scholarship of the professors."[6] Norris explained that accreditation would require ongoing oversight from the Department of Education, so any deviation from what had been reported to the State might lead to the loss of accreditation. And that, Norris reasoned, could force the closure of the school. Thus, Vick's question about the bylaws' date of origin was moot. This case was open and shut, as far as Norris was concerned, and there was nothing more that needed to be said.

A couple of weeks before the start of the 1950 fellowship meeting, Norris rounded up the seminary's trustee board for a hastily called meeting. Vick, as seminary president, was also permitted to attend, though he was given little advance notice about the meeting. Even so, Vick dropped everything to be there. He also contacted Dowell, the fellowship's president, and asked him to go along for moral support.

Norris summarized the purpose of this meeting, saying, "Since the new and permanent recognition by the State Board of Education of Texas, it was necessary for us to have a meeting by way of review and preview."[7] In other words, Norris wanted to flex his newfound authority and to set a tone for the seminary's future. He also wanted to shore up his support in advance of the coming showdown. Vick was certain to raise a fuss over Norris's maneuverings, so Norris wanted a chance to address any concerns before the fellowship meeting began. Dowell said Norris spent the entire meeting building a case for the legitimacy of his bylaws. And when the meeting was over, Norris declared an early victory. Writing in *The Fundamentalist*, he said, "The Charter and the Bylaws set forth certain very important matters that were discussed and happily agreed to by all the directors present Friday, May 4th [sic]."[8]

Norris now believed that he held complete authority over the seminary, and to prove it, he began making some changes. On the same day that the trustees left Fort Worth, Norris announced in *The Fundamentalist* his intention to expand the size of the seminary's board:

> Because of the Rapid [sic] growth of the Seminary, and in accordance with the charter and by-laws, we are adding five representative brethren to the present seven directors.
>
> The by-laws require that the trustees or directors shall be nominated by the First Baptist Church and then elected or confirmed at the annual meeting of the Fellowship.[9]

In taking this action, Norris was hedging his bets, padding the trustee board with five new allies, all of whom could be trusted to support Norris at the upcoming fellowship meeting. The move initiated some behind-the-scenes sparring between Norris and Vick. Vick was not so much concerned about the threat to his presidency. After all, he had never coveted the president's office to begin with. If Norris wanted him out, so be it. Just six weeks earlier, when the issue with Entzminger had first come to a head, Vick had confronted Norris and tried to resign on the spot. Dowell was hosting a fellowship meeting at High Street at the time, so Vick met with Norris in Dowell's office. "I'm not important enough an issue," Vick told Norris, "and I didn't want the seminary in the first place, you know that."[10] Vick claimed that he would have resigned then and there but that Norris refused to let him step down.

Once the bylaw controversy broke out, however, Vick became even more convinced that he should surrender his presidency. Yet he purposed to do so on his own terms. He would not let Norris conduct a smear campaign against his integrity, nor would he let his voice be silenced on matters concerning the needs of the seminary. Vick's objections to Norris's business practices were heartfelt, and Vick believed he owed it to the other pastors in the WFBMF to let them know how Norris operated. Then there was also the matter of the Temple Baptist Church. Vick and Norris remained co-pastors at Temple, and this squabble was sure to affect that partnership. If Norris intended to try to oust Vick from Temple the way he had ousted him from the seminary, he would be in for a real fight. And Vick made no secret of his willingness to engage in such a battle.

Of course, Norris cared little about Vick's threats. Norris rather enjoyed a good fight, and with all the cards that Norris now held in his hand, he was certain he would win. In fact, a week after expanding the size of the seminary's board, Norris ran an untitled box insert on the front page of *The Fundamentalist*. It contained a not-too-cryptic message for Vick: "Jealousy is the surest evidence of littleness," Norris wrote. "It is in bad humor. It criticizes others, and often severely. Such jealous criticism is a confession of weakness." He then added a thinly veiled threat of his own: "It is an incurable disease—only a funeral will remedy it."[11]

With the fellowship meeting now just a week away, Vick steeled himself for the promised funeral. He engaged in conversations with a number of concerned pastors and seminary students, explaining what was happening behind the scenes and telling them why he thought it was bad policy for one pastor to have full authority over a fellowship institution. At least some of these conversations had been initiated by others, not by Vick.[12] Nevertheless, Norris later lashed out at Vick in *The Fundamentalist*, calling these interactions a "campaign"[13] and a "conspiracy."[14] Dowell and others were accused of being complicit in the plot, though they consistently denied any wrongdoing. In a letter to Norris on June 13, Dowell wrote, "The fact of the business is, Dr. Norris, there was no conspiracy on our part, and I think you know that is true."[15]

Whatever the case, battle lines had been drawn before anyone ever arrived at that meeting in Fort Worth in 1950. And from Norris's perspective, Vick's allies had already been relegated to the status of persona non grata. R. O. Woodworth was one of the first to feel the sting. A week before the fellowship meeting began, Norris decided that a working relationship with Woodworth would no longer be possible. Without warning, he went to Woodworth, terminated his employment, and ordered him off the premises. Norris would later justify this action by maligning Woodworth's performance as a business manager, yet the timing of the dismissal suggests that Woodworth's chief fault was his loyalty to Vick.

Another attack—the principal one—occurred in a chapel service that same week. This was when Norris stood up before the seminary's student body and rehearsed many of the things that he had been saying in *The Fundamentalist*. In his remarks, Norris explained the significance of the bylaws, and he urged upon the students the importance of abiding by them. He also asked them to make a visible show of their support for him. If they agreed to live by the school's bylaws, they must stand to their feet. The majority stood; some did not. By most accounts, the dissenters totaled about twenty students.

The students who refused to stand comprised several individuals from the Temple Baptist Church and a handful of others. Aware of the controversy, these young people now opted to defy Norris's order and to remain in their seats. Norris showed little patience for their insubordination. Before dismissing the assembly, he ordered officials to note the names of the dissenters, and then the next day he summoned those on the list to a private meeting with him and some of his allies.

Norris reportedly began that meeting with a conciliatory tone. Some participants even said he shed tears.[16] But his message was clear: the dissenters would have to either change their votes or leave the Bible Baptist Seminary. The students in the meeting said that they had spoken to Vick and that he had advised them to hold their ground. But when they tried to do so, Norris's conciliatory tone began to change. He expelled the insurrectionists on the spot. Indeed, they were not even permitted to finish the semester. Though the summer break was just days away, all of the students from Temple received notices from Frank Godsoe, saying, "This will notify you to vacate your room in the dormitory of the Bible Baptist Seminary immediately."[17] And adding insult to injury was the fact that none of the dissenters from other churches received such notices—only the students from Temple.[18]

Norris's actions toward Vick's students angered many, including one of Norris's closest associates, Noel Smith. Smith was the heart and soul of *The Fundamentalist*. Though Norris held the official title of editor, it was Smith who did the editor's job. And Smith had strong feelings about Norris's actions against the dissenting students. By Smith's reckoning, Norris had been gunning for these students ever since the turmoil with Vick began. "Every emotional spree [Norris] has gone on," Smith charged, "he has brought to these students. The Detroit students were blamed for everything. Every Detroit student was under suspicion and everything from Detroit was bad except the senior pastor."[19]

Upon hearing that the students from Detroit had been turned out of the seminary for voting their conscience, Smith immediately found Norris and tendered his resignation. He also gave Norris a piece of his mind: "I told him that the expelling of those students under those circumstances repudiated and outraged everything I had ever been taught to believe about any constitutional principles and government, and I wouldn't stay in a place like that."[20]

Vick was likewise incensed over the expulsions. When he received word about what had happened, he told the panic-stricken students to "sit tight in the boat" until he was able to make it to Fort Worth for the fellowship meeting.[21] Then Vick fired off a telegram to Norris, saying, "Your un-Christian, illegal, bullying, brow-beating tactics toward our Detroit students will boomerang on you. Next week I shall give you detailed reasons why I will resign from Seminary, and I will meet you at Philippi."[22] This last phrase, borrowed from Shakespeare, was the warning that the ghost of Caesar had delivered to his murderer, Brutus.[23] Vick's use of the phrase was clear. If Norris wanted a war, he would have one.

Dowell happened to be in Detroit for a speaking engagement when all of this broke out. Dowell said he was with Vick when Vick learned of the expulsions. Dowell also said he watched as "an angry but calm man" penned the words of that telegram.[24] Yet once the message was written, Dowell and Vick turned their attention to their next moves. If these hostilities could not be resolved, what would become of Vick's young people? Where would they go to school? Vick felt that a branch school, one that was not controlled by Norris, might be a viable option. But opening a new institution would require a great deal of time, effort, and money, not to mention support from fellow pastors.

Neither Vick nor Dowell was sold on the idea of starting such an institution, but they were not sure whether Norris would leave them any choice in the matter. They also knew that, if Norris forced their hand, the best time to propose a new school would be during the upcoming fellowship week. So Vick decided it would be prudent to prepare for that contingency. He asked Dowell to explore options for opening a new seminary in Springfield, and he asked him to gather preliminary information that might be used in a proposal. In the last remaining days before the May meeting, then, Dowell went back to Springfield to price property, to meet with contractors, and to make inquiries at government offices. Afterward, Dowell compiled this information to bring with him to Fort Worth.[25]

As Dowell stood before those students out on that Fort Worth street corner, he suddenly wondered if all of his efforts had been for naught. It was difficult to say. What Dowell needed now was some time to think. He made yet another attempt to escape the young people's questions by hastily excusing himself. Then he ducked into the drugstore.

I'll have a Coke, please.

Stepping up to the counter, Dowell plopped himself onto a swivel stool and forced a smile at the soda jerk. The young man's narrow hat was tipped backward, revealing a tuft of black curls. These danced as the young man grabbed a glass and began pouring the drink. When the young man then slid it across the counter, he smiled at Dowell and blurted:

Here you are, sir! Enjoy!

Dowell thanked the boy and began fidgeting with the straw in his glass. Dowell had been in Fort Worth for less than two days, but already he felt drained. When he had first arrived in Fort Worth, he carried with him a measure of moral clarity. He knew—or thought he did—both the issues and the personalities in this dispute. More than that, he knew whom he could trust.

But then came the meeting. Dowell could dismiss the political chaos—the threats, the filibusters, the motions from the floor—but what of the betrayal? Like the students out on the street, Dowell had a lot of questions. He had stuck out his neck for a friend— or a man he thought was his friend—and to what end? Had Vick really sold him and the others down the river? The shock of it all made him numb. And now as he sat leaning over that countertop, he just wanted out. Indeed, that was the whole reason he had walked out of the meeting and headed down to the drugstore. He wanted to get away from it all.

But the meeting had followed him down the street. Dowell heard a voice from behind him say:

We've got some more questions for you, Brother Dowell.

Dowell smirked as he stared into the glass in front of him. Putting the straw to his lips, he mumbled:

This is the sort of thing that drives some men to drink.

Dowell, however, was not that sort of man. He just wanted a Coke.

Chapter 22: *The Pinnacle*

Dowell had hoped for some solitude when he plopped down at the drugstore counter. He wanted to sip his Coke and to ponder the week's events in peace. Instead, he found himself calming a mob of nearly sixty students.[1] There was no use trying to avoid them. So, Coke in hand, Dowell swiveled back around on his stool:

All those things you're asking me are really up to Dr. Norris.

A freckled-faced boy spoke up:

But who's going to be in charge? Is Mr. Vick going to be here?

Dowell raised his palms and said:

I have no control over any of that. We'll just have to wait and see how it all works out.

A short girl in the middle of the pack pressed him on that one:

But that's what we want to know. If it doesn't work out—if we can't come here next year, what then? Is there going to be a school for us?

Dowell wished he had the answers. Years later he told an audience, "Never will I forget that large group of students who followed me down a street in Fort Worth, Texas, at the time of the famous split, asking, 'Are you going to provide a school for us?'"[2] But Dowell had been unable to answer them. He had been forced to say, "I can't tell you anything. We'll do everything we can to help you, but right at this point I don't know where we stand, and I don't know what we're going to do." Then he added weakly, "We'll try to provide something."[3]

For Dowell, the May Fellowship Meeting was normally an uplifting experience. The week-long gathering was an annual ritual. Other fellowship meetings were held in various places throughout the year, but the May meeting was the fellowship's main event. And since part of its annual business included a commencement ceremony for the Bible Baptist Seminary, this meeting was always held in Fort Worth.

The hoopla of graduation was only one facet of this annual meeting, however. The Fellowship Week routine included preaching, ministry reports, approving new missionaries, committee meetings, and officer elections. It also included—it goes without saying—a healthy dose of fellowship. Many of the preachers, like Dowell, brought their wives and children along with them, and these families always made the most of each other's company, socializing and eating meals with their peers in the ministry.

A favorite late-night pastime among WFBMF constituents was a domino game called Forty-Two. Although fundamentalists frowned upon card games because of their longstanding associations with gambling, dominos were generally considered respectable. Consequently, the Vicks, the Dowells, and many other couples in the fellowship spent long nights competing with one another in Forty-Two tournaments.[4] One of Dowell's later partners in the game, Gaylon Randall, remembered making a special memory with him. As they played against another pair one night, Dowell and Randall grew frustrated over the fact that neither of them could draw a bidding hand. Eventually one remarked to the other that, since they could not seem to accomplish anything with their dominoes, they might just as well sing. Randall said the two of them then broke into a rendition of the gospel song "He Touched Me." It was a joke that created a lifelong bond between them, and whenever they saw each other thereafter, even while Dowell was living in a nursing home, they smiled and sang "He Touched Me" all over again.

Such was the camaraderie forged over a game of Forty-Two. Dowell and his wife loved the game so much that they also made it a regular part of Christmas gatherings with their own family. And in Dowell's eyes, fellowship meetings and family reunions were not all that different. The people of the WFBMF were, after all, a bit like extended family members.

In May of 1950, however, there was little revelry at the fellowship's family gathering. From the moment Dowell and others arrived, tensions were high. Noel Smith had seen the trouble brewing and had made a last-ditch appeal to stop it before it began. He went to Norris and urged him to hash out a "gentleman's agreement" so that Vick's presidency might end on good terms.[5] Smith said Norris seemed receptive to the idea, so on Sunday, the day before the fellowship meeting was set to begin, Smith "worked all day long" to smooth out details for a truce. Smith contacted Reg Woodworth, and the two of them in turn called Vick, seeking his support for the deal. According to Smith, all parties agreed to cooperate. If Norris would correct his wrongs, reinstate the expelled students, and retract the falsehoods he had published, Vick would exit the seminary peacefully.

Before this deal could be fully hatched, however, Norris managed to sabotage the whole affair. Smith saw early signs of the deal's demise when he came to church on Sunday night. Jock Troup, the evening speaker at the First Baptist Church, preached an entire sermon aimed at stirring up the dust, not settling it. Troup's text was a passage from the Book of Joshua. It was the story of Achan, a covetous Israelite who fell under judgment for taking something that did not belong to him. And in Smith's eyes, Troup's analogy was clear. "[I]t wasn't hard to determine who the Achans were," Smith said. Troup's criticisms became even more evident when he made reference to Entzminger in the message. Entzminger had just been taken to the hospital for a gall bladder attack,[6] and according to Troup, the blame for this illness lay at the feet of "traitors and conspirators and murderers" who had "tried to kill" both Norris and Entzminger.[7]

Hearing such words made Smith realize that the prospects for a lasting truce were not good. And he was right. The next morning Norris stunned many in the fellowship by holding an election during the fellowship meeting's opening session. Most of the pastors traveling from outside the Fort Worth area, including Vick and Dowell, were unable to attend that Monday morning session. They had to wrap up Sunday services at their respective churches before traveling to the meeting, so they were still en route. This had always been the case. No one knew better than Norris that the Monday morning crowd of the fellowship meeting was mostly seminary students and local pastors. Yet even so, Norris, without any prior warning, asked this smattering of constituents to put their stamp of approval on a new slate of seminary trustees. And after that, Norris led the board to approve a surprise nominee to take Vick's position as seminary president: the Scotsman Jock Troup.[8]

In this way, Norris managed to replace Vick before Vick had even had a chance to reach Fort Worth. The move was unprecedented. "I have been attending Fellowship Meetings regularly since 1936," Vick wrote in disgust, "and I have never known of an election of trustees, or directors, or president of the Seminary to be held before Wednesday or Thursday of the week of the annual meeting."[9] But none of that mattered to Norris. Even if the timing of this election raised some eyebrows, Norris's sway over the student body meant that his nominations were easily approved.

When other pastors in the fellowship learned about Norris's election, many of them felt that fair play had suffered a serious blow. Vick himself posed this biting question: "Was that hurried-up, 'election' an attempt to ascertain the desire and will of the brethren of the Fellowship, or was it an attempt to frustrate the will of the Fellowship and force through one more instance of one-man control, domination and dictatorship?"[10] Both Vick and Dowell thought they knew the answer. But would anyone else share their opinion?

John Rawlings certainly did. He was pastor of one of the Texas fellowship's largest churches, the Central Baptist Church in Tyler. He was also a trustee of the seminary and, by his own testimony, was a "protégé" of Entzminger's.[11] Though Rawlings also knew Vick, Rawlings said their relationship was, on the whole, less intimate than the relationship he had with Entzminger. "[W]e were acquainted," he said, "but we were not close at that time."[12]

Rawlings's closeness to Entzminger was part of the reason that Rawlings had been asked to accompany Norris and Entzminger when they went to Austin seeking accreditation. It was on that trip, Rawlings said, that he began hearing accusations about Vick. Throughout their time together, Norris and Entzminger laid out a case against Vick aimed at convincing Rawlings that Vick was "trying to take over the seminary."[13]

Rawlings later summed up that experience, calling it "a brainwashing procedure," and he said he reacted to the accusations with incredulity.[14] In Rawlings's opinion, Vick's best strategy for seizing control would have been to exert influence over the trustee board and to turn the board against Norris. But if that were so, thought Rawlings, why had Vick squandered a recent opportunity to mount a whispering campaign against Norris? Rawlings had preached for Vick in Detroit just shortly before making this trip to Austin, and during that visit, he had heard no criticisms of any kind directed at Norris or Entzminger. "Well, if [Vick] was going to try to take over, he'd have said something to me," Rawlings reasoned.[15] So Rawlings remained skeptical, and he followed up the reports that he heard from Norris and Entzminger by investigating the matters for himself. In the end, Rawlings became convinced that the charges made against Vick were trumped up.

Rawlings was so certain of his conclusions that he stood in front of his church on the night before the May Fellowship Meeting was set to begin, and he informed the crowd about the coming clash between Norris and Vick. "It could cause a break in the fellowship," he warned. Rawlings then announced which side he intended to take if it did: "If I don't learn anything else other than what I already know, I'm going to take my position with Dr. G. B. Vick because they've accused him of trying to take over the school, and I do not see one scintilla of evidence that this is true."[16] Rawlings said his congregation stood to their feet in unanimous support of his decision.

Rawlings arrived in Fort Worth the next day confident about his own views on this controversy. He was less confident about the views of the other preachers. The WFBMF had approximately three hundred participating pastors at the time,[17] and Rawlings knew that most of those did not have the inside knowledge he had about what was behind this power struggle. Some pastors, no doubt, had formed opinions based on the limited information printed in *The Fundamentalist*, while others had not yet formed an opinion at all. Still others aligned themselves based solely on the personalities involved, and Norris loyalists already viewed Vick with suspicion. After all, it was no secret that Vick had never been ordained. They had to wonder why.

Though Vick was co-pastor of one of the largest churches in America, he had never been formally recognized as a minister. Indeed, Vick would go to his grave without ever being ordained. In a 1973 interview, Vick discussed his reasons. He noted that he had carried out pastoral duties at Temple for twelve years before the title of pastor was ever conferred upon him. And after so many years of service, obtaining an ordination certificate seemed rather pointless. ". . . I didn't see any necessity for it,"[18] he said. Vick also invoked names like Moody, Spurgeon, and John the Baptist, arguing that none of them had ever been ordained. "D. L. Moody made the statement that whom God hath ordained, what can man add to?" Vick said.[19]

Then, too, Vick said that he had practical reasons for avoiding ordination. "[T]here were a lot of things I did not want to do," he confessed.[20] Weddings and baptisms were among them. Temple had many of these, and Vick did not want to have to juggle such responsibilities. He considered weddings time-consuming, and he saw performing baptisms as an unnecessary interruption to his other platform duties. Why do any of it, he reasoned, if others could be appointed to manage these tasks? So that is what he did. And it was an arrangement he liked.[21]

But Vick's decision not to be ordained prompted questions in the minds of some of his fellow ministers. Even Dowell admitted hearing frequent questions about it. "You're close to Dr. Vick," they would say to him. "You've got to know him. Why—why is it that he dismisses ordination?"[22] Dowell never approached Vick to get an answer, though he assumed that Vick's gradual ascent to the position of pastor had played a part in the decision. But others in the fellowship were quick to form their own judgments and, especially after the controversy broke out, to allege that Vick's calling into the ministry lacked legitimacy. Luther Peak, for instance, belittled Vick as "an unordained layman."[23]

As the 1950 meeting got underway, both sides in this dispute found plenty of supporters and detractors. Yet at first it was difficult to tell who was who. Rawlings said, "[Y]ou didn't know who to talk to, because you didn't know who was what side."[24] Of course, Reg Woodworth was a notable exception to that statement. Everyone knew where Woodworth stood. Rawlings once described Woodworth as "blustery," and by that he meant that one was never quite sure what Woodworth might say or do when he became upset.[25] In later years, this short fuse contributed to Woodworth's persona as an absent-minded professor. But there was nothing dotty about the warpath that Woodworth went on in 1950. When he arrived at the fellowship meeting, Woodworth found that Norris was distributing handbills about him to fellowship pastors. The fliers accused Woodworth of misappropriating over ten thousand dollars of government funds in the business office.[26] Woodworth was livid.

Norris's charges against Woodworth were, according to Vick, utterly unfounded. Though it was true that Woodworth had received a $10,500 check for GI Bill money while he was working for the seminary and that he had wrongly used that money to pay the seminary's music teachers, his actions in no way constituted a misappropriation. The teachers in question, Vick explained, were dually employed. They taught at the seminary, but they also worked at the First Baptist Church in positions such as song leader and church organist. This meant that the money for their paychecks came from two places, the church and the seminary—which is what led to Woodworth's snafu. When Woodworth forwarded the GI Bill money to the church office for the payment of these teachers, his actions made it appear that GI Bill funds were being used for church employment, not for teaching. Yet it was vital for institutions to demonstrate that benefits earmarked for education were being used to pay educational expenses only.

Fortunately Vick caught the error, and he told Woodworth that the GI Bill money belonged in "the general fund of the seminary."[27] He then tasked Woodworth with correcting the mistake. And in Vick's eyes, this ended the matter. But as Woodworth tried to straighten out his situation, things got worse. Woodworth stopped payment on the funds sent to the church, resulting in a ten-thousand-dollar overdraft at the First Baptist Church.

Now Norris, who had never been a fan of Vick's strict money management to begin with, seized an opportunity. In addition to firing Woodworth over the matter, he printed up handbills under the headline "Reg Woodworth Misappropriates $10,000."[28] Of course, Norris left the details of Woodworth's "misappropriation" to the reader's imagination, but he certainly gave the impression that Woodworth's actions had been sinister. In a follow-up article published in *The Fundamentalist*, Norris propagated the same rumor, careful to avoid any specific details. He dared readers to check out the story for themselves, saying, "I want you to investigate why Reg Woodworth was fired by the trustees." Elsewhere he wrote, "Investigate the $10,000 check that Reg gave out of Government funds that were sent to pay Brooks Morris, Walker Moore, Guy Pitner and Faye Smith. The records of the Continental National Bank are open on this transaction. And bank turned down $10,000 check [sic]."[29]

Woodworth responded to these allegations by buttonholing as many pastors at the fellowship meeting as he could. And he urged them to take action against Norris. From Woodworth's perspective, Norris's move had demonstrated that there were no limits to what he would do to win a fight. So it was time to stand up to this bully. Woodworth openly advocated selling off seminary properties and moving the whole operation to Springfield.[30] The time had come for a fresh start.

Some of the men who heard Woodworth's proposal immediately viewed it with suspicion. They believed that this was part of a conspiracy led by Vick. Norris had already begun referring to Woodworth as Vick's "stooge," and Woodworth's campaign convinced some that Norris was right.[31] Florida Pastor Bob Ingle thought the idea of selling the seminary out from under Norris was outlandish, and he wanted nothing to do with it. "I was wise enough to listen and let [Woodworth] talk," Ingle said, "but certainly not dumb enough to enter into the conspiracy."[32]

Yet others agreed with Woodworth. Wendell Zimmerman, a Kansas City pastor, may have been among the men most receptive to Woodworth's pleas. By all accounts, Zimmerman was one of the most outspoken advocates for separating from Norris and the WFBMF. According to Vick, Zimmerman urged this action even before Vick and the others were on board.[33] Rawlings likewise remembered Zimmerman as a separatist: "He's the one that continually said, 'We have to break with Dr. Norris. There's no way that we can be compatible.'"[34]

Woodworth and Zimmerman were the exceptions, however. Most of the other pastors, even those in Vick's camp, were reluctant to call it quits with J. Frank Norris. Dowell wrote that "neither Dr. Vick nor I, nor for that matter any of the other leaders, had any thought except to work cautiously and prayerfully to keep the fellowship together."[35] Vick, too, claimed that he had arrived at that meeting with a strong desire to remain with the WFBMF. "Well, I loved the old Fellowship," Vick said, "had helped build it, had been president of it, and had poured thousands of dollars into it. It was difficult to just turn it over to Norris and that crowd when we were the majority group. If the fight had been doctrinal, then I would have left it immediately; but it was essentially the crookedness of one man, who would not be around forever."[36]

It was Norris himself who ultimately convinced Vick and the others that a complete break would be necessary. A pivotal moment came on Tuesday morning of the fellowship meeting. That is when a public confrontation broke out. Norris had previously announced in *The Fundamentalist* a theme for each day of that meeting, and ironically, Tuesday was designated as Seminary Day. The events planned for that day included a large barbecue sponsored by the Norris family in celebration of the seminary's newly won accreditation. Norris had also filled the day's program with speakers who had strong ties to the seminary.

But at the last minute, some of Norris's plans changed. Vick, for instance, learned that his place on the speaking roster had been reassigned to Luther Peak. Dowell, too, had been removed from the agenda. As the fellowship's president, Dowell had been scheduled to moderate all of the morning activities, but without explanation, Norris appointed Frank Godsoe to serve in Dowell's place. Curtis Goldman, who had been a student at the seminary since 1947, remarked that "it was very evident that the program was planned to keep all opposition off the platform."[37]

Dowell and the others learned about these program changes on Monday, and afterward they held "an informal meeting," Dowell said, "to decide exactly what course [they] should follow." They concluded that sitting idly by was not an option. "As president of the Fellowship, I would be forced to challenge Dr. Norris," Dowell explained, "and insist that if he spoke on the seminary issue, Dr. Vick would also be permitted to speak as had been originally planned. Our reasoning was that it was necessary and fair for the Fellowship to hear both sides of the controversy."[38]

The next morning Vick's party arrived at the meeting and saw Godsoe preparing to take charge of the session. Vick, Zimmerman, and Rawlings then urged Dowell to make his move. "Bill, you're supposed to preside at this meeting," they said. "Go on up there, put it—you know, go on up there and just put it to a vote."[39] What occurred next is an event that John Rawlings described as the "pinnacle" of Dowell's entire ministry.[40] Dowell marched onto the platform "in spite of threats and intimidation," Rawlings said, and he took charge of the morning session. Rawlings said he was not surprised by Dowell's boldness. "I expected him to do that," Rawlings said, "because I'd known him well enough and known him long enough by then to know that he was not a pushover and he would fight to the death if he felt like he was right."[41]

Although witnesses said Dowell ascended the platform "calmly,"[42] Dowell himself remembered the moment differently. "My heart was almost in my throat as I walked up . . . ," he said.[43] This was, after all, J. Frank Norris's platform, and in committing this act of insubordination, Dowell was crossing a man of great influence and a man that he personally admired. Still, Dowell believed it was the right thing to do. In 1977, he detailed what he did when reached the top of those stairs:

> I went straight to Dr. Norris and asked him if he was going to speak on the Seminary issue. With his small piercing eyes, he looked at me and said, "Yes." I then plainly stated that as president of the Fellowship, I would insist that Dr. Vick also be given the opportunity to speak. He stated that Dr. Vick was no longer on the program and that Luther Peak would be the next speaker. I looked Dr. Norris straight in the eye and said, "Dr. Norris, in the name of fairness, I will publicly insist that Dr. Vick have the opportunity to speak." He said, "Go ahead; go ahead. Tell Dr. Frank Godsoe. He is moderating the meeting." I turned and walked straight to Dr. Godsoe and stated that since there were some issues to be resolved, as president of the Fellowship, I would moderate the meeting. Anger blazed in the eyes of Dr. Godsoe as he turned toward me and bluntly stated, "You will not!"[44]

Dowell said he then did "the only reasonable thing [he] could think of."[45] He stepped up to the podium and, without warning, began addressing those gathered in the room, an estimated crowd of fifteen hundred.[46] "I said, 'Ladies and gentlemen, I have never known it necessary before, but I must ask your permission for your president to moderate this meeting.'"[47] Just then he heard Norris, who was standing behind him, trying to cut him off. "It's Seminary Day," Norris barked, attempting to justify why Godsoe made a more logical choice for moderator. Dowell answered that objection by reminding Norris that the seminary was a fellowship institution and that he was the current president of the fellowship. "I don't know how much longer I will be," Dowell joked to the audience, "but right now I am."[48]

And with that, Dowell proposed a vote. He told the crowd, "Those in favor of my moderating this meeting and seeking to resolve the issues that are before us, please stand to your feet." Now the uncertain direction of the political winds became clearer. "In one mighty movement the audience stood," Dowell recalled. By an estimated "four to one margin," Dowell had won the vote,[49] and he turned to Godsoe triumphantly and said, "I will moderate the meeting."[50]

Some reports indicate that another vote was then taken to reinstate Vick as a morning speaker, at which time Norris insisted that he be permitted an opportunity for rebuttal.[51] Dowell agreed to let him.[52] Then when all of this haggling finally ended, the meeting got underway. As usual, the service began with congregational hymn singing. Dowell said that, while this music was going on, "two young men came to the edge of the platform and motioned" to get his attention. "I stooped down so that I could hear what they had to say," he said. "They very bluntly threatened me if I pursued the matter further." But in response, Dowell smiled and said, "You fellows take your seat; you are not scaring anyone." He confessed later that this answer may not have been "the whole truth," saying, "What we were doing was being done with fear and trembling."[53] In any event, Dowell managed to put up a bold front.

After the opening music concluded, Dowell introduced Norris as the first speaker of the morning. By many accounts, Norris did little to aid his cause. Dowell stated that, though Norris spoke for "about one hour," he "did not say a great deal nor even mention many of the issues that he had previously discussed in his accusations against Vick."[54] Vick agreed. Vick said Norris's presentation was "mostly bluffing and blustering." "He'd mention something and say, 'If I hear any more about that, I'll have more to say about it.' . . . He wasn't at his best that day by a long shot," Vick said, "but he was nervous."[55]

Whether Norris realized it or not, his age was beginning to show. Researcher Royce Measures noted that even some of Norris's sympathizers described his closing years as "confused," "disorganized in seminary," and "irrational."[56] Vick couched a similar observation in biblical language. Borrowing a statement from Judges 16:20—"he wist not that the Lord was departed from him"[57]—Vick suggested that Norris's downfall was of divine origin. Vick also invoked 2 Samuel 15:31 in the argument. There David prays that the Lord will "turn the counsel of Ahithophel into foolishness." Vick believed this was precisely what had happened to Norris. "It wasn't Beauchamp Vick licking J. Frank Norris," Vick maintained. "It was the Lord."[58]

Whatever the case, Norris's rambling speech that day was followed up by a much stronger presentation from Vick. Reportedly, even Norris's assistant, Jane Harwell, grew concerned. Harwell was seen pacing near the church switchboard as Vick spoke, and the switchboard operator heard her say, "The preacher has never lost a fight yet, but he's losing this one."[59] Vick's message went on for a full hour and a half. In it, he brought up his concerns about the Monday morning election and asked audience members to indicate by a show of hands which of them had been present to participate in that election. Fourteen hands went up. This was a far smaller number of preachers than what Norris and his allies had been claiming in their reports,[60] so after giving audience members a chance to count the uplifted hands, Vick added a brief comment. "That's peculiar," he said.[61]

Vick went on to address allegations that had gone out about him and his administration at the seminary. And as he made his case, Vick supported his claims with meticulously prepared files, which he pulled from a brown briefcase.[62] Vick answered the charges that he had mistreated Entzminger, producing copies of Norris's own letters wherein Norris himself spoke dismissively of the aging Entzminger. For dramatic effect, Vick paused periodically, turning to Norris and asking if he would deny his signature on those letters.[63] Norris did not.

Eventually, Vick got to the "real issue," which he said was Norris's "cooked up bylaws."[64] Vick pointed out the curious timing of the bylaws' emergence, as well as the fact that virtually no one, including insiders like himself, ever recalled seeing this document before the controversy broke out.[65] Vick raised concerns about the implications of these bylaws, arguing that "they gave 'Russian veto power' over the Seminary to the First Baptist Church. 'And when you say the First Baptist Church', said Vick 'you might just as well say one man'; and he turned and pointed at Norris seated behind him."[66]

Ultimately, Vick brought his speech to a dramatic climax, saying:

> Now we have no argument—we have no fight with those who want to support a school who is dominated and controlled by one church, just as well say one man. That's your right if you want to, but as for me and my house, I'm not going to support a school where one man dominates the whole thing. No matter how much money the rest of you put in, it will be controlled by one man—one church. You'd just as well say one man. The rest of you can support it if you please, but I don't choose to. For that reason—for these—for several reasons I present my resignation as president of the Bible Baptist Seminary.[67]

With that, Vick picked up his briefcase and walked away from the pulpit. And a dozen men were instantly "on their feet" seeking to pose questions, make comments, or offer recommendations.[68] Dowell recognized Wendell Zimmerman. Zimmerman held up in one hand a copy of the bylaws that Norris had distributed to the audience, and in the other hand he held up a copy of the 1948-49 Seminary Catalog.[69] This catalog, Zimmerman explained, contained a copy of the seminary's bylaws. But, as Zimmerman pointed out, the published bylaws did not match Norris's document. To illustrate, Zimmerman began a comparative reading of the two sets of bylaws, noting that the published document did not give Norris the same level of authority over the seminary. And that being the case, Zimmerman urged fellow pastors to throw their support behind the published bylaws and not Norris's version. Zimmerman also made a motion that the fellowship reject Vick's resignation from the seminary.

Immediately several others in the room attempted to speak. Dowell now called on Bob Ingle of Florida. Ingle's feeling was that the fellowship needed more information before its members could vote either for or against Vick's resignation. He proposed appointing a committee to investigate the various charges. Since conflicting bylaws were obviously in play, a committee representing all sides should determine which document was official and should make recommendations about how to proceed.[70]

But neither Ingle's motion nor Zimmerman's ever came to a vote. According to Loys Vess, when Norris heard what was being proposed, he sprang to his feet and "pushed [Dowell] away, and the others on the platform, and said, 'I don't care what the committee decides; I don't care what the Fellowship decides; everything is going to stand as it is.'"[71] Norris then demanded that he be given his promised time for rebuttal. And in deference, Dowell yielded the floor.

By this time it was late in the morning, yet many in the room hoped that, before the session ended, Norris would give answers to the charges made by Vick. Regrettably, no such answers came. Instead, Norris engaged in what Dowell referred to as a filibuster. He rehashed things that had already been stated without ever addressing Vick's concerns about the bylaws, the Monday morning election, the Detroit students, or any of the other issues. Vick maintained that Norris did not give any answers to those matters because "he couldn't."[72] To Norris, only one thing mattered. His bylaws were "on record in Austin," and they could not be changed.[73] Furthermore, Norris said he would lock the doors of his church before he would allow anyone to overturn his authority there.[74]

As Norris's filibuster hammered on, Dowell and others became exasperated. "I called him down twice," Dowell said, "and he finally turned and asked me if I wanted to blow him out of his own pulpit. I said, 'No, go right ahead Dr. Norris, go right ahead.' And then he went ahead and filibustered."[75] But eventually those ramblings came to an end. And this was when Norris announced that there was no need for any sort of committee because "Beauchamp and I can go to lunch and settle this thing between ourselves."[76]

Although no one but Norris really believed an agreement was possible, Vick agreed to go to lunch in the interest of trying to reach some sort of accord. Dowell dismissed the morning session, and the beleaguered members of the WFBMF then filed out of the First Baptist Church. Everyone would have to wait to see if a private luncheon between Norris and Vick could somehow resolve their seemingly irreconcilable differences. The fellowship meeting would reconvene at two o'clock.

In the meantime, Dowell was confident that he had done the right thing. And he never regretted doing the right thing. In 1947, Dowell received from Nola and their three children a Bible as a gift for Father's Day. In it, Nola wrote a lengthy inscription. She said, in part, "To my beloved husband, Bill Dowell, who not only believes the Bible and preaches the word, but lives it; my testimony of him is this, that he truly says with Paul—'you follow me, as I follow Christ.'"[77]

When Dowell reflected back on the turmoil of 1950, he believed that he had lived the Word. Indeed, he used the experience to exhort others to do the same. Dowell preached a sermon in the mid-1970s, urging his church to follow him as he had followed Christ on that day in Fort Worth. Borrowing words from the first chapter of Joshua, Dowell cried out, "Be strong. Stand!" Dowell then followed up that exhortation by telling his audience that he knew what it meant to face opposition:

> *I've been in many a battle. I was in, I suppose, one of the hottest contested spiritual battles or religious battles in our generation. It so happened that I was the president of the fellowship at the time that these things happened and I had to do some things that, I'll tell you, it was hard on me as a young preacher. I had to stand in a large pulpit and challenge the pastor of that church. And we had some real battle royals spiritually, religiously, over honesty and integrity and the things that were right (sic).*[78]

Dowell went on to explain that, when it came to matters such as these, backing down was not an option. "I don't ever to intend to compromise my honesty and my integrity," he told the crowd. "I'd rather lose everything else."[79]

When Dowell walked out the First Baptist Church on that difficult Tuesday morning in 1950, he knew that he had stood up for his principles and that his honesty and integrity were intact. Of course, it remained to be seen what such a moral victory would cost him. For the moment, Dowell believed it was Norris, not him, who would suffer loss. But that assumption would soon be challenged. Indeed, when the fellowship meeting reconvened, Dowell faced surprises that would shake him to his very core. And not long after that, he would be sitting on a drugstore stool questioning, for the first time, the loyalty of his friend G. B. Vick.

Chapter 23: *The Texas Hotel*

That'll be five cents, please!

The soda jerk was now wiping the counter with a towel. To Dowell, the boy's tone of voice was too upbeat for a day like today. Dowell turned and handed the boy a nickel to pay for his Coke, but he found it difficult to match the boy's enthusiasm. Dowell simply said:

Thank you, my friend.

Now the boy looked out at the crowd of students standing behind Dowell:

Can I get anyone else anything?

The students looked from side to side, and no one really responded. So Dowell said:

We'll be moving out of here pretty soon.

The boy nodded and threw the towel over his shoulder, saying in that same cheerful voice:

Okay. Ya'll have a nice day!

When Dowell left the drugstore that afternoon, he parted ways with the seminary students and spent the rest of the afternoon wandering the streets of Fort Worth with Nola. By this time he was holding back tears, he said. Remarks made by Vick at the beginning of the afternoon session had left him and others in shock.

As promised, Norris and Vick had gone to lunch for a tête-à-tête. They ate in the Westbrook Hotel, not far from Norris's church. Many of the other preachers from the fellowship, including Dowell, had been scattered throughout that same dining room. Reportedly Jock Troup at one point came over to the table where Norris and Vick were seated, but Troup's effort to get in on the conversation was rebuffed. No sooner had the Scotsman rested his palms on the tabletop than Norris shooed him off. "Get on away from here!" Norris snapped. "Beauchamp and I are busy." Vick said Troup "looked like he had thrown cold water in his face. . . ."[1]

Billy Vick Bartlett, in his book A *History of Baptist Separatism*, details the conversation that transpired between Norris and Vick. ". . . Norris broke the icy silence," Bartlett explains, "by asking Vick his terms for settlement." In reply, Vick listed three stipulations:

> Vick stated that first the expelled Temple Baptist Church students must be
> reinstated. Second, since he had resigned his position at the college, Norris must
> resign as co-pastor of the Temple Baptist Church in Detroit. Finally, Norris would
> have to acquiesce to the establishment of an additional Fellowship school which
> would be structurally within the World Fundamental Baptist Missionary
> Fellowship but would be autonomous in its management.[2]

Vick claimed that other proposals were also introduced as part of these negotiations, including an offer from Norris to take him on a trip around the world at no expense.[3] Vick had no designs on any of Norris's favors, however. What Vick wanted was a parting of ways. He also hoped that the terms of the separation would be amicable.

According to the plan that Vick outlined for Norris, the new seminary would be a sister institution to the one in Fort Worth, and it would be situated in Springfield. Vick felt that Springfield made a logical choice. It was "centrally located,"[4] Vick said, and Dowell had a large and growing church there. And since High Street was already the headquarters for the fellowship's mission giving, many in the WFBMF viewed Springfield as a key outpost for the fellowship.[5] Vick further believed that Springfield was preferable to a big city like Detroit. Whereas the motor city offered mostly eight-hour shifts for its employees, Springfield was more likely to offer students the part-time positions they needed in order to go to school.[6]

In the course of this lunch conversation, Vick showed Norris how he could save face by supporting his plan. Vick said Norris could tout the new institution as a branch school, an idea that was in line with ambitions Norris had already published in *The Fundamentalist*. The churches of the WFBMF could send students and financial support to whichever institution they chose, Vick explained, and since Norris and Vick would be running distinct seminaries, there would be no further cause for the clash of personalities that had brought them to this impasse. Their schools would operate independently, and people on both sides of this dispute could view the solution as a win.

Vick thought his luncheon with Norris went better than expected. As part of their conversation, Vick invoked the words that Abraham once spoke to Lot: "Let there be no strife, I pray you, between me and you, and between my herdsmen and your herdsmen; for we be brothers."[7] And at least in principle, Norris seemed to share the sentiment. When Norris asked if Vick would be willing to serve as a guest lecturer at the Fort Worth seminary, Vick said he would. And when Vick told Norris that he hoped he would continue to be a frequent guest in the pulpit at Temple, Norris agreed to do so.[8]

By the end of that meal at the Westbrook, it appeared that Norris and Vick had found a solution to their differences. So they returned to the First Baptist Church to announce the terms of their agreement to the rest of the fellowship. Dowell, as much as anyone, was waiting eagerly for the news. No matter the outcome, Vick's negotiations would have ramifications for Dowell and the rest of the fellowship. And if the fellowship split, Dowell knew that he and other leaders would serve as lightning rods for Norris's hostilities. "I had really stuck my neck out," Dowell explained.[9]

Dowell now waited to hear his fate. But as he listened, he got the uneasy feeling that he had risked his neck in vain. Vick told the assembled pastors that his luncheon with Norris had been "a very congenial dinner."[10] He went on to announce that he was leaving the seminary's presidency but that he had agreed to visit that institution as a guest lecturer. Vick also said that Norris was stepping down from the pastorate at Temple but that he would continue to be a regular speaker there. And as for the expelled students, they had been reinstated to the Bible Baptist Seminary.

Dowell and his fellow insurrectionists sat speechless. This was not at all the outcome that they had expected. To them it sounded like Vick had backed down, not Norris. It also appeared that Vick's allegiance to Norris had been reborn. And where did that leave them? Norris was particularly good at shaming his enemies in *The Fundamentalist*. Indeed, Bartlett dubbed the paper "Norris's usual vehicle of political execution."[11] Now that Vick had been restored to Norris's good graces, Dowell and the others had to wonder how long it would be before they would be vilified for poisoning Vick's ear against Norris. A prophecy that Wendell Zimmerman had previously made now seemed to be coming to pass. "[Norris] will knock us off one at a time if we don't stay together," Zimmerman warned. "If we don't hang together, we'll hang separately."[12]

As Dowell listened to Vick's opening remarks, it seemed that the gallows were now going up. Still in disbelief, Dowell left his seat and made his way over to John Rawlings to see if Rawlings was getting the same impression he was. Dowell asked in a low voice, "What is—what is Dr. Vick doing?"[13] Dowell hoped that Rawlings would contradict his fears. Instead he confirmed them. "Looks like Beauchamp's selling us down the river." Rawlings said grimly.[14] Dowell then turned and saw Wendell Zimmerman, and he posed to him the same question. "And Wendell made identically the same statement," Dowell said, "—used the same words."[15] All three of these men had reached the same conclusion. And Dowell said he felt like he had been "crucified."[16]

At this point Dowell decided he had heard enough. Rawlings once observed that Dowell "didn't wear his emotions on his coat sleeve as we say, but he was deeply emotional in his heart."[17] Those emotions were now running high. Dowell said he would have driven back to Springfield immediately if it had not been for the fact that he was not traveling alone. A busload of High Streeters had come to Fort Worth with him, and rounding all of them up would take some time. So for the moment, Dowell decided simply to exit the meeting. Though he could not leave town, he saw no reason to sit through the rest of those proceedings.

Dowell escorted his wife up the aisle and out the back door to the foyer. There they met Noel Smith, who stopped them and asked, "Bill, you got any integrity left?" Dowell's bitter reply was "Yeah, that's why I'm leaving."[18] Smith responded, "If you have, you are about the only one left that has."[19]

After that, Dowell exited the First Baptist Church and marched down to the corner of Fourth and Houston. This was where he sipped a Coke and pretended to offer hope to a group of worried students. He later went for a walk with Nola, and when it was over, he made his way back to the First Baptist Church. He was going to round up his church members so that they could go home.

Norris's afternoon session was just ending when Dowell returned to the church, and as the attendees began to disperse, Dowell went and found Earl Smith. Dowell instructed Smith to start loading their delegation onto the bus.[20] But a seminary student, Curtis Goldman, overheard these instructions and knew immediately that something was amiss. Fearing that there had been a breakdown in communication, Goldman darted into the auditorium to find Vick. Goldman pushed his way through a crowd of preachers on the church platform to reach Vick and to tell him what was going on.[21] Then, when Vick heard the news, he rushed out to investigate.[22]

Finding Dowell and the others, Vick now learned of his friends' reactions, and it became clear to him that there had been a grave misunderstanding. Vick's truce with Norris had been interpreted as the waving of a white flag, but Vick assured his allies that he had never capitulated. While he had attempted to work out an amicable separation from Norris, he was nevertheless committed to a separation. In further remarks that afternoon—remarks that Dowell had not heard—Vick had described his goal of starting a new school in Springfield. And even Norris was cooperating with the idea. In fact, in a show of support, Norris had stood before that assembly and repeated the same passage from Genesis that Vick had quoted to him over lunch.[23] Like Abraham and Lot, he and Vick would be two kinsmen going separate directions.

Far from capitulating, then, Vick had won for his supporters a peace deal. And as a result of his efforts, the afternoon session of the WFBMF meeting had ended warmly, with Vick and Norris embracing on the platform and with the other men of the fellowship coming to surround them in a tearful closing prayer.[24] As Vick saw the situation, then, he had managed to preserve the unity of the fellowship even while standing his ground.

Vick's explanation reassured Dowell and the other insurrectionists, and they now saw that their friend had acted honorably. Looking back on the incident, Dowell wrote, "I must state here that we had completely misjudged Dr. Vick. He was making one last desperate effort to keep the Fellowship from splitting and [to] preserve what we had gained through the years. He had no intention of deserting his friends. We have all come to appreciate the honest effort he made, but some of us felt that things had gone too far for any sort of honest reconciliation."[25]

At the end of Vick's explanation, Dowell cancelled his plans to leave Fort Worth. Instead, he and the others began strategizing with Vick. After all, Vick wanted to waste no time formulating plans for their new school in Springfield. Vick called a meeting with key leaders that evening to lay the groundwork. They would follow up this planning session, he said, with a larger meeting on Wednesday. This was when they would communicate their preliminary plans to other interested members of the WFBMF. Vick dispatched Reg Woodworth to secure a meeting space for his Wednesday gathering, and Woodworth located a suitable venue six blocks from the First Baptist Church. It was the ballroom of the Texas Hotel.[26]

After the evening service, Woodworth, Rawlings, Noel Smith, and other locals headed to their respective homes in and around Fort Worth. Meanwhile the out-of-towners—Vick, Dowell, and Zimmerman—convened a late-night planning meeting in Vick's hotel room. The night would be a long one, they suspected, so Vick had a third bed rolled into his room.

Vick's men spent that night not only making plans for their new school but also reliving the events of that day. The stress of it all had left them rather keyed up, they found. In fact, when the lights in their hotel room finally went out sometime early the next morning, the three of them lay in bed unable to fall asleep. At last, Zimmerman rolled over and moaned, "God help, God help." The words came out in a tone that made Vick begin to chuckle. Then Zimmerman called out again. He was still processing Norris's rantings from the morning session as well as the brouhaha that followed. Zimmerman concluded that it had all been the devil's doings. To make his point he referenced the biblical story where Christ casts demons into a herd of two thousand swine. "[E]nough demons to be in two thousand [hogs]," Zimmerman blurted. "Enough demons in that place there today to inhabit every one of us."[27] This outburst left Vick in a full-blown fit of hysterics. And soon Dowell and Zimmerman, too, were rolling with laughter.

Of course, all of that hilarity had faded by the time the sun came up on Wednesday morning. This was when Vick and his supporters returned to the First Baptist Church. Before the morning session of the fellowship meeting began, Vick approached Norris and informed him of his intention to host an organizational meeting for his new school at 12:30. Vick also asked permission to announce the details of his meeting to the fellowship as part of the morning's proceedings. To this, Norris offered a cold reply. "I don't think we'll make an announcement," Norris said.[28]

Vick said the support that he had witnessed from Norris a day earlier was now gone. But Vick was undeterred. After all, he was quite accustomed to working around Norris. Instead of a public announcement, Vick would have Woodworth and others spread news about their meeting by word of mouth.

In the meantime, Norris approached Dowell and instructed him to start the morning's proceedings. But Dowell was now miffed over the renewed antagonism that Norris had shown toward Vick. He responded to Norris, saying, "I want to ask you one question before I do." Dowell asked if he, as moderator, would be permitted to present matters that pertained to the fellowship, "or if things would stand as they were." Norris answered, "They will stand as they are." And upon hearing those terms, Dowell bowed out of the role of moderator. According to Dowell, Norris then turned to Luther Peak and asked him to moderate in Dowell's stead. Peak likewise declined, however, so in the end, Norris made his way to the pulpit and opened the meeting himself.[29]

Sometime around noon, the Wednesday morning meeting adjourned. That is when approximately one hundred and fifty people—including about a hundred pastors—made their way to the tall brick building on Main Street known as the Texas Hotel.[30] Attendees filed past the hotel's arched windows, through its large double doors, and into a spacious ballroom lit by heavy black chandeliers and wall sconces. This hotel would eventually be placed on the National Register of Historic Places, not because of Vick's meeting, but because of a later historic event. John F. Kennedy, on the morning of his assassination in 1963, would deliver an impromptu speech standing in front of this hotel, followed by another speech to the Fort Worth Chamber of Commerce inside the hotel's ballroom. These would be the last two speeches of Kennedy's life.[31]

Monumental as those happenings were in 1963, however, Dowell saw greater eternal value in the events that occurred at the Texas Hotel on May 24, 1950. Norris's renewed opposition that morning had put organizers of this meeting into a bit of disarray. Though their stated purpose was to launch plans for a new seminary, some leaders, including Zimmerman and Dowell, now believed it was also time to launch a new fellowship.[32] Norris called this a conspiracy, but Dowell and the others saw things differently. In their view, the spontaneous unity that erupted that week—and the joint ventures that came out of it—could only be attributed to a mighty moving of the Spirit of God. Indeed, Noel Smith described it as "the funniest conspiracy I have ever seen." By his account, not one of those who separated from Norris saw it coming. "What we are seeing is a surprise to all of us," Smith insisted.[33] Wendell Zimmerman expressed similar sentiments when he spoke to the crowd assembled in the hotel ballroom. "I do not believe in any sense of the word that this was of human appointment," Zimmerman said, "but I believe it was of divine appointment. I believe God will be pleased to bless our efforts."[34] This was Dowell's feeling, too. Looking back on that ballroom gathering, Dowell said, "I have been in the ministry for over forty years, but I have never felt the power of the Spirit of God so strong as I felt in that service."[35]

Before the pastors at the Texas Hotel began conducting their business that day, Earl Smith led them in some singing. Dowell then assumed the role of moderator. One by one, he recognized individuals in the room who wanted to offer speeches and to make motions. One of the first actions the body took was to vote on whether to organize a new Bible college. Not surprisingly, the pastors voted unanimously in favor of doing so. Next, John Rawlings made a motion to appoint Vick as the new school's president. Woodworth seconded this motion, and this too passed unanimously. Now Vick recommended that the new institution be located in Springfield. He invited Dowell to respond to that proposal. Dowell was willing to accept Vick's recommendation, yet he first wanted to allay some possible concerns. After all, what would keep the new school from becoming a one-man operation just like the old one? Dowell took the opportunity to speak to that fear, saying:

> So that everyone's mind should be clear, I had no thought of permitting any school to be started in Springfield, and I am not bidding for the school. If the group that is interested wants to start the school in Springfield, I shall do everything in my power to help get it started. The High Street Fundamental Baptist Church will not have any authority over the school but will be willing to help it. If the school should be somewhere else, I shall support it happily.[36]

Vick's meeting ran late into the afternoon, which meant a large contingent of pastors (including the president of the fellowship) missed the afternoon session of the WFBMF meeting. One preacher from the Texas Hotel went back to check on Norris's meeting, and when he returned, he reported, "You could shoot a rifle through the place and it wouldn't hurt anybody."[37] Zimmerman tagged onto the man's statement, saying, "The break has come. The very fact that we are here is proof of that. They are still having a meeting now in the First Baptist Church, and we are here."[38] Zimmerman then presented a series of motions that included starting a new fellowship and selecting Dowell as its president.

Zimmerman's proposals were followed by a lengthy discussion. If a new fellowship were formed, how would the decision be communicated to the churches? And who would draw up the new fellowship's organizational papers? And what would this decision mean for the WFMBF mission office now being housed in Dowell's church office? And most importantly, was a total break something that these men really wanted to see? Vick, in particular, was still very reluctant to make such a move.

But then, while these questions were still being discussed, a second report came from the First Baptist Church. This report, delivered by Pastor H. E. Chance of Louisiana, would change the tenor of the meeting at the Texas Hotel.[39] "They've just voted to move the Fellowship office from Springfield to Fort Worth," Chance told them, "and they're preaching Beauchamp's funeral right now."[40]

As part of the proceedings at First Baptist that afternoon, Norris not only lambasted Vick but also removed Dowell as president of the fellowship. Norris replaced Dowell with a preacher from Colorado, Harvey Springer. It was an appointment that Vick found ridiculous, since Springer's previous participation in the WFBMF had been virtually nonexistent. "Harvey's whole and sole connection with the old Fellowship, up to that time," Vick claimed, "had been he had attended one of our national meetings because he was on his way between revivals. . . ."[41] Even so, Springer was now in, and Dowell was out.

News of these actions made one thing clear to the folks in the Texas Hotel: the break with Norris had come. Consequently, when Dowell led the assembly in a vote about organizing a new fellowship, every hand was lifted. Vick himself waited until all others had voted, and then he raised his hand to make the decision unanimous.[42] A series of other motions quickly followed. Dowell was voted in as the first president of the new fellowship. Then Noel Smith was tapped to serve as the editor of a new fellowship publication, a periodical modeled after *The Fundamentalist*.

The pastors also selected names for the three entities that they had voted into existence—the college, the fellowship, and the newspaper. As it turned out, these namings required a good bit of discussion. Vick, for one, had strong opinions about what these entities would be called, mostly because of his history with the World Fundamental Baptist Missionary Fellowship. That name, in Vick's view, was one that even the organization's members could not remember.[43] "I detest a long drawn out rigmarole . . . ," Vick groused. Invoking Shakespeare again, he reminded his peers that "brevity is the soul of wit."[44]

Dowell now responded to Vick's input by proposing a name for the college. "Let's make it the Baptist Bible College," Dowell said.[45] The adjectives *Baptist* and *Bible* seemed to encapsulate everything they wanted the new school to stand for, and the appellation was also brief. Vick and the others agreed. So after this discussion, Zimmerman made a motion, and Dowell's proposal was adopted.

Names for the other institutions then fell in line with the name of the college. *Baptist Bible Fellowship* was selected as the title of the new fellowship. Fred Donnelson wondered if the term *Missionary* should be inserted into this name, but Vick argued that if the institution was both *Baptist* and *Bible*, then it would also be *Missionary*. "Let's not make it long and cumbersome," Vick insisted.[46] And with that, the shorter version was approved.

Next, Noel Smith contributed *Baptist Bible Tribune* as the name for the new periodical. Smith's suggestion came as no surprise to Vick. "Noel almost worshipped the *Chicago Tribune*," Vick jabbed. "He'd quote—in the early days we had all we could do to keep [the *Baptist Bible Tribune*] from being a reprint of the *Chicago Tribune*."[47] Even so, no one objected to the title itself, so Smith's proposal was likewise approved.

When all of this business had concluded, the pastors of the new fellowship discussed their next steps. It was obvious that they would not be participating in the remaining activities at the First Baptist Church, so John Rawlings proposed that they assemble at the Central Baptist Church in Denton instead. This church was nearby, only about thirty minutes away, and if the pastor there, Loys Vess, was willing, their group could use his regular midweek service as an impromptu fellowship gathering.

Vess, who was present in the Texas Hotel meeting, then spoke up. He thought Rawlings proposal did not go far enough. "Since I have been accused of leading the revolt in this section of the country," Vess said, "I would like to do a good job of it. We will have a fellowship meeting tonight, tomorrow, and tomorrow night."[48] And with that, Dowell led the group in another vote, and these motions passed with ease.

A sweet spirit came over this group of pastors during their afternoon deliberations. "There was weeping, laughing, and praising God," Dowell said. "Earl Smith for the first time in his life shouted." Dowell said that he too had been moved by the day's events. "The speech that lifted the meeting to its greatest heights" Dowell recalled, "was delivered by Dr. Fred Donnelson, who was elected as our Missions Director."[49] Donnelson owned a unique respect among these brethren. By the end of his life, many would know Donnelson simply as "Mr. Missions." John Rawlings hailed him as one of history's greatest missionaries. "He measures in my judgment," Rawlings said, "with Adoniram Judson, Livingston, William Carey, and the greats in the latter part of the eighteenth, nineteenth, and the early part of the twentieth century. I'd rate him right at the top with those brethren."[50]

Not surprisingly, then, Donnelson's remarks brought great inspiration to the group assembled in the Texas Hotel. His statement seemed to sum up what was on their hearts and how they felt about the things they had accomplished that afternoon. Donnelson told them that he felt as if he was "taking off an old suit, badly worn and stained, and putting on a new one."[51] He also expressed great hope for this new attire. "[T]he strong right arm of the new Fellowship," Donnelson proclaimed, "will be world missions."[52]

Amens now rang out in response to Donnelson's words. Dowell's booming voice was included in the mix. He was thrilled over what God was doing. "I think we all felt that a yoke had been taken from our necks," Dowell said. "There was a new freedom, an expectation of great things to come, a vision for a fellowship that would really have world missions as its primary aim—a vision of building great soulwinning churches all over the United States."[53]

Such excitement would continue to spread over the next day and a half. On Wednesday evening, Loys Vess stood before his congregation in Denton to explain the week's developments. "I have been in the Fellowship of Texas longer than any other preacher except Dr. Norris," Vess said, "and I have always stood with him; but this is one time my God-given conscience wouldn't let me do it."[54] After he finished this explanation, Vess invited his congregation to rise if they would support his decision to leave the WFBMF. The entire congregation stood to its feet.

The Baptist Bible Fellowship met again the next day, though Dowell himself attended very little of it. After the news media got word of the split, reporters from the Associated Press and the *Star-Telegram* came to Denton seeking interviews.[55] Vick and Dowell, as the designated spokesmen for the new fellowship, spent a good part of Thursday afternoon answering questions. Then on Friday, an article by Jack Douglass came out in the local newspaper. The article discussed Norris's "new by-laws" as well as the hasty Monday morning election by which Norris had replaced Vick with Troup. The article also outlined the Baptist Bible Fellowship's future plans. It announced the names of seven preachers selected to serve as the fellowship's first board of directors, and it presented a similar list of those who would be serving as trustees for the new college. "[N]o hardship will be worked on students who wish to attend the Springfield school," Douglass wrote in his closing sentences, "because their credits will be accepted." Then he added, "[Vick] predicted that the school would be in operation by September."[56]

Such a report must have infuriated Norris. Indeed, Norris would spend much of the next several months attempting both to thwart the efforts of the new fellowship and to discredit the men who had founded it. Yet Norris was not alone in his criticism of those men. Many Norris supporters remained firmly rooted in Norris's camp. Bob Ingle was among those who thought the actions of Vick's men had been too extreme. Ingle confronted Vick and Zimmerman in a hotel lobby, saying, "Why in the world didn't you hold on? [Norris is] not going to live more than a couple of years." But Vick was far too scrupled to go along with such a position. He shot back to Ingle, "Don't think that I'm going to stand around like a carrion crow waiting for a carcass to quit kicking."[57]

The Baptist Bible Fellowship would go on to become one of the largest Baptist movements in America, second only to the Southern Baptist Convention, according to John Rawlings.[58] But the movement did not have an easy birth. In fact, when Dowell told the story of these events in a book in 1977, he titled his work *The Birth Pangs of the Baptist Bible Fellowship, International*. And the pangs experienced at Fort Worth were just the beginning. Much toiling lay yet ahead. Dowell and the others had less than four months to start a Bible college from scratch, and it seemed inevitable that this work would be undertaken amid gale-force winds. The reason, of course, was because Dowell and his companions were now standing in the path of a raging Texas Tornado.

Chapter 24: *The Slugfest Begins*

The doorbell rang at the Dowell home on Ramsey Street. Nola opened the door to find a uniformed delivery boy standing in front of the screen door.

Telegram for Reverend W. E. Dole.

It's Dowell.

Oh sorry, Ma'am.

Nola turned and called to the back part of the house:

Bill?

This initiated a long-distance conversation:

Who is it?

There's a telegram here for you.

A what?

A telegram.

I'll be right there.

Dowell was still slipping on his suit coat when he finally stepped out onto the porch. As he adjusted his collar, he said to the boy:

You just caught me. Two minutes later, and I'da been gone.

The boy squeaked back:

Oh sorry, sir. I hope it's not a bad time.

Dowell, who was now digging in his pockets for some coins, shook his head.

Naw. I was just heading over to the church. You ever been to the High Street Fundamental Baptist Church?

No, Sir. Not yet.

Well, you ought to visit. We're starting a revival next week. You should come out for it.

As Dowell studied a palm full of coins, the boy nodded and said:

Might just do that.

Dowell smiled back at the boy.

We're in the big tent just south of Saint Louis Street over on Glenstone.

Dowell now reached out his hand and traded a set of coins for the telegram in the boy's hand. Then Dowell added:

We'll be out there every night—

That was all the boy heard. Tipping his visored cap, the youngster bounded off the porch, calling back:

Yes, Sir. Thank you! Have a nice day at church!

Dowell's eyes followed the boy momentarily, wondering if there was any chance he would see him at the revival. But when the young man was out of sight, Dowell glanced down at the telegram. And that was when the smile faded from his lips.

Just what I needed—another note from Dr. Norris.

When the 1950 meetings in Fort Worth and Denton came to an end, Dowell and his associates returned to their hometowns to carry on their ministries and to continue efforts to launch the Baptist Bible Fellowship, the Baptist Bible College, and the *Baptist Bible Tribune*. Meanwhile, J. Frank Norris waged a war that was aimed at seeing all of these efforts fail. The ensuing ugliness became what Billy Vick Bartlett described as an "ecclesiastical slugfest."[1] Throughout that summer, Dowell and the other leaders of the new fellowship endured one hit after another as Norris targeted them both in *The Fundamentalist* and in private correspondence.

These attacks were both personal and threatening. One telegram that Dowell received said simply, "Whole matter now being investigated by FBI and we will await their report."[2] Dowell's son, Bill Dowell Jr., recalled how Norris would often time the arrival of such disturbing messages so that Dowell would receive them just before going off to preach. The intent, in Dowell Jr.'s opinion, was to disrupt the elder Dowell's ministry at High Street. Whatever the case, Dowell Jr. said his father began leaving Norris's messages unread until after the day's services had ended.[3]

Of course, Norris's initial attacks that summer were aimed at G. B. Vick, not Dowell. In fact, Norris courted Dowell for a brief time, presumably hoping to win him back to the WFBMF. Dowell's first message from Norris was a letter that had been penned while Dowell was still in Denton. Its stated purpose was to inform Dowell of the decision to move the mission office away from Springfield, yet the message sounded remarkably conciliatory. "The Directors voted to move the mission office to Fort Worth," Norris wrote, "and they did this against my desire, but it is done, and was done unanimously." Norris then flattered Dowell for the work that he had done in managing the mission office. "There is not only no criticism in the way you handled these affairs of the missionary work, but everybody has nothing but praise, and I am going to in a short time write up the way you handled it from the start until now."[4] Although that promise was never kept, Norris did include some kind words for Dowell in an article published June 2. "Bill Dowell and Miss Zellota Sage, who had charge of the office at Springfield, are sending the entire records to Fort Worth," Norris wrote. "Everything is very happy in the move. Bill Dowell did a remarkable work."[5]

As time went by, Dowell saw other signs that Norris wanted to win him back. He received a conciliatory telephone call from Norris on the Sunday night following the split. Dowell said Norris's tone was pure saccharine. "[Y]ou talk about honey and cream," he remarked. Dowell reenacted Norris's call in a 1973 interview: "Hello Bill— . . . .—this is J. Frank. . . . Well, I just wanted to call you, Bill. I know a lot of things have happened. All these things fall out for the furtherment of God."[6]

In Dowell's opinion, Norris fully expected to patch things up with him. "Now, he knew he was going to lose Wendell Zimmerman and one or two others probably," Dowell said, "but he thought a bunch of us would come back to him."[7] Vick shared in that opinion. Vick said Norris even announced on radio that "John Rawlings was coming back to be with him,"[8] though Rawlings himself had no such intention. Indeed, when Rawlings heard from Reg Woodworth what Norris had broadcast, Rawlings told Woodworth, "Look, . . . If I was the only one, if all you guys went back, I never would."[9]

None of this deterred Norris from trying to mend the fences, however. On June 10, Norris wrote to Dowell, "I know that you are honest–I have never questioned that, nor will I. You have been imposed upon. This thing is the blackest conspiracy ever perpetrated and I know you are not deliberately and intentionally a part of it."[10] Three days later, Norris sent Dowell a personal invitation: "I am going to Geneva to the Congress of the International Council of Christian Churches, leaving here August 10th and then go on to Palestine for two weeks." Norris quoted to Dowell a price of only $629 for the trip, and then he said, "This is the cheapest I have ever heard from any trip. Several of the fellows are going, and I would sure love to see you get the benefit of that trip. I will have the car in Palestine and you will be under no obligation to me whatever if you accept this courtesy."[11]

Norris rounded out this lengthy letter with several attempts at diplomacy. "As I told you over the phone, these eddies come and go . . . ," Norris wrote. And in another place, "The things that have happened recently have not affected my attitude towards you, nor will it." And again, "There is a whole lot back of this that a lot of you fellows haven't understood, but . . . you will understand it more and more." Norris even extended to Dowell a helping hand, saying, "If Fred Donnelson wants to go to Hong Kong I can secure passport and visa for him."[12]

Of course, even as Norris was cozying up to Vick's associates, his relationship to Vick was becoming increasingly hostile. Upon returning to Detroit, Vick gave Temple's deacon board a full explanation of the things that had transpired at the fellowship meeting, including his and Norris's discussion about ending their co-pastor relationship. In response, some on the board immediately moved to sever relations with Norris and to designate Vick as the sole pastor. It was Vick who intervened to delay that action. "Just a minute brother," Vick told the deacon who had made the motion. "I appreciate the confidence. I tried to be honest with it and all, but you've just heard one side of the question. . . . Don't you think it would be fair to invite Mr. Norris to present his side of the thing?"[13]

At Vick's urging, then, an invitation went out to Norris asking him to meet with the deacon board and to present his version of the events. Vick said that, when the deacons contacted Norris, he asked them if Vick was aware that they were reaching out to him. The men responded by telling him that Vick was not only aware of it but that he had, in fact, orchestrated the whole thing. Even so, Norris told the story differently when he reported it in a radio broadcast, suggesting instead that Temple's board was acting without Vick's approval. He made a similar claim in a personal letter to Dowell, insisting that the deacons had contacted Norris over Vick's "protests."[14]

Norris's meeting with Temple's deacons took place on Thursday, June 1. Vick, too, was there, armed with a copy of the false letter that Norris had sent to Dowell. Vick carried plenty of other documentation as well. Yet it was Norris who took the floor first. According to Vick, the deacons warned Norris ahead of time not to let his testimony become focused on "personalities." Instead, they wanted him to limit his remarks to the events that had produced the squabble between him and Vick. This proved difficult, however. "He hadn't been going three minutes and he struck out at me," Vick said. "[O]h, it got very vitriolic."[15]

Norris's remarks now led to mutual frustration, Vick recalled. The deacons were frustrated because Norris was not giving them the answers they were seeking, and Norris was frustrated because he felt that the men were refusing to listen to him and that he was being unfairly treated. The impasse culminated in Norris exiting the meeting, saying, "Brethren, I see that you already have your minds made up. I refuse to have a part in a closed session."[16]

But after Norris's exit, the meeting carried on. Now Vick took the floor, producing documentation and witnesses to corroborate everything he said. And at the end of it all, a new motion was made to sever the relationship with Norris. This time the motion was both voted upon and passed. Norris was formally ousted from his position at Temple the following Sunday. Members of the church made the decision through a standing vote, and the widely publicized results of that vote were three thousand in favor of making Vick the sole pastor and a total of seven opposed to the move.

With this, Norris had suffered a significant defeat, though he was by no means finished fighting. Norris still believed that he could be successful in winning Dowell and others back to him. And to wage this war, Norris now packed *The Fundamentalist* with propaganda that would drive supporters away from Vick and back into his own good graces. He held nothing back. On the front page of the June 9 edition of *The Fundamentalist*, he published an article titled "Why Beauchamp Vick Refused to Have Full Proceedings before the Temple Baptist Deacons Thursday Night." In this article, Norris revealed the scandalous details about Evelyn Rae's affair with Gordon Bonner. Norris also used the story to insinuate that Vick and his wife, Eloise, had been complicit in a scheme to cover up the matter. "But the issue is whether a man is fit to be president of a great Seminary who will cover the guilty man and go in person to an innocent church at Denton and sponsor him." Norris wrote. "We can go to Denton for confirmation that Vick palmed Gordon off on them."[17]

Norris's lengthy article comments on many other facets of this conflict as well, including Vick's supposed efforts to oust Entzminger, the telephone "campaign" Vick allegedly waged to rally support against Norris's bylaws, and Woodworth's ten thousand dollar government check debacle. Norris countered Vick's objections about his bylaws by arguing that Vick had personally voted to approve those bylaws in the directors' meeting held on May 5.[18] Norris also presented testimony from two seminary students who maintained that, when Norris expelled Temple's students, he did so without the "un-Christian, illegal, bullying, brow-beating tactics" that Vick had alleged.[19]

Then in a separate article found in the same issue, Norris published an open letter written by Dallas pastor Luther Peak. In it, Peak corroborated the story told by the two students, saying, "Dr. Norris could not have approached this group of students in a more conciliatory spirit and attitude." Peak further claimed that "The students were organized for resistance. They had a spokesman, who took issue with Dr. Norris in behalf of the whole group." Peak suggested that the entire rebellion had been instigated by Vick as part of a conspiracy to overthrow Norris: "Finally, one of their number (not their spokesman) spoke out and said: 'No! We are not going to accept the by-laws. We talked to Mr. Vick last night by telephone, and he told us not to accept them.'"[20]

Vick had responded to many of these allegations when he addressed the new fellowship in Denton. "[D]id Beauchamp Vick and Bill Dowell and the Trustees approve those by-laws?" Vick asked. "NO! That is just one thing that they have misrepresented." To this he added a counterclaim. He argued that Entzminger had helped draft the 1948-49 Seminary Catalogue—the document containing Vick's version of the bylaws—and that Norris had likewise approved that document before it ever went to print.[21] Vick also disputed the claim that he had instigated an insurrection aimed at Norris and his bylaws. "They said that I told the students not to vote," Vick proclaimed. "I did not. When those heartbroken students called me, I said, 'Do not vote for anything you do not believe in. Just sit steady in the boat.'"[22]

But there was more to this dispute than conflicting versions of events. And for Dowell the most disturbing part became the personal nature of Norris's attacks. As Dowell saw it, Norris intended to embarrass, discredit, and wound his former allies—good men—at any cost. This was evident not only from Norris's distortion of the facts but also from the unnecessary attention he gave to the Bonner situation and even from his published comments about Vick's wife. In many of his writings, Norris now referred to Eloise as "Jezebel," an allusion to the wicked wife of King Ahab in scripture.[23] Commenting on the Bonner affair, Norris wrote, "One person is responsible for all this covering up—J-e-z-e-b-e-l."[24] Then in another issue, Norris explained what he meant by this term: "Jezebel was vile, lying, slanderous, scheming, vengeful—her chief trait was to tar everybody with the same tar she was tarred with."[25]

Dowell was sickened to see such malice. And it baffled him that Norris, after making such statements, thought there was any hope for the two of them to reconcile. In a sternly worded reply to one of Norris's friendly letters, Dowell chided Norris for insulting his integrity:

> *Dear Dr. Norris:*
>
> *In answer to your letter of June 10th—I have always respected you as an intelligent and wise man with your own personal convictions and the courage to stand for them. I am sorry you do not seem to feel the same about me. Your letter in which you state, 'you have been imposed upon' was not a compliment, but a slam. In other words I do not have judgment enough to make my own decisions, but am just a poor coward permitting others to lead me around at will. I am writing this letter only because I want the records straight.*

If it were not for the fact that we are dealing with sacred matters the things you are publishing and the tactics you are using would be rather laughable. And these very tactics are winning friends for the Baptist Bible Fellowship by the hundreds—and I speak the truth. Good men in the Baptist circles all over the South (such as O. K. Armstrong) are calling and writing commending us for the stand we have taken, and we are receiving word from entire State Fellowships that have voted to withdraw from the World Fundamental Baptist Missionary Fellowship and support the Baptist Bible Fellowship and the Baptist Bible College. . . .

No, Dr. Norris, your letter in which you stated, 'I know that you are honest and have never questioned that,' might have carried greater weight had you not listed me, by name, in your letter of May 27 to Beauchamp Vick, as one, along with Wendell Zimmerman and G. B. Vick, who had formed a conspiracy or agreement to move the Seminary. The fact of the business is, Dr. Norris, there was no conspiracy on our part, and I think you know that is true. Even though we pastors have put the majority of money into the Seminary buildings and have loyally supported the school, we are willing in order to be out from under the responsibility of pouring our money and our efforts into a school controlled and dominated by one church to give up all our investments in the school and start anew with a clean slate and a New Testament program.

Please believe me Dr. Norris, when I say it is not our purpose to try to hurt you in any way, even if we could. We are only interested in building New Testament Churches, sending out missionaries and winning souls to Jesus Christ. However, the things you have said and published have made it expedient for us to inform the people concerning the truth about this whole controversy.

I have all confidence in G. B. Vick. He has proved himself to be a man and a real Christian and in my opinion the attack you have made upon him involving a member of his family was the cheapest thing I have ever seen. Yes, Dr. Norris, we all knew what we were doing in Fort Worth, and we believe we were definitely led of the Lord to do it. I am an American citizen, thirty-six years old with a reasonable amount of intelligence, born again and called to preach and, (believe it or not) have some personal convictions, and I fear no living man but I fear the Lord. I can honestly say there is no ill will in my heart toward you. I just wanted to write you this open frank letter so that you would know where I stand.

Yours sincerely,
W. E. Dowell[26]

Dowell's tone became even sharper just two days later. This was when he received Norris's invitation to travel to Palestine. In reply, Dowell shot back a curt telegram: "IN ANSWER TO YOUR LETTER OF JUNE 13TH IN WHICH YOU INVITE ME TO GO TO PALESTINE WITH YOU FOR $629.00 ROUND TRIP, THANKS MY SOUL IS NOT FOR SALE."[27] Dowell shared this telegram with Noel Smith, and Smith promptly published it in the second issue of the *Baptist Bible Tribune*. After that, any warmth between Norris and Dowell seems to have evaporated.

As this summer slugfest escalated, Norris now proposed one final showdown between the two warring factions. He announced in the June 16 issue of *The Fundamentalist* that he planned to conduct an "investigation" of Vick's actions and that he would present his findings in a "hearing" to be held at the First Baptist Church in Fort Worth on Tuesday, June 27. Norris then issued several telegram "subpoenas" to summon Vick, Dowell, and others to attend the proceedings.[28] He warned in *The Fundamentalist*, "And Beauchamp Vick must be here, and I am sure he will be, for he cannot afford not to be!"[29] Then in the next issue Norris repeated that threat, adding, "Every Word WILL BE PUBLISHED."[30]

For Vick and the others, all this talk about "court proceedings" and "legal hearings" was a familiar strain. Norris had resorted to similar tactics in earlier conflicts. Joel A. Carpenter, in his work *Fundamentalism in American Religion 1880-1950*, cites a news article from 1923 that discusses another conflict wherein Norris employed this same battle plan:

> *Of late, Rev. J. Frank Norris has invented a new instrument of torture for colleges—the trial. At his recent 'world convention' of Fundamentalists, he turned his church into a courtroom and tried three Methodist institutions, the accused being Southern Methodist University at Dallas, Southwestern University at Georgetown, and the Texas Woman's College at Fort Worth. Dr. W. B. Riley, eminent Fundamentalist, presided.*

This article goes on to describe the kind of justice that Norris meted out in his kangaroo court: "Armed with college notebooks, six young folks, graduates or undergraduates of the accused, appeared as witnesses. Before a vast congregation, Rev. W. E. Hawkins, Jr., as prosecuting attorney, examined the witnesses for two and a half hours. Defense there was none. All the accused were convicted."[31]

Vick and Dowell could not doubt that a similar fate was being planned for them at the hearing Norris was now publicizing. And while they would have liked the opportunity to confront Norris and perhaps even to reach some sort of understanding with him, they had no intention of participating in a publicity stunt. Instead they reached out to Norris with an offer to meet him at a more neutral site, somewhere outside of Fort Worth.[32] Yet according to Vick, Norris refused that proposal, contending that Entzminger needed to testify and that his poor health would not permit him to travel. Reportedly Vick then suggested having a meeting elsewhere in Fort Worth. Norris again refused. "Whenever [Norris] was in a fight," Vick concluded, "he wanted all the advantage."[33]

After that, Vick's men decided that they would ignore Norris's subpoenas and would boycott the hearing. They were, after all, quite busy. The fall semester was just weeks away, and they had a new Bible college to birth. Indeed, the day before Norris's hearing was set to take place, Vick, Dowell, Woodworth, and Zimmerman were all gathering to discuss the launching of the new school. The site for their meeting was Zimmerman's church in Kansas City. Vick traveled from Detroit. Dowell and Woodworth drove up together from Springfield.

During Dowell and Woodworth's drive, the two men began discussing Norris and the hearing that was set to take place the next day. It was difficult not to be curious about what Norris was planning. They also found themselves speculating about what they would have said if they had been given the chance. Then as this conversation wore on, Woodworth finally turned to Dowell and blurted, "Bill, I think we ought to show up at the meeting." Dowell was similarly inclined. "You know, Reg," Dowell replied. "I was thinking the same thing."[34]

By the time Dowell and Woodworth reached Zimmerman's office, they were filled with "a good deal of excitement," Dowell said. They were convinced that all of them should make an unplanned road trip to attend Norris's hearing. Since Vick had not yet arrived in Kansas City, Dowell and Woodworth told Zimmerman about their proposal. And to their delight, Zimmerman was on board. "I am in full agreement," he told them. "I feel it is necessary that we be at that meeting." Then when Vick reached the church later in the day, he, too, approved of the plan. "I believe God is in it," Vick said; "gentlemen, let's prepare to leave for Fort Worth at once."[35]

Before leaving for Fort Worth, the four men decided to make a few telephone calls. Their purpose was to level the playing field at Norris's hearing and to demonstrate the strength of their numbers. They called John Rawlings and Loys Vess down in Texas and urged them to gather up a large crowd of supporters to go with them to the hearing. These forces would meet up with Vick's party in front of the Blackstone Hotel in Fort Worth the next day. Together, then, they would parade three blocks to the First Baptist Church.[36]

Once those calls had been made, Vick's men left Missouri and drove through the night, arriving at their hotel in Fort Worth early the next morning.[37] Dowell and Vick had originally expected to be in Kansas City for just a day, so they had not traveled with a change of clothing. Thus, when they awoke the next morning, the two men sent their suits out to be pressed. Unfortunately, the work took longer than expected. The delay caused Vick's party to arrive in front of the Blackstone a bit late.

This tardiness proved serendipitous, however. According to Bartlett, Vick's late arrival at Norris's church made for a spectacularly dramatic moment. Norris's meeting was already underway as Vick walked in with "some seventy-five or eighty" local supporters.[38] Norris still had no idea that any of them were coming. "It couldn't have been more perfect if we were following a Hollywood script writer," Woodworth remarked. Woodworth then went on to describe the scene:

> We were about fifteen minutes late and Norris was already in his tirade. He was screaming "where are they—the cowards—why aren't they here." At that precise moment, Beauchamp, who was in the vanguard of our group, pushed open the back door of John Birch Hall and started down the middle aisle. Norris was

caught completely by surprise. Finally he said nervously, "You come to testify Beauchamp?" and Dr. Vick replied "that's the general idea."[39]

The John Birch Hall was a three-hundred-seat auditorium in Norris's church and was already filled near to capacity. When Vick's party entered, they were forced to stand around the edges of the room. Vick carried a chair up to the platform and sat down a few feet from the podium. He announced that if Norris was going to preach his funeral, he "wanted a good seat."[40] Vick also proposed moving the session to a larger auditorium, but Norris refused, and in Vick's opinion, this was because Norris hoped that some of Vick's supporters would leave. Instead, the crowd grew larger throughout the day, Vick said. By the afternoon, Norris himself decided to move the meeting to the main auditorium.

The hearing's proceedings got underway with the appointment of Frank Godsoe as moderator. Godsoe laid out the parameters for the discussion and also summoned the witnesses to the platform one by one. Then he permitted their testimony to drone on for eight hours.[41] Several accounts suggest that, while Vick and his crowd made every effort to present the testimony that they had been summoned to give, Norris silenced them. Indeed, two large men were posted near the front of the room to prevent uninvited guests from approaching the platform. None in Vick's party was ever given an opportunity to take the floor or to ask witnesses questions.[42]

The first "witness" in Norris's case that morning was reportedly a woman from the printing office of *The Fundamentalist*. She was there to testify about the publication of the bylaws. Norris questioned her for several minutes and then dismissed her from the platform. This is when Vick interrupted. "Just a minute," he called out. ". . . You said this was going on court procedure. . . . We have the right of cross examination. You said in your own published report the right of examination and cross examination." But Norris would not hear of it. He informed Vick that he would have an opportunity to ask questions after all of the witnesses had testified. Vick again objected: "But the court procedure is to examine a witness when the testimony is still fresh in the minds of the hearers." Still Norris refused. "We're not going to do it," Norris said flatly.[43]

This exchange occurred around ten o'clock in the morning, and the testimonies continued until well into the afternoon. Dowell said he and his friends were "lambasted" all through the day.[44] In the afternoon session, Entzminger arrived by ambulance and was wheeled into the auditorium on a stretcher. Even though he was still recovering from his gall bladder surgery, he managed to testify about the deeds of the "traitors and conspirators" for nearly two hours. And then at the end of his testimony, Norris took time to receive an offering to help pay for his dear friend's medical expenses.[45] Norris "wore that thing out," lamented Vick.[46]

When it was late in the day, Norris invited esteemed evangelist Mordecai Ham to come to the platform "to close out with a great evangelistic message." Vick could not believe his ears. He immediately spoke up, insisting that his party be given an opportunity to answer the accusations that had been leveled against them and to cross examine the witnesses. "We'll continue this tomorrow," Norris replied. "We'll give you the opportunity tomorrow."[47] But this proposal was out of the question. Vick's men had obligations. They had churches to attend to and speaking engagements to fulfill. Vick told Norris, "We can go on till midnight right here, if necessary, but they can't—they can't stay over until tomorrow."[48] His words fell on deaf ears.

Vick said "a general hubbub" then broke out as various members of his party tried to reason with Norris.[49] Dowell asked Godsoe to give them "just two minutes," but Norris would not hear of it.[50] Others reportedly mounted "the mourner's bench" in order to be seen and heard as they made their pleas.[51] As part of this heated exchange, Norris issued a patronizing remark about Vick losing his battle, and in answer to that, Dowell shouted back, "3,000 to 7." This, of course, was a reference to the recent vote at Temple wherein Norris had been ousted as pastor. Such was the extent of Vick's defeat, Dowell seemed to say; three thousand were with him but only seven were against him. According to Bartlett, Dowell's sarcastic remark "evidently touched a sore point with Norris, for he ordered Ralph Toney and Bluford Finch, two seminary students, to throw Dowell out of the building." They never did. With a football player's swagger, Dowell instead "walked over to Finch and dared him to make an attempt."[52] Finch would not touch him.

In the midst of this chaos, Vick turned to Norris and said, "You're the biggest coward I ever saw in my life. You're afraid to face the facts." Still Norris would not back down. He kept insisting that Dr. Ham was going to preach and that the hearing would resume the next day. So then Vick appealed to Ham directly. Years earlier, Vick had served on Ham's evangelistic team, so now Vick urged his old friend not to "go through the mockery" of preaching under such conditions. And Vick's pleas succeeded. Ham agreed that the task would be "impossible with this spirit," and he politely declined to speak.[53]

At this point, said Vick, the meeting simply "broke up."[54] Nothing was ever resolved, and even though Norris planned to continue his hearing the next day, Vick and his associates had seen enough. They got into their car and headed home. Norris's whole hearing was, in Dowell's words, "a fake,"[55] yet even so, Dowell considered Norris's publicity stunt a boon to their cause. When Dowell returned home, he penned a strongly worded letter to Norris, saying:

> *Everyone is shocked at the tactics you used to keep us from testifying in Fort Worth. It is very evident you have something covered up and you knew we would uncover it. WE have it in print where you invited us to be there June the 27, 1950 and that we would be permitted to ask questions and give our side of the controversy. But when we ask permission to do so you threaten to throw us out, but your strong arm men were afraid to do so. Your only hope in that invitation, was that we would not come and it unnerved you so when we walked in that you had to quit speaking. You refused to even give us two minutes when I asked to make a statement, and your great anger and shouting like a maniac, liar, liar, liar at Noel Smith, gave us the greatest victory we have had so far. Preachers*

began to call me the minute I got back to my hotel room, saying, "I was on the fence but not any more."[56]

Of course, Norris was equally convinced that he had won the victory that day. He wrote to Vick, saying, "If ever a fellow and a bunch of gangsters got annihilated, this certainly happened to your crowd."[57] Then in the next issue of *The Fundamentalist*, Norris claimed victory once again. He called his hearing a "Most Pitiful Investigation," and he referred to Vick as "Poor Beauchamp," adding the insinuation that Vick had tried unsuccessfully to control and disrupt the hearing's proceedings.[58]

Norris's article about the hearing also intimated that the reason Vick and his allies had not returned the next day was because they feared the reports that he was going to give out about them.[59] Nothing could have been further from the truth. Yet as Dowell and the others were about to see, Norris certainly did have some damning reports to give. And no longer was Vick the sole target. Norris was coming after all of them. The gloves had come off, and Norris would now stop at nothing to bring his enemies to their knees.

Chapter 25: *Filthy Lucre*

A s Dowell turned down the corridor toward his office, he saw Noel Smith standing in front of his secretary's desk. Smith had stopped by to pick up a stack of mail.

Morning, Noel.

Good morning, Brother Bill.

Smith dug through his stack of envelopes as Dowell walked by and made polite conversation:

Got a pack of new subscriptions there?

Maybe so.

Dowell waved at his secretary on his way. He had just disappeared into his office when Smith called him back:

Oh, by the way, have you seen it, Bill?

Dowell stuck his head back out through the doorway.

What's that?

The Fundamentalist.

Why? Is it a good one?

Smith rolled his eyes as he answered:

Evidently Dr. Norris thinks he's Napoleon.

He does, huh?

Some such nonsense. You'll have to read it. "The Napoleon of the religious world."

Dowell sighed, shook his head, and turned back toward his desk:

You'da thought he'd have better sense than that. Napoleon's story didn't end so well.

Once the clash at the hearing broke out, Norris began publishing in *The Fundamentalist* the "record" of many of his foes. He had been threatening such a move for weeks. He wrote to Dowell on June 16 alleging that Vick was covering up instances of "sodomy and adultery" among the preachers in his camp. "I know you don't endorse that," Norris said. Norris also claimed to have embarrassing information about Noel Smith. With no elaboration, he wrote, "I have a very interesting record on No-all [sic] Smith. That will be interesting."[1] Then a couple days later, he wrote to Dowell warning him that Vick had landed in legal trouble: "The most serious thing is the indictment against Beauchamp Vick for criminal libel. The United States District Attorney has the information from Western Union."[2] In Norris's mind, such threats gave him great leverage to use in his battles. "I want you fellows to attack me," he dared Dowell. "I have been made by attacks." Then he added, "But you will come to me before it is over."[3]

Soon thereafter Norris began airing the dirty laundry of the preachers who were in cahoots with Vick. As with the Gordon Bonner story, there were elements of truth in some of these tell-all reports, even if Norris manipulated the details to serve his own agenda. One such report was about L. T. Grantham. Grantham had been tapped to teach at the new college in Springfield, and when Norris heard about it, he announced in *The Fundamentalist* that Grantham had been caught in an adulterous affair with one of his church members. Wade House was likewise accused of sexual sin. In that report, Norris wrote, "The question is asked, why didn't we give this out sooner?" Norris's only answer: "Wade House now has joined forces with the opposition."[4]

Many other men were similarly punished for aligning themselves with Vick. Loys Vess, the pastor of the church in Denton, was the subject of yet another attack. In that instance, according to Dowell, Norris sent a copy of the "false charges . . . to every person in the Denton phone book."[5] Then there was another oft-cited scandal involving Dowell's predecessor at High Street, Charley Dyer. In a letter to Dowell, Norris warned, "That case of Sodomy on the court record yonder at Phoenix, Arizona will shake the whole fellowship. They have the name of the 14 year old boy that Charley Dyer had in the park."[6] Although Norris's first published report about this incident does not mention Dyer by name, it does say that the accused is one of Vick's "lieutenants" and that "the name will be given upon request." The article also alleges that the minister involved has "a Court House record of sodomy with a fourteen year old boy."[7] What the article does not mention is the fact that the case had been closed and that Dyer had been acquitted of all charges.

Such underhandedness was abhorrent to Dowell, and he told Norris so in no uncertain terms. Writing on June 30, Dowell said:

> You know and I know that G. B. Vick is as clean and honest a man as there is in the country. And your attacks upon him are turning more people to us, by far, than anything else that is happening. I have never seen such a united church and such a happy people as I saw Sunday June 18 at the Temple Baptist Church in Detroit.
>
> In regard to what I consider your very unjust statement concerning Charley Dyer and the charge of Sodomy that was made against him. May I call your attention to the fact that at one time you were indicted for murder, but the court vindicated you. At another time you were indicted for arson, but the court vindicated you. The court in Phoenix, Ariz., vindicated Charley Dyer just as you have been vindicated in the serious charges made against you. I cannot imagine, Dr. Norris, you using such tactics. Charley Dyer is as clean a man morally as ever walked on shoe leather and it seems to me that it would be a very serious matter to make charges against a man whom the court pronounced not guilty.[8]

Even as Dowell was penning these words, however, Norris was preparing Dowell in his crosshairs. In the June 30 issue of *The Fundamentalist*, Norris repo a revival meeting in Lubbock, Texas, that was being led by Dowell's successor as president of the WFBMF, Harvey Springer. Dowell had originally been scheduled to lead that meeting, but after the split with Norris, Springer was asked to come instead. In Norris's subsequent write-up about the meeting, he bragged about Springer's "Great City-Wide Campaign" and then added a comment aimed at embarrassing Dowell: "Bill Dowell had been advertised and posters put up but his invitation was cancelled."[9]

Norris's attacks against Dowell grew sharper as time passed. On July 3, Norris wrote Dowell a letter stating:

> *You are going to have the busiest time you ever had explaining a certain matter in your conduct. Well, you will see it for I am going to publish it front page with abundance of evidence.*
>
> *I have two powerful radios and say what I please and I give it to you that the sky is the limit.*
>
> *When your record is published you will be the worst surprised man in the country. It is worse than the five immoral cases on record. You won't bellow any more when this record is published.*[10]

Then on July 7, Norris ran a boxed statement on the front page of *The Fundamentalist* containing this warning: "Most revealing article on Bill Dowell in next issue. It's worse than sins of the flesh."[11]

To these statements Dowell replied in a letter of his own:

> *Your threats to publish my record is laughable and I do not fear you any more than I would fear a field mouse. The reason is, because I am not ashamed of my record. I have lived a clean life and kept myself above reproach morally.*
>
> *For purposes of self-respect I shall not answer any more of your correspondence.*
>
> *Your cooked-up charges against honest preachers of the gospel do not deserve the attention of respectable people. All my efforts from henceforth will be put forth in the building of the High Street Baptist Church and the Baptist Bible Fellowship.*
>
> *I write this letter mainly to let you know that I am not afraid to face my record before God or man.*[12]

Whether or not that fearlessness was genuine, Dowell was determined to maintain his self-respect. So Norris attacked. In the next issue of *The Fundamentalist*, he landed several blows aimed at tarnishing Dowell's good name. One of these came in an article by Bob Ingle. With so many pastors now standing behind Vick, Norris's fellowship and school were facing a sizeable financial loss. For that reason, Norris's camp was quick to cry foul against the new fellowship wherever money was at stake. Ingle's article accused Dowell of purloining WFBMF resources. Specifically, Ingle lashed out at Dowell over a recent mailing Dowell had sent using the WFBMF mailing list. Ingle even intimated that the content of Dowell's letter had played fast and loose with the truth. It left churches with the impression, Ingle contended, that the missions office of the WFBMF was still located in Springfield and that funds sent there would still to support WFBMF missionaries.[13]

Ingle was right in assuming that churches had been confused. Although Dowell's mission office was no longer affiliated with the WFBMF and although Dowell had forwarded the old fellowship's records to Norris, all of the missionaries who had previously served in the WFBMF were now aligned with Vick and the BBF. Thus, the churches that wished to continue supporting those missionaries would need to continue sending their funds to Dowell's church in Springfield. And indeed, Dowell's letter encouraged them to do so. He wrote to them, saying, "We have adopted all the missionaries we have been supporting and we certainly do not want our mission work to suffer because of our 'house cleaning' activities at home."[14]

Dowell's letter had been aimed at eliminating existing confusion, but Ingle did not see it that way. Ingle asserted that Dowell's mailing represented a gross misuse of proprietary information (i.e., the names and addresses in the directory of the WFBMF). Ingle further alleged that Dowell's hidden purpose in all of this had been to divert support away from the WFBMF. In short, Dowell was a shyster.

To further support that charge, Norris added another indictment. According to Dowell, this charge surfaced soon after Dowell received an eleven thousand dollar check from the Temple Baptist Church. The check had been sent by Vick for the start of the new college in Springfield, yet Norris, who had not yet been discharged as the co-pastor of Temple, claimed that these funds had been earmarked for the Bible Baptist Seminary. According to Norris, Dowell had somehow misappropriated the funds, using them for a purpose that was never intended. Norris began making public statements threatening to expose Dowell's wrongful act in the same way that he had exposed Woodworth's misuse of the GI Bill funds.

Norris abandoned those efforts, Dowell said, after he learned that Dowell had received a letter along with Temple's check. The letter was from the deacons of the Temple Baptist Church, and it expressly authorized Dowell to use the funds for the Baptist Bible College. Dowell still had the letter in his possession when Norris began making his accusations, and Dowell challenged Norris to investigate for himself and see whether a copy of that letter was "in the files" at Temple. Dowell said Norris then promptly dropped the matter, realizing that he "was up a tree."[15]

But Norris was not finished with his attacks on Dowell. Another swipe at him occurred on July 20. This was when Norris wrote to Dowell notifying him that the honorary doctorate Dowell had received from the Bible Baptist Seminary was being revoked. To ensure the wound would be well salted, Norris published his letter in *The Fundamentalist*:

Dear Sir:

This is to notify you that your degree from the Bible Baptist Seminary has been canceled.

Investigation will prove that you did nothing to earn this degree but that it was given to you by Mr. Vick and he had no right to give this degree.

I am notifying the State Board of Education of Missouri of this cancellation.

Yours very truly,

J. Frank Norris[16]

Norris's most brutal attack against Dowell, however, was the one that earned for Dowell his nickname: "filthy lucre." Norris was fond of assigning embarrassing names to his enemies. Norris's successor at the First Baptist Church, Homer G. Ritchie, described this practice saying:

[H]e called various leaders in the new Baptist Bible Fellowship names so disgraceful that his antagonists considered them outrageous and even his friends felt them to be shameful. Among the infamous appellations were: 'Jezebel,' 'boot licker,' 'radio fraud,' 'Absalom,' 'traitor,' 'arch-conspirator,' 'deep freeze,' 'filthy lucre,' 'picket fence,' 'weeds and diapers,' and 'know all.' Each name related to some deed or attitude of his chief opponents. Norris considered this humorous; his enemies declared it was criminal and insane and many outsiders thought it was sad and tragic.[17]

Dowell earned his nickname for some supposed irregularities in his salary arrangement at High Street. A front-page article in *The Fundamentalist* on July 21 reported on a conversation between Norris and Vick several months earlier. According to this article, Vick told Norris that Dowell was receiving the entire Sunday morning offering at High Street as his salary, and that his earnings were now running "to many thousand dollars a year." Allegedly Vick also said that if Dowell did not put a stop to the avaricious practice, it would be his undoing. Here Norris chimed in with a pious comment for his readers: "We are thinking of that expression used twice in the first chapter of Titus, 'filthy lucre.'"[18]

The rambling paragraphs that followed this remark went on to present evidence aimed at shaming Dowell and stirring up as much trouble for him as possible:

Here's how it happened. When the church was organized it was small and the pastor then said he would take the Sunday offering for his salary. And through the years that method has been followed, and now there is a storm on in the church against the pastor, Bill Dowell, getting such a large amount.

This explains why Bill Dowell and his church have given such small amounts to the Seminary and to our mission work.

> Bill Dowell has told some people 'confidentially' that he is going to be called to the Temple Baptist Church.
>
> Maybe so.
>
> One thing is sure he is not going to break his back raising money for the new school.
>
> There are two sins which ruin the ministry and Beauchamp already has four or five that have one of them, and now Bill Dowell with the 'itching palm.'[19]

Over the next several weeks, Norris repeatedly alluded to the name "filthy lucre" as well as to Dowell's supposed greed. On July 28, Norris published an article by Bill Fraser that alleged Dowell was earning "$20,000 or more a year." Though this sum is paltry by modern standards, it far exceeded the average household income in 1950, which the US Bureau of Labor Statistics reports as $4,237.[20] Another article in the July 28 issue taunts Dowell with this statement: "Poor Bill, he is in a peck of trouble over taking the Sunday offerings of his church for his salary. So, nothing he says from now on will have any weight with many people. He had his engagement canceled on him at Lubbock."[21] Only a week later, Norris wrote to Dowell directly, saying, "You had no small stir in your church over being guilty of 'filthy lucre.'"[22] Then in the August 18 issue of *The Fundamentalist*, Norris again targeted Dowell, this time with two articles, one entitled "Poor Bill Dowell" and the other "Murder Will Out (Bill Dowell Confesses)."

Norris's attacks, by this time, were so becoming routine and belabored that the men of the Baptist Bible Fellowship were growing immune to them. Still, on August 2, Dowell made one last attempt to set the record straight. Norris was, at every turn, threatening to drag his adversaries into court and to force them to testify about their wrongdoings under oath. Dowell responded to this, saying it would be a welcomed opportunity:

> I had no intentions of answering any more of your correspondence but I am so happy I must write this word.
>
> I understand you would like for some of us to testify before the court. Since we were refused this privilege at your so-called investigation, I will be tickled to death to have that opportunity.
>
> I will also be glad to testify concerning the statement you made in the last *Fundamentalist*, that I receive all the Sunday offerings and it amounts to $20,000 or more a year. I will have the church records. I have been paid by check for many years and we have accurate financial records.
>
> Any lawyer will tell you that these false statements with intent to hurt are morally and legally libelous.
>
> I will also be glad to have you attempt to prove your charges against me which you state are worse than sodomy, adultery and other immoral crimes. We will let the court decide this.

It will also be interesting to present to the court a letter which I have from a lawyer in Phoenix concerning Charley's trial and also the testimony of the judge who tried the case in view of your rash accusations against Charley.

Yes, Dr. Norris when you get ready to subpoena me please do so for I am very anxious to testify.[23]

Dowell had faith that Norris's attempts to discredit him would, in the end, prove ineffective. And he was right. There were never any legal indictments or court cases. And as for the charges themselves, they were increasingly viewed as the unsubstantiated rantings of an irrelevant voice. When publication of the *Baptist Bible Tribune* began on June 23, 1950, Noel Smith used his newspaper to correct much of Norris's misinformation, a practice that Smith would continue for many months. For *Tribune* readers, these reports helped to dispel falsehoods and to prove that Norris's allegations were little more than propaganda. Smith also countered Norris's assaults with a great many barbs of his own. In one instance, Smith wrote with biting wit, "The other day we heard of a fellow who has from time to time, when somebody would listen to him, broadly hinted that he was to the religious world what Napoleon was to the political world. Which reminds us that every asylum has its collection of 'Napoleons,' and reservations are constantly being made for new arrivals."[24]

For his part, Dowell seems to have grown dismissive both of Norris and his accusations, and he expended little effort to wrangle with Norris any further. Years later Dowell did answer the charge of avarice, explaining that, while it was true that his initial income at High Street had been based on the offerings given during the eleven o'clock service, this policy had been implemented by Charley Dyer and had been changed at Dowell's behest. "I did not like the method," Dowell said, "and as soon as I could persuade the church, we changed it to a set salary." Dowell further claimed that his annual income in 1950 "amounted to about $8,000 a year."[25] Though this was a sizeable income for that time period, it was far less than what Norris's paper had reported, and both Dowell and his deacons knew it.

Something else that Norris seems to have wrongly assessed in 1950 was the strength of the men he was trying to assassinate. Norris once wrote to Dowell, "You little fellows have been so jealous of me—well it is pitiful."[26] Then in another letter, he wrote, "You fellows are just amateurs in a controversy."[27] Woodworth replied to Norris, saying, "I honestly believe you are one of the smartest men in many respects, living today. Your greatest weakness is underrating the abilities of others."[28] Rawlings seems to have agreed with that statement. Reflecting back on the events of 1950, Rawlings spouted, "[Norris] wasn't fighting pygmies whenever that thing took place."[29]

Dowell's boldness during that long summer may bear out the truth of Rawlings's statement. In a letter to Norris dated June 30, Dowell labeled his former mentor "a dictator who set himself up as lord over all." Dowell also said, "Dr. Norris there is one thing you must realize, and that is, people are not afraid of you any more."[30] Reg Woodworth observed a similar defiance in Dowell. After Norris published his accusations against him, Woodworth wrote to Norris, saying, "Bill Dowell has said if he had a record, he would rather confess it and ask God to forgive him for it than to live in fear of being blackmailed."[31]

Through these experiences, Dowell had discovered strength both to defy tyranny and to endure consequences. Dowell credited his wife Nola as one source of that strength. The book that Dowell wrote recounting the birth of the new fellowship was dedicated to her. Nola was a "special source of strength" during that "period of struggle," Dowell said.[32]

Norris, too, may have unwittingly played a role in strengthening Dowell for this fight. According to Vick, Norris's "biggest contribution" to many of the men in their movement was "his courage."[33] As Rawlings saw it, Norris's tutelage had ushered all of them into adulthood. "We were not pudgy-cheeked boys anymore," Rawlings remarked. "We were men, and we were standing on our own."[34]

But far greater than the strength that Dowell gained from his wife or his adversary was the strength that he found in his God. In one of the sharpest letters Dowell wrote to Norris, he quoted a verse from the fifty-fourth chapter of Isaiah: "No weapon that is formed against thee shall prosper; and every tongue that shall rise against thee in judgment thou shalt condemn. This is the heritage of the servants of the LORD, and their righteousness is of me, saith the LORD."[35] According to Vick, Norris himself often cited this verse, many times in questionable contexts. "Man, he used that [verse] to cover up more dirty work," Vick alleged. "Anybody else wasn't serving the Lord, you know. He had the corner on that."[36]

But as Dowell turned to Isaiah's verse in the summer of 1950, his faith in its promise was sincere. Norris's barrage of attacks would not prosper, Dowell believed, and in the end, Almighty God would provide vindication. This was the heritage of any true servant of the Lord. Dowell carried on, trusting in those words. And the enduring fruit of the Baptist Bible Fellowship may be the greatest evidence that Dowell's faith was rightly placed.

Chapter 26: *A Diploma Worth a Continental*

The man behind the desk wore a pencil-thin moustache that seemed frozen in place, like something drawn on a department store mannequin. The man's eyes, too, appeared lifeless. Dowell hoped this glare was not an indication of some kind of ill will. Just in case, Dowell put on his best smile and stepped confidently into the man's office. As he did, he attempted to break the ice, saying:

We sure appreciate your meeting with us. This is Reg Woodworth, our business manager. And I'm W. E. Dowell, pastor of the High Street Church in Springfield.

Woodworth followed right along behind Dowell, and he politely nodded to the man as he slipped into one of the seats in front of the man's desk. Woodworth then began digging in a briefcase. Dowell was not quite sure what Reg was searching for, perhaps some documentation that would help them make their case. In any event, Dowell continued:

We understand your office handles matters pertaining to the GI Bill of Rights?

The man's mustache seemed not to move as he spoke:

That's one of the things we do, yes.

Dowell kept smiling:

Well I'm very pleased to hear that—

Woodworth interjected:

Yes, sir. Hate to waste a trip, you know.

And before Dowell could say more, Woodworth was in a conversation all his own:

It's about a three-hour drive up here from Springfield. Did you ever get down our way?

I can't say that I have.

Oh my goodness. You've missed one of the most beautiful parts of Missouri. Especially the hills down around Branson.

I'm sure.

Woodworth's face was still buried in his briefcase. He glanced up only occasionally as he continued chatting. He was busy pulling out documents and setting them on the edge of the man's desk:

Do you like to golf?

A cup of pencils was resting near the place where Woodworth was piling his stack of documents, and the man behind the desk slid the cup out of the way. As he did, he replied rather humorlessly:

No, I'm not much of a golfer.

Woodworth took no notice of the man's disposition. He carried on, saying:

Oh that's too bad. I understand there's some good courses down our way. Of course I'm still new to Springfield myself, but Bill, here, is an excellent tour guide. Took us all over town when we went looking for the right place to set up our college.

I see.

Didn't you, Bill–?

Dowell didn't get a chance to respond because Woodworth kept going:

Oh, and the place we got is a beauty–the place where we are setting up our college, I mean. It was a city park before. You'd be amazed what we got it for. Had to talk 'em down. They wanted sixteen thousand, but we only had eleven, so that was our price.

In the years to come, the Canadian-born R. O. Woodworth would become one of the most beloved personalities on the campus of Baptist Bible College. The school's cafeteria was eventually named in his honor. Like a good meal, he was the sort of man who put a smile on people's faces, even if at times they felt ashamed of themselves for having enjoyed the experience so much. When Woodworth died in 1998, Bill Dowell Jr. described him, saying, "He worked a crowd as a master by playing the role of a bumbling, forgetful clown. But he was far from that."[1] David Stokes recalled a day in Woodworth's Personal Evangelism class when a young man was asked to lead in prayer, and then, in the midst of his prayer, Woodworth interrupted him, saying, "YOUNG MAN, STOP PRAYING RIGHT NOW!" The large class of students was "stunned," Stokes said. But then Woodworth went on to explain the error that the young man had made in his prayer: "Never pray for God to use you," Woodworth commanded, "pray for God to make you useable."[2]

According to Dowell Jr., Reg Woodworth had a certain "depth" and "passion" and an admirable "understanding of Scripture." In his description of Woodworth, Dowell Jr. said, "He had a brilliant mind. He was well read. His thoughts and insights were profound." Many of Woodworth's students would agree. Most who knew him would recall his remarkable capacity for memorizing and quoting long passages of the Bible. Yet Woodworth quoted other sources as well. Mark Twain presented a speech in 1899 in which he famously said, "I was sorry to have my name mentioned as one of the great authors, because they have a sad habit of dying off. Chaucer is dead, Spencer is dead, so is Milton, so is Shakespeare, and I'm not feeling so well myself." When Woodworth borrowed the comical statement for his sermons, he replaced Twain's list of authors with names like Abraham, Isaac, and Jacob. But Woodworth, like Twain, always got a laugh.

Sitting in that Kansas City office, Woodworth now lowered the lid of his briefcase. When he did, the end of his tie got caught. But no matter; he carried on his monologue uninterrupted even as he began working the tie free like a master clown:

We've already built us a dormitory on that property. Can you believe it? We should have brought him a picture of it, Bill. I didn't even think about that until just now. But, oh, it's a beauty. And it practically had to go up overnight because we only started working on this thing last May. But you see, when God is in a work, it shall come to pass!

On September 5, 1950, Baptist Bible College (BBC) opened its makeshift doors on the site of a former city park. The $11,000 check that Dowell had received from Detroit's Temple Baptist was used to purchase the land. The original asking price for the property had been sixteen thousand, but since eleven was all they had, the men successfully negotiated to get a lower price.[3] The rest of that summer was then spent transforming this property into a college. There was plenty to do behind the scenes as well, completing forms and submitting applications. As was reported in the *Springfield Daily News*, the college obtained its tax-exempt status near the end of June:

> A *pro forma* decree of incorporation was granted yesterday to founders of the Baptist Bible college (sic) to be opened here in September.
>
> The decree, granted by Circuit Judge William B. Collinson, allows the school to operate as a non-profit, tax-exempt, educational institution.
>
> The school is being moved to Springfield from Fort Worth, Tex., following a split among churches of the Fundamental Baptist sect.
>
> R. O. Woodworth, business manager of the new college, said 150 applications already have been received from prospective students.
>
> The college site is a five-acre tract at Kearney and Summit.[4]

Much work was left to be done when BBC opened in September. Even so, leaders of the fellowship considered their efforts that summer a remarkable success. Noel Smith ran in the *Tribune* a photograph of those present for the school's opening day ceremonies, and in the accompanying article, he wrote, "The picture you see across the top of this page, and extending clear across the top of the back page, is that of the faculty and student body of the Baptist Bible College, which opened—as it was announced that it would open—Tuesday morning, Sept. 5. There are 110 of these students from 12 states."[5]

The same issue of the *Tribune* identified BBC's seven faculty members and six special instructors.[6] The names included many of the fellowship's key leaders: Vick, Dowell, Earl Smith, Noel Smith, Woodworth, Donnelson, Zimmerman.[7] Dowell was tapped to serve as the chairman of faculty and was also assigned to teach the Pentateuch. The school's classes would be divided between the Sunday school space of the High Street Baptist Church and a set of surplus barracks that were brought over to the campus from the O'Reilly Veterans Hospital.[8]

Meanwhile students lived and slept in a new two-story dormitory.[9] A contractor in Dowell's church, James Brackley, constructed the building that summer for the sum of fifty thousand dollars.[10] Woodworth, too, because of his background in contracting and construction, became instrumental in the project's completion. Funds had not yet been raised for the project, so Dowell and Woodworth managed to secure financing that would allow the construction to go forward. Vick, in particular, wanted the dormitory ready by opening day. Such a building would serve as a "rallying point," Vick believed, convincing naysayers that the Baptist Bible College was really coming into existence.[11]

Perhaps more than anyone else, Vick wanted to convince J. Frank Norris. Norris's propaganda machine had been cranking out weekly attacks aimed at ensuring potential students would want nothing to do with the new college. *The Fundamentalist* belittled everything about the school, from its faculty to its facilities to its home town. In the June 23 issue, Norris wrote:

> The proposed new school will have an army barracks outside of Springfield. What sanitation will they have!
>
> Springfield is a small town, about one-fourth or one-fifth the size of Fort Worth, and there will be little chance of employment of the students, and that is a very vital matter.[12]

Woodworth tried to answer such pooh-poohing in a June 30 *Tribune* article, though he may have done more harm than good. Woodworth bragged about the great progress that the college was making, comparing the institution to an infant that was "growing like a weed" and "outgrowing his diapers."[13] Of course, this only served to fuel Norris's ridicule. Thereafter Norris mocked Woodworth, nicknaming him "Weeds and Diapers."

As Norris continued his weekly slams, the primary focus of his attacks became the matter of accreditation. On June 9, Norris responded to the news that Vick's camp was trying to launch a new school by saying, "That's their right, but they can't start a Seminary with Government recognition."[14] For Norris, the matter of governmental recognition was his ace in the hole. His seminary had it, and Vick's did not. And as Norris was quick to point out to anyone who would listen, without accreditation, the veterans enrolled at BBC would be cut off from their GI Bill benefits.

When Dowell had originally spoken to the group assembled at the Texas Hotel, he had told them that their prospects for obtaining veterans benefits looked very good. A summary of Dowell's report appears in the minutes of that meeting:

> Rev. W. E. Dowell called the V. A. Office and told them that we were thinking in terms of building a school, and if we should locate it in Springfield, what procedure we should go through in order to get G. I. subsistence for the boys. He received a report that all we need to do is go to Kansas City and get a contract drawn up. Several of Wendell Zimmerman's church members are working in the V. A. Office in Kansas City.[15]

But by the following fall, the hopes expressed in that original report remained unfulfilled. Indeed, every effort to secure veterans benefits had failed. And without those benefits, keeping the college's doors open was going to be next to impossible.

Dowell finally managed to get a word in, and this was when he tried to steer the conversation back on course. He looked at the man behind the desk and said:

Well, as we were saying, we have just opened a new college in Springfield—

Woodworth interjected:

And already we have over a hundred students enrolled. Can you believe that? Brand new school.

Dowell tried to keep going:

And we've been looking into getting benefits for our veterans—

Woodworth again:

A pastor friend of ours, Wendell Zimmerman, has some folks working in this building. Have you met Wendell?

The man shook his head. Dowell spoke once again:

Anyway, it's our understanding that there is some sort of waiting period now for new colleges. Is that so?

The man with the moustache was leaning back in his chair with his arms folded. He replied most matter-of-factly:

That is correct. The ruling came down from Washington, you understand. Any institution seeking benefits is to have been in existence for at least a year.

Dowell now hoped to appeal to the fellow's good sense:

Well, that's quite a concern for us because, I'll tell you, we have just about as fine a faculty down there in Springfield as you'll find anywhere. Many of us have taught previously. And until this year, the president of our school was president of another school down in Fort Worth—where many of our guys are now coming from—and that school down there has full GI benefits—

Woodworth tapped his fingers on the pile of papers sitting on the desk:

I've got our documentation if you want to see it. Our English teacher taught at the University of Greece before the war, if that gives you any idea of the kind of training our students are going to receive.

Dowell resumed:

But it would sure bring a hardship to some of our folks—not to mention the college—if they had to wait a whole year to be eligible for their benefits.

Dowell, in his book *The Birth Pangs of the Baptist Bible Fellowship, International*, recalled this early crisis. He summed it up, saying, "One of our problems after Baptist Bible College had been opened was getting support for our veterans. . . . We had a great number of veterans the first year, and they were having a rough time." Dowell went on to explain that the source of the trouble was "a government regulation [that] stated a school must be in operation for one year to be eligible for veteran support."[16] Such a waiting period was going to prove disastrous for the fellowship's fledgling college. Even Norris knew that. Norris wrote a letter to Dowell on June 16, saying, "You can't give a diploma worth a continental."[17] And throughout that summer, Norris did his best to convince the rest of the world that he was right. A front-page headline in the June 23 issue of *The Fundamentalist* read "Why No New Creditable School Can Be Established." In a different issue Norris wrote, "Unless a school is recognized by the government, the

GI boys will get no support. All the 'promises' that they are will be a delusion to the boys."[18]

But Norris did not stop there. As he reasoned with his readers and radio listeners, he told them that this matter could affect their students' futures in ways that went far beyond paying for college. There was still much unrest on the world stage. Indeed, North Korea, with the backing of China and the Soviet Union, would invade South Korea on June 25 that same summer. With so much turmoil around the globe, Norris openly wondered how long it would be before the US would once again be pulled into a war. And more to the point, he speculated that the US might soon resume drafting men for military service. If that happened, Norris said, being enrolled in the wrong Bible school might have serious ramifications, for only those enrolled in a state-recognized seminary would be exempt from military duty, he explained. Then with a note of contempt, Norris added, "No students in a Bible Institute will be exempt."[19]

Norris's ruthless efforts to undermine the new college seemed to know no end. He bragged to Dowell in a letter: "Bill, you have known something about me. I have won every fight I have ever been in." Norris was now making every effort to win this one as well. One such effort was the opening of a rival school in the city where many of Vick's students were living: Detroit. "Now a matter of information you will be interested in," Norris wrote to Dowell. "I am going to start a full fledged Seminary in Detroit and have already secured the permission of the Federal authorities for this branch Seminary, and we will give full degrees like we give here."[20] Norris then published his plans for the branch school in *The Fundamentalist* on July 7.

Later that same month, Norris tried another tactic. He published an eye-witness account aimed at exposing the embarrassing state of affairs at the school in Springfield. Among other things, the article stated that the facilities purchased from O'Reilly Veterans Hospital were "where the tubercular patients had been housed." Norris also reported that the college was situated in the "colored" section of town "five miles from the High Street Baptist Church."[21]

In Dowell's opinion, this article was not only factually incorrect (e.g., the site of the campus was less than a mile from Dowell's church), it was also an unabashed exercise in muckraking. And Dowell knew exactly who was holding the rake. Though the article was written by one of Norris's allies, Bill Fraser, Dowell was sure that the impetus for the report had been Norris himself. Just before the article was published, Fraser had come to Springfield—unannounced—and had behaved quite peculiarly. Indeed, Fraser had attempted to gather information from Dowell's assistant, Zellota Sage, under an assumed name. Sage offered to notify Dowell that he had a guest, but Fraser declined the offer. "I didn't particularly come to see him," Fraser told Sage. "I know he's busy. I just wanted to come to the church and so forth." Fraser may have expected Dowell's reception to be as cold as the one he had been given by Earl Smith. When Smith caught Fraser snooping about the college property, Smith told him, "Bill, . . . the only difference between you and a skunk is the skunk has got a white streak down his back."[22]

Sage, too, recognized a skunk when she saw one. She also recognized Fraser's face and knew that he had given her a bogus name. "No, Brother Dowell would be very disappointed not to see you," Sage told Fraser with a polite smile.[23] And over Fraser's protests, Sage then went ahead and buzzed Dowell in his office.

When Dowell emerged from his office, he recognized immediately that Fraser had come on an errand for Norris. But Dowell decided not to turn this encounter into a confrontation. Dowell wanted to take a different approach. He greeted Fraser with every ounce of courtesy he could muster, first chatting with him in the church office and then taking him out for supper. As part of their dinner conversation, Dowell made sure to ply Fraser with plenty of good news about the progress of the college.

Dowell said Fraser had a ready explanation for his unannounced visit. He was passing through on his way to start a revival meeting in Indianapolis, he said, and he was waiting for a train connection. Dowell pretended to believe the story, and he used it to his advantage. Upon hearing that Fraser was waiting for a late train, Dowell replied, "Well, you have plenty of time then to go to church."[24] Dowell was in the midst of his annual tent revival, and he insisted that Fraser come to the tent that night as his guest. Dowell wanted Fraser to get a firsthand look at the great meeting that was then underway. Professions of faith during that three-week meeting would total 112, and the church would also glean 127 new members.[25] If Fraser intended to inform Norris about the happenings in Springfield, Dowell wanted to make sure he had a good story to tell.

After that evening's service, Fraser left the tent and slipped back to the train station, Dowell said, allegedly to catch a train to Indianapolis. Meanwhile Dowell and Noel Smith went out to get a late-night snack. They met at a restaurant near the train station, one of the few places in town that was still open, and there they enjoyed some pie, some coffee, and a few laughs at the expense of Bill Fraser. In the midst of their conversation, however, Smith and Dowell heard an announcement from the train station. The Texas Special, the train that regularly ran to Fort Worth, was now boarding. This sparked an idea. "Come on, let's go," Smith said to Dowell. Then as quickly as the two men could pay their bills, they exited the restaurant and shot over to the depot. And when they arrived, they found Bill Fraser, suitcase in hand, making his way onto the Texas-bound train. It was just as they had suspected.

Dowell was now relishing the fact that Fraser had been caught in a lie. He could not resist making the most of the opportunity. Running up to Fraser, Dowell offered the poor fellow a bit of advice: "Bill, you're about to make an awful mistake, here. . . . Remember, you're going to Indianapolis to start a revival meeting. This is the Texas Special that goes to Fort Worth." Fraser's face instantly reddened, yet he never changed his course, Dowell said. He proceeded right onto the train. "And, oh, he got so mad."[26]

As Dowell sat in that Veterans Affairs office in Kansas City, he now wondered if he might soon be the one wearing a red face. Dowell nervously drummed his fingers on the official's desk as he advanced the conversation:

So many of our boys courageously served in the war, you understand. And now for them to find out that they cannot receive the benefits due them—for a whole year—I'd just hate to see that happen, wouldn't you?

Woodworth did not wait for the man to reply. He chimed in, saying:

And with the state that this country is currently in, I'd say we can use all the preachers we can get. Every last one of 'em. If anything, the government ought to do more for Bible colleges than they do for anybody else. We're giving these boys the most important training in all the world.

Hearing that, the official's thin mustache now moved for the first time:

You say you've got a Bible college?

Woodworth answered before Dowell got a chance:

One of the finest in the land. Or it will be. We just have to get all our ducks in a row, as they say. But you should know that we are one of the most mission-minded groups around, and our boys—and our young ladies, too—they're going to go out and really do something. You mark it down.

At the beginning of this conversation, Dowell had been struck with a bad feeling. The official sitting across from him and Woodworth had "seemed cold," he said, and he had responded "almost mechanically." Even so, Dowell and Woodworth had pressed on. "Dr. Woodworth and I had really prayed about this trip and had claimed God's promises," Dowell explained. In the end, Dowell said he simply stepped out by faith: "I looked at the gentleman across the desk and asked, 'Isn't there some way around the one-year rule?'"[27]

This was when God intervened. Describing the moment, Dowell said, "I saw a smile come upon his face and he answered, 'Yes, as of this morning.' He reached and picked up a telegram and said, 'I received this this morning, and the government has exempted certain schools from this rule, and listed among them are theological schools.'" The seemingly insurmountable obstacle was instantly gone. "God had answered our prayers," Dowell wrote, "and Baptist Bible College received veteran support retroactive from the opening day of school."[28]

Woodworth shot off a letter to Norris at about this same time. "I am afraid you are a poor prophet as well as a poor guesser," Woodworth wrote, "because not one thing that you have predicted concerning our school has come to pass."[29] It was true. The doors of the Baptist Bible College were open, and they were going to stay that way for many years to come. Indeed, fourteen of the students in Noel Smith's opening-day photograph transferred in as seniors and would form the college's first graduating class, the class of 1951.[30] This was the first of many such classes. In fact, the college would outlive all of its founders, including Woodworth and Dowell.

As for J. Frank Norris, he never reconciled with the men who parted ways with him in 1950. Moreover, some who aligned themselves with him during the split later regretted it. According to Vick, Jock Troup, Vick's successor at the Bible Baptist Seminary, continued working for Norris for a time, yet he too began to challenge Norris's directives. In response, Norris "got in touch with the immigration authorities." Reportedly, when Troup first came to America, Norris had assured the Scotsman that there was no need for concern about his legal status. "I'll fix it up with the authorities," Norris had promised. But he never did. And when Troup "wouldn't do everything Norris wanted him to, then he turned him in and he was deported," Vick explained. Authorities gave Troup two weeks to leave the country. "That broke his heart," Vick claimed.[31]

Despite such continuing strife, Norris's church and seminary managed to survive, though their continuation may have been aided by the fact that Norris himself quickly passed off the scene. In August 1952, while ministering in Jacksonville, Florida, J. Frank Norris collapsed and died. He was less than a month from his seventy-fifth birthday. According to Norris's successor and biographer, Homer G. Ritchie, "The disappointment of broken friendships followed Norris to the grave."[32]

Vick, Dowell, and the others would not greatly mourn Norris's death, though they did maintain a sincere respect for what Norris had accomplished. Vick remembered him as "a brilliant man" as well as a great preacher.[33] "I couldn't hold a candle to his preaching," Vick once said.[34] Another original member of the BBF, Curtis Goldman, called Norris the "Father of Fundamental Baptists" and "the greatest pulpiteer that I have ever had the pleasure of hearing." Goldman added this: "Truly J. Frank Norris was a GOOD man and a GODLY man and a GREAT man; but also JUST A MAN!"[35] With similar equilibrium, Joel A. Carpenter, in his work *Inside History of First Baptist Church, Fort Worth, and Temple Baptist Church, Detroit*, calls Norris a "magnetic and disturbing leader."[36] That dual assessment seems incontrovertible.

At the same time, Norris must be credited for his influence on the leaders of the Baptist Bible Fellowship. Although these men ultimately left him, they had spent formative years under Norris's leadership. Vick contended that Norris had done what Second Timothy instructs; he had committed the gospel "to faithful men who are able to teach others also."[37] If that is so, then it seems fair to say that the work which emerged in Springfield was on some level a continuation of Norris's efforts—only without Norris. These "heirs" of Norris's fundamentalism, as Carpenter characterizes them, were "Fervently separatist in ecclesiology, and ultraconservative in theology and politics." And like Norris, they too became highly influential. Carpenter goes on to note that, as late as 1988, their ranks represented "a large portion of the new religious right's base of support."[38] Such was the legacy of J. Frank Norris.

Dowell, of course, played a role in carrying Norris's legacy forward. And especially in the early days of the fellowship, that role was considerable. High Street Fundamental Baptist Church played host to the fellowship's first meeting in September of 1950, and though Dowell's church was pushing attendances of two thousand in the fall of 1950, the movement that he was presiding over was still relatively small.[39] Vick said those early fellowship meetings drew between one hundred and one hundred and fifty pastors. They were "cattle huddling together in the storm," Vick said.[40]

Within a quarter of a century, however, the size and influence of the Baptist Bible Fellowship would grow considerably. In 1973, Vick described the BBF as "the strongest force . . . for uncompromising, militant Christianity—I mean, evangelistic soulwinning Christianity of the twentieth century. . . ."[41] Some might dispute that assessment, but history certainly shows that the BBF left its mark.

The strength of this movement, from a human standpoint, emanated from the exceptional individuals who were a part of it. Vick continued as president of BBC and as pastor of Temple Baptist Church until his death in 1975. For most of those years, he traveled down to Springfield from Detroit one week out of the month to attend to the business of the college.

The rest of the time Woodworth ran BBC. "Vick and Woodworth were like Moses and Aaron," Rawlings said.[42] Woodworth, in addition to serving as business manager, influenced students through his teaching of courses like Personal Evangelism. According to a college catalog, Personal Evangelism was designed to teach students "how to use the Scriptures in leading men to Christ, enabling [them] to give a Scriptural answer to the excuses and arguments of the lost."[43] Woodworth brought just the right skill set to such a course.

Noel Smith was another important contributor to this movement. Smith served as a member of BBC's faculty as well as the editor of the *Baptist Bible Tribune* until his death in 1974. John Rawlings remembered Smith as "One of the great intellectuals of the twentieth century."[44] Former student Doug Kutilek called him "the philosopher, the heart and soul of the BBF."[45] And so he was.

Then there was Fred Donnelson. Donnelson was the BBF's original mission director. He also headed the mission department at the college until his retirement. Under Donnelson's leadership, this movement sent out groundbreaking missionaries like Frank and Elsie Hooge to the Philippines and Lavern and Evelyn Rodgers to Japan. In time, Donnelson's mission department would also produce such workhorses as Bob and Helen Hughes, missionaries to the Philippines, and Elmer and Mary Deal, missionaries to the Belgian Congo. Hundreds of other BBC graduates likewise saturated the globe with the gospel, fulfilling Donnelson's dream of making mission work the strong right arm of the BBF.

Wendell Zimmerman and John Rawlings, two of the college's original trustees, went on to carry out other fellowship responsibilities. Zimmerman became the second editor of the *Baptist Bible Tribune*, and Rawlings served for twenty years as the vice president of BBC.

Dowell himself served a two-year term as the first president of the BBF; he later served a second term, beginning in 1962.[46] Dowell also continued in his position as the chairman of BBC's faculty, where he served alongside men like Ford Harper, the soft-spoken dean of men. For many years, Harper and his wife, Elsie, lived and served on the ground floor of the boys' dormitory.

Dowell worked closely with Kenneth Gillming as well. Gillming joined the faculty of BBC in 1954. Gillming went on to serve as both the chairman of the Theology Department and the dean of Education.[47] When Dowell first got acquainted with Gillming, this mild-mannered twenty-nine-year-old was finishing up his graduate training at Dallas Theological Seminary. He was also looking for work. Gillming had written to Vick in November of 1953 seeking a teaching position, but he never received a reply. Then in the early months of 1954, Gillming met up with Dowell while Dowell was visiting the Castleberry Baptist Church in Fort Worth. Gillming told Dowell about the letter that he had sent to Vick, and Dowell encouraged him to write to Vick a second time. Gillming took the advice, this time mentioning Dowell by name. That second letter resulted in Gillming's twenty-eight-year tenure at BBC.[48]

Elmer L. Towns published a book in 1970 entitled *The Ten Largest Sunday Schools: And What Makes Them Grow.* Towns said he researched forty-two different denominations in creating his list.[49] The results of his research surprised even him. "Six of the Sunday Schools among the ten largest are listed in the yearbook of The Baptist Bible Fellowship, Springfield, Missouri," Towns said.[50] Towns went on to reveal that five of those BBF churches were averaging more than three thousand in attendance, and he said only two other churches in America shared that distinction.

What made the BBF so unique? Vick thought he knew. When this question was posed to him in 1974, Vick responded, "[W]e're trying to [instill] drive and verve and punch into these preachers so that they'll not be satisfied with doing a mediocre job." Vick's interviewer probed further: "So you think you have a bigger vision?" In answer to this, Vick nodded. "I think so. I think so." Vick then added, "And I think that actually spells a large part of the difference."[51]

Dowell considered himself fortunate to have played a role in casting that vision. And in the decades that followed, nothing gave Dowell more satisfaction than to watch the vision of the BBF become a reality. Indeed, Dowell ended his 1977 book on the birth of the Baptist Bible Fellowship with a note of celebration. In those remarks, Dowell credited the Lord for the successes. Yet he also acknowledged the instruments through which the Lord had done the work. "The Baptist Bible Fellowship was formed with a group of independent, Bible-believing Baptists with convictions as deep as the soul," Dowell wrote. He then brought his book to a triumphant close:

> These men had one purpose, one motive, and one goal. They were in full agreement that their movement must be completely a separatist movement. They believed in the absolute sovereignity (sic) of the local church. They were against any form of ecclesiasticism; (Dr. Donnelson's statement was, "Every church the headquarters of world missions.") yet they believed they could work together on a voluntary basis and build a school, establish churches, and fulfill Christ's commission in building a program of world missions. This they have done, and are doing. This, God has been pleased to honor and bless. To Him be the Glory![52]

PART 4: AFTERNOON

Chapter 27: *Beacons in the Night*

*D*usk already.

Dowell had reached the top of a hill, alone. He was studying the amber sky and muttering to himself:

And I didn't get a single one of 'em.

Dowell was a better fisherman than he was a hunter. He did love the outdoors, though. And when friends from the church invited him to join them for an outing, he was quick to say yes.

Dowell noted the dark valley below him.

One thing's for certain, I'm not going to be seeing any more quail tonight.

The empty-handed hunter let out a sigh.

Best be getting back to camp before it gets any darker.

Dowell turned and headed back down the hill that he had just climbed. In the daylight, the Ozark Mountains were a beautiful sight to behold, but at night, the thick, golden forests on those hills lost their luster. Dowell, now walking alone, could feel the darkness creeping over him, and it was not at all pleasant. He paused when he reached the bottom of the hill and said:

Pretty sure I came from up over there–

Dowell climbed another hill just in time to see the sun dip behind the distant ridge. A moment later he was swallowed by shadows. He spoke a quiet prayer:

Lord, I don't suppose you'd want to do me like you did ol' King Hezekiah?

This, of course, was a plea for some additional daylight, but Dowell was not counting on any Hezekiah-sized miracles.[1] In fact, he was beginning to feel a bit uneasy. He recounted the emotions of the experience in one of his sermons. "I had been quail hunting," he said, "and I waited a little too late to start back to camp. And it began to get dark and I found myself in a strange, mountainous, wooded area. I didn't know which way was north, south, east, or west."[2]

Sure would be good to see something familiar, Lord–anything.

But there was nothing. Dowell was lost. "[I]t was a terrible experience," he said.[3] As the shadows lengthened, the preacher had to ward off a full-blown panic.

There's gotta be a way out of this mess.

That was when an idea came to him. "I finally thought of a plan," Dowell said, "and I put my gun up and shot it."[4] Dowell relied on his fellow hunters to do the rest. Before long, he "heard a shot in the distance." It was the fellows at the camp. They had heard his distress call and were now guiding him through the dark with shots of their own. Dowell said this gunshot communication continued until he finally found his way back to safety.

Dowell's hunting story could serve as a metaphor for the kind of ministry that he conducted during the 1950s. In this metaphorical version, however, Dowell would no longer be the lost hunter. Instead, he would be the one stationed safely by the campfire. The High Street Baptist Church was now thriving, the Baptist Bible College was training students, and the new fellowship was alive with excitement. So as Dowell warmed himself near the blaze of such blessings, he used his new sphere of influence to fire into the air as many beacons as possible. This, of course, made a lot of noise, yet all such efforts were aimed at guiding the lost to safety.

Dowell became Springfield's first TV preacher in 1953. That is when Springfield got its first television station, KTTS-TV (later known as KOLR).[5] Dowell contracted with the station to begin broadcasting High Street's eleven o'clock Sunday morning service live. Then by October 1953, another station had been launched: KYTV. Dowell also signed a contract with that company. Dowell's second program, a half-hour Saturday evening broadcast called *Crusade for Christ*, was likewise live, but it was produced at the television station instead of the church. This program featured, in addition to Dowell's preaching, many of High Street's musical talents.[6]

Dowell developed a love-hate relationship with the television medium. In sermons he sometimes referred to the television as the "boob box." A person had to do a lot of "knob turning" to find decent programming, he alleged. "I have one in my home," Dowell confessed, "but I wish it had never been invented."[7] Even so, Dowell had been eager to take advantage of the medium when this technology first emerged. If a television broadcast meant that his message would have a broader audience, Dowell was all for it. After all, what he had to say was not just for the saints of the church; it was for the whole world. Quoting Proverbs 14:34, Dowell once proclaimed, "'Righteousness exalteth a nation, but sin is a reproach to any people.' I wish that could be inscribed in letters of gold and flashed over every major city in the United States."[8]

As Dowell entered his second decade at High Street, his efforts to denounce sin intensified. Admirers thought of him as "the conscience of Springfield."[9] Dowell was never ashamed of the stands he took on moral issues. He told an audience in 1976, "I know a lot of people like preachers who are soft-spoken, easy-going, very careful not to offend any kind of a Christian." Dowell acknowledged that he was not that sort of a preacher. And in Dowell's opinion, this put him in good company. "Jesus wasn't that kind of a preacher," Dowell told one audience. "He said, 'You generation of vipers, you are like whited sepulchers.' Did He mean to insult them? No, He meant to shock them out of their lethargy and get them to realize where they stand."[10] Dowell, too, wanted to shock people out of their lethargy.

This preacher's moral battles were wide-ranging. Some made headlines; others were barely noticed. Some battles were waged alongside fellow warriors (commonly Pastor Bill McTeer of Springfield's South Side Baptist Church); others were fought alone. Dowell's foes in these conflicts were likewise diverse. Dowell spoke out against the sale of beer at the fairgrounds and against the false teachings of faith healers at the Shrine Mosque. In March of 1952, he challenged local gambling houses. Reportedly, a "jammed" auditorium listened as Dowell stood at his pulpit and identified the "names and addresses" of individuals who were running these illegal gambling operations.[11] Kenneth Gillming recalled another group that Dowell wrangled with, a team of businessmen who wanted to bring a nudist colony to the area. Gillming said Dowell "found out who they were and openly challenged them to close it or he would publicly divulge their identity." Gillming added, "It closed."[12] Dowell's denunciations were so effective and intimidating that when Springfield opened a new high school in 1958, the principal of the school, an acquaintance of Earl Smith, took the preemptive measure of contacting Smith. "Now, sometimes the PTA will sponsor dances," the principal said, "but I don't want you and Brother Dowell down my throat."[13]

This principal had good reason to be concerned. One of Dowell's best known crusades had been mounted against a city-sponsored street dance. That dance was part of a two-day celebration welcoming President Harry S. Truman to Springfield back in June of 1952. Dowell's city had been selected to host the annual reunion of a famed military unit, the 35th Infantry Division, and Truman, who had served as an artillery captain during World War I, was among the division's veterans.

In celebration of Truman's arrival, Springfield's city leaders pulled out all the stops. Although the reunion itself would be a private gala held at the Shrine Mosque, Truman would be in town for two days and would be making public appearances both before and after the reunion dinner. Truman's visit also reeled in some 250,000 spectators, people who would line the streets for a peek at the president.[14] Event organizers shut down several streets; put up red, white and blue banners; and hosted a city parade. According to a local news report, city officials also sponsored "a double-barreled street dance held in the Public Square and on Commercial Street."[15]

This big dance was held Thursday, June 5, the night before Truman's arrival. Many of the visiting guests were already on hand, including movie stars Ronald Reagan and Nancy Davis. These celebrities blew into town to promote the premiere of their new film, *The Winning Team*, at a downtown theatre. When their flight landed, Reagan and Davis stopped by the square to make an appearance at the dance. Dowell and the High Street Baptist Church were there as well, though it goes without saying, they were not dancing.

When Dowell had originally learned about the city's dance, it had struck a nerve. In fact, on the Sunday before Truman's arrival, Dowell took out a full-page newspaper ad to denounce the event. In his ad Dowell cited a passage from Job 21 that speaks of children dancing. Dowell went on to declare that "God condemns the dance and every informed person knows that dancing leads to a break down of morals in many instances [sic]."[16]

Dowell's objections were not just about the ungodliness of the jitterbuggers, however. He was also criticizing a perceived inequity. "On one occasion the city was asked to rope off the square for a short period of time for singing of Christmas carols," Dowell explained in his ad, "but the verdict was 'We cannot afford to tie up traffic.'" Dowell pounced upon the double standard: "They could not afford to tie up traffic for the singing of Christmas carols and honoring the Christ Child for one hour but they can afford to tie up traffic for several hours of revelry in honor of a man."[17]

In addition to running this advertisement, Dowell mobilized his forces to show up to the dance. These High Streeters would bring more than the usual street evangelism, however. Summoning up the church's large youth group, Lee McLean coordinated an unsanctioned parade of automobiles through the streets surrounding the square. The windshields of these vehicles were decorated with ominous Bible verses (such as "Prepare to meet thy God"), and as the young people circled those downtown streets, they rolled down their car windows and sang out a grim warning from a familiar hymn[18]:

There's a sad day coming,
A sad day coming;
There's a sad day coming by and by,
When the sinner shall hear his doom:
Depart, I know you not!
Are you ready for that day to come?[19]

While these efforts were largely overshadowed by the excitement of a presidential visit, many in Springfield did take notice. Dowell's unorthodox methods were giving him an increasingly visible presence in his city. This was a preacher who was unafraid to confront immorality, and virtually everyone knew it.

Dowell took another strong stand a few months after that street dance, this time against lewd literature. In 1952, such literature gained national attention when Arkansas Representative Ezekiel C. Gathings formed the House Select Committee on Pornographic Materials and launched an investigation into lewd paperback books, comic books, and magazines. Gathings maintained that the widespread distribution of such works was posing a problem for the nation and that censorship at the federal level was needed.

When Dowell heard reports of Gathings' efforts, he joined the fight at the local level. Dowell ran a newspaper ad promoting a Sunday night sermon entitled "Four Urgent Needs in Springfield." In the ad, Dowell promised, "The Matter of Filthy, Leud [sic], Obscene Literature Being Sold In Springfield Will Be Dealt With."[20] Dowell then preached this fiery sermon on December 7. In his message, he denounced local merchants, the smut that they were selling, and the city officials who were allowing all of it to go on.

Dowell also took another step. He contacted Police Chief Frank Pike to urge him to enforce the law and to stop the sale of these materials. Dowell encouraged other concerned citizens to do the same. And soon thereafter, Dowell said, he got a call from Chief Pike. The chief requested that Dowell bring him copies of the materials he was concerned about.[21]

Dowell obliged this request (though the preacher was quick to point out that he did so "in the presence of many witnesses"[22]), and within days, two local newsstands, distributors of the objectionable literature, came under intense scrutiny. Springfield's mayor, Nathan Karchmer, was among the critics. A news article on December 9 reported, "Mayor Karchmer came out against 'lewd, lascivious and mischievous' books at City Council meeting this morning."[23] Other city leaders joined in, calling the confiscated works "obscene"[24] and declaring them "detrimental to character building of young America."[25]

Initially, then, it looked as though Dowell had won a victory against the sale of lewd materials. But then officials began to discuss next steps. Mayor Karchmer, who had oversight of the city's police force, wanted to avoid a law enforcement quagmire. He explained to the city council that "qualified persons are needed to rule on such literature so that expert witnesses would be available to back up the police department after arrests are made."[26] To meet this need, Karchmer wanted to form an "advisory committee," a citizens group that could assist police in rooting out corrupt materials. Yet this proposal was rebuffed by Revenue Commissioner J. Oliver Gideon and City Attorney Gerald Gleason. These men had reached the conclusion that the war on lewd literature was "impractical legally." In defense of their position, Gideon stated, "It's just as ridiculous as appointing a board to check enforcement of dog licenses."[27]

Dowell was a spectator at the city council meeting on the day that these wranglings occurred, and when public comments were heard, Dowell stood up to add his own two cents. He argued that Karchmer's advisory committee was altogether unnecessary. Dowell pointed out that the city already had an ordinance in place calling for "the arrest of anyone selling lewd or licentious literature plus a fine."[28] All that was needed, Dowell said, was for police to take action and to enforce the existing ordinance. Despite these pleas, however, the meeting ended in a stalemate. Some leaders wanted to drop the matter altogether; others wanted to find a workable solution to the problem that Dowell had identified.

At the next city council meeting, Mayor Karchmer again pushed for the formation of an advisory committee. Karchmer hoped that someone else on the city council would make a motion for its formation, but when no one did, Karchmer temporarily turned over his chairman's position to Mayor Pro Tem Ray Brown so that Karchmer could offer the motion himself. According to a newspaper report, however, this effort did him little good. No one offered a second to Karchmer's motion, so after a "highly dramatic" silence, the motion died on the floor.[29]

Dowell was on hand for these deliberations as well, and by this time, Dowell was growing impatient with the bureaucratic nonsense. He stood up once again to address the council, saying, "I'm pleading with every member of the City Council in the name of common decency . . . to take some action to rid the city of this filthy, lewd literature." In further remarks, Dowell called upon Chief Pike to uphold the existing ordinance and to confiscate the material that was being sold. Other concerned citizens offered similarly impassioned appeals. Yet according to the *Springfield Leader and Press*, the "sharpest blow" was struck by one of the men on the council, Health Commissioner D. E. Caywood. Caywood "read a prepared statement strongly criticising Karchmer for not enforcing the present ordinance covering lewd literature [sic]." As Caywood explained, "We have been informed through our city attorney that there are ordinances and statutes presently in existence which, when properly enforced, will bring a quick end to the public sale of this objectionable material. It seems to me the duty is clear."[30]

Bowing to pressure, then, Karchmer authorized Chief Pike to proceed with efforts to confiscate the objectionable materials. He also authorized Pike to bring charges in municipal court against the distributors of the literature. Thus, on December 19, charges were filed against Paul W. Jeffries of the American News Company, and brothers Adolph and Leo Forbstein of the Ozarks News Agency. The men were charged with violating the city's lewd literature ordinance, and a trial for their case was set for February 3 and 4. News reports referred to this trial as a "test" of the city's ordinance.[31]

At the beginning of January 1953, Dowell underwent a surgery to have his gall bladder removed. He was out of the pulpit for the next several weeks. In fact, following his doctor's orders, Dowell left Springfield to convalesce. He was still out of town when the lewd literature trial got underway, though many other Springfieldians were watching its developments.

During the first day of the trial, Judge John Levan heard two hours of testimony. Prosecutors entered into evidence four magazines—*Frolic*, *Beauty Parade*, *Wink*, and *Titter*—as examples of the corrupt materials that Dowell had unearthed. On the witness stand, Chief Pike was asked to name what he found objectionable in these publications, and he responded, "They don't have enough clothes, I'd say, on in the pictures."[32]

Defense Attorney Ronald Stewart had plenty to say in response to that. On the second day of arguments, Stewart spoke for nearly an hour in defense of pornography. To make his point, he offered up a health magazine, a book on modern art, and some other works possessing content that paralleled the pornographic works. The city's ordinance was flawed, Stewart reasoned, because it did not draw a line between lewd works and permissible works. Nor did it allow for the fact that such a line would be different for different people. "If you deprive all of us of what is not good for some [of] us, you'd have to do away with things like alcohol, tobacco, and labor," Stewart said, "We'd have to close up shop."[33]

All these arguments had been concluded by the time Dowell returned to Springfield in mid-February, but Springfield was still awaiting a decision from Judge Levan. Dowell read news reports to catch up on the court's proceedings. And one of those reports left him outraged. Chief Pike in his testimony had identified Dowell as the individual who had requested the confiscation of the offensive materials. Then, according to the news article, Defense Attorney Stewart had seized on Dowell's absence. Turning to the judge, Stewart had smirked, "I'd say he handed the police and the court a hot potato and then ducked out on it."[34]

Dowell was so incensed by the comment that he called Stewart to set the record straight. "The fact is I had undergone a major operation and at my doctor's orders was out of town convalescing," Dowell explained.[35] Dowell said he then told Stewart "that since he was the one who made the slanderous, unjust statement before the court, which was published on the front page of the newspaper and given out over the radio station, that I felt that he owed me an apology."[36] Dowell also wanted Stewart to contact the newspaper and to issue a retraction.

Stewart initially told Dowell that he would consider the idea, Dowell said, but no such retraction ever came. Indeed, when Dowell followed up with the lawyer a few days later, Stewart said "he had no regrets of what he had said or done in handling the trial and did not feel that he should make such a statement." So Dowell decided to publish a correction himself. He wrote up a five paragraph explanation and sent it to the *Sunday News and Leader* for publication. "At no time was I ever informed that I would be called as a witness," Dowell's article stated, "but had I known about the trial and had been physically able to appear I would have been most happy to have done so. And should the opportunity present itself in the future, I would be more than happy to respond."[37]

Dowell's rebuttal may have served to salvage his honor, yet it did nothing to help the city win its case. On February 17, Judge Levan dropped all charges against the newsstand operators. Another news report summed up the ruling: "In a four-page typewritten opinion, Judge Levan said that he believed 'that the decision belongs in a higher court.'" Levan further stated, "There might have been an easier way out. . . . I could have found them guilty and let them appeal to circuit court. But I call the shots as I see them."[38] Levan added that parents, not city government, hold the key to protecting young people. "[C]hildren properly trained at home would ignore poor literature in favor of a better class of reading for their education and enjoyment," the judge opined.[39]

Dowell was disappointed by Levan's decision, yet he remained undaunted. On the following Sunday night Dowell continued the fight, preaching a message entitled "The Lewd Literature Trial—Common Decency and Bible Prophecy." Dowell held nothing back:

> *God has prophesied that in the last days men are going to give themselves over to the lust of the flesh. They are going to become lawless, dominated by lust; and indeed in this hour in which we are living today, illegitimate perverted sex is the order of the day. Man, who has for nearly two thousand years heard the gospel, had the light shining around them, had opportunity after opportunity to honor God, to receive Jesus Christ, to walk in the light as He is in the light; but having rejected that light, having resisted that light, their judgment has become warped and their foolish heart darkened. That is why the spirit of this age is, 'Do not legislate against anything. If you legislate against it, it will only create a desire for people, out of curiosity to do it.' . . . If this is true, then God made a mistake when He gave the Ten Commandments.*[40]

Dowell's sermon went on to denounce many of the key individuals in this case. He called out the city council for being so slow to act. "The Mayor wanted to do it, but the other councilmen didn't," Dowell said. "[T]hey want to turn all the dances loose on the street, let them do as they please; they want to uphold all of that sort of filth, but they don't want any gospel preached on the streets of Springfield and that has been proven a fact."[41]

Dowell also condemned Defense Attorney Stewart, not only because he "did not have the moral courage nor the manhood" to correct the false accusations he had made about Dowell, but also because he "had the audacity to stand there and try to justify those who are handling this filthy, lewd literature in Springfield, and [to] list some books which he said were 'worse than the books under question." With obvious disbelief, Dowell then posed a question to the audience:

> And then, do you know what he listed? You do if you read the paper. He listed the King James Version of the Holy Bible! I have it in print right here before me.
>
> Oh, how far has man gone from God and from moral character that he will place the Bible alongside such filthy, lewd literature and make such a comparison just to win a case.[42]

Finally, Dowell expressed criticism for the judge in the case:

> Do you know what would have been fine? If our judge, (and I was disappointed in him, for I have always looked upon him as a real Christian gentleman, and I still think he has a lot of sincerity about him)—but if he had said, 'Well, no matter what the higher court does, this law says that every obscene, lewd, licentious book, picture, or other publication of indecent character is a violation of the law to be sent through the mail, and these things were sent through the mail. I am going to find these men guilty, and if they appeal to a higher court and are found not guilty, then the guilt is on their hands; I have delivered myself.'"[43]

Dowell reasoned that even a verdict that was later overturned might have had a positive influence. "If a few local judges would take their stand," Dowell said, "it might have some effect on the higher courts . . . ."[44]

Dowell followed up this attack with a story about a different judge:

> I got a very interesting letter this week. It is from a judge, believe it or not. He made it plain that he was not writing in the capacity of a judge but rather as one interested in cleaning up his city. He saw a write-up about this lewd literature campaign in the Kansas City Star. He says, 'I write asking for information about your recent effort to ban certain magazines. We are interested here in getting some 25 and 30c pocket books off the prominent displays in stores all over this

country, but have made little progress by voluntary means. Would you mind writing me the names of the magazines that you especially objected to in your campaign, and whether any merchants in your city cooperated in your efforts; also what stand does the Ministerial Alliance or Council of Merchants Association take?[45]

Dowell ended this story gleefully. "I am glad there is a judge that is interested in cleaning up!" Dowell exclaimed. "I am going to give him all the information he wants."[46]

Even though Dowell's moral fights would never rid the world of its corruption, Dowell believed these efforts did put corruption on notice. He also felt that, following his lead, other individuals would find new courage to stand up against evil. And in that knowledge, Dowell continued his fights, confident that he would be able to look himself in the mirror the next day. "What shall we do?" Dowell asked his audience in response to the lewd literature verdict. "Well, I'm going to carry on the fight. I don't know what you are going to do. God is my judge; the people are my witnesses; and my pulpit is my jury room! I shall continue to lift my voice against this indecent, immoral, suggestive, perverted literature until something is done about it, or at least until God calls this preacher home and says, 'Well done, you did your best.'"[47]

The same individualistic spirit can be found in many of Dowell's battles. His skirmishes with Springfield's Drury College serve as further examples. Those clashes started as early as February of 1949. That was when Dowell took aim at the college in one of his sermons. Drury was a liberal arts college but was also touted as a Christian institution. And for several months preceding his attack, Dowell had been reading reports about Drury that he considered disturbing. First, a visiting speaker at the college had claimed that "in order to learn what part of the Bible is true and what is not true, it was necessary to study many years and acquire a knowledge of Greek and other languages." Then in another published report, Richard Pope, dean of Drury's School of Religion, was quoted as saying he "had no way of knowing whether he had had a personal experience of salvation or not." Then a Christian student on the campus, Dottie Kallenbach, published a statement in the *Drury Mirror* critical of the institution and declaring that "she had found little evidence of Drury being a Christian college."[48] And finally, there were nagging reports that Drury's faculty were proponents of dancing. Dowell could be silent no more.

Dowell responded to these matters by announcing in a newspaper ad his plans to discuss an unnamed "Christian college" in his evening sermon February 27. In his ad, he posed some biting questions, which left little doubt which college he planned to talk about: "Should a Christian college have a dean of Bible religion who has not had a definite experience of Salvation?" "Is a Bible teacher in a college who endorses dancing the right kind of spiritual leader for young people?" "Should a school that sponsors dancing and fosters modernism be called a Christian school?" "What should saved students attending such a school do?"[49]

Not surprisingly, a contingent of students and faculty from Drury were on hand to hear Dowell's sermon. At least one local news reporter was also present. "Dowell Raps Drury College in Sharply-Worded Sermon" ran the headline in the *Springfield Leader and Press* the next day. According to the article, Dowell's "blast" of the school included the charge that its teachings were "'the essence of modernism.'" Dowell also chided "professors who sit in colleges and tell young people they don't need to be saved from Hell." In particular, Dowell targeted the dean of religion, saying, "If Dean Pope is what he ought to be, he'll come out with a public statement: 'I have been saved. I do feel that people need to be saved from Hell through revivals.'"[50]

Dowell's barbed remarks drew the ire of many in the community. Some of their hostility erupted even on the night that Dowell delivered his sermon. Drury students attending the service attempted to interrupt as Dowell was speaking, though Dowell said the disruption was short-lived. "Some of our men went over real quickly and popped them down and said, 'You just keep your seat,'" he recalled.[51]

Less anticipated, perhaps, was the angry response that Dowell heard from members of Springfield's religious community. One congregation reacted to Dowell's remarks by publishing an open letter to Dean Pope in the *Springfield News and Leader*: "By enthusiastic, unanimous and standing vote the church board of Central Christian Church reaffirms its absolute confidence in you and in your work." In the same statement, the church's leaders summarily dismissed Dowell and his antics, saying, "His only source of information is second, third, or fourth hand information supplied by immature minds that have been disturbed by the process of growth." To this was added, "A minister of the Gospel has the moral obligation of checking his facts and determining at first hand the truth of his statements before broadcasting them from the pulpit."[52]

While Dowell found such criticisms surprising, he never let them diminish his resolve. The charge that he had misrepresented the facts was baseless, he said, because all of his claims had been taken from published reports. Indeed, Dowell believed his remarks had been vindicated by a conversation one of his men overheard between two Drury students as they exited High Street's service. One of the students accused Dowell of lying, and in reply, the other student spoke up and said, "What that preacher said tonight was true, and you know it's true."[53]

But whether Dowell's listeners approved or disapproved, this preacher had no intention of ceasing such efforts. Indeed, Dowell would wrangle with Drury often in the years to come. Of note was Dowell's condemnation of the college for hosting Swedish-American theologian Nels F. S. Ferré as a guest lecturer.[54] Dowell railed against Ferré's teachings from his pulpit at High Street, and those remarks were subsequently published in the campus newspaper, the *Drury Mirror*. Indeed, Dowell said he received a handwritten letter from Ferré after those charges were published:

> He started the letter off by saying, "Dear Brother Dowell," said, "I want to commend you for the manner in which you gave your exposé of me. . . . One could not read it without knowing that it was from the heart of a true pastor who

was concerned for the welfare of his sheep." . . . *But in that same letter, in that same letter, Mr. Nels Ferré said, "There was a time when I believed exactly what you do about the Bible as the verbally inspired word of God, about Jesus Christ, His virgin birth, His deity, about the cross, and all the rest of it." Said, "I learned it at my mother's knee." But said, "After going to college and seminary, I had to give up what I at one time conscientiously believed and accept the philosophy that I now follow."*[55]

Dowell said he reached out to Ferré once more in a personal letter of his own, but that this correspondence was never answered. And in spite of Dowell's urgings, there was never any evidence that Ferré turned back from his heresies.

Dowell could not turn a blind eye to such heresies. Ferré "stood against everything that was fundamental," Dowell alleged. "He also commended Communism." So Dowell spoke out. He employed Ferré's own writings to substantiate his charges against him. Among other things, Ferré called into question the infallibility of the Bible and the virgin birth, Dowell said.[56] "If you're not acquainted with Nels Ferré," Dowell explained in one sermon, "he wrote a book, he wrote several books, but in one of these books that he published, he said that in all probability the father of Jesus was a mercenary soldier, that it was a very common thing for young people who lived near army camps to get in trouble morally. And that's the way he explains the birth of Christ." Dowell's disdain for such a teacher could not be masked: "Brethren, he'll not preach in my pulpit, as long as I have anything to say about it."[57]

This was ever the case. Dowell's sharpest attacks were reserved for those who undermined the Word of God. Dowell illustrated this again in the fall of 1952 when he responded to the publication of a new Bible translation, the Revised Standard Version (RSV). "It aims to correct old errors and clarify obscure usages, without losing the dignity of the King James language," a news report said. This monumental publication was the culmination of "a 15-year project, backed by 40 denominations." A million copies immediately went to the presses, "the biggest first edition in book publishing history." Newspapers announced, "American Protestants have a new Bible."[58]

Dowell himself would not soon be jumping on the bandwagon. On Saturday, October 4, Dowell published an ad announcing his plans to preach about the new translation the next day. "QUOTATIONS FROM NEW BIBLE WILL BE READ," he warned.[59] In his sermon, Dowell then called the new translation "a blatant attempt of the Devil himself, through his false prophets, to confuse and deceive and discourage and tear down that firm foundation that we sang about a little while ago."[60] Dowell also said he was alarmed that copies of the new Bible were "selling like hotcakes" because he considered the work "a deliberate attack, carefully planned, upon the Word of God itself—a plan to discredit the fundamental truths of the Bible." He added, "[T]here is nothing that is more serious than that."[61]

As promised, Dowell then proceeded to itemize the many concerns he had about this new translation. "What is wrong with this Bible?" he asked. "First of all, this Bible was put out by the National Council of Churches, whose leaders deny the deity, virgin birth, blood atonement, bodily resurrection and second coming of Christ. Don't you dare say that they do not deny it; their words are in print. I have copies of their sermons, their books, their publications."[62]

Dowell went on to show how such views had colored their translation. In Isaiah's prophecy, for instance, the statement "Behold, a *virgin* shall conceive" had been replaced with, "Behold, a *young woman* shall conceive." Dowell responded, saying, "I can understand why they want to take 'virgin' out of the Bible—because they don't believe in the virgin birth, and they don't want you to believe it."[63] Dowell also laid out evidence to show the problem with such a translation. "But the word *almah*," he said, "which is used here in Isaiah 7:14—and appears only three other times in the Old Testament—always and without exception means a virgin—a pure, unmarried female. It means that in every place it appears."[64]

Dowell's other criticisms of the RSV were wide-ranging. He found fault with some of the pronouns that this version uses for Christ and for the Holy Spirit. He noted omissions of phrases like "shall not perish" in John 3:4 and "through his blood" in Colossians 1:14.[65] He further objected to changes like the one found in Matthew 27:54, wherein the centurion's declaration—"Truly this was *the* Son of God"—becomes "Truly this was *a* son of God." Dowell's response: "Listen, I am a son of God, but I'm not the Son of God."[66]

Yale Divinity School, which was closely tied to the RSV's publication, collected historical documentation about the efforts to prepare this new translation. The library also archived the public's reaction to the work. Dowell's sermon, which was subsequently published as a pamphlet, exists as a part of that collection. Dowell would be pleased to know that his criticisms had been heard. In his view, the flaws in this translation posed serious threats to the doctrinal integrity of the church, leaving him no choice but to speak out. "God's preachers must re-affirm our faith in the Bible as the literal Word of God," Dowell once said. "There can be no compromise on the issue of the complete authenticity of the Word of God. We must believe all of it, or believe none of it."[67]

Dowell did believe, and he wanted others to believe as well. Furthermore, he wanted people to live out their beliefs and to stand for what is right. Preaching before his church in 1953, Dowell cried out:

> *What we need is an old-fashioned, heaven-sent, Holy Ghost revival that will wake up our churches—the dead, cold, formal churches, and wake up the church people, so that they will have the courage of their convictions to stand up on their hind feet and roll up their sleeves in the old-fashioned John-the-Baptist manner and stand for the truth of the Word of God and for common decency.[68]*

Not everyone who heard such cries would respond to them, of course. Yet many did. And those individuals not only heard the hunter's shots but also rallied to them, moving ever closer to the fire of God's holiness. Something else occurred as well. Dowell's listeners soon began taking up shotguns of their own, pointing them into the air and, one by one, squeezing the triggers. Inspired by Dowell, these followers began reaching out to others with hope for a darkened world. Suddenly Dowell's shots were reverberating all across the night sky. Indeed, as Dowell himself would discover, those echoes sometimes rang longer and louder than his initial blasts. But that was just fine with him. In fact, nothing could have pleased him more.

Chapter 28: *Enduring Fruit*

Dowell sat leaning over his desk. An open Bible lay in front of him. Scattered next to it were a ballpoint pen and several sheets of paper.

Brother Dowell?

The preacher was hunched over and did not see his visitor enter.

Yes?

At first he tried to answer without lifting his head. The gravitational pull of his deep Bible study was hanging on his eyes.

I was wondering if you had just a minute.

Finally the preacher was able to break free from his concentration.

What? Oh, how ya doing, Shirley? What brings you here?

Dowell's visitor was a girl of about seventeen or eighteen. She wore a bright smile on her face and giggled a bit when she spoke.

Just thought I'd stop by.

Dowell chuckled a reply:

Well, good for you!

Dowell suspected there was more to it than that, yet he played along. And after a moment, his nervous young guest told him everything.

I wanted to tell you my news.

What news?

About my dad and all.

Oh? What about him?

Dowell was surprised that Shirley had any news on the subject of her dad. Mr. Wayland had been dead for several years. Wayland and the rest of his family had moved up to Springfield from Arkansas when Shirley was eleven years old, and Dowell had known Wayland only a short while before he passed away.

In Arkansas, the Wayland family had attended a church of about two hundred and fifty people. So when they arrived in Springfield, the Waylands tried out a modest congregation located over on Glenstone Avenue. But then on their second Sunday in town, Shirley's father decided to give High Street a try. Shirley admitted that she had been "taken back" by the size of it. After the service was over, she asked her father where they would go to church the next week. That was when Wayland told his daughter, "We have found our church home."[1]

A short while later, Shirley's father was in Heaven. He died "suddenly" and "at a very early age," Shirley recalled. She also remembered the comfort that was afforded her family by her new church home. "Dr. Dowell and the members of his church put their arms around my family and helped us through one of the most difficult times of my life," she said.[2]

Well, you see, Brother Dowell, I just got back from a visit down to Arkansas.

Shirley was older now, but she had not forgotten those days following her father's death. In a way, she felt like she was seeing her dad every time she looked at her pastor. And remembering her father always made it easier for Shirley to talk to this powerful preacher.

Dowell answered her:

Arkansas? Is that where you've been? Did ya have a good time?

She nodded eagerly.

Yes. And I just had to tell you what I found out.

Shirley had struggled with a lot of emotions after her father was taken from her. Nothing could have seemed more unjust. "My dad was the most wonderful man in the world," she recalled. In fact, at the age of fifteen or so, the still-grieving daughter found herself puzzling over a verse of scripture from Exodus 20: "Honour thy father and thy mother: that thy days may be long upon the land which the LORD thy God giveth thee." The words baffled her. "I didn't know anybody that honored his mother and father any more than my dad did," she explained.[3] So the burdened girl made an appointment to talk to her pastor about what was on her mind. In that meeting, Dowell had not pretended to have all of the answers, Shirley said. He did, however, comfort her, assuring her that God was both wise and righteous. "[Y]ou probably won't know until years go by," Dowell told her, "but there's some way that the Lord used your dad's death for his glory."[4] These words helped to ease the young girl's mind, and she held onto them.

Several years had now passed, and the teenager now leaning over the edge of Dowell's desk no longer seemed to need comforting. Indeed, she was beaming.

You see, I know what it is!

The preacher's eyebrows lifted.

What do you mean?

She answered:

I know how God used my daddy's death!

After that, Shirley related to Dowell the story of how, during her trip to Arkansas, a man had come up to her. The man was someone her father had known. In fact, Mr. Wayland "had testified" to this man "quite often," Shirley said.[5] But to no avail. The man had remained an unbeliever.

Things changed after Shirley's father died, however. The suddenness of Mr. Wayland's departure had sparked in this man a new appreciation for the testimony that Wayland had shared with him. So sometime later, the man accepted Christ. "And my dad's death made him realize that he needed to become a Christian," Shirley marveled.[6] In this way, a chance meeting in Arkansas, several years after her father's death, had demonstrated to this girl the truth of Dowell's assurances as well as the reality of her Heavenly Father's love. She would never forget either of these.

Far more vital to Dowell's ministry than broadcasts, newspaper headlines, or controversies was his personal connection with people. Every sermon he preached touched the lives of real people, people with concerns and questions, people for whom Christ had died. Dowell learned that his ministry could have lasting effects on such lives. It certainly did for Shirley Wayland Hackler. She remained a lifelong member of High Street, and for many years, she served as a key member of the secretarial staff at Baptist Bible College. Writing in 2006, Hackler said, "To this day High Street is my church, and I will always be grateful to Dr. Dowell for all of the guidance I was given as a young lady growing up in his church."[7]

During the 1950s and 60s, Dowell was making such personal connections on a grand scale. Some of those connections involved men of renown. Dowell held frequent conferences with Jack Hyles and John R. Rice. He also interacted with preachers like W. A. Criswell, Lee Roberson, and Robert T. Ketcham. Yet Dowell's greatest influence seems to have been with ordinary church members and Bible college students. Indeed, through television and radio broadcasts, Dowell sometimes touched the lives of people that he never even met.

Springfieldian Eldon Harmon recalled watching Dowell's program on a Sunday morning in 1960. Harmon and his wife Faye attended a different church, but their infant son was sick that day, so Harmon sent his wife on to church, and he stayed home with the baby. Dowell's TV program aired as usual that day, but Dowell was not the featured speaker. Instead the morning message was delivered by "a converted Jew," Harmon said. The man shared his testimony, and in the process, he also presented the gospel. Then at the end of it all, Dowell "got up and gave the invitation," Harmon recalled. It was then that this young father sensed an inaudible voice speaking to him in his living room and saying, "Look what He's done for you." Harmon said his spiritual eyes were suddenly opened to the reality of Christ's sacrifice. "That's when I realized that I was truly lost," Harmon said.[8] So as a result of Dowell's television broadcast, Eldon Harmon gave his life to Christ. Harmon went on to serve for many years as a deacon in Dowell's congregation.

Such lifelong friendships were made possible because of the gospel, but they were also the result of Dowell's efforts to prioritize people. Souls mattered. Speaking in 1957, Dowell confessed that he had recently been "a little late getting to church" because he had a call to make at "the home of an unsaved man." Tardiness was of no consequence, Dowell determined, if a man's eternity was at stake. Dowell went on to relate the rest of that experience:

> *I had the privilege of opening my Bible and showing him the plan of salvation. As he got up off his knees, with the tears streaming down his cheeks, falling off on the floor, and a smile upon his face with something of Heaven in it, he reached*

over, took me by the hand, and said, "Brother Dowell, I'll thank you through all eternity for taking the time to come here and tell me about Jesus." Then he began to praise God for the new experience that had come into his life. I'll tell you, though I was a little late for church, I didn't have any trouble preaching that night. It put some fire in me. I stood and told that audience about that in the very introduction of my message and the people began to weep, and the power of God came and other souls were saved that night at the close of the service.[9]

Dowell made a habit of prioritizing people. Eldon Harmon recalled an incident that occurred after his children were in high school. Dowell was by then pastoring a different Springfield church, Baptist Temple, a congregation that also operated a Christian school, and the Harmon children were enrolled in Dowell's school. But then, due to some misbehavior, Harmon's eldest daughter found herself on the verge of being expelled. In fact, according to Harmon, some members of the school board were eager to take that action.

It was Dowell who prevented his men from making a hasty decision. Instead, Dowell called for a disciplinary committee to meet and discuss the matter. What impressed Harmon most was the extra effort that Dowell made to be present for that discussion. Harmon later heard from one of the secretaries at BBC that Dowell had instructed her not to let him miss that meeting. Dowell was a busy pastor, evangelist, and college administrator, Harmon noted, but somehow this girl's predicament had become a priority for him. "He had other things to do," Harmon observed.[10] For Harmon, Dowell's extra concern made a real difference. Indeed, Harmon credited Dowell's influence that day with keeping his daughter in school and making it possible for her to graduate. The gesture was not soon forgotten.

Dowell's concern for the needs of individuals left a lasting impression upon them. And no doubt this quality also contributed to Dowell's success as a minister. His concern came through when he preached, and many lives were changed as a result. Dowell long remembered a meeting in Akron, Ohio, in which God used him in an extraordinary way. He was there for a revival meeting at the Akron Baptist Temple pastored by Dallas Billington. On the last night of the meeting, Dowell finished his "simple message" and invited the audience to stand to their feet. Then as he looked over that vast sea of faces, he began to weep. "It's time for countless numbers of you that are unsaved to make your way to this altar and get right with God," he told them. And as an invitation song began, Dowell observed a mighty moving of God's Spirit. In an instant, the aisles were filled "from the back to the front," he said, with people seeking salvation. "No use giving an invitation," Dowell shrugged. "Dr. Billington and I sat down on the platform for forty-five minutes and watched them come. I never knew how many. I never saw so many folks come to an altar in my life. And I never felt so helpless. The service was taken out of our hands. The power of God moved upon that audience."[11] Dowell could not help but celebrate. "Dr. Dallas Billington and I just sat and wept and rejoiced and laughed and watched them come."[12]

This preacher thrilled to see such large numbers responding to his message, but it was always the individual that mattered most to him. He relished being the one to introduce people to Christ, just as his brother Ernest had done for him when was a boy. Dowell knew that, after meeting Jesus, they would never be the same. He recalled one woman who attended a meeting that he held in Rock Island, Illinois. She "was the wife of one of the department store owners there in the city," Dowell said. "She came down with all of her expensive fur coats on and bowed down on her face at an old-fashioned altar and wept her heart out and accepted the Lord Jesus as her savior." Then afterward, with "tears streaming down her cheeks," she came to shake hands with the preacher. "And she said, 'I just want to thank you for saving me today.'" This statement gave Dowell pause. "I think I knew what she meant," he said, "but I wanted to be sure. I said, 'Well, ma'am, I appreciate that, but you know I didn't save you.'" The woman's response made Dowell realize that "she understood a little more than [he] thought she did." She said, "Oh, I know that, Preacher. I don't know religious words. But you're the one that brought me the message and told me about the One Who did save me."[13]

The privilege of carrying such a message was something that Dowell never took for granted. And he did his best to live up to the responsibility. Dowell conducted another revival in 1952, this one held in Lynchburg, Virginia. It was an unlikely place for a mighty moving of God, yet Dowell called it "the greatest revival I ever conducted in my life."[14] The meeting was held at the Park Avenue Baptist Church, then pastored by Paul Donnelson. Donnelson's church was only three years old, and it was not nearly as large as High Street or many of the other churches that Dowell frequented. A former member of Park Avenue said it was "running about three hundred at the time."[15]

Even so, this congregation put months of planning and effort into the upcoming revival meeting. They hoped to build on the momentum of Dowell's first visit to their church, a revival that he had held back in June of 1951. By the end of that original meeting, the church had seen 103 people added to their congregation. The church was hoping that Dowell's return visit scheduled for September 6-19, 1952, would yield even greater fruits.[16]

Among the members of Park Avenue that year was a recent convert named Jerry Falwell. Falwell was a second year student at Lynchburg College. In January, Falwell had attended Donnelson's church and, at the age of eighteen, had accepted Christ as his savior. Falwell then became an active member of Park Avenue. He even recalled joining in the efforts to prepare for the upcoming revival meeting, though Falwell himself knew nothing about the evangelist. "[W]e would meet every morning before school," Falwell explained. "We were all heading off to different schools. We'd come by as young people and meet in the pastor's office for prayer for that revival beginning about March when the preparations were beginning."[17]

The young people did more than pray, however. "After school, and weekends, and nights we would knock on doors, carry out leaflets, invite people to a meeting months later in September," Falwell continued. "[W]e knocked on just about every door in that city. . . ."[18] The church even purchased advertising on local billboards, something that eventually caught the evangelist's attention. Dowell had never before seen his picture on a billboard.

Such efforts made it evident that this church wanted the Lord to do something extraordinary in their town. And the Lord did not disappoint. As it happened, Falwell himself attended none of that revival meeting. By the summer of 1952, God had directed this young man to give up his studies at Lynchburg College and to transfer to the Baptist Bible College in Missouri to study for the ministry. Falwell left for Springfield at the end of August, departing from Lynchburg before Dowell's revival ever began. In fact, Dowell's and Falwell's paths crossed along the way. Falwell left Lynchburg in time to attend a national fellowship meeting that was being held in Cincinnati, and Dowell attended that same meeting on his way to Lynchburg. Though both of the men were present in Cincinnati, they never met.[19]

When Dowell reached Lynchburg, he was not well. He did not know why. Four months later he would have his gall bladder removed, but for the moment, all Dowell knew was that he was sick. "[E]very night during that revival I would sit in the office just as white as a sheet, so sick I was almost afraid to go to the platform," Dowell said. "They'd go down to a drug store nearby and get some medicine, bring and give it to me and try to calm me down—my stomach." Dowell said he would hold off going into the auditorium for as long as he could. "I'd walk out on that platform after they'd sang for awhile," Dowell said, "and I'd take my Bible and open it and preach my heart out for about fifteen minutes. That's about as long as I could preach."[20]

By that time, of course, Falwell was in Springfield. But Falwell said he phoned home every night during Dowell's revival to get the latest news about the meeting. And the reports he heard left a lasting impression. "The town was shaken, and God mightily moved," Falwell recalled many years later. "The fact was that they just had a Holy Ghost visitation." To this Falwell added, "Never have heard of a local church meeting in a church that size with comparable results."[21]

Dowell too was amazed. In his weakened state, the strongest invitation that Dowell had been able to muster was this: "If you want to be saved, come on and meet us here at the altar." Yet despite his lackluster appeals, people responded. "[E]very night fifteen, twenty, thirty, forty people would just break loose from that audience and make their way down to the front and fall on their face," Dowell said. "In just a few nights we had over 202 saved and great numbers came into the church and the whole city was moved by the power of God."[22]

For Dowell, the fruits of that revival also included a lifelong friendship with Jerry Falwell. When Dowell returned to Springfield, he found an eager nineteen-year-old ready to join his church. "My pastor had already told me to join High Street Baptist Church because Bill Dowell was the pastor," Falwell admitted. "And so the first Sunday he was back, I did."[23] For the next several years, Falwell was a part of Dowell's congregation, observing Dowell as he reached out to the world around him on television, on radio, and in the pulpit. "I remember Bro. Dowell speaking out against the liquor industry," Falwell once said, "He made a great impression on me."[24] On another occasion Falwell remarked, "He quickly became my mentor and hero."[25]

Falwell learned many things under Dowell. "I will never forget my first Sunday at High Street Baptist Church in Springfield," Falwell wrote in his autobiography. Falwell said he experienced a rather uncomfortable feeling as Dowell was preaching that day. "I was only four to five days into my Bible College experience," Falwell said, "when Pastor Dowell opened the Bible to Proverbs 3:9 and preached on tithing." As it happened, Falwell's mother had presented him with a four thousand dollar gift just before he left Lynchburg. The money was intended to help Falwell pay for his first year of Bible college, but Dowell's sermon seemed woefully uninterested in such explanations. Falwell described Dowell's remarks:

> *"Thou shalt bring forth the firstfruits of all thine increase," [Dowell] ad-libbed from the Old Testament text. "A-l-l," he said again, spelling the word carefully and looking, or so it seemed straight in my direction.*
>
> *I was just nineteen. I had a check for $4,000 deep in my pocket to cover my education. Certainly I was not to tithe that money. My mother had already tithed it before placing it in her savings. That check represented approximately what the year's board, room, and my personal needs would be. How could I take 10 percent of my entire nest egg and give it to God?*
>
> *". . . the firstfruits of ALL thine increase," Pastor Dowell said again, and when the offering plate went by during the very next service, I placed my own check for $400 on the top of the pile. What I thought would be a crippling act resulted once again in a feeling of joy and liberation. God came first and the rest would follow.*[26]

Falwell learned other things during that time as well. The gift that he had received from his mother made it unnecessary for him to work a job during that first year of Bible college, so Falwell dedicated his extra time to serving in the church. Indeed, on the same day that he joined High Street, Falwell approached Dowell to find a place of service.[27] "I asked Dr. Dowell to give me a Sunday School class," Falwell recalled in a sermon. "He referred me to Max Hawkins, a local businessman who was lay superintendent of the Junior Department, boys and girls 9-11 years of age."[28] It was Hawkins who gave Falwell his first official post in the ministry.

Dowell's Sunday school program in those days was sizeable, Falwell recalled. "At that time, High Street had more than 2,000 people enrolled in Sunday School. The junior department alone included more than 150 children ages nine, ten, and eleven."[29] Yet Falwell would have to start small. Hawkins assigned to Falwell just "one 11 year old boy, a roll book and a curtained-off area in the general assembly hall." For the eager young teacher, the situation could not have been more discouraging. "I failed quickly with my new class," Falwell confessed.[30]

Falwell said he might have given up on his class entirely had it not been for some sharp words from his superintendent. When Falwell went to Hawkins with his frustrations, Hawkins set him straight. And by the end of that conversation, Falwell said, he had been persuaded to repent of his own "spiritual shallowness."[31] That was when Falwell became serious about building his new class. Falwell described the transformation in one of his sermons:

> *My experience in Christ's school of prayer actually took on a new dimension because of this tiny class. After some frustration and thoughts of resignation over the lack of numerical and spiritual growth of this class, God drove me to my knees. I began praying about this new ministry from 1 p.m. till 5 p.m. every day, after classes. These 20 hours of weekly prayer, plus weekends of aggressive visitation and soul-winning, caused my class of one 11-year-old boy to grow to an average attendance of 56 by the end of the school year.*[32]

By Falwell's own account, his "life was changed forever" because of that Sunday school class.[33] Not only did this fledgling leader see his class's numbers increase, but he also saw the lives of his boys changed. "Most of these boys, plus their brothers, sisters and parents gave their hearts to Christ that year. Revival broke out at High Street Church," Falwell said. "And I learned the power of prayer in doing effective ministry."[34]

Perhaps as never before, Falwell began to prioritize people that year. Since he had just one boy on his roster, he determined to pour himself into that one. And those efforts made an eternal difference. Indeed, nearly fifty years later, Falwell received a letter from that original youngster. His name was Philip Henderson. Falwell had long since lost touch with Henderson, but from his letter, Falwell learned that Henderson had lived a successful life. He had enjoyed a brief career as a baseball player and then went on to work as a professional contractor. Falwell read the text of Henderson's letter in a sermon. Henderson wrote:

> *Countless times I have heard men speak regarding the impact made on their lives by their Sunday School teachers as 11 year old boys. I treasured my own memories and thanked God for you many years before the USA had heard of the work you are doing. For me you were not that "right wing extremist" in Lynchburg, rather, you were the man who asked a young lost boy in an unfamiliar setting if he had a personal relationship with Jesus Christ. "Philip, are you saved?" That's what you said to me. Lots of things have happened to me in the 40+ years [since then] but I have always thought that your interest in my soul was my high water mark. To this day, you are still the only one who has ever asked me this most important of questions. I want you to know that I have asked many. You taught me well.*[35]

In 1956, Falwell graduated from BBC and returned to Lynchburg. A month later, at the age of twenty-two, Falwell launched a new church. This group met in an elementary school building that was located across town from the church on Park Avenue. Thirty-five adults attended Falwell's first service. But a year later, "more than 800 people were regularly attending" those services.[36] Lynchburg was never the same.

Falwell's new congregation, Thomas Road Baptist Church, was soon recognized as one of the fastest growing churches in America. The church's average attendance would top two thousand by the end of the 1960s,[37] and by the time of Falwell's death in 2007, the size of this congregation would exceed twenty thousand.[38] Falwell's vision also led to the creation of *The Old-Time Gospel Hour*, a television broadcast with more than fifty million regular viewers in 2007,[39] as well as the Liberty Baptist College (later Liberty University), a liberal arts institution that the *Washington Post* once described as "an evangelical mega-university with global reach."[40]

Falwell himself acknowledged Dowell's role in launching those great ministries. In August of 1985, when Falwell visited Dowell's church in Springfield, he reflected on the influence that Dowell had wielded in his life. Recalling Dowell's 1952 revival at Park Avenue, Falwell explained that ". . . much of the nucleus of the old original Thomas Road Baptist Church—thirty-five charter members of the Thomas Road Church—were converted in that September meeting in 1952. . . ." Falwell went on to note that ". . . seven of our present deacons at Thomas Road Baptist Church, including the chairman . . . made decisions for Christ in that meeting."[41]

Listening to Falwell's account, Dowell could not have missed the irony of it all. A brief revival meeting held in a seemingly inconsequential church under less-than-ideal physical conditions had somehow produced enduring fruits. "God moves in a mysterious way / His wonders to perform," goes the oft-quoted hymn by William Cowper.[42] Dowell had seen glimpses of those wonders back in 1952, yet the story had not ended there. Just as it had been with young Shirley Wayland, the extent of God's wonders took many years to unfold. Indeed, even when Dowell heard this story in 1985, he knew that there would be more to come. The full measure of the Lord's handiwork would take an eternity to behold. And that was just fine with Dowell. In the meantime, he would continue spreading the Bible's life-altering message, the message that God loves people.

Chapter 29: *Pastor on the Go*

As the hatch lifted on the side of a white and silver Delta airliner, a set of stairs began to unfold. A member of the ground crew, his hands resting on his hips, stood on the pavement ready to meet the passengers as they disembarked. The mid-afternoon sun was out, and the pilot sitting in the cockpit slid open a tiny window to get a breath of air. Nola too was feeling the warmth as she stood in the waiting area next to the terminal. Her brown, pleated dress was a terrible choice for this weather, she thought. Still, it was one of Bill's favorites, and she wanted to look her best when he stepped off the airplane.

Nola was known for her fine taste. There was much more to this woman, of course. She had a reputation for being outgoing and active, playing both softball and tennis. She also knew the Bible. For a time she taught a women's class at High Street, the Tabithian Bible Class, and many women of the church looked up to her. Evangelist Roy Kemp once said of her, ". . . she is a born leader of women, a Bible scholar—and she does it all with a feminine graciousness that dignifies womanhood."[1] Like her husband, Nola personalized her ministry, focusing on individuals instead of crowds. One longtime church member even recalled Nola's weekly efforts to wash and fold the laundry of an elderly neighbor woman.[2]

To those who did not know her, however, Nola's elegance may have been her most striking quality. According to one daughter-in-law, Nola was viewed by many in her community as a kind of "high society dame."[3] Nola always attended church smartly dressed in matching shoes, hats, and gloves. This was the way she looked even in a 1946 newspaper photo that captured her grocery shopping.[4] Then in 1955, after the Dowell family bought a home in the fashionable Brentwood Estates of South Springfield, Nola's smart style once again made the news. The newspaper ran a feature about the Dowell's new home, noting in particular a large mural that adorned one of its walls.

By this time, Nola was hiring domestic help to assist her in maintaining her home. This was a practice she continued throughout much of her life. Having such help was never a sign of snobbery. The women who worked for Nola, particularly a Mrs. Vaughn, became like extended family to her. Still, Nola developed an aura of classiness within her community. A 1958 article in the *Baptist Bible Tribune* complimented her as a woman "whose birth, training, and instinct made it unnecessary for her to take any courses on how to be courteous, kind and considerate of others."[5]

Nola forgot all about that high society image as she stood waiting on that airport tarmac. She strained on tiptoes to peer into the airplane doorway, and when she finally spotted a broad-brimmed straw hat emerging, her face lit up. She broke free of the waiting crowd and darted past the crewman onto the pavement, careful to shuffle on her toes so as not to damage her high heels. Nola reached the bottom of the stairs just as her husband started making his descent. Then, in an instant, she replaced her eager smile with furled eyebrows and a pair of pursed lips. With mock sternness, she blurted:

You're late.

That is when the traveler's face broke into a broad grin. He sheepishly replied:

Sorry. Getting around the world took a little longer than I thought it would.

In the summer of 1958, Dowell embarked on a nine-week mission trip. He traveled to five of the world's seven continents, making a complete circle around the globe. During those travels he conducted meetings, encouraged missionaries, and attended to business on behalf of the Baptist Bible Fellowship. Then when he returned home, his wife greeted him with an uncharacteristically public display of affection as he was stepping off the airplane.

Bill now wiped the lipstick off of his mouth as he said:

Wow. I think that was worth the trip.

A few days after his return, Dowell would be taking his family down to Mexico for a vacation. They deserved the extra attention, he thought. This would not be the family's first visit to Mexico. During a 1955 vacation they traveled to Acapulco, Mexico City, and the Aztec ruins. Dowell used such experiences to invest in the people he cared about most. Next to Christ, Dowell's wife and children held the top place in his heart. And as every pastor knows, no investment in people is as vital as the one that he makes in his own family.

Of course by 1958, Dowell's household was growing smaller. Janet had married in June of 1953. She married a recent graduate of BBC, Bernie Rodgers. Janet was just seventeen years old at the time, graduating from high school that same year. After she and Bernie were married, they moved to St. Louis to begin their own ministry life. Janet's father later told her that, on the day she was wed, ". . . he went out on a country road and had a big cry because he would really miss his only daughter."[6] Nola experienced a similar grief. In personal notes, she called Janet's departure her "first real heartache."[7] The Dowells loved Bernie–"They always signed birthday cards and letters, 'to our 3rd son,'" Janet recalled[8]–but the thought of losing their only daughter was difficult for them. "I shed many tears as the day of their marriage approached," Nola wrote.[9]

Of course, the Dowells' sadness did not last long. Near the end of 1953, the Dowells learned that they would soon become grandparents. Nola said she first greeted this news with "mixed emotion," fearing that a grandchild would have an aging effect on her. "[B]ut when the baby arrived I was reborn," she said, "so happy and excited that I felt much younger instead of much older (as I thought)."[10]

The Dowells' oldest son, Bill, was now likewise married. He married in May of 1958, just before his father left for his trip around the world. Bill Jr. had attended one year at BBC, but after that year, he followed a couple of his college buddies, Truman Dollar and Jerry Thorpe, down to Texas. These "three musketeers," as they were known, had originally planned to transfer to Texas Tech, yet when those plans fell through due to the cost, Bill Jr. wound up moving in with Dollar's family in Borger, Texas.[11] There Bill Jr. continued his studies at a junior college while also serving as an intern at the church where Truman's dad was pastor. It was at that church, Southside Baptist, that Bill Jr. met his bride-to-be, Joan Hunter. Then, after their wedding, this couple returned to Springfield to serve on Dowell's staff at High Street.

By August of 1958, then, Clyde was the only remaining child in the Dowells' household, though even Clyde had recently started dating the love of his life, Sharon Ward. So the Dowells were making the most of their time with their last remaining child. Clyde and his dad had always been close. Like his father, Clyde was athletically inclined, so father and son cherished a playful rivalry that developed between them. Each year at youth camp, they played on competing softball teams. Clyde pitched for the youth team; his father pitched for the pastors. Clyde relished beating his father's team, and Dowell relished watching him try.

This father-son relationship went beyond sports, of course. All throughout Dowell's world tour, Dowell and his family had corresponded through letters. In one letter, Clyde confided to his father that he had rededicated his life to the Lord during a young people's meeting. "It wasn't things, necessarily, that I had been doing," the son wrote, "it was the things that I hadn't been doing like reading my Bible very much, praying often enough, going to visitation with the right attitude, etc. But that is all different now." Clyde told his father that he had not spoken to his mother or anyone else about the experience. ". . . I figured it was kind of between me and the Lord," he said. Still, the boy did not hesitate to share the experience with his dad.[12]

Even as the number of place settings at the Dowell dinner table was dwindling, the clan itself continued to grow. Each of the Dowells' three children produced three offspring of their own. Karen was the first grandchild; then came Tonya, Kyle, Connie, Lynda, Stephen, Angie, Karla, and David. The Dowells treasured them all. Karen remembered how her grandmother dressed her in "endless rows of ruffles and lace" and took her up to sit in the balcony at High Street when she came to visit because that was Karen's favorite spot. Karen also recalled Dowell playing "horsey games" with her, bouncing her on his legs as she giggled.[13] None of the Dowell grandchildren could forget their grandmother's incessant picture-taking or their grandfather's powerful bear hugs.

Back on the tarmac, Nola emerged from Dowell's embrace with a smile:

Careful. You'll break me in two.

Dowell's hugs may have had extra intensity on the day that he stepped off of his airplane from his world tour. His trip had been a glorious experience, but he was ready to be at home with his loved ones once again. Dowell had gone on this trip at the urging of Mission Director Fred Donnelson. Indeed, Donnelson's office paid for it all.

Dowell now wore the title of Assistant Director of Missions for the BBF, so he made the trip in that capacity. At that time, the BBF was supporting a hundred and fifteen missionaries on sixteen different fields. Dowell visited ten of those fields that summer.[14]

Donnelson had asked Dowell to make this trip so that he could address several important matters. One of these related to some interpersonal conflicts that were threatening the mission work in the Philippines. Another situation had to do with Elmer and Mary Deal, new missionaries who were having difficulty gaining admittance into the Belgian Congo. It was hoped that Dowell could resolve those difficulties during his visit to Africa. Dowell's trip might also bolster efforts in the US, Donnelson believed. When Dowell returned home again, he would also be able to report back to fellowship churches about the global efforts that they were supporting. Dowell's reports would likely inspire more giving and going, and in Donnelson's mind, all such results would make the trip well worth the cost.

Dowell traveled for most of that summer, and during his extended absence from High Street, guests like Frank Collins, A. V. Henderson, and Wendell Zimmerman were asked to fill the pulpit. The church also held a Sunday school attendance campaign that summer: "The Sheep versus the Goats." The classes that reached their weekly attendance goals were added to the "sheep pen." The other classes were relegated to the "goat pen." In regular letters to Dowell, Nola and Earl Smith kept Dowell abreast of the latest church news. Earl reported in one of his letters that High Street maintained a summer average of 2,495.[15]

Dowell's church set up a large world map that summer that would allow church members to follow Dowell's progress as he moved from place to place. Dowell's journey began from Springfield on Monday, June 23. The day before he left, the local newspaper ran a story about his tour. The reporter asked if Dowell was excited about the adventure. Dowell replied with one word: "Extremely!"[16]

The Dowell family had a "prayer meeting" at their home the next morning. Then at the airport, Dowell was given a grand farewell by the members of his church. He flew from Springfield to Kansas City, where he had lunch with Wendell Zimmerman, and after that, he flew on to Los Angeles. Just before he landed in California, Dowell jotted a note to his wife. "I took out $125,000.00 insurance," Dowell said. "It cost $10.00 but it is worth it. . . . I am sure the Lord is going to see that you never collect, but that you have me instead, but it is still good to have." Dowell added, "You are my very life and you get sweeter with every passing day."[17]

From Los Angeles, Dowell caught a connection to San Francisco. He would take a flight from there to Honolulu, the first official stop on his tour. While he was waiting in San Francisco, Dowell received a telegram from Beauchamp Vick. "Just to wish you God speed and assure you of our prayers on your journey," Vick wrote.[18]

Dowell would travel to more than twenty-five foreign countries during his lifetime,[19] but it was this journey that marked many of the firsts in his life, including his first trip across an ocean. Dowell kept a diary of the experience. He noted, for instance, that, as his plane taxied out of San Francisco, the pilot detected some sort of a problem. The flight was delayed for about a half hour while the aircraft was fixed. When Dowell's plane finally got off the ground, Dowell made notes about seeing the low, dark clouds that hung over San Francisco Bay. The plane flew out about midnight, he said, and once the ocean disappeared from view, there was little else to see, so Dowell settled in for his nine-and-a-half-hour flight to the island of Oahu.

Hawaii was still a territory of the US in 1958. The Hawaiian Islands would not become America's fiftieth state until the year after Dowell's visit. Since Dowell's stay on those islands would be a brief one, he wasted no time seeing the sights. One of the first places he visited was Pearl Harbor. After that experience, Dowell wrote in his journal, "I could not help but recall that my next stop would be Japan, where now we have soldiers of the cross witnessing to the Japs of the saving grace of Jesus Christ. What a difference the gospel makes."[20]

On Dowell's second day in Hawaii, he had lunch with Ingram M. Stainback, former governor of the Hawaiian territory. The Baptist Bible Fellowship had a presence in Hawaii, the Waikiki Baptist Church, and perhaps it was through this connection that the meeting with Stainback was arranged. Whatever the case, Dowell felt honored to have such an opportunity. Stainback had been appointed governor of Hawaii during the early days of World War II, and he had held that post for the next nine years. Of his meeting with Stainback, Dowell wrote:

> Mr. Stainback was very kind to me. After taking me to lunch, he spent the rest of the afternoon driving me over the Island and explaining many things. One of the very interesting places he took me was to a crater which is called the punch bowl, and which is now a federal cemetery, dedicated by Mr. Stainback when he was governor. Many of the brave men who died on Pearl Harbor day are buried there. Before returning me to my hotel, he took me to his lovely beach home for a brief visit. I had the opportunity to witness briefly to him before he left me at the hotel.[21]

Later that day, Wednesday, June 25, Dowell visited Waikiki Baptist Church. Then the next day Dowell made ready to fly to Japan. As he was waiting for his flight, he bumped into Mr. and Mrs. Olson Hodges. They were on their way home from Japan for a furlough even as Dowell was heading to their mission field. Dowell said he was glad for a chance to visit with these missionaries, especially since he would be speaking in their church while he was in Japan.

Dowell's plane out of Hawaii stopped briefly at Wake Island. From that island, Dowell sent Nola and Clyde a postcard. Then he flew on to Tokyo, where he experienced another chance meeting. As he was going through customs, ". . . a man and his wife came over to where [he] was waiting and said, 'Hello Bro. Dowell.'" Dowell had never met the couple, but they recognized him. They were from Springfield and operated a grocery store there. In a letter to his family, Dowell remarked, "A small world, huh."[22]

While he was in Japan, Dowell spent time with several missionaries. Among them were Laverne and Evelyn Rodgers. Lavern was Bernie Rodgers's older brother and, like the Japanese people that he ministered to, this missionary was a kind and gracious host. During Dowell's week-long stay in Japan, Dowell saw everything from Shinto shrines to rice paddies. He also had the opportunity to preach "to capacity crowds in Makuhari, Chiba, Shizuoka, Ota, and Kumagaya."[23] Dowell wrote to Nola, "I am enjoying Japan, but I have been a very busy boy."[24]

In between speaking engagements, Dowell interacted informally with Japanese Christians, eating meals with them and answering their questions. "They asked all sorts of questions about our work in the States and how they could best build their work," Dowell wrote.[25] These meetings with the Japanese ranged from as little as forty-five minutes to as much as two hours. And in least one case, the forum was held "in the true Japanese fashion," Dowell wrote with a seeming groan. "We sat on the floor . . . ," he explained.[26]

All throughout Dowell's world tour, souls were saved. Indeed, in his letters he often included the number of converts that were reached at each place. But the individuals always mattered more to him than the numbers. Dowell retained a vivid memory of one of his Japanese converts. He told the story in a sermon many years later. "When I was preaching in Kumagaya, Japan, an old man was saved one night about sixty-five years of age," Dowell said. "He came and gave his testimony and they interpreted it to us. And he said, 'I've lived in Shintoism all my life,' but said, 'I've been conscious every minute of the time that there was a void in my soul and in my heart that Shintoism didn't fill.' He looked up and tears ran down his cheeks and he said, 'Tonight, Jesus filled that vacuum.'"[27]

When Dowell left Japan, he traveled on to the island nation of Taiwan, known to many as Formosa. Fred Donnelson's son-in-law, Bill Logan, was waiting for Dowell when he landed. Logan had with him a delegation of Chinese Christians to welcome Dowell. A young girl from this group carried a lei out to Dowell when he stepped off of the airplane, and as she placed it around Dowell's neck, the crowd erupted in English: "Welcome to Taipei and Formosa."[28]

On this island, Dowell interacted with worshipers in the cities of Taipei, Chai-yi, Nan Gong-Poo Tzu, and Shih Lin. At Chai-yi, Dowell assisted missionary Lee Homer in a dedication service for a new church building. Dowell had the privilege of unlocking the new building to allow the congregants to enter. And the people came in droves. "The house was packed to standing room," Dowell noted.[29] Dowell was also the guest preacher that day. His sermon was translated by two interpreters since more than one language was spoken by his audience. The service lasted three hours, Dowell said, but it was a good day. At the end of it all, Dowell was asked to baptize six converts.

Sometime later Dowell took a short ride on the back of Lee Homer's motorcycle. Homer drove Dowell up to the Tropic of Cancer. Along the way, Dowell took photographs of the sights. One photo captured a man preparing a snake to cook. Dowell was pleased that the meals he was eating were more appetizing. Dowell admitted to friends back in the US that he had experienced some difficulty learning to use chopsticks, but he said he "managed to get [his] share of the food" nonetheless.[30]

Dowell left Taiwan on July 8, 1958, his forty-fourth birthday. Before his departure, Bill Logan and others presented Dowell with a birthday cake. Dowell also opened cards, including some that had been sent over by Nola and Clyde. The meal that night was served on the bank of a river, and on the menu was wild boar. "Tasty," Dowell wrote.[31]

Dowell's next stop was the Philippines. Dowell stepped off of the airplane in Manilla to another "royal welcome," he said.[32] Once again he received a lei of orchids and plenty of warm smiles. He was even interviewed by a local newspaper reporter. Then that night, missionary Frank Hooge (HO-gee) and his family hosted Dowell for dinner. Dowell had high regard for Hooge. He was part of a strong, aggressive team of missionaries who were doing a fine work in the Philippines. Unfortunately, the team's aggressive spirit may have helped spark the friction that was now affecting some of its members. Dowell got the lowdown on this conflict over dinner, and as Hooge explained the situation, Dowell could see that he was going to have his work cut out for him.

Of course, the discord between the missionaries was just one of the challenges that Dowell faced during his stay in the Philippines. He also faced a hectic schedule, some health concerns, and a bit of disagreeable weather. Despite these things, Dowell saw the hand of God at work. On his second day in the Philippines, Dowell spoke at one of Frank Hooge's churches, and afterward he wrote in his journal, "My throat bothered me to the extent of causing me great concern. That night on my knees by my bed I claimed God's promise for the healing of my throat. God answered and I had no more trouble. The fact that I had had the same trouble for several weeks before leaving the States is all the more evidence that God has undertaken. I praise him for it."[33]

On Wednesday morning of that week, Dowell held an initial conference to try to hash out the differences between the missionaries. This conference was "not satisfying," Dowell said, in part because there was insufficient time to fully discuss the concerns.[34] Dowell had to get to his next speaking engagement. He was scheduled to speak eight times during his week in the Philippines. He would preach in three churches, in a Bible institute, and in a national fellowship meeting. At one point, Dowell recalled seeing a beautiful Filipino golf course. Dowell said he borrowed a club long enough to step out onto that course to pose for a photograph, but regrettably, there was no time for anything more than that. On the outside of a letter that he sent to Nola and Clyde, Dowell posted this return address:

W. E. Dowell
Pastor on the Go[35]

In addition to his speaking engagements, Dowell went on several personal visits with Frank Hooge. As Dowell entered those Filipino homes, he was struck by the differences that separated his culture from that of the Philippines. "Open sewers run in front of the houses on all the streets," Dowell wrote. "The smell is horrible." Dowell also noted the scantily clad "mountain people" that he saw shopping in one of the villages. He said it reminded him of the stories of headhunters that the missionaries had told him. On the subject of Filipino food, Dowell said, "Tasty but, oh, so different. If you can think of the taste and not the looks, you are o.k."[36]

Near the end of that week, Dowell held another meeting with the missionaries to try to resolve the conflicts between them. This time tempers flared. "It got pretty hot at times but I managed to keep things under control," Dowell said. And eventually Dowell witnessed a breakthrough. "I had reached a place of almost hopelessness when God moved in and took over," Dowell wrote. "He broke my heart until I could not talk for weeping. Others felt the same. Agreements were reached, apologies were made, and mutual love for each other prevailed."[37] In a report to the fellowship, Dowell celebrated the turnaround, saying, "I believe I saw evidences of a great and permanent victory."[38] Then in his journal, Dowell wrote: "The missionaries said my coming meant more to them and the work than anything that had ever happened. If this be true, I thank God and take courage. It was worth my whole trip to be able to help them."[39]

But Dowell's challenges did not end there. Dowell was now suffering from a case of dysentery. That weekend also brought to the Philippines a major rainstorm. "The streets were flooded until traffic was almost stopped," Dowell wrote. That busy weekend included preaching in two churches and helping Brother Hooge place a cornerstone for a new building. The services were "filled," Dowell said, "and God blessed with souls."[40] As Dowell's final service in the Philippines concluded, the members of Hooge's church "overwhelmed" their guest with special gifts for him and his wife. The church's affection for Nola caused Dowell to take out his billfold to show them her picture. Dowell chuckled at their reaction: ". . . after many aw's and oo's, they said, 'She is beautiful, and she looks so young,'"[41]

Dowell left the Philippines a few hours later. Just before his departure, the missionaries gathered around him and sang "God Be with You till We Meet Again."[42] Dowell then traveled to Hong Kong, where he met up with Bill Logan again. Prices in Hong Kong made this a good place for missionaries to shop for supplies, so Dowell tagged along for the experience. Logan's knowledge of the shops, language, and culture would also make it possible for Dowell to find some good bargains. "This is some place," Dowell wrote to his wife from Hong Kong. "I surely wish you were here. Though I am afraid you would break me up shopping. This is the greatest shopping center I have ever seen."[43] Dowell took full advantage of the opportunity. During his two-day visit, he shipped home a number of gifts for his family members, including two sets of intricately carved stacking tables, which he designated for the homes of Janet and Bill Jr.[44]

Dowell's health was now on the mend, and after his shopping excursion came to an end, he was ready to continue on his journey. His next appointment was in Pakistan, but on the way there, he would be making brief stops in the cities of Bangkok, Calcutta, and Delhi. As Dowell began this leg of his trip, he noted seeing from his airplane window both the South China Sea and the vast jungles of Asia.

Dowell had an overnight layover at Calcutta, India, an experience that proved to be an emotional one. First, Dowell learned that he would not be able to leave the city on schedule. He had expected to stay overnight and then leave the next morning, but officials at the airline notified him that he would not be able to fly out until seven o'clock the next evening. This delay would also cause him to miss his connection in Delhi, forcing him to have another overnight layover there, and delaying his arrival in Pakistan by a full day. When Dowell heard this news, he argued with airline officials, "but to no avail," he said. In the end, he decided he would just have to "make the most" of the situation.[45]

After checking into the Grand Hotel in Calcutta, Dowell went on a walking tour of the area around him. It was already dark by the time he went out, but he was shocked by what he was able to see. The streets were littered not only with "so-called holy cows" but also with the people who revered them. "The sight that met my eyes had been described to me," Dowell wrote, "but words cannot describe the actual fact. The streets were cluttered and dirty, but there is where thousands sleep. Some had crude cots; others nothing, not even a blanket or a quilt." Years later Dowell rehearsed the scene in a sermon:

> *I should never have been on the street but nobody told me it wasn't all right. It's a wonder I hadn't got killed while I was out there, but I went out and walked all up and down the street, and went down one dark street. I felt perfectly secure. Nothing happened, so I guess I was. I guess the Lord takes care of the foolish. But I saw—I don't know—I wouldn't dare tell you how many—people lying on the street at ten o'clock at night with a piece of wood under their head for a pillow. They had no home. One little mother had a little baby that couldn't have been over a week old, and a little dirty bottle she was holding out begging money for a little milk for her baby.*[46]

Dowell said the experience left him feeling powerless. In a letter to his family, he wrote, "Your heart cries out to help, then you look around to see the streets crowded with such cases and there is no place to begin nor to end."[47]

Dowell returned to his hotel room that night "heart-sick."[48] He wrote in his journal, "I am convinced where Christ is not known there is ignorance, poverty, and misery, as well as spiritual death." The realization reminded him both of his own blessings and of the dire need of the people around him. "As I returned to my air conditioned room," he said, "I thought it is nice in here but outside there is poverty, misery, filth and death, and worst of all, spiritual blindness. I had to fall on my knees and thank God for His blessings upon my family and I, and ask Him to help me do more for such people that they may find Christ."[49]

When the sun came up the next day, Dowell saw even more of Calcutta. "Things look a little better in the day time even on the streets but it is pitiful at best," Dowell wrote.[50] For the price of seven dollars, Dowell hired a driver to take him on an all-day tour. As they went, Dowell saw yaks standing on the sidewalks and pedestrians stepping around them with loads on their heads. "We visited the government buildings, the parks, the library, the zoo, the shipping dock, the better residential part of the city, the downtown section, the slums, etc. We also visited some religious shrines," Dowell said. One of Dowell's stops was at a Jain temple. "Their religion comes from the Hindu but still is different," Dowell explained. "Their so-called holy men never wear a stitch of clothes, not even when they preach."[51] Dowell described an encounter that he had with one of those priests:

> One of them called us over to him and spoke through my guide and said we Americans are striving for positions, wealth, and prestige, but he is striving for salvation. I told him that while that was true with some in America, that we Christians have placed our faith in Jesus Christ, the only one who is able to save, and that I have dedicated my life to trying to get others to accept Jesus Christ also. He preached some more, but I couldn't understand him and the guide told me very little.[52]

Later that day, Dowell did his best to share the gospel with his driver, and afterward, the two men parted ways. Dowell gathered his things and checked in for his flight to Delhi. Since he still had a little time before his departure, Dowell said he slipped away from the airport to see one more sight. He visited Carey Baptist Church, a work founded by famed missionary William Carey. Dowell said he took a few photos and then returned to the airport, eager to make his way to his next destination.

Delhi was a much more agreeable Indian city, Dowell said. "Just the opposite from Calcutta," he wrote. "There did not seem to be the poverty as in Calcutta. And it was clean."[53] Dowell also enjoyed his hotel stay there. Initially he was told by hotel officials that he did not have a reservation and that there were no rooms available, but when Dowell showed them the documentation that the airline had given him, they relented and gave him a room key. Dowell went up to his assigned room and opened the door to find a luxury suite inside. "Three times as large as the average hotel room," Dowell remarked. Dowell said he called the front desk to inform them that there had been a mistake, but they assured him that the upgrade was intentional. "I lived in style one night," Dowell winked.[54]

Although Dowell enjoyed his accommodations in Delhi, he was now growing concerned about his travel schedule. The recent delays had already cost him a night in Karachi, Pakistan, and there were signs that there might be additional delays. From Pakistan, Dowell was planning to go to Beirut, Lebanon, where he would meet more missionaries and would prepare to enter the Holy Land, the most highly anticipated leg of his journey. Yet Dowell was beginning to wonder if he would ever make it there. While he was in Delhi, Dowell learned that US ground forces had just occupied Beirut.

The circumstances that prompted Beirut's occupation had been brewing for several months. In February 1958, Egyptian President Gamal Abdel Nasser formed the United Arab Republic (UAR), a union between Egypt and Syria. Nasser now had designs on conquering the rest of the Arab world. Indeed, many believed that America's Cold War enemy, Russia, was poised to help Nasser succeed. Lebanon was one of the nations caught up in the turmoil. Lebanon's Christian president wanted to maintain ties with the West, but her Muslim prime minister wanted to join the UAR.

The civil unrest that ensued prompted US marines to assume control of parts of Beirut, including its airport. Dowell got the bad news just as he was preparing to board his plane for Karachi, Pakistan. "At present Beirut airport is closed to international travel and controlled by U.S. marines," Dowell wrote in his journal. He then added with some trepidation, "I do not know what awaits me when I leave Karachi."[55]

Dowell did not have the answers, yet he felt confident that Someone else did. So when he finished writing those words, Dowell closed up his notebook, boarded his plane, and prayed that the Lord would get him where he needed to be. He also asked the Lord to get him there on time. After all, Dowell chuckled, if he was late getting home, Nola was not going to like it.

Chapter 30: *Hot Spots*

The café was mostly quiet, all except for the sound of some workers banging pots and pans in the kitchen. From time to time, the workers' voices rang out as well, nothing intelligible, though it all sounded angry.

As Dowell carved another bite and popped it into his mouth, an elderly man sitting across from him asked:

How is your steak?

The chewer tried to negotiate his mouthful so as not to be impolite.

Can't complain. A little tough, maybe, but still good.

Dowell then smiled and nodded to the man's wife. She instinctively nodded back. She was Japanese. Like Dowell, this couple was en route to Lebanon. Dowell had befriended them as they were traveling. Indeed, conversations about the woman's home country had helped pass the time during what turned out to be a very long airport layover.

The man sitting across from Dowell looked away from their table.

There goes another one.

Through a large window Dowell could see what his companion was referring to. The head and shoulders of a foreign soldier were floating by. A sharp bayonet pointed out over one shoulder.

Dowell swallowed again and said:

They've got the place surrounded all right.

The man smiled in agreement and replied:

I'm just not sure whether that is a good thing or a bad thing.

As planned, Dowell had stopped briefly in Pakistan. While there, he was entertained by the Holske and Coleman families. It was a worthwhile visit, Dowell said, even though he could not be with the missionaries as long as he had originally planned. In his notes about this visit, Dowell told of a mix-up that had occurred when he first arrived. Walter Holske was supposed to pick Dowell up from Karachi's airport, but in all the confusion over Dowell's flight schedule, Holske missed him. So instead, Dowell wound up taking a bus to his hotel.

From the hotel, Dowell contacted the American Embassy to try to get help contacting the missionaries. The embassy provided Dowell with an address for the

Colemans. They also informed him that Beirut's airport had just reopened. Dowell was pleasantly surprised by the news, and after he heard it, he quickly amended his travel plans. Since he could not be certain how long flights into Beirut would continue, he decided to shorten his visit in Pakistan yet again. Instead of leaving the next day, he would catch a flight at the end of that same day.

Dowell now hung up the telephone and went to the hotel's front desk to get directions for the address that the embassy had given him. During this conversation, a call came in from Walter Holske. Holske was phoning from the airport to see if Dowell had somehow gotten past him. A short while later, Holske and Dowell made contact, and Holske gave Dowell a tour of Karachi. Dowell's photographs from that day included pictures of a man on an elephant and of himself posing next to a camel.[1]

When this tour had ended, Dowell and Holske went to the home of some Pakistani Christians, where Dowell was able to preach to a group of congregants. "I preached on the subject 'Stand fast in the liberty wherewith Christ has made you free," Dowell wrote.[2] Then that evening, Dowell enjoyed a "native" Pakistani dinner in the missionaries' home. He also spent some time discussing with them "the problems and possibilities of the work."[3]

After all of that, it was time for Dowell to catch his DC-6 for Beirut. Dowell said he slept "fairly well" on this overnight flight.[4] Unfortunately, when morning came, he heard a disappointing announcement from his pilot. The political situation had changed again, and instead of landing in Beirut, their plane would be landing in the city of Tehran, "about 1000 miles from Beirut."[5] In a matter of minutes, Dowell's plane was on the ground in Iran. And Dowell had no idea when he would be leaving or where he would be heading.

Dowell and his fellow travelers were eventually given two options. They could take a flight bound for some other destination, or, despite the uncertainty, they could try to continue on to Beirut aboard a DC-7 that would be coming into Tehran approximately three hours later. Dowell said that about ten of the passengers opted to head for Beirut, including him and his elderly friends. Dowell wrote in his journal:

> The situation in both Lebanon and Jordan seems to be quite serious. Many American marines in Lebanon, and British troops moving into Jordan, and Russia very angry and constantly bombarding the USA and England with criticism (sic). Perhaps I am foolish for going on in, but I have lived 44 years longing to visit the Holy Land. Unless they forbid me to do so, I am determined to take whatever risk there may be to carry through.[6]

Dowell said his three-hour layover in Tehran turned into nine hours. And all throughout that day, things at the airport remained tense:

> It was a strange day. The people at the airport were unfriendly, but the [Pan American Airline] officials were wonderful and did everything possible to make us comfortable. We were not permitted to go to town as we had no visa. But we

were finally taken to a little airport café and served a steak dinner. Tough but good. Soldiers with guns and bayonets were walking over the airport ground and stationed up and down the runway.[7]

In time, the DC-7 arrived, and Dowell and the other waiting travelers departed for Lebanon. As they flew out of Tehran, Dowell saw "lines of tanks near the airport." Dowell had heard rumors that Russian troops were moving into that city, so he was glad to be up in the air and out of that part of the world. He was also eager to see the end of this flight. Since his plane was traveling to Beirut by way of Damascus, there would be an additional stop to make in Syria before he would reach his destination. The pilot also had to take the long way around to get there, Dowell said. The nation of Iraq, situated between Iran and Syria, was now considered a danger zone, so the plane had to be routed around Iraq's airspace. "I do not know yet what we will face in Beirut," Dowell wrote as he traveled, "but the Lord is with me, and I am unafraid. I am still mindful that I am on a mission for Him."[8]

Dowell's flight eventually made it into Beirut, though it was late when the plane finally landed. Then, because of a nighttime curfew, no missionary was able to meet Dowell at the airport. He had to catch a cab to his hotel.

The next morning Dowell and that same elderly couple from the airport went to visit the American Embassy to get the latest report. "Of course, as was to be expected they advised us to get out as soon as possible . . . ," Dowell wrote. Dowell added that the embassy officials were "empathetic." They "did not try to discourage me too much," Dowell said. Instead they made it clear that their warning was "only advice, not an order."[9]

Hearing these things, Dowell decided to stay put and to carry on with his original plans. He made contact with missionaries Clarence Green and Clyde Aynes and even managed to preach for them while he was there. Green's church "was packed and many on the outside," Dowell wrote. "Four were saved."[10] Dowell preached for Aynes later that same day.

In between speaking engagements, the missionaries treated Dowell to some of Lebanon's tourist sights. Dowell said the missionaries took him to see Tripoli as well as the ancient city of Byblos. "[D]uring the day we were free to go and come at will except for a few hot spots," Dowell explained in his journal. At one point during these wanderings, Dowell even interacted with some of the American marines who had recently landed. In a letter to Nola and Clyde, he wrote:

> *I got some real pictures yesterday of the marines landing. Also of them digging fox holes on the beach. I was surprised that they did not stop me from taking pictures, but some of the soldiers even posed for me. Uncle Sam and the French navy had 74 battleships nearby. It is a pretty hot spot, but don't worry, I am fine, and the Lord has assured me He will take care of me and see me through.*[11]

The situation may have been more volatile than Dowell let on. In his personal notes, he wrote, "I heard much shooting, and the last night I was there I heard eleven bombs go off."[12]

On Monday, July 21, Dowell finally got out of that battle zone and flew into Jerusalem, which was then under Jordanian control. Dowell hoped to be in that city until the following Sunday, though the tensions there were much like the rest of the Middle East, and nothing could be certain. Dowell purposed to accomplish as much sightseeing as he could before any further problems developed. He was overjoyed to be in the Holy Land. Dowell would return to Jerusalem three more times during his lifetime, but this original visit remained a special memory for him. On his first night there he wrote, "It is a thrill to be in the city where my Lord ministered and was crucified. As I prayed tonight I could not help but weep. I will read the account of Christ's ministry and death here in the holy city before I go to sleep."[13]

Dowell's time in the Holy Land was spent living at the National Hotel and touring in and around Jerusalem. Dowell swam in both the Jordan River and the Dead Sea, and he visited nearby places like Bethlehem and Hebron. Dowell also made contact with Protestant missionaries Jad and Cynthia Mikhail. Jad, a native Palestinian, served as one of Dowell's tour guides that week. In return for this favor, Dowell spoke for one of the Mikhail's afternoon services. "God's power came down and six precious souls were saved," Dowell reported in his journal. "All of them grown—most of them elderly. For this I praise the Lord."[14]

On Thursday of that week, Dowell went to the Garden Tomb, which was only a few blocks away from his hotel. Dowell appreciated seeing the tomb, though his initial enjoyment of it was somewhat diminished by the crowds of people around him. What Dowell really wanted was a chance to step into that empty tomb alone.[15] So the next morning Dowell went back for a better look. And this early morning visit to tomb of Christ became one of Dowell's most treasured memories, one that he often rehearsed in his sermons. Dowell said he arrived before the site opened. It took some "maneuvering" to get in, he said, but a woman eventually came and unlocked the gate for him. Dowell lost track of time once he entered the tomb. The visit may have lasted as much as an hour, he said. Describing the experience in 1987, Dowell said:

> I stood there alone and yet I wasn't alone. I reviewed as best I could every step, every movement that I could recall of those days just preceding the resurrection of Christ. My mind went back to Calvary and I think in a new way, I think I saw the blood streaming down from his head, his hands, and his feet. I think I may have realized in a new manner why Christ died. I was tired. I'd been traveling for weeks. I'd been to many different countries. I'd studied about the gods of those countries. And as I stood there, a voice spoke to me. It was not an audible voice, but it would have been no clearer if it had been. And it said, "What are you most thankful for today?" Tears began to roll down my cheeks. I was so overcome by it I spoke out loud as if I was really answering a voice. And I said the thing that I'm most thankful for is that Jesus—the body of Jesus—is not here. This tomb is

empty and stands as an everlasting testimony to the fact that Jesus Christ arose from the dead.[16]

Later that same day, Dowell wrote to tell his family that he was going to have to cut short his visit to the Holy Land. Dowell explained, "I will leave Jerusalem tomorrow—a day earlier than I had intended. The flights from here are slowly being shut down because of the crisis."[17] Dowell's next stop was Cairo, but his direct flight from Jerusalem had already been cancelled, and now it appeared that he would have to catch a connection from Beirut if he wanted to make it on into Egypt. "It was the only connection available," Dowell wrote.[18]

Dowell said he got to see all that he wanted to see in the Holy Land, but he was disappointed that his schedule change would prevent him from attending Sunday services with the Mikhails. Still, it was clear that he needed to move on. Tensions had escalated even while Dowell was in Jerusalem. A recent coup in Baghdad had toppled the Hashimite monarchy of Iraq, a regime that had lasted for nearly four decades. During this coup, two senior Jordanian ministers visiting Baghdad had been executed. In fact, the confirmation of their deaths reached Jerusalem while Dowell was still in town, and one of the affected families lived across the street from his hotel. "I saw the commotion when the family received the news," Dowell wrote.[19]

Sensing the need to move on, Dowell boarded a flight back to Beirut. But he observed that travel was becoming increasingly difficult. Indeed, he now had to adopt a rather aggressive persona just to reach his destinations. "I arrived in Beirut," Dowell wrote, "and was informed I had no seat on the plane going to Cairo the next morning. I insisted that I had been informed in Jerusalem that my ticket was good all the way to Cairo. After some argument, they asked me to wait and at length came back and told me my ticket was confirmed."[20]

Dowell's travel headaches were far from over, however. He stayed overnight with the Green family in Beirut and the next day, after a "pretty wild night" of machine gun and artillery fire, Dowell returned to the airport to catch his flight to Cairo. "Upon entering the gate," Dowell said, "one of the guards started questioning me in his language." Dowell tried to communicate with the soldier in English, but the man seemed to know only Arabic. So the two babbled on to each other, waving their arms with growing frustration until, in the end, Dowell decided "to rattle off [his] little piece of Spanish." Dowell did this not because he or his listener could actually speak the Spanish language, but because Dowell believed the words would help him sound more belligerent. And the tactic seems to have work. "He looked at me, handed me my papers and waved me on," Dowell said.[21]

Yet there were further difficulties for Dowell at the terminal gate. "I then checked my ticket," Dowell continued, "and again was informed I had no reservations, and again I protested that my ticket had been confirmed the night before. He insisted for a minute and so did I. Then he marked my ticket and said, 'Okay. Everything is all right.' And so I finally boarded the plane for Cairo."[22]

All of this trouble may have stemmed from the anti-American sentiments that were now filling the Arab world. Dowell had witnessed hostility even while he was in Jerusalem. Speaking a few years later, Dowell said, "When we were in Jordan, we interviewed citizens among the Arabs, and they told us, 'We do not like the West, because they have not treated us right. We do not like the Communists but they are the only ones offering to help us, and it may be that we will finally have to turn to Russia for the help we need.'" Dowell added, "This is the spirit that we found nearly everywhere."[23]

As Dowell now headed for Nasser's homeland, he did not know what to expect. There were no missionaries to visit in this Muslim nation, so Dowell entered Egypt strictly as a tourist. Egyptians were "very courteous" on the whole, Dowell said.[24] (Customs officials did not even open his suitcase when he arrived, he noted.) But Dowell saw a very different side of Cairo when he stepped out of his hotel. "[W]e were shocked," Dowell later wrote, "when we saw in a large window of a downtown store a life size dummy of Uncle Sam in a vise with his tongue hanging out and blood flowing out on the ground. Standing over Uncle Sam was a dummy of Nassar [sic], head of the Egyptian government, twisting the vise tighter and tighter."[25] In a letter to his family, Dowell commented on this ill will. "Nassar has built up a great deal of prejudice against America," Dowell wrote. "In my opinion he is a modern Hitler."[26]

Given these circumstances, Dowell was careful not to stay out too late at night while he was in Egypt. On that first night, he found a restaurant, ate dinner, and then returned to his hotel room for what he hoped would be a night of rest. Unfortunately, his room was situated directly above a noisy nightclub, so even that proved a disappointment. But Dowell dismissed the sleepless night, rising the next day ready to take in Egypt's historical landmarks. Since Dowell had just one day to see those sights, he determined not to let political tensions or a lack of rest diminish his enjoyment of it all. He spent the day visiting as many archaeological ruins and museums as he could. He was even photographed atop a camel in front of the Great Pyramid of Giza. Then, when this day was over, Dowell returned to his hotel for his second and final night in Egypt.

When Dowell got back to his hotel, he received the disappointing news that his flight out of the country, scheduled for the following morning, had been cancelled. Dowell now had no way of reaching his next destination, Athens. He began calling other airlines to see what new arrangements could be made, but with little success. But then, after several calls, Dowell found a Swiss Air flight departing for Greece at 4:50 the next morning. Dowell quickly booked a seat on that plane.

Dowell arose to further difficulties the next day. As he was checking out of his hotel, Dowell tried to give the clerk a traveler's check to pay his bill. The proprietor balked. In order to accept a traveler's check, the man said, he would have to tack a heavy surcharge onto the amount owed. This revelation led to a squabble between Dowell and the hotel manager. Dowell had exhausted his supply of ready cash, but he "firmly refused" to accept the hotel's exorbitant surcharge. The manager "insisted there was no other way." After an extended debate, Dowell demanded to speak to the police.

Dowell said the man behind the desk then picked up a telephone and made a call, and when he returned after several minutes, he offered Dowell a new solution. Someone at the airport was willing to cash Dowell's traveler's check, the man said, and this would allow Dowell to pay his bill without a surcharge. The manager said he would even send a boy from the hotel to escort Dowell so that Dowell could send back his payment. Dowell quickly accepted the offer. "So that is what we did," Dowell said triumphantly in his journal. To this, Dowell added, "I will be so glad to get out of the trouble zone. It gets pretty wearing after a while."[27]

Later that day Dowell landed in Athens, where he checked in to the El Greco Hotel. During this stay, Dowell would visit the Acropolis, Mars Hill, and Old Corinth. Dowell said the life of the Apostle Paul became fresh to him as he saw such sights. "I must confess it does something to you," he wrote. But Dowell lamented one aspect of his visit to Greece. In Paul's day, Dowell observed, "[a]nyone could stand and speak his convictions. Now they have a state church and other religions are suppressed. They are not even allowed to meet in their homes for services."[28]

From Greece, Dowell proceeded on to Rome for a four-day visit. Temperatures there were soaring. "I hit Rome during the worst heat wave they have ever had," Dowell wrote. "When I left, 25 people had died of the heat. What made it worse, it did not cool off during the night."[29] Despite this discomfort, Dowell managed to take in the Coliseum, the catacombs, and St. Peter's Basilica. On the subject of St. Peter's, Dowell wrote, "The building is the most magnificent thing I have ever seen, but oh what a religious sham."[30]

Dowell's stay in Rome also included a visit to Paul's Mamertine Prison. Dowell's reaction to that site was very different from his reaction to St. Peter's Basilica. As he discussed the scene in his journal, a tone of reverence entered into the description:

> *I walked down into the dungeon where Paul was supposed to have been kept in prison awaiting his death, and I rehearsed his dying testimony: "I have fought a good fight. I have kept the faith. I have finished my course, henceforth there is laid up for me a crown of righteousness, which the Lord the righteous judge shall give me in that day, and not to me only but to all those that love His appearing." What a testimony, and there I stood where he may have been when he gave that testimony just before his head was severed from his body.[31]*

Dowell's stay in Rome included a weekend, so it goes without saying that he also attended church while he was there. He had planned to visit a nearby Baptist church, but those plans fell through when Dowell was unable to locate the meeting place. He walked for more than a mile, he said, but to no avail. Instead, Dowell settled for an English-speaking Episcopalian church. Admittedly, Dowell entered the service with low expectations. He took a dim view of the rituals and flowing robes associated with high church liturgy. But Dowell said he was pleasantly surprised by what he experienced. He was especially impressed by the content of the priest's sermon. This sermon focused on a character found in Luke 15, the prodigal son's elder brother, and Dowell liked the message so much that he openly praised it when he preached a similar message in 1982. Dowell titled his sermon "The Elder Brother."[32]

Dowell also experienced another encounter with a priest while he was visiting Rome, this one with a Catholic clergyman named Father John. Father John was a personal friend of Willa Mae Stewart-Setseck, one of Dowell's acquaintances from Springfield. Stewart-Setseck was a retired opera singer with family connections at High Street. She had even sung in Dowell's church on occasion ("very different from what was usually heard," Dowell Jr. recalled[33]). When Stewart-Setseck learned of Dowell's upcoming visit to Rome, she insisted that he visit Father John. The singer had even given Dowell a letter of introduction to help ensure that Father John would give him a proper welcome to that city. As part of her letter, Stewart-Setseck asked Father John to try to arrange an audience with Pope Pius XII.[34]

Dowell had not been keen on meeting a pope, but at the urging of his friend, he did want to make contact with Father John. And afterward, Dowell wrote, "He is very nice and treated me royally." Dowell said Father John even offered to try to set up the requested meeting with the pope. Unfortunately, such a meeting was going to have to wait until the following Wednesday, Father John told him. The eighty-two-year-old pope (who died just two months later) had suspended all interviews until the middle of the week. Dowell was forced to turn down the priest's offer. Dowell would be flying out of Rome on Monday night. "In a way I was glad," Dowell confided to Nola in a letter, "because I think the Catholic system and the Popery especially is a religious sham and an enemy to true New Testament Christianity, and I have my doubts whether real Christians ought to thus recognize him as if he was a great spiritual leader that we are to bow to. Well anyway, Rom. 8:28."[35]

That concluding remark was a reference to a familiar line from the writings of the Apostle Paul: "And we know that all things work together for good to them that love God, to them who are the called according to his purpose." This was a fitting sentiment, Dowell believed, for many of the things that he had recently experienced. Dowell had survived the troubled Middle East, he had made all of his flights, and he had dodged an awkward meeting with a pope. God was good.

Yet now it was time to leave the lands of the Bible and to get back to the business of spreading the Bible's message. In that spirit, Dowell cheerfully returned to the airport and boarded a plane headed back to the continent of Africa. This time Dowell's primary goal was not to see the sights. He was on a more serious errand. Indeed, by God's grace, Dowell would be opening a new mission field, the Belgian Congo, for the missionaries of the Baptist Bible Fellowship.

Chapter 31: *At Home and Abroad*

*T*here *he is.*

The missionary was pointing ahead. Dowell looked up and spotted, at the top of a set of stairs, a tall gray figure mounted against a clear sky. The statue's head was covered with a pith helmet; its face was dominated by a bushy moustache. The figure's curved left hand was lifted over its head, as if to block out the African sun. The other hand was clutching a tall walking stick.

Dowell was not overly impressed, but he tried to offer a polite response:

Well, isn't that somethin'.

The missionary continued:

They put this up here two years ago. It's a pretty good place for him, don't you think, way up here overlooking everything? You've got the view of the river down below and, of course, the city of Leopoldville.

Dowell snapped a quick picture of the view. He then continued his examination of the bronze statue of Henry Morton Stanley, nineteenth century journalist and explorer. Dowell tried to read the inscription on the statue's stone base, but like nearly everything in the Belgian Congo, the writing was in French. Dowell thought his missionary acquaintance might offer to translate, but the man never did. Instead, he asked Dowell a question:

Do you know much about Stanley?

Dowell had to confess his ignorance.

Not really. I know that he came to Africa. That's about all.

Dowell now stepped away from the statue to try to get a better angle for his snapshots. He continued the conversation as he moved:

I suppose just about everybody knows one thing about ol' Stanley, something he said–

The missionary did not even wait for Dowell to finish. The two men blurted the statement in unison:

"Dr. Livingstone, I presume?"

Dowell and his friend shared a chuckle as Dowell snapped another picture. Meanwhile, the missionary retrieved a handkerchief from one of his pockets. He used it to wipe the end of his nose and then leaned up against the statue's base as he launched into a well-rehearsed monologue:

Stanley actually came over to Africa more than once. The first time, of course, was when that newspaper back in New York hired him to try to locate David Livingstone. Livingstone had gone missing, you know. Stanley traveled halfway across the continent before he found him. But all of that happened far away from here.

For added emphasis, the missionary waved his handkerchief toward the meandering river below. Continuing, he said:

The thing is, Stanley kept coming back over. To Africa, I mean. He was inspired by Livingstone, I guess you might say. Traveled up and down this river. In fact, the city of Leopoldville was founded by Stanley as a trading post. At one point Stanley floated the entire length of the Congo River, nearly three thousand miles. Can you imagine?

Dowell answered with a smile:

Well, as a matter of fact, it sounds a bit like the summer I've been having.

The missionary returned a smile and tucked his handkerchief back into his pants pocket. He then turned and patted one of the statue's boots.

Well, anyway, ol' Stanley was an interesting fella'. For some people, he's sort of a controversial figure, but you have to admire his determination. At least that's what I say.

Dowell could not disagree.

Dowell landed in the Belgian Congo on Tuesday, August 5. His immediate purpose was to see what could be done to gain a permanent foothold in this country for the BBF. Fred Donnelson had been trying to get the necessary approvals for more than a year. Indeed, Donnelson had made his own trip to the Congo in 1957 but had come back emptyhanded. Donnelson was told that ". . . no new mission groups were needed."[1]

This answer left Donnelson—and an eager pair of missionaries named Elmer and Mary Deal—in a quandary. The Deals had been called by God to go to this field. They had trained at BBC, they had been approved as BBF missionaries, and they had spent the last year raising support so that they could go and minister in the Congo. Little good any of that would do them, however, if they were unable to enter the country.

As both Donnelson and the Deals were learning, navigating Congo's bureaucracy would require deep determination. Gaining entry into this place was not going to be an easy process. Indeed, that was by design. History had taught the Congolese that missionaries to Africa sometimes did more harm than good. Through the years, such guests had repeatedly instigated conflicts or subjugated the indigenous people. Such criticisms had even been leveled against the Congo's most famous visitor, Henry M. Stanley.

As a consequence, modern officials now kept their guard up. They protected Congo against such exploitation by insisting that missionaries help to educate the Congolese and to make them self-sufficient. Monitoring these efforts was the Congo Protestant Council (CPC), the entity charged with oversight of Christian mission groups.

The CPC's stated purpose was "to unite the missions at work in the Belgian Congo, to act as a liaison officer between them and the Government, to present, when necessary, matters to the Government General on behalf of the missions and to help all to work happily together in comity so that the whole of the Colony can be covered by evangelical mission work."[2] But the CPC also served as the de facto gatekeeper for new missionaries. And unfortunately, the secretary general of the CPC, V. de Carle Thompson, was reluctant to accept any missionaries from the Baptist Bible Fellowship. Thompson wrote Fred Donnelson a letter, saying, "[W]e feel that there are sufficient separate Protestant Missionary Societies engaged in work in the Colony."[3] Thompson said the Deals' best option would be to team up with some of the other entities already working in the Congo. "If some of the already established Missions were willing to accept missionaries from your Bible School and fellowship," Thompson wrote, "thus bringing support in personnel and finances, that would be a different matter. . . ."[4]

Neither the Deals nor Fred Donnelson liked this suggestion. They wanted to see the BBF working in the Congo independently, and they continued praying to that end. At the same time, the Deals began exploring some secondary options, including the possibility of forming a temporary relationship with some of those other groups. Indeed, this was the impetus for Dowell's visit to the Congo. Just weeks before Dowell left for his trip, Fred Donnelson had reached out to Carl J. Tanis, executive director of Christian Life Missions in Wheaton, Illinois, to see what partnership opportunities might present themselves. Tanis pointed Donnelson in the direction of Trevor Shaw, the publisher of an African mission magazine, *ENVOL*. Tanis also suggested the name of Ross Manning, a former missionary with the Regions Beyond Missionary Union.[5] Both of these men, Donnelson learned, were now residing in the Congolese city of Leopoldville (later known as Kinshasa), and both of them had connections, chiefly through the publication of literature, that might offer the Deals a back door into the Congo.

Dowell's itinerary afforded him eleven days to meet with these missionary contacts and with the CPC. It was hoped that, by the end of those meetings, Dowell would be able to offer a formal recommendation to the BBF about how they should proceed. He met with Trevor Shaw first. It was Shaw who came to pick Dowell up when he landed at the airport. Dowell's flight into Leopoldville arrived about an hour late, but Shaw, a gracious New Zealander, waited patiently for him. Shaw and his wife then hosted Dowell at their mission compound for the next couple of days. Dowell used this time to observe the Shaws' magazine operation and to explore the city of Leopoldville. Dowell was pleasantly surprised to find that temperatures in Africa were far cooler than they had been in Rome.

A couple of days later, Shaw took Dowell to meet Ross Manning of the Regions Beyond organization. It was Manning who orchestrated the most interesting part of Dowell's visit to the Congo. Upon meeting the American, Manning recommended that Dowell visit some of the mission stations in the interior of the country. Manning saw real possibilities for a partnership in those outlying areas, and such a trip would give Dowell a chance to experience Africa's wilderness.

Dowell readily accepted Manning's proposal, so Manning went to work making the travel arrangements. To help coordinate the trip, Manning reached out to contacts that were some seven hundred miles inland. Then, once Dowell's air and land travel arrangements had been made, Dowell jotted his family a note. "I will write you a few lines and inform you that you may not hear from me for about a week," he said. "I am leaving early in the morning for the bush country to see the real native Africa and to discuss the problem of our entering Africa with Dr. Wide of Baringa who may be in a position to help us."[6]

The next day, Thursday, Dowell flew from Leopoldville up to Basankusu. And from there he was taken by car to Baringa. Dowell took photos of the grass-covered huts that he saw along the way. "In one village," Dowell wrote, "the natives were trying to kill a very dangerous snake. My friend swerved his car and ran over the head of the snake and killed it. The natives were jubilant."[7] Dowell made sure to pose for a picture with the snake after its demise.

Dowell spent the next several days with a team of missionaries in Baringa. This group was led by a thirty-year veteran of medical missions, Dr. Wide. Wide and his wife, originally from England, not only operated a hospital but also cared for the residents of a large leper colony. Dowell said the Wides took him in "with open arms." While he was with them, he had the opportunity to watch Dr. Wide perform an operation. He was also invited to preach to a crowd of five hundred lepers, with Wide serving as his interpreter. "It was a thrill," Dowell wrote.[8]

Of course, that was where the excitement ended. Ministry in the bush was a plodding business, Dowell discovered, especially when he compared it to the breakneck schedule that he had been keeping for the last several weeks. At one point, Dowell's host offered to show him what the missionaries did for a diversion. Dowell readily accepted the offer. Dowell said he followed the doctor and his pet collie on a path down to a river, and when they got there, the missionary leaned up against a tree. That was his pastime. "That's it?" Dowell queried. "Why don't you go fishing? There's a river out there." The missionary looked at the murky African river and smiled. "The only ones that go fishing out there are the natives," the man told Dowell, "and many of them don't come back."[9]

Dowell's bushland adventure lasted five days, and at the end of it, Dowell began his trek back to Leopoldville. A Scottish missionary by the name of Campbell drove Dowell from Baringa to Boende to catch his return flight. Unfortunately, Campbell's vehicle had a flat tire on the way. The missionary attempted to put on the spare, Dowell said, but he discovered that his jack "didn't work right and would not lift the car high enough to get the wheel off." Campbell was still wrestling with this predicament when a crowd of Africans gathered around him. The blowout had occurred directly in front of their village, Dowell explained. "Of all the jabbering you have ever heard we heard it."[10]

But the circumstance proved serendipitous. When Campbell could not get his jack to work, he hired the villagers for some assistance. Some of the men promptly carried over a log and lifted the car. "Soon the tire was changed and we were on our way again," Dowell reported.[11]

When Dowell arrived back in Leopoldville, he lodged at the Union Missionnaire Hospitaliere, a sort of missionary hotel. Dowell said he also spent some additional time with Ross Manning, discussing options for getting BBF missionaries into the Congo.

"He is very sympathetic," Dowell wrote, "but the problems are many."[12] Manning thought Dowell's missionaries should join forces with one of the organizations operating in the interior, but Dowell rejected this idea. Wide and the others had been gracious hosts, but they were not fundamental Baptists. And Dowell knew that the BBF would never accept an interdenominational partnership.

Such a position left the BBF with few options, Manning said. The Congo's territories were parceled out to particular organizations, and the CPC would allow only one organization to work in each region. Since all of the regions were currently assigned, the BBF had little hope of admittance. From Manning's perspective, the Deal's best alternative might be to seek admittance into some of Congo's larger cities. In such places, shared turf was less of a concern because the needs of urban areas far exceeded the resources afforded by any one missionary organization.

Dowell agreed that Manning's idea was a worthwhile proposal, so he visited the CPC a day or so later to explore that option. And this meeting seems to have gone fairly well. Afterward Dowell wrote, "I had a very interesting conference with Mr. Sprunger, who is acting general secretary of the CPC. He concurred with me that under the existing conditions in Congo our best work as a fellowship could be done in the cities. There is a great need in the cities of Congo."[13]

Dowell now had a viable recommendation to take back to the BBF, and even though he had not obtained any official clearances, he believed his meetings had been profitable. "My contacts have been wonderful, and I feel much good has been done, but there is little more I can do now," Dowell said.[14] Dowell finished out that week relaxing in his room, dining with missionaries, shopping at an outdoor market, taking in a museum, and visiting a monument dedicated to Henry M. Stanley. Dowell also visited a local zoo. "Not as good as we have in the states" he remarked, "but interesting."[15]

As that week wore on, Dowell grew restless. "I have thoroughly enjoyed my trip," he wrote, "but I am beginning to get a little anxious to get home to my family and church."[16] Dowell even checked into the possibility of leaving Africa a bit early. Unfortunately, no airline connections were available, so Dowell had to bide his time.

Dowell finally left the Congo on Saturday, August 16. He was now headed for South America. But before crossing the Atlantic, Dowell would have to endure several layovers in French West Africa. On Saturday night Dowell stayed in Accra, Ghana, where the accommodations were "poor," he said. "But it was free," he added, "furnished by the airline."[17]

The following day Dowell traveled to the city of Abidjan in the Ivory Coast. There, Dowell struggled to communicate with the hotel staff, he said. No one working there was able to speak English. "I finally got checked in," Dowell wrote, "but it was pretty lonely not being able to speak to anyone."[18] Dowell said his situation improved a bit when another American traveler spotted him at dinnertime and offered to join him for coffee. Then, before long, the two men were joined by a third English-speaking traveler. "We three took some long walks together," Dowell wrote, "and ate together the rest of the time."[19]

Dowell left Abidjan on Monday, traveling now to the city of Dakar in Senegal. Dowell's next flight, the one crossing the Atlantic, would depart at 2:45 a.m. In the meantime, the airline provided Dowell with a posh hotel room. Dowell noted that his hotel had even been featured in an issue of *Time Magazine*. Unfortunately, as Dowell discovered, magazine photographs do not tell the whole story. Swarms of mosquitos were everywhere. "I thought I might sleep," Dowell wrote, "but mosquitoes were so bad I finally got up and put my clothes on, went downstairs and got some water and took two pills Trevor Shaw had given me to prevent malaria, found the mosquitoes were just as bad in the lobby, so I returned to my room for a brief time, and then it was time to return to the airport."[20]

Needless to say, Dowell was relieved to board that transatlantic flight. He was even more relieved when he learned that the passenger load on that plane was light and that he would be able to spread out across three seats for some needed rest. Dowell's final destination was Brazil. His plane would make a brief stop in Rio de Janeiro before continuing on to Brazil's largest city, Sao Paulo, where he would minister to another group of missionaries.

Brazil was an important stop for Dowell. In those days, each of the fellowship's mission fields was assigned to a "field representative," an American pastor who acted as a liaison and advocate for the missionaries of that country back in the US. Dowell had been serving as the field representative for Brazil for some time, but he had never yet visited that country.

Dowell was greeted in Sao Paulo by a joyous assembly of missionaries. Mr. and Mrs. Byron McCartney stepped up to serve as Dowell's hosts for the week. Dowell preached at the McCartneys' church on Tuesday night. Though his journaling was growing much less detailed now, he did manage a brief report about that Tuesday night service. "Some saved," he wrote.[21]

Dowell spent much of the next day riding in a car. Byron took him down a coastal highway to visit two mission outposts—"a dusty trip," Dowell said, but "the beach was one of the most beautiful I have ever seen."[22] Since Dowell was scheduled to speak back in Sao Paulo later that evening, the men made a return trip that same day. It was on this leg of the journey that McCartney's vehicle had a flat tire. And unfortunately, no villagers came to the rescue this time; Dowell and his host were on their own. According to Dowell, the ordeal left them "filthy," and it also put them behind schedule. "[W]e had to go directly to the church where I was to preach that night because it was time for service," he said. Fortunately, the Brazilians did not seem to mind that their evangelist had not freshened up. Dowell gave a positive report about this service in his journal. "We had a good crowd and a good service," Dowell wrote cheerfully.[23]

Dowell's itinerary the rest of the week was likewise hectic. His other meetings included two mornings of lecturing at a Brazilian Bible college and a visit to a Brazilian home owned by "a rather prosperous family." Serving in that home, Dowell said, was a boy who had attended Dowell's Tuesday night meeting at McCartney's church. In fact, this boy had been among the "Some saved" mentioned in Dowell's journal. The young man had been raised as a Catholic, so McCartney took extra time to counsel him while they were visiting, Dowell said.[24]

Later that same day, Dowell attended a dinner at the home of Missionary Jean Kruse. Then following that meal, Dowell was taken to another church to preach. So went the remainder of his week. Dowell found his stay in Brazil to be profitable, but he also found it to be exhausting. By the end of it all, the weary preacher was happy to board a Pan Am flight headed for home.

Dowell would travel back to Springfield by way of Rio, San Juan, and New York. Or at least that was his plan. His flight out of Rio did not go well. After the plane had been flying "a great while," Dowell noticed that one of the engines was not running. He flagged down a stewardess to ask about it. Dowell was then informed that, due to a mechanical problem, the pilot had turned the plane around and was heading back to Rio. "She said we would be in Rio in about two hours," Dowell wrote in his journal, "and that it was not serious."

Not everyone on board took this news so calmly. Indeed, as word of the dead engine spread, some passengers began to panic. "One woman has cried a great deal," Dowell wrote. Dowell himself managed to find comfort in his faith. "I experienced a little uneasy feeling," he admitted, "but not to any great extent. I am in the hands of the Lord and He will care for me."[25]

Dowell's greatest concern was that the delay would prevent him from reaching Springfield on schedule. He was supposed to arrive at home just in time for High Street's Sunday morning service. In fact, he had instructed Nola to bring a fresh suit of clothes to the airport so that he could go straight to church without stopping by their house to change. But those plans were looking doubtful now. Indeed, when Dowell's plane reached Rio, he and the other travelers learned that their burned-out motor was going to have to be replaced and that this repair would take at least twelve hours. The airline booked all of the passengers into a hotel, and Dowell had to wire Earl Smith to let him know that his plans had been changed. Instead of arriving Sunday morning, Dowell would be there sometime Sunday afternoon.

Dowell's second departure from Rio took place the next morning, and there were no further problems after that. "It will be so good to be on American soil again," Dowell wrote as he flew. "For one to appreciate the good old U.S.A., he has only to travel in other countries," Dowell said. "I am really looking forward to seeing my sweet family and being with my people again."[26] Dowell stepped off of a Delta airliner and into the arms of his wife in Springfield a few hours later. It had been a wonderful trip, but Dowell was grateful to be home.

As Dowell looked back on that world tour, he acknowledged its many benefits. Among other things, it had helped to solidify a friendship with Elmer and Mary Deal that would last for the rest of their lives. Back in 1957, Dowell had given this couple some helpful advice as they graduated from BBC. Elmer recorded Dowell's statement in a memoir that he wrote years later. "Right now, it doesn't look bright for you going to the Congo," Dowell had said. "If you succeed, you are going to have to be determined."

Elmer took that counsel to heart and adopted as one of his "life's themes" the words of an old song: "I am determined. I've made up my mind."[27]

This determination served the Deals' ministry well. After Elmer and Mary finished raising their support, they attended language school in Europe. They then traveled on to the Congo, departing for their new field on August 3, 1959, about a year after Dowell had visited that country. The couple arrived with nothing more than a visitor's visa, and they were still unsure how they would establish an independent mission work. Even so, they were determined to trust God and to let Him direct their steps. They were also grateful for the early help that they had received from Dowell, Donnelson, and others.

The Deals made a survey trip of the Congo, and as it happened, the Lord placed within them a strong desire to take the gospel, not to Congo's urban centers as Dowell had suggested, but to the kinds of places that Dowell had seen when he visited the interior, places with no existing gospel witness. In fact, God showed the Deals just such a place when He brought them to the town of Albertville during their survey of the country. The Deals returned to Leopoldville determined to convince the CPC to let them start a ministry in Albertville. Yet happily, no such convincing was necessary. Secretary General Thompson had "been getting letters from that area," the Deals learned, asking him for some additional help from missionaries.[28]

On February 16, 1960, the Deals telegrammed Fred Donnelson to say, "We are now officially in Congo. Received our permanent resident visas today. Prayers have been answered."[29] Thus began a ministry that spanned more than fifty years and produced more than one hundred and fifty churches.[30] Elmer, writing in his memoir, credited Dowell for helping to make those things possible. His "example, teaching, missionary burden and challenge to 'be determined,' prepared me for the struggles of African missionary work," Elmer said.[31]

Those qualities that the Deals admired in Dowell had been deepened, it seems, during his world tour. In particular, Dowell had returned from the trip with a greater "burden for world evangelism," he said.[32] And in answer to that burden, Dowell leveraged his travel experiences soon after he returned to the US. The unrest in the Middle East had piqued the interest of many Americans, Dowell found, so he now had a unique opportunity to share with them his firsthand experiences. In the process, he could also share with them the gospel.

One instance of this came when Dowell was invited to speak at a civic organization in Springfield, the University Club. Officials of this organization believed that Dowell's account of his experiences would be a real crowd-pleaser, and Dowell was happy to oblige. "I knew what they wanted," Dowel recalled, "and I told them all that I had learned about the political situations in all of the various countries that I visited." Indeed, Dowell's stories were well received. The audience "drank it up," he said.[33] Yet Dowell did not stop there.

In a different part of his life, Dowell had once misunderstood an invitation he had received to speak for a public high school graduation. Dowell had arrived thinking he was speaking at a baccalaureate service. The mix-up made little difference to Dowell, of course, but school officials grew concerned. Just before Dowell got up to speak, one official "reminded [him] publicly that this was not a church service; this was a commencement exercise." Dowell answered that admonition. ". . . I reminded *them* publicly when I got up that I was a Baptist preacher," Dowell said. "If you tell me not to preach a sermon, I won't preach a sermon, but don't you be too much surprised if what I say sounds like a sermon, 'cause that's all I know to do." Dowell finished his account of this story, saying, "I wouldn't agree to preach anywhere in the world that I couldn't preach Christ."[34]

Dowell addressed the University Club in that same spirit. He gave them the eye-witness political news that they were so interested in hearing, but then he turned their attention to Christ. "But being a Baptist preacher," Dowell told them, "the most interesting place that I visited was the Holy Land." According to Dowell, the rest was preaching. ". . . I started them in with Bethlehem of Judaea where Christ was born of a virgin and I took them all the way to the cross."[35]

Dowell received a five-minute ovation when he finished that presentation. But he also received something else. He received the satisfaction of knowing that he had obeyed a command found in Mark 16:15. In that passage the Lord states, "Go ye into all the world and preach the gospel to every creature." At home and abroad, Dowell had done just that. And he was determined to keep on doing it for as long as the Lord would give him breath.

Chapter 32: *Chest Pains*

A glass door swung open, and in walked a spry bank customer lugging a bulging zipper pouch under one arm. As he passed by, he spoke to a pair of women huddled at a desk.

Morning, ladies. It's a beautiful day out there.

The women glanced up to see that it was Earl Smith. One of the women, the one with a pair of chains dangling from her glasses, said:

Good morning, Mr. Smith.

The platinum blonde standing next to her chimed in:

Morning.

Smith stepped up to a high, open countertop in the middle of the lobby. As he dropped his zipper bag on the glassy marble, a man in a suit walked by carrying a cup of coffee. Smith greeted him, too.

How ya doin', Jerry?

Jerry paused in mid-sip.

Doing a whole lot better now that I got my joe.

Just then, Smith glanced over to his left and spotted another familiar face, a man who was standing in an open doorway.

Is that Hank back there? I thought he was still on vacation.

Hank turned and waved, and Smith called out to him:

You still owe me a round of golf, you know.

Hank answered cheerfully:

I'm ready any day you are.

Smith was now forming stacks of bills on the countertop. Over the weekend, he and his quartet had sponsored a concert down at the Shrine Mosque. Admission was a dollar, Smith said, and the proceeds would go to help out the quartet's ministry. They were hoping to get an album together pretty soon.[1]

So did you bring me a joke today, Mr. Smith?

This question came from a young woman standing behind a teller's station a few feet away. Smith immediately stopped working, set down a stack of ones, and rested his elbows on the counter in front of him.

Okay, Sally, how about this one. A visitor went into a church one day, and the sermon was terrible. The man could hardly keep his eyes open the entire time. So afterward a woman from the congregation went up to introduce herself. She said, "Hello, I'm Gladys Dunn." And the man replied, "You're not the only one."

Smith's punchline gave Sally a good laugh. The two ladies huddling at the desk were likewise laughing. The blonde one called out:

I've gotta tell my boyfriend that one!

Smith, now busy counting again, answered back:

Just so long as you tell him where you got it.

In the midst of all this revelry, there were other bank customers coming and going. One man in a pair of overalls had just finished cashing a check. He had been chatting with one of the other tellers since Smith had walked in. Then, when the man turned to leave, he spotted Smith and his pile of ones. The man in overalls instantly turned back to his teller friend to deliver a joke of his own. He pointed to Smith and said:

See that guy over there? He's countin' his cash like ol' Dowell does it.

Smith was licking his thumb just then and paused momentarily to glance over at the stranger. He said to the man:

Oh, you think so, huh?

The jokester was still chuckling.

That's what it looks like to me. I'd say your pile is just about as big as ol' Dowell's.

Smith was pretty sure he knew the answer to this next question, but he asked the man anyway:

You know who I am?

The stranger's eyes now widened.

No-o-o-o.

So Smith rested his palms on the edge of the countertop and told him:

I'm Brother Dowell's associate, and I'd like to talk to you about the remark you just made.

But according to Smith, that was the end of it. Smith had no sooner uttered those words than the wisecracker shot out the bank door.[2]

Dowell's final years at High Street were a mixed bag. There were many things to celebrate, of course. In 1959, Dowell's tent revivals morphed into something new: the Springfield Revival Crusade. It was a cooperative venture involving many of Springfield's churches, though it was spearheaded by Dowell. This meeting was conducted in a tent at the local fairgrounds. G. B. Vick was engaged to preach, and Earl Smith directed a four-hundred-voice choir for the services. The first night alone drew an estimated four thousand people, and the excitement continued for two more weeks, May 3 to May 17. Two of the services were even filmed for national broadcasts. According to a *Tribune* article, they aired "in 105 cities in 40 states."[3] Nola's parents living out in California said they were able to watch them from their home.[4]

Dowell's ministry witnessed other blessings as well. By 1960, High Street's membership had surpassed five thousand,[5] and its average attendance had reached 2,726.[6] High Street was now more than three times the size of the next largest church in the area. Indeed, it had reached the peak of its growth. Never before or since has it been any larger.

Another blessing came in 1962, when Dowell was elected to serve a second term as the president of the BBF.[7] By that time, the fellowship was rapidly growing. It included twelve hundred churches in forty-three states, and it supported a hundred and seventy-eight missionaries in twenty-seven countries.[8] Dowell considered it a unique privilege to lead such a movement for a second time.

But these blessings were accompanied by many burdens. And the heaviness of those burdens took its toll. In Springfield, Dowell's high profile made him the focus of skeptics, critics, and outright enemies. Dowell said being accused of something that he did not do "was the order of the day." Some of those falsehoods were even circulated in the press. "The newspaper was my enemy," Dowell said.[9]

Dowell recalled one newspaper report about a meeting he had with Springfield's mayor. The article left the impression that Dowell was stepping into a political office. "I went down personally to their office, and I made them eat that," Dowell snarled. "I said, 'I want you to know, personally, there's not enough money in the treasury of the Springfield government to get me to run for any office here in this town.' I said, 'I have had opportunity but I've refused to do it.' And I said, 'It isn't right for you to sit in judgment upon me based on rumor.' I said, 'That's not good journalism.'"[10]

Dowell's confrontation brought an immediate turnabout, he noted. The newspaper official "was very nice" and he even thanked Dowell for coming to speak to him. "And really, shortly after that, he sent a reporter to my office and they interviewed me and gave me a big headline write-up about my whole life and ministry and about the High Street Baptist Church. . . . And from then on," Dowell said, "I didn't have any trouble with him."[11]

But not every rumor was so easily quashed. Even more worrisome than stories about Dowell's political aspirations were the rumors that impugned his character. He found that he had to remain vigilant to protect his reputation. His most important advice for young preachers was always this: "Live an exemplary life above reproach."[12] And Dowell was careful to follow that advice. In a 1986 sermon, he told of being contacted by a car dealer to whom he had traded a vehicle. The vehicle had about seventy-eight thousand miles on it, but the dealer wanted to roll the odometer back to thirty thousand. The man called Dowell to ask him to corroborate that number if he was contacted by any potential buyers. Dowell said he was "stunned" by the man's request. He answered the dealer, "I thought I had a better reputation than that."[13] And after an awkward pause, the man apologized for making the suggestion and hung up.

While some in the community may have doubted Dowell's integrity, those who really knew him never did. Even so, certain rumors seemed to persist. One of the most stubborn was the one that Earl Smith had heard while standing in the bank. Many people believed that Dowell was becoming some sort of tycoon. Dowell said the same rumor had been reported to another man in his church, a man who happened to be a member of the FBI. This man had been told by another gentleman, "I happen to know that Bill Dowell gets fifty thousand dollars a year or more." Dowell's FBI friend—"a great big ol' burly guy"—took offense to the statement. "[H]e reached up and got him by the collar, and he said, 'I'm gonna make you eat those words.' Said, 'I happen to be a member of that church. I know what salary he gets, and it's so far away from fifty thousand dollars till there's no comparison to it." The gossiper then admitted that there was no basis for his claim. "I heard it," he confessed. And in answer to that excuse, the FBI man offered a word of advice: "Try to investigate next time."[14]

Unfortunately, not many people took the time to investigate the rumors that they heard about Dowell. As a result, a wide range of outlandish stories got passed around. "They began to attribute all sorts of things to me," Dowell said. "They had me owning interests—that I had become a very, very wealthy man—that I had interest in Consumer's Market, Clover Leaf Dairy, Heer's Incorporated [a local department store], KGBX [a radio station], and all sorts of things that I was supposed to have had some interest in."[15] Earl Smith recalled hearing one such rumor from a police officer who attended High Street. "His department head said Brother Dowell owned half of a liquor store in town," Smith recalled.[16]

Periodically people carried such rumors back to Dowell, asking if there was any truth to them. In answer, Dowell would once again assure them that the reports were complete fabrications. "Well, these folks are trying to hurt me," Dowell explained, "but I've never owned interest in any of these things or any other business in town. The only income I have is from my church and meetings that I hold from time to time."[17]

Of course, it was true that Dowell's regular income provided his family with a comfortable living. And to an extent, the Dowells' affluence showed. Dowell and his wife enjoyed fine clothing, luxurious automobiles, and even some expensive jewelry. But there was no secret fortune as was often supposed. At the time of Dowell's death, he and his wife owned just one home, the same home they had occupied for thirty years. It was a modest ranch-style residence with a two-car garage, and it was located in a middle-class neighborhood. They had enjoyed a good life, but not an extravagant one.

As for the material goodness that Dowell did experience, he glorified God for all of it. He told one audience:

> Some people think God wants His people to live in poverty. I personally don't think He wants them to. I think He permits some people to live in poverty because they wouldn't live for God if He didn't. If they had money, they'd turn away from God. But I believe—if we're real men of God—I believe God wants to supply us with abundance and plenty. And He's promised to do it. He said, "All of your needs." Somebody says, "Oh, yeah, I know God supplies just our needs, but He doesn't supply our wants." Well, I even believe God will supply our wants if we'll meet the conditions. I used to preach that, too, until I found a scripture. And in this scripture He says, "If you'll delight yourself in the Lord, He'll give you the desires of your heart." If you trust in the Lord, He'll supply your needs, but if you delight yourself in the Lord, He'll give you the desires of your heart![18]

Dowell immediately qualified that claim, saying, God "gives us wisdom even in our wants."[19] Yet Dowell stood by the basic premise. He believed there was no shame in having or enjoying a measure of personal wealth. And as for his critics, they could say what they pleased. Dowell's church members knew the truth, and they defended him. "I would've never made it if they hadn't," he said.[20]

For Dowell, the attacks that came from without were much easier to cope with than those that came from within—within the body, one might say. Dowell had seen internal strife rip apart Norris's old fellowship. He had also seen the threat that it sometimes posed to mission works. In May 1961, Dowell took another extended mission trip, this one concentrated in Central and South America. It was no "pleasure trip," Dowell said.[21] There were serious problems affecting the missionaries in these places. They ranged from interpersonal conflicts to troubling family matters. Dowell was asked to go and address the needs.

In Brazil, for instance, the missionaries were bickering with one another. Dowell gathered the missionaries of Brazil together for a meeting, telling them:

> *I was officially asked by unanimous vote of the mission committee and mission director to come at this time. They invested in me all the authority legally and scripturally possible to dissolve the disturbing conditions that have divided this field. They have placed such great confidence in me I feel compelled to leave no stone unturned in solving the problems here. This I will do, pledging my love to all, but showing preference to none.*[22]

Dowell then spent several days working to resolve the problems that had arisen in that country. He conducted private conferences with each of the missionaries, investigating a feud that had developed. Joint projects involving building construction and Christian education had produced the squabbles. Now the two major factions in these disputes were at each other's throats. Dowell sent a postcard to Nola, saying, "I will be glad when conference in Sao Paulo is over. Some real problems to work out."[23]

Once Dowell had listened to all sides, he brought the missionaries and their wives back together. In that second conference, he laid out his findings. His best hope was that the factions would cease their strife by parting ways. He listed his recommendations in his notes, saying, "That each missionary leave the other missionaries' works alone unless invited to assist," and in another place, "That all talking, criticizing, accusing, and judging be stopped."[24]

When Dowell finished laying out these recommendations, he felt satisfied that the situation had been resolved. He wrote in his notes, "To all of this they all wholeheartedly agreed and felt it was a happy solution and pledged patience and understanding in working out all the details." He further stated, "I had all the missionaries with me for dinner the day I left. There was a natural happy fellowship."[25]

But Dowell's work was not finished. Although this entire trip lasted just sixteen days, Dowell traveled to Brazil, Uruguay, Argentina, Chile, Peru, and Mexico. At Montevideo, Uruguay, Dowell comforted Lavon and Carolyn Waters, a missionary couple whose third child had been born with spina bifida. The girl died just four months after her birth. In fact, Dowell arrived in Uruguay on the day of her death. He remained with the family "through the grief of her funeral and burial," he said.[26] Then Dowell also helped them in another way. The Waters family had amassed some significant medical bills, so Dowell used his contacts in the US to try to alleviate that debt.

In Mexico, Dowell dealt with a different matter. A missionary and his family had placed themselves in a questionable situation. "They have taken a young 16-year-old Mexican boy into their home to support and educate," Dowell wrote. "I believe this is unwise. It is creating doubt if not suspicion on the part of some." Dowell sent a recommendation back to the mission committee: "Instruct him to return the boy to his parents. . . ."[27]

Troubles within the body were never pleasant to deal with, but they could not be ignored. Dowell witnessed this firsthand. Within days of coming back from his trip to South and Central America, Dowell began experiencing some chest pains. Nola summoned a physician to their home, and soon afterward, Dowell was rushed to the hospital. He had suffered a major heart attack. Dowell spent the next couple of weeks on a hospital bed and several more weeks after that convalescing at home. By order of the doctor, he had to slow down.[28]

Slowing down was a difficult pill for this patient to swallow, especially where church work was involved. Dowell had strong views about Christians even missing church services. He told a story about starting a revival in one rural place and admonishing the people to be present in every service. Afterward a farmer came to him: "He said, 'I milk forty cows every night and it takes me so long to do it I have to start at a certain time and I get through at a certain time, and by the time I am through it is too late to come to church. What are you going to say about that?'" Dowell said he gave the man a blunt answer: "I said, 'Brother, I have just one thing to say. You've got too many cows. Sell some of them.'" Dowell added gleefully, "I don't know whether he sold any or not, but he got to church every night after that!"[29]

Dowell's attitude toward faithful attendance extended even to situations involving poor health. He told one audience, "I don't think [a Christian] ought to stay home unless he's half dead."[30] And Dowell lived by this principle for much of his life, though he acknowledged that his zeal in this matter had, at times, been misguided. Dowell told his Pastoral Theology students, "When I was a young preacher I was cautioned by older preachers to slow down a bit, to which I answered in my ignorance, I would rather wear out than rust out. Because I foolishly did not listen to the wise advice of my elders by the time I was 47 I had had three major operations and a heart attack."[31]

Dowell began heeding the advice that he had heard only after he experienced that heart attack. And friends and family rallied around him to make sure that he took better care of himself. One note that Dowell received while he was convalescing came from Fred Donnelson. "It was such a shock to hear of your illness that I have been in somewhat of a daze since then," Donnelson wrote. "My insistence on your taking the South America trip and keeping you up all night during the Fellowship leaves me with a sense of responsibility for your condition." Donnelson then added a firm admonition: "Only you must learn to say 'No!' to fellows like me who keep pestering you."[32]

Dowell exercised greater caution when he returned to his office and responsibilities. Even so, he soon experienced another kind of heartache, this one affecting the church body. The situation had sinister origins, Dowell believed. He told one audience, "The devil goes to church more often than most of you members."[33] And Dowell knew whereof he spoke.

This latest crisis arose in January of 1962. The individual at the center of it all was one of Dowell's staff members, Alden Jaynes. In 1992, Dowell was asked if he had any regrets about his ministry. Dowell offered just one answer: "We talked Alden Jaynes into becoming our general superintendent and teaching one of our large adult Bible classes. And he built a great class. Added to it. He had a lot of ability, and he was a good teacher. But he wasn't loyal."[34]

Dowell had hired Jaynes away from Pilley's Dairy back in the mid-1950s. Jaynes had been a member of the dairy's upper management, and Dowell believed that someone with Jaynes's business savvy would be a great asset to his growing church. Jaynes and his family were already personal friends of the Dowells. Jaynes was a hunting and fishing enthusiast, and he and Dowell enjoyed good fellowship during their outdoor adventures together. Dowell Jr. likewise enjoyed a close bond with this family. He and Jaynes's son, Rex, were the best of friends. Consequently, Dowell Jr. was a regular guest in the Jaynes's home, and he often joined them for family outings. When Dowell Jr. was a teen, the Dowells even had their eye on Jaynes's daughter, Donna, as a possible mate for their son.

Not surprisingly, then, the entire Dowell family was in favor of bringing Jaynes on board at High Street. "I remember I thought it was a great idea," Dowell Jr. said. "I thought the world of Alden Jaynes. He was like a second dad to me at the time."[35] But getting Jaynes to accept the position took some convincing. "There was much concern in the Jaynes family," Dowell Jr. recalled. "There were many discussions." In hindsight, Dowell Jr. thought he understood the family's reluctance. "I think they had some fears about what would happen. They knew their dad perhaps better than some others did because he was very, very headstrong. Things had to be his way. And he could be very vocal about things—even critical."[36]

Despite all of this, Dowell continued his pursuit of Jaynes until Jaynes eventually accepted a position as High Street's Sunday school superintendent. Jaynes would have oversight of the various Sunday school departments. He would also be the manager of the church's finances and would carry on his role as the teacher of an adult Bible study, the Harmony Class.

Unfortunately, High Street's harmony became more delicate after Jaynes's arrival on the staff. Dowell said the situation grew out of a tense working relationship that developed between Alden Jaynes and Earl Smith.[37] Smith had already worked with Dowell for a decade, and by this time the two of them shared an implicit trust. Jaynes, as the third member of this team, found it difficult to fit in. He also objected to some of Smith's work activities. Smith's shoot-from-the-hip approach to ministry clashed with

Jaynes's "methodical" approach to business management.[38] From Jaynes's point of view, Smith was constantly overstepping his bounds. Smith, on the other hand, may have felt that Jaynes could do with a bit of common sense.

One of the first clashes between these two men occurred over picking up the church mail. This was normally a task that Smith took care of, but on one occasion, Smith was standing in the church office and heard Jaynes tell the secretary that he was going downtown. Instinctively Smith pulled out the keys to the post office box and tossed them to Jaynes, saying, "Here, pick up the mail while you're down there." According to Dowell Jr., the interpersonal subtext of that moment went something like this: "To Earl, it was just a matter of efficiency, but Alden interpreted it as if he was some kind of errand boy to Earl. His reaction was, 'You're not gonna treat me like some kind of office boy.'"[39]

Dowell Jr. said the situation between Jaynes and Smith "escalated" from there.[40] According to Dowell, Jaynes "resented Earl tremendously."[41] But Dowell defended Smith. "He was one of the best co-workers a man could ever have," Dowell once said in an interview. "And he never did one iota, one thing against his pastor."[42]

At the same time, Dowell understood the source of Jaynes's resentment. "Second to me, [Smith] had more influence than almost the whole church put together. Everybody liked him," Dowell said, "and he was just a good fellow."[43] Smith's unwritten authority at High Street undermined Jaynes at every turn, or so it seemed to Jaynes. And Dowell was well acquainted with the complaints. Dowell Jr. said Jaynes routinely carried his concerns into the pastor's office. "Alden would come and knock on the door, stick his head in and say, 'You got a minute?' And he could come in there, you know, and just ruin your day, and always expressing his deep concern about this or that. He'd sometimes stay an hour and a half," Dowell Jr. said. "He'd do Earl the same way. 'Have you got a minute?'"[44]

Jaynes's constant complaints had an observable effect on the pastor's spirit. Dowell Jr. noticed it even while he was living in Texas. He came home from Borger for a holiday visit and, for the first time in his life, heard his father express dread about going to the office.[45]

Still, Dowell was not entirely dissatisfied with Jaynes's work. Without question, Jaynes had proven himself to be an efficient manager. Even Dowell Jr. admitted that he ran "a tight ship." High Street continued to thrive for a number of years after Jaynes joined the staff, and by the early 1960s, High Street's Sunday school was larger than it had ever been. Jaynes's own Sunday school class had grown to attendances of several hundred. And Dowell had to admire such results. When, at one point, Jaynes was offered a staff position with Pastor Verle Ackerman of Florida, it was Dowell who kept him from going. "Dad took Alden out fishing and spent the day with him and talked him into not leaving," Dowell Jr. recalled. "In hindsight," Dowell Jr. added, "he might have been wise to have let him go."[46]

Over time, Jaynes's presence on the staff grew more problematic. After Dowell Jr. joined the staff in 1958, he too witnessed the tension that Jaynes produced. Jaynes seemed to feel that ". . . everybody else was kowtowing down to Earl and Dad," Dowell

Jr. said. As a consequence, Jaynes became increasingly critical, not just of Earl Smith, but of everyone, including the pastor. "[H]e made a statement to me about my dad," Dowell Jr. said, "that he can't even manage his own finances much less the finances of the church."[47]

Jaynes's criticisms also extended to Dowell Jr., who served as High Street's youth and college ministry director. On Sundays, Dowell Jr. met with the high school group for opening exercises and then taught the college class. Dowell Jr.'s other responsibilities included overseeing the high school class teachers, coordinating high school and college class activities, and directing dramatic productions for the holidays. His leadership in the college class resulted in attendances of more than two hundred students.

But Dowell Jr. found that Jaynes sometimes lorded over him in these efforts. For instance, Jaynes disagreed with Dowell Jr. on a choice that he made to fill a leadership position in his department. In Jaynes's opinion, the couple that Dowell Jr. had selected belonged elsewhere. So Jaynes had them removed. When Dowell Jr. found out about it, he reinstated them. "I turned around and put them back in there," Dowell Jr. said. This was a move that angered Jaynes.[48]

In another instance, Dowell Jr. had a man working under him who had been "caught in some bad finances" at his place of employment. "The guy was dishonest," Dowell Jr. recalled. Jaynes learned about the situation and directed Dowell Jr. to remove the man from his post. But Dowell Jr. delayed his response. While he agreed that the man had to go, this circumstance had presented itself during the fall months, and Dowell Jr.'s youth department was busy putting together a Christmas program. Furthermore, the gentleman in question had already made plans to leave Springfield over the Christmas holidays. So in defiance of Jaynes's directive, Dowell Jr. opted to "ride it out for a few more weeks." Dowell Jr. added, ". . . I was probably wrong to do it. . . ."[49]

Situations such as these left Jaynes deeply frustrated, and by January 1962, he found he could tolerate no more. He went to Dowell and told him he would be leaving High Street. Dowell, by this time, was content to let him go. Dowell called a meeting of the deacons so that Jaynes could air his grievances before leaving. He also granted a request that Jaynes put to him to stand before the church and tell them goodbye. ". . . I was just gracious enough and unwise enough that I allowed him to do it," Dowell said.[50]

The next Sunday Jaynes spoke to the congregation. Yet instead of bidding farewell, he used the opportunity to voice his complaints. "When he got up there, he just tried to tear things apart," Dowell said. "He went into things, took, oh, twenty-five minutes anyway."[51] According to Dowell Jr., the speech "Worked on sympathies a lot." The younger Dowell recalled a tone of desperation in Jaynes's appeals. "He got up in front of the whole church and said, 'I don't know what I'm going to do. I can't fight everybody else and that's why I'm gonna resign. I don't know what I'm gonna do.'"[52]

Jaynes's comments left many in the church puzzled over the situation, so after his remarks, Dowell said he would open the upcoming deacons meeting—the one planned for the next night—to the entire church. Dowell Jr. recalled that some two hundred people attended that meeting. It was held in one of High Street's large classrooms, and the room "was packed and jammed." The meeting took the form of a question and answer forum, Dowell Jr. recalled. "Each staff member got up and talked and then answered questions from the audience." And tensions ran high. "I know I was scared to death," Dowell Jr. said, "I was just trembling."[53]

Yet if that night served to accomplish anything, it was merely to deepen a rift that had already formed within the congregation. Jaynes continued his allegations, saying, "I can't do anything. They won't cooperate." And according to Dowell Jr., Jaynes's charges served to "further polarize" the people gathered.[54] In the end, many of those individuals chose to sever their ties with High Street, and Dowell had to stand by and watch as beloved friends exited his church.

High Street lost no less than five hundred members in a week's time. Among them were such respected leaders as Goy Campbell, Lee McClain, Max Hawkins, and Fred Lynn. Fred Lynn and Alden Jaynes had both built large adult classes, and when they left, they influenced many members of their classes to follow after them.

Dowell Jr., in hindsight, considered Jaynes's desperate pleas from the pulpit to be disingenuous. "Things were not as uncertain and spontaneous as they sounded . . . ," Dowell Jr. alleged.[55] Jaynes had known exactly what he was going to do when he left. "[T]he fact was, he already had a job lined up," Dowell Jr. said. "He had already made arrangements for what was the old Second Baptist Church property."[56] Jaynes and his crowd never even missed a service, Dowell Jr. recalled. The following Sunday they were meeting together in a new facility. Meanwhile, the High Street Baptist Church was recovering from a major split.

When Dowell was interviewed about these events thirty years later, he tended to downplay or even sugarcoat what had transpired. He was reluctant to call names or to vilify individuals, and his account of the story left the impression that little damage had been done. "It didn't hurt the church very much," he claimed. "We had a full house the next Sunday." In this regard, Dowell was no J. Frank Norris seeking to crush his enemies. He set the contentions aside and moved on. "We never made a public affair out of the so-called split," he said. "I was pastor long enough that I knew, too, that we should not dignify this move that they had made."[57]

Dowell said he also extended love to those who had left his side. "I even prayed," Dowell admitted, "maybe I was going too far, but I prayed and I asked God that if there was any way to keep from judging that church—for that church to go on and have a good ministry—that the Lord would help them to do it." Those prayers were offered, Dowell said, because he believed the perpetrators had put themselves in danger of such judgment. "You can't rebel against God and openly fight God's word and get by with it," Dowell declared. He added with resignation, "[N]evertheless, it came to pass even as I imagined that it would."[58]

Some of the fallout resulting from this split took the form of collateral damage. In several cases, members of the same families found themselves on opposite sides of this dispute. Jaynes's own daughter and son-in-law remained at High Street, Dowell Jr. recalled. Goy Campbell likewise had a daughter that remained behind.

But there were also troubles within the new church body, a group which took the name Victory Baptist Church. Initially, this church experienced great success, Dowell Jr. recalled. "They had some super services," he said, and their attendances may have reached as high as seven or eight hundred. Even so, the odd combination of personalities at Victory seemed to spell disaster from the start. Factions that had kept their distance from one another at High Street were now thrown into a much smaller fish bowl. "Someone commented and said, 'Boy, that's not going to last long,'" Dowell Jr. stated. "And it didn't."[59] Just four years after splitting from High Street, Victory Baptist Church experienced a split of its own. Fred Lynn and a group of his followers pulled out of the church and began a new work in another part of town.

Fortunately, this did not end the story. Over time, the fellowship between these warring parties was restored. Both Dowell and his associate, Earl Smith, acknowledged that the primary players in this conflict eventually reached out to them to patch things up. Dowell and Smith also said that they had personally dealt with the matter of forgiveness long before it was ever asked of them. Smith spoke of running into Jaynes and his wife at a local supermarket. He turned a corner and caught a glimpse of them not long after the split. "And the first quick flash that went through my mind," Smith said, "was I wish I could give him a hug." Smith found it a great relief to know that this, and not anger, had been his first impulse.[60]

Dowell usually spoke about High Street's split in general terms, but he does seem to reference this matter in some notes that he kept for his Pastoral Theology class at BBC. Describing how he dealt with the situation, Dowell said:

> I had an experience once in my ministry when I had a close associate and paid worker betray me. While I was very sick, he succeeded in leading a sizable number from the church. He continued to visit members of the church for some time. One day while I was thinking about it, I felt a tinge of jealousy and bitterness. I knew this would hurt me more than anyone else. I drove to my office, told my secretary I did not want to be disturbed. I then went into my office, locked the door, and got down on my face and prayed until the feeling was all gone, and I felt a love for the party who had injured me.[61]

God rewarded Smith and Dowell for their willingness to forgive. In the years that followed, Jaynes sought out each of them to issue an apology and to ask for their forgiveness.[62] Both men responded affirmatively, and when Dowell was asked about High Street's split in a 1972 newspaper interview, he said, "That's healed, now. There is fellowship again."[63]

Of course, such healing could not mitigate the pain of those initial wounds. Earl Smith referred to High Street's split as the "darkest days" of his ministry. In a 1993 interview, Smith pulled back his shirt to reveal a scar from an open-heart surgery. That damage, Smith believed, had stemmed from that 1962 dispute.[64]

On an emotional level, Dowell had been similarly scarred. John Rawlings witnessed in Dowell a "broken heart" following the split.[65] Dowell Jr. observed the same thing.

"Dad's spirit was crushed," the son said. And though Dowell himself never spoke much about this situation, he did make a telling statement in 1982: "I think a church split is one of the worst things that can happen."[66]

Not surprisingly, Dowell did not quickly recover from the thing that had occurred in his church. Though he continued at High Street for more than a year, his ministry there was not the same. His spirit was further affected, no doubt, when, in February 1963, he learned that his brother Ernest had passed away. It was like losing a father all over again. Dowell tried to set these heartaches aside, but they were affecting him nonetheless, and the ministry began to wane. Dowell attributed the problem to spiritual atrophy. The people became "self-satisfied," he said.[67] Whether or not that was so, High Street's ministry had lost its momentum, and Dowell was now struggling to reclaim it. "He just couldn't seem to regain [the] vision and excitement over High Street Baptist Church he once had," Dowell Jr. observed.[68]

It was clear to Dowell that something needed to change, and that feeling may have amplified the voice that he heard when he answered a telephone call in the spring of 1963. This call came from the Beaver Street Baptist Church in Jacksonville, Florida. Church leaders were looking for a new pastor. As Dowell and others knew well, Beaver Street was experiencing its own set of problems. Indeed, this congregation had reached out to Dowell because they believed he was the kind of leader who might pull them through it all. Dowell himself was not so sure about that, but he listened to what they had to say. Then as he hung up the phone, he took to his knees. Were twenty-two years of ministry at High Street Baptist Church nearing an end? Dowell certainly did not have the answer. But if the Lord had a new assignment for him, he wanted to find out.

Chapter 33: *Beaver Street*

It was breakfast time at the Dowell home in Springfield. Nola was tending to a sink full of dishes, and her husband was working on a plate of toast and eggs. The morning newspaper was on the table beside him, but it was folded off to one side. Bill was feeling uncharacteristically apathetic toward the world's news. Even though a brightly shining sun hung in the window over the sink, there was an icy silence indoors. Bill broke it when he said:

Mrs. Vaughan coming today?

Nola shot back:

Maybe a little later. I'll have to call and see.

The words had a sharp tone to them, but Bill pretended not to notice.

I can get the ladder out for you if you want her to work on the windows.

Nola was now rinsing a few plates and placing them in a rack on the counter. She shook her head, saying:

I don't think so. I'm considering having a garage sale, and if I do, I'll need help getting everything ready. We'll probably clean out one of the back rooms.

Dowell took a long sip from his coffee mug. Then he spoke again:

Have you thought about what we discussed?

Nola picked up a handful of silverware and began to scrub. She kept her eyes on her work as the conversation continued:

I've thought about it.

You want to tell me what you've been thinking?

There isn't much to say.

I'd like to know that I have your support.

I've already told you how I feel.

After rinsing her utensils, Nola plopped them down on a dishtowel. She then reached into the soapy water to retrieve some more. Bill continued with a more businesslike tone:

Well, if we're not going down there, I need to let Beaver Street know—

She cut him off.

You can go to Florida if you like. You can do whatever you want. But I'm not going, so that's that.

Beaver Street Baptist Church was a good size church located along Florida's east coast. One newspaper article described it as "one of the largest Baptist churches in the South."[1] It was not as large as High Street, but its attendances still ran over a thousand. This church was thrown into turmoil, however, when, on April 8, 1963, the congregation was struck by a tragedy. The church's founding pastor, George Hodges, had been shot and killed.

This happened on a Monday morning when Hodges, age 57, was visiting the home of a woman who had been associated with his church. There was a struggle in the home, and Hodges was shot twice in the stomach. Afterward, Hodges drove himself to his church parking lot for help. He never made it into the building. A secretary spotted him bleeding out, and though she and others tried to get him to a hospital, Hodges died en route.

In addition to pastoring Beaver Street, Hodges had been a prominent member of the BBF. He had even served a term as the fellowship's president. So understandably, pastor friends across the country were stunned when they received the news. Noel Smith ran an article in the *Tribune* to explain what was known about Hodges's death:

> Police arrested, jailed, and charged with murder Mrs. Sara Thelma Luckie, a tall, large-framed, black-haired wife and mother, 40 years old.
> Police said that Mrs. Luckie told them that Dr. Hodges was shot while struggling for the possession of a 32-caliber pistol during an argument.[2]

As Smith continued his article, he also tried to explain what had led up to Hodges's death. "A member of the Beaver Street staff told me over the telephone that Mrs. Luckie had for a dozen years been the source of incredible disturbance in the church, for which the church withdrew fellowship from her," Smith said. "My informant told me that the church had received a telephone call saying that Mrs. Luckie was threatening to kill herself. 'Dr. Hodges,' he said, 'had on a number of occasions been successful in preventing domestic tragedies, and he felt that he should go to the home and make an effort to do what he could. That's why he went.'"[3]

But much suspicion shrouded this story. In court, Mrs. Luckie and others alleged that there was more to it than that. A news report that appeared in the *Jacksonville Times-Union* stated, "Mrs. Luckie claimed in testimony at the inquest that the minister had been her lover and other witnesses offered testimony tending to substantiate this claim."[4] An article in the *Ocala Star-Banner* reported:

> Another witness, Mrs. Evelyn B. Dye, testified that the Baptist minister came to the insurance firm where Mrs. Luckie worked several times during the six weeks Mrs. Dye was employed there.
> The witness said at least six times Rev. Hodges drove into a parking lot behind the office, motioned for Mrs. Luckie to follow him and Mrs. Luckie drove off behind him in her car.[5]

This was not the story being told by Hodges's friends and family. According to the *Jacksonville Times-Union*, "Members of the church, however, testified the minister tried to avoid Mrs. Luckie, was continually pestered by her, and lived in mortal fear of her."[6]

Dowell himself was never decisive in his assessment of the case. He stopped short of pinning any guilt on Hodges, though he did acknowledge that some "dangerous sin" had crept into Hodges's church.[7] When asked about the murder case in a 1992 interview, Dowell said Hodges "was killed by a woman. All kinds of reports went out. I don't know how much of it to believe and how much not to believe."[8]

It should be noted that Sara Thelma Luckie eventually pleaded not guilty by reason of insanity. In fact, in January 1964, a psychiatrist stated in court that Luckie had "suicidal tendencies" and that "much of what she said was a delusion."[9] Luckie died while still in the care of the Florida State Hospital in Chattahoochee.

History further demonstrates that Dowell tried to honor Hodges's memory and accomplishments. At Hodges's funeral, an event that drew an estimated 5,500 mourners, Dowell paid tribute to the deceased pastor on behalf of the entire fellowship.[10] Then at a 1966 event in Jacksonville, Dowell again went on record expressing kind regards for Hodges.[11] One of Hodges's grandson's made this statement to Dowell in a 1984 letter: "I know after my grandfather passed away my dad remarked several times that if he could claim a man as his father, you would be the man. He had the greatest respect for you."[12]

Far from being a critic of George Hodges, then, Dowell became a kind of protector of this man's reputation and legacy. And part of that legacy was the Beaver Street Baptist Church. In 1963, Beaver Street was suffering. The guilt or innocence of the parties involved mattered little to the surrounding community. The mere suspicion of sexual impropriety was sufficient to do serious damage to the church's reputation. Bill Dougherty, one of the church's later staff members summed up the situation, saying, "The church was under a vicious attack from the Devil and of course the media was having a field day." According to Dougherty, the investigation into Hodges's murder became a high-profile spectacle, and as a consequence, the church's name was dragged "through the mud."[13]

It was during the early stages of this fallout that Beaver Street reached out to Dowell. The church needed help. Not only were they grieving but they were also without a pastor. They needed a strong leader who could restore stability and help salvage the church's reputation. And Dowell seemed well suited for the job.

After receiving the church's invitation, Dowell took up the matter in prayer. He also pitched the idea to his wife. But Nola was not receptive. This was the one time in their marriage, Dowell said, when she "bowed her neck a little bit" in defiance of his leadership. "And she said, 'You can go down there if you want to, but I'm not going,'" Dowell recalled. "She didn't mean it, but that's what she said." In answer to this statement, Dowell told his wife, "Well, honey, you know that I'm not going without you. God's not going to lead me down there and not lead you down there, too. Until He leads both of us, none of us are going."[14]

Dowell said he then went to his office and, after "considerable thought," decided to "pick up the phone and call Jacksonville" to turn down their invitation. Yet a telephone call from Nola prevented him from doing so. He reenacted the conversation in an interview: "She said, 'When are we leaving for Jacksonville?'" I said, 'I thought you weren't going?' She said, 'Aw, I've had a little talk with the Lord. If He's leading you down there, I'm going with you.'"[15]

Soon thereafter, in July 1963, Dowell resigned as the pastor of High Street. Not surprisingly, many were grieved by the news, including Earl Smith. Before Dowell had a chance to tell Smith about his plans, Smith got wind of the decision from Reg Woodworth. They were playing a round of golf, Smith said, and Woodworth let the information slip. "Of course, Reg sometimes talks without thinking," Smith remarked.[16]

Smith confessed that he wrestled with Dowell's decision. "If I ever met a man I thought God laid his hand upon, it was him," Smith said. "That's why I'll never understand why he left here—fully." When Smith was asked if he had been hurt by Dowell's departure, he replied, "Oh, I was hurt. Oh yeah. But he told me, 'The Lord led me,' so I accepted it."[17]

Some in Springfield wondered if Dowell might take Smith with him when he left, but according to Smith, that idea was never given serious consideration. Smith said he knew from the start that the Lord did not want him to go. "I can't explain it," Smith said, "It's just that still small voice. I knew I wasn't supposed to."[18] And in time, Dowell helped to confirm that voice. Dowell asked Smith to stay at High Street for at least a year to help ease the transition. "He said it would be a disaster if we both left," Smith recalled.[19]

Once Dowell's resignation from High Street became public, there was also speculation that Dowell's departure had been the result of the 1962 split. Dowell himself tried to dispel such rumors. In his formal resignation to the church, Dowell was adamant that his leaving was the result of God's direction in his life, nothing else. His statement to the church appeared as part of a *Tribune* article:

> "I want it clearly understood" he said in somber tones, "that my decision to leave High Street is based entirely upon the definite conviction that God has called me to this new field. . . . When I came to Springfield 22 years ago," he said, "it was with the definite conviction that God had called me to this field. I think the unity of this church and the progress it has made through these years have confirmed the conviction I had. I have the same conviction with respect to Jacksonville."[20]

Dowell's remarks were heartfelt, no doubt, yet perhaps a bit self-deceiving. Looking back on this same decision in 1972, Dowell told a newspaper reporter that he left Springfield "because of 'personality problems' in High Street."[21] Regardless of his motives, however, Dowell decided to move on. And for some citizens of Springfield, the city would never be the same. Earl Smith related a statement made to him by a local businessman. "Earl, the city is going to miss him worse than the church," the man said.

"You can get somebody else to take the church, but they'll never do for the city what he did."[22] A congressman from Springfield, Durward G. Hall, expressed similar sentiments. Hall was also a medical doctor and had served as Dowell's physician before being elected to office. He wrote Dowell a note, saying, "It is certainly with mingled emotion that I address you as a dear friend, a cherished citizen and a patient, as well as constituent. Certainly I hate to lose you to Florida, but it is their gain and Missouri's loss. No one has built it better than you have in the Lord's Kingdom."[23]

The Dowells' last Sunday at High Street was August 25, 1963, and that afternoon, the church hosted an open house to allow well-wishers to say their goodbyes. In addition to parting with the church, the Dowells were bidding farewell to some of their own family members. Even though Bernie and Janet were now ministering in southern Florida and would be closer to Janet's parents, the Dowells would be seeing much less of their two sons and their families. Clyde and Sharon and their daughter would remain in Springfield for several more years. Bill Jr. and his family had recently left High Street to move to Springdale, Arkansas.

Dowell Jr. said it was commonly assumed that his move to Arkansas had been prompted by his father's departure from High Street, but that was not the case. The timing of Dowell Jr.'s exit was more of "a God thing," he said. When a pastor friend resigned from a church in Springdale, the man called Dowell Jr. "out of the blue" to see if the younger Dowell might want to candidate.[24] Soon Dowell Jr.'s family was headed to Arkansas. They left Springfield within weeks of the Dowells' move to Jacksonville, but none of it had been by human design.

Of course, God was also at work in the life of High Street Baptist Church. Months passed before the church selected a new pastor, and in that time, several candidates were considered. Jack Hyles of Indiana was one of these. According to Dowell, Hyles wanted the church "very badly."[25] Unfortunately, some remarks Hyles made when he visited the church hurt his chances. G. B. Vick explained, "[H]e got up there and wisecracked, and he told them what a sacrifice it was going to be away from his own church, and what a favor, I mean in essence, what a favor he was doing them by coming there."[26] The people of High Street were not impressed. "He only got fifteen votes," Dowell said.[27]

Yet by March 1964, God's will for this congregation had become clear. And to Dowell's delight, the church selected one of his good friends, David A. Cavin, to take his place. Dowell was pleased not only by the choice but also by the transition process. Years later, Dowell told an interviewer, "I like to leave a church like I left High Street." He elaborated, saying, "If a man builds around a dynamic personality, and 'I'm it,' well, the church begins to sort of accept this. Then when he's gone, why, things—there's not a stabilization there."[28]

But this had not been the case at High Street. According to Dowell, High Street's ministry had been built "around Christ and around the word of God"—not the pastor.[29] One great evidence of this was the way the church continued to thrive under Cavin. Indeed, Cavin's pastorate lasted just as long as Dowell's, twenty-two years. And no one was happier to see those post-Dowell successes than Dowell himself.

After exiting Springfield, Dowell and his wife shifted their attention to their new place of service: Beaver Street Baptist Church. The Dowells' first official Sunday in Jacksonville was September 8, 1963. They had their work cut out for them. Bill Dougherty recalled, "[W]hen we would knock on doors and say we were from Beaver Street there was normally a very cold response."[30] Dowell, too, remembered those initial difficulties. "We'd get new people out," Dowell said, "but it was hard to get them to join the church for about two or three years after I went there."[31]

Dowell's first few years in Jacksonville were difficult in other ways as well. Dowell and his wife suffered a string of personal setbacks during that time. Less than a month after they arrived in Jacksonville, Dowell got word that another one of his brothers, Louis, had died. Only four months later, they heard the news that Bill Jr.'s newest addition, a son, had arrived with a birth defect. The boy's cleft lip and palate required immediate surgery.

Then came September 1964, and Jacksonville was struck by Hurricane Dora. It was the first hurricane on record to make a direct hit on that city. Jacksonville was pounded with strong winds for fifteen hours. Sea levels rose ten feet, and the city's power was out for nearly a week. The resulting damage was estimated at $280 million.[32] Though the Dowells' home and church were largely spared, the city around them had suffered a tremendous blow.

It was less than a year later, July 3, 1965, when Nola got word that her father had died of a heart attack in Delano, California. Nola took this news especially hard. The Dowells attended the funeral, and then Nola spent some additional time tending to her mother afterward. But the stress of it all began to affect Nola's health. Upon returning to Jacksonville, she experienced some heart ailments of her own. In fact, she "grieved herself into the hospital," one family member said.[33]

Nola's health was still fragile when, a month later, the Dowells got word about another loss. Dowell's brother and sister-in-law, Lester and Estelle Dowell, were killed in an automobile accident near Dimmitt, Texas. The accident had occurred as Lester and Estelle were traveling home from their daughter's wedding. A third passenger in their vehicle, Estelle's sister, was also killed in the head-on collision. Dowell was unable to attend the funeral services because of his wife's unstable health.

Dowell faced these difficulties with characteristic faith, of course. He told one audience, "[I]t takes some of the sting out of death when we understand that for the believer, in reality, there isn't any death. Jesus said, 'I am the resurrection and the life. He that believeth in me, though he were dead, yet shall he live. And he that liveth and believeth in me shall never die.' There is no real death for the believer. He only sleeps in Jesus Christ."[34]

There was comfort in such words, but even for Dowell, the promise of Heaven could not keep life on earth from becoming wearisome. And Dowell's new life at Beaver Street was certainly that. "Some of the old-timers couldn't forget the former pastor," Dowell recalled about his church. Dowell said he got past such resistance by simply ignoring it: "[W]e just didn't let those things bother us. We turned those things over to the Lord."[35]

But the weight of these burdens and the ceaseless effort that Dowell was pouring into Beaver Street grew concerning to some. Nola's mother, writing in January 1964, said, "I can not believe God expects his dear children to over tax their physical strength or over work them selves, and I fear both you and Bill are doing just that [sic]."[36] Two months later Mrs. Callahan issued another warning: "Bill, I fear you too are driving your self too hard and are not getting enough rest, and will eventually get you down [sic]."[37] Dowell's associate, Bill Dougherty, shared Callahan's concern. Dougherty said he began insisting that Dowell let him drive him to his speaking engagements just so his boss could get some rest. "Many times he pushed himself too much," Dougherty observed, "but he was a very determined man of men."[38]

In those early days at Beaver Street, Dowell channeled his determination into strengthening his church's image and into getting his message out into the community. Dougherty recalled one strategy the pastor employed in this effort. Instead of publishing standard newspaper advertisements, Dowell bought space for a weekly article that he called "As I See It." "It had a one inch square picture of himself at the top," Dougherty said, "and it usually was about 6 to 8 inches long." Each article was different, but each recorded the pastor's take on some contemporary issue, often a controversial one. "He would give his conservative view of important matters in the city, state, country and the world," Dougherty said. "It drew a lot of attention and he had a very large following. He received letters and phone calls letting him know they read his article each week before they read anything else in the paper."[39]

In time, Dowell's prominence in Jacksonville grew. He bought radio time over station WAYR, and he made occasional television appearances. In July 1966, for instance, Dowell was asked to participate in a televised program, *Religion Is Relevant*, sponsored by the local ministerial alliance. Dowell appeared as part of a panel of ministers discussing capital punishment.[40]

In another instance, Dowell made the news when he was asked to offer the invocation at a groundbreaking ceremony for a new fire station. This episode became newsworthy not only because of the groundbreaking but also because of what happened during Dowell's invocation. According to the *Florida Times-Union*: "The minister was interrupted by the squawk from—yes, you guessed it—the fire radio calling the volunteers to answer a house fire call." Reportedly Dowell remained unfazed. "Dr. Dowell continued his invocation," the article states, "but Lake Shore Chief W. D. Estes marshaled his men to duty. The alarm turned out to be false, and Chief Estes and his men returned to the ceremonies in time to hear Dr. Dowell's amen, and help County Commissioner Julian Warren turn the first spadeful of earth."[41]

Dowell's coolheaded approach to ministry was likewise helping him guide Beaver Street back to a state of health. One of the most important decisions Dowell made along the way was the decision to build a new auditorium. This decision had not been an easy one. The new building had been Hodges's vision, not Dowell's, and it was an ambitious project, "one of the modern architectural marvels of its day," according to Bill Dougherty.[42]

304 - *Cry Aloud, Spare Not*

Yet church members disagreed about how to go forward with the project after Hodges's death. "Many of us felt the need to relocate and build a different style building and change the name of the church," Dougherty said. Others held a different opinion. "There was a lot of pressure from family and long time friends to build the facility [that Hodges had originally proposed]," Dougherty explained. Those who urged Dowell to stay the course argued that to do anything else "would be admitting to the public that Dr. Hodges was guilty." Dowell and his church endured "agonizing debate and opinions" on these matters, Dougherty said, but Dowell remained "a very wise and gracious man of God during all this turmoil."[43]

In the end, Dowell settled on a middle ground. The church would go forward with its original building plans, but when the new facility opened, the congregation would adopt a new name: Jacksonville Baptist Temple. This name change was needed, Dowell explained, not just so the church could move past the Hodges tragedy, but also so it could rebrand itself in the city. Beaver Street Baptist was no neighborhood operation; it was a ministry to the entire city of Jacksonville. "[The church] was truly drawing its membership from all over the city," Dougherty said.[44] So Dowell decided it was time to let the city know.

Construction on Beaver Street's new sanctuary began in 1965 and was completed the following summer. In the meantime, Dowell and his wife helped celebrate the completion of another construction project. Back in Springfield, High Street was dedicating a half-million dollar Sunday school building. To mark the occasion, the Cavins invited the Dowells back to Springfield for a series of special events. Dowell conducted a week-long revival, May 15 through 22, 1966. He also preached the dedication sermon for High Street's new facility. As part of the festivities, Cavin led his church to give the Dowells special honor. Cavin dubbed Sunday, May 22, "Bill Dowell Day," and he treated the Dowells to a reception as well as a scrapbook of photos from their time at High Street. Dowell greatly enjoyed the fellowship of that week. But what pleased him more was the thirty-nine new believers who were added to the Kingdom of God under his preaching.[45]

Dowell and his wife returned to Jacksonville, and later that summer, they hosted their own building dedication. Beaver Street's new sanctuary opened August 14, 1966. In a newspaper ad, Dowell touted the structure as the "Most Unique Church Building in the United States."[46] It was, indeed, unusual. The circular building had a fanfold roof and angular outer walls. Its exterior was bejeweled by large panels of stained glass. One reporter described the structure as "strikingly beautiful."[47] And it was.

Dowell's 37,000-square-foot sanctuary cost nearly three-quarters of a million dollars to construct, and it provided his church with seating for three thousand people. Yet despite the facility's massive size, the interior felt surprisingly intimate.[48] Dowell told a local newspaper, "Just as the Jacksonville Coliseum is round, to seat as many persons as possible without having anyone too far away from the center of interest, so is our sanctuary building."[49]

Dowell inaugurated his new building with a series of events like the ones he had attended back at High Street. He hosted a dedication service followed by a week-long revival meeting. The dedication was attended by a crowd of twenty-five hundred spectators, including Jacksonville's mayor, Louis H. Ritter. As part of those proceedings, George Hodges's widow was also honored. Dowell then preached a dedicatory sermon out of a text in 2 Chronicles 7.

The remainder of that week featured a memorable revival led by John Rawlings. Rawlings preached nightly, August 15 through 21, and thankfully, attendees could ignore the summertime heat. Dowell's new building included a much anticipated feature: air conditioning.

When Dowell summed up his time in Florida, he said simply, "The Lord gave us a real good, outstanding ministry there."[50] But it is evident that a pivotal moment in that ministry came when Dowell opened his new sanctuary. Beaver Street transitioned to its new name, Jacksonville Baptist Temple, at about the same time, and together these changes ushered in a new day. Average attendances were now approaching fourteen hundred, and Dowell's ministry was again on a forward trajectory.

Of course, these successes had been hard-won, and Dowell knew that they were the result of deep dependence upon God. In a 1976 sermon, Dowell thought back to a small room that he had often visited in Jacksonville's new sanctuary. It was a windowless room, a storage area, Dowell said, just off to one side of the platform. In the floor of this room was a secret compartment where the church's sound equipment was stored. "They'd steal our microphones," Dowell explained, "and we had pretty expensive microphones, so we'd take those microphones and after everybody was gone, we'd take them in and put them in that hole and cover it up and put the carpet over it and try to keep the thieves from stealing."[51]

Dowell had another purpose for that room, however. "It was handy," Dowell said, "and just at the close of the Sunday school hour, after I taught my class, I always walked over on that side and walked in that door and shut it. And I spent a time alone with my Lord before I went on the platform. I think it's good to go from prayer to the platform." To this, Dowell added, "That place was a sacred place to me because I used it only for prayer."[52]

Sacred rooms such as this had helped carry the Dowells through some difficult days. And quite frankly, it felt good to them to be celebrating some victories once again. For the first time in a long time, they were looking forward to seeing what the Lord would bring next. So even as they basked in their present blessings, they bowed and asked God to continue directing their steps. And He did.

Chapter 34: *The Man for the Job*

Crickets were beginning to chirp as long shadows draped across the campground. Scores of teenage campers were packed onto benches beneath a pavilion. The summer air around them was stagnant, but the young people were now used to it. They had been at this Baptist camp for most of the week. Indeed, tonight was their last night—a fact that made the preacher's remarks all the more poignant.

This isn't fantasy. I'm not telling you about a myth. I'm telling you about something that's literally going to occur when the trump of God sounds.[1]

A pin drop might have shattered the silence.

When that trumpet sounds, announcers will stand and announce over the television and radio stations and flare upon the headline of the newspapers, "Millions of People Have Disappeared from Earth Mysteriously."

The speaker had made references to that same trumpet throughout his message.

For the trumpet shall sound and the dead shall be raised. . . .

For the Lord himself shall descend from heaven with a shout, with the voice of the archangel, and with the trump of God. . . .

The speaker's booming voice seared onto the minds of those young listeners the horrors that would take place when that trumpet blared.

All over this nation there'll be husbands and wives looking into that empty bed where their precious little curly-headed baby girl had been placed the night before. Mysteriously gone! And no one knows where she is.

But the preacher did not stop there. He also told of the glorious hope that will accompany the trumpet's sound.

In a moment, in the twinkling of an eye, that cemetery that has been a place of mourning, a place of tears, a place of heartbreak, suddenly as you look—if God would give you eyes that could see fast enough to view the scene—you'd see coming up out of those graves the bodies of mothers and dads and wives and husbands and children that have been planted together there in the cemetery to await the morning of the resurrection. And now you suddenly lose sight of the trees, the grass, the tombstones, the graves, and you see that cemetery decorated with the glorified bodies of God's saints. And it'll become the most beautiful place on this earth. At the sound of the trumpet this event will take place.

From every corner of that camp pavilion, young eyes were tracking the preacher's slightest move. But now their eyes came to a halt. The speaker's hands dropped to his sides, and he stood motionless. And as the young people studied him, the preacher looked back at them with eyes that welled with emotion. He then put to them an earnest thought:

Suppose right now, at this moment, when I'm just ready to give an invitation, suppose that trumpet should sound.

The preacher paused, waiting for the words to sink in. Quietly he added:

Would you be ready?

Even as this piercing question left his lips, the timbre of the speaker's voice was joined by a different melody, one that came out of nowhere. The source was someplace outside the pavilion, but the landscape's reverberations made it impossible to determine a point of origin. There was no mistaking the instrument, however. This was the slow, reverent cry of a trumpet.

In the mid-1960s, Dowell's influence among fundamental Baptists echoed far beyond the walls of the Jacksonville Baptist Temple. Dowell remained much in demand as a guest speaker and evangelist. He was regularly heard in revivals, fellowship meetings, commencement services, and youth camps. Dave Drury recalled hearing him at a 1967 camp. The camp was held at a place situated on the border of Texas and Oklahoma, Lake Texoma. Writing nearly forty years later, Drury said:

> *I remember one night in particular, when Dr. Dowell spoke on The Second Coming of Christ. He began his message by telling the young people that the coming of our Lord would be announced by Gabriel blowing his horn. All throughout his message he kept reminding them of the trumpet, and that it could happen at any time. At the close of his message, and at the precise time, he had a man ready to blow a trumpet. When he did, a chill came over that service that was unbelievable.*[2]

Drury also recalled the crowd's reaction: "Needless to say, the altars were filled that night, and an indelible mark was made on all who were in that service."[3] Dowell's sound effect had achieved its intended purpose.

Dowell was able to touch countless lives through meetings such as this. Pastor Rick L. Carter shared his story when he wrote to Dowell in 1984:

> *I first became acquainted with you in the summer of 1965 when you were preaching at the Rolling Hills Youth Camp in Citronelle, Alabama. It was the month of July and I had been saved about four months. I am from a poor family and all week I sat on the back row because I was ashamed of my clothes. On Thursday night you preached on Acts 9:6, 'Lord, what wilt thou have me to do?' That night I came forward and dedicated my life to God and His service.*[4]

Scores of other lives were similarly affected. Dowell's work as an evangelist amplified his influence in inestimable ways. It allowed his preaching to shake, not one congregation, but hundreds. And though Dowell could not see what the outcome of these efforts would be, he was firm in the belief that God's word would never return to Him void.[5] In that confidence, then, Dowell continued planting the seed and trusting God to give the increase.

In addition to fulfilling regular speaking engagements during this time, Dowell served as a mainstay of the Baptist Bible Fellowship. He did all that he could to promote BBF interests from his post in Jacksonville. This included hosting fellowship meetings at his church. Dowell's daughter recalled traveling to Jacksonville to attend such a meeting. During a break, she "rushed down to the front of the church" to greet her father, she said. "[H]e just lit up and gave me one of his bear hugs and a big kiss." Only afterwards did the preacher stop to think about the implications that these actions might have for his congregation. It was the enlarged eyes of several bewildered bystanders that helped remind him that his church did not yet know his daughter. Janet said her father quickly introduced her to the people standing around, and afterward, "We all had a big laugh."[6]

Dowell's presence in the BBF was more than social, of course. He participated in many of the fellowship's joint undertakings, both at the national and state levels. In one instance, Dowell and other Florida pastors joined together to save a sister church. Pastor Dennis Wheeler described the circumstance. A congregation in Melbourne, Bethany Baptist Church, had fallen on hard times. "Their pastor had resigned and they had a tremendous debt," Wheeler explained. Wheeler, who was then pastoring in Hialeah, spearheaded an effort to try to keep the work afloat. Wheeler became the church's interim pastor, and Dowell and others pitched in to help him fill the pulpit, raise funds, and even canvass the neighborhoods of Melbourne. Then, once the church had selected a permanent pastor, Dowell went down and held a week-long revival to make sure the new man, Ron Schaffer, would get off to a good start. The church was saved, Wheeler said, and Schaffer went on to do "an outstanding work in Melbourne."[7]

Dowell's service to his generation manifested itself in other ways as well. Although the activities of the BBF kept him quite busy, Dowell was also part of a broader, informal network of fundamentalist leaders, many of whom were not a part of the BBF. Dowell's long association with John R. Rice, for instance, continued throughout the 1960s. In addition to being a regular speaker at Rice's conferences, Dowell was named to the advisory board of Rice's publication, *The Sword of the Lord*, based in Murfreesboro, Tennessee. Dowell also aided Rice in other ways. One typical example is found in a letter that Dowell received from Rice's assistant in February 1966:

> *Dr. Rice's latest book, Why Our Churches Do Not Win Souls, has comments and approval of pastors of five great soul-winning churches–Dr. Lee Roberson, Dr. Jack Hyles, Dr. Tom Malone, Dr. Harold Sightler, and Dr. Bob Gray.*
>
> *I would consider it a real kindness if you would send me your comment on this book, so I can show it to Dr. Rice when he returns from the Holy Land. He values your opinion very much.*[8]

Another fundamentalist leader who held Dowell in high esteem was Bob Jones Jr., president of Bob Jones University in Greenville, South Carolina. In November 1966, Jones wrote to Dowell saying, "I would like to propose your name to the Executive Committee for an honorary degree to be presented at Commencement. . . ." Dowell accepted that invitation, and six months later, at BJU's fortieth annual commencement exercises, Dowell was honored with a doctor of divinity degree. This recognition was the third such honor that Dowell had received. His first honorary degree had been conferred and then subsequently revoked by J. Frank Norris. The second had been conferred in 1950 by a small institution in Rockford, Illinois, Lighthouse Bible College. But this third degree was the one that Dowell cherished most. BJU graduated nearly four hundred students that year, and in addition to receiving his honorary degree, Dowell was honored to be the speaker at the baccalaureate service.[9] Dowell said he spoke to forty-five hundred people packed into three auditoriums.[10] He spoke again at this institution in 1972 and 1976. Each time was, for Dowell, a distinct honor.

Of course, it was another college, one halfway across the country, that would always claim Dowell's greatest allegiance. And in 1966, Dowell was contacted by that institution as well. Baptist Bible College was then experiencing some remarkable growth. In the fall of 1966, BBC's enrollment topped a thousand, up from six hundred just five years earlier.[11]

BBC's rapid growth was at once gratifying and troubling for her president and vice president, G. B. Vick and John Rawlings. A growing student body meant growing needs. And by the mid-1960s, BBC's needs included just about everything: faculty, classrooms, and housing. The school was constructing buildings at a pace of about one structure per year, but even at that, the facilities were having trouble keeping up with the enrollment. Indeed, BBC was now so large that its commencement exercises had to be held off-site at Southwest Missouri State College. Plans were in the works for a new 5,500-seat fieldhouse on campus. In fact, Dallas Billington's church in Akron, Ohio, had donated funds for the purchase of the land for this facility. But the only way that this or any other project at BBC could go forward was for the rest of the fellowship's churches to follow suit, enlarging both their vision for the school and their support.

One reason BBC faced such a predicament, of course, was because it was tuition free. Students paid for their books and for room and board, but the tuition costs were underwritten by the supporting churches of the fellowship. The fellowship viewed the college as a mission project, a means of fulfilling the church's Great Commission, and as such, it seemed reasonable that the churches should pick up the tab. But the college's rapid growth was now outpacing Vick and Rawlings' ability to generate new revenue to cover that tab. They needed additional help raising funds, and this need was fast becoming a dire one.

BBC had another need as well. In the fall of 1966, BBC was experiencing some significant internal struggles among its faculty. From Vick's perspective, this turmoil was mostly due to a lack of strong leadership on campus. Vick himself was able to be in Springfield only one week a month. The rest of the time Reg Woodworth ran things.

And that seems to have been a significant part of the problem. By all accounts, whenever interpersonal conflicts arose, Woodworth was usually involved.

In the midst of these difficulties, Rawlings came to Vick with a suggestion. He encouraged Vick to try to bring Dowell back to Springfield. Dowell's history with the school made him the ideal candidate to serve both as a fundraiser off campus and as a stabilizing force on campus. Vick reacted to the idea with skepticism. Though he would have welcomed Dowell's return to BBC, Vick saw little chance of that ever happening. Rawlings reenacted their conversation: "[H]e said, 'Well, Bill won't come.' I said, 'How do you know?' 'Well,' he said, 'I just didn't think so.' He said, 'What do you know that I don't know?' And I said, 'Well, maybe I know the Lord in a way that you don't know Him.'"[12]

At the end of this banter, Vick gave Rawlings the green light to pursue Dowell directly. And Rawlings did so. Yet just as Vick had anticipated, Dowell was quite reluctant. Dowell's concerns about the proposal were many. What would his departure from Florida mean for the Jacksonville Baptist Temple? And what would his return to Springfield mean for the High Street Baptist Church and for his relationship with David Cavin? And what would this new role at BBC look like? And could such a position be as fulfilling for him as pastoring?

Rawlings recognized that this was not going to be an easy sell, but he did not give up. According to Dowell, "Dr. Vick and Dr. John Rawlings just hung on my neck constantly wanting me to come back [to Springfield] and work at the college."[13] In fact, the arm-twisting continued throughout the spring of 1967 until, at last, Dowell's reluctance began to soften. On June 19, Dowell sent a letter to David Cavin exploring the possibility of returning to Springfield:

> *Dear Dave:*
>
> *This letter is strictly confidential. I would appreciate it if for now you will not mention it to a soul.*
>
> *There is the possibility that I will accept a position with the college of great importance. I would be in meetings a great deal of the time, but it would be necessary for me to live in Springfield. I would be there regularly one week out of the month and other times when necessary.*
>
> *I have not fully decided to accept this position, but I am challenged and giving it very serious consideration. In fact it may develop into the fulfillment of a call I have felt all my ministry. I would be free for all kinds of meetings.*
>
> *The reason I am writing you even before I have made a decision is because I wanted to know how you would feel about my living in Springfield.*
>
> *I think you know me well enough to know I would never under any circumstances hinder your ministry there, nor would I tolerate anyone to criticize you to me.*
>
> *I do not believe there would be any conflict. But I wanted to know how you would feel about it. Please be perfectly frank in your answer.*

I would rather you would not discuss this to anyone including Bro. Vick until I am certain of my answer.

Nola and I have prayed much about it and I will confess we are both deeply impressed. Please write me at our home address, 1637 Westminister Ave. Jacksonville, Florida 32210.[14]

Cavin wrote back three days later, and if Dowell was anticipating some resistance, he was mistaken. Cavin answered Dowell's letter with characteristic graciousness:

Dear Bill and Nola,

Just received your letter and I hasten to reply, and to assure you its contents shall be held in confidence.

I would be delighted to have you back in Springfield and of course in High St. Church. You can be sure I would not feel your presence here would hinder, but rather help. Our friendship has been such that there would be a personal blessing to us to have you here.

For Maxine and me, may we assure you of the prayers daily from us, that you may know the Lord's will, and that from here the 'Welcome' mat is out.[15]

During that same month Dowell was also in communication with Vick about this proposed move. Dowell sent Vick a list of questions, which Vick promptly answered. In his lengthy reply, Vick said that Dowell would have full control of the types of meetings he conducted. He would also be supplied with secretarial help at the college. As Vick saw it, Dowell's primary work would be promotional, "laying the needs of the School upon the hearts of the pastors" and "interviewing prospective students." But Dowell would also work on campus one week out of the month. "If you were there one week, and I was there one week," Vick explained, "I am sure that certain problems with the Faculty would be eliminated."[16]

As for Dowell's new title, this would be worked out in cooperation with others, but Vick said he had a plan in mind. "I believe you should be Vice President of the College," Vick wrote. "and John [Rawlings] suggested it. Then it would be just a natural thing for you to step into the Presidency, one of these days. We could change the College By-Laws to enlarge the Board of Trustees and make John Chairman of the Board. What do you think of it?"[17]

Vick went on to explain that he would consider Dowell's role on campus to be an extension of his own. "You and I would work together as one," Vick said, "and when you would speak it would be with the voice of authority—not as the scribes and Pharisees."[18] Then, near the end of this letter, Vick once again tried to demonstrate the benefits of such a proposal:

I think I can understand a little about how you would feel not being in the pastorate. However, think of this side of it: While there are problems wherever you deal with human nature, yet in your position in the College there would not be the thousand-and-one nagging, worrisome problems, and tales-of-woe that you constantly confront as a pastor. I think there would be a relief from those things that is inestimable.[19]

Of course, Vick's written appeals were coupled with other solicitations. Later that same month Reg Woodworth wrote to Dowell, saying, "We are all still praying that the Lord will give you to the college. The need for such a ministry increases every day."[20] Then in mid-July, Vick brought Dowell to Temple Baptist as a guest speaker. All throughout that visit, conversations about Dowell returning to Springfield continued. In fact, Dowell and Vick reached a loose agreement that Dowell would wrap things up in Jacksonville by the end of the year and then relocate to Springfield at the beginning of 1968.

After Dowell got back to Jacksonville, however, he had a change of heart. Dowell wrote to Vick, saying:

> *In many respects this is one of the hardest letters I have ever written. I feel highly honored that you would invite me to work with you and the college. I feel if I have a specialized ministry it would be the type of ministry involved in your offer. I also believe I would thoroughly injoy [sic] this work and receive great satisfaction from it.*
>
> *However since returning home, I have looked into our [church's] finances thoroughly along with certain other things that must be done here before I can leave in good conscience.*
>
> *While I was up there I thought I might be able to leave here by the first of the year. But after careful consideration and investigation and after spending a night of agony and striving with the Lord in earnest prayer, I feel it would be a major mistake for me to leave the church before May or possibly September of next year. If you could see our circumstances here in the overall picture, I am sure you would agree with me.*
>
> *This is too long I know to ask you to hold the position open for me and I do not ask you to do so. If you find a man that can do the job, I will understand completely. I know the need is very great.*
>
> *If however the position is not filled at the time I can get away from here, and if in your good graces you should feel inclined to renew your offer, it would be my great pleasure to consider it.*[21]

In reply to Dowell's letter, Vick wrote this:

> *Thanks for your good letter. While I, too, was hoping that you could be with us by the first of the year, yet I feel so strongly that you are the man for the job that I*

cannot even think of any one else who would adequately meet our needs as I believe you can.

I am so strongly convinced that it is of the Lord that I am holding open the place until such time as you feel that you can conscientiously leave the work there and come to us.[22]

At the end of all these conversations, Dowell finally decided to leave Jacksonville. Still, he did so with trepidation. "I never prayed as hard in my life as I prayed over that," Dowell confessed.[23] Nola was visiting her mother in California just before Dowell broke the news to his church. He wrote her a letter, saying, "I will sure be glad when the ordeal down here is over. I hope the church takes my resignation in the right spirit, and that God will lead the right man here very quickly."[24]

Dowell saw no resistance from his wife when he made this decision, even though, by this time, Nola had grown comfortable in Jacksonville. For her, there would be advantages and disadvantages no matter which place she lived. Nola loved Springfield, but she knew her life there would not be the same as it was. Indeed, Dowell's new post at the college would mean that Nola would have to give up her role as a pastor's wife, a role that she loved. It would also mean seeing less of her husband. So in the end, Nola decided to let the Lord direct her husband as He saw fit. She told Dowell that she would support him no matter what he decided. Dowell expressed appreciation for that support in his letter. "I am glad you feel as you do about our future work," he said. "You have been a great encouragement to me during my struggle trying to be sure of His will. Only the Lord knows the inner surging of my soul as I have wrestled with this radical change in my ministry."[25]

Dowell announced his resignation from the church in Jacksonville on Wednesday, March 20. He scripted his remarks in full:

I address you tonight with mingled feelings. There is joy, and there is sorrow.

I left a ministry of 22 years at the High Street Baptist Church of Springfield, Missouri, and came here nearly five years ago to become your pastor, because I felt led, yea compelled, by the Holy Spirit to do so. God had a work for me to do here, and I have sought to do that work the best I knew how.

God has increasingly opened doors of opportunity among the churches of our fellowship for my council and ministry. These have not only been doors of opportunity, but there has been a compelling power within me that has all but forced me to answer these calls. Hence I find myself more and more being drawn away from the pastorate which has been my first responsibility for 33 years.

I am now being urged by the President, the Vice President, and the Trustee board of the Baptist Bible College, as well as the leaders of our fellowship, to accept an executive position with the college, and spend a great deal of time with the pastors and churches of the fellowship.

To say I have not had a struggle within myself would be something less than the truth.

> Mrs. Dowell and I love the church here, and we like Jacksonville very much. We have never worked with a finer people, and you have been wonderful to us.
>
> After much prayer, and earnestly seeking the will of the Lord, and laying my own feelings and desires aside, I have without any question found God's leadership for my ministry at this time.
>
> Tonight, I am resigning my position as pastor of the Jacksonville Baptist Temple, to become effective when a new pastor is called, or at such a time as the church and myself mutually agree it would be appropriate for me to step aside.[26]

After Dowell finished this announcement, a motion was made to reject his resignation, but Dowell hastened to quell the effort. "I told them it wouldn't do any good to do that," Dowell said.[27] And in time, God helped this congregation both to accept Dowell's decision and to find a worthy replacement for him. In fact, they selected one of Dowell's close friends, Wendell Zimmerman of Kansas City. Zimmerman finished out his career in Jacksonville, retiring in 1987.

The Jacksonville Baptist Temple graced the Dowells with a warm farewell, even hosting a banquet in their honor. And soon thereafter the Dowells were on their way back to Springfield. According to John Rawlings, Vick "was thrilled to death" over their return.[28] Vick immediately published the news in the *Tribune*. He explained in his article that fellowship leaders had decided to differentiate Dowell's new title from the badge that John Rawlings had worn. Instead of making him vice president, the trustees had conferred upon Dowell the title of executive vice president. Vick also made it clear this popular evangelist would now be available for bookings. "Dr. Dowell's duties will include public relations work," Vick proclaimed, "and he will be constantly speaking at churches, conferences, and various kinds of assemblies."[29] Vick hoped the announcement would generate for Dowell a full schedule of summer meetings. As far as Vick was concerned, the sooner Dowell began raising money for the college, the better off everyone would be.

The Dowells reached Springfield just in time for the 1968 May Fellowship Meeting, and the couple moved into a residence on South Barnes Avenue. They also rejoined the High Street Baptist Church. Their son Clyde was graduating from BBC with a music degree that year, and Dowell was asked to serve as the commencement speaker. Though BBC's fieldhouse was still under construction, officials decided to pray for good weather and to hold graduation in the unfinished building. Thus, Dowell became the first person to speak in that spacious new facility, a fact that seems fitting in retrospect. Many years later, this fieldhouse was renamed in Dowell's honor.

Of course, Dowell's real work at BBC would begin after those graduation festivities were over. Indeed, Dowell and his wife were apart for most of that summer. Nola stayed busy setting up their new home, opening bank accounts, registering their automobiles, and the like. She also served as babysitter for Clyde's two daughters, thus allowing Clyde and Sharon to pack up their belongings for a move to Denver, Colorado. Meanwhile, Dowell poured himself into his new work for the college and was occupied with nonstop travel and speaking engagements. In 1968, the BBF included nearly two thousand churches in fifty states and thirty foreign countries, so there was never any shortage of speaking opportunities.

Nola wrote her husband a note of encouragement as Dowell's summer travels got underway. "Please take good care of yourself," she wrote, "and your only obligation is 'Preach the Word' and it is up to our Lord to save souls and convict the lost and bring backsliders to repentance."[30] Dowell took those words to heart, and the summer of 1968 proved to be a fruitful one. Dowell conducted six youth camps, a revival, a Bible conference, and several Sunday services, and through those efforts he saw two hundred and eighty people saved, more than a hundred people surrender for fulltime Christian service, and over seven hundred other public decisions.[31] By the end of 1968, Dowell had conducted meetings in California, Delaware, Florida, Illinois, Michigan, Missouri, New Mexico, Ohio, Oklahoma, Tennessee, and Texas.[32]

Vick, of course, was delighted to see such effort. He wrote Dowell a note on August 4, saying, "You are doing a great job—just exactly what we need. I thank God for you." At the same time, Vick was candid about BBC's ongoing financial woes. "If our May pledges for the College would come in we would be OK," Vick told Dowell, "but they are slow. I have had to borrow more than $100,000 more since graduation and yet our sub-contractors are hollering for their balances which total over $170,000 additional. I wish all our Pastors realized our situation."[33]

Dowell had no easy solutions for such problems, but he did have a plan of action. It was the same three-pronged solution that he brought to most of life's challenges: go hard, preach hard, and pray hard. And this was exactly what he intended to do. The rest, Dowell decided, would have to be left to the Lord.

Chapter 35: *But God!*

The morning's coolness was fading as Dowell stared through the curved windshield of a boxy sedan. He was riding in the vehicle's passenger seat. This car had been white when Dowell's preacher friend had picked him up from his motel that morning, but after several home visits along dusty Texas roads, it was now more of a hazy brown.

The vehicle slowed as it pulled up in front of a farmhouse.

Here we are, Dr. Dowell.

Dowell's host was the pastor of a church in the town of Canyon—the same part of Texas where Dowell had been saved as a boy. It was a Wednesday, and Dowell was midway through a revival meeting at that church. Dowell and his friend had spent the morning visiting families from both inside and outside the church, people whom the preacher had met somewhere along the way or those he had heard about through a church member or those he had prayed over in a hospital bed. Whatever the case, they were folks that the preacher thought would benefit from a personal invitation to the revival. He and Dowell might even have an opportunity to lead some of them to the Lord.

Spotting a pickup truck parked next to the house, Dowell said:

Looks like we caught 'em at home.

The two men opened their doors and peeled themselves off of the vehicle's vinyl seats. Dowell did not wait for his preacher friend to come around the front of the car. He immediately made his way toward a gate that opened into the farmer's front yard.

Back in those days, most folks in rural Texas considered it an honor to have guests such as these show up on their doorstep. When the clergy arrived, other activities in the home ceased. Quite often the visitors were invited in, where they were offered a seat on the couch and a cup of coffee or a glass of lemonade. But Dowell was beginning to think this was not that kind of a home. As he reached the farmer's front gate, the farmer came running off of the porch, waving his arms and saying:

Stay back! Stay back!

Dowell stopped in his tracks, as did the pastor behind him. And just then, Dowell heard the thing that had prompted the farmer's actions. It was a low, sinister rattling coming from the other side of the gate. Moments later the farmer was aiming a gun at the source of the sound. And once the gun's trigger had been squeezed, Dowell opened the gate to get a look at the snaky trouble that had been coiled on the other side.

Recounting this story in a letter, Dowell appended this exclamation: "But God! I don't think I can ever doubt him again."[1] Dowell was now finding many opportunities to exclaim "But God!" in his new life at BBC.[2] Certainly there was much to be thankful for. In April 1969, BBC launched a new radio station, KWFC. Then a month later the fellowship gathered in the recently completed fieldhouse for its May Fellowship Meeting. Composer John W. Peterson joined that conference to conduct his new missionary cantata *So Send I You.* BBC's enrollment was also doing well. By the fall of 1969, the number of full-time students had grown to over thirteen hundred. And within three years that number would top two thousand. "We had more people than we had rooms," Dowell recalled. "But we'd put them in the hallways and say, 'There'll be some leave, and we'll get you in a room.'"[3]

Dowell was seeing blessings in his travels as well. BBC's money problems were far from over, but Dowell's efforts were helping the cause, and more than seven hundred churches were now sending regular monthly support. In a *Tribune* article, Dowell called the summer of 1969 "One of His Best Summers of His 35 Years' Ministry." "I averaged speaking a little over twice daily seven days a week," Dowell said in his article. And those efforts did more than raise money. According to Dowell, "hundreds" were saved, and over ninety others surrendered to full-time Christian work.[4]

Then, too, Dowell's travels were helping him build strong relationships with pastors all over the US. Even before Dowell moved back to Springfield from Jacksonville, one of his friends from California, Jimmie Combs, sent him a note of congratulations. As part of his remarks, Combs made this prediction: "We pastors will consider you our pastor. We all need a pastor to counsel with."[5] In Dowell's new role as a traveling representative for the college, he watched Combs's words become a reality. Writing from a hotel in 1970, Dowell said, "Two preachers from Denton Tex. came to my room. One of them actually has been working for Clarence Green as song leader and youth director, but wants to pastor. They came over to enlist my help in finding a church for him. Soon after they left, Bro. Edd Hill came over and stayed quite a while. I think he just wanted to talk to me for encouragement."[6] Dowell wrote another letter from Stamford, Texas. "I visit some each day with the Pastor," Dowell said. "He is young and likes to spend as much time with me as possible and pick my brain."[7]

Dowell's efforts among these younger men would never be forgotten. Pastor Billy Hamm once wrote, "My memories are warm of how Dr. Dowell spent time mentoring me when he preached a meeting in my first church in 1971."[8] Ronald Schaffer told Dowell, ". . . I have never made a major move in the ministry without counseling from you.'"[9] Paul Duckett of Fort Worth went so far as to send Nola a thank-you note for the time that she allowed her husband to spend with him. "I know that God will reward you abundantly for your willingness to share his life and ministry with so many pastors like myself, who need the blessing of his counsel and preaching," Duckett wrote.[10]

A newspaper article written about Dowell in 1999 celebrated him as the "Pastors' Pastor."[11] This was a well-deserved title. Dowell spent many years pouring into the ministries of his fellow preachers, often in ways that even they did not expect. Writing to Dowell in 1984, Pastor Ray Brinson recalled, "About eleven years ago you made a phone call to me in Memphis, Tennessee. As far as I was concerned no one understood what had happened to me. When you called me, I was never so surprised but was so glad to know that you did care. I want you to know that I love you in the Lord for that very reason, you cared."[12]

Another preacher friend, Terry Allcorn, recalled the special effort Dowell made to come visit him at his "storefront church." "Dr. Dowell was in revival with Pastor John Tucker in Kansas City," Allcorn wrote. "One afternoon Dr. Dowell and Pastor Tucker drove out to Richmond, about 50 miles east of Kansas City, to meet with me and to look at the work that God had called me to pastor." Allcorn said Dowell's visit left him "totally surprised and appreciative."[13]

Dowell was seemingly tireless when it came to the lives and ministries of his fellow pastors. Back in 1969, Dowell conducted a revival for Ellis Leslie Sharpe of Richmond, Virginia. He did much more, however. Dowell's visit to Richmond coincided with a major religious controversy that was brewing in the Southern Baptist Convention, and the situation held particular significance for the people of Richmond. SBC leader W. A. Criswell had recently published a book entitled *Why I Preach That the Bible Is Literally True*. Yet there were some in the Convention, including three professors from the University of Richmond, who tried to discredit Criswell for taking this fundamentalist position.

Pastor Sharpe decided to seize the opportunity. Not only did he bring Dowell to his church as a revivalist, but he also placed him in front of every media microphone he could conjure. "I have never been so busy in a meeting," Dowell told his wife from Richmond. "I am on two radio programs daily, one television program daily; I have two interviews on radio, I was interviewed on television this morning, and I will be on three radio stations Sunday, one live and two taped."[14] As Sharpe had anticipated. Dowell's outspoken views in support of Criswell caught fire that week. Indeed, by the time it was over, Dowell had "preached 42 times in 8 days."[15]

Dowell was routinely called upon to fight the good fight in his new ministry, and he was happy to do it. In an era that included the Vietnam War, unrest in the Middle East, assassinations, and urban riots, Dowell felt compelled to do all he could to push back against the forces of evil. When he visited Arlington, Texas, Dowell lent his aid to local pastors trying to stop a 1970 proposition that would legalize by-the-drink liquor sales. In San Angelo, Texas, in 1972, Dowell stood before a youthful crowd gathered in a football stadium and articulated the differences between Jesus Christ of Nazareth and *Jesus Christ Superstar* of Broadway.[16]

Dowell weighed in on other matters as well. In November of 1969, he sent a letter to President Richard Nixon on behalf of the college expressing support for the war effort. G. B. Vick had recently delivered an address to BBC's student body in which he lambasted the anti-war protests occurring on many college campuses. While Vick believed the US should never have entered Vietnam, he said it would be disastrous to abandon that effort midway through. Dowell sent Nixon a copy of Vick's address, and in his cover letter, Dowell offered the college's official position:

> *We stand unitedly against those who would divide our country, against the type of anti-Viet Nam demonstrations being held over this country.*
>
> *We are behind our country and behind you, Mr. President, in seeking to work out an honorable peace in Viet Nam.*[17]

Then in 1971, Dowell wrote Nixon another letter. This one urged an "immediate withdrawal of the United States from the United Nations." At issue, Dowell explained, was the UN's seating of Communist China. Such an action, Dowell said, "should convince our national leaders that membership in the United Nations can no longer serve any useful purpose, but rather creates a threat to world peace." Dowell concluded his statement, saying, "It is our strong conviction that the headquarters of the world organization should be removed from our shores."[18]

Of course, Dowell did not approach every issue of his day with the same fervor. Neither he nor his fellowship was ever very outspoken on matters of race. Though not by design, the BBF was a white man's institution. It could also be argued that, to one degree or another, most of the fellowship's founders, including Dowell, were influenced by Jim-Crow-era thinking. When Dowell conversed with people of other races, his manner and speech could sometimes become awkward. Dowell also employed expressions like "colored man" in his sermons long after such language had passed out of favor with the general public.[19]

Such trappings were not indicative of any racial hatred, however. To the contrary, Dowell was warm and welcoming toward the members of other races. He accepted such individuals both as members of his churches and as students at the Baptist Bible College. Dwight E. Scott was one of the earliest African Americans to graduate from BBC. In 1978, Scott's respect on the campus of BBC earned him a term as fourth-year class president. Scott also managed to earn Dowell's respect. The two men remained friends for many years, and indeed, when Dowell passed away in 2002, Pastor Scott and his wife were among the mourners at Dowell's funeral.

Even if Dowell could not be described as a Civil Rights activist, then, it is clear that he was a preacher who loved and valued all people. From Dowell's perspective, the Bible demanded no less. Dowell told a racially mixed crowd in Brazil in 1961, "I am very happy to be privileged to have this mutual fellowship with you in Christ. Our blessed Lord cuts through all color and language barriers. He has made all men of one blood. Constantly we find the scriptures confirming that in God's great plan, there is no difference. There is no difference for all have sinned. There is no difference for Christ died for all."[20]

Dowell viewed all of the world's controversies through such spiritual eyes. Reflecting on America's decline in the early 1980s, Dowell said:

The League of Nations was formed and the biggest mistake America ever made—
and we've been going downhill ever since—when Russia said, "I will not agree to
open this session with prayer," and the United States said—after some discussion—
"All right we'll not open with prayer, we'll open with silence." That's what they
said about this school prayer situation. They said, "Well, it'll be all right to pray
silently, just have silent prayer." Nobody can give you silence. We've already got
that. America ought to have stood up on her hind legs and said, "Everything that
we do, that we're involved in—I don't care what you do, but we pray before we go
into it and whether you pray or not, we're gonna pray!" But she didn't.[21]

Such words were not mere rhetoric. Dowell was passionate in his belief that
America's best hope was a return to God. On the day that Bobby Kennedy was
assassinated, Dowell wrote to his wife, saying, "It's too bad about Robert Kennedy. I
don't know what it is going to take to wake America up and cause her to turn back to
God. It looks like God's judgment, or revival. Pray for God to open the door wide for
me to have some influence in helping turn people back to God."[22] Then, in a revival
sermon from that same era, Dowell said:

It's not my purpose to deal with the political or the economic aspect of the
problem, because our problem, oh I wish I knew how to say this. I'm talking
about the race problem; I'm talking about the war problem; I'm talking about the
poverty problem; I'm talking about the education problem and all the rest of it.
Our problem is not political; it's spiritual. When you solve the spiritual problem,
you'll solve the other problems that's brought about the chaos that we have in our
land today.[23]

Those same spiritual eyes now guided Dowell as he approached his new career at
BBC. The world's desperate need made it incumbent upon him to send more laborers
into the harvest fields. "The absolute necessity of B.B.C. becomes more evident every
day," Dowell told Reg Woodworth in a letter.[24] And Dowell preached that same urgency
to his fellow pastors. In a fundraising letter for the college, Dowell wrote, "God has
placed an awesome responsibility upon our Baptist Bible Fellowship pastors and
churches in these last days."[25]

This sense of responsibility magnified for Dowell the importance of BBC's
financial needs. Even after a year of fundraising, those needs remained pressing.
Writing to Woodworth in the summer of 1969, Dowell said, "I am deeply concerned
about our general expenses. We still have a long way to go. We will find a way, but I do
not know at present what the answer is. Our preachers must come through. It is this
need that keeps driving me on day and night."[26]

Dowell was greatly concerned about another need at the college as well. In fact, by
the summer of 1969, he was preparing to make a major shift in his responsibilities in
order to address it. Dowell wrote to BBF pastors in August to let them know what was
being planned. "Recently Dr. Vick the distinguished President of the College asked me

to spend more time at the College," Dowell wrote. "I have consented to spend two weeks and if necessary three weeks of each month doing administrative work and some teaching at the College."[27]

Dowell's increased presence on campus had become necessary because of the continuing internal problems at BBC. And the epicenter of the trouble was Reg Woodworth. Dowell wrote to his wife from Beaumont, Texas, in August of 1969, just before returning to Springfield. "I will have a busy week next week," Dowell told her. "I must get some things done about Reg. It can go no longer. It will take a lot of wisdom. Please pray real hard."[28]

Woodworth had been a great friend to Vick, Rawlings, and Dowell since their earliest days as foot soldiers for J. Frank Norris. He had also become an icon at BBC. As Mike Randall once put it, Woodworth served as "the resident executive of the college under the title of Business Manager."[29] In other words, Woodworth did it all. "He was a jack of all trades," Bill Dowell Jr. remembered.[30] Woodworth taught classes, he handled finances, and he served as the general contractor for building projects. Indeed, he had been doing so since the college first opened its doors.

By 1969, however, Woodworth's presence at BBC was becoming increasingly problematic. Part of the concern was doctrinal. Pastor Keith Gillming recalled a statement that Woodworth once made out on a golf course. Just before taking a swing with a club, Woodworth mentioned that there were some in the BBF who had accused him of being a Calvinist. According to Gillming, Woodworth issued a four-word answer to the accusation just as his club met the ball: "And they were right."[31]

In those days, few things could start a brawl at a Baptist meeting faster than a discussion of the five points of Calvinism. Though all Baptists embraced some of John Calvin's ideas, a great number, including Dowell, rejected Calvin's teachings on irresistible grace and limited atonement. But the vote was by no means unanimous. Within the BBF, conflicting views on these matters were the source of much contention. In fact, Calvinism was such a hot-button issue that Vick once found it necessary to ban campus debates about it. "I say that these things which mar or disrupt good Christian fellowship and destroy the unity of the Spirit are not of God!" Vick railed.[32]

Dowell, too, developed a sensitivity to this topic's divisiveness. Writing to a teaching candidate in 1972, Dowell was careful to ask the man about the disputed elements of Calvinism. "Please know that I am not trying to overly question you on your doctrines," Dowell wrote, "but these two areas have created some problems in the past and we want to avoid it in the future if possible."[33]

As brothers in Christ and co-laborers in the BBF, Dowell and Woodworth could easily look past their differences on Calvinism. Yet for Dowell, it was more difficult to ignore the trouble that brewed whenever Woodworth plied students with his hyper-Calvinist leanings. Such teachings—or even the suspicion of them—were sufficient to keep the fellowship's dust stirred up. And it was Dowell, the college's traveling representative, who often heard the complaints from fellow pastors.

Doctrine was not the only concern, however. Woodworth was also affecting
As Bill Dowell Jr. explained, "[Woodworth] did some things that upset a lot of people.
He would walk into a classroom and rebuke the teacher publicly before his entire class.
He was impulsive and was not noted for being consistent and certainly not gracious."[34]
Dowell Sr. was well aware of the concerns. Indeed, in preparation for a meeting with
Vick, Dowell once made a list of the complaints he was hearing: "(1) Demanded that
Bro. Burks fire two young men. When asked why, he said, 'I just don't like their looks.'
(2) Faculty member told he could not fail a certain student, even though he was not
making his grades. (3) He goes into office and changes grades from that turned in by the
professor." The sixteen-point list of grievances ranged from the mistreatment of faculty
members to public criticisms of the cafeteria. The list ended with one of Dowell's own
concerns: "(16) I am never informed of changes or actions that are made in my absence,
& I am embarrassed continually because of this neglect. Preachers wonder why changes
are made and I know nothing about it. I sometimes even deny it and then find out I was
wrong."[35]

Concerns about Woodworth's behavior were widely known, and though Dowell
was not the only one who held such concerns, he may have been the individual who
suffered most because of them. According to Dowell Jr., "The faculty members came to
Dad and threatened to resign if something was not done in regard to Dr.
Woodworth."[36] So in the fall of 1969, Woodworth was reassigned to the position of
national field representative. Woodworth would now represent the college in revivals,
conferences, and fellowship meetings. He would also continue to lecture in some
courses and would even serve as a student adviser.[37] He would not, however, have a
major role in BBC's day-to-day operations.

This was a difficult transition in many ways, yet it seemed a good use of
Woodworth's remaining years. He was beloved by many, "even by those who hated
him," Dowell Jr. remarked. Woodworth was also a capable communicator. "He was a
good teacher and was a good speaker," Dowell Jr. said. "He knew God's word
thoroughly and memorized large portions of it and quoted them in his messages." And
such qualities won him many admirers. "[P]astors who did not want him in [the
business manager] position at BBC still would welcome him into their pulpits to
promote BBC," Dowell Jr. explained.[38]

As Dowell Jr. recalled, it was Vick who broke the news. "Dr. Vick talked to Dr.
Woodworth privately," Dowell Jr. said.[39] John Rawlings then took ownership of the
blame. In a 2007 interview, Rawlings insisted that it was he who had led the effort to
have Woodworth reassigned. "I'm the only one that fired Woodworth," Rawlings
declared. Rawlings added that Woodworth forgave him for it: "Reg Woodworth said
before he died, said I'm one of the two best friends he ever had—Vick and Rawlings."[40]
Woodworth also seems to have forgiven Dowell. Rawlings recalled "some controversy"
between the two of them, but he said their differences were eventually resolved. "It
wasn't major, just turf-building, I suppose."[41]

But others in the fellowship had a stronger reaction. And according to Dowell Jr.,
his father caught most of the flack. "I know Dr. Vic Sears wrote Dad a letter and

basically said shame on you and attacked Dad in a very hurtful and inaccurate way for getting rid of Dr. Woodworth," Dowell Jr. said.[42]

Dowell himself managed to set aside such criticisms. If this was the price of preserving the health of the institution, so be it. Dowell believed the changes would prove beneficial, and he was right. Richard A. Burks succeeded Woodworth as BBC's new business manager, and under Burks watch, BBC continued to grow. Meanwhile, Woodworth assumed the role of field representative and did an admirable job. In fact, he continued in that capacity until his retirement in 1983. According to Dowell Jr., "Dr. Woodworth was loved and respected as a man and preacher till the time of his death."[43]

Of course, this shakeup also affected Dowell's responsibilities. Though Vick retained the title of president, Dowell now became the school's operational manager. And Dowell's oversight of the campus involved matters large and small. Indeed, Vick liked it that way. "At first, I'd mention the details to [Vick]," Dowell explained, "and he'd say, 'Look, that's what I've got you down there for.'" So Dowell took a new approach. He consulted with Vick on the "important decisions," he said, but he managed everything else himself.[44]

Now, as BBC's troubles rattled their tails from behind the fence, Dowell became the man designated to squeeze the trigger. And such troubles seemed to slither onto Dowell's path with increasing frequency. Dowell dealt with everything from faculty grievances to student disciplinary matters. On at least one occasion, he even sent a letter to a former student in Ohio to try to retrieve an overdue book for the Springfield Public Library.[45]

Then in 1971, Dowell found it necessary to address a renegade preacher, R. B. Thieme. Thieme's unconventional teachings included his opposition to church visitation, his acceptance of alcohol consumption, his position that men with long hair should be shot, and his belief that fetuses are not human beings. Thieme caught Dowell's attention when his taped Bible studies made their way into the hands of some of the students at BBC. Before long, Dowell was hearing reports that Thieme's ideas were being promoted on campus. Dowell promptly addressed both the tapes and the rumors. Responding to one concerned pastor, Dowell wrote, "We have not forbidden anyone to have [Thieme's] Bible studies individually, but we do forbid them to promote it among the students."[46]

Dowell's defense of BBC took other forms as well. In 1974, he sent a letter to one of the school's graduates, Jerry Sloan. Sloan, by that time, had become head of the Universal Fellowship of Metropolitan Community Church in Des Moines, Iowa. Sloan was also openly gay. When Dowell learned of the situation, he wrote to Sloan reminding him of a pledge that he had taken on the day of his graduation. As part of graduation exercises, all BBC graduates promised to return their diplomas if, at some future time, they departed from the doctrine they had been taught. On that basis, then, Dowell revoked Sloan's degree, saying, "We deplore your stand and will be praying for God to change your thinking and lead you back to faith or destroy your influence from the earth."[47] According to Dowell, this action brought him "international news coverage" as well as "letters from all over the United States damning [him] as narrow-minded." In answer to that charge, Dowell held up a Bible and declared, "I'm as narrow-minded as this Book is."[48]

Of course, at times, Dowell's hard-hitting efforts were unsuccessful. Such was the case when he fought the US Department of Health, Education, and Welfare (HEW). In October 1969, Dowell wrote to Senator Thomas F. Eagleton to denounce an HEW policy that was preventing BBC graduates from becoming military chaplains. "There has been some discrimination practiced against our conservative colleges and seminaries," Dowell wrote, "and we believe it is time for this to be brought to an end. Senator Gurney of Florida and Senator Strom Thurmond both have been very sympathetic to our aims. We are earnestly requesting you to use your influence in every way possible to assist us in this matter."[49]

At issue was BBC's accreditation. For many years BBC operated without any recognition from an outside accrediting body. This protected the institution from outside interference, pastors believed, though it also limited students in matters like credit portability. It created another problem as well. Graduates who tried to enter the military chaplaincy were denied admittance because they did not have degrees from an accredited institution.

At first, Dowell tried to overcome this hurdle by challenging the system. He spent several months pressuring the HEW to drop its accreditation requirement and to give BBC students the necessary approval. Yet those efforts failed. That was when Dowell and other administrators determined that it was time to change course. BBC, for the first time, would pursue outside accreditation. These efforts, which began in 1971, were spearheaded by Academic Dean Kenneth Gillming. The work was completed in 1978, when BBC was granted full accreditation from the American Association of Bible Colleges.[50] A few years later, BBC went on to earn a second accreditation from the prestigious Higher Learning Commission. No longer would BBC's graduates have any trouble entering the chaplaincy of the US military.

There were other challenges, of course. And the most difficult were always those involving Dowell's brothers in Christ. Indeed, in one instance BBC found itself at cross-purposes with David Cavin and the High Street Baptist Church, leaving Dowell caught in the middle. Back in 1970, High Street had launched an effort to sell its current property and to build a new facility along a state highway. To help make that move possible, Cavin had appealed to BBC to annex his existing buildings. Dowell and others initially supported the idea. In fact, the entire fellowship took a vote in the fall of 1970 giving approval to purchase High Street's property at a cost of approximately one million dollars.[51] On that promise, High Street went forward with plans to relocate. Indeed, two and a half years later, on Easter Sunday 1973, the church had a groundbreaking ceremony on its new site.

Less than a month before that groundbreaking ceremony, Dowell had assured Cavin that BBC remained committed to purchasing High Street's property. "We feel that we are morally bound to go through with the purchase," Dowell wrote, "with certain stipulations that are spelled out in the minutes of our trustee meeting following our joint meeting."[52] Those stipulations proved difficult to satisfy, however. The sale was contingent upon both parties acquiring the necessary financing. Additionally, High Street had to turn over its property not later than August 1, 1975. These issues ultimately caused the collapse of the deal in the fall of 1973. Lenders wanted unencumbered property as security, and since BBC's property was already mortgaged, Dowell was unable to obtain a loan.[53] There were also indications that High Street would be unable to turn over its property by the August 1975 deadline.[54] For those reasons, then, the college trustees made the unanimous decision "to terminate all agreements in regard to the purchase of the High Street property."[55]

Cavin's plans were now dashed. Without a buyer for High Street's facilities, his entire building program would have to be reevaluated. Cavin explained the situation to his church in a newsletter, saying, "This was a great disappointment to all of us, and your deacons and pastor have met and are trying to determine what will be the proper procedure for us to follow from this point on." As part of his explanation, Cavin alleged that the college had "broken the contract."[56]

Dowell, too, was perplexed by this situation, and he certainly understood Cavin's disappointment. At the same time, Dowell disagreed with Cavin's characterization of what had taken place. Dowell wrote in the *Tribune* in December 1973, saying, "It has been suggested that the college broke the contract with the church, but, of course, this is not true since we did not have such a contract and since neither of the parties were able to meet the stipulations that had been set forth. . . ."[57] It was regrettable that the college could not obtain the necessary financing, but as far as Dowell was concerned, none of the college's actions had demonstrated bad faith.

Fortunately, the strong Christian character of both Dowell and Cavin prevented this matter from doing any lasting damage to their friendship. Cavin eventually found a new buyer for his church's facilities, and he remained an ally of the fellowship and of the college. Indeed, Cavin went on to serve a term as the fellowship's president, and in 1976, he joined Dowell for a ribbon-cutting ceremony on the campus of BBC. The college was opening a new parking lot, and Cavin had led his church to donate forty thousand dollars for the project.[58]

Not all of Dowell's skirmishes saw such satisfying resolutions, of course. Dowell's efforts to shield BBC's fundraising efforts from competition proved, in the end, ineffective. For many years, the fellowship had been dominated by just one Bible college. Yet in the 1960s, this began to change. Of particular concern was a new college that sprang up in Southern California, the Pacific Coast Baptist Bible College (PCBBC). At its inception in 1966, PCBBC had only a loose connection to the national fellowship and was not under fellowship control. Furthermore, its appeal was mainly to West Coast students, many of whom already found the distance to Springfield a deterrent for attending Bible college. For these reasons, BBF leaders offered no serious objections when the new college came on the scene. To the extent that PCBBC would further God's kingdom, they were even supportive of the effort.

Yet by 1971, PCBBC was branching out. Dowell began receiving reports that this college was soliciting financial support, not just from West Coast churches, but from the entire fellowship. In effect, PCBBC was becoming a competitor of BBC. For Dowell, this revelation was most disturbing. He contacted PCBBC's executive vice president, Jack Baskin, to voice his opposition. He also took up the matter with Vick, who issued a sternly worded letter to Baskin. In his remarks, Vick said that he found it "entirely unbecoming and unethical for anyone to use the Fellowship list to promote anything other than a Fellowship enterprise." He added, "Dr. Dowell is constantly on the go throughout the land, and he stated to me that pastors all over the country who have received communications from you have deeply resented the same."[59]

Dowell's efforts on this issue may have helped slow the damage, but history demonstrates that the problem was far from over. Competition from sister institutions was a factor that would nag at the health of BBC for years to come. And if anything, the problem only grew worse. Even so, Dowell felt responsible to confront such snaky challenges to the best of his ability. And so he did.

Dowell was happy in his work at BBC, and he would have done it all again. Of course, on that second time around, it seems likely he would have chuckled at Vick's assurances that he was going to escape the "thousand-and-one nagging, worrisome problems, and tales-of-woe that you constantly confront as a pastor."[60] Still, Dowell did not mind those things too much. For him, what made the work meaningful was knowing that his efforts were having an impact on future pastors and missionaries.

This was also what made Dowell appreciate his time in the classroom. He became a noted lecturer in courses such as Personal Evangelism, Preaching Workshop, and Pastoral Theology. Through such courses, he found that he could invest himself in the next generation. Pastor David Stokes hailed Dowell's Pastoral Theology course as the most beneficial class he took at BBC. "In fact," Stokes said, "throughout my academic career I never had a more powerful and practical learning experience. Not only were his notes invaluable but on the occasion when we could get him off track it was even more inspiring. You know . . . the personal side of things."[61]

Dowell's colleague, James Sewell, once illustrated that "personal" side. Sewell recalled a time when Dowell was speaking to a large group of men in a Pastoral Theology course. A young man asked, "What's the last thing you do before you preach?" In answer, Dowell replied, "Honestly, I check my zipper." This remark was met with laughter, of course, but Sewell said the real enjoyment came after class. That was when a red-faced Dowell realized that a group of wives and girlfriends had been assembled outside his classroom door and had heard the whole thing.[62]

Dowell brought smiles to many student faces through the years. Missionary Naim Khoury would never forget a personal recommendation Dowell once gave him. Khoury's future father-in-law contacted Dowell to get his opinion of him. Dowell reportedly told the man, "If I had a daughter, I would give her to him with my eyes closed."[63] Khoury had to wonder if this was the recommendation that helped him win his father-in-law over.

Keith Bassham related a different memory, a time when Dowell made a telephone call on his behalf. Bassham said he was facing a "situation with a local police officer." It was a "routine traffic stop," Bassham explained. "It was nothing serious, but I felt some intervention would help." So Bassham brought the matter to Dowell's attention, and

Dowell did not hesitate to lend his aid. "I was in Mr. Dowell's office," Bassham wrote, "when he phoned the police department and said simply, 'I want to talk with the chief. This is Brother Dowell.'" Minutes later, Bassham remarked, "the problem had vanished."[64]

Neither Dowell nor his students would ever know all the ways that he blessed them, but there is no question that he did. From her days as a secretary at BBC, Shirley Hackler recalled one instance when Dowell helped "a young BBC student who was struggling financially by anonymously buying groceries for the family."[65] For Dowell, it was not so important that the students knew *how* he had blessed them. What mattered was *that* he had blessed them. And so he carried on, coping with problems large and small, and blessing the people around him in the process. Then, at the end of each day, Dowell looked up into the heavens and whispered once again, "But God!"

Chapter 36: *Nothing Is Impossible*

A balding man was poring over a set of documents behind a large desk. The man's office was also large. Furthermore, it was tastefully decorated. Indeed, the man, too, seemed to be well furnished. His rings and cufflinks marked him as a man of means, and his gold wristwatch glittered in the light that was spilling in through his office window.

On the other side of this executive's desk sat another man, a man of much more modest means. He was also younger. The younger man looked on while the older man worked on the documents, and from time to time, the older man would grunt:

Yes. Uh-huh. All right. I see.

The older man was using a fountain pen to mark various items on the documents. He was also clipping and unclipping pages, retrieving forms from file folders—that sort of thing. It may be that the visitor on the other side of the desk had come in seeking to apply for a job or a loan. Or perhaps the young man was just getting assistance with a tax return or a legal case. Admittedly, some of the details of this episode have grown murky.

But as the young man sat studying the walls of that office, he spotted something. Hanging from the rich brown paneling was a photograph of W. E. Dowell. Naturally, the young man's curiosity was piqued. After all, he was one of the students at Dowell's college. The student pondered the situation for a moment and then deduced that he must be sitting in the office of one of Dowell's congregants. To confirm the theory, the young man asked:

Do you belong to Brother Dowell's church?

The interruption caused the businessman to look up from his paperwork. The man then turned to spy the picture that had prompted the question. He chuckled as he returned to his work:

No. I never have.

Now the younger man was embarrassed.

Oh, I just thought—when I saw that picture—that maybe—

The businessman laughed again as he closed the file folder in front of him. Then he said to his client:

No, no. I just keep that picture as a reminder—

330 - *Cry Aloud, Spare Not*

The older man leaned forward to finish the remark. He said with a wink:

–*A reminder that nothing is impossible.*

Near the end of 1973, Dowell was contacted by Harry Vickery, pastor of Springfield's Baptist Temple. Vickery needed help. His north Springfield church, which he had organized back in 1957, was facing foreclosure. This is not to say that Vickery had failed in his job. On the contrary, Vickery had done an admirable work. His congregation, which began in a two-story house, grew to attendances of more than nine hundred people in just sixteen years. The church had also acquired sixteen acres of property, had built several buildings, and had launched a Christian school.[1]

But then this ministry hit a wall. Like so many other churches of that era, Baptist Temple had managed its rapid growth, at least in part, through the sale of church bonds. Bond sales were an alternative to traditional mortgage loans. Investors—often church members—purchased the bonds through a broker-dealer at a fixed term and a fixed rate of interest. For the church, the conditions of these notes were usually more favorable than traditional loans, so this was an attractive way of financing church construction projects.

Bond programs could be problematic, however. At times, bonds reached maturity before a church was fully prepared to repay them. In those instances, churches frequently issued new bonds and used the proceeds to cover the old ones. Thus, instead of retiring their debts, some churches floated them indefinitely. And since succeeding bond sales usually grew larger, these churches found themselves going deeper and deeper in debt.

In the early 1970s, this situation came under scrutiny from federal and state authorities. Jerry Falwell's church in Lynchburg, Virginia, was taken to court in the summer of 1973 over its sale of bonds. As was reported in the *Washington Post*, ". . . the Securities and Exchange Commission charged Falwell's ministries with 'fraud and deceit' and 'gross insolvency' in the sale of $6.6 million in church bonds to raise money for Falwell's operation."[2] The situation became a nightmare. "The really scary part of it all," Falwell said in his autobiography, "was the possibility that the S.E.C. might force our church into bankruptcy, put us in 'receivership,' and padlock our sanctuary and office doors."[3]

A major element in Falwell's case was the fact that he had sold his bonds across state lines. It should also be noted that Falwell's ministry eventually "entered into a consent decree" with the SEC, and under the terms of that decree, the words *fraud* and *deceit* were dropped from the SEC's complaint.[4] Even so, this and other cases prompted governing bodies to take a closer look at regulations affecting church bond sales. And the consensus they reached was that investors needed greater protections from ministries that might take their money and then go defunct.

As new controls on bond sales began to be implemented, many churches, including Springfield's Baptist Temple, found themselves in a serious predicament. Vickery and his church had recently financed a half-million dollar fieldhouse through a construction loan, but they had planned to pay off that loan with proceeds from a subsequent church bond sale. Then state authorities stepped in and prohibited the bond sale. The church's total debt (which included some existing church bonds, some other debts, and the recent construction loan) was approaching 1.5 million dollars. Officials refused to let investors take on any further risks until the church brought its debt under control.

Suddenly Baptist Temple found itself overextended with no way to pay, and Vickery was in a catch-22. The church could not sell bonds until its debt was restructured, but banks refused to issue a restructuring loan because the church was so greatly in debt. Making matters worse was the fact that word got out about this church's financial woes. Baptist Temple began losing both members and income. The average attendance in 1972 was 927, but by 1973, that number had fallen to 576.[5] The once-thriving ministry that Vickery had built from scratch was now in a tailspin. And foreclosure was all but certain.

In an effort to preserve his church, Vickery decided it was time for him to leave. But first he contacted Dowell, a preacher friend who had helped him to organize the church back in 1957. According to Dowell Jr., Vickery's appeal to his father went something like this: "Dr. Dowell, you're the only man in the world who can save this church. And I'd like to resign and have you come and take over the church."[6] Vickery believed Dowell was uniquely equipped to prevent a foreclosure because of Dowell's prestige in Springfield. Not only might Dowell's presence in the pulpit draw people back to Baptist Temple, but it might also change the attitude of lenders, buying the church much-needed time to emerge from its debts.

After hearing Vickery's appeal, Dowell wanted to help. He did not, however, want to become Baptist Temple's permanent pastor. He was willing to step in as an interim but only to buoy the congregation during this difficult time. His presence in the pulpit would help boost attendances and bring in additional money, and hopefully this would allow the church time to work through its financial crisis.

But Dowell wanted a limited involvement in the crisis itself. He would offer his services as an adviser and as a short-term guest speaker, but he would not take on the full responsibilities of a permanent pastor. Larry Smith, Vickery's assistant pastor, wrote to Etsyl Sparkman, president of Empire Bank, to explain the agreement. "[Dowell] will not be involved in the financial responsibilities by his request," Smith told the banker.[7]

Dowell's oldest son, who was now back in Springfield and working as a professor at BBC, was quite concerned over Dowell's decision to get involved with Baptist Temple. Dowell Jr. voiced those concerns after he learned that his father was considering taking the church. "I went into his office and I was crying," Dowell Jr. recalled. "I said, 'Dad, you've had a fantastic ministry. You're going to take this church, the church is going to go under, and it's going to drag you under with it. And you're going to be remembered as the one that ended up with this.' And I pleaded with him not to take the church." But the elder Dowell could not be dissuaded, and Dowell Jr. decided he would have to defer to his father's wisdom. After further reflection, the son returned to his father's office, saying, "If you don't know God's will by now, you never will."[8]

Vickery resigned from Baptist Temple on November 11, 1973, and he wrapped up his responsibilities by the end of that month. Dowell was then recommended and approved as the church's interim pastor. He began his work on December 2. It had been more than five years since Dowell had last pastored a congregation, so despite the bleak circumstances, Dowell was thrilled to be leading a church again. In February 1974, his daughter wrote to Mrs. Callahan in California, saying, "Mother and Dad seem so very happy to be back in the pastorate."[9]

Dowell served without a salary from Baptist Temple during that first year of service.[10] Instead he put money into the church's radio ministry. Dowell had a weekday program on KWFC at 8:30 a.m. He also broadcast his Sunday evening services over the radio each week. These and other efforts now caused Baptist Temple's attendances and offerings to begin to climb. Nola wrote to her mother on Valentine's Day 1974, saying, "We have new people join the church every service, even on Wed. nights."[11] Indeed, between December 1973 and April 1974, average attendances at Baptist Temple grew from 533 to 661.[12]

Dowell's church was now moving in a positive direction, but even so, the immediate crisis remained. The church had no permanent pastor, and demands from creditors gave the congregation little time for a financial recovery. Dowell's presence was a plus, but his loose connection to the situation did not inspire confidence from lenders. Bank officials were forthright in telling Dowell that they were willing to give his church additional time only if he stepped in on a more permanent basis.

Dowell answered those appeals by accepting a unanimous call to become Baptist Temple's second pastor on Easter Sunday 1974. Yet this decision was driven by more than pragmatism. Dowell saw God's leading in it. "I had no intention of accepting such a position in the beginning," Dowell stated in a *Tribune* article. "I wanted to help, but it was my feeling that my ministry would be of about a year's duration, and then the church would call a permanent pastor." Dowell went on to state that God had changed his mind. "I am now convinced, beyond any doubt, that God has called me to be pastor of Baptist Temple. The acceptance of the church has given me the greatest peace I have known for years."[13]

Within days of accepting this new role, Dowell had a luncheon with Etsyl Sparkman of Empire Bank. Together they negotiated a tentative plan for restructuring the church's debt. Of course, Sparkman was quick to point out that the bank could not solve the crisis singlehandedly. "Our loan would be only one-half of the package," Sparkman noted, "and would work only if you had a solution for the other half."[14]

Addressing the "other half" of this problem, Dowell learned, would require a complex series of steps. The church would have to sell off some of its current property. Furthermore, since the total debt exceeded the amount that the bank could legally finance for a single borrower, the church would have to seek out some additional financing. Dowell hoped to bring in this additional financing through a new bond sale, but he had no guarantees that such a sale would be approved. Getting the state's permission would require the preparation of many forms and reports, and there was no way of knowing if any of it would pay off. The only thing that was certain was that Empire Bank would go through with its half of the financing only if Dowell managed to take care of the remainder of the debt. And Sparkman also wanted something else. "We look upon you as a very important element in this over-all picture," Sparkman told

Dowell. "If you are insurable we would ask that the church take out life insurance on you and the proceeds be assigned to the bank in connection with the proposed loan."[15]

Dowell and his staff spent that next summer taking care of the necessary transactions and paperwork, and then, in September 1974, Baptist Temple filed an application with the state securities commissioner for a $634,000 first mortgage bond issue. Dowell went to Missouri's capital, Jefferson City, to make a personal appeal for the application's approval. During that conversation a state official raised concerns about Dowell's ability to see such a debt repaid. Dowell said the official "was a little dried up man," and Dowell was not impressed. "I've tried to thinks of some way to describe him," Dowell told one audience. "If you ever saw a little mouse—I mean, he was mousey. He really was. And he was determined we weren't going to get a permit."[16]

The state official was particularly concerned, Dowell said, about the fact that Dowell was now past sixty years of age. "You know, that would make a difference," the mousey man said. Dowell countered the barb with one of his own. "I leaned over and looked at him. I said, 'You know, something occurs to me.' I said, 'I've been preaching for almost forty years, and I've buried a lot more men your age than I have my age.'"[17] According to Dowell, the mousy fellow then "turned white and green" as he started to wonder "what he had ahold of."[18]

From Dowell's perspective, his remark brought a turning point to their conversation. Dowell may have been right. Within a few weeks, Baptist Temple had approval for its bond sale. Dowell said the news arrived in the nick of time. The church's 1963 bond issue was, by then, past due, and the church had exhausted the broker's patience. "The fact is," Dowell stated in an interview, "when I got things worked out for this [new] bond program, I called the fellow who was head of the other bond program, and he said, 'As of this morning I had a letter—dictated a letter—to have them foreclose on our portion of the bonds—the buildings, the property.' But he said, 'It looks like you've got it worked out.' So they went along with us."[19]

Of course, the news was not all good. The bond sale's approval came during the last quarter of 1974, and in Dowell's opinion, the timing was dismal. The holiday season, the weak economy, and the recent bad press over church bond issues made this "one of the worst times for bond sales that there'd ever been," Dowell stated.[20] And that was not all. The state securities commissioner had mandated strict requirements that would almost certainly spell the doom of Dowell's sale. The $634,000 sale was set to begin December 2, and if the church did not raise at least $400,000 by the end of December, the program would have to be suspended and all of the money returned to the church's donors.[21] Furthermore, the prospectus had to contain strong cautions for investors:

- *THESE SECURITIES INVOLVE A HIGH DEGREE OF RISK.*
- *The Church may or may not receive sufficient funds to meet these obligations.*
- *The Church has substantial debt, in addition to the Bonds. The Church has generally not been able to meet payments required under notes falling due, and has substantial obligations which are overdue. The Church has made attempts to secure private financing, but has been unable to do so; consequently the Church has no other option*

but to sell Bonds to the public to provide necessary funds to permit it to operate and to continue to exist.

- *The Church issued mortgage bonds in 1963, which came due in 1973. The Church was unable to pay the bonds when they came due in 1973, and secured a one-year extension; those bonds are due on January 15, 1975. If the proposed Bonds are not sold, the Church will probably not be able to pay the 1963 Bonds when they become due.*

- *The Church suffered a substantial decrease in income in 1973, which was a result of decreased membership. Membership has increased in 1974, and so has the Church's income. The Church attributes this increase in income and membership to the efforts of Dr. Dowell. Dr. Dowell is not under any employment agreement with the Church; and although he has expressed his intention to continue with the Church, there is no assurance of a continued affiliation.*

- *There is no public market for the Bonds, and there is no assurance that a market will develop.*

- *The financial statements of the Church included in this offering Circular have not been audited, because the Church did not maintain a double entry bookkeeping system, and because the property, plant and equipment are stated at appraised or estimated values, which are not in accordance with generally accepted accounting practices.*[22]

Dowell Jr. said the state's requirements were designed "to make sure [the bond sale] was a failure."[23] His father shared the opinion. Speaking of that mousey state official in Jefferson City, Dowell said, "Now I'm as sure as I'm standing here that he thought we couldn't do it. And he thought this would be a way out without saying no." Dowell said the approval was intended to appease Dowell and his church, but the official believed it would do nothing to delay the church's inevitable demise. After all, no reasonable investor would accept risks such as these.

Dowell himself was unwilling to concede defeat, however. Indeed, Dowell dismissed the state's cynicism and approached the situation from a heart of faith, telling his congregation, "[W]e need to recognize the fact that this church is not here just coincidentally. It was planted here by the hand of Almighty God."[24] And in that confidence, the people of Baptist Temple went to work selling their bonds.

Those efforts were not only blessed, but they were blessed quickly. "[I]n twenty-nine days, we had sold four hundred and twenty-six thousand dollars in bonds," Dowell recalled.[25] Shortly after the first of the year, the church completed the entire sale.[26] Buyers stepped up from both inside and outside the church, some investing large amounts and some very little. But at every turn, Dowell and his church saw the hand of God at work. In one instance, Dowell met with a contractor at a large electrical company, a company to which the church already owed thirty thousand dollars. The contractor decided to turn that existing debt into an investment by purchasing thirty thousand dollars in bonds. In response,, Dowell took out a prospectus and said to the man, "Now I've got to show you here—they've made us print this, that there's no evidence this will ever be paid back." But the contractor waved off the warning.

"Brother Dowell, I don't care what's on there," the contractor answered. "If you say it's good, give me thirty thousand of them."[27]

Similar stories played out in sale after sale, and Dowell and his church watched as the impossible was made possible. Indeed, this was what had prompted a Springfield businessman to hang Dowell's photo on his wall. Dowell recounted the story on the day that Baptist Temple celebrated its twentieth anniversary:

> *One of our students that is attending Baptist Bible College happened to be in one of the big businessmen's office downtown one day about that time, and he looked and saw up on the wall my picture. And so the first thing that came to this man's mind: "I suppose this man belongs to Brother Dowell's church." So he asked him, said, "Do you belong to Brother Dowell's church?" He said, "No. I never have." He said, "I put that picture up there for one reason." Said, "When Brother Dowell announced on the radio that he was going to sell four hundred thousand dollars in bonds in thirty days, at this particular time, I said, 'He's a fool. It's impossible to do.'" But he said, "When he made the announcement that he had sold four hundred and twenty-six thousand in twenty-nine days," said, "I put his picture up there to remind me that nothing is impossible."[28]*

Dowell was pleased to know that his step of faith was influencing the community around him. But Dowell knew too much to be cocky. "Boast not thyself of to morrow;" the scripture says, "for thou knowest not what a day may bring forth."[29] Dowell was mindful that his church was not yet out of the woods. The bond sale was merely the first step. In order for Baptist Temple to emerge from its indebtedness, it would need a great many more miracles. And there were no guarantees that the church would see them.

Dowell was also humbled by the responsibility that he was now carrying. While Dowell understood that he was not the source of the miracles that God was doing at Baptist Temple, he also recognized that many people were looking to him as if he were. From bankers to investors, Dowell's community was counting on him to keep this church afloat. And Dowell could feel the weight of it all. His response was to take it one day at a time, avoiding thoughts of the tomorrows that were ahead of him.

Something else that Dowell tried to dismiss from his mind was the picture hanging on that businessman's wall. It was "a pretty good testimony," Dowell said in retrospect, but that was the extent of it.[30] Dowell had his sights set on Someone far greater than himself. The Lord had led Dowell down this new path of service, so Dowell wanted to leave it to the Lord to sustain him along the way. The Lord knows "the end from the beginning," Isaiah assures, and His "counsel shall stand."[31] Dowell held on to such promises as he now led his new church. And it was fortunate that he did. Soon Dowell would be facing some of the greatest challenges of his ministry.

Chapter 37: *Carrying Water on Both Shoulders*

Dowell leaned around the corner, a briefcase hanging from one hand. He said sheepishly:

Mary Jane . . . could I ask you a small favor?

A bright-faced secretary looked up from behind her desk at BBC.

Certainly, Dr. Dowell. What can I—

Then it dawned upon her. She laughed and said:

You need me to unlock your office again, don't you?

Dowell nodded.

I'm so sorry to trouble you. I guess I left my keys over at the church.

Mary Jane grabbed a set of keys from her desk. She was not the least bit annoyed.

Don't be silly. It's no trouble at all. Did things go well at the funeral?

Dowell followed her down a short hallway.

Seemed to. There was quite a few guests from out of town, and I got to give a real clear gospel message. The family seemed appreciative.

As Mary Jane inserted a key into a door marked "Executive Vice President," she answered:

I'm so glad.

Then as she swung the door open, she said:

There you are, Brother Dowell.

Dowell now passed into the room, still embarrassed that he had forgotten his keys. He said as he went:

Sure glad I had you to call upon. Thanks a million, Mary Jane—

A brief disturbance from the hallway interrupted his statement.

Oh! I didn't see you there, Dr. Bartlett.

Dowell heard a deep voice say in reply:

Morning, Mary Jane.

As the secretary's giggles trailed off, Dowell turned to see Bill Bartlett standing in his office doorway. Bartlett was a faculty member and an administrator at BBC. He was also G. B. Vick's grandson. Bartlett and Dowell shared a brief conversation as Dowell hung up his suitcoat.

Hello, Brother Dowell.

Oh, hello, Bill.

Just stopped by to see about our administration meeting. Are we still on for this afternoon?

As far as I know. You might check with your granddad. I had a funeral this morning, and I haven't yet had a chance to speak to him.

Very good.

Bartlett turned and headed in the direction of his grandfather's office. Meanwhile Dowell settled into his chair and unfastened the strap on his leather briefcase. He was still digging inside of it when he heard Bartlett again speaking from the doorway. This time Bartlett's deep resonance was overtaken by a peculiar trembling:

Dr. Dowell, I need your help. Granddaddy's on the floor.

Dowell became the pastor of Baptist Temple at a pivotal moment in his career—even more so than he understood. And just when it seemed he was doing all he could do, the Lord seemed to ask for more. As every pastor understands, preaching is only a small part of a pastor's job. The meetings, the phone calls, and the hospital visits are never ending. There are also many weddings, and even more funerals.

For Dowell, these duties had to be factored into an already-busy calendar. Dowell's work at the college and his efforts within the fellowship placed great demands on him. He credited his wife and coworkers for making it all work. People like Larry Smith, Dowell's associate at Baptist Temple, and Sandy Huntsman, Dowell's newly hired music minister, did much to lighten his load and to help keep his church running smoothly whenever he was away. Mary Jane Cotter and others played a similar role at BBC.

But even with such help, there were elements of this schizophrenic life that Dowell had to shoulder alone. The meetings with bankers and regulators to prevent foreclosure on Baptist Temple were the pastor's burden to bear. And only Dowell could fulfill the responsibilities that came with being a fellowship leader and the executive vice president of BBC.

It was Dowell, for instance, who had been asked to deliver the eulogy at Noel Smith's funeral. Dowell did so, not as Smith's pastor, but as his friend and fellow-laborer in the BBF. Smith had served as the *Tribune's* editor until the day he died, January 12, 1974. Indeed, Smith was the only editor that this newspaper had ever known. One admirer noted that Smith was also "the first of the pre-eminent founders of the BBF to depart this life."[1]

Smith died just a month after Dowell began his ministry at Baptist Temple, and when the news got out, Dowell was among the many who were grieved by the loss. Though Smith had recently been admitted to the hospital, he was subsequently released, and most of his friends thought he was on the mend. This made the news of Smith's death all the more shocking. Dowell himself was saddened to know that his friend was gone. But Dowell had to set his own feelings aside while others mourned. As a leader in the BBF, it was Dowell's job to bring comfort. And so he did. Smith's son Charles later commented that Dowell's eulogy was "obviously straight from the heart."[2]

The death of Noel Smith was actually the first in a string of losses that year, all within a two-month period. The second came on February 9. That was when Fred Donnelson died. Donnelson had been retired since 1968, but he would always be viewed by Dowell and the BBF as "Mr. Missions." Once again Dowell took part in the funeral services, speaking on the program alongside family members Paul Donnelson and Bill Logan.

Then, less than a week later, the Dowell family experienced a third loss, one that was even more personal. Nola's mother died of a heart attack on February 15. Nola said that when she got the news over the telephone, she "screamed and said, 'No!'"[3] Nola's husband had to help carry that load, too. Within a few days he was accompanying his grieving wife to California, and there he helped to officiate yet another funeral.

Not all of Dowell's duties from this period were so grief-ridden, of course. Dowell spent the summer of 1974 preaching at youth camps in Arkansas, North Dakota, Oklahoma, Texas, and Washington. He also had the privilege of leading a ten-day revival in Canton, Ohio. Then, when the new school year began, Dowell joined with others to help celebrate BBC's silver anniversary. There was much to celebrate. BBC's enrollment had grown to 2,061,[4] and the fellowship now included twenty-four hundred churches,[5] representing an estimated 1.3 million people.[6] Missouri Governor Kit Bond honored these achievements in the spring of 1975 by declaring May 19 through May 26 "Baptist Bible College and Baptist Bible Fellowship Week." US President Gerald Ford likewise marked the occasion by sending a letter of congratulations.

With so much going on, the demands on Dowell's time had never been greater, yet he made every effort to juggle it all. And for the most part, he did it honorably. BBC's academic dean, Kenneth Gillming, recalled an incident in which a young professor came to Gillming seeking to be excused from some of his duties. The man explained that he would be speaking out of town and would not be back in Springfield until Sunday at midnight; therefore he wanted to be excused from his Monday morning classes. But Gillming denied the request. And in answer, the man said he would go over Gillming's head and put the request to Dowell. "Fine," Gillming replied. "Just go ahead and ask him, but I happen to know that Dr. Dowell is preaching away from here this weekend as well, and he will not be in until much later than mid-night. But he expects to meet his classes as usual on Monday morning."[7]

Dowell's 1975 calendar was again filled with meetings and speaking engagements, but that year also included two overseas trips. In January, Pastor James L. Reid brought Dowell to Australia, where he preached a fellowship meeting in Penrith and then conducted an eight-day Bible conference in Adelaide. Dowell also made stops in New Zealand, Fiji, and Hawaii as part of this trip. Afterwards, he called the tour one of his "most historic preaching missions abroad."[8] In fact, when he was interviewed in 1996, Dowell listed this trip as one of the five highlights of his entire ministry.[9] "Although the Australian preachers were somewhat skeptical of me at the beginning," Dowell explained, "I saw them melt and some of them even came to the altar and before the end of the week, they were responding wonderfully to my preaching."[10]

Dowell's other overseas trip that year occurred during the summer. That was when Dowell spent ten days in Peru. He preached revivals in four different churches. In a meeting at El Bosque, a television producer was saved, and then later that same week, one of the producer's contacts—a man that Dowell described as "a television star of international fame"—was likewise saved.[11]

In September of 1975, Dowell and his wife celebrated their forty-first anniversary. As a gift, Dowell replaced Nola's yellow gold wedding rings with a new set in white gold. The card that accompanied the gift said this: "God has given me a reasonable amount of success in the ministry. I give Him the glory for it, but humanly speaking, I would have failed without you. I know myself, and you have been a necessity for me. When the rewards are passed out, I am sure the greatest reward will be given to you."[12]

Dowell's ministries had, indeed, enjoyed good success. As the 1975-76 school year got underway, BBC's enrollment was approaching twenty-two hundred students. And Baptist Temple was likewise thriving. Its attendances that fall averaged over twelve hundred, roughly double what they had been when Dowell became pastor. Along with those attendances came some much-needed financial relief. Weekly offerings were now averaging eight thousand dollars, up from twenty-two hundred dollars when Dowell first came.[13]

Dowell was especially pleased to see this turnaround at his church. He once wrote an article describing his philosophy on church finances. "The credit of a church should be unquestionable," he said. "A church should pay their bills and be honest in every respect with the community." Dowell conceded that even a church might experience financial hardships, but when those situations arose, he believed it was imperative for the church to protect its integrity at all costs. "If a church should run into financial difficulty," Dowell continued, "they should get in touch with their creditors and make satisfactory arrangements." For Dowell, this was not just about good business practices; the gospel's message was at stake. Invoking a phrase from 2 Corinthians 3:2, Dowell said, "God's people are 'living epistles known and read of all men.'"[14]

Dowell's high profile in the BBF meant that his own epistle was now being read more widely than ever. And Dowell was careful to guard its contents. One of Dowell's staff members at Baptist Temple, Tony Isaacs, remembered the strong character exhibited by this preacher. Standing in an outer office one day, Isaacs saw Dowell in a back room using a photocopier. No one else was around, and according to Isaacs, Dowell did not know that he was being watched. But after Dowell made a small set of photocopies, he reached into his pocket and counted out three nickels, which he laid down next to the copier. This was in keeping with a procedure that had been set up for church employees who needed to make personal copies. And Dowell had been copying some personal tax forms. Isaacs said Dowell's authority and status would have made it unthinkable for anyone to question him for making a few copies at no cost. But for Isaacs, it was meaningful to watch Dowell surrender those nickels. Even in the little things, Isaacs noted, this was a man of integrity.[15]

On September 29, 1975, this man of integrity, and his fellowship, experienced a seismic jolt. As it happened, God was preparing to write a new chapter in Dowell's epistle. That was the day that Bill Bartlett, after stopping by Dowell's office, walked down a hallway to find G. B. Vick, age seventy-four, collapsed at his desk. Standing over Vick's body two days later, Dowell described the events:

> *Last Monday morning I arrived at the school, after having had a funeral, at twelve o'clock. I had a momentary visit with Brother Bill Bartlett, Dr. Vick's grandson, about a meeting we were to have in just a few moments. He stepped out of the office and was gone only a few seconds and came running back and said, "Dr. Dowell, come, Granddaddy's on the floor." We went into his office and we found him lying on the floor. Everything that could be done from a human standpoint was done to preserve his life—if he was still alive—until the coronary unit arrived. And then they took over and did what they could and took him to an emergency ward in Cox Medical Center, and four of the best doctors in the city worked on him for thirty minutes. And they did not get any response, and finally at 1:41, they pronounced him dead. It was a tremendous shock to all of us.*[16]

Dowell presided over a campus memorial service for Vick in BBC's fieldhouse, and then Dowell traveled to Detroit to moderate Vick's funeral at Temple Baptist. Condolences poured in from people around the world, including Strom Thurmond, senator from South Carolina, and Raymond W. Barber, president of the World Baptist Fellowship. Dowell, too, was struck by the loss. As he looked into the casket, he told the crowd of mourners, "I say without any reservation that lying before us this morning is my greatest friend with whom I've worked for 34 years very intimately." Dowell said that, in all of that time, he and Vick had "never had a cross word with each other."[17]

Vick served as the president of BBC for twenty-five years, and his death left a great void at the college. It also raised some perplexities. The corporate charter included provisions for a vice president to take over after a president's death, but those provisions were out of step with recent changes in BBC's administration. John Rawlings had, by this time, resigned his long-held position as BBC's vice president, so there was no longer anyone serving under the vice president's title. And Dowell's title, executive vice president, was never a part of the founding documents, so there was no constitutional basis for Dowell to step in to the presidency.[18]

Given these circumstances, the trustee board voted to leave the president's office open for the 1975-76 school year. This would give them time both to revise the school's constitution and to select the right candidate to fill the vacancy. Dowell would continue to run the campus, but the trustees asked him not to implement any major changes until after the presidency question had been decided.[19]

Dowell and the trustee board had another conversation a few weeks later. This time, the board wanted to gauge Dowell's interest in becoming the next president. Of course, to many of the fellowship's constituents, Dowell seemed a logical successor. But his appointment was never assumed to be automatic. Nor was it without its concerns. So the board sent three representatives to Dowell's office in November of 1975 to try to work through the issues. The men approached Dowell with a proposal, explaining that the board was ready to name him to the presidency if he would agree to one stipulation. They wanted him to resign Baptist Temple.[20]

Dowell recalled that conversation in a 1991 interview. He said that some on the board had questioned his ability to make quick decisions, but he noted that those concerns were quickly allayed when he heard their proposal. "Very quickly I told them, I said, 'If that's your criterion then you go back and tell them to begin looking for someone else because I'm not resigning Baptist Temple.'"[21] The subcommittee carried back a report to their fellow board members telling them not to worry about Dowell's ability to make snap judgments. "We didn't have it all out of our mouth," they said, "till he told us to go look for somebody else."[22]

After hearing Dowell's refusal, the board members returned to their deliberations and gave the matter further consideration. And by the beginning of December, they decided to amend their offer. They would invite Dowell to serve as president with no strings attached. He could serve as both president and pastor, just as Vick had done for twenty-five years. And for these services, the college would raise Dowell's salary to $25,000 a year plus benefits. Parker Dailey of Kansas City would be invited to join Dowell as the institution's vice president.[23]

Dowell and Dailey both accepted their new appointments, and the two of them were formally installed into office during the May Fellowship Meeting of 1976. A crowd of over five thousand attended that event. Bob Jones Jr. delivered the ceremony's opening prayer, and Tom Malone of Midwestern Bible College in Pontiac, Michigan, brought the charge.[24] John Rawlings framed the occasion in biblical terms. "God never takes away a Moses," Rawlings said, "without raising up a Joshua to take his place."[25]

Whether or not Dowell would have made such a comparison, he did find this new chapter in his life momentous. When Dowell listed the highlights of his ministry in a 1996 interview, he ranked his presidency at BBC as number two, second only to his years at High Street. Dowell went on to say that his 1983 retirement from the college—which was prompted by declining health—was the "greatest disappointment" of his life.[26]

This was because Dowell enjoyed his presidency and because he was proud of his accomplishments at the college. In his first year in office, BBC's enrollment jumped to 2,414, the highest number on record. Then BBC won accreditation in 1978. Under Dowell's administration, BBC also phased out the three-year degrees that it had offered for many years. Now all of BBC's bachelor's programs would be aligned with those at other four-year institutions. In both 1978 and 1981, BBC's basketball team, the Patriots, won the NCCAA Division II national championships. And one other accomplishment that brought Dowell satisfaction was a 1982 ribbon-cutting ceremony. That was when several members of the Vick family joined Dowell to open the G. B. Vick Memorial Library, a new facility that was made possible by generosity of the Temple Baptist Church of Detroit and their new pastor, A. V. Henderson.

Of course, Dowell's closeness to Vick assured not only a respect for Vick's legacy but also a continuation of Vick's vision. There was no daylight between Vick and Dowell on the purpose of the college. BBC existed to equip men and women to fulfill the Great Commission. Two nights after he assumed the president's title, Dowell delivered the college's twenty-sixth annual commencement address. Dowell took that opportunity to make his position clear. "Someone says the main emphasis of a Bible college is academic," Dowell stated. "Let me shout back with all the fervor of my soul. NO! The main interest of a Bible college is evangelism. We try to place the academic tools in the student's hand, but only to prepare him for his evangelistic task."[27]

Dowell continued to preside over that evangelistic training ground for the next seven years, and even as he did, he carried out his own evangelistic work from the pulpit of Baptist Temple. He made good progress. In 1978, Dowell resumed publication of his weekly newspaper article "As I See It," and in those advertisements, he touted Baptist Temple as "Springfield's fastest growing church."[28] He wrote in July of that year, "Baptist Temple has grown in the past five years from 500 in Sunday School to an average of nearly 1300. The weekly offering has become five times as large as it was five years ago. There is a reason why! Soulwinning – excellent music – Bible preaching."[29] Baptist Temple was doing so well, in fact, that by 1979 the church began televising its Sunday morning worship services over station KMTC. Dowell's church also hosted a number of special guests, including best-selling author Charles "Tremendous" Jones and evangelist Jerry Johnston.

Of course, some of Baptist Temple's greatest moments would come years later. In June 1985, the church paid off the last of its bonds, an accomplishment that prompted Jerry Falwell to refer to Baptist Temple as "a miracle work."[30] The church went on to consolidate its remaining debts through Empire Bank, and when that consolidation loan was paid off in 1996, the church was finally debt-free. To celebrate, Dowell and Vickery, both retired by that time, joined with bankers, friends, and church members for a grand homecoming and a note-burning ceremony. Dowell could only thank God and bless the people. The congregation had "stood like the rock of Gibraltar," he said.[31]

Dowell, too, had exhibited Gibraltar-like fortitude when, within a two-year timespan, 1974 and 1975, he had answered calls from both Baptist Temple and the Baptist Bible College. As one preacher friend expressed it, Dowell was "carrying water on both shoulders."[32] His role at each institution would be fraught with many difficulties, but he would also see many victories. And Dowell chose to focus on the latter. On the first Sunday of 1976, Dowell told his church: "I believe as we face a new year with all of its problems and its complications along with all of its opportunities, I believe if this church believes God and we'll claim God's promise and we'll not lean upon the arm of the flesh, I believe God will give us victory just like he gave Caleb victory."[33]

If Dowell himself was rock-like, it was because he had learned to lean upon the Rock. He believed victory was possible, even in a time of loss, because there was Someone greater and stronger to call upon. And in Dowell's new capacity as both pastor and president, he was calling upon that One with increasing frequency. Indeed, Dowell would soon be treading waters that were as deep as any that he had yet experienced, yet those waters would not go over his soul. When Dowell called upon his God, the Lord's hand would be there to uphold him. And with the Psalmist, Dowell would look back on it all and declare victory, saying:

> *If it had not been the Lord who was on our side, now may Israel say;*
> *If it had not been the Lord who was on our side, when men rose up against us:*
> *Then they had swallowed us up quick, when their wrath was kindled against us:*
> *Then the waters had overwhelmed us, the stream had gone over our soul:*
> *Then the proud waters had gone over our soul.*
> *Blessed be the Lord, who hath not given us as a prey to their teeth.*
> *Our soul is escaped as a bird out of the snare of the fowlers: the snare is broken, and we are escaped.*
> *Our help is in the name of the Lord, who made heaven and earth.*[34]

PART 5: SUNSET

Chapter 38: *Body Troubles*

A flight attendant covered in blue and white emerged through the terminal door. Her tightly pinned hair and her brisk manner announced to onlookers that she was all business. She glanced at Nola, Bill Jr., and Joan as she propped open the door. The empty wheelchair parked in front of them made it clear which passenger this trio had come to pick up. The woman adopted a professional tone, neither warm nor indifferent, as she spoke to them.

They're bringing him out now.

Seconds later a tired-looking Dowell stepped into view. The left side of his face was hanging as if partially melted. This was May 21, 1977.

How you doing, Dad?

Bill Jr. tried not to look too alarmed by his father's mushy response.

Nyot tu gud.

Nola's eyebrows furled. She said impatiently:

What did you say?

Dowell tried again.

Nyot tu gud.

Nola watched her son guide the patient into his wheelchair, and as Dowell plopped into the seat, Nola reached over to tuck the collar of his white shirt back under his suitcoat. In situations like this, Nola's emotions came out as fastidiousness. Instead of crying over her problems, she strong-armed them. She issued the next command in that same spirit:

Speak clearly. We can't understand you.

Dowell's left eye was hidden behind a sagging eyelid, but he tried to make visual contact using the other eye. He needed his wife to understand.

I can'dt. I wizh I cud.

Dowell reached up to take Nola's hand and said it again:

Budt I jus' can'dt.

Battles within the body had always been the toughest for Dowell endure. And nothing had changed—except for the fact that such battles were occurring with greater frequency now. Sometimes these battles manifested themselves in the physical body. Yet they also occurred within the body of believers or within the body of the fellowship. The troubles were neither welcome nor pleasant, but they could not be ignored. The longer they were left untreated, the more dangerous they became.

One ailment that Dowell hated to see within the body of Christ was the "namby-pamby" Christian. Dowell's cornball nomenclature notwithstanding, he found this problem rampant and quite serious during the 1970s. Christianity seemed to be turning up everywhere, from Hollywood to the White House, yet the Christianity of popular culture was a strange, knock-off brand, one that cheapened Christ's sacrifice. In one sermon, Dowell said:

> I'll be very frank to tell you, I am sick–I am horrified–I deplore the manner in which the new birth is being used by the masses in the world today. A fellow gets up and says, "I'm born again!" Preaches it. Then goes to Las Vegas to entertain at a nightclub. I don't care if your name is Pat Boone or whoever you are. It just doesn't make sense. We do what our nature dictates to us. And going to a nightclub and entertaining at a nightclub–I'll guarantee you the Spirit of God will never lead you to do that. Don't you make any mistake about it, that's of the devil. That's of sin.[1]

Dowell observed a similar sickness in the political world. Presidential Candidate Jimmy Carter was touting himself as a Southern Baptist, yet critics of Carter were skeptical. The liberal platform that Carter had aligned himself with, including his party's support of both abortion and the Equal Rights Amendment, certainly did not coincide with the views of many fundamentalists. But Dowell had yet another concern. During Carter's campaign, the candidate's staff had contacted Dowell at BBC to lodge a surprising complaint. Dowell explained the episode in a sermon:

> Some few days ago I received a phone call from Jimmy Carter's press secretary asking about a short article written by a student at Baptist Bible College and published in the Banner–that's the BBC student paper. I was rather shocked that attention would be called to a small college paper nestled in the foot of the Ozarks. They said in this telephone call, said, "Mr. Carter's disturbed about that article." I thought, "That isn't possible." He said, "He may want to answer it." And I said, "I'd be very happy to have him answer it and we'll publish it word for word as he writes it in the Banner." What I didn't tell him was that I would have had my answer under it probably. But I would have published it. This article was an article objecting–it was a very short article–I edited it three times before I let it go into the paper. It was very mild and yet it condemned a circular that had been widely distributed. Six thousand were handed out during the Democratic Convention. It had a picture of Carter that had him dressed up where he's supposed to look like Jesus Christ. And underneath it had the caption, "J.C. will save you." That's blasphemy. I didn't let this student say it was blasphemy in the paper, but I did let the student lift a voice of protest against anyone having that kind of association. Now Carter didn't have anything to do

with that, I don't imagine, but he knew it was done. And if I'd have been him, I'd have objected to it, too. If they'd object to a little article that long in the Banner, it looks to me like they'd object to six thousand circulars like that that was passed out at the Democratic Convention.[2]

Dowell devoted relatively little time to criticizing fellow believers, but he did not hesitate to condemn those whose actions he considered damaging to the body of Christ. Usually Dowell's focus was on the behavior instead of the personalities. Dowell said little about Evangelist Billy Graham, for instance, though he was no fan of Graham's ecumenism. Dowell conceded that Graham's crusades won great numbers to Christ, but he noted that afterward those converts were cast to the denominational winds. Catholics, Presbyterians, Methodists—Graham seemed to lock arms with all such groups.[3] And the practice left Dowell alarmed. Still, Dowell emphasized the practice, not the personality. Denouncing ecumenism in a 1965 sermon, Dowell said:

> *The ecumenical movement today teaches unity at any price. There's a great effort being made, "Oh, let's all join together; let's have a great brotherhood. One for all and all for one." And it sounds good, but the Word of God teaches unity based only upon truth and never unity based upon compromise. God has a great deal to say about those who compromise His Word. He says if you take from it, your part will be taken from the Holy City and from the Book of Life. If you add to it, the plagues that are written in this book will be added unto you. Let God be true and every man a liar.*[4]

Upholding the truth was important to Dowell, and whether listeners liked it or not, Dowell aimed to level with them. Not always was such straight talk well received, of course. In 1977, at the urging of many in the BBF, Dowell published a brief account of the 1950 split with J. Frank Norris, and after this book came out, Raymond W. Barber, then head of Norris's fellowship, shot back a two-and-a-half-page letter condemning Dowell's work. The letter said in part:

> *To say the least I am saddened by it—not because you recalled the history of your movement, to which you gave very little space as far as specific history of the Fellowship is concerned, but because of the tragic consequences of your approach.*
>
> *It appears to the reader that you were not nearly so concerned with the development of the Baptist Bible Fellowship, International, as you were with the degrading of the man to whom you, your fellow pastors, and your constituency owe a great deal—indeed, your identity as independent, fundamental Baptists.*
>
> *It seems that the "resurrection" and the "second death" of J. Frank Norris are the keynotes of your treatise. While we all admit Dr. Norris was not impeccable, and while he employed tactics which most of us would not and could*

not use, he did give his time, energy, ability, and life to the cause we all espouse—
the cause of fundamentalism, and in a greater sense, the cause of Jesus Christ.[5]

Dowell took exception to Barber's criticisms, believing that his motives had been misinterpreted. Dowell wrote back to Barber explaining that his document was "strictly a background history" of the BBF and that he had taken no potshots. Indeed, Dowell said that he had truthfully shared his own actions even though, in retrospect, he was ashamed of some of them. As evidence of the balanced position he had taken, Dowell pointed out a statement found on page 45 of his book: "In spite of all the things Dr. Norris did under the pressure of seeing many of his best friends and associates leave him, I still must recognize him as one of the greatest spiritual leaders of his day." Far from "degrading" Norris or anyone else, Dowell had told the truth in what he believed to be a fair and balanced way. "I really think if you would reread the book you might change your opinion as to what the purpose of the book was," Dowell told Barber.[6]

Dowell avoided such preacher-to-preacher squabbles to the extent possible. At times, however, circumstances compelled him to express opposition even toward men that he admired. One example was Dowell's falling out with John R. Rice. It started in 1973 when Rice published an article in *The Sword of the Lord* under the title "Must All Tithes Go to Church Treasury?" In his article, Rice quoted Malachi 3:10, "Bring ye all the tithes into the storehouse." Rice then posed and answered his essay's central question: "Does that mean that Christians ought to bring their tithes to the church house? It certainly does not. It means nothing of the kind." Rice maintained that paying the tithe to other gospel organizations, including *The Sword of the Lord*, was equally scriptural. "Christians ought to give God tithes and offerings," Rice went on to say. "But the tithe is the Lord's, not the church's. And every Christian ought to get instruction from God as to where and how his money should be given."[7]

Of course, Dowell and many of his peers held a very different opinion on this subject. Yet for most of those preachers, agreeing to disagree was a workable solution. This was not the case for Dowell. Dowell was a member of Rice's advisory board, and his name was listed in every issue of *The Sword of the Lord*. To remain silent, Dowell believed, was tantamount to endorsing Rice's attack on storehouse tithing. Dowell decided to clear the air by publishing in the *Tribune* a letter that he had also sent to Rice:

> *Dear Dr. Rice—*
> *May I begin by saying there is no man I respect more and love more than I do you; hence, what I am doing is not personal.*
> *Every preacher that I know in the Baptist Bible Fellowship believes in storehouse tithing, and the reaction to your articles has been such that it has created a problem since I, too, believe very strongly that above our tithes we should support other fine Christian movements, papers, and radio stations that are doing a good work for God.*

> *May I make it very plain that what I am doing is not because of what you believe but because of the nature of your articles and the reaction they have caused.*
>
> *With great regret I request that my name be removed from your Advisory Board.*[8]

For some time afterward, Dowell and Rice remained on friendly terms. In fact, Dowell was once again a featured speaker at a conference sponsored by Rice's newspaper in 1975.[9] But then in 1977, this controversy flared up again, this time with greater hostility. In the June 10 issue of *The Sword of the Lord*, Rice launched the same argument, now under the provocative title "Storehouse Tithing: A New Heresy by Selfish Preachers." Rice's attack on his fellow preachers angered many of Dowell's close allies, including Wendell Zimmerman. Zimmerman published a lengthy reply to Rice's article in the July 1 issue of the *Tribune*.[10] Others spoke out about it in succeeding issues of the *Tribune*. Then on August 12, Rice returned fire, using statements made by Dowell to advance his own arguments. Rice intimated that Dowell's storehouse tithing position made Dowell an enemy of evangelists, television ministries, print publications, and the like. Rice further suggested that Dowell wanted no one but local churches to win souls.[11]

To refute these charges, Dowell now drafted "An Open Letter to All Fundamental Baptists," a lengthy piece that appeared in the September 16 issue of the *Tribune*. Dowell stated in part:

> *In a recent Sword of the Lord, my good friend, Dr. John R. Rice, gave much of the space of his paper to an article based upon a statement I made in a recent issue of the Baptist Bible Tribune.*
>
> *I was saddened because most of the article was based upon a misinterpretation of what I believe.*
>
> *For many years, I have preached my convictions on the local church in Sword of the Lord Conferences with Dr. Rice sitting on the front seat or on the platform.*
>
> *I have wondered why he waited so long to write such an article. What are his intentions?*
>
> *I would fight for Dr. Rice to have the privilege of printing his convictions even though I do not agree with some of them.*
>
> *Dr. Rice believes the Great Commission was given to individuals. I believe the Great Commission was given to the church. If the Great Commission was given to individuals, then the authority for baptism is the individual. I believe the authority for baptism . . . is the church.*
>
> *Dr. Rice believes the church started on the day of Pentecost. I believe the church was started during the personal ministry of Christ.*

> *Dr. Rice believes that all believers are in the church. I believe that all*
> *believers are in the family of God and will be in Heaven, but that the church is a*
> *called-out assembly of scripturally baptized believers.*
>
> *Yet, I still love and respect Dr. Rice, and I would never have lifted my voice*
> *if he had only stated his convictions. But when he began to condemn my brethren*
> *who believe the tithe should go to the local church stating that they were selfish*
> *money grabbers and making many other accusations, I felt it necessary to resign*
> *from his board. I did it, however, in a very gracious manner, and he was very*
> *gracious to me.*
>
> *Some preacher friends said to me the other day, "I admire you that you can*
> *be so gracious to Dr. Rice." I told them that I love him; he is a great man of God.*
>
> *Now Dr. Rice feels compelled to try to hurt me. I forgive him, and I still love*
> *him as a brother in the Lord and have no desire to hurt him. Because of the*
> *unkind and untrue things he said about my position, I feel obligated to set forth*
> *my convictions so people may know what I really believe. . . .*
>
> *Dr. Rice says church members are taught to feel that soul-winning is only the*
> *official business of the church and its officers, not individuals.*
>
> *I know most of the pastors in our Baptist Bible Fellowship, and I do not*
> *know of a single one that teaches this. The fact is, I never knew a Baptist*
> *preacher anywhere that did teach it. . . .*
>
> *When I stated that God chose to use the church to evangelize the world, I*
> *think everyone understood that I meant that the church was the only institution*
> *He founded and gave the worldwide commission.*
>
> *He did not start a denomination, a college, a newspaper, nor even an*
> *evangelistic association; he started the church.*[12]

Rice and Dowell had little, if any, contact after the publication of that 1977 article. And then Rice died in 1980. For Dowell, all of this served as a disappointing end to a long friendship. Still, Dowell believed that he had done the right thing. To Dowell, letting people know where he stood was more important than the political fallout. So Dowell stood his ground. And if he had lost a friend, he had at least retained his self-respect.

Dowell faced similar disputes within the ranks of the BBF. As it was with Paul and Barnabas, Dowell and his fellow laborers did not always see eye to eye. Most such battles were fought on behalf of the college. As executive vice president of BBC, for instance, Dowell had sparred with the BBF's directors over teaching appointments to his mission department. Fred Donnelson, for many years, had served both as director of BBF missions and as chairman of BBC's mission department. But this situation changed after Donnelson passed off the scene. In fact, a later mission director, Carl Boonstra, was given a directive from fellowship officials in 1974, prohibiting him and others from doing teaching in the missions department. Dowell considered the move "disastrous to our college." Reacting to the news, Dowell sent a letter to G. B. Vick urging Vick to intervene. "To my great surprise," Dowell told Vick, "it appears that the directors have instructed Brother Boonstra that he is not to become involved in teaching responsibilities and that Brother Brown could only teach through December; and that they told Brother Deal that he could teach one year and then he would have to decide whether he would be a missionary or a college professor." Dowell had but one reaction to this new ruling: "If they follow through with this policy, we will be hard put to find qualified missions teachers."[13]

Over the next decade, such turf disputes cropped up with increasing regularity. They were indicative of a new landscape now facing the college and fellowship. Growth within the fellowship had spawned competing interests. As Dowell had already seen with the Pacific Coast Baptist Bible College, these changes frequently put ministry partners at cross-purposes. In 1977, the fellowship formally recognized another BBF college, Baptist Bible College East, and then in 1978, six additional schools were approved for the training of BBF missionaries. Fellowship students now had more options than ever before, as did the churches who were underwriting their education.

BBC had the most to lose in all of this, but even so, Dowell saw little point in trying to stop it. He told his faculty in May 1977:

> BBC's attitude should be that we are deceiving ourselves when we think there are not going to be other schools started. Whether it is right or wrong is an issue for the pastors of our Fellowship to determine. Our position should be that we are BBF people and we are going to see to it that this school is operated on a high level and make it the best school in the United States, and depend upon God to do what He has always done and bless us and supply our needs.[14]

BBC was heading into a perfect storm even as Dowell uttered those words. Indeed, new colleges were but one part of the financial squall. Stagnant economic growth and an out-of-control inflation rate were likewise serving to deplete the school's coffers. In March 1978, Dowell reported in the *Tribune*:

> In the past three years, our utility bill went up 99.1%. The minimum wage went up this January and will go up again next January—an increase of 26% in one year; and of course, the cost of food has risen sharply. Almost all of our hourly workers who enjoy the benefits of the increased minimum wage are students, so we're happy they earn more—but it also places a major financial burden on the College because of the tremendous increase.[15]

As a result of these things, BBC ended its 1977-78 school year with a $300,000 deficit. Dowell mailed out three thousand letters to churches to try to recoup that loss, but he received back just forty-one responses—"not enough increased finances to even make a dent," he said.[16]

As Dowell and his trustees approached a new school year, then, they knew they had to weigh their options carefully. And this was when they decided that the time had come to begin charging BBC students tuition. Starting in the fall of 1978, students would pay a nominal fee, $248 per semester.

Dowell and his trustees understood that this was a risky move. Tuition charges might drive away students, anger pastors, or even lead supporting churches to conclude that their money was no longer needed. Before finalizing the decision, Dowell directed his office to mail out nearly twelve hundred surveys to supporting churches. In his mailing, Dowell explained to these pastors the situation and asked for their reaction to the proposed change. Dowell received about half of those surveys back, he said, and a little over half of the respondents said they were willing to support the board's decision.[17] On that basis, then, the new tuition plan was implemented.

Dowell tried to bolster support for his tuition charge even as the announcement went out to the fellowship constituency. The decision had not been a unilateral one, Dowell explained in a *Tribune* article, nor had it been made lightly. "The overwhelming feeling of the Trustees was that they had no choice," Dowell said. Dowell also noted that this change had been under consideration for several years. "Dr. Vick, although a firm advocate of the 'no tuition' philosophy at the founding of the school, had decided to start charging $125.00 per semester tuition just before his death," Dowell wrote. "In fact, he told Dr. Bartlett of his plans on the way to his BBC office the day he died."[18]

Ironically, Vick's untimely death was what had stayed the action. Dowell was not installed as president until May of 1976, and launching an unpopular fee during Dowell's first year in office would have been unthinkable. Yet this delay only worsened the problem. By the time BBC's tuition program was finally implemented, the nation was entering its second major energy crisis, and inflation was approaching the highest levels since World War I. Consequently, almost as soon as the new tuition charge went into effect, it became evident that this new revenue stream was going to be inadequate.

So Dowell took further action that same school year. "Few colleges have escaped the devastating effect of inflation upon the economy," Dowell explained in February 1979. "BBC is no exception. For this reason I have slashed over $500,000 from our 1978-79 budget in order to operate the school in the black for the coming year."[19] As part of those mid-year cutbacks, custodial crews were reduced, and faculty were asked to begin vacuuming their own offices and emptying their own trash containers.[20] But even these measures did not stabilize the financial situation at BBC.

Adding to the stress of those days was the fact that BBC's enrollment was now beginning to decline. Dowell saw that further cuts would be necessary. Word went out in the fall of 1980 that several full-time faculty members would not be returning the following semester. Academic Dean Hunter Sherman explained the situation in a letter:

> The administrative committee of the Baptist Bible College made the following recommendation. Based upon the current financial condition at the college, the national economic situation, the continued decline in student enrollment, and the rate of inflation, it is recommended that the faculty of Baptist Bible College be reduced by several full-time professors."[21]

Such things were a burden to Dowell. He once said of himself, "I have a nature that I just about love everybody."[22] And that loving nature made decisions like these difficult for him. Mary Herman, a longtime faculty member at BBC, said that if Dowell had a fault, it was in confronting such matters. When the difficult decisions needed to be made, Herman said, Dowell did so only with great reluctance.[23]

John Rawlings noted another fault in Dowell's tenure at the college. Rawlings said Dowell should have walked away sooner. "My honesty forces me to say that he would have done well to have resigned the college before his health broke down," Rawlings remarked, "because we older people have a tendency to be blinded by the needs as we grow older."[24]

Excuse me. My husband—W. E. Dowell—needs to see a doctor right away.

The Dowell family had reached the emergency room at Cox Hospital, and Nola was now standing at a sliding glass window under a sign that read "REGISTRATION." Since the woman on the other side was occupied with some documents, Nola had taken the liberty of sliding the window open for her. The woman at the desk looked put off by Nola's forwardness. She folded her hands in front of her and said:

Oh? What seems to be the problem?

Nola's eyebrows furled again.

We don't know. That's why we need to see a doctor. His body is not working properly.

Bill Jr. spoke up from behind his mother.

His face is drooping, and his speech is slurred. And he doesn't seem to have much energy.

The woman reached for a clipboard.

What did you say the name was?

Nola answered:

W. E. Dowell. D-O-W-E-L-L. He's president over at the Baptist Bible College, and he's the pastor of a large church. He was preaching out of town this week, and they had to fly him back here because there's something seriously the matter with him.

The woman behind the desk answered as she wrote:

Yes, ma'am. Let me see what we can do to get him treated.

Nola nodded and said:

And please hurry. I mean if your body isn't working properly, that's a real emergency.

The woman glanced up at her.

Yes, ma'am. It certainly is.

Chapter 39: *Complex Organisms*

So it was not a stroke?

Nola seemed more surprised than grateful. She was sitting in a chair next to her husband's bed, and she was finding it difficult to take everything in. She was also having a hard time tuning out the incessant beeping and buzzing that went along with intensive care. She sat forward in her chair to better hear the doctor's reply.

It does not appear so, ma'am, no.

The sigh that followed was not the sound of relief. It was an indication that Nola was both nervous and frustrated. She reached up to pat her husband's lower leg on the bed, taking a sort of motherly tone as she asked:

Well then, what in the world is wrong with you, Boy?

Dowell, who was now on a feeding tube, answered nothing. Instead he looked back at his wife with an eerie stare. The lids of his eyes were taped open. Dowell could no longer hold his eyes open on his own, and it was evident that whatever was afflicting him was progressing. The feeding tube had become necessary because Dowell was also having difficulty swallowing.

The doctor spoke again:

The good news is we've ruled out several possibilities: stroke, Bell's Palsy—.

This prompted a matter-of-fact exchange, initiated by Nola:

I can't see what good any of that does him.

Uh-huh.

I mean, wouldn't you agree, Doctor, that he's getting worse rather than better?

His condition is—

Nola kept going.

He can't speak, can't eat. I mean, how much worse are things going to get? Or how much worse can they get?

The doctor waited for permission to speak again, and when it seemed that he had it, he tried again.

Well, of course, the body is a pretty complex organism, Mrs. Dowell. And with so many systems interacting with one another, it can take time to figure things out. There's just a lot to look at.

As the president of BBC, Dowell was well-versed in complex organisms. BBC was operated by a fellowship of more than two thousand churches, which meant that the college president had plenty of overlords. Fellowship pastors felt a special ownership of BBC. Indeed, one of the frequent objections that Dowell heard about the idea of charging tuition at the school was that it would spell the end of pastoral control.[1] And pastors enjoyed running the show. Dowell learned that they had opinions about every aspect of BBC's operation, from music styles to dress codes. And of course, all such opinions were routinely shared with the school's president.

Keeping everyone happy was an impossible task, though Dowell made a noble effort. In a 1978 chapel message, for instance, Dowell addressed ongoing concerns about the type of music that was being allowed on campus. Because the fellowship was seeing a "trend toward what is called contemporary music," Dowell explained in his statement, the trustee board wanted him "to publicly express their desire to protect Baptist Bible College from this seeming trend."[2] Dowell's full statement, published in the *Tribune*, made a case for diplomacy:

> It is understood there are different opinions among pastors and people, and we do not sit in judgment in relation to the local churches nor the type music they may use. A church is a sovereign, indigenous body, and no one has authority over the church but Christ.
>
> The Baptist Bible College is a Fellowship-controlled school, however. It is not controlled by any one church, it is controlled by all of the churches of the Baptist Bible Fellowship. The music produced by our representative groups sent out by the College, and our own music department within the college, should be acceptable to all of our churches. I do not mean that the music we use would be preferable to every church, but it should not be offensive to any.[3]

Dowell went on to itemized specific guidelines that seemed to him in line with the expectations of most of the BBF churches at that time. "The melody and text should dominate the harmony and the rhythm," he said. "Any lyric that refers to God as 'somebody up there' or 'the man upstairs' is not appropriate. . . . Rock music of any kind is not to be performed or listened to at Baptist Bible College."[4]

Dowell was not without strong personal convictions about music and other divisive issues, but he was never fond of superintending such things. For him, complaints over these matters were a nuisance, a distraction from the real gospel ministry. In one appeal to pastors, Dowell wrote, "Oh, my friends, the world is dying. We don't have time for foolish controversies; we must be about our Master's business."[5] Then in 1975, Dowell told an audience, "You can't legislate righteousness—I tried it for twenty years. You can't legislate people to do right."[6]

Even so, running a Bible college demanded a certain amount of attention to such matters. Expectations had to be defined for the students, and Dowell understood that. What wore on him was the endless nitpicking from pastors. The minutes for a 1977 administration meeting at BBC capture some of Dowell's frustration: "Dr. Dowell began the meeting by restating his determination to be less influenced by complaints from pastors. He outlined his philosophy regarding accepting suggestions and complaints but stated that he was going to personally make an effort to reduce the amount of influence on his thinking that complaints normally produce."[7]

Dowell could not easily dismiss, however, critics who questioned BBC's commitment to its central textbook, the Bible. Since the earliest days of the fellowship, BBF constituents had been deeply loyal to a single English translation, the King James Version (KJV). Indeed, most BBF pastors, including Dowell, preached from nothing else. But recent developments in American churches were now bearing down upon Dowell and his college, demanding from them a more firm commitment to the KJV on the campus of BBC.

Though Dowell was fond of the KJV and had at times sharply criticized some of the alternative translations, Dowell stopped short of saying that the KJV was the only translation with any merit. Even men in Dowell's own circle had voiced praises for certain alternatives. It was widely known, for instance, that Noel Smith admired both the KJV and the American Standard Version (ASV). In a 1968 *Tribune* article, Smith explained his point of view, citing concern over the KJV's phrasing of Romans 8:16, "The Spirit itself beareth witness with our spirit, that we are the children of God." This rendering was not just inaccurate, Smith said; it was patently offensive. "How can you refer to any personality, not to mention the Third Person of the Trinity, as 'it'?" Smith wrote. "It is unpardonable. It is obscene."[8]

Of course, Smith never advocated abandoning the KJV in favor of something else. The ASV too was "not perfect," Smith said.[9] Smith advocated instead a kind of thoughtful scholarship. Continuing his article, he wrote:

> But you don't have to go from one extreme to another. You don't have to follow the fanatics. You have the King James Version, the American Standard Version, and The New Scofield Reference Bible. You don't have to discard your King James. You have all three (and of course, again, The New Scofield Reference Bible is printed in the King James text). You can keep on using your King James Version, as I do. But you should have the American Standard Version, if you are a real Bible student and an authentic and accurate expositor of the Word of God. You should use the American Standard Version as a commentary on the King James Version.[10]

Dowell voiced no objections to that kind of scholarship, nor did he oppose pastors who consulted commentaries or other translations to help them prepare their sermons. Dowell himself preached from C. I. Scofield's edition of the Bible and regularly consulted Scofield's marginal notes. But Dowell was careful not let such materials steer him off course. When Dowell's own study of the Bible contradicted Scofield's findings, Dowell was quick to say so. Dowell published his second book in 1980, a work titled *The Church: It's [sic] Meaning, Message and Method*. In the conclusion of that work, Dowell wrote, "C.I. Scofield gives outstanding helps in the Scofield Bible, but he is wrong when he refers to the true church being the universal body or all of the saved. The universal body of all the saved can by no stretch of the imagination be called a church."[11]

It is clear, then, that Dowell believed a faithful Christian might dispute Scofield on one hand while benefitting from him on another. And Dowell saw no need to abandon Scofield's text altogether just because he did not see eye to eye with Scofield on every point. Likewise, Dowell made no effort to abandon those like Smith who raised concerns about the KJV. In fact, if Dowell objected to Smith's criticisms at all, he said little about the matter publicly. Dowell also never voiced any concern about Smith's presence in the classrooms of BBC.

Yet by the end of the 1970s, things had changed. The BBF had been overtaken by a new sensitivity toward Bible translations, and criticisms of the KJV were now clearly out of favor. This new climate resulted from a wave of fresh Bible publications that had recently hit the market, including a paraphrase called *The Living Bible* and a translation called the New International Version (NIV). Churches saw rank-and-file Christians (particularly young people) abandoning the KJV in favor of such works, and in some cases, the newly adopted texts contained serious flaws. Some pastors believed that the thoughtful-scholarship approach had gone awry. And to fix the problem, they wanted to take a more hardline stance. The BBF needed to adopt a KJV-*only* position.[12]

In answer to those outcries, a resolution was introduced at a 1979 fellowship meeting held in Bangor, Maine. According to Pastor Billy Hamm, the push for the resolution came from a segment of preachers that Hamm characterized as "radical disciples of Ruckmanism." According to Hamm, these men "demanded that fellowship colleges use only one translation of scripture on campus." And to that end, the following resolution was proposed: "We believe that the King James Version of the Bible is God's Word preserved for the English-speaking people."[13]

For most in the BBF, including Dowell, this was not a difficult position to accept. In July 1978, Dowell described the KJV, saying it was "by far the most beautiful and the most dependable translation and is from the most accurate manuscript."[14] Most of the rest of the fellowship shared a similar opinion. And that being the case, the Bangor resolution was quickly adopted.

Upon returning to BBC, Dowell communicated the fellowship's position to faculty and students at the college. Dowell stated:

> *The twentieth century has seen a proliferation of many new Bible versions. Some are translations, some are paraphrases, and some are commentaries. This proliferation of versions has led to confusion and has raised the question, "Which Bible?" Realizing that there is such a question, the faculties and administration of Baptist Bible College and Baptist Bible Institute East recommend only the King James Version to their students. The King James Version is used exclusively in the classroom and the Greek text studied in Greek courses is the Trinitarian Bible Society text (textus receptus), which is the Greek text underlying the English Authorized Version of 1611.*[15]

Of course, if Dowell thought this would settle the matter, he was mistaken. Hamm summed up the fallout from the Bangor resolution, saying, "We conferred . . . most thought it would do no harm . . . the leaders acquiesced . . . the body approved, and yet nothing has caused more division in our fellowship."[16] Dowell learned this lesson better than anyone. In December 1979, no doubt in answer to complaints, Dowell found it necessary to issue a fresh proclamation to his faculty:

> *While we believe there are one or two other translations that may be studied with great profit, the textbook of Baptist Bible College is the Authorized Version, and we believe that all of God's Word has been preserved in that blessed book.*
>
> *Therefore I am giving a mandate from the office of president that the Authorized Version of the Bible must not be criticized nor attempts made to correct its truth.*[17]

Even this did not silence the critics. By the fall of 1980, members of Dowell's faculty were once again under fire for allegedly undermining the school's KJV-only position. The criticisms were so severe that Dowell now enlisted the help of BBF President David Cavin to conduct a formal inquiry. Dowell hoped that, even if no actions were deemed necessary, the investigation's formality would assure constituents that their concerns were being taken seriously. Dowell issued a summary report to his faculty after the investigation concluded:

> *Dr. Cavin and I have made a thorough investigation of the misunderstanding concerning our English Bible being the Word of God. We have interviewed faculty and students alike, and we do not find any reason for specific action. The testimony of the students was very weak, and all of the faculty we interviewed declared that they believed our Bible is the Word of God.*
>
> *I am instructing each one of you in language very much akin to a mandate, that you must be careful in teaching the courses that deal with this, and be sure that you are communicating properly with the students and keep them reminded often that you believe our Bible is the Word of God.*
>
> *We must stop the controversy that is coming to us from the pastors or else some action would have to be taken one way or another. We will be instructing the students at a future chapel service that they are to cease making such an issue of this thing, but please let us be very careful.*[18]

Dowell went on to publish his and Cavin's findings in the *Tribune*. Dowell explained in his article that, one by one, his faculty members had held up a copy of a KJV Bible and had affirmed their confidence in it, saying, "I believe that this is indeed the inerrant Word of God." Not a single faculty member declined to do so. Dowell said he and Cavin had also interviewed the students whose testimony had sparked the investigation. "In each case the students said, 'Well, I know I said that, but I probably misunderstood the professor,'" Dowell wrote. Then, near the end of this article, Dowell reaffirmed his own position on this matter: "I say this without any reservation whatsoever: I would not retain a professor at Baptist Bible College who does not believe that our translation of the Bible is the inspired Word of God."[19]

In this and other statements, Dowell was careful not to denounce all alternatives to the KJV. Dowell's position was not so extreme. He once told an audience in Mississippi, "I believe the Bible is inspired from the first 'In' of Genesis to the last 'Amen' of Revelation. And I believe every jot and tittle of it's inspired. And I believe God has preserved all of His truth even through proper translation in the English language. And I use the King James Version." Then he added, "I'm not a nut, but I use it and I believe it."[20]

The "nuts" were what Dowell found to be worrisome, often more so than the other translations. Dowell once told his student body in an orientation meeting, "Do not become glassy eyed about the King James Version being the only Bible from the only true manuscript. We use the King James Version as our basic translation. But there are one or two other translations that are basically good. Just don't make a big issue of it."[21] Those words were necessary, of course, because of individuals who *would* "make a big issue of it." The fundamentalist movement was teeming with the kind of sounding-brass-and-tinkling-cymbal virtuosos that Paul wrote about in 1 Corinthians 13. "I've heard people preach the truth like they were tickled to death they had it and glad nobody else did," Dowell once said.[22]

Though Dowell was never of that spirit, he did attempt to get along with such folks. And this was an undertaking that, at times, made his job at the college quite difficult. According to Doug Kutilek, BBC faculty member from 1981 to 1983, Dowell once told him that "under the then-current circumstances, Dr. [Noel] Smith in fact could not teach at BBC were he still living."[23] Dowell had no personal objection to Smith's affinity for the ASV, but he could no longer afford to let such teachings go on at BBC. The issue had simply become too divisive. And in the face of so many other problems, Dowell needed no further distractions.

The doctor leaned over Dowell's hospital bed.

Now, Mr. Dowell, what we'd like to do next, with your permission, is to try an injection.

Dowell trained his tired stare on the physician, and the doctor continued:

It's a procedure that should be able to tell us whether there's a problem within the muscles themselves. Can we give that a try, Sir?

Dowell replied with a slow nod, so the doctor tapped the bedrail as if to signal the end of the meeting. The doctor then gave a polite wink to Nola and turned to go. As he exited the room, Nola sighed again, saying to her husband:

More poking and prodding. You'll be ready for your glorified body before all this is over, won't you, Boy?

Dowell was given an injection later that same day. It produced instant results. His drooping eyes regained their strength almost immediately. The injection was only a temporary fix, but it did provide doctors with the information they needed to make a diagnosis. Dowell had a form of muscular dystrophy called Myasthenia Gravis.[24] The cause and cure of this illness were still unknown back in 1977, but what was known was rather discouraging. Only about ten to fifteen percent of Myasthenics ever went into remission.[25] And while there was no way to know if Dowell might fall into that percentage, it was clear that without further treatment, his outlook was very bleak. This disorder could attack not only the facial and throat muscles but also the lungs. In other words, it could be fatal.

The proposed treatment for Myasthenia Gravis was a steroid shot called ACTH. Doctors cautioned that the treatment might be as deadly as the illness. Doctors also indicated that Dowell's condition would likely worsen before it improved. Even so, since there were no better options on the table, Dowell and his family agreed to begin the medication. Dowell would receive treatments twice weekly, and he would be in the hospital no less than a month.

Happily, things began to turn around after Dowell's treatments began. The feeding tube was removed, and by the beginning of June, Dowell was well enough to draft this note for the *Tribune*:

> At the present time I am hospitalized with a muscle disease known as *Myasthenia Gravis*. It is a disease that the medical profession do not know a great deal about. However, they do have a series of shot treatments which has in many cases successfully arrested the disease for many years or sometimes permanently.
>
> I am in the process of taking those shots. I will be hospitalized for some three or four weeks for these treatments. During that time the patient's condition seems to worsen to a certain extent, and then to improve. It is my hope and trust that following these treatments I will be back 100 percent to fulfill my duties and responsibilities at the college.[26]

When Dowell became strong enough to leave intensive care, he was transferred to a large VIP suite. His new room was twice the size of ordinary hospital accommodations, and it included several couches and chairs for guests. Although these luxuries had never been requested by the family, it was clear that hospital staff wanted to make sure Dowell was well cared for.

Nola steadied her emotions as she went through this ordeal with her husband. Her daughter-in-law Joan observed, "She's always had so much faith."[27] In personal notes, Nola once wrote, "One day in our immediate family we will have to go through that sadness [of death]. Only the grace of God will see us through." The assurances of the Bible offered solace, Nola said. "The Bible has precious promises for every event of our life," she wrote, "and every hardship, and every trial, and every heartbreak."[28]

Dowell too managed to rely on his faith during this illness, though he admitted that his bout with Myasthenia Gravis was one of the darkest periods of his life. Dowell thought back to the experience in an interview, saying, "I couldn't speak, I couldn't see good. I wasn't in severe pain, but I was as miserable as I've ever been in my whole life because I had just got down where I was not functioning." Part of the devastation,

Dowell noted, was mental and emotional. "There are no human words adequate to describe what myasthenia gravis does to you," he explained. "A person could get very despondent with it, but I was determined that I was not going to."[29]

Dowell confessed that this mental determination was not easily forged. "I did have about two very dark hours," he said. "Victory came out of it." Dowell said it was prayer that sustained him. He "pleaded" with the Lord from his hospital bed, asking Him for healing "because I felt that my work wasn't done." As part of his prayers, Dowell said he lifted up the words of Job: "Though he slay me, yet will I trust in him."[30]

Dowell's prayers were, of course, joined by the prayers of many others. In accordance with James 5:14, Dowell summoned the elders of Baptist Temple to his room for a special season of prayer.[31] Then in his *Tribune* article, Dowell had appealed to the BBF to lend their prayer support as well. "I urge all of our people to pray for me," he wrote, "that this medication will be effective and bring about my complete restoration." People around the world responded. Many assured him of their prayers through cards and telephone calls. R. O. Woodworth commented about the fervency of the prayers that were being lifted up on Dowell's behalf. "The Pentecostals have nothing on us," Woodworth remarked.[32]

During this illness, Dowell also received other kinds of assistance. His vice president at BBC, Parker Dailey, arranged to spend more time on campus. Dailey pledged to come to Springfield from Kansas City at least every other week "as long as Dowell was incapacitated."[33] At Baptist Temple, Woodworth and other guest speakers stepped in to help carry Dowell's preaching load.[34] Then Dowell's son, Bill Jr., answered yet another need. Dowell's associate at Baptist Temple, Larry Smith, had recently moved to another ministry, so Dowell asked his son to consider stepping in as his co-pastor.

Dowell Jr. said it was "difficult" to render an immediate response to this request. He and his family were members at High Street, and Dowell Jr. was serving under David Cavin as the teacher of a large adult Sunday school class and as a part-time staff member. Before making this decision, Dowell Jr. wanted to speak both to Cavin and to his family. Cavin not only expressed understanding, Dowell Jr. recalled, but "even encouraged" him go to his father's aid.[35] Dowell Jr.'s family likewise offered their support. So later that summer, Dowell Jr.'s candidacy was put to a church vote, and much to his father's relief, Dowell Jr. was called to share the role of pastor at Baptist Temple.

The remainder of 1977 brought Dowell the physical healing for which he had prayed, though his recovery proved to be an extended one. Dowell was discharged from the hospital in mid-June, and by August, the *Tribune* reported that he was "well on the road to recovery."[36] But then in September, Dowell experienced a temporary setback. As his medication dosage was cut back, he suffered a relapse. Dowell was advised by his doctor to re-enter the hospital for a second round of ACTH treatments, something that was often necessary in Myasthenia cases.

Unfortunately, two days before Dowell's second round of treatments were set to begin, he started experiencing chest pains. Dowell was admitted to the hospital at once, though it was quickly determined that the pains had been brought on by Dowell's medications and not by his heart. Dowell remained hospitalized for the next ten days, receiving the second round of ACTH treatments, and by the end of it all, things were looking up. Dowell was feeling better, and the fact that he had gone from June to September before needing a second treatment was a positive sign, the doctor said. Dowell forwarded this news to the BBF in a *Tribune* article. "My doctor believes we are on the right track and can expect good results," Dowell wrote.[37]

Dowell's condition continued to improve, and he was eventually weaned of his medication. In fact, his Myasthenia Gravis stayed in remission for the last twenty-five years of his life. Even so, Dowell believed the disease had left behind some lasting damage. Dowell's muscles remained in a permanently weakened state. It was this weakness, Dowell believed, that compounded the effects of his later illnesses, including an excruciating case of shingles that hospitalized him in the fall of 1982.[38]

During that bout with shingles, Dowell decided to announce his resignation from the college presidency. BBC's enrollment by that time had dropped to just under fifteen hundred students, and the school's steady decline, combined with Dowell's ongoing health concerns, convinced Dowell that it was time for him to step down. He was unwell even at the time of the announcement, so he asked his son to deliver the message to the student body. Dowell Jr. read his father's statement in a chapel service just before the Thanksgiving break:

> I would like to express my sincere thanks for the large card sent to me with so many names while I was in the hospital, and for the dozens of individual cards and flowers sent to me by the students, faculty, and administration.
>
> You are my family and my kids, and I love you. I have had to make a very important decision during the past few weeks. I am sure my decision is right.
>
> Because of the heavy pressure and responsibilities of the office, and because of my illness, I have resigned as president to be effective in May of this coming year.
>
> It is my purpose to continue connections with the college. I hope, as chancellor, to have an office here and to work primarily in development, to raise money for the college, and possibly, teach one class.
>
> I want all of you to be mature and accept this as of the Lord and give your full cooperation in every way as the Fellowship seeks to replace me and provide new leadership for the college.
>
> Thanks for your love and loyalty through the years.[39]

A couple of weeks later, Dowell met with his trustees and with BBF President Verle Ackerman to formally present his resignation. According to the minutes of that meeting, "Dr. Dowell stipulated that he was not resigning from Baptist Bible College or Baptist Bible Fellowship International—just the Presidency."[40] Ackerman recommended that Dowell be honored at the upcoming May Fellowship Meeting and also that he be awarded the title of "Honorary Chancellor." Ackerman's recommendations were then followed by several other motions, all of which were unanimously approved. Dowell's college-owned house would be gifted to him and his wife; their utilities, property taxes, and insurance would be paid by the college; Dowell would continue to have an office and secretarial help at the college; and Dowell would receive a pension equal to fifty percent of his base salary until his death.[41] Dowell's successor, A. V. Henderson, formalized these arrangements as part of a consulting agreement signed in October 1984.

The generosity of these provisions speaks to the esteem that Dowell had earned on the campus of BBC. He loved the college, and the college loved him. One of BBC's longtime faculty members, Shirley McCullough, recalled an incident that, she said, illustrated the kind of loyalty President Dowell had engendered. For many years, BBC's graduating classes numbered over four hundred students, and during commencement ceremonies, the graduates' chairs were arranged in the shape of a cross. This image stretched across the full length and breadth of the fieldhouse floor, and at the beginning of each year's ceremony, administrators, faculty, and graduates marched in from the back of the facility in two lines. The path of their procession outlined the two sides of this cross-shaped seating area.

One year Dowell was unable to attend the graduation rehearsal, McCullough said, and when he showed up to lead the left side of the processional on graduation night, he got confused. Dowell made the first couple of ninety-degree turns as expected, but then, when it was time to turn back toward the center of the room, he missed his turn. The group on the right side continued marching the planned route even as Dowell, on the left side, carved out his own diagonal approach to the platform, meandering through the graduation orchestra. The blunder made for a laughable entrance, but for McCullough, the episode also signaled something deeper. None of the people in Dowell's line deviated from the path that he had set for them. This, McCullough said, was because they did not wish to make their beloved leader look foolish.[42]

Of course, the world has seen many dictators who bullied their followers into a similar kind of lockstep. But Dowell was never that sort of leader. The people who followed him were neither browbeaten nor mindless. Dowell had simply earned their loyalty. Throughout his career he had demonstrated care and concern for the BBF body, and now, in return, that body wanted to offer its care and concern back to him. The day was approaching when, sitting in that same fieldhouse, the fellowship would mourn the loss of W. E. Dowell. But such a day had not yet come. For now, both the fellowship and the man would continue to enjoy a very special bond.

Chapter 40: *And Then We'll Fight Again*

T he crowd erupted with applause as a tall, broad-shouldered man strode to the lectern to begin his speech. Dowell and some thirty other dignitaries applauded the man from behind. They stood in three rows, their black and gray three-piece suits contrasting the blue draperies that stretched across the back of the platform. The entire scene was aglow with television lights and flashbulbs, and Dowell's position in the spectacle was front and center. His seat was just to the left of the lectern. The event's driving force, Jerry Falwell, was seated just to the right.

As the applause faded, Falwell, Dowell, and the other platform guests sat down, eagerly anticipating the words of the featured speaker.

Reverend Falwell, ladies and gentlemen, thank you very much, for there are no words to describe a welcome such as you've given me here.[1]

The speaker's chiseled cheekbones made it seem that he was wearing a permanent smile. There was also a meekness in his voice, a quality that gently commanded the audience's good will. This was no preacher, yet his words were no less impassioned.

It's a real pleasure to be with so many who firmly believe that the answers to the world's problems can be found in the word of God.

This remark prompted cheers and another round of applause. During the pause, the television cameras panned the convention center. According to the *New York Times*, ten thousand people had filled that arena.[2] The BBF was well represented in the crowd, but they were not alone. Other groups, likewise conservative and Baptist, were mingled among them.

This was Baptist Fundamentalism '84. It took place April 11 through 13, 1984, in Washington, D.C. Some nineteen fundamentalist leaders, including Dowell, had joined forces with Falwell to launch these meetings. Their inspiration may have come from the kindred meetings that Dowell and G. B. Vick had helped to coordinate back in the 1960s and 70s. Those earlier meetings were referred to as the Fundamental Baptist Congress of North America. The first was held at Vick's church in 1963. Unlike ordinary fellowship meetings, the Baptist Congress gatherings brought together fundamentalists from different organizations across the US and Canada. None of the usual fellowship business took place. The preaching and camaraderie were aimed at strengthening, not a single organization, but the broader cause of fundamentalism.

Over the next decade similar meetings took place about every three years. Then in November 1973, the Baptist Congress took on a new dimension as its meeting moved from North America to Europe. Now billed as the First International Fundamental Baptist Congress, the European meeting was held in London's Metropolitan Tabernacle, the historic church once pastored by Charles Haddon Spurgeon. Twenty-six hundred people came together from the US, Great Britain, Continental Europe, and Australia to be a part of the experience. Dowell and his wife were among them.

Dowell did something else on that trip. He served as an international diplomat for the City of Springfield. On behalf of Springfield's mayor, Jim Payne, Dowell carried the Key to the City of Springfield to London's Lord Mayor, Alan Mais.[3] Dowell made the presentation to Captain Duncan Knight, a member of Lord Mais's staff, and his effort was rewarded by a personal tour of the Lord Mayor's official residence, Mansion House.[4]

The broad-shouldered speaker brought laughter when he said this:

I'm only sorry I can't spend the entire evening with you, but I'm expected across town.

Just as Dowell had done while he was in London, organizers of Baptist Fundamentalism '84 reached out to political officials in Washington, D.C. And several of these individuals responded, some even joining the roster of speakers for the event. But the speaker now standing before this audience was no mayor. His lectern was adorned with a presidential seal. And his name was Reagan.

I'm not going to talk to you about some of the things we've talked about before and some of the things that we've tried to accomplish and that we haven't yet. With regard to that, I will only say let us all heed the words of an old Scotch ballad, "For those defeats that we've had so far, we are hurt; we are not slain. We'll lie us down and rest a bit, and then we'll fight again."

Cheers followed Reagan's rhyme, and Dowell heartily joined in. If he had been born a poet, Dowell might have written those words himself. That year, 1984, marked his fiftieth year in the ministry, and throughout his career Dowell, too, had been a fighter. Indeed, even after so many health challenges, there was still a good bit of fight left in him. When his 1982 bout with shingles finally came to an end, Dowell wrote a family member saying he was "feeling unusually well." As for the parts of him that were not so well, Dowell simply chose to ignore them. "I still have some hurting in my shoulder and neck," he confessed, "but I have decided not to let it bother me."[5]

This was a characteristic response. The aches and pains would have to wait. Dowell's energies were reserved for more important battles. And Baptist Fundamentalism '84 was something that demanded his attention. Whether he felt like it or not, Dowell would not have missed it. More than ever before, Dowell believe, the nation needed to hear from fundamentalists.

Dowell, like Reagan and Falwell, was attuned to his world's social and political condition. And he wanted to make a difference. Back in 1960, Dowell had joined a thousand other BBF pastors who unanimously passed a resolution opposing the candidacy of John F. Kennedy. According to that resolution, Kennedy's Catholicism had become "a basic issue" of his campaign, and for non-Catholics, this was a serious problem. Dowell and his peers claimed that the Roman Catholic Church was "a totalitarian religio-politico institution," which would put American freedoms at risk. "The basic proposition of the Roman Catholic Church" the resolution asserted, "is that religious freedom for non-Catholics is 'tolerated' as a necessary evil. . . ."[6]

Dowell's side lost that fight, of course, along with many others through the years, but even so, Dowell would not stop waging such battles. His more recent campaigns during the 1970s and 80s were aimed at abortion, liquor, pornography, homosexuality, and the Equal Rights Amendment. In 1977, Dowell cited Ephesians 5 and reasoned, "The church has as much right to demand equal rights with God as the woman has to demand equal rights with her husband."[7] All such efforts achieved mixed results, of course, but Dowell did not back down.

In 1974, Dowell worked to block the repeal of a local liquor ordinance. The ordinance under consideration limited the number of liquor licenses in Springfield according to the size of the city's population. And when Dowell learned that a repeal of the ordinance was under consideration, he spoke out, saying in a newspaper article that liquor "has broken more homes, caused more wrecks, resulted in more immorality and hung more crepe than any other evil that has ever invaded our city."[8]

Dowell voiced another strong opinion in a 1976 sermon. This time he lambasted the decision of Roe v. Wade, saying:

> *Our Supreme Court, for instance, has ruled in favor of abortion. But God's word teaches that it's murder. You say, "Will you back the ruling of the Supreme Court?" No, I will not back it. I condemn them. I cry out aloud and spare not and tell them that they have blasphemed the name of the Lord God of Heaven. And they'll have the blood of millions of little unborn babies on their hands when they stand before the judgment of Almighty God!*[9]

Dowell targeted yet another social issue in 1977. Singer-Spokeswoman Anita Bryant came to Springfield's Shrine Mosque as part of a national campaign, "Save Our Children." Bryant's rallies were aimed at defeating the legislative endeavors of homosexual activists. Dowell not only supported Bryant's objective, but he used his influence to encourage as many others as he could—including the student body of BBC—to go and attend her rally.[10]

Dowell viewed all such efforts through spiritual eyes. In February 1979 he declared in an "As I See It" article, "The E.R.A.–abortion–homosexuality–are all in direct rebellion against God's laws. They are in effect saying 'What God says does not matter, we are more knowledgeable than God.' What blasphemy!"[11] Then in July of that year, Dowell wrote:

> *Springfield needs to examine her conscience. It is a tragedy that we condition to sin so quickly.*

> *Do you think Springfield would have allowed an abortion clinic fifteen years ago? Or allow our city to become a distributing center for raw pornography? Or allowed and licensed motels with X-rated movies?*
>
> *Springfield has been known as a good conservative, moral city.*
>
> *Will we be led down the path to corruption?*
>
> *I hope not, there is an awful price to pay.*[12]

Dowell's protests were frequently carried out in the media, so it seems ironic that much of his outrage was directed at the media itself. When in December 1973, for instance, the ABC Television Network began airing a series of special programs called *Primal Man*, Dowell was quoted in the newspaper calling the material "evolutionary filth," and "an affront to Almighty God." In response to that broadcast, Dowell lodged a complaint with ABC's vice president of programming, Martin Starger, wherein he "requested and insisted" that the network give equal time to scientists who could expose the "hoax of paleontology."[13]

Those outcries went largely unheeded, of course, though Springfield's ABC affiliate, KMTC, did offer to sell Dowell some airtime if he wished to mount his own response to *Primal Man*. Not surprisingly, Dowell took them up on the offer. With the financial help of local supporters, Dowell hosted an hour-long program, *Rebuttal to Primal Man*, which aired Thursday, March 7, 1974, at 7 PM. Dowell's program was presented just a few days after the third broadcast in the ABC series, and it featured testimony from guests Henry Morris and Duane Gish, two scientists from the Institute for Creation Research in San Diego. Dowell followed up their presentations with ten minutes of his own preaching. "Evolution denies the Bible; it denies God; it denies Christ; it denies heaven; it denies Hell; and it denies a hereafter," Dowell railed. "That is what antagonizes me about it."[14]

Local newspaper critic Bil Tatum was not swayed by Dowell's broadcast. "Surely these learned men cannot ask us to believe that thousands of scientists have for decades devoted their energies to studying a science that can in a one-hour tv show be so easily labeled a fraud," Tatum stated. At the same time, Tatum acknowledged that the broadcast's arguments could not be dismissed outright. "In stating their case, however, the men do scrupulously document their evidence," Tatum said. "Quoting experts (and evolutionists) from Simon to Leakey, they do not make idle claims."[15]

Whether or not others would find those arguments convincing, Dowell did all that he could to keep such conversations alive. When cable television was introduced to Springfield in the mid-1970s, Dowell once again tried to influence his fellow citizens with a self-produced television broadcast. Dowell's objection in that instance was over the R-rated films that the cable industry would be piping into local homes. "Springfield should not allow cable television to subject the good people of our city to this kind of smut," Dowell said.[16]

Of course, Dowell handily lost that battle as well. (And indeed, many years later he became a cable subscriber himself.) But even so, Dowell believed his fight had been worthwhile. With reference to that cable TV campaign, interviewer Bob Burke, a journalist for *Springfield! Magazine*, said in a 1988 article, "Dowell hasn't mellowed all that much with age either. . . ."[17] Burke was correct. Dowell had seen cable TV encroach upon the moral health of his city, and he believed his efforts to stop it had only been vindicated. Dowell noted that when cable had first been introduced, he had been "assured" that Springfield would see no more than six to ten R-rated movies in any given month. Yet as early as August 1978, that number had more than doubled.[18] And soon thereafter, cable companies were even offering X-rated channels in answer to consumer demands.

Dowell fought such moral encroachment at every turn, even when he had no hope of winning and even when his strong opinions got him into trouble. In September 1978, Dowell used a sermon to lash out against "a high law enforcement officer's son." The man in question, the son of Assistant Police Chief Les Reynolds, was reportedly running an adult movie motel, the Key Host Inn. Dowell condemned the motel's "illegal and immoral activity," but he also lamented the fact that "nothing is done about it" by local law enforcement. "It leads one to wonder," Dowell remarked, "who is paying off who?"[19]

Dowell's sermon, which aired live on the radio, drew fire from Reynolds. Reynolds's son had never been the motel's operator. He had operated an adjacent discotheque, the Minor Attraction, which had recently gone defunct. Furthermore, Dowell had misspoken on air when he made his accusations. Although Dowell never called the police official by name, his reference to Reynolds was unmistakable. The man was a "high official" who had "resigned recently," Dowell said. Reynolds had announced his retirement only days earlier. And what outraged Reynolds most was the fact that, as Dowell laid out his case, he omitted the word *son*, leaving the impression that it was the "high official" himself who owned the motel.

Reynolds, three days after this broadcast, made a visit to Dowell's office. He brought with him Detective Lieutenant Richard Moses, and he asked Dowell for a retraction. The meeting was not a particularly warm one. Dowell conceded to the men that he may have made a mistake. "I was reading verbatim from my notes, and the notes said the son of a high official," Dowell later told a newspaper reporter. "If I said the other, it was a slip of the tongue." Dowell also told the reporter that he did not believe Reynolds and other officers were, in fact, "taking payoffs."[20]

But that was as far as Dowell was willing to go. The two businesses in question had operated side by side, and in Dowell's mind, they had conveyed the appearance of a joint enterprise. From Dowell's point of view, any effort to differentiate the two was hairsplitting. "I did not apologize to Mr. Reynolds for the campaign I'm carrying on. I will continue to carry it on," Dowell told the reporter. "I know what's going on. They know what's going on, and they know I know what's going on."[21]

Dowell told one audience, "If you throw a stone down an alley, and some old hound dog yells, you know you've hit him."[22] Dowell was tossing a good many stones in those days, though not every rock was directed at illicit activities. Affronts to Dowell's church were just as likely to provoke his ire. In March 1979, Dowell wrote another "As I See It" article, saying:

> *Some time ago at the Battlefield Mall, they had a group of disco singers and*
> *dancers known as the Rock 99 disco performing to raise money for Easter Seals.*
> *It was so bad I received calls from people who were indignant.*
> *Some time later Baptist Temple called the mall to get permission to put on a*
> *gospel concert and raise money for the March of Dimes.*
> *We were told since we were religious in nature it would be too controversial.*
> *Strange, as if Rock disco is not controversial.*
> *This also indicates that Christian people are not to support benevolent*
> *causes. Is this what they want?*
> *This is a strange world!*[23]

In another instance, Dowell had a public spat with city officials over nine zoning and building code citations received by Baptist Temple. The situation began in the summer of 1976 when Dowell's church trucked in gravel to turn some of its vacant property into bus parking. A complaint from a neighbor triggered a visit from Springfield's building inspector, who determined that the church was creating its new parking area without the necessary building permit. The inspector ordered the work to halt until a permit could be obtained.

Dowell's associate, Larry Smith, sought to comply with the city's request, but Smith's application for a building permit was subsequently denied. The proposed lot went "above and beyond what the board of adjustment normally would allow," the church was told. This put Dowell in a difficult spot. His church owned adequate land for additional parking, and it needed such parking, and it had begun work on such parking, yet now city officials were blocking the land's development. "A growing church must have adequate parking," Dowell reasoned. "The people come and they are going to park somewhere."[24] Dowell saw no choice but to ignore the city's order.

This was a departure for Dowell. As a rule, he sought to cooperate with authorities. In 1982 Dowell received a letter from a Catholic hospital, St. John's, leveling a different complaint against his church. The letter drew attention to the evangelistic efforts of some of Baptist Temple's members and requested that the church refrain from distributing tracts to patients and visitors who were not already a part of their congregation. To say the least, Dowell was dismayed at receiving such a request from a Christian organization. He saw no possible benefit in inhibiting the spread of the gospel. But even so, Dowell announced to his church that the hospital was "their institution," and whether he liked it or not, he thought it best to "honor authority" and to comply with the hospital's wishes.[25]

Dowell was not so amenable, however, when it came to Springfield's demands on his own church property. Believing the city inspector had given him little choice, Dowell ignored the city's order and continued the development and use of his new parking lot. This in turn led to more complaints and more visits from city officials. And in the end, Dowell received a stack of directives ordering him to bring his church "into compliance with city regulations."[26]

Those "notices of correction," as they were called, were generated from the office of Dick Nichols, Springfield's director of building regulations. They were sent out in December 1976, and they identified concerns not only with Dowell's gravel parking lot but also with many other aspects of his church's facilities. In total, Baptist Temple received twenty-three pages of instructions. And they had just three months to address the identified problems.[27]

Dowell became indignant over the matter. He believed his church was now being targeted by city officials. He stated in a newspaper interview, "I have openly accused them of harassing us, and they have."[28] Among the city's demands, Dowell explained, were orders to cease using an eighteen-foot extension on the back of the church parking lot and to remove another forty-six foot section of parking from the front of that lot "and replace it with grass."[29] Dowell blasted the requirements as "unreasonable."[30] Those same parking areas had been in use since before Dowell came to the church in 1973, he said. Moreover, they had been put into use with the city's approval. "The city told us where to put our parking lot and how big to make it," Dowell alleged. "They're making demands on things they originally gave us permission to do."[31]

For those reasons, Dowell again refused to comply. He maintained that the city's expectations were unjustified and that his church did not have the resources to fulfill them. Furthermore, complying with the requests would hamper his church's operations. "'I'm not going out to plow up all of our parking lot.' he said. 'I'm not about to do that. We wouldn't have enough parking left.'"[32] Dowell also stated that his congregation fully supported him in this decision. When the matter was presented for a vote, "the church voted unanimously 1000 to nothing not to attempt to meet the requirements," Dowell said.[33] So as far as he was concerned, then, the matter was settled.

Of course, the City of Springfield saw things differently. This is why, on March 18, 1977, Baptist Temple found itself in municipal court faced with nine citations. At that initial hearing, the church's attorney, Jim Ferguson, entered an innocent plea. The judge then scheduled a trial for May 10. Yet surprisingly, that trial never took place. In the intervening weeks, City Attorney Larry Woodward had a change of heart. He "dismissed the complaints" and announced that he would instead "seek an injunction" in the Greene County Circuit Court. "The Municipal Court can't order compliance," Woodward explained. "All it can do is penalize people by a fine or imprisonment."[34]

With this action, Woodward made it apparent that the city wanted to put a growing public relations debacle to rest. Most certainly city officials did not want to fine a financially strapped church or to imprison one of the city's best-known preachers. Seeking compliance via court injunction was a much better option, Woodward believed, so he announced that he would file for that injunction "probably" within the next month.[35] Yet even this plan was upended. Just days after Woodward made this announcement, Dowell landed in intensive care with Myasthenia Gravis. And it was then that the city showed a renewed willingness to return to the negotiating table.

This new round of negotiations was facilitated by one of Baptist Temple's deacons, Eldon Harmon. Larry Smith had recently moved away, and Harmon's background as a building contractor made him a good substitute to act as liaison. Harmon not only had a good rapport with Dick Nichols, but he also had insights into building processes that Larry Smith may never have had. Harmon noted, for instance, that the church's buildings had originally been treated as separate units and that the church's parking needs had been figured for each unit individually. When Harmon redrew the plans, he based the parking needs on the combined occupancy of the church's facilities, which were all used on Sundays. In so doing, Harmon found justification for the continued use of all of the church's existing parking spaces. And when Nichols saw what Harmon had done, he agreed with him. In the end, Harmon brokered a deal that would require just one change from the church. They would have to relocate their buses from one part of their property to another. And to this requirement Dowell and his church could readily agree.[36]

Of course, in this and other standoffs, Dowell was not always viewed as a hero. His campaigns and opinions attracted plenty of critics. In 1971, an anonymous citizen sent to the newspaper a letter to the editor responding to statements that Dowell had made in a recent interview. The reporter had asked Dowell about his views on things like faith healing and speaking in tongues, and Dowell had responded candidly, explaining that Baptists reject such beliefs as they are taught by Pentecostals.[37] The anonymous letter writer called Dowell's statements an "attack" on other churches. "I would advise him to stick to a salvation message," the writer groused, "as this is the only one I've ever heard him get right."[38]

Sentiments like those were particularly vigorous whenever Dowell began meddling in politics. Even so, Dowell was unapologetic about voicing his opinions. He told one reporter, "A preacher has the right to speak out on any issue—moral, political, or religious."[39] And Dowell most certainly exercised that right. When, in 1979, Iranians took more than sixty Americans hostage to try to force the US to return their deposed shah for trial, Dowell made his opinion known. "The United States should not permit Iran or any other country to take hostages and blackmail this country," Dowell stated in a newspaper ad. "Whatever measures that are necessary to free these hostages should be taken at once."[40]

Dowell was offended by the notion that preachers should not contribute to such political conversations. Speaking in 1976, he said, "The only second class citizens there are in the United States today are preachers. Everybody else, they say get involved in politics. Be a part of the political process. To preachers, they say, 'You're in religion. You don't speak out on politics. You don't get involved in politics.'"[41]

Dowell made that statement during the 1976 presidential campaign, a heated contest that sometimes put preachers and candidates at odds. In fact, just days before preaching that sermon, Dowell—together with John R. Rice, Jack Hyles, and John Rawlings—participated in a press conference conducted by Jerry Falwell. Appearing in front of cameras from all three major television networks as well as reporters from the *New York Times*, the *Washington Post*, and many other news outlets, Falwell read a statement denouncing a recent action taken by Democratic candidate Jimmy Carter. Falwell began by saying:

We are here today because of the flagrant violation of the basic American freedom of speech and religion. These violations have arisen in recent weeks during the presidential campaign. Each week I preach to 15 million Americans over the Old-Time Gospel Hour television program. As a Christian, as a preacher, as a pastor, and as an American, it is my obligation to speak out on moral issues which may affect the spiritual strength of the nation, particularly when national leaders are involved. Politics is not our interest, but when the morality of Americans and our leaders are involved, then it is my duty as a Christian and pastor to preach against sin. That is what I do. And I will continue to do so with every breath. In my sermons in recent weeks which were videotaped in my church in Lynchburg, Virginia, I have objected to Governor Carter's interview with Playboy Magazine. I objected to his use of obscenities and vulgarity. I objected to his comments that hurt the fiber and fabric of the American home, which is the basic unit of American society. As a Christian and a minister, I objected to Governor Carter's stated concept in the interview when he indicated it is all a matter of philosophy as to whether a man is faithful to his wife or has affairs with many women. He indicated we should not look down upon persons who have illicit relationships.[42]

As Falwell continued his statement, he discussed an egregious action taken by Carter's staff in retaliation for Falwell's remarks. Dowell discussed that same situation in a subsequent sermon. Dowell said, "Mr. Carter's group–those that work directly under him–immediately got on the telephone and called those 260 television stations [those that carried Falwell's weekly program] and threatened them with two things: first, we'll sue for equal time if you allow this sermon to go on, and we'll appeal to the FCC." According to Dowell, the move was little more than an attempt to silence preachers. "I don't get angry," Dowell told his congregation, "but I get righteously indignant when I think about it."[43]

Like Falwell, Dowell maintained that preachers had, not just a right, but a duty to speak out on such matters. Dowell further claimed that such preaching had no political motive. As evidence, Dowell pointed to his own longstanding criticisms of First Lady Betty Ford, wife of a Republican, for her support of the Equal Rights Amendment. Dowell said preachers were obliged to point out moral failings wherever they found them, regardless of the political party. And in Dowell's eyes, granting an interview to a pornographic magazine fully qualified as a moral failing. "It doesn't matter who it is!" Dowell shouted in his sermon. "We're not talking about individuals now; we're talking about principles."[44]

In that same sermon, Dowell expressed a sentiment that seems to mark him as a harbinger of a new development in American politics. "All the way through the Old Testament," Dowell stated, "it was the prophets of God that told the king God's message. I think it's time we wake up in America and preachers begin to play their role as prophets!"[45] Many Christians of this era agreed with Dowell, including Jerry Falwell.

Indeed, Falwell adopted a similar position in 1979, when he launched a new nationwide political organization, the Moral Majority.

Missouri's chapter of the Moral Majority was organized in the spring of 1980, and its first major rally, featuring guest speaker Tim LaHaye, was held on the campus of BBC. Dowell's good friend Kenneth Gillming became the chapter's executive director, although Dowell too served as an unofficial spokesman. Explaining the group's purpose to a newspaper reporter, Dowell said, "It's really an organization whereby we preachers are going to try to influence our people to register so they can vote their conviction." Dowell also stated that the organization would be interviewing and endorsing political candidates whose views aligned with their own. "There isn't any question about it, it involves politics," Dowell stated. "But it wasn't formed because of politics. It was formed because of moral issues."[46]

The Moral Majority sprang up just in time for the 1980 presidential election, the same election that would remove President Jimmy Carter from power and would initiate twelve years of conservative leadership in America, first under Ronald Reagan and then under George H. W. Bush. The Moral Majority played a significant role in that political shift. During the first year of its existence, for instance, the Moral Majority helped to register more than three million voters nationwide, creating a powerful new caucus in American politics and giving rise to the expression "religious right."[47] The organization went on to enjoy nine more years of success before Falwell disbanded the group to give greater attention to his own ministries.

For Dowell, of course, it was the spiritual aspects of those political victories that really mattered. "I don't fight liberals," Dowell once said. "I fight what they teach and what they stand for."[48] Either way, liberals were none too happy. Indeed, in October 1980, the Associated Press ran an article about the Moral Majority's growing strength and quoted the Congressional Black Caucus, a group that had become alarmed by the work of Falwell's group. "The distortion of religious principles which the Moral Majority perpetrates and the political pressure they maintain is reminiscent of the foundation which paved the way for the advent of the Ayatollah Khomeini in Iran," the Caucus alleged.[49] Dowell offered an answer to that charge at a rally for the Moral Majority. The rally was held at the Indianapolis Baptist Temple, and reportedly, Dowell's remark was "cheered and applauded."[50] With biting wit, Dowell told the audience:

> *Newspapers asking Brother Jerry Falwell today, several times they've asked him this. "Well, won't it be something like it is over in Iran—you religious people taking over—become a religious system." I said, I don't know what he said, but if it had been me I'd said, "Well, the other crowd's had it long enough and they failed, and made such a terrible blot of it, it's time somebody take over."*[51]

At times Dowell took fire for expressing such views. Some argued that Dowell's profession disqualified him from voicing political positions. But Dowell was dismissive of such critics. In one sermon, Dowell openly wondered if groups like the Congressional

Black Caucus would hurl the same criticisms at religious leaders like Martin Luther King, Jr., or Jesse Jackson.[52] Dowell believed he had as much right as anyone to take a political stand, and for him, the expression of such views was the purest form of nationalism.

Dowell had always been a patriot, but that patriotism sharpened in the second half of his ministry as he watched the morals of his country deteriorate. Dowell wished that more Christians would love their country as he did. In February 1982, he had an experience that helped him see afresh the importance of loving one's country. That was when Dowell took his final trip to the Holy Land, this time as a guest of Jerry Falwell. Because of Falwell's vocal support for Israel, Falwell had received a personal invitation from the Israeli government asking him to visit Israel and to bring along a group of his conservative associates. Falwell accepted the invitation, and Dowell became a member of the entourage.

While in Israel, Falwell's group enjoyed five-star hotels and government-sponsored tours. They also visited the Knesset (the Jewish legislature) and the Golan Heights (a disputed territory that had been annexed by Israel on December 14, 1981). At the Knesset, the American visitors were briefed by three Israeli officials: Secretary General Nathan (Netan'el) Lorch, Foreign Ministry Diplomat Asher Naim, and Knesset Member Ehud Olmert. Each spent about a half hour with Falwell's group, discussing the current political situation and explaining Israel's recent actions.[53]

This trip to Israel was Dowell's fourth, but he called the experience "a most unusual trip" and "a fabulous tour." Indeed, Dowell compared the insights he gained to a "college course on the Middle East." And of course, Dowell was a most willing student. If Israel's purpose in orchestrating this tour had been to promote good will (and this seems likely given the international tensions they were facing because of the Golan Heights annexation), then Israel had summoned the right audience. Dowell framed the reasons for his support of Israel, saying, "There's one thing that makes me a friend of Israel, and that's the fact that they're the friend of God. They're God's chosen people. And God gave them the land by covenant. Whatever the United States does, whatever the United Nations do, whatever the Arab states may do, you can be sure of one thing: God is going to keep that covenant."[54]

But Dowell returned from that Holy Land experience with another cause to love Israel. Speaking of the Israelis that he had encountered along the way, Dowell said, "They have a deep sense of loyalty such as I have never experienced in all of my life. I said to the preachers that were around me as I listened, I said, 'Oh, that we could have that kind of loyalty and nationalism in the United States.'" Dowell confessed that not every preacher shared his opinion. One pastor who went on this trip told Dowell that, though he tried to be a good citizen, he did not feel a personal allegiance to the US. Dowell felt very differently. "This is the land that God has given us," Dowell told his congregation. "This is the land of our heritage. God bless America, and God help us to bless it and honor it and be loyal to it!"[55]

It was with that same spirit that Dowell listened to Reagan's speech at Baptist Fundamentalism '84. Dowell had first met Reagan back in 1976 when he came through

Springfield on a campaign tour. Dowell had been invited to pray at that political rally, and Dowell was seated with Reagan at the head table. Even then, Dowell found Reagan to be a likeable man.[56] But Dowell was a Reagan supporter only insofar as Reagan's policies aligned with God's word. "Andrew Jackson said the Bible is 'a rock upon which our republic rests,'" Dowell told an audience in 1983. "I wish President Reagan would say that a little more clearly. I wish all of our presidents could understand that. It's a rock upon which our republic rests."[57]

Reagan's speech at that 1984 convention never went as far as Jackson's. Indeed, most of Reagan's twenty-minute address was a reading from a work by a Jewish rabbi, a US Navy chaplain by the name of Arnold E. Resnicoff. Resnicoff was among the first to reach the Beirut airport after it had been struck by a terrorist truck bomb six months earlier. Resnicoff's account of the attack—which claimed the lives of 241 marines, soldiers, and sailors—elucidated the honorable deeds and interfaith cooperation that took place in the aftermath as survivors were pulled from the rubble.

Reagan began his reading of Resnicoff's story, but then he was forced to pause. Anti-war protestors were shouting from an upper level in the convention center. "Bread, not bombs!" they chanted.[58] Security guards had to be mobilized to silence the interruption. In the meantime, Reagan ad-libbed, saying, "Wouldn't it be nice if a little bit of that marine spirit would rub off, and they would listen about brotherly love?" A moment later, he said, "I've got more decibels at work for me than they have." And finally, "I think they're leaving."[59] Each of these remarks brought Falwell's crowd to its feet with applause, cheers, and laughter. After that, Reagan continued with the rest of his speech. And when it was over, Dowell and other platform guests shook the president's hand and thanked him for his leadership.

A few months later, Reagan went on to win his second national election in a landslide. He lost only two places in the nation: Washington, D.C., and Minnesota. Dowell was pleased to see those results. Following the election, Dowell was quoted in *USA Today*, saying, "This country is brighter and stronger than it was four years ago. Reagan has made this country shine again."[60] Dowell and other campaign supporters were thanked for their efforts with invitations to Reagan's second inauguration. Dowell opted not to attend, but he was happy to know that the voice of fundamentalism had been heard by one of the world's most powerful leaders. For as long as God would give him breath, Dowell intended to continue lifting up that voice.

Of course, Dowell's political fervor was always powered by an evangelistic heartbeat. The real fight was always for the souls of people. After a trip to Brazil in the summer of 1982, Dowell returned to the US more burdened for souls than ever. He told his church:

> *I stood over there in downtown Campinas and again in downtown Sao Paolo—two great cities—and you had to stand there like this because you were crowded with people, just thousands of them flocking to and fro. I counted the missionaries on my hand—four of them missionary families from this church—and*

*I said, "Oh God, the laborers are so few. What about these teeming thousands
that's never heard?"*[61]

Dowell's political outcries were marked by a similar concern. Dowell wrote an
article in December 1979, saying, "America is still faced with a great crisis in Iran. . . .
However, there is another crisis in America. It is a moral and a spiritual crisis. We are
headed the wrong direction." Dowell had but one solution for such a crisis: "America
needs a cleansing revival that will turn the hearts of the people back to God."[62]

This call for revival would be a recurring strain in Dowell's closing years. From his
perspective, no need in America was so dire. Dowell urged revival upon every audience
that would listen, though his message may never have been clearer than it was in an "As
I See It" article that he published in October 1979. Dowell began the piece by
comparing America's past and present:

> *In the latter part of the 18th and the early part of the 19th centuries, infidelity
> reigned, a moral stupor paralyzed Christianity. Sin had intoxicated the nations,
> higher criticism had dipped her pen in venom and poisoned the age, principles
> were disregarded and passion was unbridled. To millions the Bible was no more
> than a book of fables, the people were bewildered and confused. There was no
> message of hope and assurance.*
>
> *In man's desperate need, in his hopeless condition, he turned to God and
> wailed out his piteous cry for help.*
>
> *The people sick, forlorn, hungry-hearted and needy turned to God and the
> great American Revival followed.*
>
> *This describes the condition of America today.*

But then Dowell ended this article with a four-word exclamation, a statement that
underscored his deep desire to see a similar victory in his own generation. "Our prayer
is," Dowell wrote, "Lord do it again!"[63]

Chapter 41: *Strength I Find*

A chime rang out in the Dowell residence. It was a genteel sound, classier than the doorbells heard in most homes. That should not be taken to mean that life in this home was particularly elegant. The Dowell house was full of the mundane. Indeed, Nola was attending paperwork at a cluttered kitchen table when the doorbell's interruption came. Nola was meticulous where paper was concerned. She religiously clipped, labeled, photocopied, and filed. And this she did with bills, letters, newspapers, church bulletins—just about any kind of paper that came her way. Some of what she saved was meaningful; much of it had no meaning whatsoever to anyone but her. Nola's constant frustration was that she could never get caught up on all of her paperwork. Still, she never would have dreamed of abandoning the effort.

When that doorbell rang in June 1989, Nola's husband was seated only a few feet away from the front door. He was in a recliner with a tray of food on his lap. Some sort of sports or news program was blaring on the television in front of him. The reason that he did not bother getting up to answer the door was because he was certain that Nola would do so. And of course, he was right.

It was unusual for Nola to be up and about so early. She was not much of a morning person. But things being as they were, she could not sleep. Wearing a flowery floor-length housedress, Nola flowed past a framed wall hanging on her way to the front door. This glass-covered print showed Jesus standing at a door and knocking. The image hung in the Dowells' entryway every day, but on this particular day it seemed to possess a latent irony. When Jesus knocks, He brings only good news.

Nola left the safety chain in place as she eased open the door to peer through the crack. Then, when she saw that she was safe, she quickly removed the chain and opened the door. Standing on the other side were Bill Jr. and Joan. They were regular visitors to this house, even more so as the Dowells began to age. While all three of the Dowell children stayed in close contact with their parents, only Bill Jr. and Joan lived nearby. Thus, it fell to them to tend to those day-to-day needs that elderly parents often have. They assisted with everything from doctor visits to VCR instructions. (Oh, those blasted instructions.)

Nola called out to announce the visitors.

It's Bill and Joan, Dear.

On most other days, Nola's eyes would have lit up to see this couple standing on her front porch. Not so on this day. Her eyes clouded over the instant she spotted them. Their visit was an unexpected one—the second in two days—and Nola dreaded knowing its meaning. That familiar fastidiousness took over her voice as she said:

Have you heard something from Clyde?

Nola received an affirmative response to that question. She then led her guests into the living space so that they could share their news. They walked past that same ironic wall hanging as they went. The television was switched off, and the family members settled into various couches and chairs, the implication being that this news was best received sitting down.

Dowell and his wife listened intently as Bill Jr. told them what he had heard from his brother that morning. As expected, the information concerned Clyde's oldest daughter, Lynda. The news was not good. The injuries that Lynda had suffered from an auto accident a day earlier had claimed her life.

In the hours that followed, the Dowell home would be filled with much weeping. Fortunately, the tears were a temporary sort, the kind that would, on some future day, be eternally wiped away. The Dowells' gospel was not for others only. It was personal. It sustained them through difficult times, granting them a perspective that was not unlike the words of an old hymn:

> *Day by day, and with each passing moment,*
> *Strength I find, to meet my trials here;*
> *Trusting in my Father's wise bestowment,*
> *I've no cause for worry or for fear.*
> *He whose heart is kind beyond all measure*
> *Gives unto each day what He deems best—*
> *Lovingly, its part of pain and pleasure,*
> *Mingling toil with peace and rest.*[1]

During their lifetime, Dowell and his wife would experience the full gamut of human sorrows, from heartaches to betrayals. Yet those experiences would not shake their faith. Rather they would cause them to lean more heavily upon what they knew to be true. Whatever suffering might come their way, God had allowed it. Whatever burden they might carry, God would go with them. And whatever sorrow they might endure, God would bring them through.

One example of such an experience occurred years earlier, back in 1977. That was when the Dowells suffered a financial setback. It was not the sort of ruinous calamity that some families experience, but it was difficult nonetheless. One thing that made it so was the fact that it occurred about the same time that Dowell was being diagnosed with Myasthenia Gravis. For months before being given that diagnoses, Dowell had experienced health problems, particularly with his eyes. In fact, at the beginning of that year he had spent three weeks at a clinic in Virginia trying to get some answers. The situation was serious enough that Dowell became concerned that he might soon be forced into an early retirement.

This concern was double-edged, of course. Dowell was worried about the loss of his health, but he was also worried about the loss of his livelihood. While both of Dowell's Springfield employers, BBC and Baptist Temple, would be quite generous to him during his retirement years, Dowell had no guarantees of any such blessings in 1977. Indeed, given the financial situations facing these institutions, Dowell had no reason to believe either of these employers would be able to offer him any benefits when he retired. And this meant that the burden of retirement might fall squarely upon his own shoulders. Eventually Dowell would be eligible to receive social security benefits, but his full benefits would not be available until his sixty-fifth birthday in July 1979. Consequently, the prospect of retiring in 1977 raised some troubling financial questions.

Of course, Dowell had already taken some steps to begin preparing for his retirement years. One of those steps was an investment in an enterprise called PFA Farmers Market Association. PFA operated a chain of grocery and appliance stores across the Midwest. One of Dowell's acquaintances had introduced him to the venture, and Dowell liked the business model. PFA was noted for cutting out the middle man and for saving consumers money. Better still, PFA promised a good return on Dowell's investment. So Dowell joined with thousands of other private investors and put money into the association.

According to Dowell Jr., his father's PFA investment totaled about ten thousand dollars.[2] Dowell may not have understood what he was getting himself into when he made that investment. PFA cut out not only the middle man but also government regulators. The organization took advantage of laws that were originally intended to help members of the farming community. Those laws allowed farmers to set up cooperatives without having to register with the state securities office, something that minimized the amount of scrutiny and red tape small-scale farming operations had to endure. Yet PFA used such laws to dodge both governmental oversight and the regulatory agencies aimed at protecting investors.

This explains why Dowell and many others were blindsided when the enterprise went belly-up. On April 18, 1977, PFA filed for bankruptcy. None of the usual red flags had shown up ahead of time because no one was looking over the organization's shoulders. Investors lost a reported twelve million dollars overnight. According to Dowell, the devastation caused one elderly man, an individual who had lost his life's savings, to commit suicide.[3]

As the facts about PFA came to light, Dowell concluded that he and other investors had been swindled. Good laws had been used to cover up bad business practices. "This is an extremely sophisticated fraud," one state securities commissioner alleged. "They set it up to put it quite literally outside the control of anybody."[4] Dowell maintained that even he had been "lied to" by the organization. "[T]he week before they folded, one of the top directors came to my home and swore the company was solvent," Dowell said.[5]

When Dowell heard about the bankruptcy, he took action to try to save his investment. He wrote to Carl Bledsoe, President of PFA, requesting the return of his capital. "The money I invested I cannot afford to lose," Dowell told Bledsoe. "I have serious health problems at the present and could have to retire."[6] Dowell also sent a letter to the judge in the case, Bankruptcy Court Judge Jack C. Jones. But to no avail. Dowell lost his entire investment. And adding insult to injury was the fact that most of the perpetrators escaped punishment. When the verdict in the case came down in 1979, Dowell responded by saying, "Certain things in the legal system inadvertently seems [sic] to protect the criminal."[7]

But there was little more that Dowell could say or do. He was among a great host of victims, and like the rest, he would be forced to cut his losses and to move on. So he did, trusting God to meet his financial needs. "I have been young, and now am old;" the psalmist says, "yet have I not seen the righteous forsaken, nor his seed begging bread."[8] For Dowell, such promises were enough.

Dowell made another financial misstep in 1977, though in this other instance, Dowell was not the primary victim; BBC was. The situation began when Dowell hired CPA Wayne Edwards to help with BBC's finances. Edwards was one half of a local accounting firm, Edwards and Swaim. Dowell had hired him to serve as a financial adviser in 1977, but then when Richard Burks left BBC in 1979, Dowell asked Edwards to step in as the new business manager.

For several years, Edwards seemed to do outstanding work. Despite the many financial challenges that were then facing the college, Edwards managed to keep BBC afloat. According to Dowell Jr., Edwards "was hailed as a kind of financial genius."[9] Indeed, he was viewed by many as "the one who saved BBC from financial ruin," Dowell Jr. said.[10]

Edwards also helped the fellowship in other ways. He offered financial seminars for pastors, and he taught classes in money management for students. "Numerous people at BBC and pastors had him do their tax returns for them," Dowell Jr. recalled. "He knew how to save them a lot of money in taxes."[11]

BBC's president was among the people who benefitted from Edwards's expertise. In fact, Dowell and Edwards formed a close personal bond. A thank-you note sent to Edwards in 1981 captures some of Dowell's appreciation for his friend:

> *I am not always too good at expressing strong words of appreciation in person. Therefore, I wanted to take this opportunity to write you a brief note and express to you my deep appreciation for your assistance in bringing Baptist Bible College in line financially with our budget. You have been of immeasurable help to me, and you have been universally accepted by the pastors of our fellowship.*
>
> *A mere "thanks" would not be sufficient to express my appreciation for what you have done in providing the necessary furniture for my office and making it an office I can always be proud of. However, I don't know of a stronger word, so I guess I will just say "thanks a million." You have been a wonderful friend.[12]*

In addition to helping Dowell manage things at BBC, Edwards prepared Dowell's personal taxes and drew up his estate plans. Edwards also had a hand in creating the generous retirement package that Dowell received in 1983. According to longtime staff member Shirley Hackler, such efforts were motivated by a genuine love and respect for Dowell. "You know, truly, I think Wayne loved Dr. Dowell," Hackler said. "I really do."[13] Dowell Jr. agreed. "He loved Dad and Dad totally trusted him . . . ," Dowell Jr. stated.[14]

Dowell Jr. went on to say that his own opinion of Edwards had been more guarded than his father's. "He was a very likeable man and I enjoyed his friendship," Dowell Jr. explained, "but I never trusted him."[15] Dowell Jr. said Nola was likewise skeptical. When Edwards had set up Dowell's estate plans, Edwards named himself as the executor of Dowell's will and gave himself power of attorney. Nola "was furious" over the matter, Dowell Jr. said.[16] In the event of her husband's death, Edwards would have had complete control over her assets, potentially leaving her penniless. So at Nola's insistence, the paperwork was revised, substituting Dowell Jr.'s name for Edwards's.

Notwithstanding these doubters, Edwards commanded great respect within the BBF. He also enjoyed much freedom and authority at BBC, serving under both Dowell and Dowell's successor, A. V. Henderson. Dowell had so much confidence in Edwards that he permitted him to move the college's bookkeeping operations away from the campus and into his own office. That move generated "much controversy," according to Dowell Jr, but Edwards managed to get it done.[17]

President Henderson likewise trusted Edwards. Henderson reportedly made a practice of issuing Edwards stacks of check requests, documents that were blank except for Henderson's signature. These forms were prepared so that Edwards could write checks as necessary whenever his boss was out of town.[18]

A couple of years after Dowell's retirement from BBC, Edwards also finagled an institutional change. It occurred near the beginning of 1985. Edwards notified Shirley Hackler that he wanted her to become BBC's new corporate secretary. Edwards had previously held this title himself, but he said he now believed someone else should assume the position. Edwards explained that it was a conflict of interest for him to serve both as corporate secretary and as the institution's auditor.

While Hackler had never before held such a title, she agreed to step in. After all, she too trusted Edwards implicitly. The Hacklers and the Edwards were close personal friends. Both couples attended High Street Baptist, and they had even vacationed in Europe together. In fact, later in 1985 these couples would plan to take yet another joint vacation, a Caribbean cruise scheduled for December.

Nineteen eighty-five did not go as planned, however. Indeed, it turned out to be a very bad year for BBC. Henderson pushed to have a new fourteen-hundred-seat chapel building constructed on campus, but the fundraising for that project had gone poorly.[19] Edwards maintained that the expense was now threatening to drag BBC under. When Edwards spoke about the project at a fellowship meeting in February, he warned BBF leaders that the college would be lucky to open its doors the following school year.[20]

BBC did manage to reopen that next fall, but it continued to struggle. In fact, the college would eventually abandon Henderson's chapel project altogether, selling the unfinished facility to the BBF Mission Office as a means of getting out from under the debt. Of course, that sale was yet in the future, and it did nothing for the college's immediate needs. And those needs were considerable. Just a few weeks into the fall semester of 1985, Edwards told some of BBC's staff members that the college did not even have the funds to meet its next payroll. Edwards said he planned to give the college some money from his own resources as a temporary fix. Hackler urged Edwards not to go through with that plan, but Edwards insisted, and he gave Hackler nine personal checks, each written in the amount of nine thousand dollars, to take care of the need. Hackler saw to it that these were taken to the bank and deposited into the school's account.[21]

Not long afterward, on October 13, Hackler was at her office at BBC. She had just returned to campus after attending a financial aid seminar, and she answered a call from Commerce Bank. Bank officials needed her to come to their office right away, they said. Hackler left the campus and went to the bank, and while she was there, she learned that Edwards's nine checks had caught the attention of an alert bank employee. The deposit had seemed odd to him, even suspicious. At that time, banks were required to report to the IRS any check exceeding ten thousand dollars, and the extra effort that Edwards had taken to write nine smaller checks instead of one large check made it appear that perhaps he was trying to avoid IRS detection.[22]

There were other concerns as well. When bank officials looked further into BBC's accounts, they discovered other questionable activity, including several checks written from BBC to Edwards. And making matters worse was the fact that Hackler could explain very little about it. When bank officials showed her the documentation, she had few answers. She was neither a CPA nor the issuer of the checks, she explained, and as for her role as corporate secretary, she carried out those duties at Edwards's behest, often not understanding the reasons for what she was doing.[23]

When Hackler's interview at the bank came to an end, Commerce officials advised her to stop payment on Edwards's checks. With so many unanswered questions, they said it would be best for BBC to draw on its line of credit to cover its current expenditures. Hackler listened to that advice and signed the necessary forms. She then returned to her office to await further instructions. She was told not to discuss any of these matters with Edwards.

A few minutes later, Hackler was back in her office, and Edwards walked in. He chatted with her briefly, and as they were speaking, Hackler got another telephone call. It was the officials from the bank trying to track Edwards down. Hackler put Edwards on the telephone, and he was likewise summoned to the bank for a meeting.

According to Hackler, Edwards returned from that meeting very distraught. "He was sweating like crazy," she recalled. "His head was wet. Shirt was undone. Took his tie off."[24] He told Hackler that he was going to have to resign his position at BBC. He then confessed to her that he was guilty of kiting checks. But Edwards maintained that this was "the only thing" he was guilty of, Hackler said.[25] Edwards also promised to explain the situation further if Hackler would meet him at his office the next morning. He then left the campus.

That afternoon Commerce President Alvin D. Meeker and some others from the bank asked to meet with Henderson at BBC. Hackler sat in on that meeting. In it, two things became evident. First, there were serious irregularities in Edwards's management of the college's finances. Second, the college's coffers were virtually empty. When the meeting ended, Henderson told Hackler that he felt like he had been stabbed through the heart.

Hackler went to Edwards's office the next day to get the explanation that had been promised to her. She waited from eight o'clock until eleven thirty, she said, but Edwards never showed. Edwards's wife eventually called and said he was unable to make it to work because of a migraine.

In the days that followed, President Meeker of Commerce requested an independent audit of BBC's finances. He also asked that BBC's property be assigned as security for its unsecured debt. Hackler said she never had another conversation with Edwards, but she and another BBC employee did manage to pick up the college's records from Edwards's office.

Meanwhile Henderson called a meeting of several key leaders within the BBF, including Jerry Falwell, John Rawlings, David Cavin, and the pastor of Temple Baptist in Detroit, Truman Dollar. Henderson used that meeting to share what he knew about the situation and to try to answer questions. He also allowed the men to question Shirley Hackler. Hackler recalled faltering under the pressure of it all. In addition to the stress she was facing at BBC, she was coping with the news that her newest grandchild, born that same week, had cerebral palsy.

Hackler said she was contacted by one of the participants in that meeting after it was all over. He called to check on her and to give her some advice. Her close association with Edwards, he said, was causing some in the BBF to suspect that she had conspired with Edwards to embezzle money. Hackler's friend advised her to leave town to give time for the dust to settle. In response to that suggestion, Hackler mentioned her upcoming cruise. The Edwards family had already canceled their reservations, she said, and the Hackler family was planning to do the same. But Hackler's friend encouraged her to keep those travel plans instead.

Following that advice, Hackler and her husband left town in December. But then, while they were away, Hackler got a message from President Henderson. In her absence, one of the pastors had alerted government officials about the situation at BBC, prompting a federal investigation. Henderson told Hackler that officials from the FBI, the IRS, and the Treasury Department had "invaded" BBC's campus.[26] Henderson needed Hackler to return to Springfield as soon as possible.

When Hackler got back to campus, she was tasked with facilitating the investigation. For the next eighteen months, she worked closely with a team of governmental officials. These investigators told her that Edwards had likely placed her in the position of corporate secretary so that she would have "to take the fall" for any criminal activity.[27] Fortunately, that did not occur. Hackler was exonerated of any wrongdoing and was instead groomed to become a star witness in the case against Edwards.

Prosecutors had a laundry list of accusations to bring against Edwards. In addition to kiting checks, he was said to have set up "dummy corporations" by which he purchased personal real estate.[28] Hackler said she and Henderson also stumbled onto a BBC bank account that they never knew existed. This was uncovered when, following advice from Al Meeker, they took steps to safeguard BBC's bank accounts from further activity by Edwards. Hackler knew of an account that had been set up at Metropolitan Bank for employee Christmas bonuses, so she and Henderson went to Metropolitan to close out that account. But when they did, they were told that the college had two accounts. They also learned that they were not authorized to access that second account. The only names on the signature card, Hackler said, were Edwards and his wife.

Looking back on it all, Dowell Jr. took a dim view of Wayne Edwards, calling him "a smooth talking, convincing con man."[29] The elder Dowell, though less direct in saying so, seems to have reached that same conclusion. Indeed, as the reality of Edwards's actions began to sink in, Dowell was deeply wounded. Hackler described a telephone call that she got from Dowell after he first heard the news. "He said, 'Shirley, I love Wayne like my son,'" Hackler recalled. "I said, 'I know you do, Dr. Dowell.' And he started crying and he said, 'But he's in trouble, isn't he?' And I said, 'Yes, he is.'"[30]

Edwards's trial was set for the fourth week of September in 1987. But Edwards never made it to court. On September 22, he visited a branch office of his business located in the nearby town of Lebanon. On the way back, he pulled over to the side of the road and took his own life.

After Edwards's death, Hackler discovered paperwork that showed the Dowells' home had been deeded, not to the Dowells, but to Baptist Bible College and Wayne Edwards. It was Hackler who later had the deed revised. Even so, Hackler did not believe Edwards would have ever used such power against his old friend. In her opinion, Edwards's feelings for Dowell were genuine. "I think it really hurt him that Dr. Dowell knew what he had done," Hackler said.[31] Hackler also suspected that, after Edwards's actions became known, he took comfort in the fact that Dowell was no longer the president of the college. Edwards's relationship with Henderson had not been nearly as warm, Hackler said, and she believed that this made Edwards's betrayal a bit easier on his conscience.

For Dowell's part, this entire episode was difficult to fathom. Hackler thought she understood why. "He did the right thing, and he thought everybody else did," she said.[32] Dowell's only recourse had been to turn the situation over to the Lord, saying with the righteous man Job, "My friends scorn me: but mine eye poureth out tears unto God."[33] Dowell also seems to have taken to heart Christ's instruction to "pray for them which despitefully use you."[34] The month after Edwards's activities became public, Dowell preached a sermon at Baptist Temple entitled "What Is a Friend?" In that message Dowell may have alluded to Edwards without naming him. "I've had friends even recently," Dowell remarked, "friends who have dishonored God, hurt the ministry, hurt my own life, and I deplore what they did—but I talked to them on the phone and said, 'I want you to know I love you, and I'll be praying for you.'"[35]

This was a pattern for Dowell. He cared for his friends even when they disappointed him. In the spring of 1987, Dowell watched as another friend made a serious mistake. That was when reports emerged that Televangelist Jim Bakker was turning the PTL Television Network over to Jerry Falwell. Bakker's infidelity with a church secretary, Jessica Hahn, was now forcing him to step down as the leader of that global ministry. According to rules established by Bakker's denomination, the Assemblies of God (AG), Bakker's actions required him to leave the ministry for a period of not less than two years before he could be restored to leadership. To minimize the impact that this would have on his ministry, Bakker selected his own replacement. Bakker reportedly passed over AG celebrities John Ankerberg and Jimmy Swaggart, choosing instead Jerry Falwell, a Baptist with whom Bakker had no prior relationship.

Falwell wrote about this experience in his autobiography, *Strength for the Journey*, stating that he was "shocked and surprised" by the call he got from Bakker's camp.[36] Yet Falwell took pity on those who were affected by this scandal. "Because we were brothers and sisters in Christ," Falwell wrote, "their suffering had already become my suffering. And if I could do something to help, I must do it."[37]

There was another reason Falwell wanted to intervene, however. Bakker's situation had implications for Falwell's own ministry. Falwell said he "knew that this calamity, coupled with the possible collapse of a major television ministry, would do great harm to every other media ministry in America, and perhaps even to every Gospel-preaching church in America." For these reasons, then, Falwell felt compelled to step in. "I could not say no and walk away." he stated.[38]

Once Bakker's handover was made public in March 1987, Falwell immediately heard from many people. Vice President George Bush and Evangelist Billy Graham were among the callers. Both of those leaders, Falwell said, offered him their encouragement and support. There were many others, however, who told Falwell that they thought this move was a blunder, if not an outright betrayal of his Baptist roots. "Friends and foes alike were also taking me to task for associating with PTL at any time let alone during their time of scandal," Falwell wrote.[39]

Dowell delivered no such chastisement, sharing instead some fatherly advice. Dowell wrote Falwell "a long letter" counseling him not to go through with the agreement. "He didn't listen," Dowell said bluntly. "He usually does."[40] According to Dowell, Falwell's reply to him was, "I have to do what I feel I have to do."[41]

Falwell may have regretted that answer. In the weeks that followed, Falwell found himself trapped in a quagmire. The atmosphere at PTL was "cultic," Falwell said, and as he studied his new surroundings, Falwell learned that Jim Bakker's misdeeds went far beyond a one-time sexual indiscretion.[42] There was widespread corruption at PTL, corruption that would eventually result in a forty-five year prison sentence for Bakker for mail and wire fraud.[43]

According to a work coauthored by Falwell's wife in 2008, these discoveries forced Falwell to reevaluate God's purpose for bringing him into this situation. "Jerry's reason for stepping into the PTL scandal had been to save the ministry and minimize the damage to the gospel of Christ," Macel Falwell wrote. "But after it all played out, Jerry began to feel that God hadn't sent him to save PTL but to put a stop to the immorality and financial fraud."[44]

390 - *Cry Aloud, Spare Not*

Falwell left PTL less than seven months after he took control of it. During that time, he endured Chapter 11 proceedings as well as some very public efforts by the Bakkers to regain control of their ministry. At the end of it all, in October 1987, Falwell and his board resigned and walked away. Falwell was quoted in the *New York Times* as saying, "We really are tired . . . and really do feel that our contribution has been made."[45]

Three months later Dowell was interviewed by *Springfield! Magazine*. The reporter asked Dowell about his connection to Falwell, and Dowell readily acknowledged their friendship. "He's been my boy," Dowell said. Falwell's actions had disappointed Dowell, but they had not diminished his affection. And Dowell believed that even Falwell had come to the conclusion that his involvement with PTL had been a mistake. "He knows better now," Dowell said.[46]

Those remarks were published in 1988. They were part of an article written in anticipation of Dowell's retirement from Baptist Temple. After fifty-four years in the ministry, Dowell was stepping down from his role as a pastor and would be turning the leadership of his church over to his son.

Dowell had no intention of giving up preaching, of course. "Preaching is my life," he once said. He described his pulpit ministry as "the one thing that I love to do, the one thing that I'm called to do, and the one thing that I hope I can do until the day God calls me home."[47] And Dowell would have no trouble staying busy after his retirement. He was still much in demand as a special speaker, and he expected to carry on regular evangelistic meetings for many years to come. A newspaper editorial published shortly before his retirement stated it this way: "Dowell's idea of slowing down might well exhaust younger pastors."[48]

A farewell celebration was planned for Dowell in May of that year. Those plans had to be delayed, however. On the eve of that event, Dowell was rushed to the hospital for emergency surgery. He was suffering from an intestinal blockage. Baptist Temple rescheduled Dowell's retirement celebration for June 19, and this second event went on as it was planned. The celebration was attended by Missouri Secretary of State Roy Blunt as well as other dignitaries, and Blunt read a proclamation from Governor John Ashcroft honoring Dowell for his contributions to the State of Missouri. The Missouri Senate likewise recognized Dowell with a formal resolution. Baptist Temple then honored Dowell by conferring upon him the title of Pastor Emeritus.

After all of those accolades, Dowell settled in to preach. His text came from the second chapter of Haggai. It was a fitting charge for those who would be carrying on in his stead: "Yet now be strong, O Zerubbabel, saith the LORD; and be strong, O Joshua, son of Josedech, the high priest; and be strong, all ye people of the land, saith the LORD, and work: for I am with you, saith the LORD of hosts."[49]

The Lord of hosts would likewise remain with Dowell and his wife. Indeed, it was His comfort that they would rest upon exactly one year later when they received the news that their granddaughter had been involved in an automobile accident. Lynda was living just west of Pueblo, Colorado. She was a happily married young mother with a six-month-old son, Colin, and a devoted husband, Brian. Lynda worked at a nearby credit union, and her family was active at the Lighthouse Baptist Church.

On that Monday morning—June 19, 1989—Lynda rose early to get to her job in Pueblo. She strapped Colin into his car seat and was headed to drop him off at childcare. A day before, Lynda had called her parents to wish them a happy anniversary and a happy Father's Day. She was also excited to give her parents the news that Colin "had pulled himself up in his crib for the first time."[50] The family members then went on to chat about other news. Clyde was still recovering from a major back surgery that he had undergone three weeks earlier, and Lynda's sister Angie was having difficulty with a pregnancy and was now on bedrest. Lynda's youngest sister, Karla, had recently graduated high school.

Lynda and her parents finished catching up on the latest news, and then they hung up the telephone. And the next day, as Lynda drove east toward Pueblo, she veered off the road and landed in a ravine some fifteen or twenty feet below. No one was ever quite sure what caused the accident. The road was straight, traffic was light, and no other vehicles were involved. Tire marks showed that Lynda had driven to the left side of the road before going off of the embankment on the right. Brian suspected that Lynda had fallen asleep at the wheel. Lynda's parents thought perhaps the early morning sun had played a role in the accident.

Lynda's car landed upside down. The wreck was discovered minutes later by a couple of alert highway patrolmen traveling the same route. It was impossible for them to see the wreck from the road, but they noticed "a cloud of dust" and stopped to check it out.[51] They found Lynda and her baby several feet from the vehicle. Lynda was unconscious but had managed to get her infant out of the wreckage before she passed out. Colin was unharmed and was found sleeping next to his mother.

Unfortunately, Lynda's condition was worse than her child's. She had suffered a trauma to her head. Her rescuers called for an ambulance, and when Brian reached her side at the hospital, Lynda seemed restless. She calmed down only after Brian assured her that their baby was fine. Brian stayed with his wife throughout that day and into the night. The doctor told him that Lynda had a long recovery ahead of her but that she was going to be okay. Brian then conveyed those things to the rest of the family, and Clyde, in turn, relayed the news to the Dowells. He contacted Bill Jr. to ask him to tell his parents in person because he did not want them to hear about it over the telephone.

At the end of that long day, Brian was urged by Lynda's doctor to leave the hospital and to get some needed rest. Brian was again assured that his wife was going to be all right, so he left and spent the night with his parents. Then, early the next morning, Brian received troubling news. A blood clot had broken loose and had lodged in Lynda's carotid artery. She was now on life support, and there was no hope of saving her.

Clyde and Sharon were living in Texas at that time, and they had not yet left to come to Colorado. Brian had asked them not to make an immediate trip. He believed they might be needed during Lynda's long recovery, so he had asked them to wait until he knew more. When he learned about the blood clot, however, Brian called them back to tell them that if they wanted to see Lynda alive, they needed to come at once. Lynda's parents flew to Colorado that same day, though they opted not to see their daughter before the life support was removed. They did not want that to be their last memory of her.

In the meantime, Clyde asked his brother to go back to the Dowells' home to break the news of Lynda's death. The Dowells were heartbroken, of course. Lynda had enjoyed a special bond with them. She had been born in Springfield, and she had also attended BBC for a time. Now she was gone.

Just a few days after receiving this news, Dowell and his wife joined other members of Lynda's family—all except her pregnant sister, Angie—for a funeral in Colorado. On the day of that service, a team of executives came down from Denver to run Lynda's credit union so that all of her coworkers could attend. It was evident to Dowell that his granddaughter had maintained a strong Christian testimony in her church and community. As he and Nola stood in the receiving line at the end of the service, they listened proudly to the stories and comments that people shared about their granddaughter.

The Dowells were equally proud of the way that their son and daughter-in-law, Clyde and Sharon, had responded to this great loss. Sharon recalled how her in-laws openly commended her and Clyde at a family reunion the next year. Like the Dowells, Lynda's parents had exhibited strong faith in the midst of their sorrow. Clyde acknowledged that he did not understand the reasons for Lynda's death. Still, he believed God had a purpose. He said he took comfort in the words of Isaiah: "For my thoughts are not your thoughts, neither are your ways my ways, saith the Lord."[52] These words helped to assure the grieving father that he did not need to understand Lynda's death; he only needed to trust God's understanding of it. ". . . I believe with all my heart," Clyde said, "that God is always good and makes no mistakes."[53]

Clyde's wife took a similar perspective. Even many years after this tragedy, Sharon considered herself blessed by it all. "I could write a book on God's comfort and what he has done for me through this experience," she said.[54] Sharon's faith had been equally strong on the day that she buried her daughter. As she was leaving the cemetery, she commented "that God's grace really was sufficient."[55]

Perhaps Sharon's father-in-law overheard that remark. If so, he would have agreed most heartily. After all, Dowell was a beneficiary of that same grace. And it may be that, as Dowell exited the cemetery, he looked up into the heavens and affirmed Sharon's statement. The utterance would have come forth as a breathless whisper, no doubt, given the solemnity of the hour. But Dowell never knew a hushed voice, so even at a whisper, his affirmation must have reverberated across the cemetery:

Amen and Amen.

A pronouncement such as this does not intrude upon such sorrow-filled days. It only blesses them. And Dowell's voice must have adorned that day like a genteel chime, ringing out to all those around him. It was a simple sound, yet its meaning was clear. A Guest had arrived. He had brought with Him a supply of never-ending grace. And He would gladly enter in if only the occupants would throw open the door. A more magnificent chime was never heard.

Amen and Amen.

Chapter 42: *Passing the Torch*

Colorful international flags had just paraded through the W. E. Dowell Fieldhouse. This procession was then followed by the posting of the American flag and the singing of "The Star-Spangled Banner." Now as the crowd looked on, four men wearing suits and ties formed a relay team. They were Harold DeVilbiss, Lavern Rodgers, R. O. Woodworth, and W. E. Dowell, all founding members of the BBF. DeVilbiss and Rodgers were two of the fellowship's original missionaries. Woodworth and Dowell had been stateside leaders of the movement.

This was the Global Fellowship Meeting, conducted May 15 through 20, 1994. It was the forty-fourth time that BBC had hosted the fellowship's May meeting. But the 1994 event was unique. It celebrated the fact that the BBF was now an international institution. Indeed, the organization was now known as the Baptist Bible Fellowship *International* (BBFI). The fellowship had seen tremendous growth in its forty-four years of existence. Between 1950 and 1994, the BBFI had expanded from less than two hundred participating churches to over eight thousand worldwide. The number of missionary families supported by the organization had grown from seven to over eight hundred.

Another important development witnessed by the BBFI was its own diversification. US churches were no longer the sole driving force in this movement. In some cases, second- and third-generation national pastors on the mission field were now leading ministries that had once been led by American missionaries. By the 1990s countries like Mexico and Japan had their own networks of churches. And like their American counterpart, these organizations were training up missionaries and sending them out to the rest of the world.

Organizers of the BBFI's Global Meeting reached out to those international constituents, hoping to draw them to the US for this special gathering. And many responded. That year's slate of speakers included preachers from seventeen different countries, including Argentina, Australia, Ethiopia, Japan, Korea, and Thailand. Two hundred foreign delegates joined an estimated seven thousand other attendees. Crowds were so large that rooms with closed-circuit television screens had to be set up to accommodate the overflow. The *Tribune* called it "one of the best attended meetings ever."[1]

Dowell participated in a symbolic relay occurred on the opening night of that meeting. It was a ceremony that required no translation. The theme for the week was "Champions of the Light," and Olympic images blanketed the week's promotional literature and decor. On one of the fieldhouse walls, for instance, was a massive mural depicting an Olympic runner. Next to the runner were dollar figures climbing to the sum of one million dollars. BBC President Leland Kennedy, successor to A. V. Henderson, was hoping to raise a large offering for the college that week. He had commissioned the mural in support of this effort, a visual challenge to his donors to go the distance. Kennedy needed all the help he could get. If he managed to reach his one million dollar goal, it would be a record achievement.

In keeping with this theme, Dowell's relay was likewise styled after the Olympics. The "runners" in this spectacle served as symbols of the entire BBFI. Like Olympic torchbearers, preachers have the job of carrying light around the world.

The relay was initiated by DeVilbiss. He carried an artificial torch from the back of the facility and passed it off to Rodgers. Rodgers then handed it off to Woodworth. Woodworth, like Dowell, did not have many years left on the earth. He would enter Heaven in 1998. Even so, he was a faithful torchbearer to the end.

Ready, Dad?

Dowell held the relay's anchor position. His son Dowell Jr. was standing next to him as he received the torch from Woodworth. Dowell had been tasked with carrying the light up to the highest part of the fieldhouse platform, but since he was no longer steady on his feet, and since there were a number of stairs between him and his destination, Dowell Jr. served as an escort. The two of them ascended the platform, and when they reached the top, Dowell held up his torch to a tall gold stand. The top of that stand then came alive with red lights and blowing strings. The Olympic flame was aglow.

Dowell's retirement from BBC and from Baptist Temple ushered him into a new phase of his life. No longer was he a leader of a fellowship or a church. Now he was an elder statesman. This was a status that had its perks, of course. It freed Dowell from much of the pressure that came with leadership responsibility. Instead of planning the fellowship meeting, he got to wield the cardboard torch.

That is not to suggest that Dowell had not been cast aside. He led a full life and continued to be revered by the BBFI. He kept close tabs on the happenings of the fellowship and was frequently seen at fellowship meetings and at BBC basketball games. At other times, Dowell was busy spending time with his family. His two remaining siblings, Ruth and Gladys, each came to visit him during his retirement years, as did his children, grandchildren, and even great grandchildren.

Even in retirement, Dowell could never settle for a life of relaxation. He was adamant about remaining productive during his closing years. "There's no way I'd just retire and coast," he told a newspaper reporter in 1988. "I've got a lot I want to do."[2] In 1990, Dowell wrote an article admonishing all seniors to lead full and meaningful lives.

"In my travels, and at home, I find many senior citizens sitting at home discouraged, despondent, and not knowing what to do with themselves," Dowell wrote. Dowell advocated a three-part remedy for that problem: "First, remember your relationship with God. Spend time each day in prayer and the reading of the Word of God. Second, stay active in your church in whatever capacity you are able. Third, find plenty of work to do to keep you busy. This might include doing things around the house and the yard, giving out tracts, and witnessing to people in your city or community."[3]

Dowell filled his own closing years with as much preaching as he could. On the day of his retirement from Baptist Temple, he announced that he had upcoming speaking engagements in Texas, California, Nevada, Canada, and many other places. That schedule thinned out as the years passed by, but Dowell never lost his love of standing in a pulpit. In September 1995, at the age of 81, he preached at a national fellowship meeting for the last time. That meeting was held at the Bible Baptist Church in Matthews, North Carolina, and Dowell and Dowell Jr. traveled there together. The Saturday before they flew out, Dowell wrote a letter to one of his sisters, saying, "I have just finished my sermon this morning." He went on to explain the purpose of his trip. "They are featuring the living presidents of the Baptist Bible Fellowship as special speakers," Dowell wrote. "I was the first president, and have been president once since then."[4]

Dowell also served as a frequent guest speaker at Baptist Temple during those years. On New Year's Eve in 1997, he preached a seven-point sermon entitled, "God's Call to Man." He neglected to mention to his audience that he had preached this message before. It was the same outline that Dowell had used when he preached his first sermon at the age of nineteen. "God laid it on my heart," he told his audience.[5]

Dowell carried out other ministerial duties as well. He officiated at weddings, funerals, and other special events. In 1994 he stood on the ordination council for a young minister named Dave Taylor. This may have been the last time Dowell participated in such an event. Taylor found the experience meaningful. "His 'laying on of hands' was, and continues to be, a tremendous blessing to me," Taylor wrote in 2006.[6]

Dowell also made frequent calls on the sick and elderly. He described one visit that he made to a man named Gilmore. Gilmore's wife had died while he was being treated for an illness, and Dowell had been tasked with breaking the news to the widower in the hospital. With as much tenderness as Dowell could muster, he spoke to Gilmore and told him, "Your wife went home to Heaven." But Dowell never anticipated the exasperated response that he would hear in answer. "Aw, what did she do that for?" Gilmore spouted. Dowell had to chuckle as he told the story.[7]

One of Dowell's most selfless undertakings during those closing years of his life was a letter-writing ministry. At Dowell Jr.'s request, Dowell began spending an hour a day at the offices of Baptist Temple, replying to the many letters that the church received from missionaries. "It is a joy to answer your recent letter," Dowell wrote in answer to a letter from Costa Rica, "and we are glad to know what good results you are having,"[8] To a family in Mexico, Dowell wrote, "It always blesses us and the church to receive your letters and to know we are having a part in building great missionary churches in Mexico."[9] Many recipients of these letters found them both meaningful and encouraging. Russ Ivison wrote back from England, saying, "Received your 3 February letter only just this morning. Your kind thoughtfulness to write really made the day to Faye and I! That's the truth. The post here comes about 7 AM. What a way to start the day!"[10]

Dowell's retirement activities also included some political activism. In 1996, Dowell sent a large mailing to a group of Missouri pastors cautioning them about a state bill aimed at licensing daycares. A decade earlier, in 1986, Dowell stood for the last time before the Springfield's City Council. A new citizens group, Concerned Citizens for Community Standards, was then pushing for stricter regulation of pornography. Dowell joined in the effort. The organization gathered twelve thousand signatures to urge the council to take action. Participants then packed the council's chambers to see what would come of it all. Dowell listened to those deliberations and heard Mayor George Scruggs take a rather dismissive tone toward the citizens group. Scruggs advised them to get legal counsel and suggested that they did not understand the limits of the city's authority. According to a newspaper report, Dowell "resented the antagonistic attitude exhibited by the mayor." In response, Dowell stood and addressed the assembly. "'Listen to us,' Dowell pleaded with the council. 'We're citizens. We're taxpayers.'"[11]

Another important outlet for Dowell's political energies during those last years of his life was his work with Missouri Governor John Ashcroft. Ashcroft's long career in public service included not only two terms as the governor (1985-1993) but also an appointment to the office of US Attorney General (2001-2005) under George W. Bush. It is also worth noting that Ashcroft was a devout member of the Assemblies of God and that he had grown up in Springfield listening to Dowell preach on the radio. During Ashcroft's first gubernatorial campaign, Dowell sent him a letter of support, and Ashcroft sent back a handwritten response:

> Dear Brother Dowell
> Thanks for your most kind letter of August 10. I am grateful for your prayers and support.
> Brother Dowell, you have been, and continue to be an inspiration to me.
> Please continue to remember me in your prayers! I'll be in contact with you as the campaign unfolds.
> Best wishes
> John[12]

After that campaign ended, Ashcroft took office as Missouri's new governor. He then instituted the "Governor's Prayer Breakfast for Missouri," held each year in January. Dowell became a member of that event's honorary sponsoring committee. Dowell also participated in a special prayer service that Ashcroft hosted at the beginning of his second term, the "Inaugural Service of Dedication and Consecration." This event was held at the First Assembly of God in Jefferson City in January 1989. During the service, ten special guests offered up prayers for the governor. They were each assigned to pray over a distinct aspect of the governor's life and leadership. Dowell was asked to concentrate his prayer on the citizens of Missouri.

Because Ashcroft's inaugural service was being televised, this event was heavily scripted. The script for Dowell's prayer began by saying, "Heavenly Father, we boldly enter your throne room made confident by the shed blood of Jesus Christ. We rejoice in our relationship with You and acknowledge our utter dependence on You." Dowell edited the next line. The script read, "As we humble ourselves and turn from our wicked ways and seek your face, we petition you to shower your blessings upon the United States of America." For added emphasis, Dowell tacked four handwritten words onto the end of that line: "our country, our home!"[13]

Dowell's prayer then continued:

> We ask for your blessings upon the state of Missouri. May this be a state where your many gifts flourish, the laws of democracy are obeyed, absolute values are protected, and every citizen lives fully in Your Will.
>
> Almighty God, we trust in the power of the Holy Spirit to blanket this state with peace and prosperity. Grant Wisdom from above to Governor Ashcroft and his administration. May they fulfill their scriptural duties to be ministers of God for Your Will in this state.
>
> We thank you for hearing our requests and honoring them in the name of your Son, Jesus Christ.
>
> Amen.[14]

Ashcroft was clearly moved by what was said and done that day. In his thank-you note to Dowell afterward, Ashcroft called the service "a tremendous worship experience." The governor went on to note that the course of his leadership had been affected by it. "For me," Ashcroft wrote, "it served to reaffirm the proposition that the Lord must come first in everything I do."[15]

Far from being cast aside, then, Dowell remained busy in meaningful and productive work during his closing years. And those years were also enriched by many personal honors. On the campus of BBC, Dowell's name was placed on the fieldhouse. Elsewhere on campus, the BBC Alumni Association recognized Dowell by planting a tree in his honor.[16] At the Sagmount Baptist Camp near Joplin, Missouri, an athletic field was named after Dowell. Then in 1984, an antique Bible collector, Jewell E. Smith, honored Dowell by giving him a complete 1640 edition of the Bible. The present came in celebration of Dowell's fiftieth year in the ministry.

As part of that same fiftieth-anniversary celebration, Dowell received over a hundred and fifty letters of commendation. These came from well-known preacher friends, such as Lee Roberson of Tennessee Temple, and from political figures, including Fred Lynn of the Missouri House of Representatives, Missouri Governor Kit Bond, US Congressman Gene Taylor, US Senators John Danforth and Thomas Eagleton, and President Ronald Reagan.

Dowell appreciated all such well-wishes, but he may have taken the greatest joy in the letters that he received from ordinary pastors. Dowell still had a special love for them, and the feeling appears to have been mutual. A message that Dowell received from Steve Chittenden of Kerrville, Texas, said, "I do not write today to shower you with flowery words, but rather to thank you from my heart for giving me a glimpse of what Jesus must have been when He walked among men."[17] Jack J. Dinsbeer of the University Baptist Church in Jacksonville, Florida, wrote to tell Dowell how his preaching had recently impacted his life:

> *I have heard you preach many great messages over the years on numerous occasions. However, I think the most outstanding was the most recent one that I heard you preach, and that was at the Denver fellowship meeting of the Baptist Bible Fellowship. Without doubt, this message had as profound an effect upon my life as any that I have ever heard. Following that message I knelt, along with many others, and rededicated my life anew to the Lord. It was not just a shallow, emotional jaunt to the altar, but indeed things have been different than they have been for many, many years. Our church has enjoyed a great spirit of revival since then, and our Sunday School is growing, and in general things are on the move.[18]*

Dowell's notable influence also made him the subject of many magazine and newspaper articles during his closing years. In 1999, he was featured in Springfield's *News-Leader* as part of a series called "100 Ozarkers." The resulting article, four columns wide, rivaled articles that were published about some of Springfield's biggest names, including real estate developer John Q. Hammons.

Dowell had to watch how he handled such opportunities. As Nola aged, she grew increasingly jealous of any attention that was lavished upon her husband. In a 1996 interview with *The Baptist Preacher*, Dowell was careful to state, "The greatest thing in my life, next to salvation, is my wife and with her, my family. We fell in love sixty-three years ago. She has been my companion, a strength and an encouragement for my ministry all these years. She has stood by me and helped make my ministry possible."[19]

Dowell was sincere in those words, but he also knew the importance that such sentiments held for his wife. When people praised him and ignored her, Nola became genuinely offended. She had been quick to note, for instance, an oversight on a placemat that was printed for Dowell's fiftieth-year-in-the-ministry celebration. That placemat showed a timeline of Dowell's life with a caption that stated, "Dr. Dowell has three children—two sons who are both pastors, and one daughter who is a pastor's wife." Nola was not even mentioned. She corrected the omission on her own copy of that placemat, which she later filed away. Amending the printed text, she inserted her name next to her husband's and then added this statement: "Nola has stood by him and served the Lord all these 50 years, and been a wonderful wife and mother."

Nola's sensitivities only increased as the years passed, and Dowell learned to protect her feelings. Such efforts included regulating the time that he spent away from her. According to Dowell, Nola disapproved of the busy schedule that he maintained when he first entered retirement. "In the closing part of my ministry, she did resent me being gone so much," Dowell explained. "And rightly so, because her health had begun to fail also. And I'd tried to retire, and I just kept going for meetings all the time."[20] A line from Proverbs 5:18 became Nola's new favorite scripture: ". . . rejoice with the wife of thy youth." Each time she quoted the statement, she emphasized the word *with.*

Dowell came to agree that he needed to curb his travels, though he stopped short of saying that he did so at Nola's insistence. Dowell maintained that his wife complained about this matter relatively little. "She bore the brunt of it in herself," he said, "till I saw what was happening, and then I regulated it."[21]

Yet even after he made these adjustments, Dowell stayed active. In the spring of 1989, Dowell was invited to preach at the Ozark Baptist Temple in the city of Ozark, Missouri, just nineteen miles from his home. This church was virtually on life support. A former pastor had "stayed with it too long and people left," Dowell explained. "There wasn't but seven or eight you could depend on that was still down there."[22] Indeed, only seven people attended Dowell's first service.

The dwindling congregation was only part of the problem, however. Dowell indicated that the real problems surfaced when, on the night of his visit, the church conducted a business meeting. "And I got the whole ball of wax at one time," Dowell remarked. Though he did not elaborate on the situation, Dowell did say that he made some telephone calls later that week. He called "the two main men in the church" and asked to meet them for dinner. Then, in the course of their meeting, Dowell laid out a proposal: "I don't know whether you're interested at all or not, but I'm interested if you would like for me to do it. I'm not pastoring now, and I'm interested in taking that church as pastor and getting it on a good solid foundation where it'll go."[23] The men accepted Dowell's offer.

In April 1989, then, Dowell and his wife stepped out of retirement and began their ninth and final pastorate. Both of the men that Dowell originally met with eventually left the congregation, Dowell said. "They didn't leave bucking the church," he explained. "They just said we feel it would be better if we'd get out. I tried to talk them out of it, but they insisted that's what the Lord wanted them to do, so I let them go." And according to Dowell, those departures proved a blessing in disguise. The men "had been a hindrance in the church," Dowell claimed, "and I didn't know anything about it."[24]

After those former members were gone, however, Ozark Baptist Temple began to thrive. Though Dowell would turn seventy-five years old just three months after taking this church, he still managed to cast a vision that got results. He took out a weekly ad for his church in the local newspaper. He also started up a fifteen-minute Saturday morning radio broadcast on KWFC. And within a few months, Ozark Baptist Temple's attendances grew from seven to seventy.

And Dowell's vibrant leadership was bringing to this church, not just greater numbers, but also purpose and vitality. During his first summer as pastor, Dowell left town to fulfill a speaking engagement at the Lighthouse Children's Home in Kosciusko, Mississippi, and when he returned, he presented his church with a new goal. He wanted to raise two hundred dollars to help the children's home purchase a dishwashing machine. The reenergized church quickly got on board.

Dowell and his wife were personally invigorated by these efforts as well. Nola was happy to have her husband home again, and Dowell was happy to have regular preaching opportunities. He further enjoyed having his wife back by his side in the ministry. Though Nola no longer enjoyed traveling long distances, she happily engaged in the activities of this local church. On at least one occasion, she accompanied her husband to the parking lot of an Ozark shopping center to place church advertisements on the windshields of parked cars. Then in August 1989, she served as part of a team of carpet movers. Church member June Cox had secured a large rug for Dowell's church office, and Nola and her husband showed up to assist Cox in unloading it. "We met her at the church," Nola recalled in some of her personal notes, "and the 3 of us labored hard to bring it in at the front door of church. . . ." Unfortunately, the effort was not without its mishaps. "[E]nded up breaking glass in the front door," Nola reported.[25]

But even in the face of such troubles, the Dowells delighted in this new ministry, sometimes at the expense of their own health. Dowell and his wife celebrated their fifty-fifth wedding anniversary in September of that year, and their new congregation surprised them with an anniversary cake. Regrettably, Nola missed the surprise. She and June Cox had staffed the church nursery that morning, and Nola suffered a flare-up of angina the rest of the day. She was soon back on her feet, though, and according to her personal notes, she was down at the church meeting a piano tuner later that same month. The church's piano needed servicing, and Nola wanted everything to be in order for an upcoming revival meeting.[26]

Dowell too was taking great pleasure in these labors—and in seeing people respond to his preaching. In January 1990, Nola sent a letter to one of Dowell's nieces relating some of the recent news. "Last Sunday we had 81 in attendance," Nola wrote. "We now have 7 waiting baptism. So God has really blessed."[27] Similar blessings continued into the spring. The Dowells' first anniversary at Ozark came in April 1990, and to mark the day, Dowell engaged Earl Smith to come and minister in music. Governor Ashcroft acknowledged the occasion with a letter. "As Governor, it is my pleasure to extend congratulations to you as you celebrate your first anniversary as pastor of the Ozark Baptist Temple," Ashcroft wrote. "I commend you for your devotion in sharing Christ's love."[28] For that anniversary service, Dowell pushed to have an attendance of one hundred and seven—exactly one hundred more than the attendance at his first service. On special days, Ozark Baptist Temple was now seeing such attendances.

One family that was added to the church while Dowell was there went by the name of Neal. The Neal clan included Mr. and Mrs. Jim Neal, their son Terry and his wife, and a young grandson. Dowell quickly tapped Terry to be the church's song leader. But soon afterward, Dowell began to see greater potential in this young ministry partner.

From the start, Dowell had intended to work himself out of a job. He considered himself "a missionary out of Baptist Temple," and his plan all along had been to build up the Ozark Baptist Temple and then to hand it over to a younger leader.[29] Dowell was beginning to think that Terry Neal might be that leader. To seek God's will in the matter, Dowell and his wife took the Neals to dinner. But Dowell said he had second thoughts about stating what was on his heart after he and the others got seated at the restaurant. Dowell was not sure if he should discuss such a subject in front of the Neals' young son. Dowell instead decided to write his question on a napkin and to hand it across the table: "Would you be interested in taking the Ozark Baptist Temple?" Seeing the message, Neal paused momentarily. Then the young man came back with an answer. He told Dowell, "Yes. If God leads in it and that's what you want, I would be interested in the church."[30]

After that dinner, Dowell led the Ozark Baptist Temple in a smooth transition. Terry Neal became the new pastor, and Dowell and his wife returned to their retirement. Dowell was quite pleased with the handoff. "The church is doing real well under his leadership," Dowell said of Neal in 1992.[31] And those good reports continued for years to come. Although other pastors eventually stepped in, the Ozark Baptist Temple had been saved from closure. Indeed, this congregation outlived both Dowell and his wife. The torch had been successfully passed.

Successful transitions were important to Dowell. And he did all that he could to fan the flames of those who were coming after him. Dowell's oldest granddaughter, Karen Carreiro, recalled sitting with Dowell in a McDonald's restaurant in Ottumwa, Iowa, when her two boys were young. Karen said she had been "reading the Old Testament where oftentimes the aging fathers would bless the children. . . ." She wondered if such practices would be considered acceptable in modern times. Carreiro was hesitant to raise the subject, but when she finally did, Dowell responded enthusiastically. "[H]e took Ryan and Kyle right there in the McDonald's and held their hands and prayed a blessing on them that they would love and honor God," she said. Carreiro never forgot the moment. "That meant so much to me as a young mother," she stated.[32]

Dowell's life blessed many others as well. And in turn, Dowell was blessed to see his successors living out their faith. A good example occurred back at Baptist Temple. Shortly after Dowell handed the reins of that church over to his son, Dowell Jr. called his father telling him that the church was facing another financial crisis. Of course, financial needs were nothing new at Baptist Temple. Even though Dowell had completed paying off his bond program back in 1985, the church would not finish repaying its consolidation loan until 1996. And throughout those intervening years, Baptist Temple would remain financially strapped.

This latest situation was especially dire, however. Dowell Jr. had learned about it earlier that same day, when the church's bookkeeper came and announced that the church was unable to meet its weekly payroll. At first Dowell Jr. thought the woman was telling him there was a shortage in a particular church bank account. The church had several accounts, and payroll represented but one of these. The church's mission fund, a different account, normally maintained a balance of about thirty thousand dollars.

Yet Dowell Jr. had misunderstood. "We had no money at all," he recalled.[33] Without Dowell Jr.'s knowledge, the bookkeeper had used even the missions money to pay some of the church's obligations. Every account had been depleted. To say the least,

Dowell Jr. was alarmed by the news. This shortfall would affect more than the church's staff. It would also affect the staff and faculty of Baptist Temple's large daycare and private school, Christian Schools of Springfield. And many of those employees could ill afford to have their paychecks delayed. "I felt the whole thing would quickly snowball," Dowell Jr. said, "and the church would go under and drag the Christian school down with it since it was dependent upon the church financially."[34]

Like his father, however, Dowell Jr. had seen the hand of God work in this congregation many times before. The memory of Clarence Wheeler's visit to the church in the mid-1980s was still fresh in Dowell Jr.'s mind. Wheeler was the owner of a local grocery chain, Consumer's Market. He had attended Baptist Temple just one time, but on that first visit he slipped into the offering a check for twenty-five thousand dollars. The money had come "at a time the church was in great peril financially," Dowell Jr. recalled.[35] So God had used Wheeler to meet the need.

A motto oft-cited by the elder Dowell during those difficult years was this: "Ask God, and tell the people." Dowell Sr. maintained that, since the work was the Lord's, the Lord could be trusted to provide for it. Thus, whenever a special need arose, Dowell presented it first to God, and then to God's people.

Dowell Jr. took a similar approach when this payroll crisis arose. He alerted his associate, Bob Pentecost, along with the chairman of his deacon board, Gary Longstaff. He also contacted his father. And these four men met in Dowell Jr.'s office to lift up their special need before God. According to Longstaff, the prayer meeting began about two o'clock. They knelt around a glass table in Dowell Jr.'s office, and each of them called out to God on behalf of the church. Dowell Jr. recalled the tears that were shed as the men "pleaded with God to save [their] church."[36] But those tears were eventually replaced by something else. Longstaff remembered the perfect peace that settled over that room as the elder Dowell finished his prayer. "I have never felt the assurance of God's provision like I did that day," Longstaff said.[37]

The next day Longstaff received a telephone call from Dowell Jr. The conversation began with Dowell Jr. asking, "Guess what?" Longstaff's reply was "How much was it for?" Dowell Jr. then related the details about God's latest miracle. An elderly gentleman in the church, Mr. Harvey, had lost his wife about four months earlier. The life insurance check had just arrived, and Harvey had used his windfall to present a special offering to the church. Harvey's five-thousand-dollar check was delivered to the church within twenty-four hours of Dowell Jr.'s prayer meeting. And further investigation revealed that Harvey had written that check the same hour that the four men were kneeling in Dowell Jr.'s office. Dowell Jr. and his men could not help but marvel at the timing of it all. Longstaff described the experience as "life changing."[38]

For the elder Dowell, of course, the most satisfying part of this miracle may not have been the money or the timing. Instead, it may have been the recipients. Men who, for so many years, had watched Dowell's generation bask in heavenly miracles were now experiencing those miracles in their own lives and ministries.

Dowell was seeing the same thing within the greater body of the BBFI. Leland Kennedy's 1994 Global Fellowship Meeting raised more than $1.1 million for BBC, and when Kennedy wrote up his report about that meeting, he titled the article "God Still Performs Miracles."[39] The dollars raised in Kennedy's meeting told only part of the story, however. Over six hundred churches participated in Kennedy's record-setting offering, and those congregations represented but a fraction of the BBFI's ongoing efforts worldwide. Around the globe, churches were being built, colleges were being sustained, and lives were being changed. And though all of it had started with just a handful of preachers, it was evident that the torch had been passed.

Dowell must certainly have been mindful of this reality as he viewed the closing candle lighting ceremony at that Global Fellowship Meeting. For that ceremony, approximately two hundred international guests and about two hundred more American missionaries gathered near the front of the W. E. Dowell Fieldhouse. According to *Tribune* contributor Mike Randall, their candles symbolized "a commitment to continue carrying the light to the uttermost part of the world."[40] Dowell knew better than anyone that such an effort would never be easy. Still, it must have thrilled him to see that his torch had been taken up. More satisfying still was the knowledge that its light was shining brighter than ever before.

Chapter 43: *The Brush Arbor*

Children dashed about the tree-lined yard, their youthful limbs flailing in and out of the sun's rays and casting lively shadows over the freshly mowed grass. Like the daylight, summer was nearing an end, but that end had not yet come. There was still an ample supply of summer color and music—and life—for everyone to drink in. Even church folk, seated in the nearby shade, could imbibe such a cocktail. And they did. The taste of it all was pure joy.

Sowing in the morning,
Sowing seeds of kindness,
Sowing in the noontide
And the dewy eve—

Two aged singers—Bill and Nola Dowell—stood harmonizing at a microphone in front of a low platform. Bill was eighty-seven. Nola was almost eighty-nine. Though this was an outdoor service, the Dowells were attired only slightly less formally than they would have been on any other Sunday. He had shed his tie and jacket. She, though decked in a typical print dress, had added to her ensemble a bulky pair of shades that covered her regular eyeglasses. Such overblown eye gear could not have gone unnoticed under any circumstances, but these dark plastic sunglasses were especially conspicuous next to Nola's crown of white hair.

Waiting for the harvest,
And the time of reaping,
We shall come rejoicing,
Bringing in the sheaves.

Just behind these singers was a structure that had been fashioned to resemble the old brush arbors of yesteryear. Instead of actual brush, sheets of lattice had been stretched across the wooden posts, forming a kind of roof. The sight of the structure must surely have carried the Dowells back to the brush arbor revival meetings that they had attended as youngsters. Perhaps it was those memories that added such gusto to their singing.

Bringing in the sheaves,
Bringing in the sheaves,
We shall come rejoicing,

Bringing in the sheaves.

This was August 19, 2001, Baptist Temple's forty-fourth church anniversary. Dowell Jr. had dubbed the event Harvest Sunday, and hay bales and scarecrows were the order of the day. In keeping with the old-timey theme, many in the congregation traded in their usual suits and dresses for overalls and bonnets. The church carried on its morning worship activities in its regular church building, but all of its afternoon activities occurred out of doors on a vacant part of the church's property.

A good time was had by all, as the saying goes. The dunking booth was a big hit with the children, and a "tractor" race entertained the adults. This latter contest did not involve any actual tractors, of course. Instead, blindfolded wives were tasked with driving a riding lawnmower around a special course. Meanwhile their husbands were tapped to sit in a wagon hitched to the back of that mower and to spout off driving directions: Turn!—Go straight!—Other way!

Dowell and his wife had been lawn-chair spectators for most of those activities. At their age they needed to stay in the shade, shielded from the brightness of the sun. They also needed to conserve their strength for the late afternoon program. Nola was scheduled to sing "Bringing in the Sheaves" with her grandson and his wife, Steve and Robin. Her husband was slated to preach.

The duet that the Dowells sang that day had never been a part of any formal agenda. It was more of a command performance. When Nola's trio finished their song, Steve spoke into the microphone and told the audience that his granddad had been a behind-the-scenes participant in the group's rehearsals. "Pretty much told us what to do," the grandson joked.[1] Steve then invited his grandparents to sing an extra verse of "Bringing in the Sheaves" as an impromptu duet. Fortunately, the Dowells obliged.

Bringing in the sheaves,
Bringing in the sheaves,
We shall come rejoicing,
Bringing in the sheaves.

The years had weakened Dowell's voice somewhat, but on that day he sounded remarkably strong. Nola, too, gave a respectable performance. It was clear that she still had a good ear for alto harmony. Yet it was the pairing of these voices that made the moment so special. The singers' blend, though far from perfect, was somehow—right. The Dowells were just days away from their sixty-seventh wedding anniversary, and no listener could miss the fact that this couple had indeed become "one flesh."[2] Though the Dowells' coexistence could not always be called blissful, their marriage never ceased to be loving. Love "[b]eareth all things," the Apostle Paul explains.[3] The Dowells now spent virtually all of their time together, and between health crises and personal foibles, they offered each other plenty to bear, though they did so happily.

Nola, for instance, had little patience for any kind of television. Even so, she sat next to her husband night after night as he lounged in front of the latest episodes of *Who Wants to Be a Millionaire?* When Regis Philbin was on the air, Dowell was careful to tune in, so Nola too became a regular viewer. Nola kept a laminated placemat on a lampstand that stood between the recliners in their living room. A map of the United

States was printed on one side of that placemat, and she referred to this map during TV news and weather reports to help her visualize the places being discussed. But she also had another use for it. When it was not being employed as a weather map, it stood upright against the lamp, serving as a partition between her and her husband. Nola found the incessant drumming of Dowell's fingertips an insufferable distraction, and since her nagging had failed to curb Dowell of the habit, she devised this alternative as a means of bearing the burden.

In a similar way, Dowell learned to bear his wife's quirks. And they were many. In fact, within the Dowell family, Nola's idiosyncrasies were somewhat legendary. Whenever Nola's daughter-in-law held a garage sale, for example, it was a foregone conclusion that some of Joan's discarded property would make its way back to Nola's house. Indeed, that was how Nola had acquired an eight-track tape player back in the early 1990s. A fifth wheel might have been added to her automobile with greater purpose, but there was no point in trying to convince Nola of that. Nola felt duty-bound to preserve items that were cast off by others. She was not the extreme kind of hoarder that is sometimes depicted in news reports, but her household did accumulate its fair share of clutter. She was particularly fond of reusing rubbish. She retained empty medicine bottles so that she could turn them into storage containers. She also cut off the elastic from old pairs of nylon hosiery. These she used as giant rubber bands. Most of what Nola saved was never used by her or anyone else, of course. Instead it was packed away in trash bags or empty shoe boxes and piled atop kindred items within the many closets and store rooms of the Dowells' four-bedroom home.

Nola's other quirks included her insistence that she be called *Grandmother* by her grandchildren, never *Granny* or *Grandma*. This was not in any way indicative of a cold or formal relationship with her grandchildren. After all, these were the same youngsters whom Nola had once hired to pluck away her gray hairs at a wage of a penny per hair. Nola's grandchildren found her company delightful, and her peculiarities endeared her to them all the more. But to them, she was always *Grandmother*.

Nola's grandchildren chuckled as they studied their grandmother's kitchen. She stored potato chips in the freezer, transferred milk from plastic jugs to glass bottles, refrigerated leftover coffee for later consumption, and insisted that the juice from a can of green beans was too nutritious a drink to be discarded. All of her family members learned to cooperate with such oddities, if for no other reason than to keep the peace. Even when the family meals took place at Joan's house, the kitchen staff understood that it was their job to preclude any of Nola's lectures ("[Y]ou didn't throw away the green bean juice, did you?!?!?!"). For this reason, Nola's family either sent the juice home with her in a jar, or else–heaven help them–they poured the liquid out "behind the scenes," hoping that Nola would forget to ask about it this time.[4]

Meal experiences with Nola always landed somewhere between exasperating and entertaining. Nola was the family photographer, and at holiday meals, family members knew to expect a spate of obligatory snapshots before any food could be passed. The same was true whenever the Dowells ate at a restaurant, though this latter situation proved more worrisome for the rest of the family. If the people dining next to Nola's table were preventing her from getting a good snapshot, she had no qualms asking them to get up from their meal and to step out of the way.

This was typical Nola. Her brash picture-taking could even rear its head at funerals. Nola's daughter-in-law Sharon recalled the relief that she felt when, after the death of her daughter Lynda, Nola honored her wishes not to have Lynda's body photographed as it lay in the casket. This subject had come up, of course, because Nola had asked.[5]

Dowell's wife had always been a bit of a handful, but she became increasingly demanding and outspoken as she aged. Dowell once apologized to a tax preparer for her overbearing behavior. "She was okay the first seventy-five years of her life," Dowell explained.[6] Nola had been more than okay, of course. Her oldest son remembered her as "a loving, helpful, companion to Dad involved in the choir, quartets, and other things at church and a wonderful, generous Mom who loved and cared for her husband and children." Dowell Jr. went on to say, "She was a clear thinking and practical woman who enjoyed life and was full of fun. Her grandchildren loved to be around her. She was generous and kind and always provoked laughter and joy to those about her."[7] All of that was true.

Yet aging affected Nola. She became increasingly troubled by dementia. Dowell Jr. recalled his father's expression for the illness: "the disease in her head." It created a "personality change" in her, Dowell Jr. said, and "made her more difficult to deal with." Though she was still loving toward those around her, her moments of frustration and impatience grew more severe, and at times she could be quite headstrong.

To those who did not know her, Dowell's wife could seem overbearing and rude. Fortunately, most strangers managed to take her cheekiness in stride. Healthcare providers seemed especially well versed in grappling with the Nolas of this world. Dowell laughed when he recalled a nurse that Nola encountered during one of her hospital stays. Nola groused at the nurse, saying, "What do you do with all the blood you take?" Then, without cracking a smile, the nurse looked back and answered, "We sell it."[8]

Joan recalled an episode that occurred at one of Dowell's doctor visits. After Dowell's health began to fail, Nola and Joan commonly accompanied Dowell back to the examination room for his appointments. Unfortunately, Nola was woefully impatient once they arrived. Instead of sitting in the examination room to wait, she stood outside the door or even wandered the hallway. This was her not-so-subtle way of reminding caregivers that her husband was now waiting to be served. On one occasion, however, Nola hurried back to the examination room. She had spotted a rather disturbing sign at the nurse's station. It read, "Notice: If you are grouchy, you will be charged an extra $15.00."[9] Thereafter Nola decided it would be best to wait with her husband.

Nola could be both charming and consternating, but there was no mistaking the fact that she was the love of Dowell's life. When Dowell and his wife were at home alone, they regularly engaged in their favorite domino game, Forty-Two. And since Forty-Two requires two sets of players, Nola worked out a system whereby she and Dowell could play for both teams. They each alternated between two hands of dominoes. On the scorecards for these games, Nola listed the two teams as "Bill and Nola" and

"Stephen and David" (the names of Bill Jr.'s two sons), and whenever the Dowells saw these ghost players at church, they updated them on how well they had been playing during their recent matches.

Such sweetness and joy was a regular part of the Dowells' marriage, but there was far more to this relationship than fun and games. The Dowells shared a spiritual connection. Their daughter Janet recalled a bedtime ritual that she observed whenever she came to visit them. Each night after the lights went out, the Dowells sang some of their favorite hymns as they lay in bed.[10]

Dowell and his wife also prayed together, and they spoke often of the scriptures. During one such conversation, Nola reacted to some of the reading that she had been doing in her Bible. "If you'd gone through what Paul went through," she was heard saying to her husband, "you'd about give up, wouldn't you?" Dowell answered back, "No. I have the same God he did."[11]

Nola could not argue with that. For she too shared a relationship with that God. In fact, it seems safe to say that Nola's faith was as deep as her husband's. She outlived Dowell by more than two and half years, and during that time, she steadied herself in God's promises.[12] Her husband was not gone. He had simply gone ahead. "[A]bsent from the body" means "present with the Lord," the Scriptures assure.[13] Nola kept a firm grasp on such promises as she awaited her own departure from this earth. And even as her health faded during her final years, her faith never did. With the Apostle Paul, Nola held that "the sufferings of this present time are not worthy to be compared with the glory which shall be revealed in us."[14]

Isn't this a great experience?[15]

Dowell was now speaking from the brush arbor platform. And he was clearly enjoying himself. His impromptu duet with his wife had won cheers from the audience, and a twinkle had now entered his receding eyes. He was especially glad for the opportunity to preach. In fact, when Dowell Jr. had extended to him the invitation, Dowell had replied, "I told Nola the other day, 'I wish I had somewhere to preach.'"[16]

As it happened, this would be Dowell's final sermon. Already his body was weakening. Indeed, Dowell had to rest one of his hands against a post of the brush arbor structure just to remain standing during his message. He explained that he had awoken that morning with a bit of dizziness and needed the extra support to keep steady on his feet.

During his final decade of life, Dowell learned to set aside health challenges and to just carry on. He wrote to his sister Ruth in 1993, saying, "Nola and I are both ill most of the time." To this, he added, "We do attend church regularly."[17] That seeming contradiction became the new norm for the Dowells in their closing years. Although they rarely felt good, they tried to make the best of it, remaining hopeful that things would soon improve. "Nola and I are not feeling very well," Dowell wrote on another occasion. "We are expecting greater things in the future, with God's help."[18]

Some of Dowell's most serious health concerns began near the end of 1991. He had been experiencing some weakness and confusion, but then on top of that, he contracted pneumonia and had to be hospitalized. While there, doctors discovered that Dowell's blood sugar level was nearly 800 milligrams per deciliter. Since 70 to 140 milligrams is the normal range, Dowell's condition was considered quite serious.[19] Dowell was immediately given a new diet, and he was even taught to inject himself with insulin, though happily, he was later able to wean himself of those injections and to control his sugar levels through diet alone.

But Dowell remained unwell even after he recovered from this initial crisis. He found it difficult to put his symptoms into words, but he often used the phrase "nervous nausea" to explain what he was experiencing. Doctors and family members puzzled over what was causing it. By the summer of 1992, Dowell had weakened to the point that he was barely able to walk. This was when family members decided to take him to Mayo Clinic in Rochester, Minnesota, for evaluation.

Dowell was accompanied on that trip by Nola, Janet, and Joan. During the first week of his evaluation, all four of them stayed together at a hotel. But after that, Dowell was admitted into the hospital for treatment. He remained there for the next four weeks. Physicians believed that much of Dowell's problem was depression, though a definitive diagnosis was never reached. To try to help him, physicians explored the usual adjustments to medications. They also prescribed a variety of activities for Dowell to participate in—crafts, games, exercises, picnics—anything that might pique his interest. Dowell cooperated with all of it, but he benefitted little. He referred to the craft projects as "little women's work," and it was clear that he considered the activities demeaning.[20]

Eventually doctors proposed another solution, one that Nola and the rest of the family found alarming. The doctors wanted to give Dowell shock treatments. The family was assured that these treatments were not the agonizing, mind-altering jolts sometimes depicted in old Hollywood films. Instead, Dowell would receive electrical stimulation under anesthesia. There would be no pain whatsoever, and after six to eight treatments, Dowell stood a good chance of seeing a marked improvement in his condition. In fact, the doctors said that ninety-seven percent of the patients who received such treatments were helped by them.

As it turned out, Dowell's case fell outside of that ninety-seventh percentile. Though Dowell consented to undergo the treatments, his condition saw little improvement. And after five weeks in Rochester, Dowell and his family members finally returned to Springfield. Dowell had regained a bit of his strength, but the nervous nausea never left him.

There was, however, one important benefit that came from Dowell's visit to Mayo. During his time there, he was alerted to a serious health concern. Doctors had discovered polyps in his colon. The polyps were widespread, Dowell was told, and some of them were cancerous. So soon after he returned to Springfield, Dowell underwent surgery to have eighty percent of his colon removed. Fortunately, this took care of the problem, and Dowell faced no further battles with cancer.[21]

But Dowell did battle many other physical ailments. He had angioplasty in 1996, for instance, and thereafter he wore a pacemaker. During all such battles, Dowell's sustainer was the Great Physician. Dowell was incapable of seeing it any other way. When young admirers walked up to him and asked him to sign the pages of their Bibles,

Dowell often added beneath his signature the reference for Jeremiah 33:3. In that verse the Lord says, "Call unto me, and I will answer thee, and shew thee great and mighty things, which thou knowest not." Dowell made regular use of doctors, but it was promises such as this that he clung to during times of crisis.

To supplement his own prayers, Dowell routinely summoned Earl Smith to pray over him when he was ill. These men lived less than a mile apart, yet they seldom saw each other anymore. On the few occasions when they did get together, it was because Smith had stopped by with some garden tomatoes or simply to say hello. On one occasion, Smith took Dowell out for a drive around Springfield. They drove for about an hour, Smith said. Another time, Smith brought Dowell a copy of a new recording that he had made. As Smith and the Dowells sat in the living room listening to it play, they wept, relishing old times.[22]

But Smith said Dowell especially wanted to see him whenever he was in the hospital. During Dowell's younger years, Smith's prayers had yielded remarkable results, so from that time forward, Dowell made it a practice to contact Smith whenever he faced a serious illness. On one occasion, as Smith was entering the hospital room, Dowell looked up at him and said, "You're just like a ray of sunshine."[23]

All such sunshine was fading now. Dowell told the audience that was sitting in lawn chairs:

I'm here to preach for you today, and I'm not going to waste any of the time.

Dowell's final sermon lasted a mere six minutes, perhaps a record for him. But Dowell made the most of the time he had.

I want to tell you and emphasize to you one of the most important things in all of the word of God. And aren't you glad we have this book, this blessed old book that has stood the test through time and through all eternity, and will continue to stand the test until Jesus comes back again and on through eternity?

To emphasize his point, Dowell's frail left hand waved his Bible in the air. Dowell never read from the Bible that day. Nor did he read from any notes. His eyes had grown too dim. Instead, Dowell relied upon his memory, reciting even the words of his scriptural text. That text was taken from Jeremiah 8: "The harvest is past, the summer is ended, and we are not saved."[24]

Dowell followed up that text by saying, "I think those are some of the most serious words that any person or persons could speak." Dowell then delivered to his audience a warning. He first addressed those who had "waited and waited" to accept Christ, cautioning them that they were quickly running out of time. He then turned his attention to Christians, reminding them that it was their responsibility to reach lost friends and loved ones with the gospel. This part of the message was laced with gravitas. "I'm not going to apologize for mentioning the fact that there is a terrible Hell," Dowell said. Then he drove home his point:

> *And every man and woman who does not accept Jesus Christ and His shed blood for their salvation, every one of them will be plunged into Hell without hope and without mercy, and you stand and look on and see their destiny, and say, "I'm to*

blame. I should have witnessed to these people. I am responsible for these people, but the summer is ended, the harvest is past, and they're not saved."

Dowell's message was heartfelt. He believed in Hell, and he believed lost people will spend all eternity there. By his own admission, Dowell was no prophecy expert. He told one audience, "I've studied prophecy for fifty years and if there was two books written— one on what I know and one on what I don't know—the one on what I don't know would be the biggest."[25] Still, wherever Dowell found clear scriptural teachings about the end times, he was bold in declaring them. And Dowell found no ambiguity in the Bible's teachings about a literal Hell.

Dowell also believed it was possible to escape that damnation. Dowell was firm in his belief that the church will be caught up, raptured away from the coming judgment. Christians will be protected from God's wrath just as Noah's family was protected from the flood. According to Dowell Jr., Dowell, in the early days of his ministry, had taught that even the church would experience the first half of the Tribulation, that terrible seven-year judgment that will bring an end to Satan's reign upon the earth. But further study changed Dowell's mind on this matter. Dowell found the words of 1 Thessalonians 5:9, where Paul writes, "For God hath not appointed us to wrath, but to obtain salvation by our Lord Jesus Christ." This and other scriptures helped to reshape Dowell's thinking. He abandoned the midtribulationist position and instead became a pretribulationist.[26]

Like other pretribulationists, Dowell believed that the next event on God's prophetic calendar will be the Rapture. And Dowell awaited that event expectantly. He told one church member that he hoped to be "standing beside the biggest cemetery in the world" on the day of the Rapture. He wanted a good view of the dead in Christ coming up to meet the Lord in the air.[27]

Cemeteries were never morbid places for Dowell. Indeed, he viewed death as a blessing. He borrowed one sermon title from Philippians 1:21, "To Die Is Gain." In the notes for that sermon, Dowell listed some of death's benefits. "We gain the loss of our labors," Dowell wrote. "We gain the loss of sickness, pain, and sorrow." "We gain entrance into Heaven, the perfect paradise of God."[28]

Dowell used his final sermon to try, one last time, to steer human souls away from God's wrath and toward those everlasting benefits. Then, at the end of his six-minute sermon, Dowell stepped down from under the brush arbor shelter. Like the Apostle Paul, he had finished his course.[29] In fact, less than three months after he had delivered that sermon, Dowell's fragile health took a turn for the worse, and he was hospitalized for three weeks. Nola celebrated her eighty-ninth birthday at the rehabilitation facility where her husband was convalescing.

Dowell was now growing weaker by the day, so in December 2001, doctors persuaded the family that he needed round-the-clock medical care. Dowell was admitted to the Maranatha Village, a Christian-operated nursing facility located about a mile and a half from the Dowells' home. Although Dowell's fading health made it appear that he would not live through the holidays, this turned out not to be the case. Indeed, Dowell mustered enough strength to spend both Christmas and Easter at Dowell Jr.'s home. In between those times, he lived at Maranatha, where he was comforted by family and friends. Jerry Falwell was one of those who telephoned. John Ashcroft made a few personal visits to Dowell's room. Ashcroft's mother was then living in that same facility, so he made a point to greet Dowell whenever he came to see his mother.

Earl Smith likewise made regular treks to visit Dowell. Smith himself was now suffering from Alzheimer's disease, but he was still well enough to bring in some recorded music. As the old friends listened to those beloved songs, they waved handkerchiefs and sang along.

Dowell likewise ministered to others during his time at Maranatha. Some of this occurred as visitors stopped by to see him. Dowell Jr. and his young associate, Heath Marion, periodically came to his room. On one of those occasions, Dowell referenced Acts 2:17 during their conversation, Marion recalled. Dowell said that he was "an old man praying that [Marion] would see great visions while [Dowell] dreamed great dreams for [him]." Reflecting on those words years later, Marion said, "I will never forget that moment."[30]

Former BBC Professor James Sewell met someone else whom Dowell impacted while he was living at Maranatha. Sewell said he met this woman as he was shopping one day at a Walmart. During the course of their conversation, the woman learned that Sewell was affiliated with BBC. "Is that where Dr. Dowell was president?" she asked. The woman then went on to explain that she had worked at Maranatha while Dowell was a patient there. She had accepted Christ as Savior, she said, as a result of Dowell's witness to her.[31]

If Dowell's strength had not failed him, he would have been content to continue such ministry. In the last few weeks before his death, he even spoke of attending the May Fellowship Meeting at BBC. But Dowell never made it to that meeting. Indeed, by April he was completely bedfast. When Shirley Hackler came to visit him, Dowell told her "I want to go see my master, Shirley. I'm tired."[32]

Dowell lost the strength to speak around the end of April. He was unable to converse with family members for several days. But then on Thursday, May 2, with some of his family gathered around him, Dowell spoke out "as clear as a bell," his son said. Dowell then told his family members, "I love you."[33]

Later that same evening, W. E. Dowell entered Heaven. His oldest son wrote an email to the extended family, saying, "Dad passed away tonight about 8:05 p.m. at the Maranatha Resthome [sic]. Mother and my wife and I were present when he died. He died suddenly and peacefully."[34] Springfield's *News-Leader* ran a front-page article two days later under the headline "W. E. Dowell, Noted Baptist Luminary, Dies." The article featured quotations from Jerry Falwell and from John Ashcroft. Falwell stated, "A might oak as fallen." Ashcroft called Dowell "a towering spiritual and moral presence in Springfield."[35]

On Monday, May 6, the Dowell family hosted a visitation for their patriarch in the fieldhouse bearing his name. Mourners lined up for four hours, and many poignant stories emerged as friends passed through to offer their condolences and to share their remembrances. No story was more moving than the one related by a woman who was unknown to the Dowell family. The woman said that she was now living in the Springfield area but that she had grown up in St. Louis. She explained that, during the 1950s, Dowell had preaching a revival in St. Louis. Her mother, who had heard Dowell preach in Springfield, contacted the sponsoring church on a whim. She wanted to invite Dowell to their home for dinner.

To the family's surprise, the visiting evangelist accepted their invitation. Then at dinner, Dowell asked the man of the house about his spiritual condition. This man had never been a church-goer, the daughter said, but on that day she heard him acknowledge to Dowell a personal relationship with Jesus Christ. It was the first time she had ever heard her father make such a declaration.

This woman went on to say that her father was a changed man after that encounter. Indeed, he began a faithful walk with God that lasted until his death in the 1960s. So decades later, when she heard that Dowell had passed away, the woman was moved to come and tell her story. She wanted to express her gratitude for that memorable visit and to let Dowell's family know that her life had been greatly affected by his.

On Tuesday, May 7, more than a thousand such admirers attended Dowell's funeral service. The service was held in that same fieldhouse, and Dowell's family sat on the front few rows. Dowell left behind not only his wife and children but also eight living grandchildren, twenty-two great-grandchildren, and three great-great-grandchildren. The Dowell grandchildren formed an ensemble that day, singing "At the Crossing" and "I Will Meet You in the Morning." Dowell's two sons and his son-in-law, Bernie Rodgers, were also part of the program. Bernie read the obituary, Clyde delivered the eulogy, and Bill Jr. preached the funeral sermon.

Additional tributes were presented throughout that morning. John Rawlings, the last remaining member of that inner circle of BBFI founders, spoke warmly of his dear friend. Mike Randall, President of BBC, also shared some thoughts. Then the President of the BBFI, Kenneth Gillming, added further remarks.

Dowell had once told an audience how he hoped he would be eulogized after his departure from the earth. He pictured people standing over his casket, and he said, "I hope they'll be able to come around, whether they liked me or whether they didn't like me—I hope they'll be able to say 'He stood fast for the faith.' I'd rather have that said about me than any other compliment. 'He did not compromise the truth of God. He declared it without apology!'"[36] All of those who spoke on Dowell's behalf that day seemed united in their affirmation of those words.

But perhaps a more telling eulogy than any of those is the one that was never presented at Dowell's funeral. Indeed, it was never intended as a eulogy at all, nor was it intended for public consumption. This eulogy came to Dowell in a letter back in 1967. Dowell was then pastoring in Jacksonville, Florida, and he was wrestling with G. B. Vick's invitation to move back to Springfield. Dowell's son, Dowell Jr., was pastoring in Tampa, Florida, at that time, and on a recent visit, father and son had discussed the proposed move. Dowell was quite torn by the matter, still trying to discern God's will, so

Dowell Jr., without trying to sway his father one way or the other, offered his own perspective.

After that conversation concluded, Dowell Jr. wondered if his impromptu remarks had been clear. To make sure, he sent his mother and dad a letter to follow up. "It makes me lonesome already to think that you may move back to Springfield," the son wrote, "but I guess that is life. And anyway I know you will not make such a move unless you feel God is clearly and without question leading you to do so. We do not question God's leadership." Dowell Jr. then launched into a fuller explanation of the point that he had tried to make a few days earlier:

> Dad, in our conversation Friday night I started a train of thought and I don't think I ever really finished what I started to say. We were talking about the unique position you hold in the eyes of the fellowship pastors as a whole. You quoted Dr. Vick as saying that "no one else in the world can do the job needing to be done in the B.B.F. but you." I agreed but then proceeded to analyze why this was true. The following was my line of thought:
>
> You have much wisdom, but you are not the only one having wisdom.
>
> You are a man of integrity, but you are not the only man of integrity.
>
> You have built a large church, but you are not the only man who has built a large church.
>
> You are an organizer, but others are too.
>
> You are diplomatic, but so are others.
>
> You are an outstanding preacher, yet not the only one.
>
> We could go on and speak of such things as a sense of fair play, self sacrificing spirit, courage and boldness, common sense and balance, a wealth of practical knowledge, unquestioning faith in God, good taste in judgment, a love for others, a willingness to do much more than your share of the work, a tenacious persistency, unlimited vision, enthusiasm, humility unfeigned, etc. Take any one of these excellent qualities and you will find it true of many preachers.
>
> The rare thing is to find all of these qualities existing at once in one man. And what is rarer still is that such a man possessed of all these qualities should have the public image of a man possessed of all these qualities. You are such a rare man whose public image matches your exceptional qualities. That is why you alone can do what needs to be done in our fellowship.[37]

Dowell kept that letter the rest of his life. It was meaningful to know that those close to him held him in such high regard, even in their private correspondence. Dowell cherished that love and respect. However, Dowell would have been the first to say that his righteousnesses were "as filthy rags."[38] Any good that he had accomplished in his life was accomplished by God's grace. And Dowell not only wanted others to see that grace; he wanted them to partake of it. If Dowell himself could have addressed the crowd that assembled for his funeral, he would have told them just that.

It also seems plausible that Dowell would have closed those remarks the same way that he had often closed his sermons—with the words of some beloved hymn. And while it is difficult to speculate which hymn he would have chosen, one possibility is the song found written in Dowell's 1949 Bible. Near the back cover of that Bible, Dowell scribbled the lyrics to a well-known chorus, one originally penned by hymn writer Julia H. Johnston:

> *Hallelujah, what a Saviour!*
> *Who can take a poor lost sinner,*
> *Lift him from the miry clay and set him free;*
> *I will ever tell the story,*
> *Shouting glory, glory, glory,*
> *Hallelujah! Jesus ransomed me.*[39]

Would Dowell would have chosen those lines as his departing words? Perhaps. Perhaps they are on his lips even today, as he continues to cry aloud, singing praises to God from his eternal home. Whatever the case, one thing is certain. Dowell has left the shade of the old brush arbor. His sheaves have been gathered, and he has come rejoicing. And forevermore he will bask in the light—the light of a bright and glorious Son.

Afterword

My grandfather concluded his sermons with an invitation to listeners, and it seems fitting to end a book about his life with a similar appeal. I know of no more fitting statement than the one that Dowell himself made in a 1965 sermon, "To Stand for Principles." I leave you with those words, dear reader, and urge you to let my grandfather's powerful voice be heard one last time. Perhaps its sound will prompt you, too, to see a spiritual need and to respond to the gospel message. Such a response is the most important thing you will ever do.

My grandfather said it this way:

> *I believe every word of the Bible. I believe there's a literal Heaven; I don't believe it's an imaginary Heaven; I believe it's a literal Heaven. I believe that its streets will be made out of pure gold as of transparent glass. I believe that its walls will be jasper and its gates will be pearl. I believe the River of Life shall go out from the throne of God and the Tree of Life bearing twelve manner of fruits yielding its fruit every season will be growing on the riverbanks. I believe that the saints of God robed in white raiment will walk up and down those golden streets and shout glory because of all that they've received by the wonderful Savior that has redeemed them from their sins. I believe it'll be a place where there'll be no sin, no sorrow, no funeral trains, no heartache, no war, no distress, no anxiety; it'll be a place of perfect peace and joy and everlasting happiness throughout the ceaseless ages of eternity.*
>
> *But in believing that I must of necessity believe there is a literal Hell. Not an imaginary Hell. But a literal Hell of fire and brimstone where every unbeliever and every wicked man and woman will be cast and will be tormented day and night forever and ever, that their existence will be eternal and that their torture and torment will be eternal because they rejected the only provision that God made through His son Jesus Christ. There's a Heaven to gain and a Hell to shun.*
>
> *I would not close this message without, from the very depths of my heart tonight, pointing every one of you to that Christ and to that cross and to that*

Heaven. Only the cross leads home. Only Christ can save. Only faith can pave the way to Heaven. Only believers who have genuinely repented of their sins and claimed by faith the Lord Jesus Christ as their personal Savior can ever hear the glad voice, "Well done. Enter into the joy of thy Lord." Those who reject Him must be forever banished from His presence. I offer Him to you tonight as a representative of Jesus Christ, as an ambassador of Jesus Christ, and plead for you in the name of our Lord Jesus to stand up as a true soldier of the cross and be counted and place your faith and trust in Him, stand for your convictions, uphold the Word of God, and refuse to compromise with that which is evil and wrong, and you'll have the blessings of God upon your life.[1]

Photo Gallery

(above) Albin, Lizzie, and Ernest Dowell

(below) Bill at age 16

(above) Gladys and Bill

(below) Normangee Panthers 1932-33

(above left)
Dowell and his
brown Bible

(above right)
Dowell in
La Habra,
c. 1938

(left) Bill
and Nola,
1947

(above) Dowell prepares for a radio broadcast at High Street Fundamental Baptist Church. Photo courtesy of the John E. Craig, Jr., family.

(below) Dowell and his airplane, c. 1945.

(above) High Street Baptist tent revival. Photo courtesy of the *Baptist Bible Tribune*.

(right) 1948 newspaper ad featuring Dowell and Earl Smith

(below) High Street Baptist river baptism

426 – *Cry Aloud, Spare Not*

(left) Dowell and Charley Dyer

(below) G. B. Vick and
J. Frank Norris (1 to r)

(below) Earl Smith

(below) John Rawlings, W. E. Dowell,
and R. O. Woodworth (1 to r). Photo
courtesy of the *Baptist Bible Tribune*.

(above) The Dowell family in 1952—
Clyde, Janet, Bill Jr., Nola, and Bill Sr. (l to r)

(above) Dowell in Egypt, 1958

(above) Dowell in
Taiwan, 1958

(right) Dedication of the
High Street Baptist
auditorium, 1950.
Photo courtesy of the
John E. Craig, Jr., family.

(above) Opening day of classes at Baptist Bible College, 1950. Photo courtesy of the John E. Craig, Jr., family.

(right) Baptist Bible College graduation, c. 1978. Photo courtesy of the *Baptist Bible Tribune.*

(below) Baptist Fundamentalism '84
Jerry Falwell, W. E. Dowell, and Ronald Reagan (l to r)
Photo by Les Schofer / Liberty University.

(above) Dowell receives honorary doctorate from Bob Jones Jr., 1967. Photo by Unusual Films, Bob Jones University, Greeneville, SC.

(right) Bernie Rodgers, Bill Dowell Jr., W. E. Dowell (l to r), and Stephen Dowell (fr.), 1969.

(above) Dowell speaks at Baptist Temple, c. 1985.

(below) Bill and Nola Dowell at Baptist Bible College, c. 1997. Photo courtesy of the *Baptist Bible Tribune*.

About the Author

Stephen E. Dowell is the grandson of W. E. Dowell. He teaches general studies courses at Baptist Bible College in Springfield, Missouri. Dowell is also a worship leader and Sunday school teacher at Springfield's Baptist Temple, and he has extensive experience as a dramatist. His dramatic works include The Bob Hughes Story and Donnelson's Dream. Dowell has been married to Robin since 1987. The Dowells have three children, Matthew, Nicole, and Isaac.

Selected Bibliography

Books

Bartlett, Billy Vick. *A History of Baptist Separatism*. Springfield: Baptist Bible Fellowship, 1972.

Brokaw, Tom. *The Greatest Generation*. New York: Random House, 1998.

Carpenter, Joel A., ed. *Inside History of First Baptist Church, Fort Worth, and Temple Baptist Church, Detroit: Life Story of Dr. J. Frank Norris*. Vol. 33, *Fundamentalism in American Religion 1880-1950*. New York: Garland, 1988.

Deal, Elmer, and Mike Randall. *Out of the Mouth of the Lion*. Vols. 1 and 2. N.p.: Elmer Deal, 2009.

Dowell, W. E. *The Birth Pangs of the Baptist Bible Fellowship, International*. Springfield: Baptist Bible College, 1977.

Dowell, W. E. *The Church: It's Meaning, Message and Method*. Springfield: Temple, 1980.

Dyer, Frederick H. *A Compendium of the War of the Rebellion*. Des Moines: Dyer Publishing, 1908. archive.org/stream/08697590.3359.emory.edu/08697590_3359#page/n171/mode/2up/search/litt le+rock.

Entzminger, Louis. *The J. Frank Norris I Have Known for 34 Years*. St. John: Larry Harrison, Christian Book Gallery, [c. 1947].

Falwell, Jerry. *Strength for the Journey*. New York: Simon and Schuster, 1987.

Falwell, Macel, and Melanie Hemry. *Jerry Falwell: His Life and Legacy*. New York: Simon, 2008.

Goldman, Curtis. *50 Goldman Years*. N.p.: n.p., 2000.

Hankins, Barry. *God's Rascal: J. Frank Norris and the Beginnings of Southern Fundamentalism*. Lexington: UP of Kentucky, 1996.

Kutilek, Doug. *J. Frank Norris and His Heirs: The Bible Translation Controversy*. Pasadena: Pilgrim, 1999.

Melton, J. H. *The Clergyman of the Century*. Vol. 1. Springfield: Fellowship, 1976.

Phillips, Arthur Edward. *Natural Drills in Expression*. Chicago: Newton, 1927.

Randall, Mike. *G. B. Vick*. n.p.: Michael Anthony Randall, 1987.

Ritchie, Homer G. *The Life and Legend of J. Frank Norris: The Fighting Parson*. Fort Worth: Homer G. Ritchie, 1991.

Stokes, David. *Apparent Danger: The Pastor of America's First Megachurch and the Texas Murder Trial of the Decade in the 1920s*. Minneapolis: Bascom Hill, 2010.

Towns, Elmer L. *The Ten Largest Sunday Schools: And What Makes Them Grow*. Grand Rapids: Baker, 1970. elmertowns.com/wp-content/uploads/2013/10/10_Largest_SSETowns.pdf.

Dowell Sermon Recordings

"A Mother's Influence." Baptist Temple, Springfield, 12 May 1985.

"A Mother's Love." Baptist Temple, Springfield, 9 May 1982.

"A Soul-Destroying Evil." Baptist Temple, Springfield, 15 Jan. 1978.
"A Strange Cure for the Sting of Death." Baptist Temple, Springfield, 7 Feb. 1982.
"Apostasy." Baptist Temple, Springfield, 27 July 1977.
"Assurance." Baptist Temple, Springfield, 11 Aug. 1985.
"Baptism." Baptist Temple, Springfield, 25 Aug. 1985.
"Be Thankful." Baptist Temple, Springfield, 25 Nov. 1981.
"Bloody Hands." Baptist Temple, Springfield, 2 Oct. 1977.
"Born Again." Baptist Temple, Springfield, 23 Apr. 1978.
"Come Now, Let Us Reason." Baptist Temple, Springfield, 26 Sept. 1976.
"Dangerous Mistakes." Baptist Temple, Springfield, 7 Sept. 1986.
"Divine Invitation." Baptist Temple, Springfield, 13 July 1986.
"Give Me This Mountain." Baptist Temple, Springfield, 1976.
"Give Me This Mountain." Baptist Temple, Springfield, c. 1976.
"Harvest Sunday," Baptist Temple, Springfield, 19 Aug. 2001.
"How Important Is the Resurrection?" Baptist Temple, Springfield, 19 Apr. 1987.
"Israel: God's Miracle Nation." Baptist Temple, Springfield, 28 Feb. 1982.
"Jesus Christ Revealed." Baptist Temple, Springfield, 1 Aug. 1982.
"Jesus Christ Revealed." Baptist Temple, Springfield, 1 Aug. 1982.
"Justification Comes from God." Baptist Temple, Springfield, 13 Mar. 1983.
"Looking Down from the Cross." Baptist Temple, Springfield, 13 Apr. 1986.
"Love Is the Fulfillment of the Law." Baptist Temple, Springfield, 2 Nov. 1986.
"Morality and City Government." Baptist Temple, Springfield, 14 Aug. 1977.
"Politics and Religious Freedom." Baptist Temple, Springfield, n.d.
"Quit Ye Like Men." Baptist Temple, Springfield, 7 July 1985.
"Revive Us Again." Baptist Temple, Springfield, 29 Aug. 1976.
"Set Your Affections." Baptist Temple, Springfield, 30 Nov. 1977.
"Tears." Baptist Temple, Springfield, 2 Feb. 1976.
"The Betrayal of Jesus." Baptist Temple, Springfield, 22 Feb. 1976.
"The Book of All Books." Baptist Temple, Springfield, 23 Jan. 1983.
"The Elder Brother." Baptist Temple, Springfield, 17 Jan. 1982.
"The Fatal Mistake of Feminists." Baptist Temple, Springfield, 4 Dec. 1977.
"The Fields Are White Already unto Harvest." Baptist Temple, Springfield, 18 July 1982.
"The Last Days." Baptist Temple, Springfield, 3 Aug. 1980.
"The Ministry of the Holy Spirit." Baptist Temple, Springfield, 24 Aug. 1977.
"The Power of the Word of God." Baptist Temple, Springfield, 12 Oct. 1986.
"The Struggle for Freedom." Baptist Temple, Springfield, 4 Oct. 1981.
"The Substitutionary Atonement of Jesus Christ." Tabernacle Baptist Church, Farmington, c. 1984.
"Things Christ Left Behind." Baptist Temple, Springfield, 2 Jan. 1983.
"Twentieth Anniversary." Baptist Temple, Springfield, 28 Aug. 1977.
"We Need God's Power." Baptist Temple, Springfield, n.d.
"What Is a Friend?" Baptist Temple, Springfield, 10 Nov. 1985.
"What Is a Good Mother?" Baptist Temple, Springfield, 11 May 1986.
"What Is Expected of the Church This Year?" Baptist Temple, Springfield, 4 Jan. 1976.
"What Think Ye of Christ?" Baptist Temple, Springfield, 22 June 1986.
"When Love Is the Motive." Baptist Temple, Springfield, 10 Aug. 1986.
"Why God Permits His People to Suffer." Baptist Temple, Springfield, 20 June 1982.
"Wisdom Excelleth Folly." Baptist Temple, Springfield, 3 Mar. 1985.

Dowell Sermon Transcripts

"Attitude of the Heart Transplant." 21 Jan. 1968.
"Battle of Armageddon." [1968].

"Doing Something about It." N.d.
"Doing Something about It." N.d.
"God's Marching Orders." N.d.
"Lewd Literature in Springfield." 22 Feb. 1953.
"Revival Sermon." N.d.
"The Bible Preacher in a Day of Peril." N.d.
"The Communist Infiltration of the Church." N.d.
"The Revised Standard Version." 5 Oct. 1952.
"The Trump of God." N.d.
"To Stand for Principles." Feb. 1965.

Periodicals

Baptist Bible Tribune
Baptist Preacher
BBC Banner
Daily News [Springfield]
Florida Times-Union [Jacksonville]
Fundamentalist
Guide to Light [High Street Fundamental Baptist Church]
New York Times
News-Leader [Springfield]
Saturday News and Leader [Springfield]
Soul Winner [High Street Fundamental Baptist Church]
Springfield Daily News
Springfield Leader and Press
Springfield News and Leader
Springfield! Magazine
Star-Telegram [Fort Worth]
Sunday News and Leader [Springfield]
Sword of the Lord
USA Today

Notes

Abbreviations

BBT	*Baptist Bible Tribune*
BDJ	Bill Dowell Jr.
BP	*The Birth Pangs of the Baptist Bible Fellowship* by W. E. Dowell
BT	Baptist Temple, Springfield, MO.
BVB	Billy Vick Bartlett
DFP	Dowell Family Papers
DN	*Daily News* [Springfield]
ES	Earl Smith
FDML	*Fundamentalist*
GBV	G. Beauchamp Vick
IOH	"Oral Memoirs of George Beauchamp Vick," Institute of Oral History, Baylor University
JF	Jerry Falwell
JFN	J. Frank Norris
JR	John Rawlings
MR	Mike Randall
NCD	Nola [Callahan] Dowell
NL	*News-Leader* [Springfield]
SBHLA	Southern Baptist Historical Library Archives, Nashville, TN
BBT	*Baptist Bible Tribune*
SDN	Springfield Daily News
SLP	Springfield Leader and Press
SANL	*Saturday News and Leader* [Springfield]
SPNL	Springfield News and Leader
SUNL	*Sunday News and Leader* [Springfield]
BBT	*Baptist Bible Tribune*
SOTL	*Sword of the Lord*
VMLA	G. B. Vick Memorial Library Archives, Springfield, MO.
WED	W. E. [Bill] Dowell
SLP	Springfield Leader and Press

Endnotes

CHAPTER 1

1   Ps. 19:1.
2   Tom Brokaw, *The Greatest Generation* (New York: Random, 1998).
3   Ps. 127:5.
4   "Funeral Rites for Rev. A. M. Dowell Held Here Monday," news clipping, March 1945, DFP.
5   Frederick H. Dyer, *A Compendium of the War of the Rebellion*, (Des Moines: Dyer Publishing, 1908), 1308.
6   Ibid.
7   Dyer's record indicates that 355 of the 382 deaths associated with this regiment were the result of disease.
8   "Family Record," n.d., DFP.
9   Ibid.
10 A phrase borrowed from a letter that Eliza received from an aunt and uncle. M. L. Bradford, R. B. Bradford, and W. H. Bradford to Eliza Jane Dowell and all the family, 29 Sept. 1872, DFP.
11 James Dowell to Louis Marion Dowell, 27 Apr. 1873, DFP.
12 Louise Wilson Anderson, summary of Louis Marion Dowell's family history, 28 Feb. 1978, DFP.
13 Albin's baptism (1892) and wedding (1893) also occurred in this church. "Family Record," n.d., DFP.
14 Isa. 58:1.
15 "Funeral Rites for Rev. A. M. Dowell Held Here Monday," news clipping, March 1945, DFP.
16 This instance of the phrase was borrowed from WED, "A New Testament Preacher," *SOTL*, 1 Nov. 1957, 7.
17 Luke 9:62.
18 Isa. 58:1.

CHAPTER 2

1   "Funeral Rites for Rev. A. M. Dowell Held Here Monday," news clipping, March 1945, DFP.
2   Gladys Todd and WED, interview with the author, 24 May 1993.
3   Elizabeth A. Dowell to WED, 5 May 1943, DFP.
4   WED, "What Is a Good Mother?" BT, 11 May 1986, audiocassette.
5   WED, interview with the author, 7 Nov. 1991.
6   Gladys Todd and WED, interview with the author, 24 May 1993.
7   WED, interview with the author, 7 Nov. 1991.
8   Ibid.
9   Ibid.
10 Elizabeth A. Dowell to WED, 5 May 1943, DFP.
11 WED, interview with the author, 7 Nov. 1991.
12 Ibid.
13 Ibid.
14 Ibid.
15 WED, "A Mother's Influence," BT, 12 May 1985, audiocassette.
16 Ibid.
17 WED, "A Great Mother," *The Soul Winner*, High Street Fundamental Baptist Church, Aug. 1945.

18   WED, "In Memory of a Great Father—Rev. A. M. Dowell," *The Soul Winner*, High Street Fundamental Baptist Church, Apr. 1945.

CHAPTER 3

1   WED, interview with the author, 7 Nov. 1991.
2   Gladys Todd, interview with the author, 24 May 1993.
3   WED to Mr. and Mrs. Leonel B. McConathy, 16 Dec. 1980, VMLA.
4   WED, interview with the author, 7 Nov. 1991.
5   Ibid.
6   Ibid.
7   Ibid.
8   Ibid.
9   WED, "Baptism," BT, 25 Aug. 1985, audiocassette.
10   WED, interview with the author, 7 Nov. 1991.
11   Ibid.
12   Ibid.
13   Heb. 9:27.
14   WED, "Battle of Armageddon," transcript, c. 1968, DFP.
15   WED to Jerry Belton, 16 Oct. 1980, DFP.
16   WED, interview with the author, 7 Nov. 1991.
17   WED to Jerry Belton, 16 Oct. 1980, DFP.
18   Ibid.
19   Ibid.
20   WED, interview with the author, 7 Nov. 1991.
21   WED to Jerry Belton, 16 Oct. 1980, DFP.

CHAPTER 4

1   WED, "A New Testament Preacher," *SOTL*, 1 Nov. 1957, 7.
2   WED, "Assurance," BT, 11 Aug. 1985, audiocassette.
3   Gladys Todd, interview with the author, 24 May 1993.
4   WED, interview with the author, 24 May 1993.
5   WED, interview with the author, 7 Nov. 1991.
6   Ibid.
7   Ibid.
8   Ibid.
9   Ibid.
10   Ibid.
11   Ibid.
12   Ibid.
13   Ibid.
14   Dowell had been a fan of Zane Grey western novels as a young man. WED, "Born Again," BT, 23 Apr. 1978, audiocassette.
15   WED, interview with the author, 24 May 1993.
16   Ibid.
17   WED, "Bloody Hands," BT, 2 Oct. 1977, audiocassette.
18   Qtd. in Steve Hilton, "Rev. W. E. Dowell: BBC Executive Vice President Keeps Faith in Fundamentalism," *SUNL*, 16 Jan. 1972, C2.
19   Ibid.
20   WED, interview with the author, 15 Oct. 1992.
21   Ibid.
22   WED, "Born Again," BT, 23 Apr. 1978, audiocassette.
23   WED, interview with the author, 15 Oct. 1992.

CHAPTER 5

1   WED, interview with the author, 7 Nov. 1991.
2   Ibid.
3   Ibid.
4   Gladys Todd, interview with the author, 24 May 1993.
5   WED, interview with the author, 24 May 1993.
6   WED, interview with the author, 24 Oct. 1991.
7   NCD, interview with the author, 24 May 1993.
8   Noma Lea Callahan to NCD, 31 Aug. 1965, DFP.

9   NCD, interview with the author, 24 May 1993.
10   Ibid.
11   Sharon Dowell, e-mail message to the author, 18 July 2009.
12   NCD, personal notes, 16 Oct. 1979, DFP.
13   Ibid.
14   NCD, personal notes, n.d., DFP.
15   NCD to WED, 6 May 1934, DFP.
16   WED, interview with the author, 14 Feb. 1992.
17   NCD, interview with the author, 24 May 1993.

CHAPTER 6

1   BVB, *A History of Baptist Separatism*, 21. Bartlett credits a 1969 interview with WED for this characterization.
2   WED, "A New Testament Preacher," *SOTL*, 1 Nov. 1957, 7.
3   Untitled news clipping, c. 1934, DFP.
4   WED, "A New Testament Preacher," *SOTL*, 1 Nov. 1957, 7.
5   Ibid.
6   WED, interview with the author, 14 Feb. 1992.
7   Ibid.
8   Ibid. Dowell liked the message sufficiently to reprise the theme when he spoke at a New Year's Eve service at Baptist Temple in Springfield, Missouri, in 1997. In this latter version, his outline covered God's call in creation, in the Garden, in the commandments, in the sacrifices, in Israel's rebellion, in the gospels, and in the church.
9   Ibid.
10   WED, interview with the author, 7 Nov. 1991.
11   WED, interview with the author, 24 May 1993.
12   The source for this oration may have been Arthur Edward Phillips' *Natural Drills in Expression*, a textbook discovered in Dowell's library after his death. This 1927 volume contains a range of short selections from the Bible, Shakespeare, Daniel Webster, Edgar Allen Poe, and others, including four selections by Ingersoll. One of Ingersoll's texts, "Shakespeare's Imagination," is pencil-marked with a young interpreter's notes. For instance, next to the name "Pericles" he wrote, "Prince of Tyre," Next to the unfamiliar adjective "peripatetic" are the words "moving about."
13   WED, interview with the author, 7 Nov. 1991.
14   This pulpit was later donated to Baptist Bible College where it was used in one of the classrooms. A plaque was added that read, "Pulpit where Dr. Dowell preached his first sermon 1934."
15   WED, interview with the author, 14 Feb. 1992.
16   Ibid.
17   Untitled news clipping, c. 1934, DFP.
18   WED, "A New Testament Preacher," *SOTL*, 1 Nov. 1957, 1.
19   WED, interview with the author, 15 Oct. 1992.
20   WED, "A New Testament Preacher," *SOTL*, 1 Nov. 1957, 1.

CHAPTER 7

1   WED to NCD, c. May 1934, DFP.
2   "By 1931 the church reported 12,000 members, with 6,000 attending Sunday school, and property valued at $1.5 million." Karen O'Dell Bullock, "First Baptist Church, Fort Worth," *The Handbook of Texas Online*, 2001, tshaonline.org/handbook/online/articles/ibf01.
3   BVB, *A History of Baptist Separatism*, 10.
4   Ibid., 23.
5   Louis Entzminger, "The Outlook for the Sixth Session of Our Premillennial Bible School May 1-15, Is by Far the Brightest Yet," *FDML*, 23 Mar. 1934, 4.
6   Qtd in BVB, *A History of Baptist Separatism*, 23.
7   Ibid., 24.
8   WED to NCD, 1 May 1934, DFP.
9   Jack Gordon, "Prayer Heard at Night Club Tables. Patrons Stare into Beer Steins as Young Pastors Search for Converts," *Fort Worth Press*, 2 May 1934. Article reprinted in *FDML*, 4 May 1934, 8.
10   Qtd in "Daily Newspapers Front-Paging Soul Winning Campaign," *FDML*, 4 May 1934.
11   WED to NCD, 8 May 1934, DFP.
12   WED to NCD, 5 May 1934, DFP.
13   NCD to WED, 3 May 1934, DFP.
14   Jack Gordon, "Prayer Heard at Night Club Tables. Patrons Stare into Beer Steins as Young Pastors Search for Converts," *Fort Worth Press*, 2 May 1934. Article reprinted in *FDML*, 4 May 1934, 8.
15   NCD to WED, 6 May 1934, DFP.
16   NCD to WED, 13 May 1934, DFP.
17   Jack Gordon, "Prayer Heard at Night Club Tables. Patrons Stare into Beer Steins as Young Pastors Search for Converts," *Fort Worth Press*, 2 May 1934. Article reprinted in *FDML*, 4 May 1934, 8.

18   WED, *BP*, 9.
19   BVB, *A History of Baptist Separatism*, 23.
20   Ibid., 21.
21   JFN, "Fifteen Signs of the Second Coming of Christ," *The Gospel of Dynamite*, 4th ed., (n.p., n.d.), 3-26.
22   WED to NCD, 8 May 1934, DFP.
23   Elizabeth K. Mills, "We'll Work Till Jesus Comes," *HymnTime.com*, accessed 27 Mar. 2017, www.hymntime.com/tch/htm/w/e/l/wellwork.htm.

CHAPTER 8

1   BVB, *A History of Baptist Separatism*, 8.
2   Ibid., 8-9.
3   "John Franklyn Norris," *Jesus-Is-Savior.com*, accessed 19 Jan. 2017, www.jesus-is-savior.com/Great%20Men%20of%20God/dr_john_frank_norris.htm.
4   Ibid.
5   "Norris, J. Frank 1877-1952," *American Decades*, 2001, *Encyclopedia.com*, accessed 8 Jun. 2010.
6   BVB, *A History of Baptist Separatism*, 15.
7   WED, *BP*, 8-9.
8   Dowell concedes that "it is doubtful that Dr. Norris ever completely recovered from this awful tragedy," WED, *BP*, 9.
9   "Norris, J. Frank 1877-1952," *American Decades*, 2001, *Encyclopedia.com*, accessed 8 Jun. 2010.
10   David Stokes, *Apparent Danger*, book jacket notes.
11   "More than Three Times as Many Letters for Bible School than Ever Before," *FDML*, 27 Apr. 1934, 1.
12   "This Is by Far the Greatest of All Bible Schools," *FDML*, 11 May 1934, 7.
13   GBV, interview with Royce Measures, 26 July 1973, transcript, IOH, 12-13.
14   MR, *G. B. Vick*, 8.
15   Homer G. Ritchie, *The Life and Legend of J. Frank Norris*, 184.
16   GBV, interview with Royce Measures, 26 July 1973, transcript, IOH, 15.
17   MR, *G. B. Vick*, 8.
18   Ibid., 6-8.
19   Ibid., 6.
20   Ibid., 8.
21   Vick's role remained virtually unchanged until that time, but his title changed in 1948, when he was name co-pastor. See BVB, *A History of Baptist Separatism*, 33.
22   "The World's Three Largest Sunday Schools," *FDML*, 12 May 1950, 7.
23   Delnay[?] qtd. in BVB, *A History of Baptist Separatism*, 8.
24   Leiann Simpson, "Fort Worth's Top 100 Movers and Shakers," *Fort Worth, Texas: The City's Magazine*, June 1999, p. 31-41.
25   WED, *BP*, 9.
26   "This Is by Far the Greatest of All Bible Schools," *FDML*, 11 May 1934, 7.
27   "The Bible School and My Impressions," *FDML*, 9 Nov. 1934, 5.
28   NCD to WED, 6 May 1934, DFP.
29   Elisha A. Hoffman, "Are You Washed in the Blood?" *HymnTime.com*, accessed 27 Mar. 2017, www.hymntime.com/tch/htm/a/r/u/aruwashd.htm.

CHAPTER 9

1   NCD to WED, 5 May 1934, DFP.
2   NCD to WED, 10 May 1934, DFP.
3   WED to NCD, 8 May 1934, DFP.
4   NCD to WED, 6 May 1934, DFP.
5   NCD to WED, 10 May 1934, DFP.
6   NCD to WED, 12 May 1934, DFP.
7   NCD to WED, 5 May 1934, DFP.
8   NCD to WED, 6 May 1934, DFP.
9   NCD to WED, 10 May 1934, DFP.
10   Ibid.
11   WED to NCD, 8 May 1934, DFP.
12   WED to NCD, 9 May 1934, DFP.
13   WED to NCD, 1 May 1934, DFP.
14   WED to NCD, 11 May 1934, DFP.
15   NCD to WED, 3 May 1934, DFP.
16   NCD to WED, 6 May 1934, DFP.
17   NCD, personal notes, 16 Oct. 1979, DFP.
18   NCD to WED, 6 May 1934, DFP.
19   "The Bible School and My Impressions," *FDML*, 9 Nov. 1934, 5.
20   "Northside Missionary Baptist Church," n.d., DFP.

21   NCD to WED, 11 Nov. 1934, DFP.
22   NCD to WED, 13 May 1934, DFP.
23   WED, notes for Pastoral Theology, n.d., VMLA.
24   NCD, interview with the author, 24 May 1993.
25   Untitled article, n.d., DFP.
26   WED, interview with the author, 24 May 1993.
27   NCD, personal notes, n.d., DFP.
28   WED, interview with the author, 24 Oct. 1991.

CHAPTER 10

1   WED, interview with the author, 14 Feb. 1992.
2   Ibid.
3   WED, notes for Pastoral Theology, n.d., VMLA.
4   MR, *G. B. Vick*, 14.
5   Qtd. in Steve Hilton, "Rev. W. E. Dowell: BBC Executive Vice President Keeps Faith in Fundamentalism," *SUNL*, 16 Jan. 1972, C2.
6   Ibid.
7   WED, "To Stand for Principles," transcript, 1965, DFP.
8   WED, "Jesus Christ Revealed," BT, 1 Aug. 1982, audiocassette.
9   WED, "To Stand for Principles," transcript, 1965, DFP.
10   WED, notes for Pastoral Theology, n.d., VMLA.
11   "Heads Baptist Church Formed at Corcoran," newspaper clipping, 1 Mar. 1937, DFP.
12   WED, notes for Pastoral Theology, n.d., VMLA.
13   WED, interview with the author, 14 Feb. 1992.
14   Qtd. in "From the President's Desk," Baptist Bible College e-newsletter, 6 July 2007. See also WED, "The Ministry of the Holy Spirit," BT, 24 Aug. 1977, audiocassette.
15   WED, "Born Again," BT, 23 Apr. 1978, audiocassette.
16   WED, "A Strange Cure for the Sting of Death," BT, 7 Feb. 1982, audiocassette.
17   WED, *Pastoral Theology*, n.d., 19.
18   WED, "Attitude of the Heart Transplant," transcript, 21 Jan. 1968, DFP.
19   WED, "Doing Something about It," transcript, n.d., DFP.
20   Handwritten in Dowell's copy of the 1927 textbook *Natural Drills in Expression* by Arthur Edward Phillips.
21   Ibid.
22   WED, *Pastoral Theology*, n.d., 17.
23   Terry Allcorn, e-mail message to the author, 8 June 2006.
24   Arthur Edward Phillips, *Natural Drills in Expression*, (Chicago: Newton, 1927).
25   Handwritten in Dowell's copy of the 1927 textbook *Natural Drills in Expression* by Arthur Edward Phillips.
26   WED, "The Elder Brother," BT, 17 Jan. 1982, audiocassette.
27   WED, "God's Marching Orders," transcript, n.d., DFP.
28   Terry Allcorn, e-mail message to the author, 8 June 2006.
29   Tony Isaacs, untitled sermon, Baptist Bible College, 24 Sept. 2015.
30   Terry Allcorn, e-mail message to the author, 8 June 2006.
31   WED, "Politics and Religious Freedom," BT, n.d., audiocassette.
32   Keith Stoller, interview with the author, 6 May 2014.
33   WED, "Divine Invitation," BT, 13 July 1986, audiocassette.
34   WED, "Doing Something about It," transcript, n.d., DFP.
35   Kevin Carson, e-mail message to the author, 25 May 2006.
36   WED, "A New Testament Preacher," *SOTL*, 1 Nov. 1957, 7.
37   WED, "The Power of the Word of God," BT, 12 Oct. 1986, audiocassette.
38   Exod. 32:29.

CHAPTER 11

1   "History of Landmark Baptists of California, Part II, The Twentieth Century," *Cooperative Association Missionary Baptist Churches of California*, accessed 9 June 2009, calcoopassochac.org/book/part-2/schools.htm.
2   WED, interview with the author, 24 Oct. 1991.
3   "History of Landmark Baptists of California, Part II, The Twentieth Century," *Cooperative Association Missionary Baptist Churches of California*, accessed 9 June 2009, calcoopassochac.org/book/part-2/schools.htm.
4   Ibid.
5   NCD, personal notes, 16 Oct. 1979, DFP.
6   "Surprise Minister with Birthday Picnic," newspaper clipping, n.d., DFP.
7   NCD, personal notes, n.d., DFP.
8   NCD, interview with the author, 24 May 1993.
9   NCD, personal notes, 16 Oct. 1979, DFP.

10   Ibid.
11   Ibid.
12   Ibid.
13   qtd. in WED, "Things Christ Left Behind," BT, 2 Jan. 1983, audiocassette.
14   WED, interview with the author, 15 Oct. 1992.
15   Ibid.
16   WED, "Bloody Hands," BT, 2 Oct. 1977, audiocassette.
17   "DeWitte Thomas Dowell," *Find a Grave*, 22 Feb. 2013, accessed 15 Aug. 2014, www.findagrave.com/cgi-bin/fg.cgi?page=gr&GRid=105651008.
18   WED, "Bloody Hands," BT, 2 Oct. 1977, audiocassette.
19   Ibid.
20   Ibid.
21   "Lynwood," undated clipping, DFP.
22   Ibid.
23   "Baptists Plan Active Program," *Lynwood Press*, Jan. 1941, n. pag., DFP.
24   WED, interview with the author, 14 Feb. 1992.
25   Ibid.
26   Ibid.
27   Ibid.
28   WED to NCD, 4 Nov. 1940, DFP.
29   NCD, personal notes, 16 Oct. 1979, DFP.
30   WED to NCD, 4 Nov. 1940, DFP.
31   WED, interview with the author, 14 Feb. 1992.
32   WED, interview with the author, 24 Oct. 1991.
33   Ibid.
34   WED, interview with the author, 14 Feb. 1992.
35   Ibid.
36   Ibid.

CHAPTER 12

1   WED, interview with the author, 24 Oct. 1991.
2   Ibid.
3   Ibid.
4   NCD, personal notes, 16 Oct. 1979, DFP.
5   WED, interview with the author, 15 Oct. 1992.
6   WED, notes for Pastoral Theology, n.d., VMLA.
7   Ibid.
8   Ibid.
9   Ibid.
10   Ritchie, *The Life and Legend of J. Frank Norris*, 178.
11   Ibid., 193.
12   M. H. Wolfe, "Great Fellowship Meeting," *FDML*, 17 Oct. 1941, 1.
13   BVB, *A History of Baptist Separatism*, 26.
14   As of 1937. Ritchie, *The Life and Legend of J. Frank Norris*, 16.
15   Norris himself made this claim in JFN to C. Oscar Johnson, 18 Apr. 1947, SBHLA.
16   Several reports in *FDML* indicate that auto makers provided Norris with vehicles to use on his trips, and in some cases, they gave him vehicles as personal gifts.
17   Barry Hankins, *God's Rascal*, 113.
18   Ritchie, *The Life and Legend of J. Frank Norris*, 18-19.
19   Hankins, *God's Rascal*, 82.
20   Qtd. in Ritchie, *The Life and Legend of J. Frank Norris*, 19.
21   M. H. Wolfe, "Great Fellowship Meeting," *FDML*, 17 Oct. 1941, 1.
22   JFN, "Happy Visit with Jock, Katy and the Three Bairns," *FDML*, 10 Oct. 1941, 1.
23   "'Declare War' He Cables to Roosevelt," *London Evening Standard*, reprinted in *FDML*, 3 Oct. 1941, 5.
24   Louis Entzminger, "The Next Annual Meeting of the World Fundamental Baptist Missionary Fellowship and Annual Bible School, Fort Worth, October 5-12," *FDML*, 19 Sept. 1941, 1.
25   M. H. Wolf, "Great Fellowship Meeting," *FDML*, 17 Oct. 1941, 1.
26   Ibid.
27   Ibid.
28   D. B. Clapp, "Over 22,000 at All Services of First Baptist Church Sunday, Oct. 12," *FDML*, 24 Oct. 1941, 1.
29   WED, interview with the author, 24 Oct. 1991.
30   Louis Entzminger, *The J. Frank Norris I Have Known for 34 Years*, circa 1947, 11.
31   Qtd. in WED, interview with the author, 24 Oct. 1991.
32   Ibid.

33 JFN, "With Only Few Hours Notice Overflowing Crowd Came from Every Direction—See Picture of Part of Huge Crowd in This Issue," *FDML*, 14 Nov. 1941, 1.
34 Ibid.
35 "Wake Up to War Before Too Late, Norris Begs U S," *DN*, 5 Nov. 1941, 1+.
36 JFN, "With Only Few Hours Notice Overflowing Crowd Came from Every Direction—See Picture of Part of Huge Crowd in This Issue," *FDML*, 14 Nov. 1941, 4.
37 Ibid., 1.
38 Ps. 37:23.

CHAPTER 13

1 WED, interview with the author, 15 Oct. 1992.
2 Ibid.
3 Ibid.
4 WED, "Corporal EARL SMITH Begins Full-Time Christian Work at the High Street Fundamental Baptist Church," *The Soul Winner*, May 1946, 1.
5 ES, interview with the author, 9 Nov. 1993.
6 WED, "Corporal EARL SMITH Begins Full-Time Christian Work at the High Street Fundamental Baptist Church," *The Soul Winner*, May 1946, 1.
7 ES, interview with the author, 9 Nov. 1993.
8 Ibid.
9 Ibid.
10 WED, "Dangerous Mistakes," BT, 7 Sept. 1986, audiocassette.
11 WED, "Overflow Crowds at High Street Fundamental Baptist Church," *The Guide to Light*, Feb. 1944, 1.
12 WED, interview with the author, 15 Oct. 1992.
13 Ibid.
14 Ibid.
15 WED, interview with the author, 14 Feb. 1992.
16 Janet Rodgers, e-mail message to the author, 24 July 2007.
17 ES, interview with the author, 9 Nov. 1993.
18 WED, interview with the author, 24 Oct. 1991.
19 WED, "Great Downtown Tent Revival Aug. 22 to Sept. 12," *The Guide to Light*, Sept. 1943, 1.
20 WED, from GBV, interview with Royce Measures, 26 July 1973, transcript, IOH, 60.
21 WED, interview with the author, 24 Oct. 1991.
22 WED, "The Last Days," BT, 3 Aug. 1980, audiocassette.
23 WED, interview with the author, 14 Feb. 1992.
24 WED, "Overflow Crowds at High Street Fundamental Baptist Church," *The Guide to Light*, High Street Fundamental Baptist Church. Feb. 1944, 1.
25 Ibid.
26 WED, "100 Additions in Rawlings' High St. Revival," *BBT*, 30 Mar. 1951, 3.
27 JR, telephone interview with the author, 24 July 2007.
28 WED, "3700 People in Evening Service to Hear Dr. Fred Donnelson," *The Guide to Light*, Jan. 1944, 1.
29 WED, interview with the author, 14 Feb. 1992.

CHAPTER 14

1 Eph. 6:12.
2 WED, "Quit Ye Like Men," BT, 7 July 1985, audiocassette.
3 WED, interview with the author, 15 Oct. 1992.
4 Ibid.
5 Ibid.
6 Ibid.
7 "Southwest Missouri Teachers Association Openly Encourages Juvenile Delinquency," *SLP*, 14 Oct. 1944, 2.
8 WED, interview with the author, 15 Oct. 1992.
9 Qtd. in Docia Karell, "Teachers Call Their Dancing 'Innocent Fun,'" *SLP*, 16 Oct. 1944, 1.
10 Docia Karell, "Teachers Call Their Dancing 'Innocent Fun,'" *SLP*, 16 Oct. 1944, 1.
11 WED, interview with the author, 15 Oct. 1992.
12 H. L. Lawhon, "'Biggest Factor in Delinquency,'" *SUNL*, 22 Oct. 1944, B7.
13 S. O., "Sorry She Went to 'Hell Hole,'" *SUNL*, 22 Oct. 1944, B7.
14 WED, interview with the author, 15 Oct. 1992.
15 Stokes, *Apparent Danger*, 6.
16 Hankins. *God's Rascal*, 141.
17 WED, interview with the author, 15 Oct. 1992.
18 Ibid.
19 Hankins. *God's Rascal*, 15.

20   WED, interview with the author, 15 Oct. 1992.
21   Ibid.
22   Eldon Harmon, interview with the author, 21 Nov. 1993.
23   John Ashcroft to WED, 28 Feb. 1984, DFP.
24   WED, "Why the Coming of V-Day Has Been Prolonged," *The Soul Winner*, Apr. 1945, 1.
25   Ibid., 2.
26   Ibid., 2.
27   WED, "In Memory of a Great Father—Rev. A. M. Dowell," *The Soul Winner*, Apr. 1945, 1.
28   II Tim. 4:7-8.
29   WED, interview with the author, 15 Oct. 1992.

CHAPTER 15

1   Frederick E. Weatherly and Stephen Adams, "The Holy City," 1891. This song was recorded by ES on *The Longer I Serve Him, the Sweeter He Grows*, compact disc, Knight, 1993.
2   ES, interview with the author, 9 Nov. 1993.
3   ES to WED, 15 May 1943, DFP.
4   ES to WED and NCD, 12 Jun. 1943, DFP.
5   ES to WED, 15 May 1943, DFP.
6   Ibid.
7   ES to WED and NCD, 12 Jun. 1943, DFP.
8   ES to WED, 15 May 1943, DFP.
9   ES to WED and NCD, 12 Jun. 1943, DFP.
10   Shirley Hackler, e-mail message to the author, 6 June 2006.
11   WED, "A New Testament Preacher," *SOTL*, 1 Nov. 1957, 11.
12   ES, interview with the author, 9 Nov. 1993.
13   WED, "Corporal Earl Smith Begins Full-Time Christian Work at the High Street Fundamental Baptist Church," *The Soul Winner*, May 1946, 1.
14   ES, interview with the author, 9 Nov. 1993.
15   WED, "Corporal Earl Smith Begins Full-Time Christian Work at the High Street Fundamental Baptist Church," *The Soul Winner*, May 1946, 1.
16   BDJ, interview with the author, 25 Nov. 1993.
17   ES, interview with the author, 9 Nov. 1993.
18   Ibid.
19   NCD, personal notes, 16 Oct. 1979, DFP.
20   Janet Rodgers, e-mail message to the author, 24 July 2007.
21   ES, interview with the author, 9 Nov. 1993.
22   Ibid.
23   Ibid.
24   Ibid.
25   Ibid.
26   Ibid.
27   Ibid.
28   Ibid.
29   Ibid.
30   Ibid.
31   Ibid.
32   WED, "Dangerous Mistakes," BT, 7 Sept. 1986, audiocassette. See also 2 Tim. 4:5.
33   ES, interview with the author, 9 Nov. 1993.
34   Ibid.
35   Ibid.
36   Ibid.
37   Ibid.

CHAPTER 16

1   WED, "We Need God's Power," BT, n.d., audiocassette.
2   WED, "The Worth of a Soul," *SOTL*, 3 Aug. 1975, 11.
3   WED, interview with the author, 14 Feb. 1992.
4   2 Cor. 6:2.
5   WED, interview with the author, 14 Feb. 1992.
6   WED, "We Need God's Power," BT, n.d., audiocassette.
7   WED, interview with the author, 14 Feb. 1992.
8   WED, "A New Testament Preacher," *SOTL*, 1 Nov. 1957, 12.
9   Ibid., 11.

10 Roy A. Kemp, "Two Weeks with Bill Dowell and the High Street Baptist Church . . . ," *The Soul Winner*, July 1948, 1.
11 WED, interview with the author, 15 Oct. 1992.
12 Mary Ritchie, "He's Pastor to 4500 Persons," *SUNL*, 9 Nov. 1952, D2.
13 WED, "Overflow Crowds at High Street Fundamental Baptist Church," *The Guide to Light*, Feb. 1944, 1.
14 Ibid.
15 Clyde Dowell, e-mail message to the author, 4 Aug. 2010.
16 BDJ, e-mail message to the author, 3 Aug. 2010.
17 WED, "A Mother's Love," BT, 9 May 1982, audiocassette.
18 Roy A. Kemp, "Two Weeks with Bill Dowell and the High Street Baptist Church . . . ," *The Soul Winner*, July 1948, 1.
19 High Street Baptist Church, *Years of Blessing 1936:1967*, 1967, 68.
20 Ibid., 4.
21 WED, "How the High Street Fundamental Baptist Church Will Build a Sunday School of Fifteen Hundred," *The Soul Winner*, May 1946, 4.
22 WED, interview with the author, 15 Oct. 1992.
23 WED, "How the High Street Fundamental Baptist Church Will Build a Sunday School of Fifteen Hundred," *The Soul Winner*, May 1946, 4.
24 WED, interview with the author, 15 Oct. 1992.
25 WED, "Is the 'Soul Winner' Worth While?" *The Soul Winner*, Oct. 1947, 1.
26 "High Street Fundamental Baptist Church," advertisement, *SDN*, 21 Sept. 1947, 12.
27 "High St. Fundamental Baptist Church," advertisement, *SDN*, 28 Dec. 1946, 10.
28 "High Street Fundamental Baptist Church," advertisement, *SLP*, 21 Sept. 1946, 5.
29 Bob Barker to the author, 30 May 2006, DFP.
30 "Temple Baptist Celebrates 59th Anniversary," *BBT*, Oct. 2009, 29.
31 High Street Baptist Church, *Years of Blessing 1936:1967*, 1967, 68.
32 WED, "The Last Days," BT, 3 Aug. 1980, audiocassette.
33 WED, "The Substitutionary Atonement of Jesus Christ," Tabernacle Baptist Church [Farmington, N.M.], c. 1984.
34 WED, "Overflow Crowds at High Street Fundamental Baptist Church," *The Guide to Light*, Feb. 1944, 1.
35 Ibid.
36 Ibid.

CHAPTER 17

1 WED, "Overflow Crowds at High Street Fundamental Baptist Church," *The Guide to Light*, Feb. 1944, 1.
2 Roy A. Kemp, "Two Weeks with Bill Dowell and the High Street Baptist Church . . . ," *The Soul Winner*, July 1948, 1.
3 This facility's balcony expansion never came about; however, High Street's next facility did include a horseshoe balcony.
4 "Springfield's Easter Services Set New Attendance Records," *SLP*, 29 Mar. 1948, 9.
5 1 Pet. 2:5-7.
6 "Dowell's Church Ready to Start Construction Job," *SLP*, 22 Feb. 1949, 10.
7 "Cornerstone Laid," *SLP*, 16 May 1949, 9.
8 "High Street's Building Ready," *SUNL*, 8 Jan. 1950, C6.
9 WED, "Dedication of High Street Fundamental Baptist Auditorium," *FDML*, 10 Mar. 1950, 5.
10 "Great Revival," advertisement, *SLP*, 4 Feb. 1950, 8.
11 WED, "Dedication of High Street Fundamental Baptist Auditorium," *FDML*, 10 Mar. 1950, 5.
12 ES, interview with the author, 9 Nov. 1993.
13 Verle S. Ackerman, "Tributes to W. E. Dowell," *BBT*, 15 Mar. 2000, 15.
14 J. Curtis Goldman to Baptist Temple (commemorating WED's fifty years in ministry), 25 Jan. 1984, DFP.
15 JFN to WED, 22 July 1948, SBHLA.
16 WED to JFN, 26 July 1948, SBHLA.
17 See *McCullom v. Board of Education*, 1948.
18 WED, "Work of the Holy Spirit," *The Soul Winner*, Feb. 1947, 1.
19 Referenced in JFN to Walter R. Mayne (Atty), 26 Apr. 1947, SBHLA. Dowell was likewise critical of President Roosevelt and the New Deal, though he confessed that he voted for Roosevelt the first time he was elected.
20 WED, *The Communist Infiltration of the Church*, 11.
21 Ibid., 9.
22 JFN to C. Oscar Johnson, 18 Apr. 1947, SBHLA.
23 WED, *The Communist Infiltration of the Church*, 12.
24 Qtd. in Louis Entzminger, *The J. Frank Norris I Have Known for 34 Years*, 227.
25 JFN to John R. Green, 24 Apr. 1947, SBHLA.
26 JFN to WED, 7 Jan. 1947, SBHLA.
27 JFN to Boyle, Priest, and Elliott, 10 Apr. 1947, SBHLA.
28 JFN to Harry B. Boyer, 11 Apr. 1947, SBHLA.
29 William Fraser to JFN, 12 Apr. 1947, SBHLA.
30 Qtd. in Louis Entzminger, *The J. Frank Norris I Have Known for 34 Years*, 225-26.
31 NCD to Noma Callahan, 12 May 1947, DFP.
32 "W. E. (Bill) Dowell, Beauchamp Vick, Wendell Zimmerman and J. Frank Norris Make Trip to Tampico and Mexico City on Mission Work," *FDML*, 3 Mar. 1950, 1.

CHAPTER 18

1   Shakespeare, *King Lear*, 1.1.135-36.
2   GBV, interview with Royce Measures, 26 July 1973, transcript, IOH, 51.
3   BVB, *A History of Baptist Separatism*, 30.
4   Qtd. in Hankins. *God's Rascal*, 129.
5   Ibid.
6   GBV, "Chapter XIII," *The J. Frank Norris I Have Known for 34 Years* by Louis Entzminger, 335.
7   Ritchie, *The Life and Legend of J. Frank Norris*, 238.
8   Ibid., 240.
9   JFN to WED, 21 May 1944, SBHLA.
10 WED to JFN, 31 May 1944, SBHLA.
11 JFN to WED, 28 Jan. 1947, SBHLA.
12 BVB, *A History of Baptist Separatism*, 33.
13 JFN to WED, 1 Aug. 1944, SBHLA.
14 JFN to WED, 3 Feb. 1947, SBHLA.
15 GBV, interview with Royce Measures, 28 Feb. 1974, transcript, IOH, 187.
16 JFN to WED, 28 Jan. 1948, SBHLA.
17 JFN to WED, 8 Apr. 1948, SBHLA.
18 BVB, *A History of Baptist Separatism*, 28.
19 GBV, interview with Royce Measures, 26 Sept. 1973, transcript, IOH, 156.
20 Ibid., 158.
21 JFN to WED, 18 Jan. 1947, SBHLA.
22 JFN to WED, 13 July 1947, SBHLA.
23 Qtd. in GBV. "Separation from WFBMF and the Organization of the Baptist Bible Fellowship and Baptist Bible College: The Real Issues Involved," *BBT*, 23 June 1950, 5.
24 WED, *BP*, 11.
25 Qtd in. BVB, *A History of Baptist Separatism*, 31.
26 MR, *G. B. Vick*, 13.
27 GBV, interview with Royce Measures, 26 Sept. 1973, transcript, IOH, 152.
28 Ibid., 155.
29 MR, *G. B. Vick*, 13.
30 BVB, *A History of Baptist Separatism*, 34.
31 GBV, interview with Royce Measures, 26 Sept. 1973, transcript, IOH, 151.
32 JR, from GBV, interview with Royce Measures, 26 Sept. 1973, transcript, IOH, 151.
33 GBV, interview with Royce Measures, 26 Sept. 1973, transcript, IOH, 158.
34 JFN to WED, 23 Dec. 1947, SBHLA.
35 JFN to WED, 13 July 1948, SBHLA.
36 JFN to WED, 24 Apr. 1948, SBHLA.
37 JFN to WED, 23 Dec. 1947, SBHLA.

CHAPTER 19

1   WED, *BP*, 11-12.
2   Ibid., 12.
3   Qtd. in BVB, *A History of Baptist Separatism*, 36.
4   BVB, *A History of Baptist Separatism*, 37.
5   Ibid.
6   WED, *BP*, 12.
7   MR, *G. B. Vick*, 15.
8   BVB, *A History of Baptist Separatism*, 37.
9   JFN to WED, 20 Dec. 1947, SBHLA.
10 JFN to WED, 8 Apr. 1948, SBHLA.
11 GBV, interview with Royce Measures, 28 Feb. 1974, transcript, IOH, 190.
12 JFN to WED, 26 July 1947, SBHLA.
13 Ibid.
14 WED to JFN, 29 July 1947, SBHLA.
15 WED to JFN, 20 Jan. 1948, SBHLA.
16 Ibid.
17 GBV, interview with Royce Measures, 28 Feb. 1974, transcript, IOH, 190-91.
18 GBV, interview with Royce Measures, 27 July 1973, transcript, IOH, 104.
19 Ibid.
20 Ibid., 90.
21 WED, from GBV, interview with Royce Measures, 27 July 1973, transcript, IOH, 90.

22   Ibid., 91.
23   Qtd. in GBV, interview with Royce Measures, 26 Sept. 1973, transcript, IOH, 159.
24   WED, from GBV, interview with Royce Measures, 26 Sept. 1973, transcript, IOH, 159.
25   GBV, interview with Royce Measures, 26 Sept. 1973, transcript, IOH, 159.
26   Ritchie, *The Life and Legend of J. Frank Norris*, 198.
27   Ibid., 199.
28   Ibid., 196.
29   GBV, interview with Royce Measures, 28 Feb. 1974, transcript, IOH, 187.
30   Ritchie, *The Life and Legend of J. Frank Norris*, 207.

CHAPTER 20

1   BVB, *A History of Baptist Separatism*, 68.
2   Ibid., 39.
3   WED, interview with the author, 24 Oct. 1991.
4   GBV, "Separation from WFBMF and the Organization of the Baptist Bible Fellowship and Baptist Bible College: The Real Issues Involved," *BBT*, 23 June 1950, 1.
5   Ibid., 5.
6   "Flowers for the Living, But Not for the Dead: A Simple Statement of Facts Concerning Louis Entzminger," *FDML*, 10 Apr. 1950, 1.
7   "Greatest Sorrow of My Life that I Trusted a Man Who Turned Out to Be the Worst Traitor in My Whole Ministry," *FDML*, 16 June 1950, 5.
8   "Luther Peak Enthusiastic Over Dallas Branch of the Seminary," *FDML*, 5 May 1950, 7.
9   JR, from GBV, interview with Royce Measures, 26 Sept. 1973, transcript, IOH, 144.
10   Ibid.
11   Jock Troup, "Personal Impressions of the First Baptist Church and the Bible Baptist Seminary," *FDML*, 13 Jan. 1950, 1.
12   "Jock Troup, Britain's Most Noted Evangelist, Arrived Dec. 28th," *FDML*, 6 Jan. 1950, 1.
13   "Rev. Jock Troup to Be the Commencement Speaker of the Seminary May 28 [sic]," *FDML*, 20 Jan. 1950, 1.
14   "First Baptist Church Calls Jock Troup as Joint Pastor," *FDML*, 27 Jan. 1950, 1.
15   "Why Beauchamp Vick Refused to Have Full Proceedings Before the Temple Baptist Deacons Thursday Night," *FDML*, 9 June 1950, 2.
16   Ibid.
17   Untitled box insert, *FDML*, 23 June 1950, 8. (Another reference, found on page 2 of the 9 June 1950 issue of *FDML*, suggests that Bonner "had been running a harem in Detroit.")
18   "Why Beauchamp Vick Refused to Have Full Proceedings Before the Temple Baptist Deacons Thursday Night," *FDML*, 9 June 1950, 2.
19   "Dr. Entzminger Very Low," *FDML*, 2 June 1950, 1.
20   GBV, "Separation from WFBMF and the Organization of the Baptist Bible Fellowship and Baptist Bible College: The Real Issues Involved," *BBT*, 23 June 1950, 6.
21   Ibid.
22   JR, from GBV, interview with Royce Measures, 26 Sept. 1973, transcript, IOH, 139. Vick was also present during this interview.
23   GBV, "Separation from WFBMF and the Organization of the Baptist Bible Fellowship and Baptist Bible College: The Real Issues Involved," *BBT*, 23 June 1950, 6.
24   "Dr. Entzminger Improving Slowing—Still in Hospital. Cost of Operation and Hospital Will Be over $500," *FDML*, 16 June 1950, 3.
25   Though Godsoe signed this title with his name in May 1950, Vick said he had never been given such a title by the seminary's president or its trustees. See GBV, "Separation from WFBMF and the Organization of the Baptist Bible Fellowship and Baptist Bible College: The Real Issues Involved," *BBT*, 23 June 1950, 7.
26   GBV, "Separation from WFBMF and the Organization of the Baptist Bible Fellowship and Baptist Bible College: The Real Issues Involved," *BBT*, 23 June 1950, 5.
27   "Why Beauchamp Vick Refused to Have Full Proceedings Before the Temple Baptist Deacons Thursday Night," *FDML*, 9 June 1950, 4.
28   "How Entzminger Saved Seminary," *FDML*, 21 Apr. 1950, 1. (See also "Entzminger Very Low," *FDML*, 2 June 1950, 1.)
29   "Four Men Expected to Be Pastors of Temple Baptist Church of Detroit," *FDML*, 16 June 1950, 8.
30   GBV, "Separation from WFBMF and the Organization of the Baptist Bible Fellowship and Baptist Bible College: The Real Issues Involved," *BBT*, 23 June 1950, 5-6.
31   Ibid., 6.
32   Qtd. in "How Entzminger Saved Seminary," *FDML*, 21 Apr. 1950, 5.
33   Ibid.
34   "An Approved Theological or Divinity School within the Purview of the Federal Law," *FDML*, 2 June 1950, 4.
35   "We Will Not Serve Thy Gods," *FDML*, 21 Apr. 1950, 6.
36   JR, from GBV, interview with Royce Measures, 26 Sept. 1973, transcript, IOH, 138.
37   "We Will Not Serve Thy Gods," *FDML*, 21 Apr. 1950, 6.
38   Ibid.

CHAPTER 21

1   "State Board Confirms Our Statement of Faith," *FDML*, 28 Apr. 1950, 2.
2   Ibid., 7.
3   GBV, "Separation from WFBMF and the Organization of the Baptist Bible Fellowship and Baptist Bible College: The Real Issues Involved," *BBT*, 23 June 1950, 7.
4   "State Board Confirms Our Statement of Faith," *FDML*, 28 Apr. 1950, 2.
5   Ibid.
6   "Letter to Mr. Vick," *FDML*, 28 Apr. 1950, 4.
7   "Very Happy and Profitable Meeting of the Directors of the Bible Baptist Seminary," *FDML*, 19 May 1950, 1.
8   Ibid. (May 4, 1950, was a Thursday. Other records indicate that this meeting concluded on Friday, May 5.)
9   "Enlarged Responsibility—Five New Directors Added," *FDML*, 5 May 1950, 3.
10   GBV, interview with Royce Measures, 26 Sept. 1973, transcript, IOH, 148.
11   Untitled article, *FDML*, 12 May 1950, 1.
12   No one disputes that the expelled Temple students contacted Vick.
13   "Why Beauchamp Vick Refused to Have Full Proceedings Before the Temple Baptist Deacons Thursday Night," *FDML*, 9 June 1950, 2.
14   "Greatest Sorrow of My Life that I Trusted a Man Who Turned Out to Be the Worst Traitor in My Whole Ministry," *FDML*, 16 June 1950, 5.
15   WED to JFN, 13 June 1950, SBHLA.
16   Luther C. Peak, open letter dated 29 May 1950, *FDML*, 9 June 1950, 6.
17   GBV, "Separation from WFBMF and the Organization of the Baptist Bible Fellowship and Baptist Bible College: The Real Issues Involved," *BBT*, 23 June 1950, 7.
18   Ibid.
19   Qtd. in WED, *BP*, 37.
20   Ibid.
21   BVB, *A History of Baptist Separatism*, 39-40.
22   GBV, telegram to JFN, 17 May 1950, SBHLA.
23   See Shakespeare, *Julius Caesar*, 4.3.224.
24   WED, *BP*, 13.
25   See Texas Hotel Meeting Minutes qtd. in Curtis Goldman, *50 Goldman Years*, 16-17.

CHAPTER 22

1   WED, from GBV, interview with Royce Measures, 27 July 1973, transcript, IOH, 99.
2   WED, "Staff Meeting Notes," Sept. 1977, VMLA.
3   WED, from GBV, interview with Royce Measures, 27 July 1973, transcript, IOH, 100.
4   Norris mentions the game in JFN to Dowell, 5 Aug. 1950, SBHLA.
5   Qtd. in WED, *BP*, 39.
6   Curtis Goldman's account of this illness suggests that Entzminger's surgery was not any kind of emergency but instead was treatment for an ongoing medical condition. Goldman reports that a seminary classmate, Charles Johnson, drove to Entzminger's home that same week and found him mowing his lawn after his surgery. Goldman said that Johnson also heard Entzminger tell a visiting pastor that Norris had encouraged him to time his surgery for the beginning of the fellowship meeting. See Curtis Goldman, *50 Goldman Years*, 11.
7   Qtd. in WED, *BP*, 40.
8   GBV, interview with Royce Measures, 28 Feb. 1974, transcript, IOH, 169.
9   GBV, "Separation from WFBMF and the Organization of the Baptist Bible Fellowship and Baptist Bible College: The Real Issues Involved," *BBT*, 23 June 1950, 7.
10   Ibid., 8.
11   JR, from GBV, interview with Royce Measures, 26 Sept. 1973, transcript, IOH, 137.
12   Ibid.
13   Ibid., 136.
14   Ibid., 137.
15   Ibid.
16   Ibid., 140.
17   GBV, interview with Royce Measures, 27 July 1973, transcript, IOH, 82.
18   Ibid., 122.
19   Ibid., 119.
20   Ibid.
21   Ibid., 119-20.
22   WED, from GBV, interview with Royce Measures, 27 July 1973, transcript, IOH, 122.
23   Peak, Luther. "Luther Peak Gives Knock-Out Blow to the Treacherous Conspirator," *FDML*, 21 July 1950, 4-5.
24   JR, from GBV, interview with Royce Measures, 26 Sept. 1973, transcript, IOH, 140.
25   JR, telephone interview with the author, 24 July 2007.

26   BVB, *A History of Baptist Separatism*, 40.
27   GBV, interview with Royce Measures, 26 Sept. 1973, transcript, IOH, 153.
28   Ibid., 153.
29   "Why Beauchamp Vick Refused to Have Full Proceedings Before the Temple Baptist Deacons Thursday Night," *FDML*, 9 June 1950, 4.
30   R. D. Ingle, "The Truth about the Seminary and the Fellowship," *FDML*, 21 July 1950, 6.
31   Untitled box insert, *FDML*, 16 June 1950, 1.
32   R. D. Ingle, "The Truth about the Seminary and the Fellowship," *FDML*, 21 July 1950, 6.
33   GBV, interview with Royce Measures, 27 July 1973, transcript, IOH, 101.
34   JR, telephone interview with the author, 24 July 2007.
35   WED, *BP*, 12-13.
36   Qtd. in BVB, *A History of Baptist Separatism*, 48-49.
37   J. Curtis Goldman, *50 Goldman Years*, 13.
38   WED, *BP*, 14.
39   GBV, interview with Royce Measures, 27 July 1973, transcript, IOH, 81.
40   JR. "The Pinnacle of Bill Dowell's Labors," *BBT*, 15 Mar. 2000, 15.
41   JR, telephone interview with the author, 24 July 2007.
42   BVB, *A History of Baptist Separatism*, 41.
43   WED, *BP*, 14.
44   Ibid., 14-15.
45   Ibid., 15.
46   BVB, *A History of Baptist Separatism*, 41.
47   WED, *BP*, 15.
48   BVB, *A History of Baptist Separatism*, 41.
49   Ibid., 41.
50   WED, *BP*, 15.
51   WED, qtd in BVB, *A History of Baptist Separatism*, 41.
52   WED, *BP*, 16.
53   Ibid., 15.
54   Ibid., 15-16.
55   Royce Measures, interview with GBV, 27 July 1973, transcript, IOH, 81.
56   Ibid., 170.
57   GBV, interview with Royce Measures, 26 July 1973, transcript, IOH, 14, 43.
58   Ibid., 51.
59   Ibid., 49-50.
60   Noel Smith, "Reasons for Baptist Bible Fellowship," *BBT*, 23 June 1950, 3.
61   GBV, interview with Royce Measures, 27 July 1973, transcript, IOH, 82.
62   BVB, *A History of Baptist Separatism*, 42.
63   Noel Smith, "Reasons for Baptist Bible Fellowship," *BBT*, 23 June 1950, 3.
64   GBV, interview with Royce Measures, 27 July 1973, transcript, IOH, 82-83.
65   Ibid., 82-83.
66   Here BVB cites an interview with WED. See BVB, *A History of Baptist Separatism*, 43.
67   GBV, interview with Royce Measures, 27 July 1973, transcript, IOH, 83.
68   Ibid.
69   WED, *BP*, 16.
70   GBV, "Separation from WFBMF and the Organization of the Baptist Bible Fellowship and Baptist Bible College: The Real Issues Involved," *BBT*, 23 June 1950, 7.
71   Qtd. in WED, *BP*, 34.
72   GBV, interview with Royce Measures, 27 July 1973, transcript, IOH, 84.
73   Noel Smith, "Reasons for Baptist Bible Fellowship," *BBT*, 23 June 1950, 3.
74   GBV, interview with Royce Measures, 27 July 1973, transcript, IOH, 94.
75   WED, from GBV, interview with Royce Measures, 27 July 1973, transcript, IOH, 84.
76   Qtd. in GBV, interview with Royce Measures, 27 July 1973, transcript, IOH, 85.
77   This Bible was among Dowell's belongings when he died. Nearly every page had personal markings written on it. A note found in the margin of John 1 reminded Dowell how Christ led others. It said, "Pastor should say come on, not go on,"
78   WED, "Give Me This Mountain," BT, c. 1976, audiocassette.
79   Ibid.

CHAPTER 23

1   GBV, interview with Royce Measures, 27 July 1973, transcript, IOH, 85.
2   BVB, *A History of Baptist Separatism*, 45-46.
3   GBV, interview with Royce Measures, 27 July 1973, transcript, IOH, 94.
4   GBV, interview with Royce Measures, 28 Feb. 1974, transcript, IOH, 187.
5   BVB, *A History of Baptist Separatism*, 46.
6   GBV, interview with Royce Measures, 28 Feb. 1974, transcript, IOH, 188-89.

7   Gen. 13:8.
8   GBV, interview with Royce Measures, 28 Feb. 1974, transcript, IOH, 169.
9   WED, from GBV, interview with Royce Measures, 27 July 1973, transcript, IOH, 98.
10 WED, *BP*, 18.
11 BVB, *A History of Baptist Separatism*, 51.
12 Qtd. in JR, telephone interview with the author, 24 July 2007.
13 WED, from GBV, interview with Royce Measures, 27 July 1973, transcript, IOH, 98.
14 Qtd. in WED, from GBV, interview with Royce Measures, 27 July 1973, transcript, IOH, 99.
15 WED, from GBV, interview with Royce Measures, 27 July 1973, transcript, IOH, 99.
16 Ibid., 99.
17 JR, telephone interview with the author, 24 July 2007.
18 WED, from GBV, interview with Royce Measures, 27 July 1973, transcript, IOH, 99.
19 WED, *BP*, 19.
20 Curtis Goldman, *50 Goldman Years*, 4.
21 BVB, *A History of Baptist Separatism*, 47.
22 Curtis Goldman, *50 Goldman Years*, 4.
23 See GBV, interview with Royce Measures, 26 Sept. 1973, transcript, IOH, 95, and 28 Feb. 1974, transcript, IOH, 168.
24 GBV, interview with Royce Measures, 27 July 1973, transcript, IOH, 97-98.
25 WED, *BP*, 19.
26 BVB, *A History of Baptist Separatism*, 48.
27 Qtd. in GBV, interview with Royce Measures, 27 July 1973, transcript, IOH, 101.
28 Qtd. in GBV, interview with Royce Measures, 27 July 1973, transcript, IOH, 101.
29 Dowell's two accounts of this story show some discrepancies. One account shows that it occurred on Tuesday afternoon; the other indicates Wednesday morning. See WED, from GBV, interview with Royce Measures, 27 July 1973, transcript, IOH, 101, and WED, *BP*, 17.
30 F. S. Donnelson, "What Happened at Fellowship at Fort Worth," *BBT*, 23 June 1950, 3.
31 "President Kennedy in Fort Worth, Texas, on November 22, 1963 (His Last Two Speeches)," *DVP's JFK Archives*, accessed 23 Mar. 2017, jfk-archives.blogspot.com/2011/12/jfk-in-fort-worth-on-11-22-63.html.
32 WED, from GBV, interview with Royce Measures, 27 July 1973, transcript, IOH, 104.
33 WED, *BP*, 44.
34 Ibid., 22.
35 Ibid., 27.
36 Ibid., 24.
37 GBV, interview with Royce Measures, 27 July 1973, transcript, IOH, 102.
38 Qtd. in WED, *BP*, 24.
39 WED, *BP*, 25.
40 Qtd. in BVB, *A History of Baptist Separatism*, 50.
41 GBV, interview with Royce Measures, 27 July 1973, transcript, IOH, 103.
42 BVB, *A History of Baptist Separatism*, 50-51.
43 GBV, interview with Royce Measures, 26 July 1973, transcript, IOH, 40.
44 Shakespeare, *Hamlet*, 2.2.90. See GBV, interview with Royce Measures, 26 Sept. 1973, transcript, IOH, 160.
45 WED, interview with Royce Measures, 27 July 1973, transcript, IOH, 104-05.
46 GBV, interview with Royce Measures, 27 July 1973, transcript, IOH, 105.
47 Ibid.
48 Qtd. in WED, *BP*, 26.
49 WED, *BP*, 26.
50 JR, telephone interview with the author, 24 July 2007.
51 F. S. Donnelson, "What Happened at Fellowship at Fort Worth," *BBT*, 23 June 1950, 2.
52 WED, *BP*, 27.
53 Ibid., 27.
54 Ibid., 35.
55 Ibid., 33.
56 Jack Douglass, "Separatist Group Forms New Baptist Organization," *The Star-Telegram* [Fort Worth], 26 May 1950, n.p.
57 GBV, interview with Royce Measures, 26 Sept. 1973, transcript, IOH, 147.
58 JR, telephone interview with the author, 24 July 2007.

CHAPTER 24

1   BVB, *A History of Baptist Separatism*, 57-58.
2   JFN, Telegram to WED, SBHLA. 21 June 1950.
3   BDJ, interview with the author, 25 Nov. 1993.
4   JFN to WED, 25 May 1950, SBHLA.
5   "Mission Office Moved to Fort Worth," *FDML*, 2 June 1950, 3.
6   Qtd. in WED, from GBV, interview with Royce Measures, 26 July 1973, transcript, IOH, 62.
7   WED, from GBV, interview with Royce Measures, 26 July 1973, transcript, IOH, 62.
8   GBV, interview with Royce Measures, 26 July 1973, transcript, IOH, 63.

9   Qtd. in GBV, interview with Royce Measures, 26 July 1973, transcript, IOH, 63.
10   JFN to WED, 10 June 1950, SBHLA.
11   JFN to WED, 13 June 1950, SBHLA.
12   Ibid.
13   GBV, interview with Royce Measures, 26 July 1973, transcript, IOH, 54.
14   Ibid., 55.
15   Ibid., 56.
16   Qtd. in GBV, interview with Royce Measures, 26 July 1973, transcript, IOH, 57.
17   "Why Beauchamp Vick Refused to Have Full Proceedings Before the Temple Baptist Deacons Thursday Night," *FDML*, 9 June 1950, 2.
18   Ibid.
19   Ibid.
20   Luther C. Peak, open letter dated 29 May 1950, *FDML*, 9 June 1950, 6.
21   GBV, "Separation from WFBMF and the Organization of the Baptist Bible Fellowship and Baptist Bible College: The Real Issues Involved," *BBT*, 23 June 1950, 6. (Noel Smith said Verle Ackerman was likewise prepared to testify about Entzminger's involvement. See Noel Smith, "Frank Norris' 'Hearing,'" *BBT*, 7 July 1950, 2.)
22   Qtd. in Curtis Goldman, *50 Goldman Years*, 29.
23   Norris's use of this name was veiled at first, but direct references to Eloise appear in a letter from JFN to GBV, 29 June 1950, SBHLA. Similar references occur in the 7 July 1950 issue of *FDML*.
24   Untitled box insert, *FDML*, 23 June 1950, 8.
25   "When Jezebel Rules the Roost," *FDML*, 9 June 1950, 6.
26   WED to JFN, 13 June 1950, SBHLA.
27   "Bill Dowell's Soul Not on the Market," *BBT*, 30 June 1950, 2.
28   GBV, interview with Royce Measures, 27 July 1973, transcript, IOH, 104.
29   "Four Men Expected to be Pastors of Temple Baptist Church of Detroit," *FDML*, 16 June 1950, 8.
30   "Why No New Creditable School Can Be Established," *FDML*, 23 June 1950, 1.
31   From "Fundamentalists War among the Churches," *The World's Work of New York*, Oct. 1923. Qtd. in Joel A. Carpenter, ed., *Inside History of First Baptist Church, Fort Worth, and Temple Baptist Church, Detroit: Life Story of Dr. J. Frank Norris*, 10.
32   GBV and WED, telegram to JFN, 21 June 1950, SBHLA.
33   GBV, interview with Royce Measures, 26 July 1973, transcript, IOH, 43.
34   WED, *BP*, 47-48.
35   Ibid.
36   GBV, interview with Royce Measures, 26 July 1973, transcript, IOH, 44-45.
37   Accounts of this event mention both the Blackstone and the Texas Hotels. The earliest reports, however, suggest that the group gathered at the Blackstone.
38   BVB, *A History of Baptist Separatism*, 53.
39   Qtd. in BVB, *A History of Baptist Separatism*, 53.
40   BVB, *A History of Baptist Separatism*, 53.
41   "Frank Norris Has His 'Hearing'—Takes 6 Hours; Refuses Other Side 2 Minutes," *BBT*, 7 July 1950, 1-2.
42   Curtis Goldman, *50 Goldman Years*, 30.
43   GBV, interview with Royce Measures, 26 July 1973, transcript, IOH, 46-47.
44   WED to JFN, 30 June 1950, SBHLA.
45   "Frank Norris Has His 'Hearing'—Takes 6 Hours; Refuses Other Side 2 Minutes," *BBT*, 7 July 1950, 1-2.
46   GBV, interview with Royce Measures, 26 July 1973, transcript, IOH, 47.
47   Ibid.
48   Ibid.
49   Ibid.
50   "Frank Norris Has His 'Hearing'—Takes 6 Hours; Refuses Other Side 2 Minutes," *BBT*, 7 July 1950, 1-2.
51   BVB, *A History of Baptist Separatism*, 54-55.
52   Ibid., 55.
53   GBV, interview with Royce Measures, 27 July 1973, transcript, IOH, 47.
54   GBV, interview with Royce Measures, 26 July 1973, transcript, IOH, 47.
55   WED, from GBV, interview with Royce Measures, 27 July 1973, transcript, IOH, 94.
56   WED to JFN, 30 June 1950, SBHLA.
57   JFN to GBV, 29 June 1950, SBHLA.
58   "Most Pitiful Investigation," *FDML*, 7 July 1950, 3.
59   Ibid.

CHAPTER 25

1   JFN to WED, 16 June 1950, SBHLA.
2   JFN to WED, 18 June 1950, SBHLA.
3   JFN to WED, 16 June 1950, SBHLA.
4   "L. T. Grantham's Record of Adultery," *FDML*, 7 July 1950, 8.
5   WED, *BP*, 45.
6   JFN to WED, 18 June 1950, SBHLA.

7   Untitled boxed insert. *FDML*, 30 June 1950, 1.
8   WED to JFN, 30 June 1950, SBHLA.
9   "Harvey Springer in Great City-Wide Campaign at Lubbock," *FDML*, 30 June 1950, 1.
10   JFN to WED, 3 July 1950, SBHLA.
11   Untitled boxed insert, *FDML*, 7 July 1950, 1.
12   WED to JFN, 5 July 1950, SBHLA.
13   Bob Ingle, "The Truth about the Fellowship and the Seminary," *FDML*, 21 July 1950, 6.
14   WED to JFN, 28 June 1950, SBHLA.
15   WED, from GBV, interview with Royce Measures, 26 Sept. 1973, transcript, IOH, 153.
16   "Letter to Bill Dowell Canceling Degree from Seminary," *FDML*, 28 July 1950, 1.
17   Ritchie, *The Life and Legend of J. Frank Norris*, 22.
18   "Unless Bill Dowell Changes and Quits Taking Sunday Collection for His Salary It Will Ruin Him' – Beauchamp Vick," *FDML*, 21 July 1950, 1.
19   Ibid.
20   US Bureau of Labor Statistics, "1950," *Bureau of Labor Statistics*, accessed 23 Mar. 2017, www.bls.gov/opub/uscs/1950.pdf.
21   "My Last Trip Rather Strenuous but Happy," *FDML*, 28 July 1950, 1.
22   JFN to WED, 5 August 1950, SBHLA.
23   WED to JFN, 2 August 1950, SBHLA.
24   "Napoleons," *BBT*, 22 Sept. 1950, 4.
25   WED, *BP*, 46.
26   JFN to WED, 5 Aug. 1950, SBHLA.
27   JFN to WED, 3 July 1950, SBHLA.
28   R. O. Woodworth to JFN, 16 Sept. 1950, SBHLA.
29   JR, from GBV, interview with Royce Measures, 26 Sept. 1973, transcript, IOH, 133.
30   WED to JFN, 30 June 1950, SBHLA.
31   R. O. Woodworth to JFN, 22 Sept. 1950, SBHLA.
32   WED, *BP*, iii.
33   GBV, interview with Royce Measures, 26 Sept. 1973, transcript, IOH, 133.
34   JR, from GBV, interview with Royce Measures, 26 Sept. 1973, transcript, IOH, 144.
35   Isa. 54:17.
36   GBV, interview with Royce Measures, 26 Sept. 1973, transcript, IOH, 141.

CHAPTER 26

1   Qtd. in "He Is 'Running around the Streets of Gold Kicking Up Gold Dust!'" *BBT*, 15 Sept. 1998, 13.
2   Ibid.
3   BVB, *A History of Baptist Separatism*, 60.
4   "New Bible College Is Granted Decree," reprinted from *DN* in *BBT*, 30 June 1950, 1.
5   "Baptist Bible College Opens as It Said It Would," *BBT*, 15 Sept. 1950, 1.
6   L. T. Grantham, the pastor accused of adultery in Norris's publication, was not listed as part of the 1950 faculty of BBC. See "Baptist Bible College," *BBT*, 15 Sept. 1950, 7.
7   "Baptist Bible College," *BBT*, 15 Sept. 1950, 7.
8   Curtis Goldman, *50 Goldman Years*, 17.
9   "First Term of College Begins Sept. 5," *BBT*, 25 Aug. 1950, 1.
10   "Ground Broken for Baptist Bible College Dormitory," *BBT*, 28 July 1950, 1.
11   BVB, *A History of Baptist Separatism*, 61.
12   "Why No New Creditable School Can Be Established," *FDML*, 23 June 1950, 1.
13   R. O. Woodworth, "In the News of the Week," *BBT*, 30 June 1950, 8.
14   "Why Beauchamp Vick Refused to Have Full Proceedings Before the Temple Baptist Deacons Thursday Night," *FDML*, 9 June 1950, 2.
15   Minutes of the Texas Hotel meeting, qtd. in Curtis Goldman, *50 Goldman Years*, 17.
16   WED, *BP*, 51.
17   JFN to WED, 16 June 1950, SBHLA.
18   "For the Welfare of the GI Boys," *FDML*, 2 June 1950, 1.
19   "The Old Draft Law Re-Passed," *FDML*, 2 June 1950, 1.
20   JFN to WED, 18 June 1950, SBHLA.
21   Bill Fraser, "My Visit to Springfield," *FDML*, 28 July 1950, 2.
22   Ibid.
23   Qtd. in WED, from GBV, interview with Royce Measures, 26 July 1973, transcript, IOH, 59.
24   WED, interview with Royce Measures, 26 July 1973, transcript, IOH, 60.
25   Mildred Newton, "W. E. Dowell," *BBT*, 15 Sept. 1950, 7.
26   WED, interview with Royce Measures, 26 July 1973, transcript, IOH, 61.
27   Ibid., 51.
28   Ibid.
29   R. O. Woodworth to JFN, 22 Sept. 1950, SBHLA.

30   MR, *G. B. Vick*, 118. An earlier article listing the names of the class of 1951 shows seventeen total graduates. See "Founders' Week at BBC, May 20-23, 1985," *BBT*, 1 Mar. 1985, 12.

31   GBV, interview with Royce Measures, 27 July 1973, transcript, IOH, 87-88.

32   Ritchie, *The Life and Legend of J. Frank Norris*, 207.

33   GBV, interview with Royce Measures, 26 July 1973, transcript, IOH, 36.

34   Ibid., 33.

35   Curtis Goldman, *50 Goldman Years*, 5.

36   Joel A. Carpenter, ed., *Inside History of First Baptist Church, Fort Worth, and Temple Baptist Church, Detroit: Life Story of Dr. J. Frank Norris*, editor's note.

37   GBV, interview with Royce Measures, 28 Feb. 1974, transcript, IOH, 173.

38   Joel A. Carpenter, ed., *Inside History of First Baptist Church, Fort Worth, and Temple Baptist Church, Detroit: Life Story of Dr. J. Frank Norris*, editor's note.

39   R. O. Woodworth to JFN, 16 Sept. 1950, SBHLA.

40   GBV, interview with Royce Measures, 26 July 1973, transcript, IOH, 61.

41   Ibid., 37.

42   JR, telephone interview with the author, 24 July 2007.

43   *Baptist Bible College Catalog*, 1958-59.

44   JR, telephone interview with the author, 24 July 2007.

45   Doug Kutilek, "I Remember Noel Smith," *The Biblical Evangelist*, Jan.-Feb. 2007, www.biblicalevangelist.org/index.php?view=Sermons&id=520&issue=Volume%2038,%20Number%201.

46   Each of Dowell's two terms as president was two years long.

47   "Dr. Kenneth Gillming—Obituary," *NL*, 9 Feb. 2014, www.legacy.com/obituaries/news-leader/obituary.aspx?n=kenneth-gillming&pid=169558581&fhid=2196.

48   Kenneth Gillming to GBV, 4 Feb. 1954, VMLA.

49   Elmer L. Towns, *The Ten Largest Sunday Schools: And What Makes Them Grow*, (Grand Rapids: Baker, 1970), 40, elmertowns.com/wp-content/uploads/2013/10/10_Largest_SSETowns.pdf.

50   Ibid., 6.

51   GBV, interview with Royce Measures, 28 Feb. 1974, transcript, IOH, 183.

52   WED, *BP*, 56-57.

CHAPTER 27

1   Isa. 38:7-8.

2   WED, "Wisdom Excelleth Folly," BT, 3 Mar. 1985, audiocassette.

3   Ibid.

4   Ibid.

5   Bob Burke, "Watch Out Florida! Here Comes Bill Dowell," *Springfield! Magazine*, Jan. 1988, 49.

6   BDJ, e-mail message to the author, 29 June 2010.

7   WED, "Love Is the Fulfillment of the Law," BT, 2 Nov. 1986, audiocassette.

8   WED, "Politics and Religious Freedom," BT, n.d., audiocassette.

9   Kenneth E. Gillming, "Dr. W. E. Dowell: A Man Who Made a Difference," *BBT*, June/July 2002, 4.

10   WED, "I Charge Thee," *BBT*, 18 June 1976, 3+.

11   R. O. Woodworth, "In the News of the Week," *BBT*, 21 March 1952, 5.

12   Kenneth E. Gillming, "Dr. W. E. Dowell: A Man Who Made a Difference," *BBT*, June/July 2002, 4.

13   ES, interview with the author, 9 Nov. 1993.

14   "President Truman Arrives Here Today," *DN*, 6 June 1952, 1.

15   Ibid.

16   "Current Street Dance Condemned," *SUNL*, 1 June 1952, D5.

17   Ibid.

18   BDJ, e-mail message to the author, 15 July 2015.

19   Will L. Thompson, "There's a Great Day Coming," *HymnTime.com*, accessed 20 May 2016, www.hymntime.com/tch/htm/t/g/r/tgreatda.htm.

20   Newspaper advertisement, *DN*, 6 Dec. 1952, 2.

21   WED, "Didn't Know about Trial," *SUNL*, 22 Feb. 1953, B5.

22   Ibid.

23   "'Lewd' Books Worry Council," *SLP*, 9 Dec. 1952, 17.

24   "'Lewd Literature' Test Decision Set Feb. 17," *DN*, 4 Feb. 1953, 1.

25   J. Oliver Gideon, qtd. in "No Sense in Censorship?" *SLP*, 12 Dec. 1952, 1.

26   Ibid.

27   "No Sense in Censorship?" *SLP*, 12 Dec. 1952, 1.

28   Ibid.

29   "Heavy Silence Kills Plea for Censorship," *SLP*, 16 Dec. 1952, 1.

30   Ibid.

31   "'Lewd' Books Test Underway," *SLP*, 20 Dec. 1952, 8.

32   "'Lewd Literature' Test Decision Set Feb. 17," *DN*, 4 Feb. 1953, 1.

33   Ibid.

34   Ibid.
35   WED, "Didn't Know about Trial," *SUNL*, 22 Feb. 1953, B5.
36   WED, "Lewd Literature in Springfield," High Street Baptist Church, 22 Feb. 1953, transcript, 12.
37   WED, "Didn't Know about Trial," *SUNL*, 22 Feb. 1953, B5.
38   "Lewd Reading Case Dropped," *SLP*, 17 Feb. 1953, 1.
39   "3 Dealers Acquitted of 'Lewd Book' Sales," *DN*, 18 Feb. 1953, 1.
40   WED, "Lewd Literature in Springfield," High Street Baptist Church, 22 Feb. 1953, transcript, 10.
41   Ibid., 11.
42   Ibid., 13.
43   Ibid., 15.
44   Ibid.
45   Ibid.
46   Ibid., 16.
47   Ibid., 16-17.
48   "Dowell Raps Drury College in Sharply-Worded Sermon," *SLP*, 28 Feb. 1949, 8.
49   "High Street Fundamental Baptist Church," Advertisement. *SLP*, 26 Feb. 1949, 4.
50   "Dowell Raps Drury College in Sharply-Worded Sermon," *SLP*, 28 Feb. 1949, 8.
51   WED, interview with the author, 15 Oct. 1992.
52   Rex Thompson, Fred Carr, and Roy Fields. "Church Sends Assurances of Support to Drury Dean," *SPNL*, 6 Mar. 1949, B5.
53   WED, interview with the author, 15 Oct. 1992.
54   "Ferré to Be Drury Speaker," *DN*, 16 Feb. 1963, 2.
55   WED, "Apostasy," BT, 27 July 1977, audiocassette.
56   e.g., Ferré's work *The Sun and the Umbrella*.
57   WED, "To Stand for Principles," Feb. 1965, transcript, 3, DFP.
58   George Cornell, "New Bible Version Published," *SLP*, 28 Sept. 1952, A2.
59   "High Street Fundamental Baptist Church," advertisement, *SDN*, 4 Oct. 1952, 2.
60   WED, "The Revised Standard Version," High Street Baptist Church, 5 Oct. 1952, transcript, 15.
61   Ibid., 9.
62   Ibid., 10.
63   Ibid.
64   Ibid., 13.
65   Ibid., 13-14.
66   Ibid., 14.
67   WED, "The Bible Preacher in a Day of Peril," transcript, n.d, 5, DFP.
68   WED, "Lewd Literature in Springfield," High Street Baptist Church, 22 Feb. 1953, transcript, 18.

CHAPTER 28

1   Shirley Hackler, e-mail message to the author, 6 June 2006.
2   Ibid.
3   Shirley Hackler, interview with the author, 14 Jan. 2008.
4   qtd. in Shirley Hackler, interview with the author, 14 Jan. 2008.
5   Shirley Hackler, interview with the author, 14 Jan. 2008.
6   Ibid.
7   Shirley Hackler, e-mail message to the author, 6 June 2006.
8   Eldon Harmon, interview with the author, 21 Nov. 1993.
9   WED, "A New Testament Preacher," *SOTL*, 1 Nov. 1957, 11.
10   Ibid.
11   WED, "We Need God's Power," BT, n.d., audiocassette.
12   WED, "Tears," BT, 2 Feb. 1976, audiocassette.
13   WED, "Looking Down from the Cross," BT, 13 Apr. 1986, audiocassette.
14   WED, "We Need God's Power," BT, n.d., audiocassette.
15   JF, untitled sermon, BT, 26 Aug. 1985, videotape.
16   WED, "150 Additions in Lynchburg Revival," *BBT*, 17 Oct. 1952, 3.
17   JF, untitled sermon, BT, 26 Aug. 1985, videotape.
18   Ibid.
19   Ibid.
20   WED, "We Need God's Power," BT, n.d., audiocassette.
21   Ibid.
22   Ibid.
23   JF, untitled sermon, BT, 26 Aug. 1985, videotape.
24   Ibid.
25   qtd. in Linda Leicht, "W. E. Dowell, Noted Baptist Luminary, Dies," *NL*, 4 May 2002, 13A.
26   JF, *Strength for the Journey*, 152-53.
27   Ibid., 142.
28   JF, "Prayer Because of Easter," *Thomas Road Baptist Church*, 24 Mar. 2002, accessed 10 June 2010.

29   JF, *Strength for the Journey*, 142.

30   JF, "Prayer Because of Easter," *Thomas Road Baptist Church*, 24 Mar. 2002, accessed 10 June 2010.

31   Ibid.

32   JF, "Ye Have Not Because Ye Ask Not," *WND*, 19 Feb. 2000, www.wnd.com/2000/02/4375/.

33   JF, "Prayer Because of Easter," *Thomas Road Baptist Church*, 24 Mar. 2002, accessed 10 June 2010.

34   JF, "Ye Have Not Because Ye Ask Not," *WND*, 19 Feb. 2000, www.wnd.com/2000/02/4375/.

35   JF, "Prayer Because of Easter," *Thomas Road Baptist Church*, 24 Mar. 2002, accessed 10 June 2010.

36   Jonathan Falwell, "Remembering My Father and Mentor," *National Liberty Journal*, July 2007, 2.

37   "History," *Thomas Road Baptist Church*, accessed 23 Mar. 2017, trbc.org/history/.

38   "Jerry Falwell," *Britannica Academic*, accessed March 20, 2017, academic.eb.com/levels/collegiate/article/Jerry-Falwell/438085.

39   Ibid.

40   Nick Anderson, "Virginia's Liberty Transforms into Evangelical Mega-University," *The Washington Post*, 4 Mar. 2013, www.washingtonpost.com/local/education/virginias-liberty-transforms-into-evangelical-mega-university/2013/03/04/931cb116-7d09-11e2-9a75-dab0201670da_story.html?utm_term=.2b3ada390648.

41   JF, untitled sermon, BT, 26 Aug. 1985, videotape.

42   William Cowper, "God Moves in a Mysterious Way [1774]," *Net Hymnal*, 2011, www.cyberhymnal.org/htm/g/m/gmovesmw.htm.

CHAPTER 29

1   Roy A. Kemp, "Two Weeks with Bill Dowell and the High Street Baptist Church . . . ," *The Soul Winner*, July 1948, 1.

2   Jim Arthur, interview with the author, 19 Dec. 2008.

3   Joan Dowell, interview with the author, 25 Nov. 1993.

4   "No Meat?" *SLP*, 1 May 1946, 1.

5   "Dr. and Mrs. W. E. Dowell," *BBT*, 21 Mar. 1958, 3.

6   Janet Rodgers, e-mail message to the author, 24 July 2007.

7   NCD, personal notes, 16 Oct. 1979, DFP.

8   Janet Rodgers, e-mail message to the author, 24 July 2007.

9   NCD, personal notes, 16 Oct. 1979, DFP.

10   Ibid.

11   BDJ, e-mail message to the author, 1 July 2015.

12   Clyde Dowell to WED, 30 June 1958, DFP.

13   Karen Lyn Carreiro to the author, 2 Mar. 1994, DFP.

14   "Dowell Starts World Junket," *SUNL*, 22 June 1958, C7.

15   ES to WED, 11 August 1958, DFP.

16   "Dowell Starts World Junket," *SUNL*, 22 June 1958, C7.

17   WED to NCD, 23 June 1958, DFP.

18   GBV, telegram to WED, 23 June 1958, DFP.

19   WED to Jerry Belton, 16 Oct. 1980, DFP.

20   WED, journal, summer 1958, DFP.

21   Ibid.

22   WED to NCD and Clyde Dowell, n.d., DFP.

23   WED, journal, summer 1958, DFP.

24   WED to NCD and Clyde Dowell, n.d., DFP.

25   Ibid.

26   WED, journal, summer 1958, DFP.

27   WED, sermon, BT, c. 1976, audiocassette.

28   WED, "Dowell Has a Grand Time with Missionaries in Japan," *BBT*, 8 Aug. 1958, 3.

29   WED to NCD and Clyde Dowell, n.d., DFP.

30   WED, "Dowell Has a Grand Time with Missionaries in Japan," *BBT*, 8 Aug. 1958, 3.

31   Ibid.

32   WED to NCD and Clyde Dowell, n.d., DFP.

33   WED, journal, summer 1958, DFP.

34   Ibid.

35   WED to NCD and Clyde Dowell, n.d., DFP.

36   WED, journal, summer 1958, DFP.

37   Ibid.

38   WED, "Dowell Visits 'Pearl of the Orient,'" *BBT*, 22 Aug. 1958, 1.

39   WED, journal, summer 1958, DFP.

40   WED, "Dowell Visits 'Pearl of the Orient,'" *BBT*, 22 Aug. 1958, 1.

41   WED, journal, summer 1958, DFP.

42   WED, "Dowell Visits 'Pearl of the Orient,'" *BBT*, 22 Aug. 1958, 1.

43   WED to NCD and Clyde Dowell, n.d., DFP.

44   WED to NCD and Clyde Dowell, 14 July 1958, DFP.

45   WED, journal, summer 1958, DFP.

46   WED, "Be Thankful," BT, 25 Nov. 1981, audiocassette.

47   WED to NCD and Clyde Dowell, n.d., DFP.
48   WED, "Dowell Accepts Unanimous Call to Beaver Street Pastorate,'" *BBT*, 2 Aug. 1963, 3.
49   WED, journal, summer 1958, DFP.
50   WED to NCD and Clyde Dowell, n.d., DFP.
51   WED, journal, summer 1958, DFP.
52   WED to NCD and Clyde Dowell, n.d., DFP.
53   WED, journal, summer 1958, DFP.
54   Ibid.
55   Ibid.

CHAPTER 30

1   WED, journal, summer 1958, DFP.
2   Ibid.
3   Ibid.
4   Ibid.
5   WED to NCD and Clyde Dowell, 20 July 1958, DFP.
6   WED, journal, summer 1958, DFP.
7   Ibid.
8   Ibid.
9   Ibid.
10   Ibid.
11   WED to NCD and Clyde Dowell, 20 July 1958, DFP.
12   WED, journal, summer 1958, DFP.
13   Ibid.
14   Ibid.
15   WED, "What Think Ye of Christ?" BT, 22 June 1986, audiocassette.
16   WED, "How Important Is the Resurrection?" BT, 19 Apr. 1987, audiocassette.
17   WED to NCD and Clyde Dowell, 27 July 1958, DFP.
18   WED, journal, summer 1958, DFP.
19   WED to NCD and Clyde Dowell, 27 July 1958, DFP.
20   WED, journal, summer 1958, DFP.
21   Ibid.
22   Ibid.
23   WED, *The Communist Infiltration of the Church*, 17.
24   WED, journal, summer 1958, DFP.
25   WED, *The Communist Infiltration of the Church*, 17-18.
26   WED to NCD and Clyde Dowell, n.d., DFP.
27   WED, journal, summer 1958, DFP.
28   Ibid.
29   Ibid.
30   WED to NCD and Clyde Dowell, n.d., DFP.
31   WED, journal, summer 1958, DFP.
32   WED, "The Elder Brother," BT, 17 Jan. 1982, audiocassette.
33   BDJ, e-mail message to the author, 18 July 2015.
34   Willa Mae Stewart-Setseck to Father John, n.d., DFP.
35   WED to NCD and Clyde Dowell, n.d., DFP.

CHAPTER 31

1   Elmer Deal and MR, *Out of the Mouth of the Lion*, 28.
2   V. de Carle Thompson to F. S. Donnelson, 26 Mar. 1958, *VMLA*.
3   Ibid.
4   Ibid.
5   Carl J. Tanis to F. S. Donnelson, 18 June 1958, *VMLA*.
6   WED to NCD and Clyde Dowell, n.d., DFP.
7   WED, journal, summer 1958, DFP.
8   Ibid.
9   Qtd. in WED, "What Is Expected of the Church This Year?" BT, 4 Jan. 1976, audiocassette.
10   WED, journal, summer 1958, DFP.
11   Ibid.
12   Ibid.
13   Ibid.
14   Ibid.
15   Ibid.

16   Ibid.
17   Ibid.
18   Ibid.
19   Ibid.
20   Ibid.
21   Ibid.
22   Ibid.
23   Ibid.
24   Ibid.
25   Ibid.
26   Ibid.
27   Elmer Deal and MR, *Out of the Mouth of the Lion*, 20.
28   Ibid., 51.
29   Ibid., 52.
30   Ibid., 473-79.
31   Elmer Deal and MR, *Out of the Mouth of the Lion*, XIII.
32   "W. E. Dowell Sr. Reflects on Over Sixty Years of Ministry," *The Baptist Preacher*, May/June 1996, 11.
33   WED, sermon, BT, c. 1976, audiocassette.
34   Ibid.
35   Ibid.

CHAPTER 32

1   ES, interview with the author, 9 Nov. 1993.
2   Ibid.
3   Norma Gillming, "The Springfield Revival Crusade," *BBT*, 15 May 1959, 1.
4   Noma Lea Callahan to NCD, 29 May 1959, DFP.
5   "Dr. and Mrs. W. E. Dowell," *BBT*, 21 Mar. 1958, 3.
6   WED, interview with the author, 24 Oct. 1991.
7   "Dowell and Alexander Head the Fellowship; Next Year, Detroit," *BBT*, 21 Sept. 1962, 1.
8   "Dowell Wants More of Everything," *BBT*, 21 Sept. 1962, 2, and "Fellowship Wants Nuclear Weapons and Doesn't Want Communist Propaganda," *BBT*, 21 Sept. 1962, 6.
9   WED, interview with the author, 15 Oct. 1992.
10   Ibid.
11   Ibid.
12   WED, personal notes, n.d., VMLA.
13   WED, "When Love Is the Motive," BT, 10 Aug. 1986, audiocassette.
14   Qtd. in WED, interview with the author, 15 Oct. 1992.
15   Ibid.
16   ES, interview with the author, 9 Nov. 1993.
17   WED, interview with the author, 15 Oct. 1992.
18   WED, "Give Me This Mountain," BT, 1976, audiocassette.
19   Ibid.
20   WED, interview with the author, 15 Oct. 1992.
21   WED, personal notes, 1961, DFP.
22   Ibid.
23   WED, postcard to NCD, 5 May 1961, DFP.
24   WED, personal notes, n.d., DFP.
25   Ibid.
26   Ibid.
27   Ibid.
28   Sharon Dowell, e-mail message to the author, 18 July 2009.
29   WED, "A New Testament Preacher," *SOTL*, 1 Nov. 1957, 11.
30   WED, "Divine Invitation," BT, 13 July 1986, audiocassette.
31   WED, *Pastoral Theology*, 61.
32   F. S. Donnelson to WED, 7 June 1961, DFP.
33   WED, "A Soul-Destroying Evil," BT, 15 Jan. 1978, audiocassette.
34   WED, interview with the author, 15 Oct. 1992.
35   BDJ, interview with the author, 25 Nov. 1993.
36   Ibid.
37   WED, interview with the author, 24 Oct. 1991.
38   Ibid.
39   Ibid.
40   Ibid.
41   WED, interview with the author, 15 Oct. 1992.
42   WED, interview with the author, 24 Oct. 1991.

43   Ibid.
44   BDJ, interview with the author, 25 Nov. 1993.
45   Ibid.
46   Ibid.
47   Ibid.
48   Ibid.
49   Ibid.
50   WED, interview with the author, 24 Oct. 1991.
51   Ibid.
52   BDJ, interview with the author, 25 Nov. 1993.
53   Ibid.
54   Ibid.
55   BDJ, e-mail message to the author, 9 June 2016.
56   BDJ, interview with the author, 25 Nov. 1993.
57   WED, interview with the author, 24 Oct. 1991.
58   Ibid.
59   BDJ, interview with the author, 25 Nov. 1993.
60   ES, interview with the author, 9 Nov. 1993.
61   WED, personal notes, n.d., VMLA.
62   WED, interview with the author, 24 Oct. 1991.
63   Qtd. in Steve Hilton, "Rev. W. E. Dowell: BBC Executive Vice President Keeps Faith in Fundamentalism," *SUNL*, 16 Jan. 1972, C2.
64   ES, interview with the author, 9 Nov. 1993.
65   JR, telephone interview with the author, 24 July 2007.
66   WED, "Jesus Christ Revealed," BT, 1 Aug. 1982, audiocassette.
67   WED, interview with the author, 14 Feb. 1992.
68   BDJ, e-mail message to the author, 4 July 2015.

CHAPTER 33

1   "Baptist Pastor Is Fatally Shot," *Sarasota Journal*, 9 Apr. 1963, 5.
2   Noel Smith, "George Hodges," *BBT*, 19 Apr. 1963, 1.
3   Ibid.
4   "Mrs. Luckie Indicted for Manslaughter," rpt. from *Jacksonville Times Union* in *BBT*, 6 Sept. 1963, 2.
5   "Earlier Threat Was Made by Woman Who Killed Pastor," *Ocala Star-Banner*, 3 May 1963, 3.
6   "Mrs. Luckie Indicted for Manslaughter," rpt. from *Jacksonville Times Union* in *BBT*, 6 Sept. 1963, 2.
7   WED, interview with the author, 14 Feb. 1992.
8   Ibid.
9   "Mrs. Luckie Reported Insane, Forcing Murder Trial's Delay," *Sarasota Herald-Tribune*, 21 Jan. 1964, 7.
10   "He Lies Under the Spreading Oaks, By the Sid of His Dear Elizabeth," *BBT*, 26 Apr. 1963, 1.
11   James R. Ward, "Beaver Street Baptist Church Sanctuary Solemnly Dedicated," *The Florida Times-Union* [Jacksonville], 15 Aug. 1966, B-1.
12   Mark D. Hodges to WED, 2 Feb. 1984, DFP.
13   Bill Dougherty, e-mail message to the author, 17 July 2007.
14   WED, interview with the author, 14 Feb. 1992.
15   Ibid.
16   ES, interview with the author, 9 Nov. 1993.
17   Ibid.
18   Ibid.
19   Qtd. in ES, interview with the author, 9 Nov. 1993.
20   "W. E. Dowell Accepts Unanimous Call to Beaver Street Pastorate," *BBT*, 2 Aug. 1963, 2.
21   Steve Hilton, "Rev. W. E. Dowell: BBC Executive Vice President Keeps Faith in Fundamentalism," *SUNL*, 16 Jan. 1972, C2.
22   Qtd. in ES, interview with the author, 9 Nov. 1993.
23   Durward G. Hall to WED, 24 July 1963.
24   BDJ, e-mail message to the author, 4 July 2015.
25   WED, from GBV, interview with Royce Measures, 27 July 1973, transcript, IOH, 113.
26   GBV, interview with Royce Measures, 27 July 1973, transcript, IOH, 114.
27   WED, from GBV, interview with Royce Measures, 27 July 1973, transcript, IOH, 114.
28   Ibid., 118-19.
29   Ibid., 119.
30   Bill Dougherty, e-mail message to the author, 17 July 2007.
31   WED, interview with the author, 14 Feb. 1992.
32   "Remembering Hurricane Dora," *The Jacksonville Historical Society*, 2015, www.jaxhistory.org/remembering-hurricane-dora/.
33   Sharon Dowell, e-mail message to the author, 19 July 2009.
34   WED, "The Trump of God," n.d., transcript, 4, DFP.
35   WED, interview with the author, 14 Feb. 1992.

36   Noma Lea Callahan to WED and NCD, 26 Jan. 1964, DFP.
37   Noma Lea Callahan to WED and NCD, 24 Mar. 1964, DFP.
38   Bill Dougherty, e-mail message to the author, 17 July 2007.
39   Ibid.
40   "Death Penalty to Be Discussed by 3 Ministers," *Florida Times-Union* [Jacksonville], 24 July 1966, n.p.
41   "Ground Broken Anyway," *Florida Times-Union* [Jacksonville], 10 Sept. 1965, n.p.
42   Bill Dougherty, e-mail message to the author, 17 July 2007.
43   Ibid.
44   Ibid.
45   "Climaxed a Week's Meeting," *BBT*, 10 June 1966, 8.
46   "Most Unique Church Building in the United States," *Jacksonville Journal*, 13 Aug. 1966, 3.
47   "Jacksonville Landmark," *The Financial News* [Jacksonville], 3 Mar. 1967, 6.
48   James R. Ward, "Beaver Street Baptist Church Sanctuary Solemnly Dedicated," *Florida Times-Union* [Jacksonville], 15 Aug. 1966, B-1.
49   Qtd. in "Jacksonville Landmark," *The Financial News* [Jacksonville], 3 Mar. 1967, 6.
50   WED, interview with the author, 14 Feb. 1992.
51   WED, "The Betrayal of Jesus," BT, 22 Feb. 1976, audiocassette.
52   Ibid.

CHAPTER 34

1   The dialogue in this section has been adapted from a mid-1960's sermon by Dowell called "The Trump of God." The sermon has been preserved in transcript form and is part of the DFP.
2   Dave Drury, e-mail message to the author, 25 May 2006.
3   Ibid.
4   Rick L. Carter to WED, 30 Jan. 1984.
5   Isa. 55:11.
6   Janet Rodgers, e-mail message to the author, 24 July 2007.
7   "A Biographical History of Dennis E. Wheeler," *Dennis Wheeler*, accessed 30 June 2010, home.att.net/~dwheesaved/memoirs/personal.htm.
8   Viola Walden to WED, 25 Feb. 1966, DFP.
9   Jack Norris, "Nearly 400 Earn Degrees at BJU," *Greenville News*, 1 June 1967, 1.
10   WED to David A. Cavin, 19 June 1967, DFP.
11   MR, *G. B. Vick*, 118.
12   JR, telephone interview with the author, 24 July 2007.
13   WED, interview with the author, 14 Feb. 1992.
14   WED to David A. Cavin, 19 June 1967, DFP.
15   D. A. Cavin to WED and NCD, 22 June 1967, DFP.
16   GBV to WED, 14 June 1967, DFP.
17   Ibid.
18   Ibid.
19   Ibid.
20   R. O. Woodworth to WED, 29 June 1967, DFP.
21   WED to GBV, 22 July 1967, DFP.
22   GBV to WED, 27 July 1967, DFP.
23   WED, interview with the author, 14 Feb. 1992.
24   WED to NCD, 7 Mar. 1968, DFP.
25   Ibid.
26   WED, personal notes, 20 Mar. 1968, DFP.
27   WED, interview with the author, 14 Feb. 1992.
28   JR, telephone interview with the author, 24 July 2007.
29   "W. E. Dowell – He Is Now Executive Vice-President of Baptist Bible College," *BBT*, 5 Apr. 1968, 1.
30   NCD to WED, 31 May 1968, DFP.
31   WED, "Dowell's Summer of Evangelism," *BBT*, 4 Oct. 1968, 5.
32   Information gleaned from Dowell's 1968 planner, DFP.
33   GBV to WED, 4 Aug. 1968, DFP.

CHAPTER 35

1   WED to NCD, 29 May 1968, DFP.
2   "But God!" is an expression found in Eph. 2:4.
3   WED, interview with the author, 24 Oct. 1991.
4   WED, "Dowell Has One of His Best Summers of His 35 Years' Ministry," *BBT*, 12 Sept. 1969, 3.
5   Qtd. in WED to NCD, 3 Mar. 1968, DFP.
6   WED to NCD, 29 June 1970, DFP.

7   WED to NCD, 16 July 1971, DFP.
8   Billy Hamm, "Independence in the BBFI," *Baptist Bible Fellowship International*, accessed 11 Jan. 2008, www.bbfi.org/archives/news/page023.htm.
9   Ronald Schaffer to WED, 30 Jan. 1984, DFP.
10   Paul Duckett to NCD, 10 May 1971, DFP.
11   Laura Bauer Menner, "Pastors' Pastor Leads Way," *NL*, 10 Oct. 1999, 34.
12   Ray Brinson to WED, 24 Feb. 1984, DFP.
13   Terry Allcorn, e-mail message to the author, 8 June 2006.
14   WED to NCD, 2 July 1969, DFP.
15   WED, "Dowell Has One of His Best Summers of His 35 Years' Ministry," *BBT*, 12 Sept. 1969, 3.
16   "Bible College Official Guest Baptist Evangelist," *San Angelo Standard-Times*, 21 June 1972, 10A.
17   WED to President Richard Nixon, 14 Nov. 1969, VMLA.
18   WED and BBC Faculty to President Richard Nixon, 27 Oct. 1971, VMLA.
19   e.g., WED, "Set Your Affections," BT, 30 Nov. 1977, audiocassette. Also "The First Commandment," BT, n.d., audiocassette.
20   WED, personal notes, 1961, DFP.
21   WED, "The Substitutionary Atonement of Jesus Christ," Tabernacle Baptist Church [Farmington, N.M.], c. 1984.
22   WED to NCD, 6 June 1968, DFP.
23   WED, "Revival Sermon," n.d., transcript, 6, DFP.
24   WED to R. O. Woodworth, DFP.
25   WED to pastors of the Baptist Bible Fellowship, 18 Aug. 1969, VMLA.
26   WED to R. O. Woodworth, n.d., VMLA.
27   WED to pastors of the Baptist Bible Fellowship, 18 Aug. 1969, VMLA.
28   WED to NCD, 27 Aug. 1969, DFP.
29   MR, "R. O. Woodworth Graduates at Age 93," *BBT*, 15 Aug. 1998, 21.
30   BDJ, e-mail message to the author, 10 July 2015.
31   Keith Gillming, untitled sermon, Baptist Bible College, 29 Mar. 2016.
32   GBV, untitled notes, n.d., VMLA.
33   WED to Richard Ostella, 16 Feb. 1972, DFP.
34   BDJ, e-mail message to the author, 10 July 2015.
35   WED, personal notes. n.d., DFP.
36   BDJ, e-mail message to the author, 10 July 2015.
37   MR, "R. O. Woodworth Graduates at Age 93," *BBT*, 15 Aug. 1998, 21.
38   BDJ, e-mail message to the author, 10 July 2015.
39   Ibid.
40   JR, telephone interview with the author, 24 July 2007.
41   Ibid.
42   BDJ, e-mail message to the author, 10 July 2015.
43   Ibid.
44   WED, interview with the author, 14 Feb. 1992.
45   WED to an individual in N. Olmsted, Ohio, 12 July 1972, VMLA.
46   WED to a pastor, 9 Dec. 1971, VMLA.
47   Qtd. in "The Nth Degree," *Integrity USA*, Nov. 1974, www.integrityusa.org/archive/voice/1974/November1974.htm.
48   WED, "The Worth of a Soul," *SOTL*, 3 Aug. 1975, 11.
49   WED to Senator Thomas F. Eagleton, 30 Oct. 1969, VMLA.
50   "Accreditation," *BBC Banner*, 5 Dec. 1978, 1.
51   "College Authorized to Purchase High Street Properties," *BBT*, 16 Oct. 1970, 1-2.
52   WED to David A. Cavin, 28 Mar. 1973, VMLA.
53   WED, "A Statement," *BBT*, 7 Dec. 1973, 2.
54   Richard A. Burks, "BBC Trustee Minutes," 26 Sept. 1973, VMLA.
55   WED to David A. Cavin, 16 Oct. 1973, VMLA.
56   David A. Cavin, "The Pastor's Desk . . ," *High Street Baptist News*, 25 Oct. 1973, 1.
57   WED, "A Statement," *BBT*, 7 Dec. 1973, 2.
58   "Parking Lot Opens," *SLP*, 11 Nov. 1976, 19.
59   GBV to Jack Baskin, 11 Sept. 1971, VMLA.
60   GBV to WED, 14 June 1967, DFP.
61   David Stokes, "Tribute to W. E. Dowell," *Masterpubmag.com*, 13 Sept. 2004, accessed 30 June 2010, masterpubmag.com/comments.php?id=30_0_1_0_C.
62   James Sewell, interview with the author, 26 Oct. 2009.
63   Naim Khoury, untitled sermon, BT, 19 May 2002.
64   Keith Bassham, "Remembering 'Brother Dowell,'" *BBT*, Special Insert, June/July 2002, 2.
65   Linda Leicht, "W. E. Dowell, Noted Baptist Luminary, Dies," *NL*, 4 May 2002, 1A.

CHAPTER 36

1   "Dowell Accepts the Call to Be Permanent Pastor," *BBT*, 10 May 1974, 2.

2   Myra MacPherson, "The Rise of the Falwell Empire," *The Washington Post*, 26 Sept. 1984, www.washingtonpost.com/archive/lifestyle/1984/09/26/the-rise-of-the-falwell-empire/9dda636e-3475-4b64-899a-650a1d6dbb89/?utm_term=.fa198f537494.

3   JF, *Strength for the Journey*, 327.

4   JF, "Statement by Jerry Falwell," *BBT*, 31 Aug. 1973, 9.

5   "Baptist Temple Offering Circular," 2 Dec. 1974, 4.

6   BDJ, interview with the author, 25 Nov. 1993.

7   Larry Smith to Etsyl Sparkman, 7 Nov. 1973, DFP.

8   Ibid.

9   Janet Rodgers to Noma Lea Callahan, 14 Feb. 1974, DFP.

10   "W. E. Dowell Retirement Service," BT, 19 June 1988, videotape.

11   NCD to Noma Lea Callahan, 14 Feb. 1974, DFP.

12   "Dowell Accepts the Call to Be Permanent Pastor," *BBT*, 10 May 1974, 2.

13   Ibid.

14   Etsyl Sparkman to WED, 3 May 1974, DFP.

15   Ibid.

16   WED, "Twentieth Anniversary," BT, 28 Aug. 1977, audiocassette.

17   Ibid.

18   Ibid.

19   WED, interview with the author, 14 Feb. 1992.

20   Ibid.

21   "Baptist Temple Offering Circular," 2 Dec. 1974, 1.

22   Ibid., 1-2.

23   BDJ, interview with the author, 25 Nov. 1993.

24   WED, untitled sermon, BT, 4 Jan. 1976, audiocassette.

25   WED, "Twentieth Anniversary," BT, 28 Aug. 1977, audiocassette.

26   Ken Howard, "The Miracle$ at Baptist Temple—A Ten-Year Project," *BBT*, 5 July 1985, 1-2.

27   Qtd. in BDJ, interview with the author, 25 Nov. 1993.

28   WED, "Twentieth Anniversary," BT, 28 Aug. 1977, audiocassette.

29   Prov. 27:1.

30   WED, "Twentieth Anniversary," BT, 28 Aug. 1977, audiocassette.

31   Isa. 46:10.

CHAPTER 37

1   Doug Kutilek, "I Remember Noel Smith," *The Biblical Evangelist*, Jan.-Feb. 2007, www.biblicalevangelist.org/index.php?view=Sermons&id=520&issue=Volume%2038,%20Number%201.

2   Charles Smith to WED, 20 Jan. 1974, VMLA.

3   NCD, personal notes, 16 Oct. 1979, DFP.

4   MR, *G. B. Vick*, 119.

5   J. H. Melton, *The Clergyman of the Century*, vol. 1, 1976, vii.

6   WED, from GBV, interview with Royce Measures, 26 July 1973, transcript, IOH, 74.

7   Kenneth E. Gillming, "Dr. Dowell: A Man Who Made a Difference," *BBT*, June/July 2002, 4.

8   WED, "Dowell Visits Australia," *BBT*, 7 Mar. 1975, 7.

9   "W. E. Dowell Sr. Reflects on Over Sixty Years of Ministry," *The Baptist Preacher*, May/June 1996, 10-11.

10   WED, "Dowell Visits Australia," *BBT*, 7 Mar. 1975, 7.

11   WED, "Dowell Visits Peru," *BBT*, 31 Oct. 1975, 13.

12   WED to NCD, 16 Sept. 1975, DFP.

13   Larry Smith to Jay Edwards, 24 Nov. 1975, DFP.

14   WED, "As I See It," *NL*, 8 Dec. 1979, 5A.

15   Tony Isaacs, untitled sermon, Baptist Bible College, 24 Sept. 2015.

16   "Memorial Service in Springfield, Mo," *BBT*, 24 Oct. 1975, 3.

17   Ibid.

18   Dorothy Y. Burks, BBC Faculty Meeting Minutes, 7 Oct. 1975, VMLA.

19   Ibid.

20   "W. E. Dowell Sr. Reflects on Over Sixty Years of Ministry," *The Baptist Preacher*, May/June 1996, 10-11.

21   WED, interview with the author, 24 Oct. 1991.

22   Qtd. in WED, interview with the author, 24 Oct. 1991.

23   Don Woodworth, Minutes of Trustee Meeting, Baptist Bible College, 2 Dec. 1975.

24   Mary Ritchie. "Dowell Established as College's Chief During Ceremonies," *SLP*, 19 May 1976, 49.

25   "Dowell to Take BBC Leadership Officially Tonight," *SLP*, 18 May 1976, 13.

26   "W. E. Dowell Sr. Reflects on Over Sixty Years of Ministry," *The Baptist Preacher*, May/June 1996, 11.

27   WED, "I Charge Thee," *BBT*, 18 June 1976, 6.

28   WED, "As I See It," *NL*, 12 Aug. 1978, 7A.

29   WED, "As I See It," *NL*, 29 July 1978, 5A.

30   JF, untitled sermon, BT, 26 Aug. 1985, videotape.

31   WED, interview with the author, 14 Feb. 1992.
32   Monroe Parker to WED, 14 Apr. 1976, DFP.
33   WED, "What Is Expected of the Church This Year?" BT, 4 Jan. 1976, audiocassette.
34   Ps. 124:1-5.

CHAPTER 38

1   WED, "Born Again," BT, 23 Apr. 1978, audiocassette.
2   WED, "Politics and Religious Freedom," BT, 31 Oct. 1976, audiocassette.
3   Leland R. Kennedy, "Precious Memories of the BBFI," BBT, 15 Jan. 2000, 49.
4   WED, "To Stand for Principles," transcript, Feb. 1965, 10, DFP.
5   Raymond W. Barber to WED, 8 Mar. 1978, VMLA.
6   WED to Raymond W. Barber, 15 Mar. 1978, VMLA.
7   John R. Rice, "Must All Tithes Go to Church Treasury?" SOTL, 4 May 1973, 1.
8   WED, "Dowell Resigns from Rice's Board," BBT, 24 Aug. 1973, 3.
9   WED, "The Worth of a Soul," SOTL, 3 Aug. 1975, 11.
10   Wendell Zimmerman, "Tribune Editor Answers John R. Rice," BBT, 1 July 1977, 1+.
11   WED, "W. E. Dowell, BBC President, Responds to John R. Rice," BBT, 16 Sept. 1977, 1+.
12   Ibid.
13   WED to GBV, 31 May 1974, VMLA.
14   Qtd. in Mary Jane Cotter, BBC Faculty Meeting Minutes, 5 May 1977, VMLA.
15   WED, "Baptist Bible College Trustees Chart the Future," BBT, 17 Mar. 1978, 1+.
16   WED, personal notes. n.d., DFP.
17   WED, "Baptist Bible College Trustees Chart the Future," BBT, 17 Mar. 1978, 4.
18   Ibid.
19   WED, "Banner Year Expected at BBC," BBT, 23 Feb. 1979, 1.
20   Shirley McCullough, BBC Faculty Meeting Minutes, 15 Mar. 1979, VMLA.
21   Hunter Sherman to Mark Mills, 8 Oct. 1980, VMLA.
22   WED, "Assurance," BT, 11 Aug. 1985, audiocassette.
23   Mary Herman, interview with the author, 29 Dec. 2007.
24   JR, telephone interview with the author, 24 July 2007.

CHAPTER 39

1   WED, "Baptist Bible College Trustees Chart the Future," BBT, 17 Mar. 1978, 4.
2   WED, "BBC Philosophy of Music," BBT, 22 Dec. 1978, 12.
3   Ibid.
4   Ibid.
5   WED, "An Open Letter to All Fundamental Baptists," n.d., DFP.
6   WED, "The Worth of a Soul," SOTL, 3 Aug. 1975, 11.
7   BBC Administration Meeting Minutes, 9 Nov. 1977, VMLA.
8   Noel Smith, "Translations of Our English Bible," BBT, 13 Dec. 1968, 6.
9   Ibid.
10   Ibid., 7.
11   WED, The Church: It's Meaning, Message and Method, 1980, 42.
12   See Doug Kutilek, "I Remember Noel Smith," The Biblical Evangelist, Jan.-Feb. 2007, www.biblicalevangelist.org/index.php?view=Sermons&id=520&issue=Volume%2038,%20Number%201.
13   "BBC and BBIE Issue Statement Concerning Scriptures," BBT, 30 Jan. 1981, 1.
14   WED, "As I See It," SPNL, 1 July 1978, 4.
15   WED, personal notes, n.d., VMLA.
16   Billy Hamm, "Independence in the BBFI," Baptist Bible Fellowship International, accessed 10 June 2010, www.bbfi.org/archives/news/page023.htm.
17   WED, personal notes, 11 Dec. 1979, VMLA.
18   WED, memo to Fred Moody, 22 Oct. 1980, VMLA.
19   WED, "A College Where They Enter to Learn and Go Forth to Serve," BBT, 12 Dec. 1980, 12.
20   WED, untitled sermon, Lighthouse Children's Home [Kosciusko, MS], n.d., videotape.
21   WED, "Message for Orientation," transcript, Baptist Bible College, n.d., VMLA.
22   WED, "Revive Us Again," BT, 29 Aug. 1976, audiocassette.
23   Doug Kutilek, J. Frank Norris and His Heirs: The Bible Translation Controversy, (Pasadena: Pilgrim, 1999), 111.
24   Joan Dowell, interview with the author, 25 Nov. 1993.
25   Help Is on the Way: A Handbook for Patients, (New York: Myasthenia Gravis Foundation, n.d.), 12.
26   WED, "Most Successful Fellowship Week," BBT, 1 July 1977, 5.
27   Joan Dowell, interview with the author, 25 Nov. 1993.
28   NCD, personal notes, 16 Oct. 1979, DFP.
29   WED, interview with Zimmerman, transcript, c. 1978. Interview was conducted when Dowell was age 64.

30   Ibid.
31   Ibid.
32   R. O. Woodworth, "Fellowship Circuit," *BBT*, 5 Aug. 1977, 12.
33   Minutes of Administrative Staff Meeting, 2 June 1977, VMLA.
34   R. O. Woodworth, "Fellowship Circuit," *BBT*, 5 Aug. 1977, 12.
35   BDJ, e-mail message to the author, 8 July 2016.
36   R. O. Woodworth, "Fellowship Circuit," *BBT*, 5 Aug. 1977, 12.
37   WED, "Letter from Dr. Dowell," *BBT*, 23 Sept. 1977, 6.
38   Joan Dowell, interview with the author, 25 Nov. 1993.
39   "BBC to Have New President," *BBT*, 10 Dec. 1982, 2.
40   Minutes of the BBC Trustee Meeting, 8 Dec. 1982, VMLA.
41   Ibid.
42   Shirley McCullough, interview with the author, 2008.

CHAPTER 40

1   The dialogue in this chapter is taken from Reagan's actual speech. See Ronald Reagan, "Remarks at the Baptist Fundamentalism Annual Convention," *Ronald Reagan Presidential Library and Museum*, 13 Apr. 1984, www.reaganlibrary.archives.gov/archives/speeches/1984/41384h.htm.
2   Francis X. Clines. "Hecklers Interrupt Reagan Speech at Gathering of Fundamentalists," *New York Times*, 14 Apr. 1984, www.nytimes.com/1984/04/14/us/hecklers-interrupt-reagan-speech-at-gathering-of-fundamentalists.html.
3   "Key to Lord Mayor," *BBT*, 7 Dec. 1973, 3.
4   "50 MPH Limit Is Questioned in Mayor's Letter to Nixon," *SLP*, 16 Nov. 1973, 20.
5   WED to the author, 18 Mar. 1983, DFP.
6   "Religious News Service Report," *BBT*, 16 Sept. 1960, 5.
7   WED, "The Fatal Mistake of Feminists," BT, 4 Dec. 1977, audiocassette.
8   "Claims Sickening, Rev. Dowell Says," *NL*, 20 Oct. 1974, A21.
9   WED, "Politics and Religious Freedom," BT, 31 Oct. 1976, audiocassette.
10   BBC Administration Meeting Minutes, 21 Oct. 1977, VMLA.
11   WED, "As I See It," *SPNL*, 17 Feb. 1979, 7A.
12   WED, "As I See It," *SPNL*, 14 July 1979, 5A.
13   WED, "Dowell Asks Equal Time," *SUNL*, 16 Dec. 1973, A35.
14   Qtd. in Bil Tatum, "'Rebuttal to Primal Man' Something Else: Critic," *SLP*, 7 Mar. 1974, 23.
15   Bil Tatum, "'Rebuttal to Primal Man' Something Else: Critic," *SLP*, 7 Mar. 1974, 23.
16   WED, "As I See It," *SPNL*, 30 Sept. 1978, 4A.
17   Bob Burke. "Watch Out Florida! Here Comes Bill Dowell," *Springfield! Magazine*, Jan. 1988, 48.
18   WED, "As I See It," *SPNL*, 30 Sept. 1978, 4A.
19   WED, "As I See It," *SPNL*, 2 Sept. 1978, 4A.
20   Vicki Allen, "Dowell Cites 'Slip of Tongue,'" *SLP*, 7 Sept. 1978, 1C.
21   Ibid., 2C.
22   WED, "Morality and City Government," BT, 14 Aug. 1977, audiocassette.
23   WED, "As I See It," *SPNL*, 24 Mar. 1979, 5A.
24   Gale Baldwin, "Church Charges City 'Harassment,'" *SANL*, 19 Mar. 1977, 1.
25   WED, "Why God Permits His People to Suffer," BT, 20 June 1982, audiocassette.
26   Gale Baldwin, "Church Charges City 'Harassment,'" *SANL*, 19 Mar. 1977, 1.
27   Ibid., 1-2.
28   Gale Baldwin, "Lawsuit Seen against Church," *SLP*, 11 May 1977, 26.
29   Ibid.
30   Gale Baldwin, "Church Charges City 'Harassment,'" *SANL*, 19 Mar. 1977, 2.
31   Gale Baldwin, "Lawsuit Seen against Church," *SLP*, 11 May 1977, 26.
32   Ibid.
33   Gale Baldwin, "Church Charges City 'Harassment,'" *SANL*, 19 Mar. 1977, 2.
34   Gale Baldwin, "Lawsuit Seen against Church," *SLP*, 11 May 1977, 26.
35   Ibid.
36   Eldon Harmon, interview with the author, 19 July 2015.
37   Steve Hilton, "Rev. W. E. Dowell: BBC Executive Vice President Keeps Faith in Fundamentalism," *SUNL*, 16 Jan. 1972, C2.
38   "Don't Knock Others," *SLP*, 28 Jan. 1972, 12.
39   Qtd. in Steve Hilton, "Rev. W. E. Dowell: BBC Executive Vice President Keeps Faith in Fundamentalism," *SUNL*, 16 Jan. 1972, C7.
40   WED, "As I See It," *NL*, 1 Dec. 1979, 5A.
41   WED, "Politics and Religious Freedom," BT, 31 Oct. 1976, audiocassette.
42   Qtd. in ibid.
43   WED, "Politics and Religious Freedom," BT, 31 Oct. 1976, audiocassette.
44   Ibid.
45   Ibid.
46   Qtd. in Clara Tuma, "Ministers Join Morals Battle to Save Families," *SLP*, 16 June 1980, 1B.

47 "Thomas Road Baptist Church Celebrates 50 Years of Ministry," *TRBC Update*, Golden Anniversary Edition, June/July 2006, TR6.

48 Qtd. in Linda Leicht, "W. E. Dowell, Noted Baptist Luminary, Dies," *NL*, 4 May 2002, 13A.

49 Qtd. in "Fundamentalists Fight Liberals," *Spartanburg Herald-Journal*, 28 Sept. 1980, A6.

50 Jim Peron, "Ayatollahs in America: The Genesis," *Institute for Liberal Values*, 9 June 2005, accessed 9 July 2009, www.liberalvalues.org.nz/index.php?action=view_journal&journal_id=163. See also freestudents.blogspot.com/2007/05/lies-of-jerry-falwell-jerry-falwell-was.html.

51 Qtd. in Jim Peron, "Ayatollahs in America: The Genesis," *Institute for Liberal Values*, 9 June 2005, accessed 9 July 2009. See also freestudents.blogspot.com/2007/05/lies-of-jerry-falwell-jerry-falwell-was.html.

52 WED, "The Struggle for Freedom," BT, 4 Oct. 1981, audiocassette.

53 WED, "Israel: God's Miracle Nation," BT, 28 Feb. 1982, audiocassette.

54 Ibid.

55 Ibid.

56 WED, "Come Now, Let Us Reason," BT, 26 Sept. 1976, audiocassette.

57 WED, "The Book of All Books," BT, 23 Jan. 1983, audiocassette.

58 Francis X. Clines. "Hecklers Interrupt Reagan Speech at Gathering of Fundamentalists," *New York Times*, 14 Apr. 1984, www.nytimes.com/1984/04/14/us/hecklers-interrupt-reagan-speech-at-gathering-of-fundamentalists.html.

59 Ronald Reagan, "Remarks at the Baptist Fundamentalism Annual Convention," *Ronald Reagan Presidential Library and Museum*, 13 Apr. 1984, www.reaganlibrary.archives.gov/archives/speeches/1984/41384h.htm.

60 Qtd. in "The Voters' Voices," *USA Today*, 7 Nov. 1984, 15A.

61 WED, "The Fields Are White Already unto Harvest," BT, 18 July 1982, audiocassette.

62 WED, "As I See It," *NL*, 15 Dec. 1979, 6A.

63 WED, "As I See It," *NL*, 27 Oct. 1979, 5A.

CHAPTER 41

1 Karolina W. Sandell-Berg, "Day by Day [1865]," trans. Andrew L. Skoog, *HymnTime.com*, 2001, www.hymntime.com/tch/htm/d/a/y/daybyday.htm.

2 BDJ, e-mail message to the author, 17 June 2009.

3 WED, "As I See It," *NL*, 12 May 1979, 5A.

4 Qtd. in "Sophisticated Fraud Cheats Thousands," *Lubbock Avalanche-Journal*, 20 May 1977, 36.

5 WED, "As I See It," *NL*, 12 May 1979, 5A.

6 WED to Carl Bledsoe, 20 Apr. 1977, VMLA.

7 WED, "As I See It," *NL*, 12 May 1979, 5A.

8 Ps. 37:25.

9 BDJ, e-mail message to the author, 7 Jan. 2008.

10 BDJ, e-mail message to the author, 4 July 2015.

11 Ibid.

12 WED to Wayne Edwards, 1 May 1981, VMLA.

13 Shirley Hackler, interview with the author, 14 Jan. 2008.

14 BDJ, e-mail message to the author, 7 Jan. 2008.

15 Ibid.

16 BDJ, message to the author, 4 July 2015.

17 Ibid.

18 Shirley Hackler, interview with the author, 14 Jan. 2008.

19 "Construction Progresses on New BBC Chapel," *BBT*, 25 Oct. 1985, 5.

20 Shirley Hackler, interview with the author, 14 Jan. 2008.

21 Ibid.

22 Ibid.

23 Ibid.

24 Ibid.

25 Qtd. in Shirley Hackler, interview with the author, 14 Jan. 2008.

26 Ibid.

27 Shirley Hackler, interview with the author, 14 Jan. 2008.

28 Ibid.

29 BDJ, e-mail message to the author, 7 Jan. 2008.

30 Shirley Hackler, interview with the author, 14 Jan. 2008.

31 Ibid.

32 Ibid.

33 Job 16:20.

34 Matt. 5:44.

35 WED, "What Is a Friend?" BT, 10 Nov. 1985, audiocassette.

36 JF, *Strength for the Journey*, 407.

37 Ibid., 416.

38 Ibid., 408-09.

39 Ibid., 418.

40   Bob Burke, "Watch Out Florida! Here Comes Bill Dowell," *Springfield! Magazine*, Jan. 1988, 50.

41   Ibid.

42   JF, *Strength for the Journey*, 417.

43   "Jim Bakker Is Indicted on Federal Charges," *History*, 2016, www.history.com/this-day-in-history/jim-bakker-is-indicted-on-federal-charges.

44   Macel Falwell and Melanie Hemry, *Jerry Falwell: His Life and Legacy*, (New York: Simon, 2008), 197.

45   "Falwell Quits, Warning PTL Ministry May End," *New York Times*, 9 Oct. 1987, www.nytimes.com/1987/10/09/us/falwell-quits-warning-ptl-ministry-may-end.html.

46   Bob Burke, "Watch Out Florida! Here Comes Bill Dowell," *Springfield! Magazine*, Jan. 1988, 50.

47   WED, "Justification Comes from God," BT, 13 Mar. 1983, audiocassette.

48   "A Voice Worth Heeding," *NL*, editorial, 12 May 1988, 10A.

49   Hag. 2:4.

50   Sharon Dowell. e-mail message to the author, 18 July 2009.

51   Ibid.

52   Isa. 55:8.

53   Clyde Dowell, e-mail message to the author, 18 July 2009.

54   Sharon Dowell, e-mail message to the author, 18 July 2009.

55   BDJ, e-mail message to the author, 25 July 2016.

CHAPTER 42

1   "The '94 Global Meeting: A Collage," *BBT*, June/July 1994, 4-5.

2   Qtd. in Terry Lemons, "Longtime Minister Steps Down," *NL*, 7 May 1988, 1B.

3   WED, "Awake Senior Citizens," 21 Apr. 1990, DFP.

4   WED to Ruth and Mac McConathy, 23 Sept. 1995, DFP.

5   WED, "God's Call to Man," BT, 31 Dec. 1997.

6   Dave Taylor, e-mail message to the author, 25 May 2006.

7   WED, interview with the author, c. 1995.

8   WED to Rev. and Mrs. Ramon Perez, 15 Mar. 1994, DFP.

9   WED to Rev. and Mrs. Don Swearingin, 15 Mar. 1994, DFP.

10   Russ Ivison to WED, 1 Mar. 1994, DFP.

11   Gloria Sunderman, "City Council Plans Meeting on Porn Issues," *SLP*, 13 May 1986, 2A.

12   John Ashcroft to WED, n.d., DFP.

13   WED, prayer transcript, n.d., DFP.

14   Ibid.

15   John Ashcroft to WED, 13 Jan. 1989, DFP.

16   "BBC Alumni Association Honors Dowell, Woodworth," *BBT*, 15 Sept. 1997, 28.

17   Steve Chittenden to WED, 2 Feb. 1984, DFP.

18   Jack Dinsbeer to WED, 14 Feb. 1984, DFP.

19   Qtd. in "W. E. Dowell Sr. Reflects on Over Sixty Years of Ministry," *The Baptist Preacher*, May/June 1996, 10-11.

20   WED, interview with the author, 14 Feb. 1992.

21   Ibid.

22   Ibid.

23   Ibid.

24   Ibid.

25   NCD, personal notes, 25 Aug. 1989, DFP.

26   NCD, personal notes, 12 Sept. 1989, DFP.

27   NCD to Jim and Marie Studstill, 23 Jan. 1990, DFP.

28   John Ashcroft to WED, 8 Apr. 1990, DFP.

29   WED, notes for radio broadcast, 22 Apr. 1989, DFP.

30   Qtd. in WED, interview with the author, 14 Feb. 1992.

31   WED, interview with the author, 14 Feb. 1992, DFP.

32   Karen Lyn Carreiro to the author, 2 Mar. 1994, DFP.

33   BDJ, e-mail message to the author, 13 July 2016.

34   Ibid.

35   Ibid.

36   Ibid.

37   Gary Longstaff, Facebook message to the author, 3 Aug. 2016.

38   Gary Longstaff, telephone interview with the author, 3 Aug. 2016.

39   Leland R. Kennedy, "God Still Performs Miracles," *BBT*, June/July 1994, 6.

40   MR, "It Was a Meeting like No Other," *BBT*, June/July 1994, 6-7.

CHAPTER 43

1   "Harvest Sunday," BT, 19 Aug. 2001, videotape.

2   Gen. 2:24.
3   1 Cor. 13:7.
4   Connie Allison, "Sure thing. . . ," Facebook comment, 5 Sept. 2016.
5   Sharon Dowell, e-mail message to the author, 18 July 2009.
6   Author's notes, n.d.
7   BDJ, e-mail message to the author, 7 Jan. 2017.
8   Author's notes, n.d.
9   Qtd. in Joan Dowell, interview with the author, 18 July 2010.
10   Janet Rodgers, e-mail message to the author, 24 July 2007.
11   Author's notes, n.d.
12   Nola died 8 Jan. 2005.
13   2 Cor. 5:8.
14   Rom. 8:18.
15   WED, "Harvest Sunday," BT, 19 Aug. 2001, videotape.
16   Qtd. in BDJ, "Harvest Sunday," BT, 19 Aug. 2001, videotape.
17   WED to Ruth and Mac McConathy, 2 Oct. 1993, DFP.
18   WED to Gladys Todd, 7 Nov. 1994, DFP.
19   Edward S. Horton, "What Is the Normal Range for Blood Sugar Levels, and What Blood Sugar Level Constitutes a True Emergency?" *ABC News*, 14 Aug. 2008, abcnews.go.com/Health/DiabetesScreening/story?id=3812946.
20   Qtd. in Joan Dowell, interview with the author, 25 Nov. 1993.
21   Joan Dowell, interview with the author, 25 Nov. 1993.
22   ES, interview with the author, 9 Nov. 1993.
23   Ibid.
24   Jer. 8:20.
25   WED, "The Substitutionary Atonement of Jesus Christ," Tabernacle Baptist Church [Farmington, N.M.], c. 1984.
26   BDJ, "Studies in Daniel—Part IV: Daniel 12," BT, 23 Oct. 2013.
27   Qtd. in BDJ, funeral sermon for John Robert Hartley, 19 Aug. 2006.
28   WED, "To Die Is Gain," sermon notes, n.d., DFP.
29   2 Tim. 4:7.
30   Heath Marion, Facebook comment to BDJ, 13 June 2014.
31   James Sewell, interview with the author, 17 Aug. 2009.
32   Qtd. in Linda Leicht, "W. E. Dowell, Noted Baptist Luminary, Dies," *NL*, 4 May 2002, 13A.
33   Ibid.
34   BDJ, e-mail message to the author, 2 May 2002.
35   Linda Leicht, "W. E. Dowell, Noted Baptist Luminary, Dies," *NL*, 4 May 2002, 1A.
36   WED, "Quit Ye Like Men," BT, 7 July 1985, audiocassette.
37   BDJ to WED and NCD, 24 June 1967, DFP.
38   Isa. 64:6.
39   See also Julia H. Johnston, "He Ransomed Me [1944]," *All-American Church Hymnal*, compiled by Earl Smith and John T. Benson, (Nashville: Benson, n.d.), 66.

AFTERWORD

1   WED, "To Stand for Principles," transcript, Feb. 1965, 12-13, DFP.

Made in the USA
San Bernardino, CA
04 May 2017